R Charlesworth

BIOLOGY ALIVE

John Bushell and Pam Nicholson

COLLINS EDUCATIONAL

ACKNOWLEDGEMENTS

Many of the questions used in this book are drawn from past examination papers. The authors and publishers would like to thank the Examinations Boards for allowing their questions to be reproduced, and have acknowledged each question individually as follows.

Associated Lancashire Schools Examining Board *(ALSEB)*
East Anglian Examinations Board *(EAEB)*
East Midland Regional Examinations Board *(EMREB)*
London Regional Examining Board *(LREB)*
North Regional Examinations Board *(NREB)*
Northern Examining Association *(NEA)*
South-East Regional Examinations Board *(SEREB)*
Southern Regional Examinations Board *(SREB)*
University of London Entrance and Schools Examinations Council *(ULESEC)*
Welsh Joint Education Committee *(WJEC)*

The publishers are grateful to the following sources for permission to reproduce photographs in this book.
Aspect Picture Library, page 133
S. Beaufoy, Ipswich, page 278
Birds Eye, Walls, page 100
The Guardian (London and Manchester), page 197
A.C. Hudson, pages 30, 32, 33, 34, 48, 50, 60, 61, 124, 150, 189, 253
National Coal Board, page 92
The Press Association, page 50
Sunday Times Picture Library, page 132
Syndicate International, pages 103
Topham Picture Library, pages 132, 134, 277
Which Consumer Magazine, page 208
D.P. Wilson/Eric and David Hosking, page 123

The publishers have made every effort to trace copyright holders, but if they have inadvertently overlooked any they will be pleased to make the necessary arrangements at the first opportunity.

ISBN 0 00327757-7

First published 1985 by Collins Educational
8 Grafton Street, London W1X 3LA

Reprinted 1986, 1987, 1988

Designed, typeset and illustrated by
Logos Design and Advertising, Datchet, Berkshire

Printed in Great Britain by
R.J. Acford, Chichester, Sussex

CONTENTS

TO THE STUDENT

'Biology Alive' introduces you to the important ideas of biology and shows you how these ideas can help you to understand your world.

The book is intended for CSE examinations, as a basis for most 'O' level courses and for the common-core syllabus of a common examination at 16+.

Biology has many 'scientific' words of its own and it is important that you should know these words. All the important 'scientific' words which you need to know have been included. You will find however that the 'ordinary' non-scientific words are simple and straightforward. This is to help you to understand the biology.

Important words are printed in *italics* and there is a collection of these, together with a summary of important facts, at the end of each topic. The questions at the end of each topic range from filling in the missing word, to questions which ask you to think carefully. Many of these questions are CSE or 16+ questions set by different Examination Boards.

There are suggestions for 'Things to do' many of which you can try out at home. You may also be amazed by some of the facts in 'Fancy that'!

When you have finished a topic, this is what you should do:

1. Think about how it might help you to understand other topics you have finished. *'Diffusion and Osmosis'*, for example, will help you to understand other topics such as *'Cells at Work'*, *'Transport and* Transpiration' and *'Digestion'*. The topic *'How Green Plants Feed'* will help you to understand *'Connections'*, *'The Carbon Cycle'* and *The Nitrogen Cycle'*.

2. Look at and learn the 'Important words'. Say a sentence to yourself which contains each word.

3. Read the 'Summary'.

4. Try some of the *different* types of questions.

TOPIC 1

CELLS

Houses are built of house bricks, and living organisms are built of 'bricks' called *cells*. Because cells are so small we have to use a *microscope* to see them. If we want to see the smallest parts of a cell we must use a special microscope called an electron microscope. The electron microscope magnifies cells more than an ordinary light microscope.

All cells are like each other in some ways, but they also have differences. The most important differences are between plant cells and animals cells (figures 1.1–1.3).

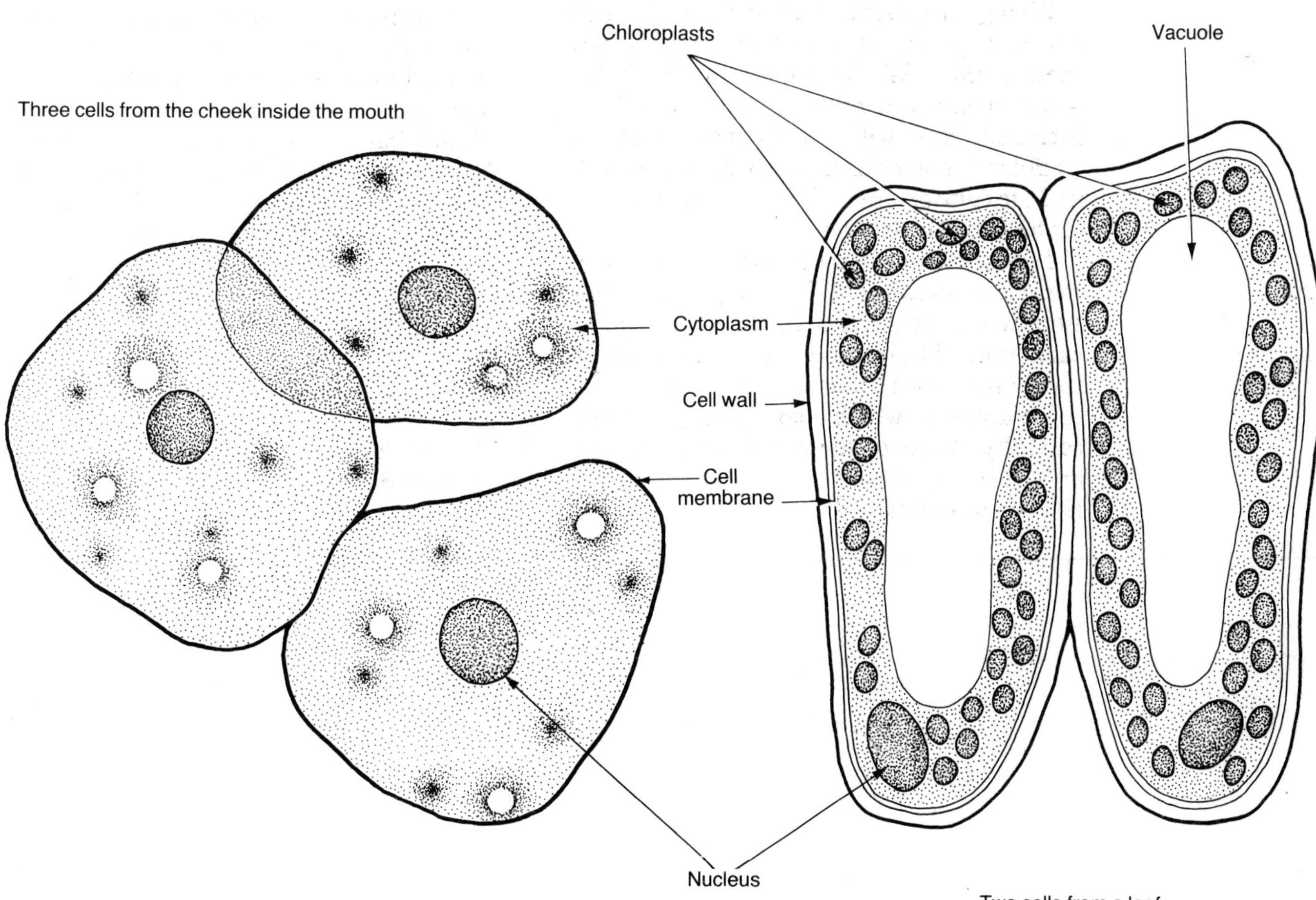

Figure 1.1 Plant and animal cells

Nucleus – controls all the chemical reactions in the cells. The nucleus contains chromosomes which come from the parents.

Cell membrane – a thin 'skin' between the cytoplasm and the outside of the cell. It lets some substances go through but not others.

Cytoplasm – looks like the runny part of a raw egg. It is a clear liquid in which many chemical reactions happen. These reactions keep the cell alive.

Figure 1.2 All cells have these structures

Chloroplasts – contain a green substance called *chlorophyll.* Chlorophyll absorbs energy from sunlight. The energy is used in photosynthesis to make food.

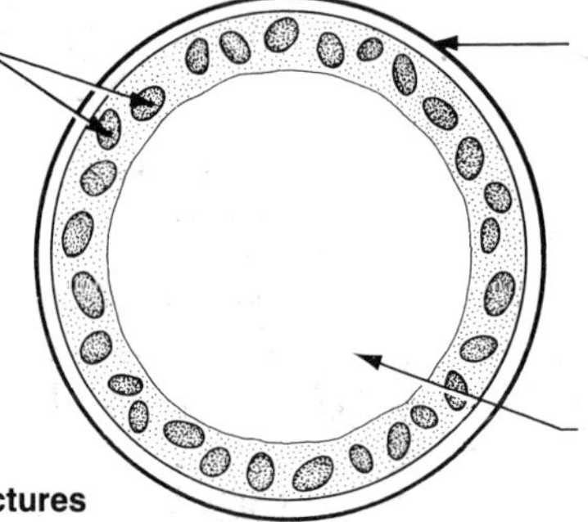

Cellulose cell wall – a stiff 'case' which keeps the shape of the cell and supports it.

Vacuole – a large space filled with a clear liquid called *cell sap.* The cell sap has sugar, salts and other substances dissolved in it.

Figure 1.3 Only plant cells have these structures

Difference between plant and animal cells

PLANT CELLS	ANIMAL CELLS
Often have chloroplasts	Never have chloroplasts
Have cell walls made of cellulose	Never have cell walls made of cellulose
Have a large vacuole	Any vacuoles are usually small
Have a thin lining of cytoplasm	Most of the cell is filled with cytoplasm

ONE-CELLED AND MANY-CELLED ORGANISMS

Some simple organisms are made of only one cell and we call these unicellular organisms. Other organisms are made of many cells and are called multicellular organisms.

Unicellular organisms live on their own without other cells to help them. So one cell does all the jobs which are needed to keep the organism alive. The cell feeds, reproduces, excretes and respires. It is also sensitive and may move.

The cells of multicellular organisms live together with other cells which they need to help them. This is because the cells are adapted for doing one job very well. A muscle cell does not get its own oxygen and food. It is adapted for doing one job – movement. Other cells in the organism are adapting for absorbing oxygen and other for collecting food. Blood cells are adapted for bringing oxygen to all the other cells.

In multicellular organisms cells which do the same job group together to make *tissues*. Blood and bone in animals, and 'wood' and pith in plants are all examples of tissues. Each tissue is made of a particular kind of cell. Bone tissue in animals is made only of bone cells. Pith tissue in plants is made only of pith cells. All the cells in a tissue do the *same* kind of job.

Tissues which do *different* jobs group together to make *organs*. Eyes and lungs, leaves and stems are all examples of organs. An eye is made of muscle tissue, nerve tissue and some other tissues. A leaf is made of tissue which carries liquids, tissue which makes food and some other tissues. (See figure 1.4.)

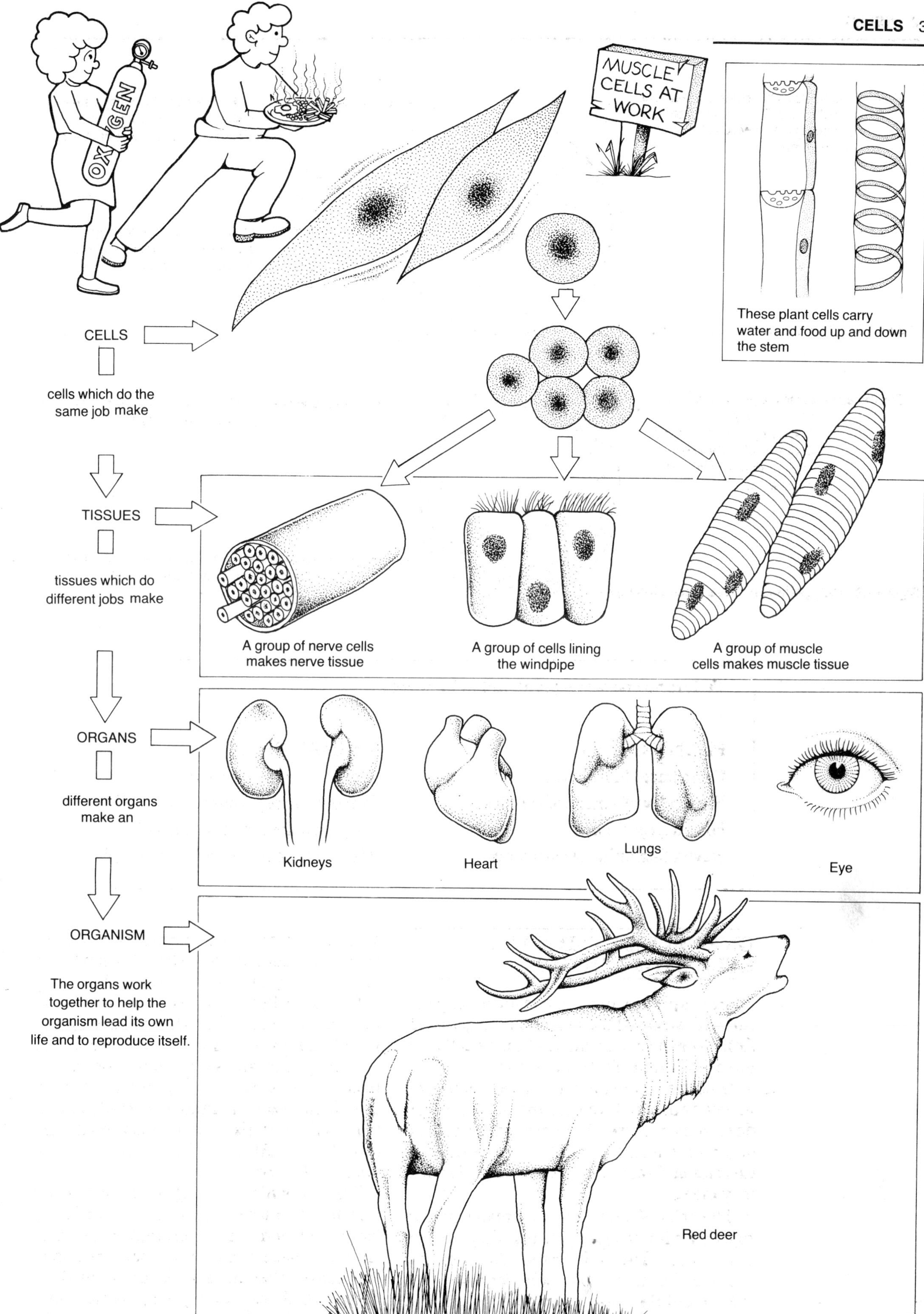
OXYGEN
MUSCLE CELLS AT WORK
These plant cells carry water and food up and down the stem
CELLS
cells which do the same job make
TISSUES
A group of nerve cells makes nerve tissue
A group of cells lining the windpipe
A group of muscle cells makes muscle tissue
tissues which do different jobs make
ORGANS
Kidneys
Heart
Lungs
Eye
different organs make an
ORGANISM
The organs work together to help the organism lead its own life and to reproduce itself.
Red deer

Figure 1.4

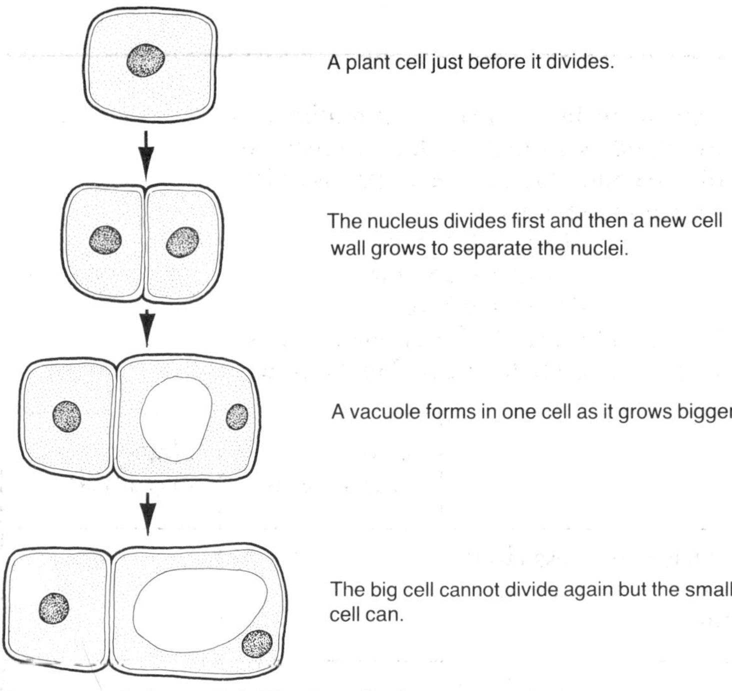

Figure 1.5 A plant cell dividing by mitosis

CELL DIVISION

Organisms must be able to grow and so cells divide to make more cells. When a cell divides into two, the new cell grows bigger. When this happens in thousands of cells the organism starts to grow.

Organisms must also be able to repair damaged tissues and, to do this, cell division continues in organisms which have stopped growing.

Not all cells can divide to make new cells. In plants, most cell division happens at the growing points or meristems. These are at the tip of the shoot and just behind the tip of the root.

In vertebrate animals cell division in the bones causes growth in length.

This kind of cell division is called *mitosis* (see figure 1.5). It is discussed again in Topic 41 together with another kind of cell division.

Fancy that!

Cells in your body measure between 0.005 mm and 0.02 mm across. If they were 1000 times bigger, the smallest would be this size:

and the biggest this size:

Of course, this would mean that you were 1000 times bigger as well!

Summary

Living organisms are made of *cells*. These can only be seen with a *microscope*. *Unicellular* organisms are made of one cell.

Most organisms are made of many cells and are *multicellular*. In these organisms different cells do different jobs: there are cells for movement, cells for reproduction, etc. Groups of cells which do the same job are *tissues*. Blood, muscles, 'wood' and pith are tissues. *Organs* like eyes, lungs, leaves and stems are groups of different tissues. An *organism* is made of groups of organs which do different jobs but work together.

Plant and animal cells are different. Plant cells have a *cellulose cell wall*, a large *vacuole* and often have *chloroplasts*. Animal cells do not have cellulose cell walls or chloroplasts.

All cells have *cytoplasm* and a *nucleus*. The nucleus controls the chemical reactions in a cell and contains the *chromosomes*. Organisms grow by cell division or *mitosis*. Mitosis happens at the growing points.

Important words

Microscope	an instrument which magnifies very small objects (makes them look bigger).
Cell	has a nucleus, cytoplasm and a cell membrane. Multicellular animals and plants are made of many cells.
Tissue	a group of cells which do the same job.
Organ	part of a plant or animal made from a group of tissues.
Nucleus	controls all the activities of a cell.
Cytoplasm	a jelly-like substance around the nucleus.
Chlorophyll	a green substance which helps plants to make their food.
Chloroplast	part of a plant cell containing chlorophyll.
Cell membrane	a very thin layer around a plant or animal cell.
Vacuole	a space in the cytoplasm of a cell.

Things to do

1. Cells are very small but it is not difficult to measure them. Put your microscope on the lowest magnification. Put a clear plastic ruler on the stage. Now look at the mm lines on your ruler through the microscope. Measure how far it is from one side of the circle of light to the other. Now put the microscope on a higher magnification. Measure how far it is across the circle of light again. Fill in row 1 in the table.

2. Peel off a bit of the thin white skin from a piece of the inside of an onion. Put the skin onto a microscope slide and put one drop of water on top of it. Put a coverslip on top of the piece of skin. Look at the skin under the low magnification of the microscope. You should be able to see the cells quite easily. Try to find the length of the cells. You may have to measure the length of a row of cells and divide by the number of cells. This will give you the average length of one cell. Try to measure the cells under a higher magnification in the same way. Fill in row 2 in the table.

3. Cells are really too small to use millimetres to try and measure them. If a millimetre is divided into 1000 parts, each part is called a micrometre (μm) So:

$500\ \mu m = 0.5\ mm$
$250\ \mu m = 0.25\ mm$
$100\ \mu m = 0.1\ mm$

Work out the length of your onion cells in micrometres and fill in row 3 in the table.

	Low magnification	Higher magnification
1. Distance across circle of light in millimetres (mm)		
2. Average length of cell in millimetres (mm)		
3. Average length of cell in micrometres (μm)		

Questions

A.

Write out each sentence in your book. Fill in the missing words from those in the box. Some words may be used more than once.

cellulose — chromosomes — microscope — vacuole — organs — selectively permeable — electron microscope — cells — cytoplasm — chlorophyll — nucleus

1. Cells can only be seen with a ....
2. The smallest parts of a cell can be seen with an ....
3. Plant cells often have chloroplasts containing ....
4. Cell membranes let some substances go through and are ....
5. ...... are structures in a nucleus which come from the parents.
6. All cells contain a clear substance called ...... in which many chemical reactions happen.
7. The clear liquid inside plant cells is found in the ....
8. Plant cells have stiff cell walls made of ....
9. Lungs are ...... because they are made of different tissues.
10. Muscles are tissues because they are groups of ...... which do the same job.
11. The ...... controls what happens in a cell.

B.

Put each of these parts of sentences into the correct order.

1. when a cell / divides first and then a new cell / wall is made / divides the nucleus
2. when organisms stop / tissue needs to be repaired / mitosis does not stop / growing because damaged
3. at the growing points / in plants mitosis only happens / not all cells can divide / to make new cells and
4. after a new plant / cell has been made by / cell division a vacuole / begins to appear in it

C.

1. Why do plant cells have a cellulose cell wall when animal cells do not?
2. Why do plant cells often have chloroplasts when animal cells never have them?
3. Why is blood called a tissue?
4. The cell membrane is very thin. Why is it important?
5. How do cells divide in mitosis?
6. What is the difference between an organ and an organism?
7. Figure 1.6 was made by a scientist looking at a cell collected from another planet. The scientist has made a few notes on the drawing.
   (a) Do you think that the cell has come from an animal, a plant or a 'plant-animal'? Give reasons for your answer.
   (b) What is unusual about the cell?
   (c) The scientist thinks that the cell has come from a very large organism. Say why you agree or disagree with this.

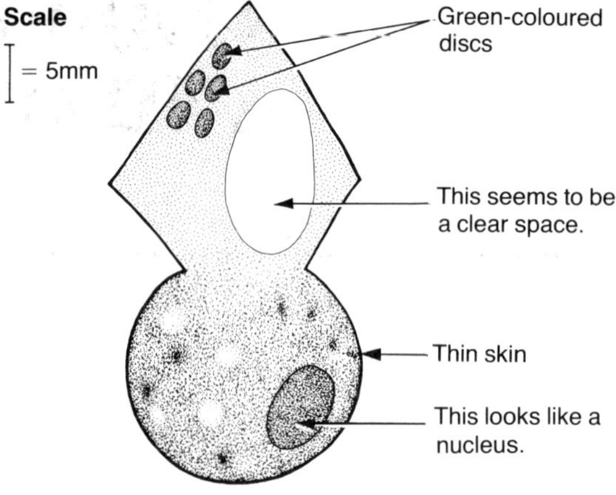

Figure 1.6

(*ALSEB*)

D.

Study figures 1.7 and 1.8. Figure 1.7 shows a stinging cell from the tentacle of a jelly-fish, as seen under the microscope. Groups of these cells are used to capture small organisms in the water for food. Figure 1.6 shows a stinging cell from the epidermis of a nettle leaf. These cells are used to protect the plant from animals which would eat it.

1. Using *all* labels given in the two figures, explain how you think each cell works.
2. Give *one* feature of the nettle cell which shows it is from a plant.
3. The nettle sting cell does *not* contain chlorophyll.
   (a) Where exactly is its food made?
   (b) Name the process by which the nettle sting cell obtains food.
4. Neither the nettle cell nor jelly-fish cell could exist by itself. Name one cell, found in pond water, which can live an independent life.

(*NREB*)

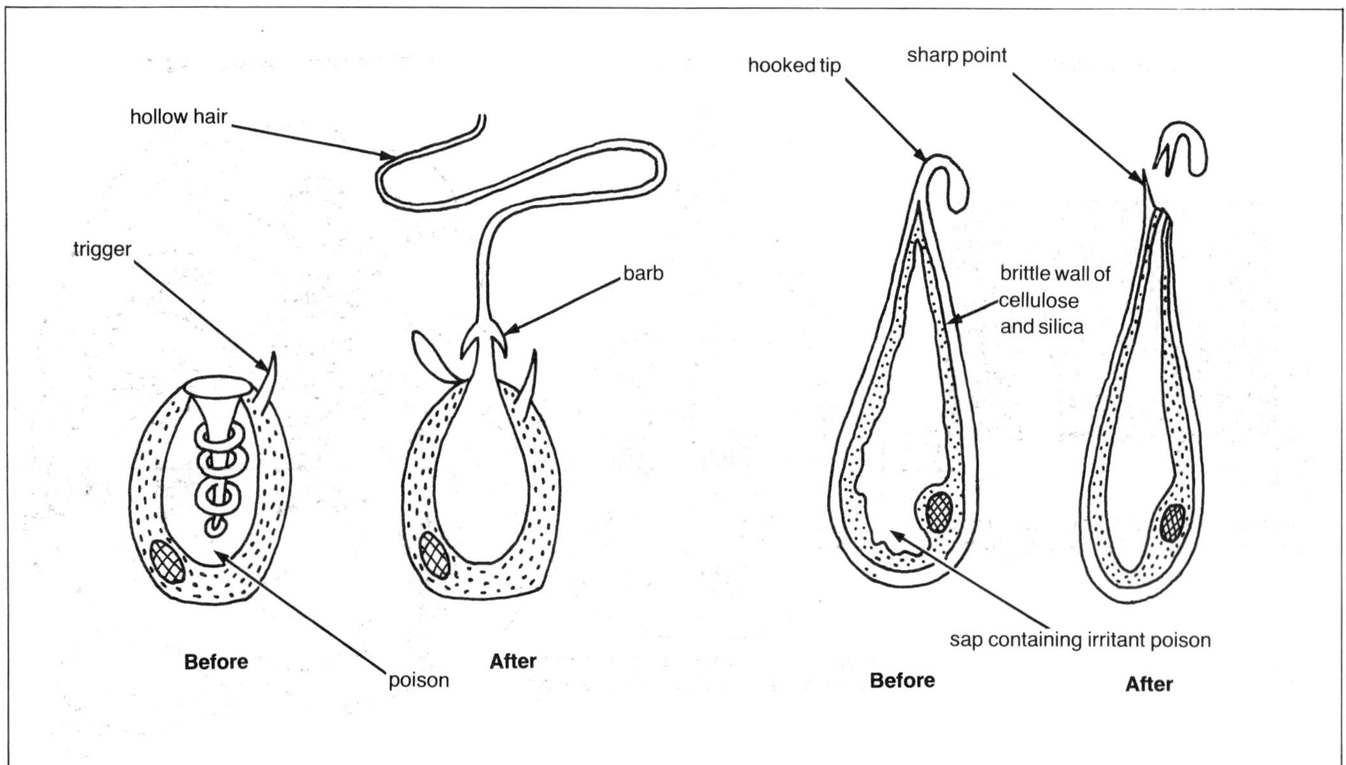

Figure 1.7 Sting cell of jellyfish before and after it is touched

Figure 1.8 Sting cell of a nettle before and after it is touched

TOPIC 2

DIFFUSION AND OSMOSIS

All substances are made of many millions of tiny molecules. These molecules are too small to be seen even with the most powerful microscope in the world. In some substances the molecules are more closely packed together than in others.

DIFFUSION IN GASES

Gas molecules move about all the time, bumping into each other. Because of this, gas molecules always spread themselves out evenly and quickly. (See figure 2.1.)

The gas molecules inside this tin (figure 2.2) have spread themselves out to fill it. The distance between each gas molecule is about the same.

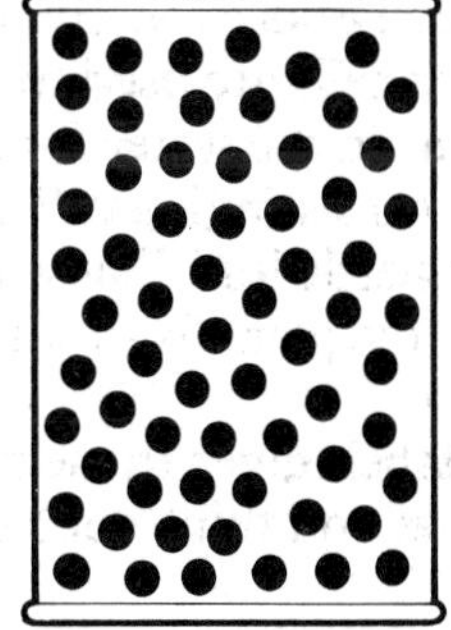

Diffusion in gases

Figure 2.2

Figure 2.1

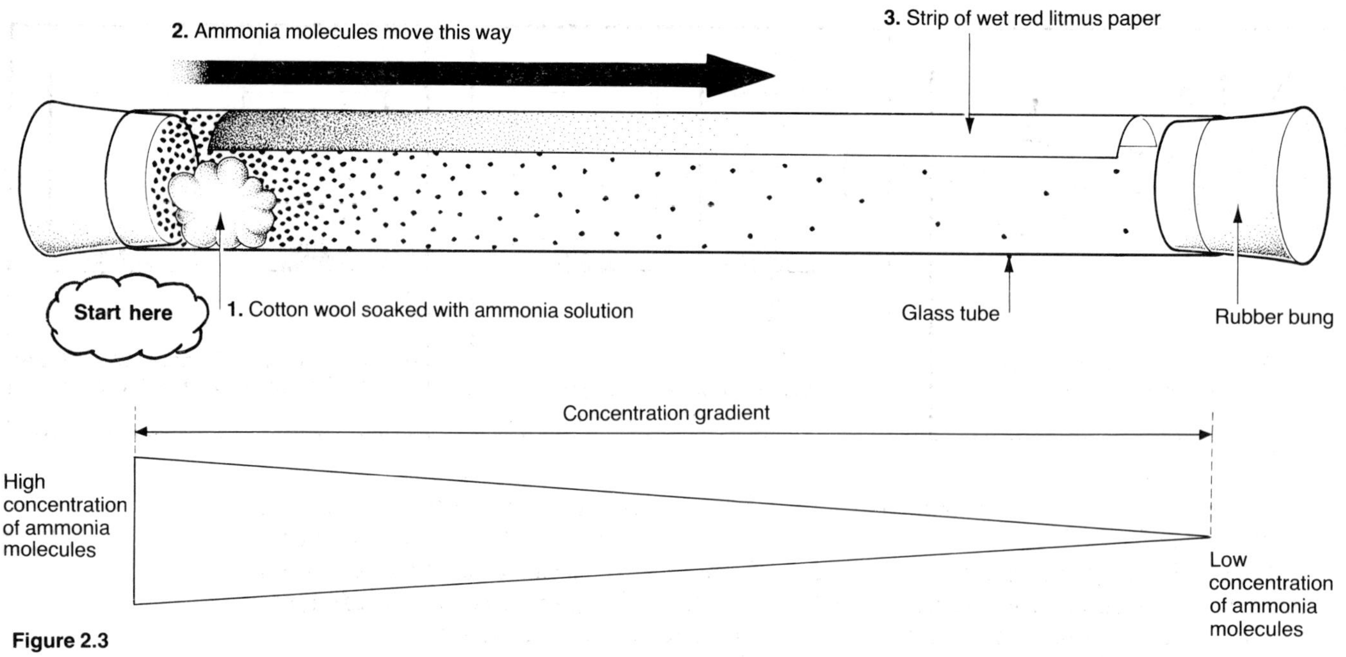

2. Ammonia molecules move this way

3. Strip of wet red litmus paper

Start here

1. Cotton wool soaked with ammonia solution

Glass tube

Rubber bung

Concentration gradient

High concentration of ammonia molecules

Low concentration of ammonia molecules

Figure 2.3

If you set up a tube like the one in Figure 2.3 all the ammonia molecules will be concentrated at one end of the tube. There will be no ammonia molecules at the other end of the tube. We call this difference in the number of molecules a *concentration gradient*. The ammonia molecules will slowly begin to move along the tube. The litmus paper changes colour as the molecules move.

After a few minutes the ammonia molecules will have spaced themselves out evenly in the tube. When this has happened there is no concentration gradient.

The same thing happens with solids which dissolve in liquids. The molecules of the solid move about between the molecules of the liquid. All the molecules bump into each other as they move about.

If you drop sugar into a cup of tea it will be concentrated at the bottom of the cup at first. The tea at the top of the cup will have no sugar in it. There will be a concentration gradient between the tea and the sugar.

After a few minutes the sugar will dissolve and the molecules will slowly spread through the tea. The sugar and tea molecules mix together evenly. Each sip of tea will now taste sweet because the concentration gradient has disappeared.

We call the movement of molecules in gases and liquids *diffusion*. Molecules diffuse from high concentrations (where there are many molecules) to low concentrations (where there are few molecules). Diffusion makes the molecules mix together and spread out evenly. In Figure 2.3 the ammonia molecules will diffuse along the tube and mix with the air. In Figure 2.4 the sugar molecules will diffuse through the liquid and mix with the tea.

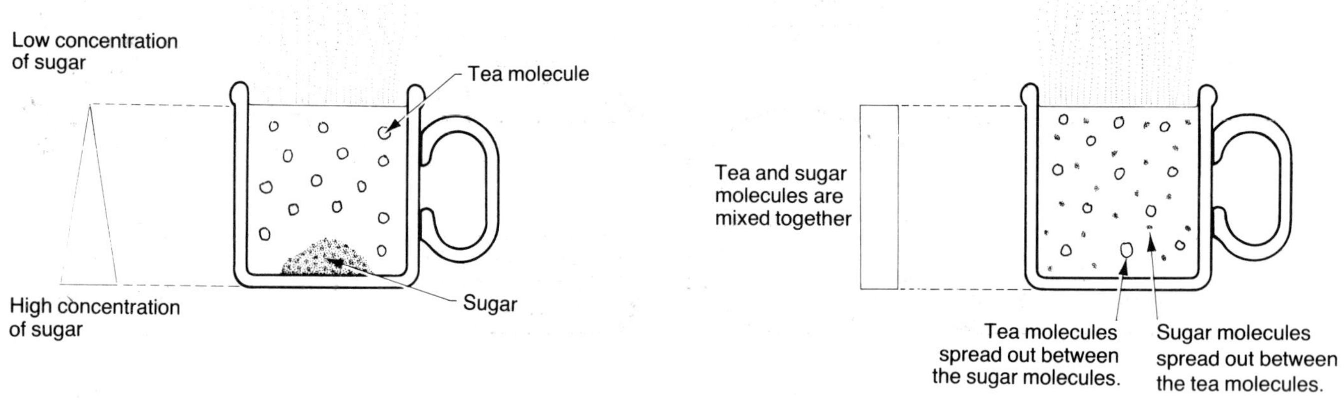

Figure 2.4 What happens when you put sugar in ...... **......and after you have stirred your tea.**

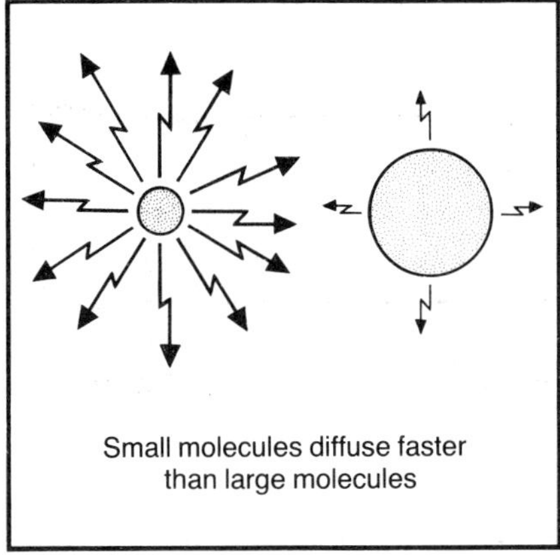
Small molecules diffuse faster than large molecules

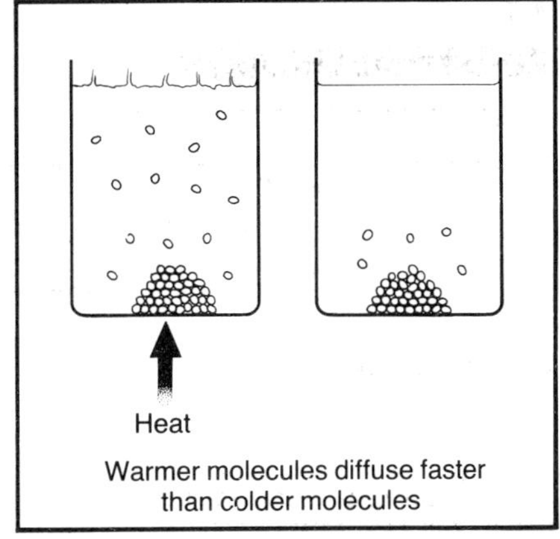

Warmer molecules diffuse faster than colder molecules

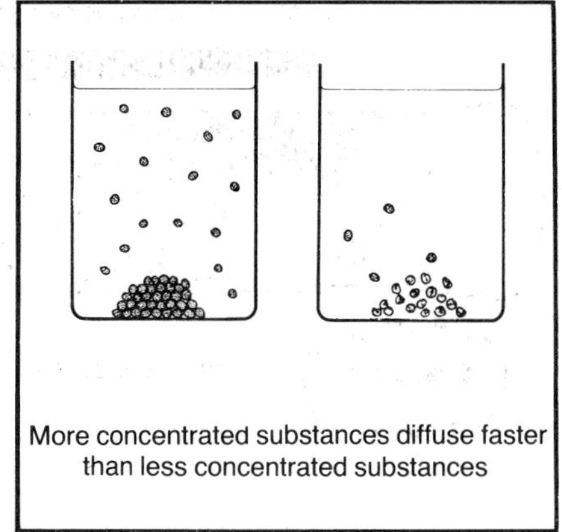
More concentrated substances diffuse faster than less concentrated substances

Figure 2.5

Some substances diffuse more quickly than others (see figure 2.5).

Diffusion is very important in living organisms. Many substances are exchanged between living organisms and their surroundings by diffusion.

Substances also move from cell to cell and from one part of a cell to another by diffusion.

Substances move by diffusion in the directions shown by the arrows in figures 2.6 and 2.7. You can find out more about diffusion in living organisms by reading the pages listed on these diagrams.

Some useful substances which diffuse into cells are oxygen, food, mineral salts and water. Carbon dioxide is a harmful substance which diffuses out of cells.

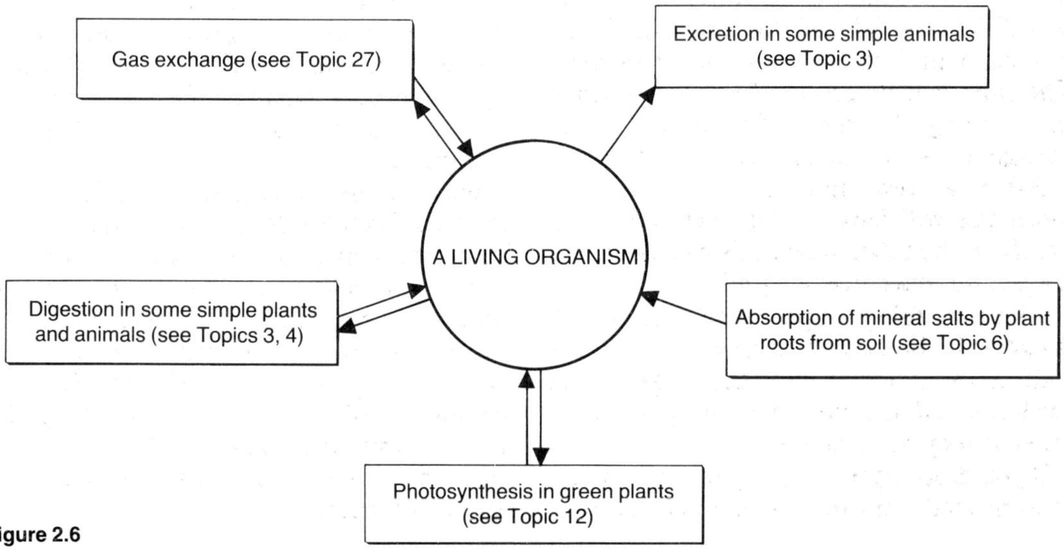

Gas exchange (see Topic 27)

Excretion in some simple animals (see Topic 3)

A LIVING ORGANISM

Digestion in some simple plants and animals (see Topics 3, 4)

Absorption of mineral salts by plant roots from soil (see Topic 6)

Photosynthesis in green plants (see Topic 12)

Figure 2.6

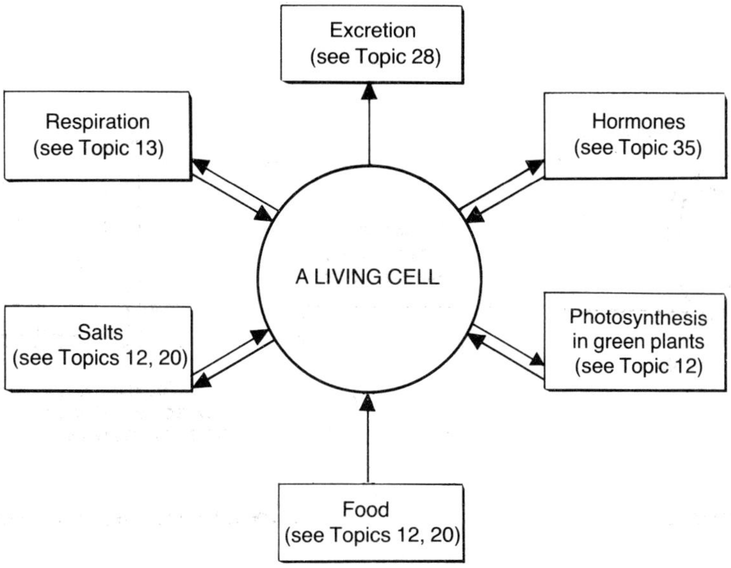

Excretion (see Topic 28)

Respiration (see Topic 13)

Hormones (see Topic 35)

A LIVING CELL

Salts (see Topics 12, 20)

Photosynthesis in green plants (see Topic 12)

Food (see Topics 12, 20)

Figure 2.7

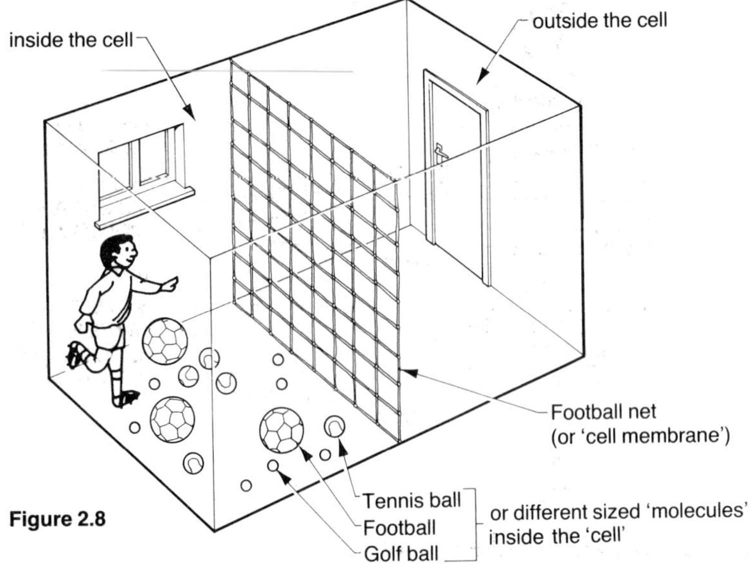

Figure 2.8

CELL MEMBRANES

Cells are surrounded by thin membranes. These membranes have many tiny holes in them and are like nets. Molecules which are small enough can diffuse through the holes in the membranes to the other side. Large molecules cannot diffuse through the holes and are held back.

The room (see figure 2.8) has a football net fixed across the middle. The net is the 'cell membrane'. One half of the room has footballs, tennis balls and golf balls in it. These are different 'molecules' inside the 'cell'.

If you kick all the balls at the net…

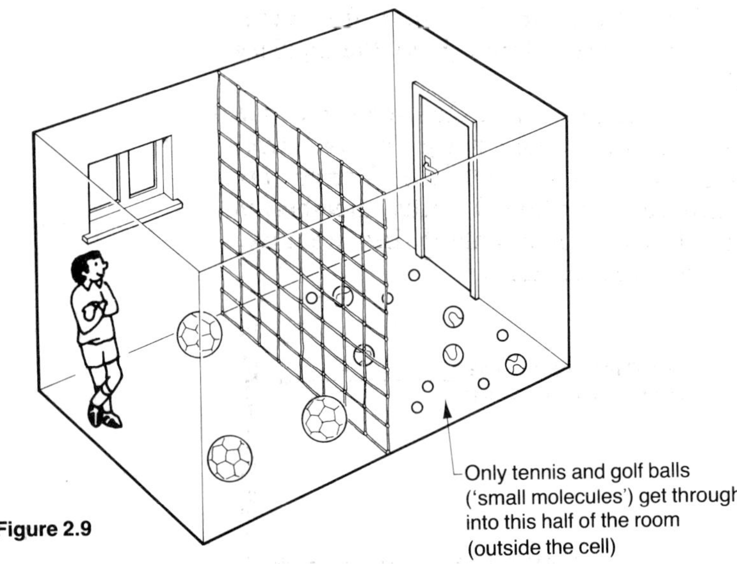

Figure 2.9

…only the golf balls and tennis balls would go through. The footballs are too big and cannot go through. The net lets some balls go through and is *permeable* to these, but not others. The net 'selects' or sorts out what size of ball gets through. It is *selectively permeable*.

Cell membranes are selectively permeable.

Figure 2.10 shows how you can make a model cell by using Visking tubing. This is a selectively permeable substance.

Weigh the model cell before you put it into the water. After 30 minutes take it out, carefully dry it and weigh it again.

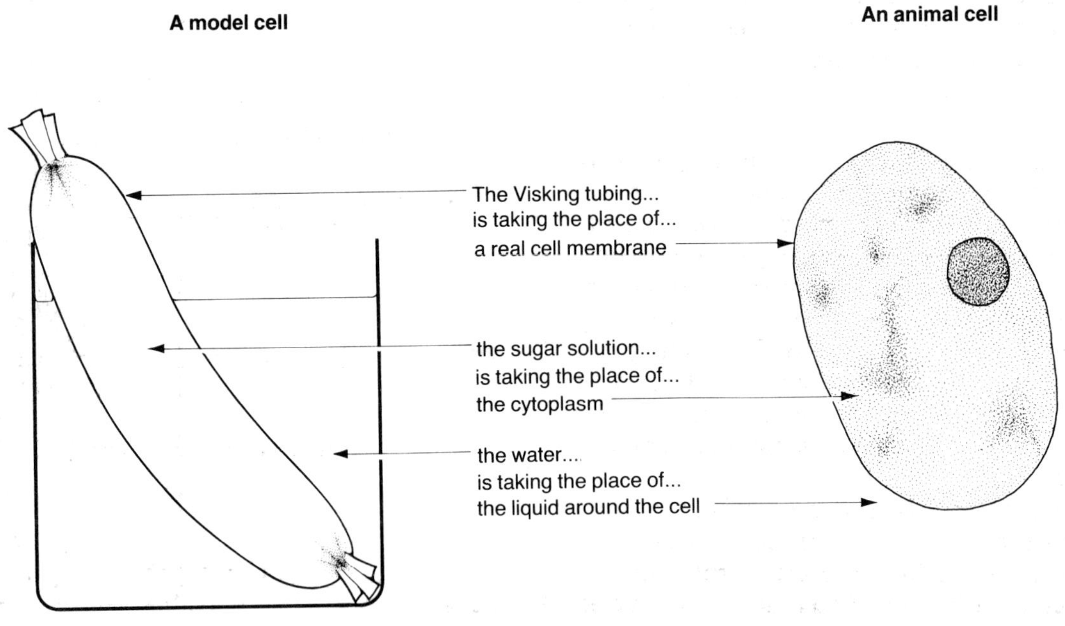

Figure 2.10

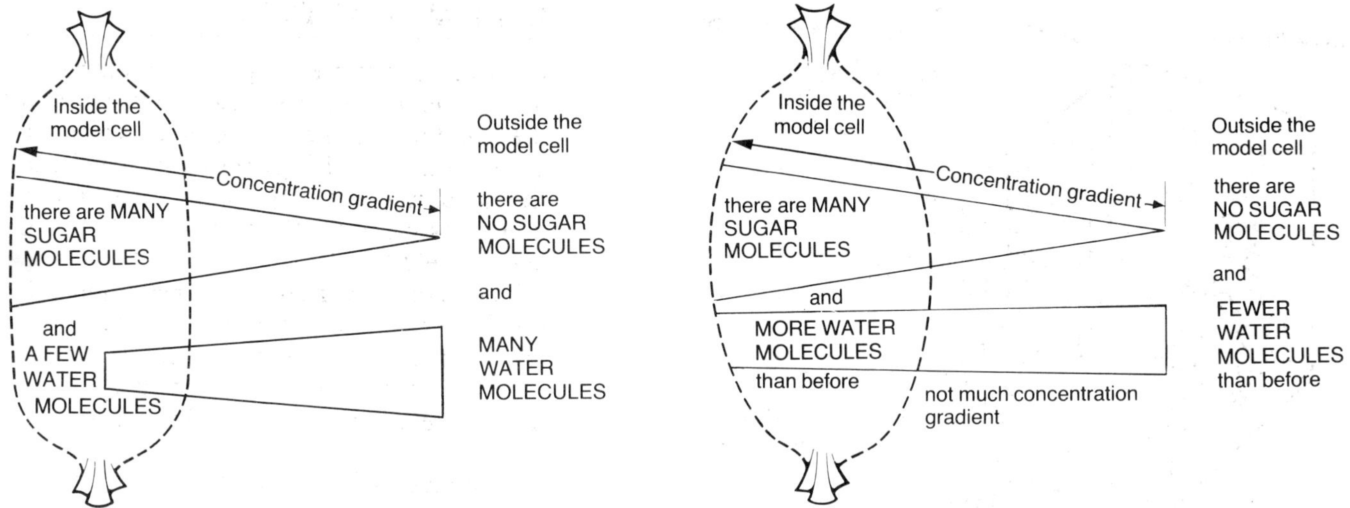

Figure 2.11 At the start of the experiment

Figure 2.12 At the end of the experiment

There are different numbers of molecules (a concentration gradient) inside and outside the model cell. (See figure 2.11.)

The water molecules are small enough to go through the Visking tubing and they diffuse into the model cell (figure 2.12). The sugar molecules are too large to go through the Visking tubing. They cannot diffuse out of the cell into the water. The model cell will get heavier because water molecules diffuse into it, through the tubing, by *osmosis*.

Osmosis is a kind of diffusion which happens through a selectively permeable membrane. A weak solution has more water molecules in it than a strong solution. Osmosis happens when a weak solution is separated from a strong solution by a selectively permeable membrane.

Osmosis is the movement of water from a weaker solution to a stronger solution through a selectively permeable membrane.

In Figure 2.11 and 2.12 a model cell was used to show osmosis. Figure 2.13 shows osmosis in a *living* organism – a fresh carrot. A teacher poured a strong sugar solution into a hole made in the carrot with a cork borer. The teacher fixed a piece of capillary tubing into the hole using a tightly fitting bung and put the carrot into a beaker of water. After about 30 minutes, the sugar solution had risen several centimetres up the capillary tube.

The carrot cells have selectively permeable membranes. The membranes separate the strong sugar solution in the carrot from the water in the beaker. Water moves by osmosis from cell to cell across the carrot to the sugar solution. Water moving into the carrot makes the sugar solution go up the capillary tube.

If the teacher boiled the carrot first, the sugar solution would not go up the tube. This is because cell membranes are destroyed by boiling. In cells, membranes are selectively permeable if they are alive, but not if they are dead.

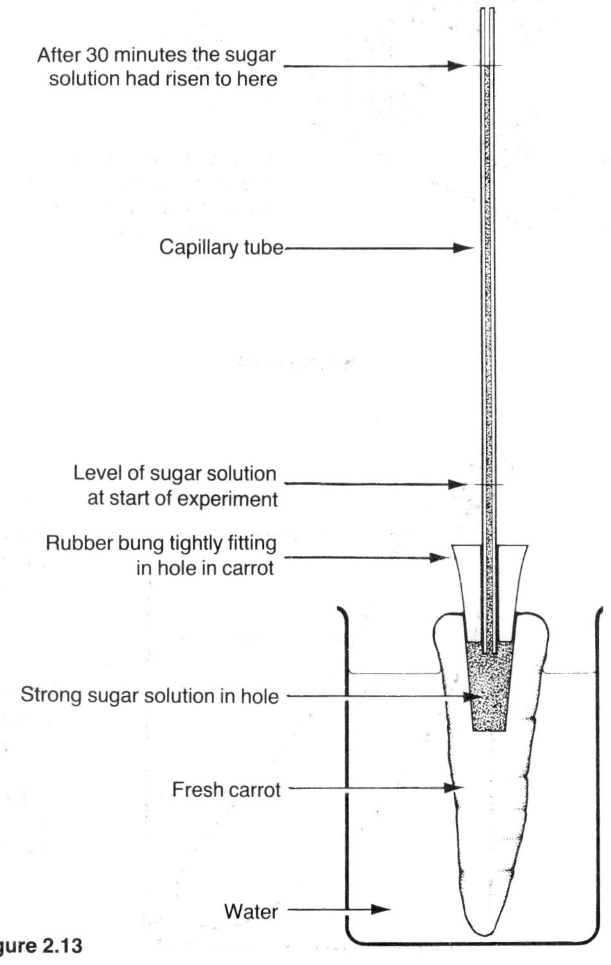

Figure 2.13

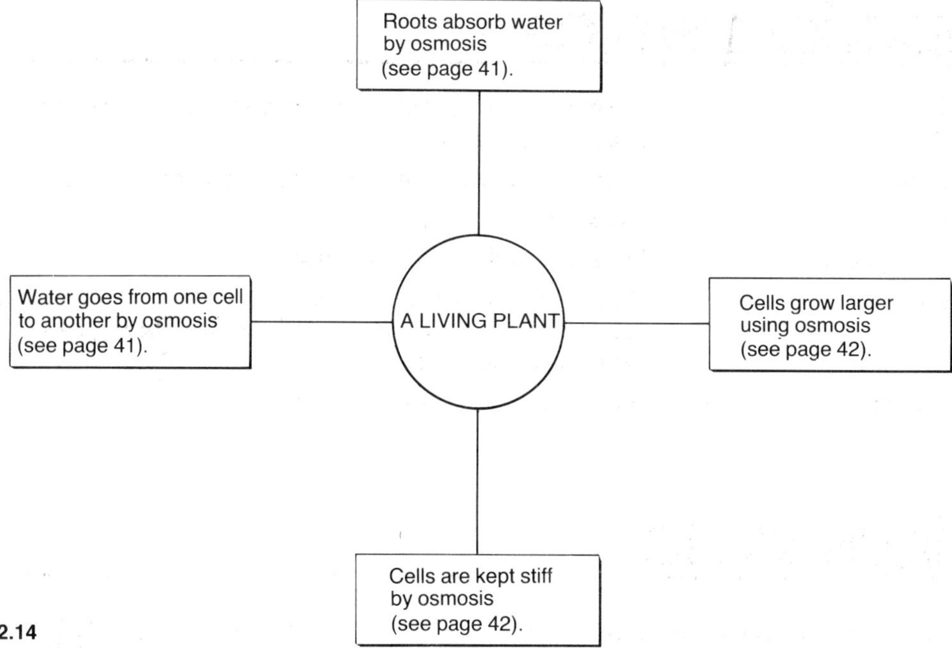

Figure 2.14

OSMOSIS IN PLANTS

Osmosis is important in all living things. Figure 2.14 shows how osmosis is important in plants.

You can find out more about osmosis in plants on the pages listed in figure 2.14.

OSMOSIS IN ANIMALS

Many animals which live in water have selectively permeable skin. The cytoplasm of animals which live in ponds and rivers is a stronger solution than the water around the animals. Because of this water diffuses *into* their bodies by osmosis. If they do not pump some of this water out the animals will die. We call the process of pumping out this water *osmo-regulation*. Fish and frogs use their kidneys for osmo-regulation. Their kidneys get rid of the extra water as a weak solution called urine.

Sea water is stronger than the cytoplasm of many fish that live in the sea. Because of this water diffuses *out* of their bodies by osmosis. If they do not replace this water they will die. The fish drink sea water to replace the water they lose by osmosis! They have to get rid of the salts in the sea water they drink.

Animals which live on land lose water by evaporation. They gain water from their food and drink. Osmo-regulation in mammals is done mainly by their kidneys.

Summary

All substances are made of *molecules*. In *solids* the molecules are closely packed together and cannot move much. In *gases* the molecules can move about easily.

Molecules move from *high* concentrations (where there are many of them) to *low* concentrations (where there are fewer of them). This is called *diffusion*. Living organisms exchange substances with their surroundings by diffusion and substances go from cell to cell by diffusion. Cell membranes are *selectively permeable*: they let some molecules go through but hold others back.

The solution *inside* a cell may be more concentrated (have fewer water molecules) than the solution outside it. Water molecules then go *into* the cell by *osmosis*. This happens until the solution inside the cell is the same concentration as the solution outside it. The solution *outside* a cell may be more concentrated than the solution inside it (which has more water molecules). Water molecules then go *out* of the cell by osmosis.

Animals get rid of extra water by *osmo-regulation*. Vertebrates osmo-regulate by using their kidneys to make urine.

Important words

Diffusion	the movement of molecules from a high concentration to a lower concentration.
Concentrated	many molecules crowded together in a small space.
Permeable	lets all molecules go through.
Selectively permeable	lets some molecules go through.
Osmosis	the movement of water molecules from a less concentrated solution to a more concentrated solution through a selectively permeable membrane.
Osmo-regulation	the control of the amount of water in organisms.

Things to do

1. Make a working model to show how a selectively permeable membrane works in osmosis.
   You will need:
   a disposable plastic petri dish (ask your teacher if there is one to spare);
   Plasticine;
   a few marbles or ball bearings of different sizes.
   Stick a strip of Plasticine across the middle of the dish. Make a 'gate' in the Plasticine wide enough to let only the small ball bearings get through. Put the large marbles in one half of the dish. Put the small ball bearings in the other half. Add two ball bearings to the marbles.
   Shake the dish gently from side to side. Some ball bearings will go through the gate and mix with the marbles. What happens to the marbles? If you stand the dish on an overhead projector everyone can see what happens!

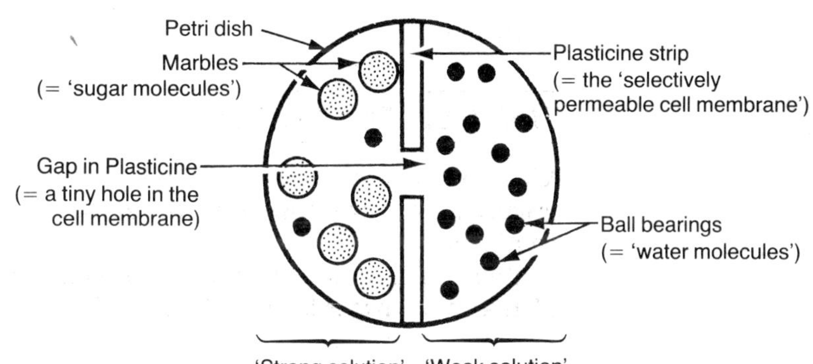

Figure 2.15

2. Cut a potato into chips. Choose two chips and cut them to the same length. Try to get them the same weight. Measure them carefully. Put one chip into water and the other into strong sugar solution. Leave them for 24 hours. Take out the chips and dry them carefully with a paper tissue. Weigh and measure them. What has happened and why?

Questions

A.
Join these sentences together using either the word 'and' or the word 'because', whichever is correct.

1. Living cell membranes are selectively permeable. They are alive.
2. Fish which live in the sea drink the water. They lose water by osmosis.
3. Water goes into the cells of fish which live in fresh water. They get rid of this extra water as urine.
4. Cells have selectively permeable membranes. They need to exchange substances with their surroundings.

B.
Explain each of the following: (a) the smell of food being cooked in your kitchen soon fills the house. (b) If you wash lettuce leaves in slightly salted water you kill any insects on the leaves but the leaves go limp. (c) If you sprinkle sugar onto a dish of strawberries, liquid collects in the dish. If you do the same with raisins, nothing happens.

C.
In an experiment to investigate osmosis using potato tissue, twelve cylinders of potato tissue were cut to a length of 50 mm. Three of these cylinders were placed in each of the following solutions:
(A) water,
(B) 10% sucrose (sugar) solution;
(C) 20% sucrose (sugar) solution; and
(D) 30% sucrose (sugar) solution.

After two hours the cylinders were taken out of the solutions, dried and placed on 2 mm graph paper to measure their lengths. The outline of each cylinder is shown in figure 2.16.

Solution	Average length of cylinders (mm)	Average change in length of cylinders (mm) + or –
(a) Water		
(b) 10% sucrose		
(c) 20% sucrose		
(d) 30% sucrose		

1. Find the average length of the cylinders from each of the four solutions and record your results in a table like the one shown. Then work out the average change in length of the cylinders from each of the four solutions and record your results in the table, using + for an increase in length and – for a decrease in length.

2. Plot the average change in the length of the cylinders against the concentration of sucrose, on graph paper.

3. (a) Why did the cylinders in sucrose solutions C and D change in length?
(b) Why did the cylinders in sucrose solution B stay the same average length?

4. At the end of the experiment the cylinders from the water would feel different from those which had been in sucrose solution D.
(a) What would be the differences in feel?
(b) Explain why these two would feel different.

(NREB)

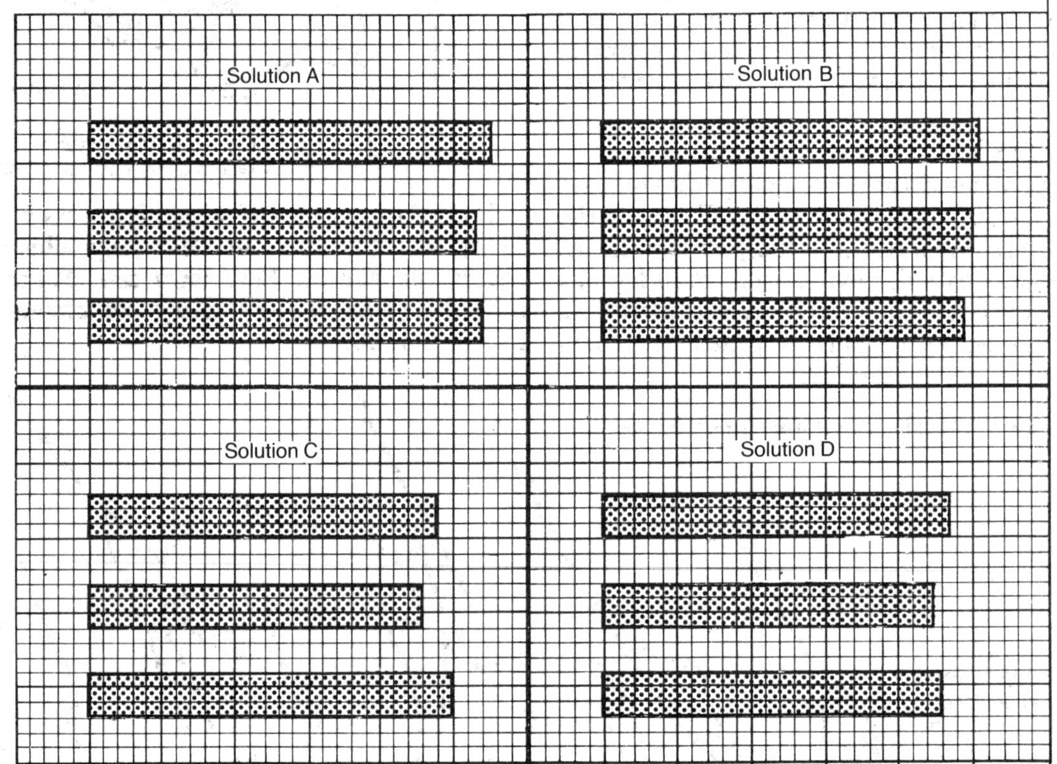

Figure 2.16

TOPIC 3

CELLS AT WORK

Unicellular organisms are made of only one cell. This cell does all the jobs needed to keep it alive. Most of these tiny organisms can only be seen with a microscope.

AMOEBA

Amoeba is a very simple unicellular animal (figure 3.1.). You can find it on mud at the bottom of ponds and in sewage filters. Amoeba looks like a drop of the runny part of a raw egg.Amoeba moves, feeds, respires, reproduces, excretes, grows and is sensitive.

Movement

A bulge called a *pseudopodium* pushes out and the cytoplasm flows into it. When all the cytoplasm has run into the pseudopodium, the amoeba will have moved. Pseudopodia can push out in any direction from anywhere on an amoeba. This is called amoeboid movement. (Figure 3.2.)

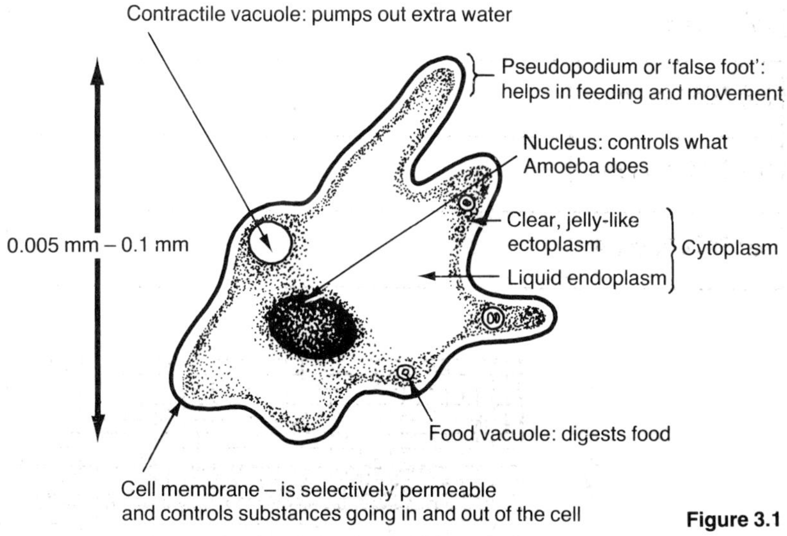

Contractile vacuole: pumps out extra water
Pseudopodium or 'false foot': helps in feeding and movement
Nucleus: controls what Amoeba does
Clear, jelly-like ectoplasm
Liquid endoplasm
Cytoplasm
0.005 mm – 0.1 mm
Food vacuole: digests food
Cell membrane – is selectively permeable and controls substances going in and out of the cell

Figure 3.1

Endoplasm is a liquid which flows easily. Ectoplasm is a kind of clear jelly which covers the animal. Ectoplasm can change into endoplasm and endoplasm can change into ectoplasm.

Figure 3.2 Watching amoeba move from above

Direction of movement of amoeba
Streaming movements of the endoplasm
Pseudopodia
1.
2.
3.
4.
5.

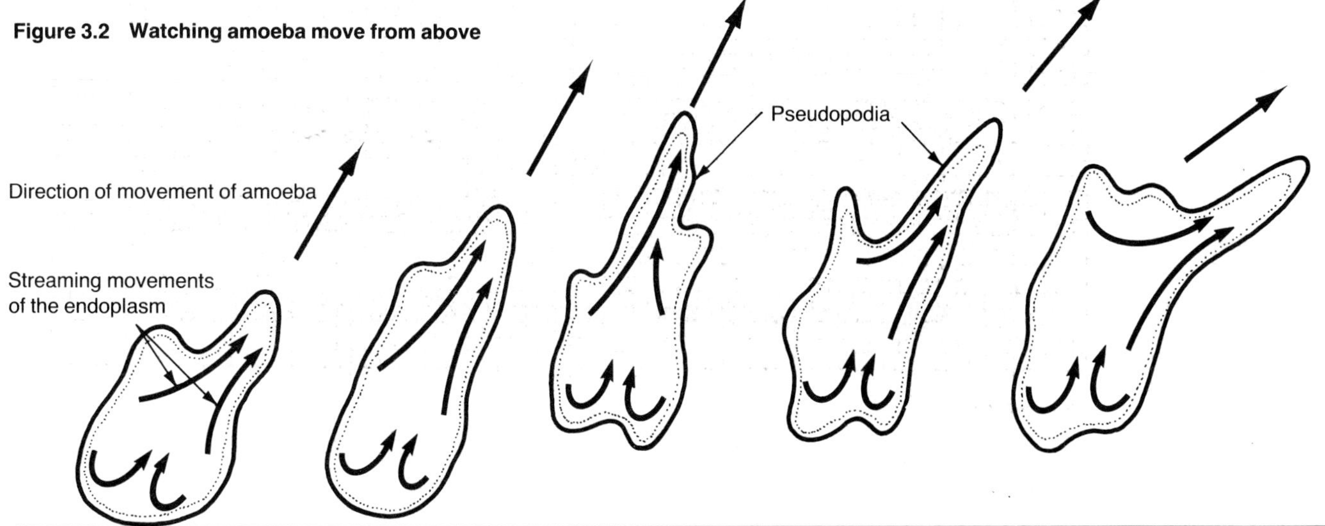

Endoplasm flows into a pseudopodium and changes to ectoplasm when it touches water. This happens at the tip of the pseudopodium where endoplasm spurts out like a fountain and then sets like a jelly.

Feeding

Amoeba feeds on bacteria, microscopic algae and small unicellular organisms. Amoeba surrounds its food with pseudopodia and forms a *food vacuole* around it. If you drip paste (the 'amoeba') over a blob of plasticine (the 'food') the paste flows around the plasticine. Amoeba feeds like this. Chemicals from the cytoplasm surround the food and digest it. The Amoeba absorbs the digested food and leaves the waste food behind when it moves away. (See figure 3.3.)

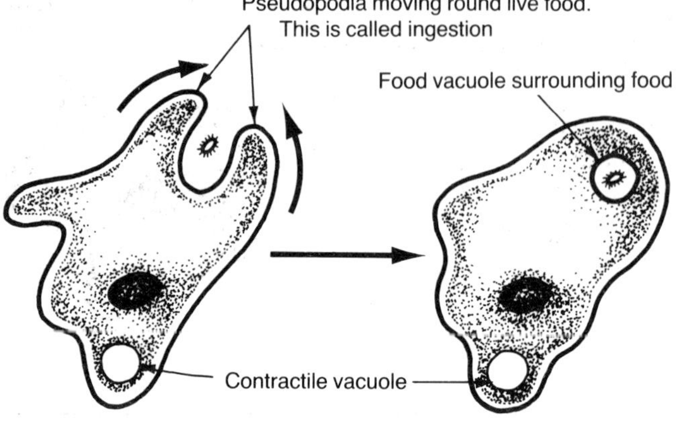

Figure 3.3

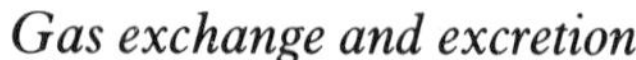

Gas exchange and excretion

Both gas exchange and excretion in Amoeba happen by diffusion. An Amoeba needs oxygen to set free the energy in its food. This is called respiration. Oxygen diffuses into Amoeba from the higher concentration of oxygen in the water (figure 3.4a).

An Amoeba makes waste substances during its life. These wastes must be removed (or excreted). This is called excretion. Waste substances such as carbon dioxide diffuse out of Amoeba from the higher concentration of carbon dioxide inside the animal (figure 3.4b).

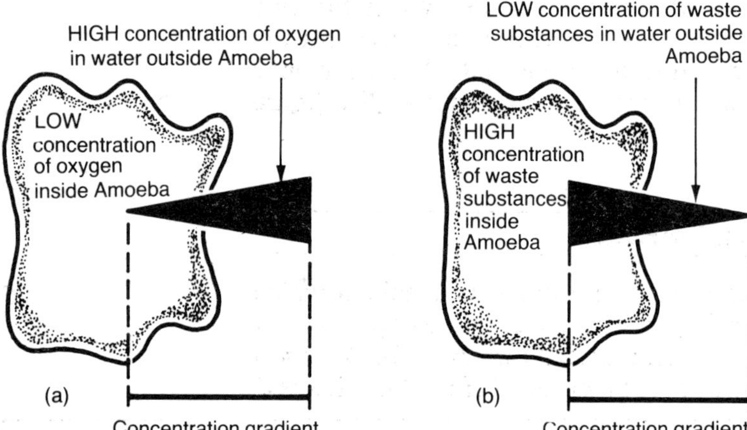

Figure 3.4

The contractile vacuole

What flows into Amoeba by osmosis. This water must be pumped out, or the cell will 'flood'. The water drains into a *contractile vacuole*, which gets bigger as more water flows in. The contractile vacuole bursts like a pricked balloon when it is full and the water is pumped out. The contractile vacuole then starts to grow again. Getting rid of extra water like this is called *osmo-regulation*.

In figure 3.5 an Amoeba is drawn from the side as it moves over some mud. It shows how an Amoeba might look to a bacterium that is just about to be eaten! The arrows

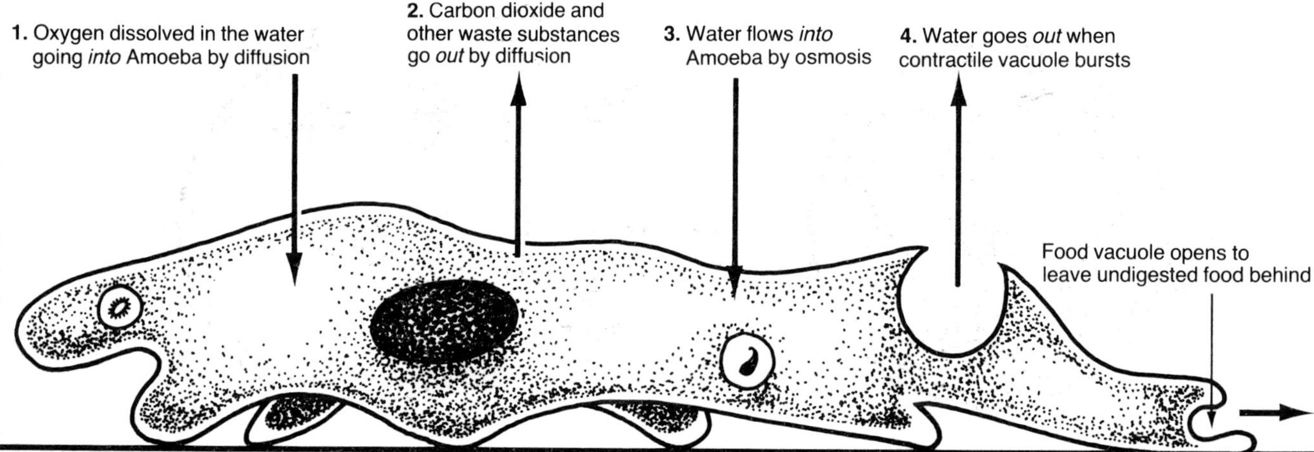

Figure 3.5

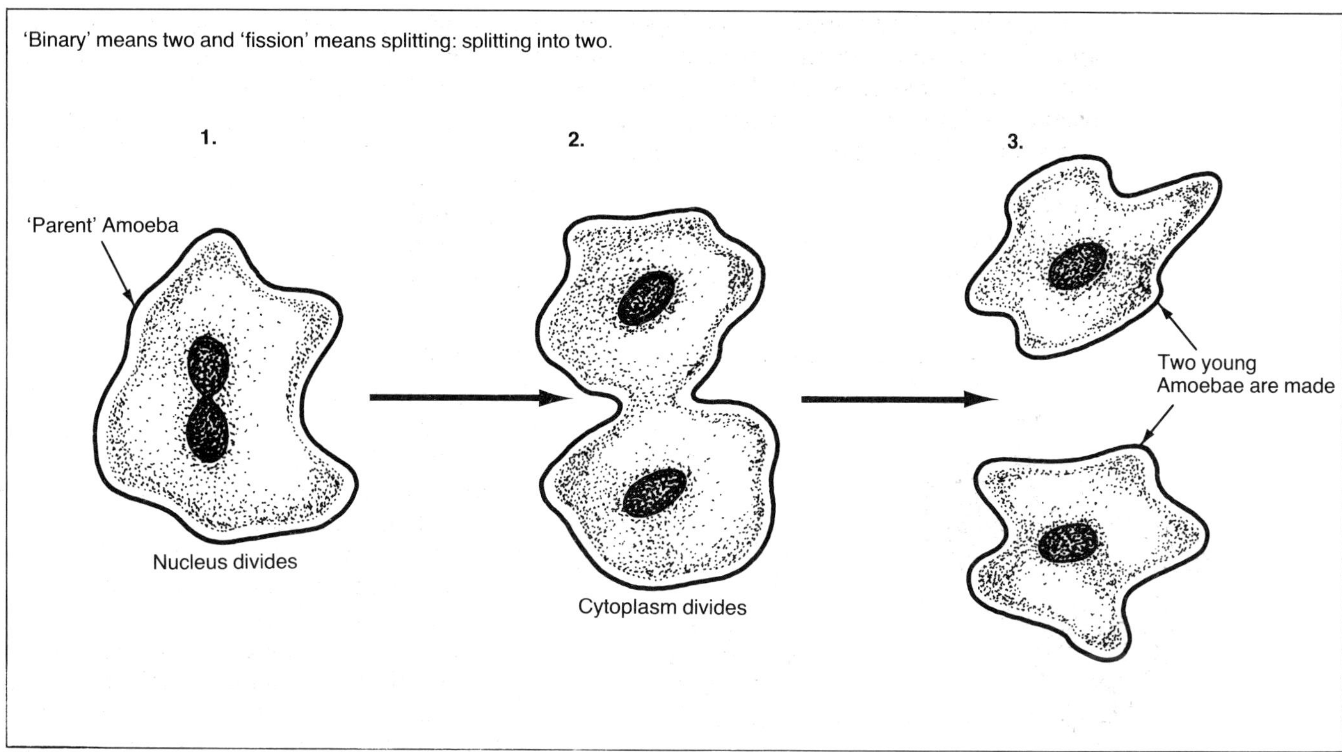

Figure 3.6 Binary fission in Amoeba

show how substances are exchanged with the water.
(bacterium = singular; bacteria = plural)

Reproduction

A well-fed Amoeba reproduces by splitting into two halves. The nucleus divides first and the cytoplasm divides later. In this way the 'parent' Amoeba makes two smaller Amoebae. This kind of asexual reproduction is called binary fission. (Figure 3.6.)

If there is not enough water or if the temperature rises too high, an Amoeba will make a cyst. This is a tough coat around the outside of the animal. Inside the cyst a lot of small Amoebae are made. When the cyst reaches better conditions it bursts and the small Amoebae come out. The wind may blow the cyst to another pond. (See figure 3.7.)

PARAMECIUM

Paramecium is a unicellular animal which lives in puddles, ponds and sewage filters. It is more complicated than Amoeba. It swims using short hairs called *cilia*. The cilia also

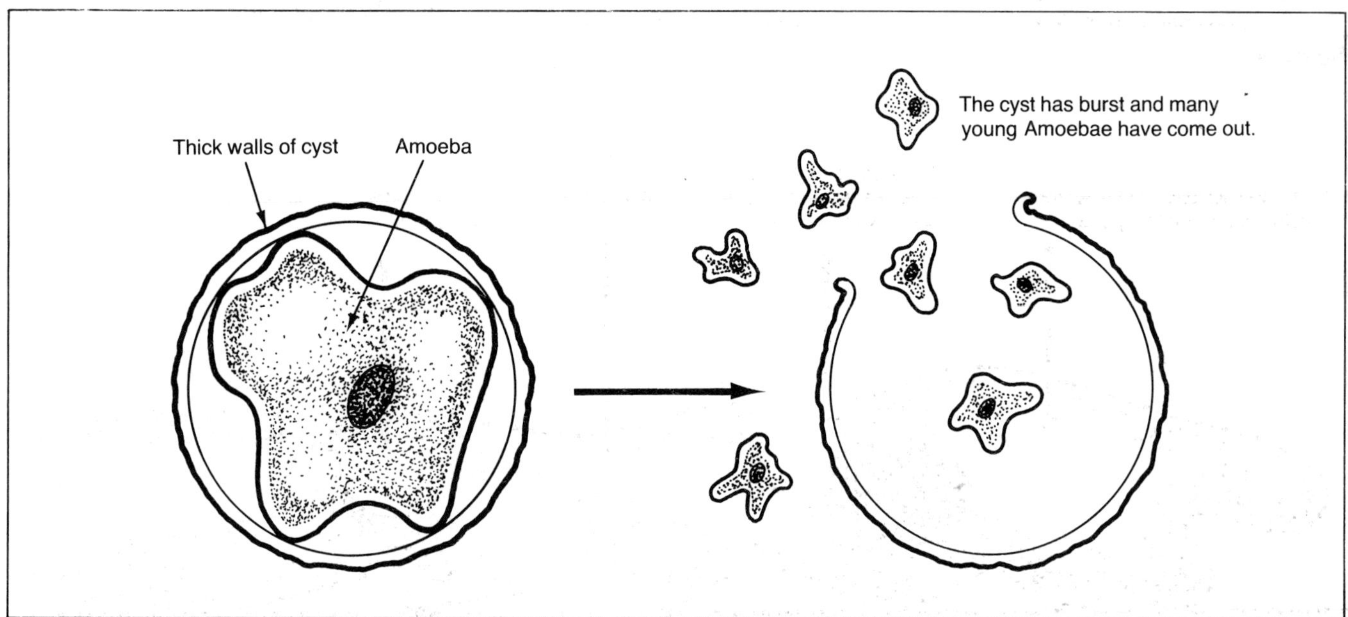

Figure 3.7 How Amoeba makes a cyst

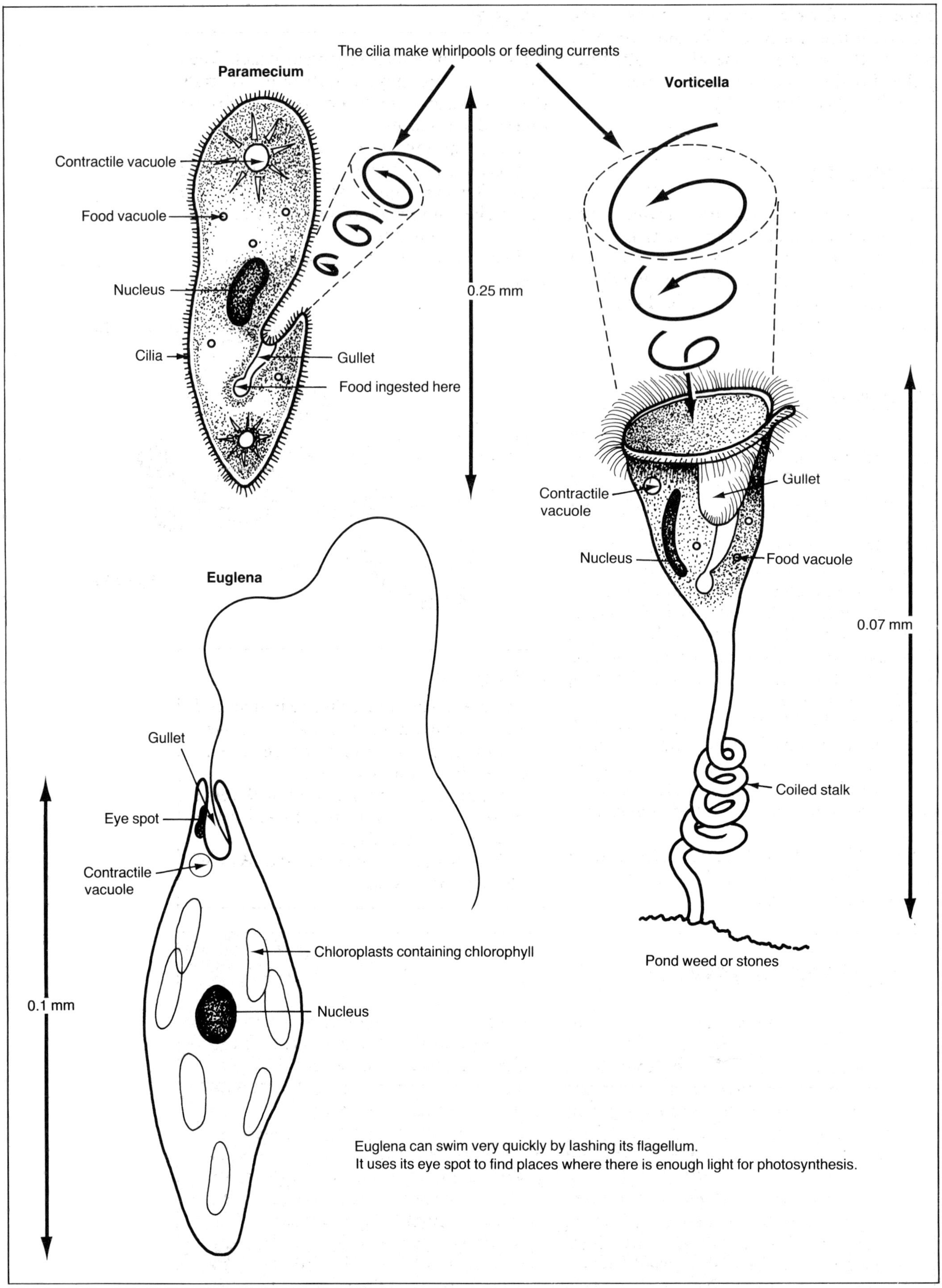

Figure 3.8 Some unicellular organisms

make a small whirlpool which sucks in the bacteria it uses for food. The food can only get into the animal at one place, called the gullet. Food vacuoles are made at the end of the gullet. (See figure 3.8.)

VORTICELLA

Vorticella is a unicellular animal which lives in ponds and sewage filters. It is fixed to weeds or stones by a long stalk. The stalk can be coiled like a telephone cable. Vorticella uses cilia to suck in the bacteria that are its food. (See figure 3.8.)

EUGLENA

Euglena is a unicellular organism which you can find in ponds, puddles and sewage filters. Sometimes there are so many that they make the water green. Euglena is not really an animal or a plant. It is a mixture of both. It swims by using a long whip or *flagellum*. Movement like this is usually found only in animals. (See figure 3.8.)

Some kinds of Euglena feed like green plants by using photosynthesis. In sunlight they make starch from carbon dioxide and water. Another name for this kind of feeding is *holophytic nutrition*.

Other kinds of Euglena feed by absorbing substances dissolved in the water. These dissolved substances come from dead animals and plants. This kind of feeding does not need light and is called *saprophytic nutrition*.

Some kinds of Euglena can take in solid food. This is how most animals feed and is called *holozoic nutrition*.

YEAST

Yeast is a unicellular organism which feeds by using saprophytic nutrition. It puts digestive juices onto its food and absorbs the digested substances.

Yeast reproduces asexually by budding. New cells grow as small buds from the parent cells. This can happen so quickly that one cell makes thousands of new cells in a few days! (See figure 3.9.)

Yeast is important in making beer and bread.

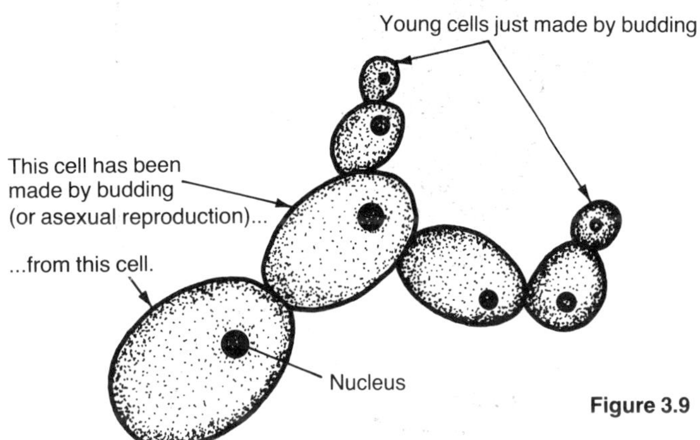

Figure 3.9

Fancy that!

Some Amoebae cause disease in man and animals. One kind of Amoeba can live in our digestive system, where it can cause ulcers and dysentery.

Damp moss from a wall will often produce a lot of Amoebae if you leave it in water for a few days!

The white 'powder' on the skin of black grapes is yeast!

Summary

Amoeba, *Paramecium*, *Euglena*, *Vorticella* and *yeast* are *unicellular* organisms. All the jobs needed to keep these organisms alive are done by one cell. The cells of each of these organisms are very different from each other. They move, feed and reproduce in different ways.

Amoeba changes shape as it moves, using *pseudopodia*. It is an animal which feeds on bacteria and unicellular organisms. Its food is digested in *food vacuoles* and a *contractile vacuole* gets rid of extra water. This is called *osmo-regulation*. Amoeba reproduces by splitting into two (*binary fission*). It can make a *cyst* if conditions get too difficult.

Paramecium swims using *cilia*. It is an animal and feeds on bacteria.

Euglena swims using a *flagellum*. Some kinds of Euglena have *holophytic* nutrition and others have *saprophytic* or *holozoic* nutrition. Euglena seems to be partly an animal and partly a plant.

Yeast is a *fungus* which feeds using saprophytic nutrition. It reproduces by *budding*. All unicellular organisms use *diffusion* for gas exchange and excretion.

Important words

Pseudopodium	part of an Amoeba used for feeding and moving (plural: pseudopodia).
Food vacuole	a small space in the cytoplasm where food is digested.
Contractile vacuole	a large space in the cytoplasm which controls the amount of water in a cell.
Osmo-regulation	the control of the amount of water in a cell.
Cilia	are like hairs and wave backwards and forwards to cause movement.
Flagellum	a long thread growing from a cell; used to cause movement (plural: flagella).
Holophytic nutrition	feeding like green plants; making food from simple substances.
Holozoic nutrition	feeding like animals; eating food and digesting it inside the body.
Saprophytic nutrition	feeding like fungi on dead or decaying organisms.

Things to do

Make a model Amoeba.

You will need:

- two pieces of cardboard, 7 cm x 9 cm, 1-2 mm thick
- one piece of polythene, 7 cm x 9 cm
- four paper clips
- sharp scissors
- Vaseline
- clear-setting glue (Gloy P.V.A. is suitable)

What to do

1. Draw the outline of an Amoeba on one piece of cardboard

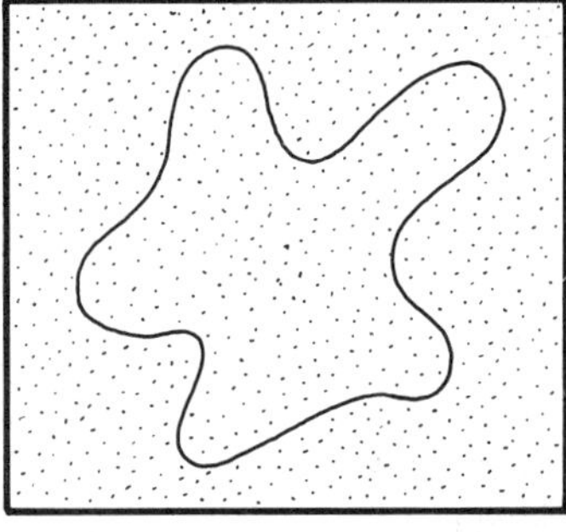

2. Cut the shape from the *middle* of the card – do not cut around the outside

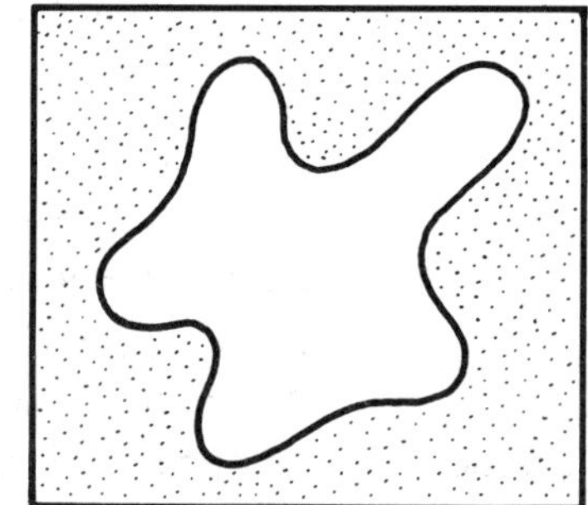

3. Smear Vaseline over the cut edges and over one side of the card. Put the polythene on this side.

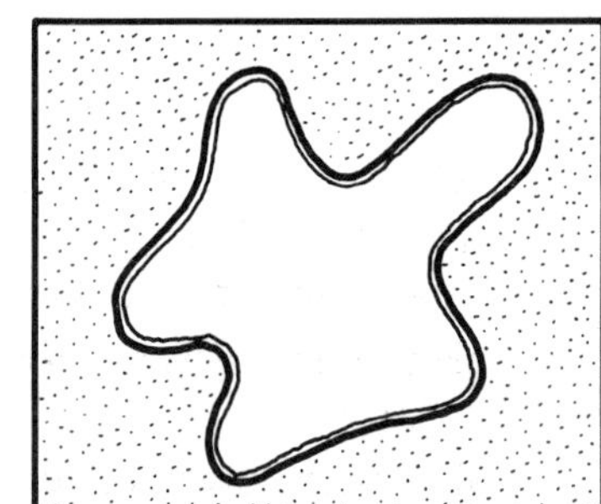

4. Place the other piece of card against the polythene.
5. Fasten the 'sandwich' with paper clips.
6. Pour a *thin* layer of glue into the shape.
7. Put a small circle of polythene into the glue. This is the 'contractile vacuole'.

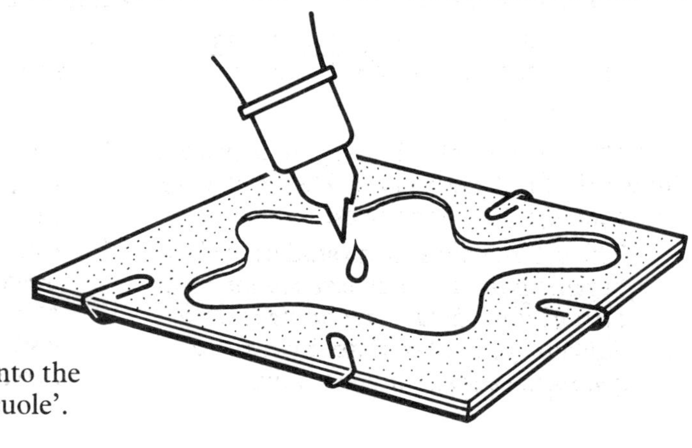

8. Put one or two smaller paper circles into the glue. These are 'food vacuoles'. The discs from a paper punch are good for this.
9. Put a disc of a different colour into the glue for the 'nucleus'.
10. Now put a thin layer of glue on top of the discs.
11. Leave the model to set for 24 hours when the glue should have cleared.
12. *Carefully* remove the glue from the mould. You may need scissors to cut the mould away.
13. Now stick the model Amoeba into your book with a little more of the same glue. Label all the parts.

Questions

A.

Write out each sentence in your book. Fill in the missing words from those in the box. Some words may be used more than once.

osmo-regulation — ectoplasm — flagellum — ingestion — higher — holozoic — food vacuoles — endoplasm — holophytic — pseudopodia — bacteria — contractile vacuole — saprophytic — fungus — cilia — diffusion — carbon dioxide — osmosis — holozoic — asexual reproduction

1. Amoeba moves using ....
2. Amoeba uses a ...... to get rid of water.
3. Water goes into Amoeba by ....
4. ...... is how Amoeba controls the water inside it.
5. Cytoplasm in Amoeba is made of ...... and ....
6. ...... is a runny liquid but ...... is jelly-like.
7. Amoeba takes in food by ....
8. In Amoeba food is digested inside ....
9. Gas exchange and excretion in unicellular organisms happen by ....
10. There is a ...... concentration of oxygen in the water outside an Amoeba than there is inside it.
11. There is a ...... concentration of carbon dioxide inside an Amoeba than in the water outside.
12. ...... is a waste substance which diffuses out of Amoeba.
13. Paramecium swims using ....
14. Euglena swims using a ....
15. Paramecium feeds on ....
16. Paramecium, Amoeba and Vorticella all feed using ...... nutrition.
17. Different sorts of Euglena can feed like plants (...... nutrition), like fungi (...... nutrition) or like animals (...... nutrition).
18. Yeast is a ...... which feeds using ...... nutrition.
19. Yeast uses a kind of ...... called budding.
20. Amoeba uses a kind of ...... called binary fission.

B.

Put each of these parts of sentences into the correct order.

1.	when the animal just by asexual reproduction	divides into two Amoeba reproduces
2.	yeast makes new cells by a kind of	asexual reproduction budding which is
3.	all of them have to catch their food and Amoeba feed	using holozoic nutrition and Paramecium, Vorticella
4.	Euglena use saprophytic nutrition and absorb dissolved substances	from their surroundings yeast and some kinds of

C.

Copy this into your book using another word (or words) for those *in italics*. Do not change the meaning of the sentences.

1. The cell membrance around unicellular organisms is *able to let some substances go through it but holds other substances back*.
2. Amoeba gets rid of water by using *a contractile vacuole to pump it out*.
3. Although unicellular organisms are *very small* they can be seen by using *an instrument which makes them look bigger*.
4. Gas exchange and excretion in unicellular organisms happen by *oxygen, carbon dioxide and wastes moving from a higher concentration to a lower concentration*.

D.

1. Write down two ways in which you think Paramecium is more complicated than Amoeba.
2. Name one sort of organism which Amoeba, Paramecium and Vorticella all use for food.
3. What is another name for photosynthesis?
4. Name all the organisms in this topic which use (a) holozoic nutrition, (b) saprophytic nutrition.

E.

1. Copy figure 3.9 into your book and label the parts (a) to (d).

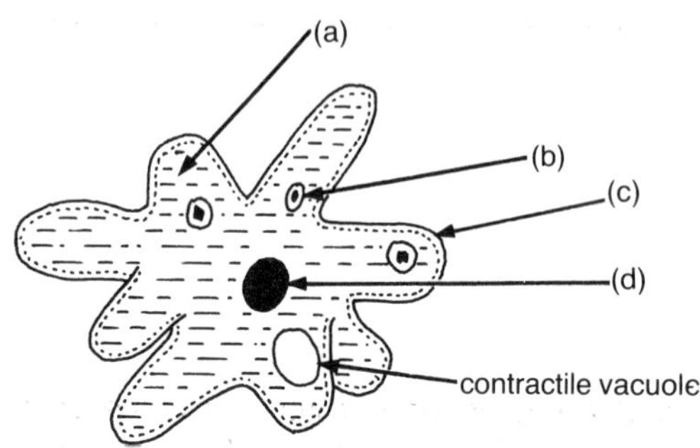

Figure 3.9

2. Explain why Amoeba needs a contractile vacuole.
3. The graph shows the rate at which the contractile vacuole empties when an organism such as Amoeba is placed in salt water of increasing concentrations. From the graph, work out the strength of the salt solution which results in the Amoeba emptying its contractile vacuole 240 times in an hour. Why did the contractile vacuole not empty when the solution was more than 3.5% salt?

(SREB)

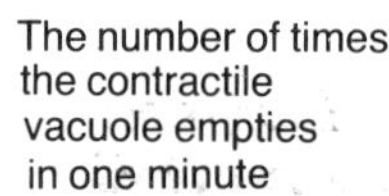

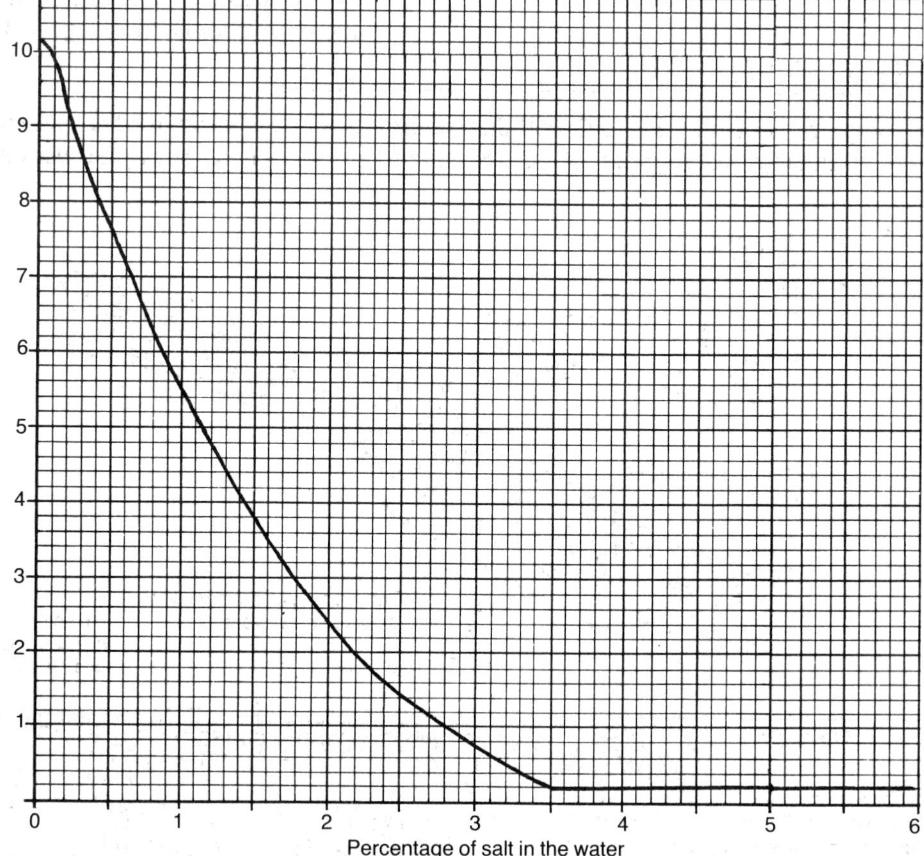

Figure 3.10

TOPIC 4

SIMPLE PLANTS

Amoeba, Paramecium and yeast are simple organisms made of one cell (unicellular). Multicellular organisms are made of many cells and often have cells adapted for doing different jobs.

SPIROGYRA

Spirogyra is a simple multicellular plant which belongs to a group of plants called *algae*. It floats at the surface of the water in ponds and ditches. It is made of bright green threads or filaments. Each filament looks like a piece of cotton and is made of long rows of cells. Each cell in a filament is the same.

Each cell could live by itself if it was cut off from a filament. The filaments have no roots and do not move. (See figure 4.1.)

Feeding

Spirogyra feeds by *photosynthesis*. Like other green plants, Spirogyra uses its chlorophyll

Figure 4.1

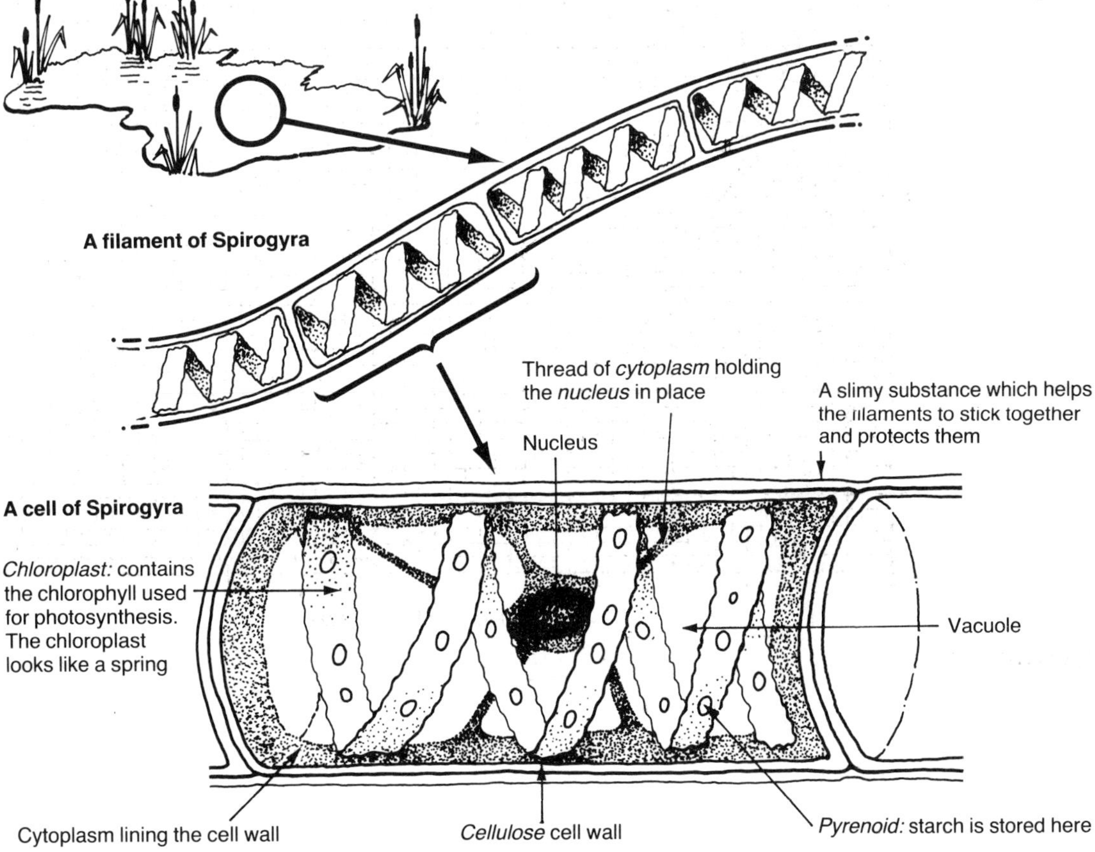

A filament of Spirogyra

A cell of Spirogyra

Chloroplast: contains the chlorophyll used for photosynthesis. The chloroplast looks like a spring

Thread of *cytoplasm* holding the *nucleus* in place

Nucleus

A slimy substance which helps the filaments to stick together and protects them

Vacuole

Cytoplasm lining the cell wall

Cellulose cell wall

Pyrenoid: starch is stored here

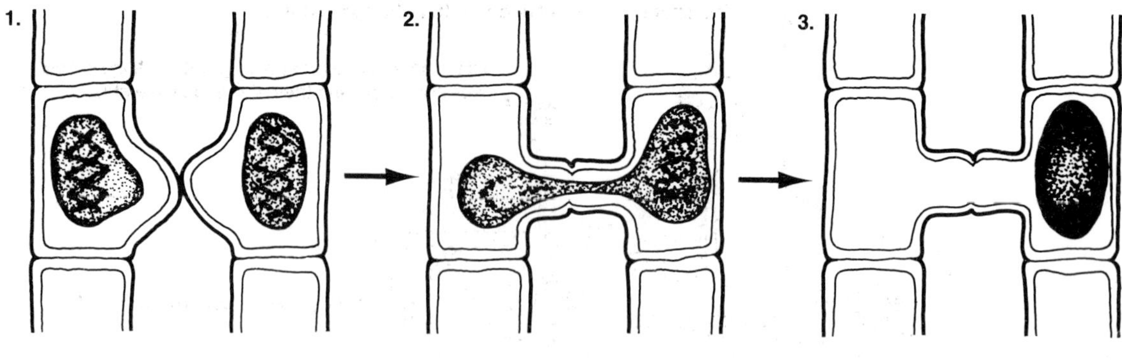

Figure 4.2

to catch the energy of sunlight. This energy is used to make starch from carbon dioxide and water.

Reproduction

Spirogyra reproduces *sexually* by conjugation. (See figure 4.2.)

The zygospore may not grow for a long time and is not affected by bad conditions. When conditions in the pool are good the zygospore splits open (germinates) and a new filament grows out. (See figure 4.3.)

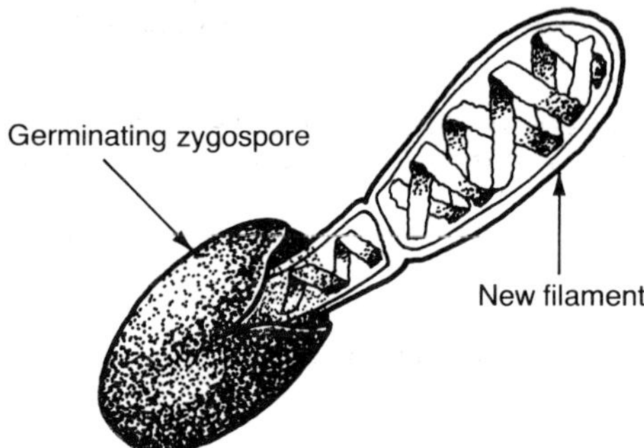

Figure 4.3

MOSSES

Mosses are green multicellular plants which live in wet places on land. Look for them in the joins between paving stones, on walls and on wet soil. Most of them have stems no longer than 5 cm.

Unlike Spirogyra mosses have cells adapted to do different jobs. Some cells help to make leaves and others help to make simple roots (rhizoids). Other cells help to make the reproductive organs.

Mosses have male and female sexual reproductive organs. The male organs make sperms which swim to the female organs and fertilise the eggs. The fertilised eggs grow into spore cases on long stalks. *Spores* are set free from the spore cases and grow into green threads. New moss plants grow from the threads. (See figure 4.4.)

Mosses need to live in damp places so that their sperms can swim in water.

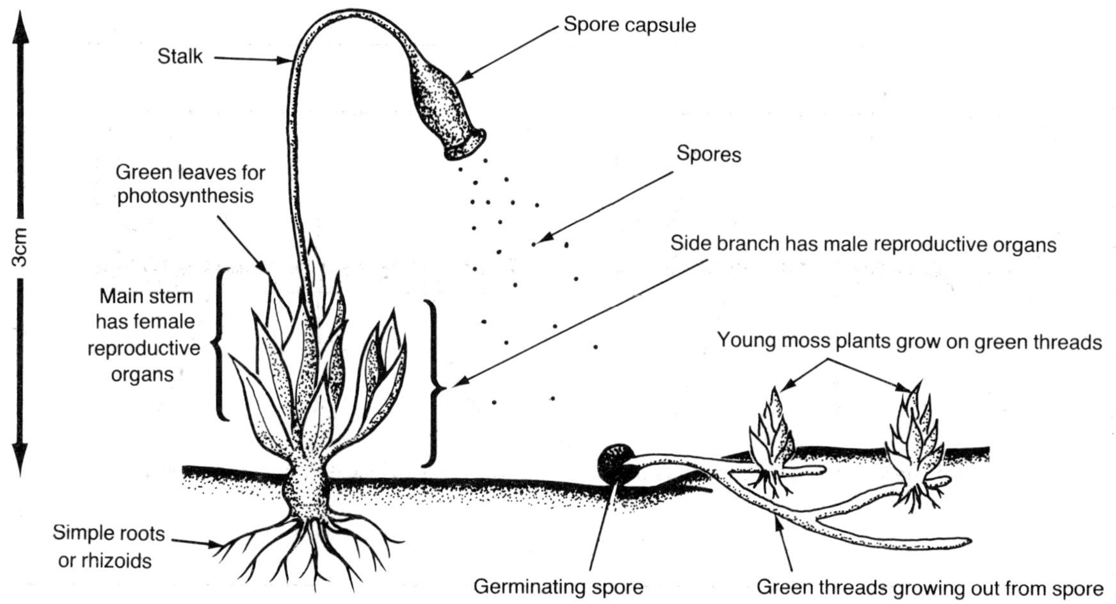

Figure 4.4 A moss plant

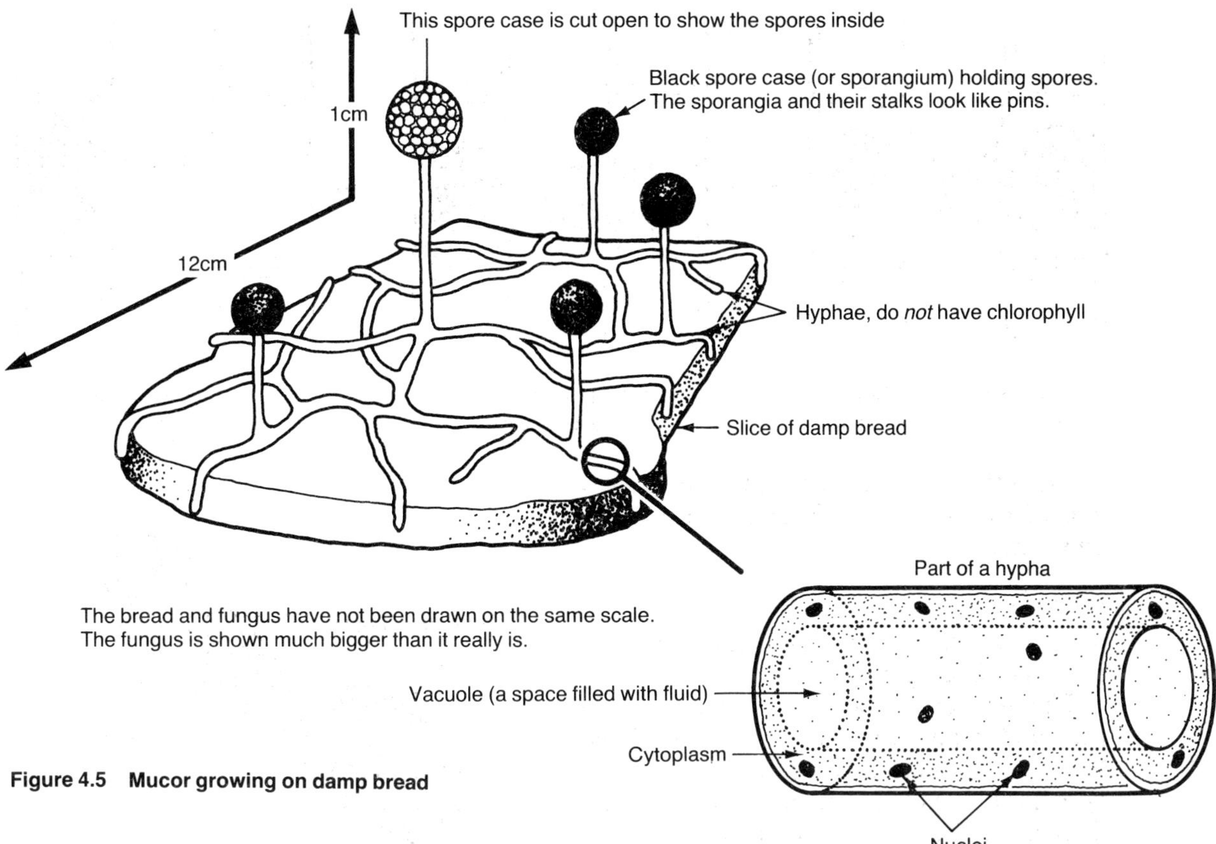

Figure 4.5 Mucor growing on damp bread

MUCOR

Mucor is a small, fluffy, white *fungus*, sometimes called pin mould. It grows on damp bread, leather and many other things.

Mucor is made of many small threads called *hyphae*. Each hypha is too small for you to see it without a microscope. The *mycelium* is the name we give to all the hyphae together. You can see the mycelium without a microscope. The mycelium grows in and on the food. (See figure 4.5.)

Feeding

Like all other fungi Mucor has no chlorophyll and it cannot feed by photosynthesis. Mucor is a *saprophyte*. Saprophytes feed on dead organisms by using chemicals called enzymes. The enzymes are set free on to the food and they digest it. The digested food is soaked up (or absorbed) by the hyphae. This is called extracellular digestion because it happens outside Mucor. (See figure 4.6.)

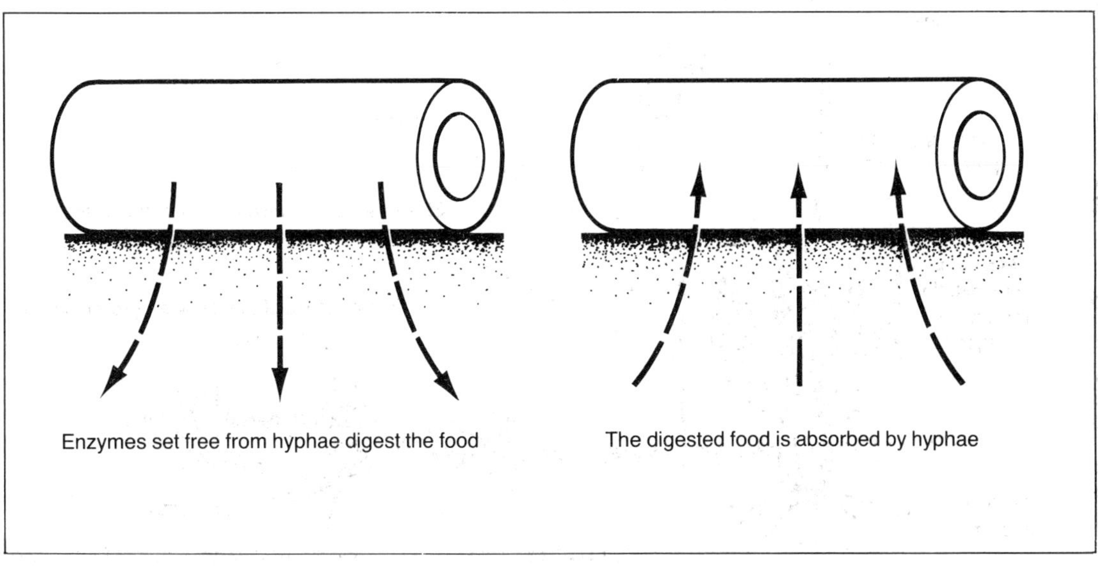

Figure 4.6

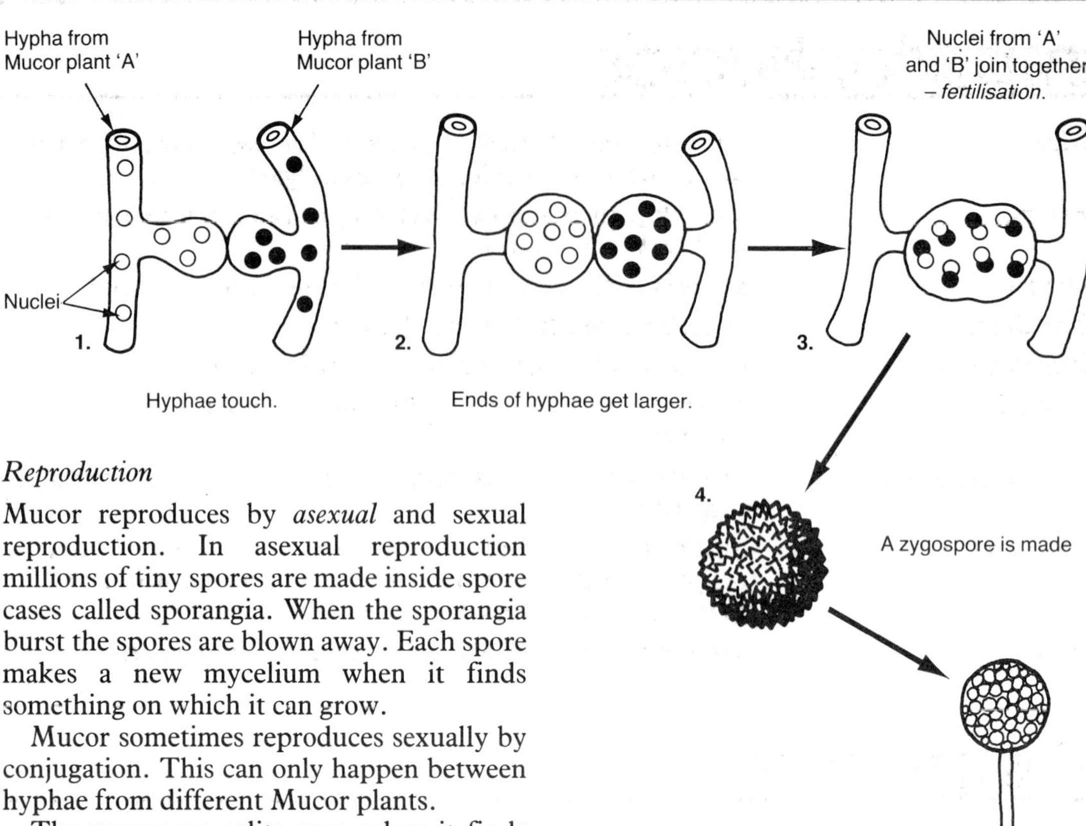

Figure 4.7 Sexual reproduction in Mucor

Reproduction

Mucor reproduces by *asexual* and sexual reproduction. In asexual reproduction millions of tiny spores are made inside spore cases called sporangia. When the sporangia burst the spores are blown away. Each spore makes a new mycelium when it finds something on which it can grow.

Mucor sometimes reproduces sexually by conjugation. This can only happen between hyphae from different Mucor plants.

The zygospore splits open when it finds good conditions for growth. It makes a spore case with many spores inside. Each spore can grow into a new mycelium when it is set free from the spore case. (See figure 4.7.)

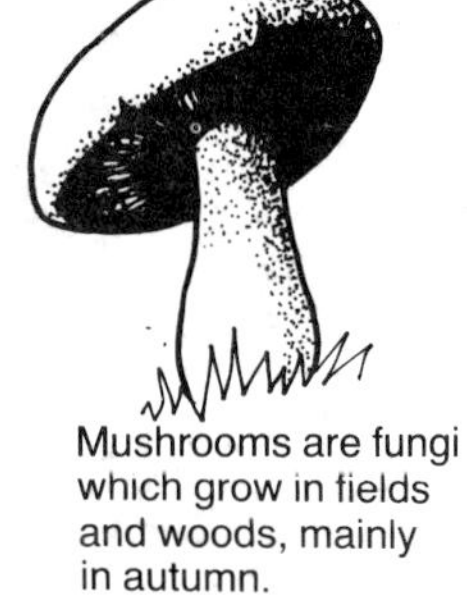

Mushrooms are fungi which grow in fields and woods, mainly in autumn.

Bracket fungus grows on trees

Figure 4.8

Saprophytes keep things going!

Saprophytes such as fungi (and some bacteria) are important organisms. Animals and plants are made of many chemical substances such as nitrogen, phosphorus and carbon. By feeding on dead animals and plants, saprophytes set free these substances. Other organisms can then use them to build-up their own bodies. (See figure 4.8.)

Many important antibiotics (substances which kill harmful bacteria) are made by saprophytic fungi. Saprophytic bacteria and fungi are important in sewage treatment. They change harmful substances in sewage to less harmful ones.

Summary

Many simple plants do not have proper roots, stems or leaves. They do not reproduce by using flowers like flowering plants. Most reproduce using *spores*. Some spores are made by *asexual reproduction* and others are made by *sexual reproduction*.

Some simple plants are *unicellular* and other are *multicellular*. Multicellular plants often have different cells which do different jobs.

Spirogyra is a multicellular *alga* but each cell does the same jobs. Spirogyra feeds by *photosynthesis* and reproduces by sexual reproduction.

Mosses live in wet places on land and feed by photosynthesis.

Mucor is a *fungus* which grows on damp bread etc. Mucor is a *saprophyte* and uses *enzymes* to digest its food. Mucor reproduces by asexual and sexual reproduction. Saprophytes are important because they cause decay.

Important words

Alga	a simple green plant, made of one cell or many cells, but which has no roots, stems or leaves (plural: algae).
Fungus	a simple plant which has no chlorophyll and which is made of hyphae (plural: fungi).
Hypha	a very small thread-like part of a fungus (plural: hyphae).
Mycelium	all the hyphae which make a fungus.
Photosynthesis	the way in which green plants make their food.
Saprophyte	an organism which feeds on dead or decaying animals and plants.
Asexual reproduction	making new organisms from one parent without using sex cells (eggs and sperms).
Sexual reproduction	making new organisms using two parents (a male and a female); the parents make sex cells (eggs and sperms) which join together to make a new organism.
Spore	a reproductive cell which can grow into a new organism.

Things to do

Make a model of a Spirogyra cell (see figure 4.9).

You will need:

- 3 pieces of clear cellulose acetate film (your teacher may use this for the overhead projector): 13 cm x 13 cm; 13 cm x 12 cm; 13 cm x 5 cm;
- 2 pieces of 'Clingfilm' about 5 cm^2 each
- Sellotape or clear-setting glue
- small piece of green tissue paper
- sharp scissors
- a spirit marker pen

1.

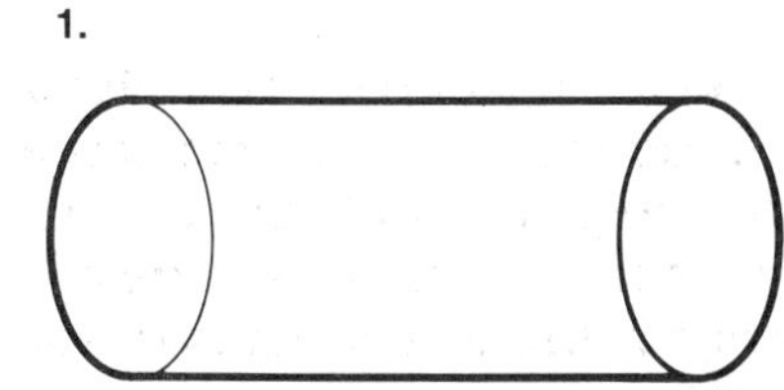

Take the 13 cm x 13 cm piece of cellulose acetate. Roll it up and glue it into a cylinder. This is the 'cellulose cell wall'.

2.

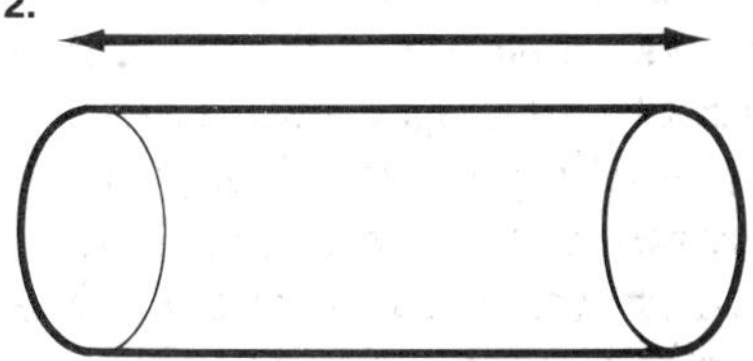

Do the same with the 13 cm x 12 cm piece of acetate. This is the 'cytoplasm' lining the cell wall.

3.

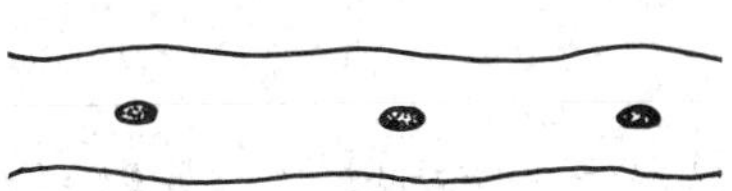

Cut a strip of green tissue paper 40 cm x 1.5 cm. Cut the edges as shown. Mark in some dots in pencil. This is the 'chloroplast' with 'pyrenoids'.

4.

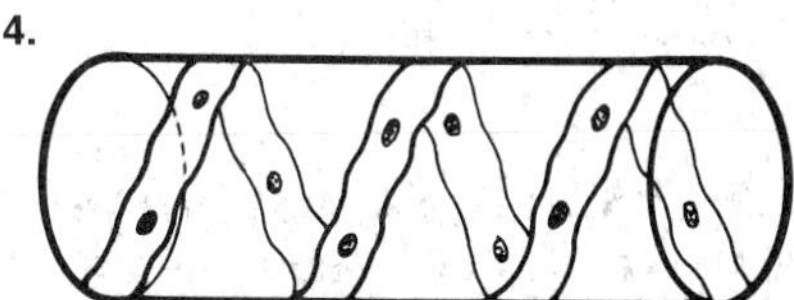

Glue the 'chloroplast' round the 'cytoplasm' from **2**.

5.
Carefully slide the 'cytoplasm' inside the 'cellulose cell wall'.

6.

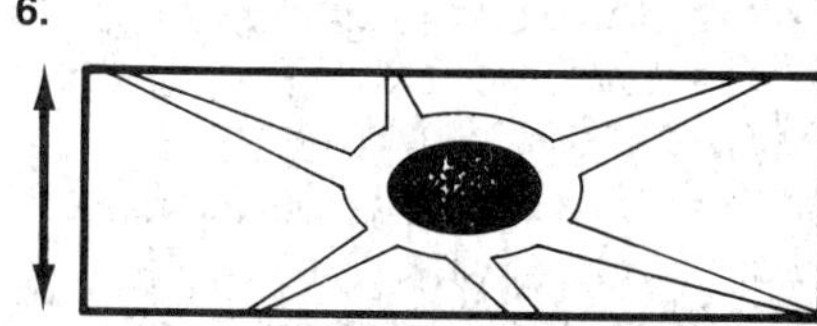

Draw this shape on the 13 cm x 5 cm piece of acetate using the spirit master pen. Cut round it carefully and push it inside the cell. It should stay upright in the middle of the cell. This is the 'nucleus and 'supporting cytoplasm'.

7.
Cover the ends of the cell with clingfilm. These are the 'end walls' of the cell. If several cells have been made they can be fixed together with Sellotape to make a 'filament'.

Figure 4.9

Make a moss garden. Mosses are attractive plants to look at. Make this moss garden and watch them grow!
You will need:
a wide-mouthed bottle (such as a large salad-cream jar)
some soil (potting compost is best)
a thin stick or wire
Collect as many different kinds of moss as you can. Collect them with soil still fixed to them. Put some soil into your bottle. If you lay the bottle on its side you can plant more mosses in it. Push the mosses into the soil with the stick.

It may help if you split the end of the stick. Make sure that the soil is damp but not soaked. Close the bottle with the lid or with Clingfilm and put it in the light. You should not have to water your moss garden. Put some small stones or clay animals in it.

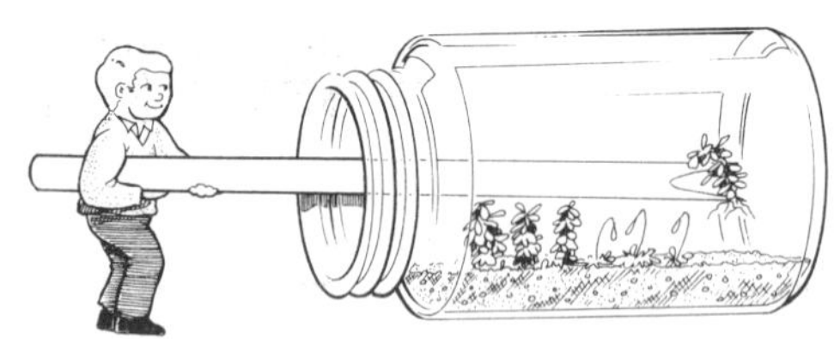

Questions

A.
Put each of these parts of sentences into the correct order.

1. different hyphae join together / nuclei from two / in mucor a zygospore / is made when
2. a new filament / Spirogyra grows into / in the right conditions / a zygospore of
3. in mosses spores are made / and grow into green threads / which make new moss plants / by sexual reproduction
4. Mucor grows into / with many spores inside / a zygospore of / a spore case

B.
1. Which of these organisms has cells adapted for doing different jobs: Amoeba, Spirogyra, yeast, mosses, Mucor?
2. What is a chloroplast and what does it do?
3. Explain why saprophytes are important.
4. What is the difference between: (a) a spore and a zygospore, (b) a hypha and a mycelium?
5. A strange new plant is found growing on the walls of a dark cave. It is white in colour and is made of tiny threads. What sort of plant is it? Give two reasons for your answer.

C. Experiment corner
1. Spirogyra gives off a gas when it is photosynthesising. Think how you could collect this gas to test if it is oxygen. Draw your apparatus and explain how it works.
2. How could you show that the spores of Mucor are carried from place to place by air currents? Write about how your experiment would work.
3. Suppose that you have two slices of bread. How could you use them to show that Mucor grows best on damp substances? Write about how you would set up your experiment.

D.
A housewife placed some damp bread in a bread bin. After a few days she noticed that the piece of bread was covered with a grey pin mould (Mucor).
1. Where did the mould come from?
2. Draw a diagram to show the structure of this type of mould. Label the spore cases (sporangia), hyphae and spores.
3. Explain why the piece of bread is likely to become smaller as the mould grows.
4. This mould can reproduce asexually.
(a) State the essential difference between asexual and sexual reproduction.
(b) State one advantage to the mould of producing a large number of spores.
5. Explain why it would be wise for the housewife to clean the bread bin thoroughly before placing fresh bread within it.

(EAEB)

TOPIC 5

THE STEM, ROOT AND LEAF

Flowering plants are made up of roots, stems, leaves and flowers. (See figure 5.1.)

THE STEM

Most stems grow upwards towards the light but some creep sideways over the soil and are called runners. Strawberry plants have runners. Other stems are found underground and never grow above the soil. Crocus stems are found underground. They are called corms.

Some stems, like those of beans and peas, cannot grow upwards by themselves. They need a support because they have no cells which give strength to the stem. Bean stems pull themselves up by twisting round the support. Peas have small shoots called tendrils which grip the support. (See figure 5.2.)

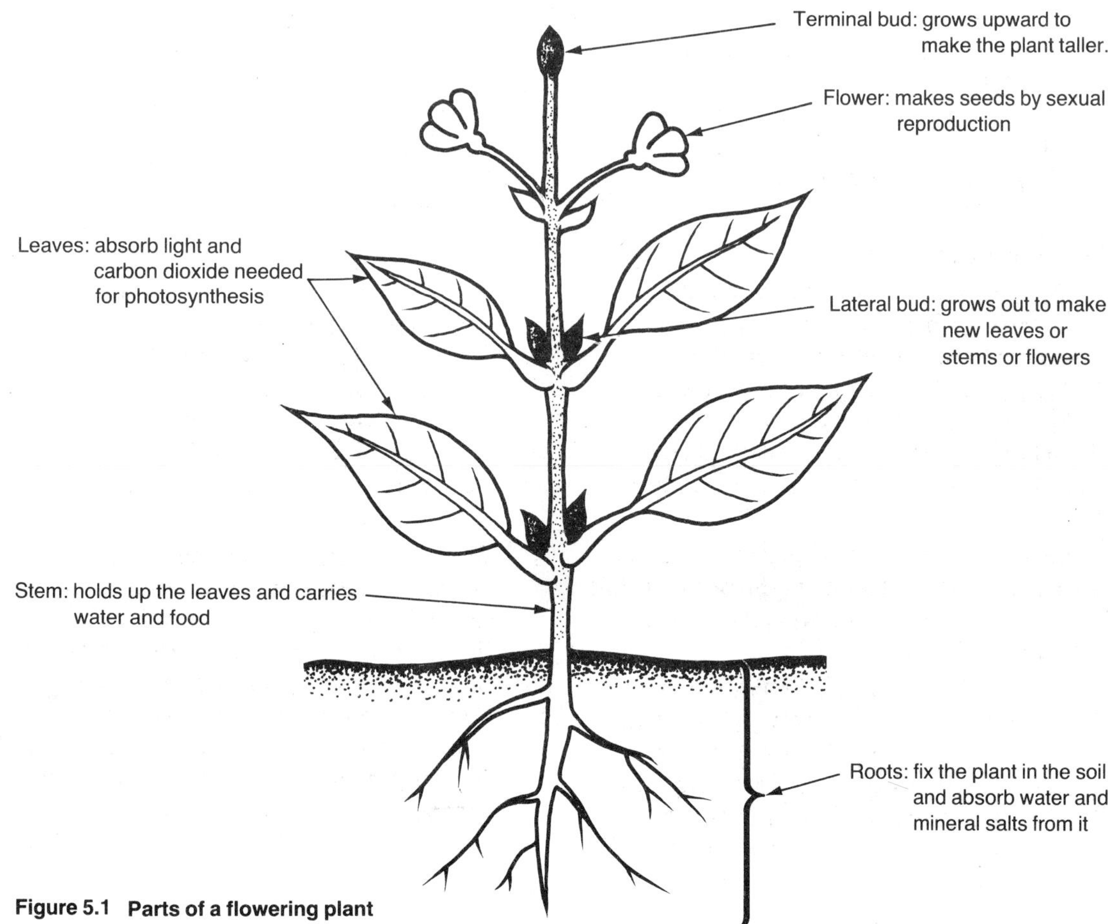

Figure 5.1 Parts of a flowering plant

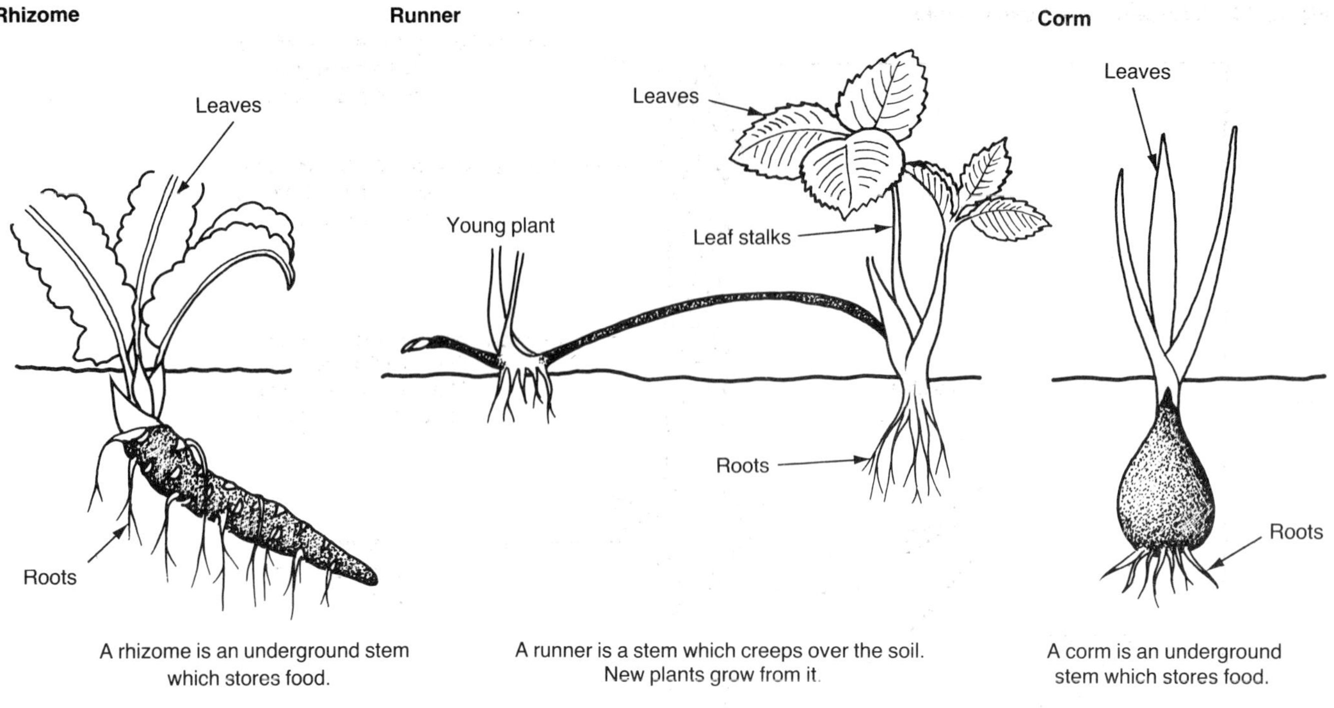

A rhizome is an underground stem which stores food.

A runner is a stem which creeps over the soil. New plants grow from it.

A corm is an underground stem which stores food.

A runner bean stem

Stem twisting round a stick

Bindweed climbing up a support. It has reached a height of about 2.5 metres. Does it climb in a clockwise or anticlockwise direction?

A pea stem

Tendrils twisting around a twig

Main stem

Figure 5.2 Different sorts of stems

Figure 5.3 A horse chestnut twig in winter

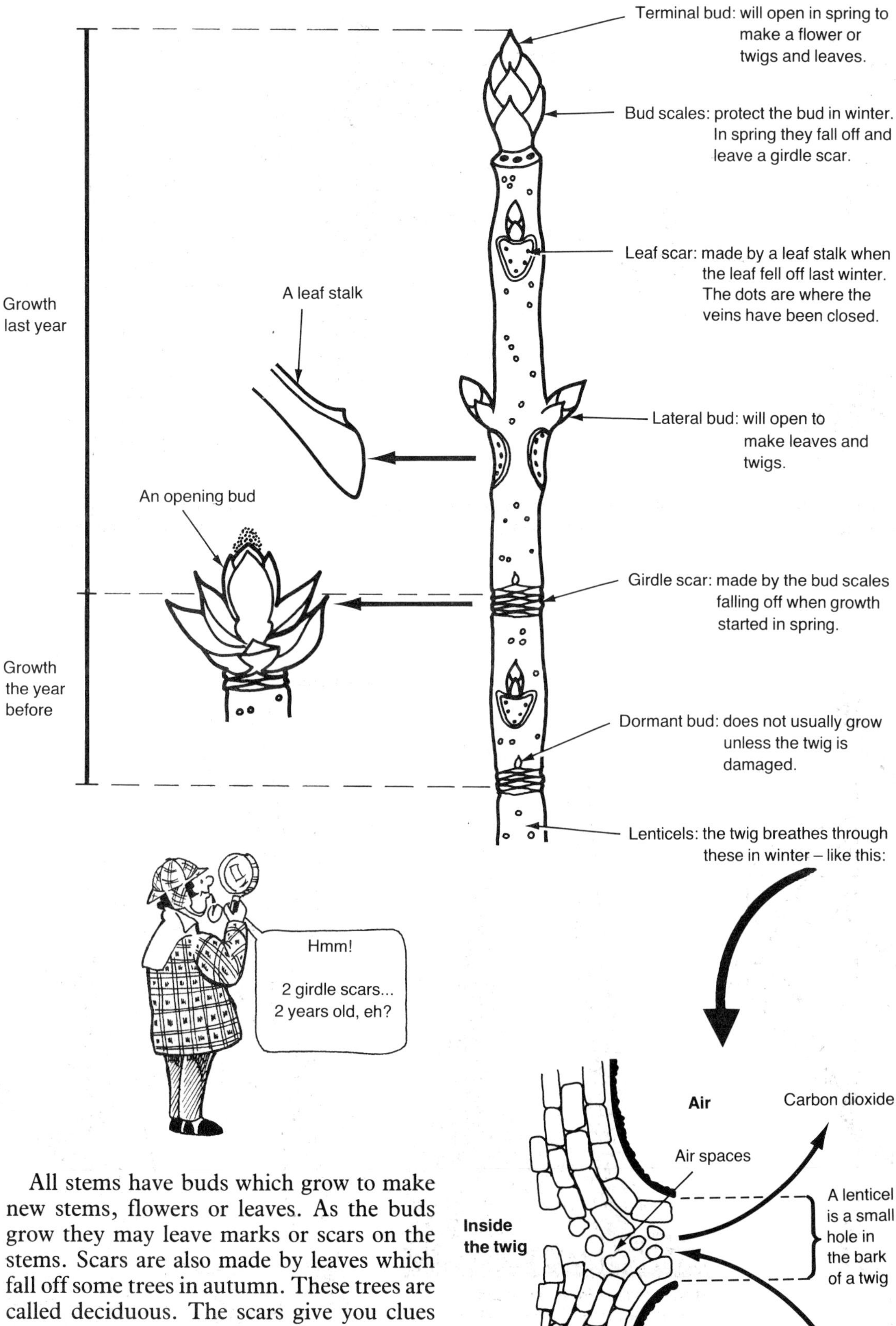

Figure 5.4 Section through a lenticel

All stems have buds which grow to make new stems, flowers or leaves. As the buds grow they may leave marks or scars on the stems. Scars are also made by leaves which fall off some trees in autumn. These trees are called deciduous. The scars give you clues about the age of a twig. (See figure 5.3.)

INSIDE A STEM

Stems do the important job of carrying water, minerals and sugar to other parts of the plant. They are carried inside small cells like tubes in the stem. The tubes are in groups called *vascular bundles*. Each vascular bundle has two sorts of tubes, called *xylem* and *phloem*. (See figure 5.5.)

When xylem and phloem tubes have been made they cannot divide to make new tubes. As the plant grows, new xylem and phloem tubes are made by the *cambium* instead.

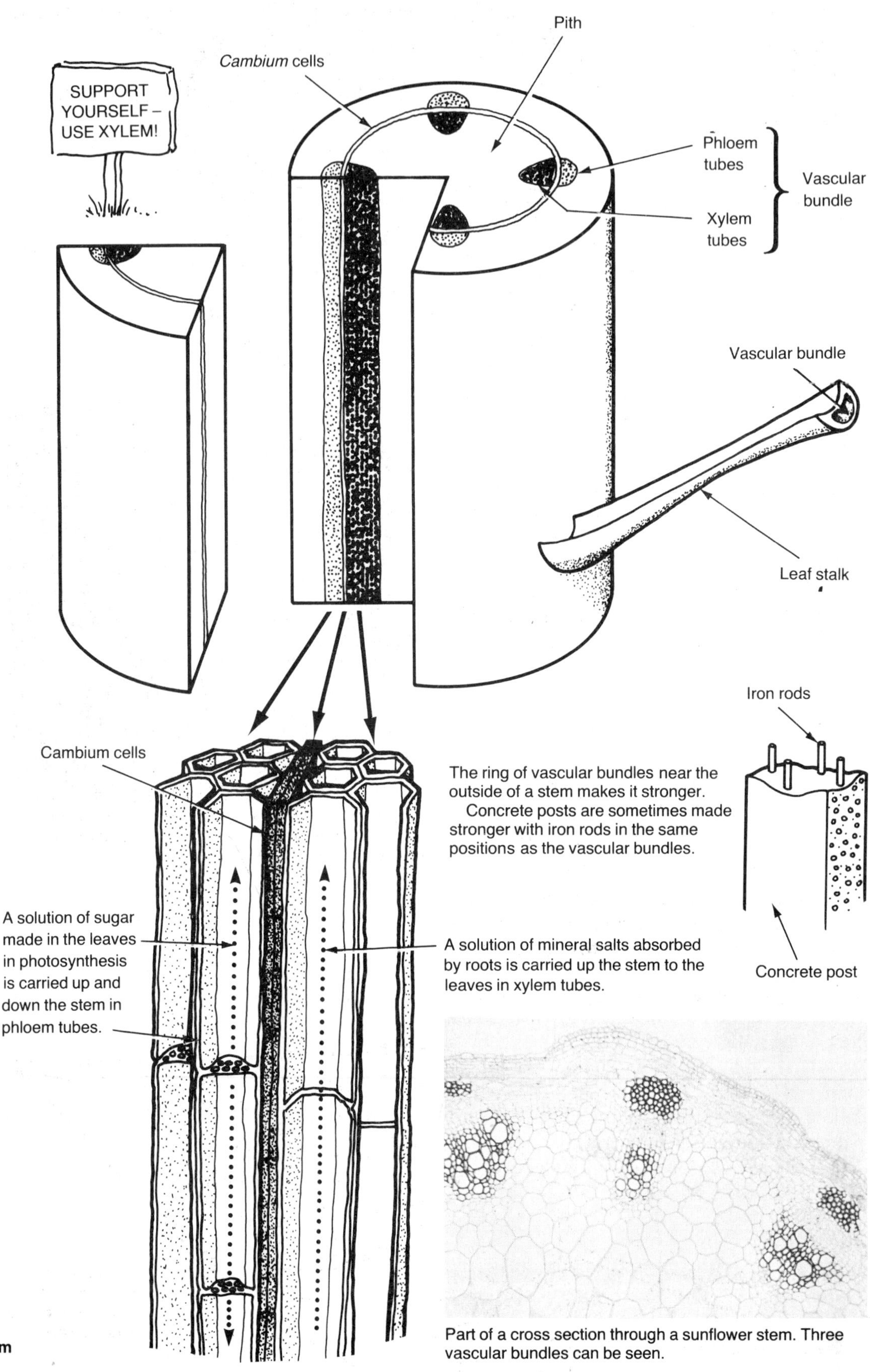

Part of a cross section through a sunflower stem. Three vascular bundles can be seen.

Figure 5.5 A plant stem

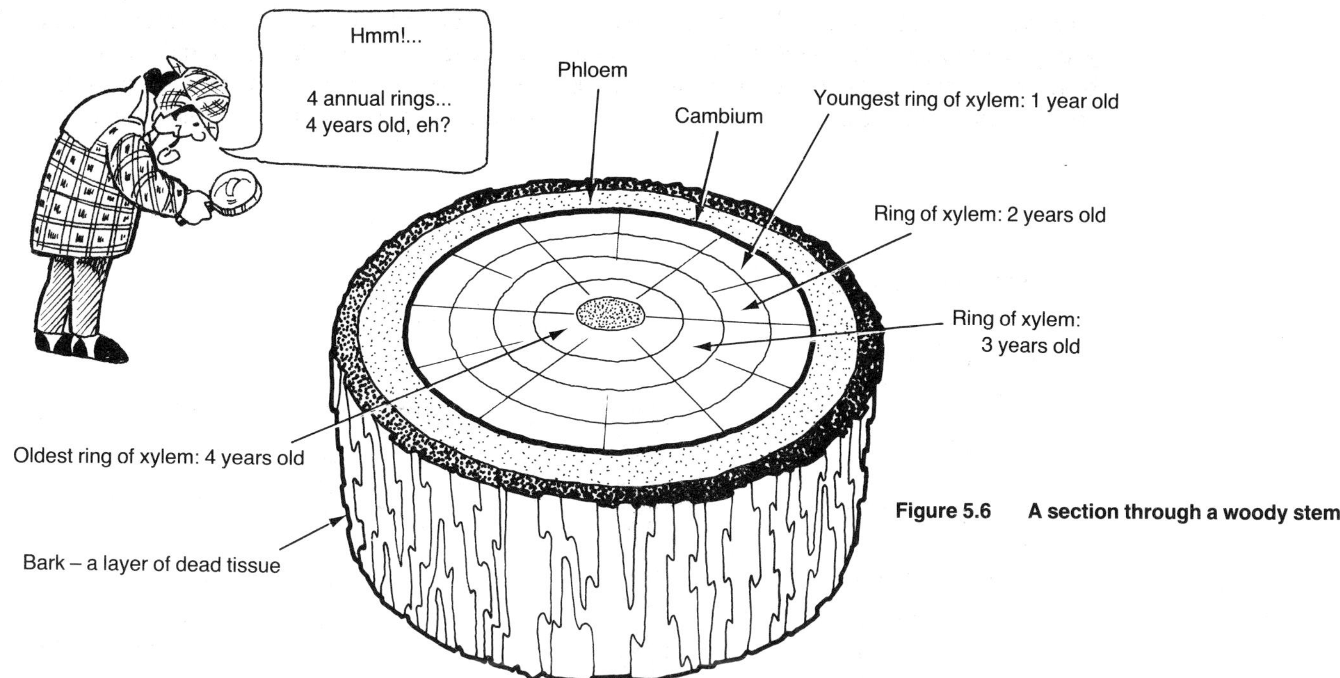

Figure 5.6 A section through a woody stem

WHAT HAPPENS AS STEMS GROW

The cambium makes one new ring of xylem and phloem tubes each year of growth. This makes the stem grow thicker and it is called *secondary thickening.*

The rings of xylem are called *annual rings*. By counting them you can find the age of a tree. The tree in figure 5.6 was four years old when it was cut down.

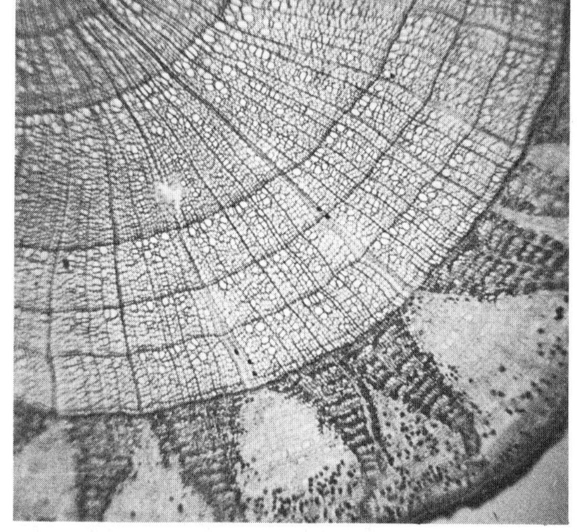

Part of a cross section through a lime twig. How many annual rings can you find? The phloem cells make up the cone shapes which you can see in the outer ring.

LEAVES

Leaves are thin, flat and green (figure 5.7). They are made of soft cells with thin walls. Leaves may be fixed to the stem with a stalk called a petiole. Leaves have three main jobs:

1. they absorb sunlight for photosynthesis,
2. they exchange oxygen and carbon dioxide with the air during photosynthesis and respiration,
3. they give off water during transpiration.

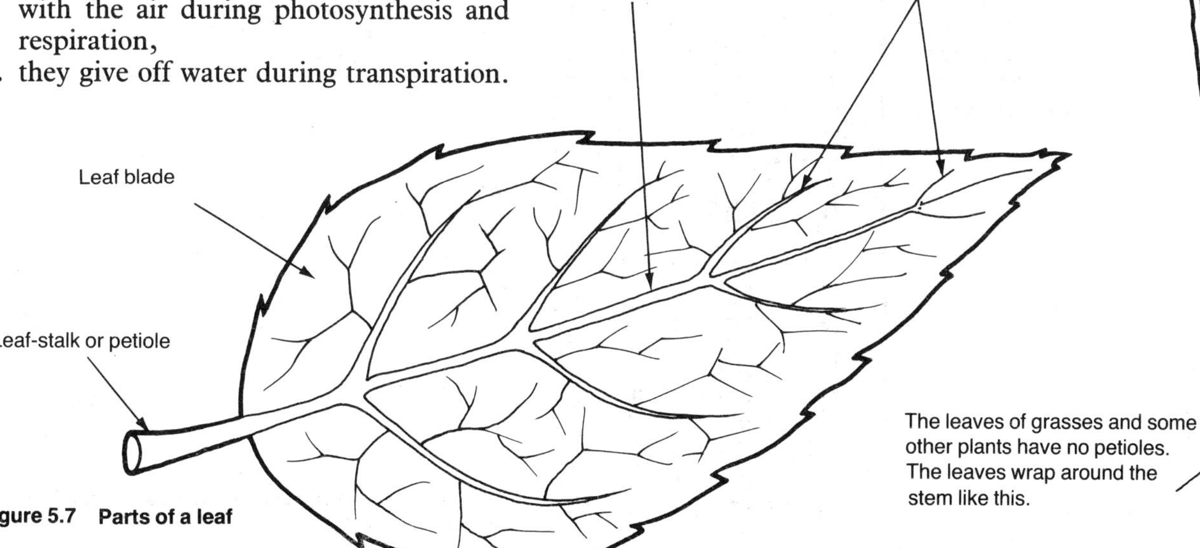

Figure 5.7 Parts of a leaf

The leaves of grasses and some other plants have no petioles. The leaves wrap around the stem like this.

The petiole carries water and mineral salts from the stem into the leaf. It also takes away sugar which is made in the leaf. The sugar is taken to other parts of the plant and stored or used in respiration.

The mid-rib supports the leaf. It has vascular bundles inside it which carry water and solutions of mineral salts and sugar.

Veins are small vascular bundles. They carry water, mineral salts and sugar to and from every part of the leaf.

The leaf blade is wide, thin and flat. It has a large surface area which absorbs the sunlight needed for photosynthesis. This thin, flat shape is also good for exchanging carbon dioxide and oxygen in respiration and photosynthesis.

Figure 5.8 Inside a leaf

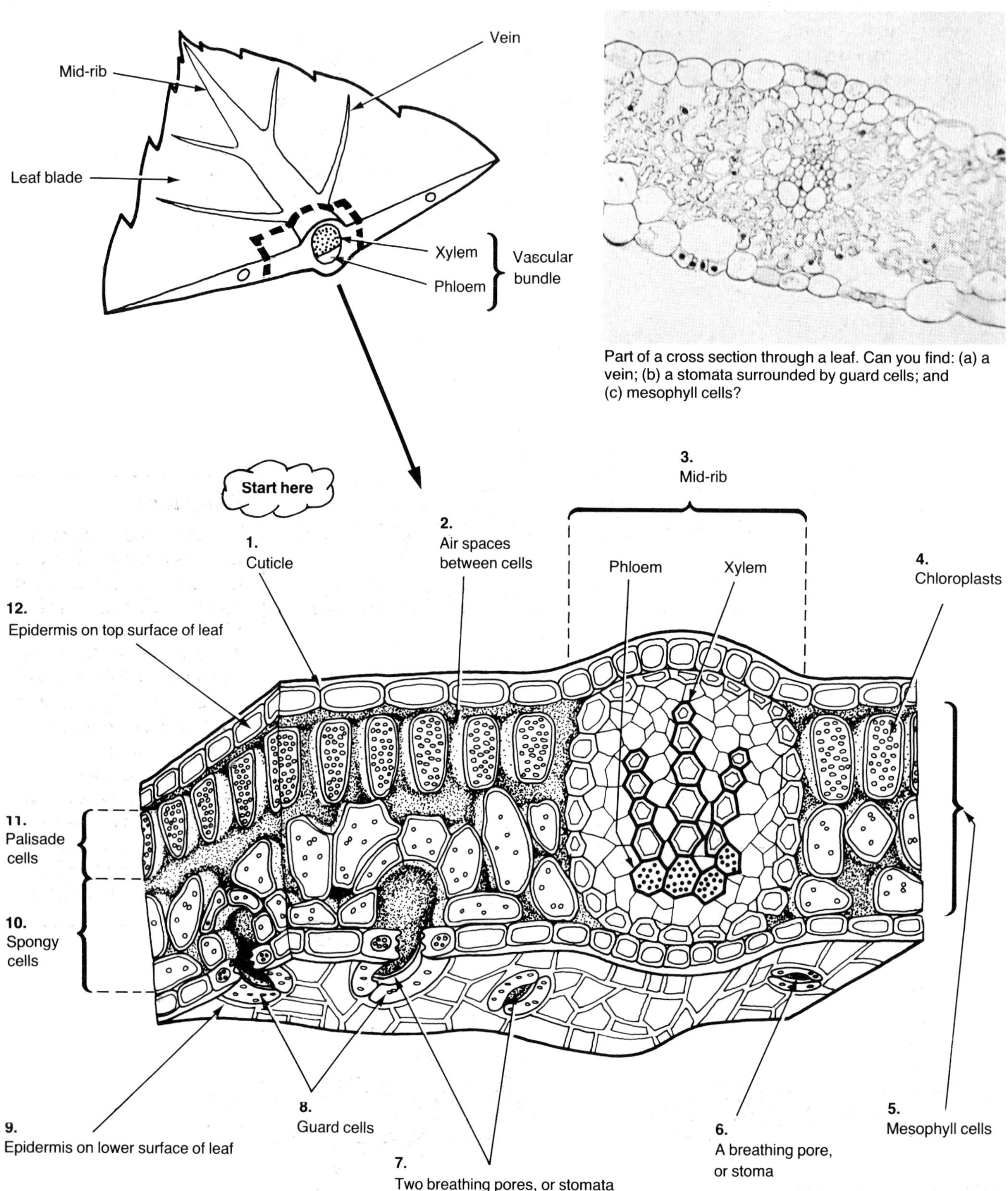

Part of a cross section through a leaf. Can you find: (a) a vein; (b) a stomata surrounded by guard cells; and (c) mesophyll cells?

Figure 5.8 shows the different parts of a leaf, listed here.

1. The cuticle is a layer of wax. The wax stops rain from getting into the leaf. It also stops the leaf losing water.
2. Air spaces between the cells let air get to every cell in the leaf.
3. The phloem and xylem in the mid-rib join onto the phloem and xylem in the stem.
4. Chloroplasts are small discs containing chlorophyll. Photosynthesis happens in the chloroplasts.
5. The mesophyll is made up of tall palisade cells and spongy cells.
6. and 7. *Stomata* are tiny holes or pores which let air and water vapour in and out of the leaf. (Singular: stoma)
8. Guard cells have chloroplasts and are on each side of the stomata. The guard cells make the stomata open and close. Most cells in the epidermis do not have chloroplasts.
9. The lower epidermis has most of the stomata in it.
10. The spongy cells fit together loosely and have many air spaces between them.
11. The palisade cells have many chloroplasts for photosynthesis.
12. The top epidermis of the leaf does not always have stomata in it.

HOW STOMATA WORK

Guard cells are the only cells in the epidermis that can make sugar. The sugar makes water from other cells go into the guard cells by osmosis. This makes the guard cells swell. Because they have a special shape they move further apart and the stoma opens.(See figure 5.9.)

Stoma open

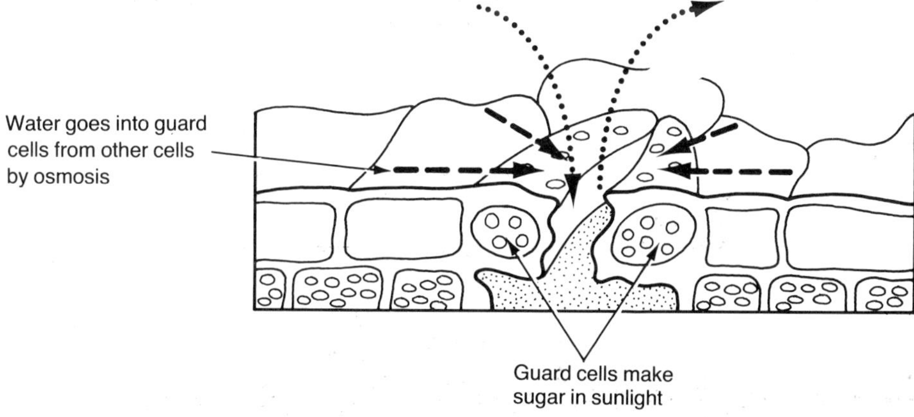

Stoma closed

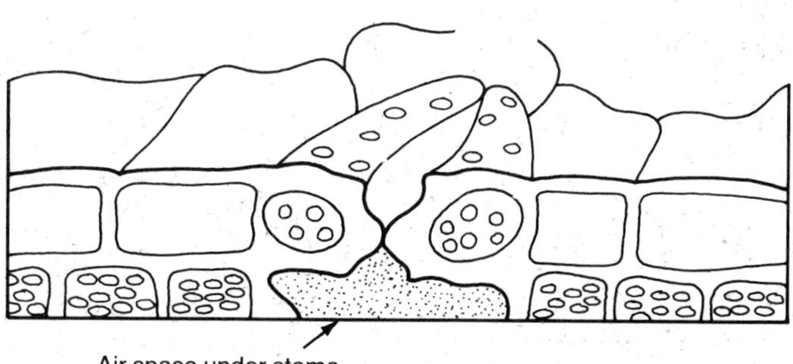

A model stoma

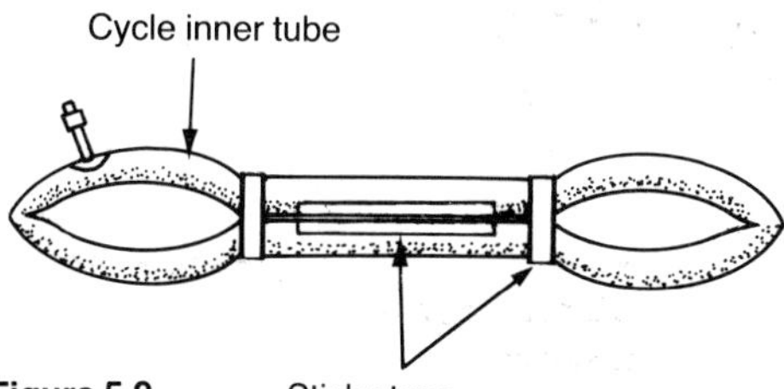

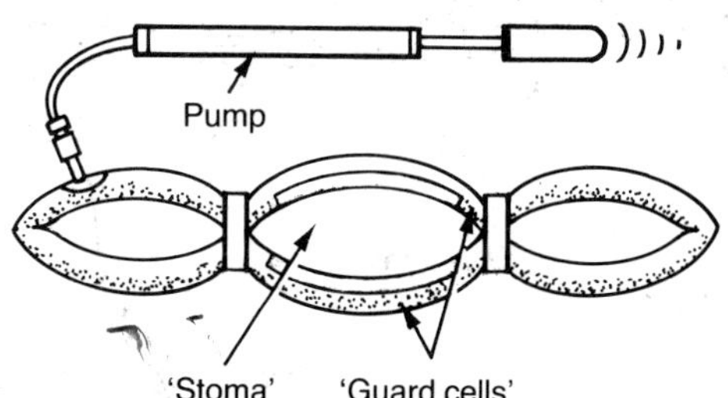

Figure 5.9

> **Fancy that!**
>
> The biggest organism on Earth is a redwood tree in California, U.S.A., called 'General Sherman'. It is 83 m tall, measures 24.11 m round the trunk and weights 2030 tonnes!
>
> The roots of a fig tree in South Africa grew to a depth of 120 m!
>
> The largest leaves of any plant are those of the bamboo palm of South America. The leaf blades are 19.81 m long and the petioles are 3.96 m long!

ROOTS

Roots have two main jobs:

1. They fix the plant firmly in the soil.
2. They absorb water and mineral salts from the soil. Xylem tubes carry these into the stem and up into the leaves.

Some roots store the food which is made by leaves. Roots do not have chlorophyll and do not have buds or leaves.

Figure 5.10 shows the parts of a root listed here.

1. The vascular bundles of the root join onto the vascular bundles of the stem.
2. Root hairs are tiny. They absorb water and mineral salts from the soil.
3. The meristem is just behind the root tip. It is the place where new cells are made by cell division.
4. The root cap protects the tip of the root as it pushes through the soil.

When the wind pushes a stem *sideways* this force is carried down to the roots and pulls *upwards*. The roots must hold the plant without breaking or it will be blown over. (See figure 5.11.)

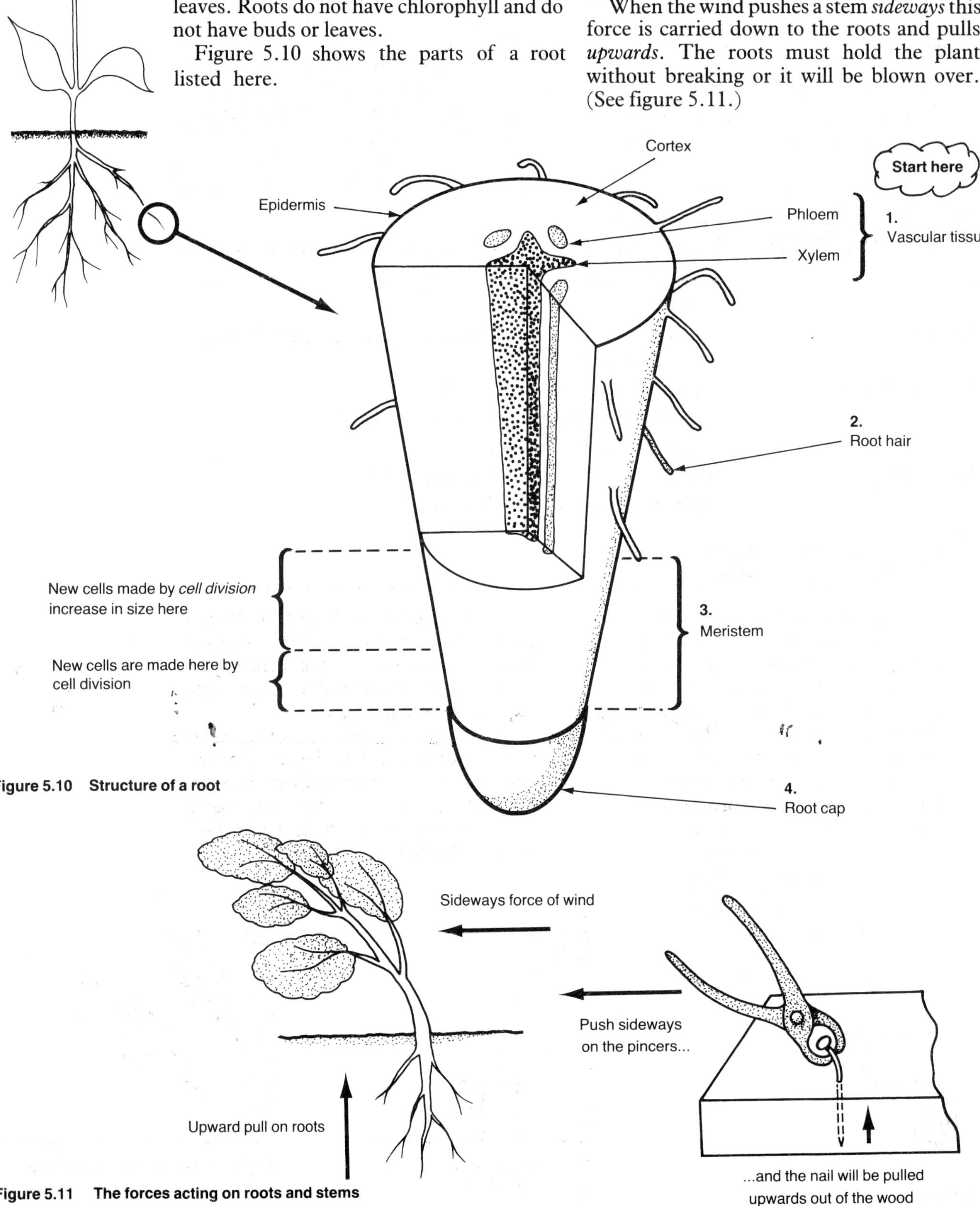

Figure 5.10 Structure of a root

Figure 5.11 The forces acting on roots and stems

Summary

Stems have *buds* which grow into leaves, flowers or new stems. Underground stems store food. The age of twigs of *deciduous* trees can be found by counting the number of girdle scars on the twigs.

Groups of *xylem* and *phloem* tubes in *vascular bundles* carry food up and down stems. A new *annual ring* of xylem and phloem is made each year of growth by the *cambium*. This makes stems grow in thickness and is called *secondary thickening*. Xylem tubes also help to support stems.

Leaves absorb sunlight for photosynthesis. They exchange carbon dioxide and oxygen with the air during photosynthesis and breathing. These gases go in and out of the leaves through the breathing pores or *stomata*. Leaves also give off water vapour in transpiration.

Plants are firmly fixed in soil by their roots which also absorb water and mineral salts from the soil. Some roots store food made by the leaves.

Important words

Xylem	small tubes which carry water and mineral salts up stems, roots and leaves.
Phloem	small tubes which carry sugar and mineral salts up and down stems, roots and leaves.
Vascular bundle	a group of xylem and phloem cells.
Cambium	cells which make new xylem and phloem cells.
Secondary thickening	growth in thickness of a stem.
Annual rings	rings of xylem made in each year of growth.
Stoma	a small pore in a leaf (plural: stomata).

Things to do

1. Cut lengths of stem about 20 cm long from different plants. Choose some woody stems and some softer green stems. Fix 3 cm of one end of a stem into a retort stand clamped to the bench. Tie a piece of string to the other end of the stem. Hook a spring balance into a loop in the string and pull sideways gently. When the stem breaks or folds, note the reading on the balance.

   Ask someone to hold a clear protractor against the stem as you pull. Measure the angle reached just before the stem breaks or folds. Make a graph like that in figure 5.12 to show your results.

   Could any stems be bent more than 90% without breaking? Did the woody stems need more force to break them than the softer stems? Did the softer stems bend more than the woody stems before they broke or folded?

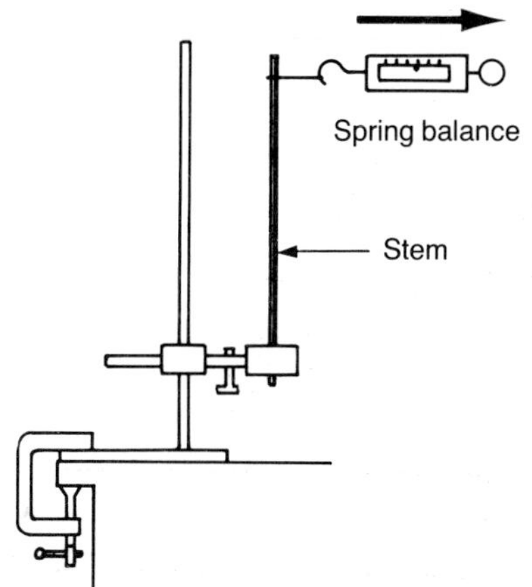

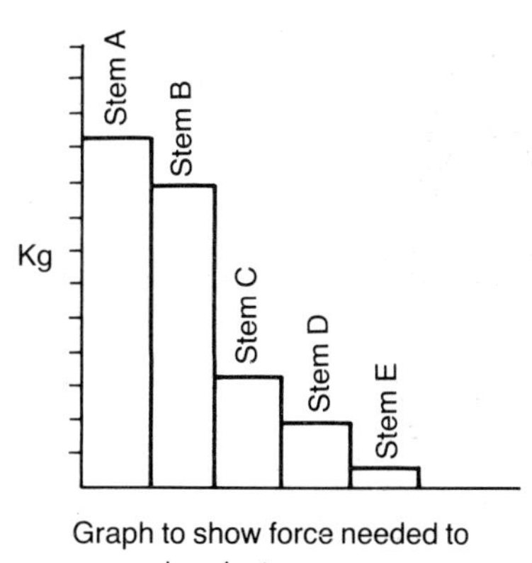

Graph to show force needed to break stems

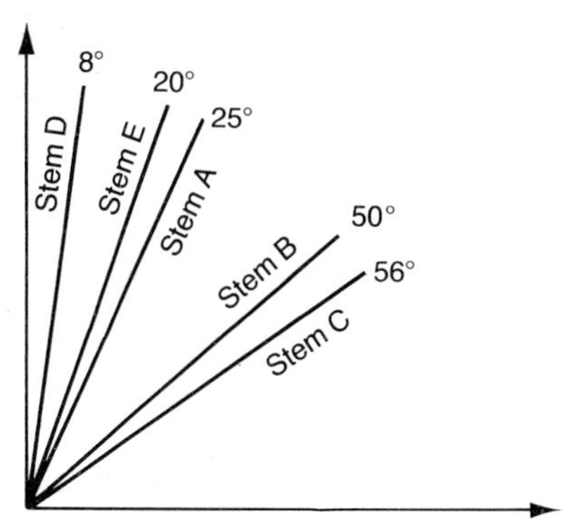

Angles at which stems broke or folded

Figure 5.12

2. Put one layer of clear nail varnish on the underside of a privet leaf. When it is dry, carefully peel off the varnish. The epidermis of the leaf will stick to the varnish layer. Put the varnish peel into a drop of water on a slide and look at it under a microscope. You should be able to see the stomata quite clearly. Does the top epidermis of a privet leaf have any stomata?

3. You will need help from an adult for this investigation. You need a complete slice of a cross section cut through a tree trunk. The slice should be smoothed on one surface with a power sander. If you know when the tree was cut down, work out how old it is by counting the annual rings. Stick paper flags in the rings to show something interesting or important that happened in each year.

Questions

A.

Write out each sentence in your book. Fill in the missing words from those in the box. Some words may be used more than once.

lenticels — air spaces — guard cells — vascular bundles — corm — buds — stomata — cambium — phloem — secondary thickening — xylem — bud scales — petioles — root hairs — meristem — mesophyll — deciduous — runners — palisade

1. A ...... is an underground stem.
2. ...... are stems which creep sideways over the soil.
3. All stems have ...... on them.
4. Trees which drop their leaves in winter are ....
5. Buds are protected by ...... in winter.
6. Girdle scars are made by ...... falling off.
7. In winter twigs of deciduous trees breathe through ....
8. Water and mineral salts move up stems in the ....
9. Sugar moves up and down stems in the ....
10. A vascular bundle in a stem is made of ...... , ... and ....
11. The ...... makes new xylem and phloem cells.
12. Annual rings are made of rings of ....
13. Twigs grow in thickness by ....
14. Most leaves have stalks or ....
15. Palisade cells are spongy cells which make the ......layer of a leaf.
16. Most chloroplasts in leaves are found in the ...... cells.
18. ...... are found on each side of a stoma.
19. Spongy cells have a lot of ...... between them.
20. ...... are found in the centre of roots.
21. Water and mineral salts are absorbed by ....
22. The ...... is the part of a root where new cells are made and growth happens.

B.

Join these sentences together using either the word 'and' or the word 'because', whichever is correct.

1. Leaf scars are made in autumn. Girdle scars are made in spring.
2. Pea plants use tendrils to support their stems. They do not have much strength.
3. Rhizomes are underground stems. They have buds.
4. Palisade cells do most of the photosynthesis in a leaf. They have many chloroplasts.
5. You can find lateral buds on the sides of stems. Terminal buds are found at the end of stems.

C.

1. Explain why air spaces are needed in the tissues of a root.
2. Suggest *one* reason why there is more supporting tissue in a stem than a root.
3. Name *two* substances transported by xylem.
4. Name *one* substance transported by phloem.

D.

Study figure 5.13 of a cross section of the centre of a leaf blade and answer the following questions.

1. Use words from the box to label the parts A to F in figure 5.13.

epidermis — cuticle — xylem — palisade layer — spongy layer — guard cell

2. Use the letters A to F to answer the following questions. Which cells:
(a) allow gases into the leaf?
(b) bring water into the leaf?
(c) control the amount of water transpired from the leaf?
(d) provide spaces for diffusion of gases inside the leaf?
(e) are the main photosynthetic cells?
(f) support the veins of the leaf?

3. Copy figure 5.14 of a section of a palisade cell into your book. Complete the figure and label the nucleus, chloroplasts, cellulose wall, cytoplasm and sap vacuole.
Name three features of this cell which would not be found in an animal cell, such as a cheek cell.

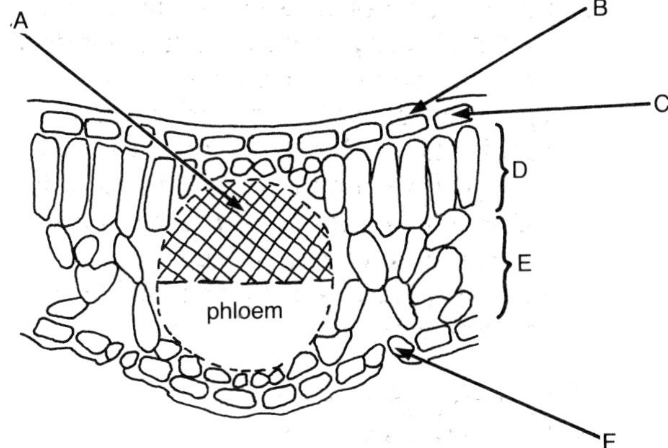

Figure 5.13

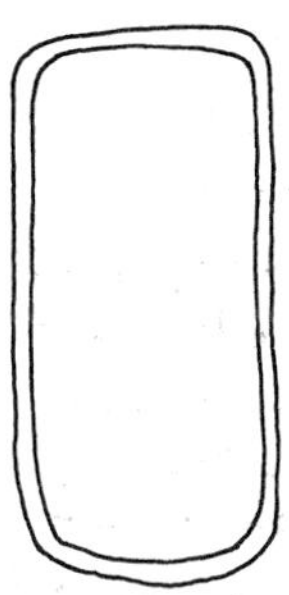

Figure 5.14

(NREB)

TOPIC 6

TRANSPORT AND TRANSPIRATION

All living plant cells need water, mineral salts and sugar. A plant's roots absorb a weak solution of water and mineral salts from the soil. The xylem tubes inside the roots and stems take this solution to all parts of the plant.

A plant's leaves make sugar, which the phloem tubes take to every part of the plant.

The xylem and phloem tubes are the *transport system* of a plant. Plants lose water into the air through the stomata in their leaves. This is called *transpiration*. The water is lost as water vapour which is an invisible gas. The water lost in transpiration moves from the soil, up the transport system and out of the leaves. (See figure 6.1.)

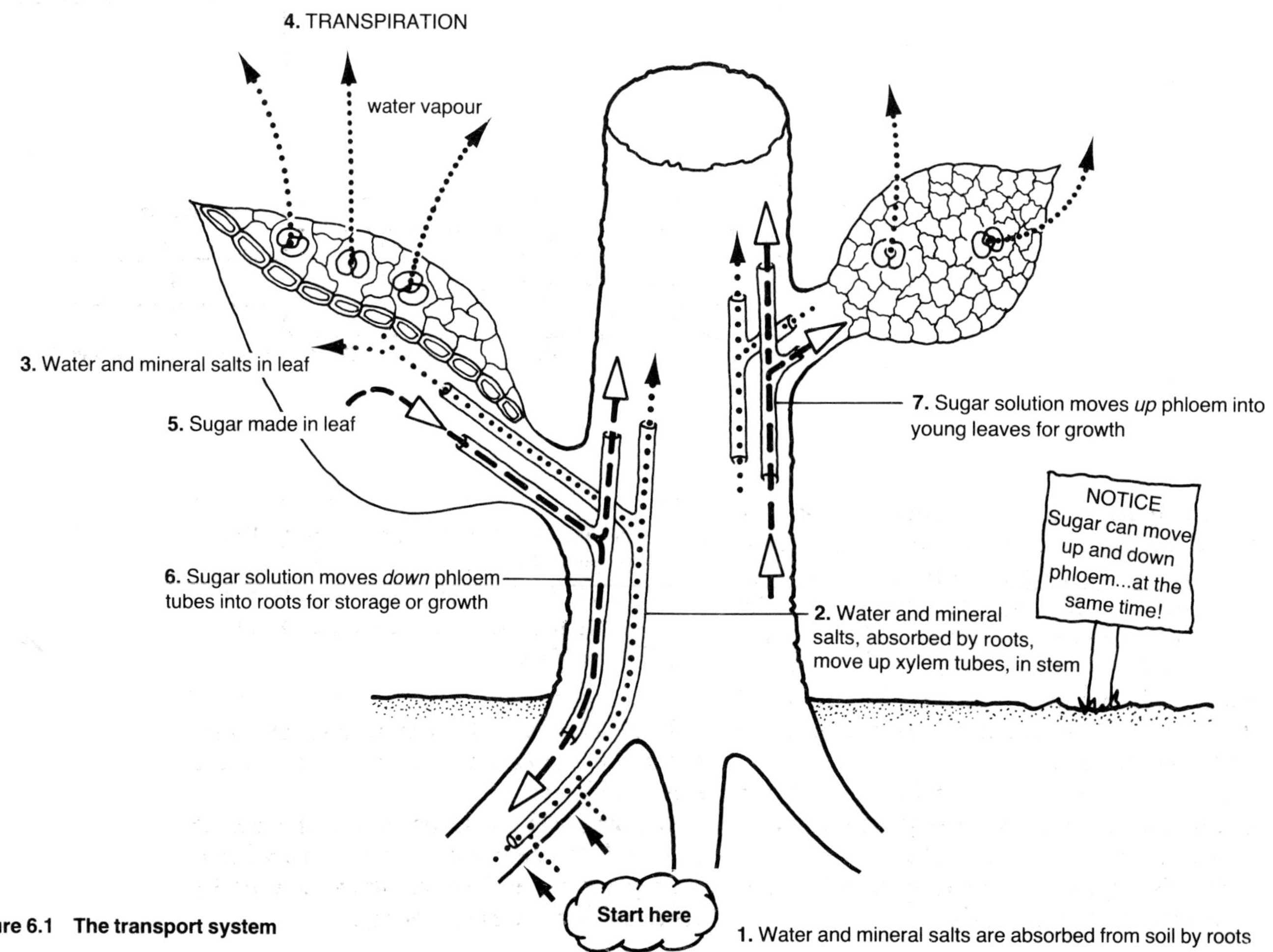

Figure 6.1 The transport system

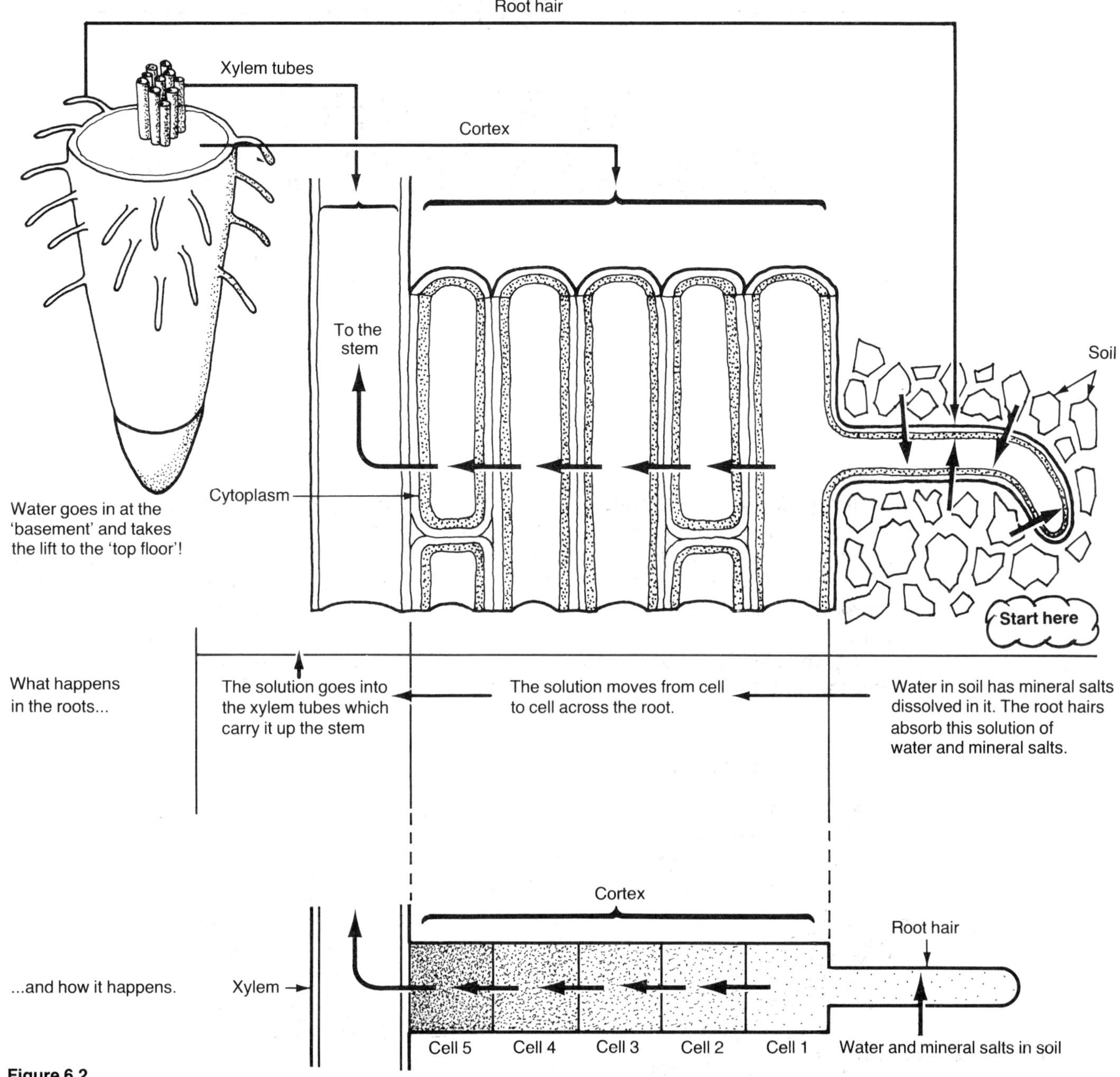

Figure 6.2

The solution of mineral salts in soil is very weak. The solution in the cytoplasm of root hair cells is stronger than this weak soil solution. Because of this, water moves into the root hair cells (**cell 1**, figure 6.2) by *osmosis*.

The solution in **cell 1** now contains more water and is weaker than the solution in **cell 2**. Because of this, water moves from **cell 1** to **cell 2** by osmosis.

Loss of water to **cell 2** makes the solution in **cell 1** stronger. Because of this more water moves from the soil into **cell 1**.

In this way, water moves from cell to cell across the root by osmosis.

As water moves into a cell, the solution inside that cell gets WEAKER. As water moves out of a cell, the solution inside that cell gets STRONGER.

In the middle of the root, water moves into the xylem tubes which carry it up into the stem and leaves.

Osmosis only tells us how *water* moves from cell-to-cell across a root. *Mineral salts* may get into and move across a root by *diffusion*. This uses up energy.

TRANSPIRATION

As soon as the leaves lose some water, the roots absorb more water. This flow of water from roots to leaves is called the *transpiration stream*.

On hot days hundreds of litres of water are carried to the leaves of large trees. On cold days much less water is carried upwards in the transpiration stream.

The transpiration stream is important because:

1. it cools the plant in hot weather when water is lost from the leaves;
2. it carries mineral salts to the leaves for making proteins;
3. it carries water to the leaves for making sugar by photosynthesis (See figure 6.1);
4. it takes water to the cells to keep them stiff.

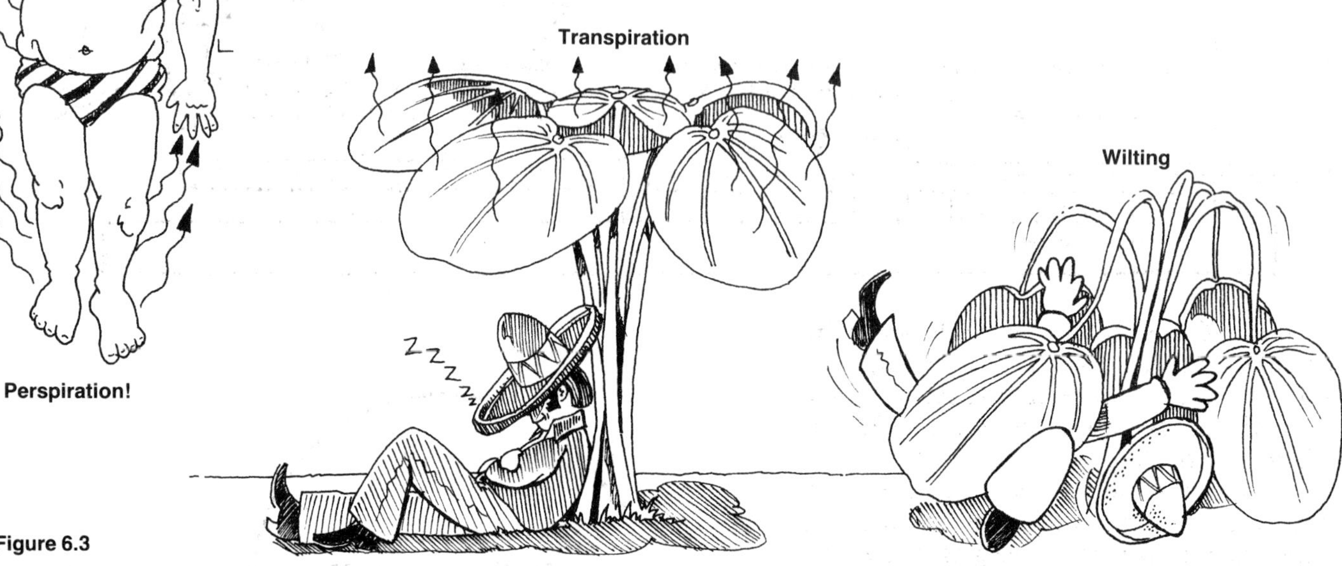

Figure 6.3

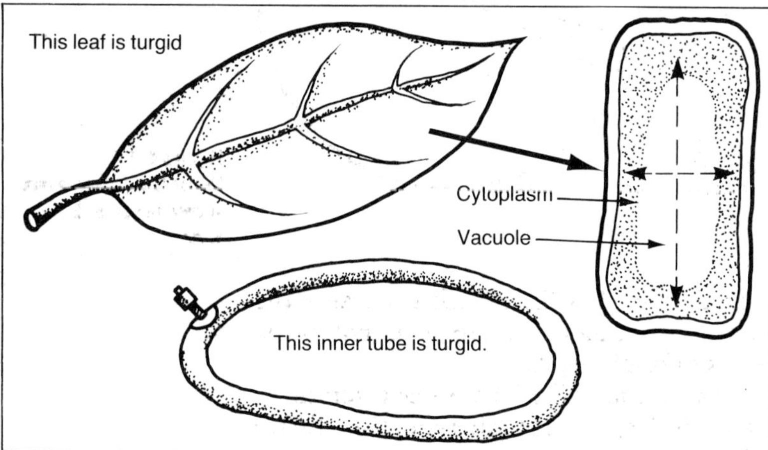

Figure 6.4

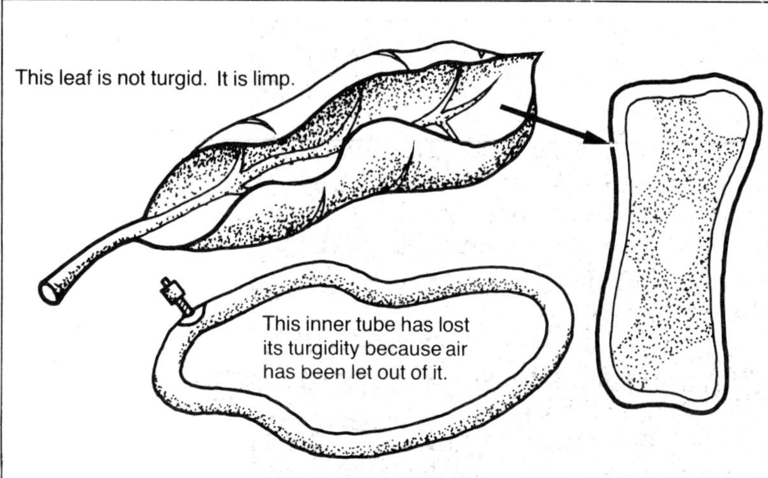

Figure 6.5

Leaves sometimes lose water faster than roots can absorb it from the soil. When this happens the leaves and stems lose their stiffness and the plant *wilts*. (See figure 6.3.) Wilting happens when cells are short of water. Water makes cells stiff or *turgid*. The air in a cycle inner tube makes the tube turgid.

Water moves into cells by osmosis. The extra water in the cells increases the pressure inside them. This pressure is called *turgor pressure*. It pushes outwards on the cell walls and this makes the cells turgid. (See figure 6.4.)

The cells in figure 6.5 have lost their turgidity because they are short of water. This makes the turgor pressure less and the cell wall goes limp. This also happens when cells are put into a strong sugar solution. Water leaves the cells by osmosis and they become *plasmolysed*. A plasmolysed cell looks like the one on the right of figure 6.5.

Young plants get most of their support from turgid cells. In some older plants most support comes from the woody tissue or xylem.

Transpiration happens faster in some conditions than in others. The speed of transpiration of a shoot under different conditions can be compared using a *potometer*. (See figure 6.6.)

Figure 6.6 **A potometer**

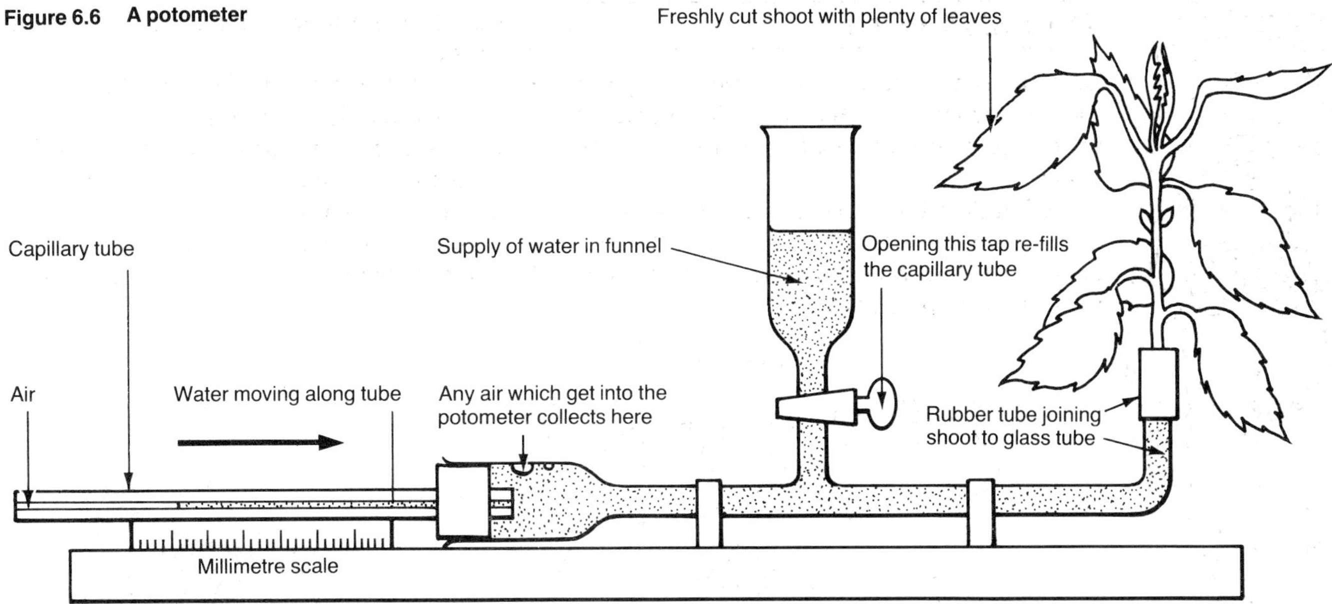

First fill the potometer with water by opening the tap. Cut a leafy stem from a plant and push it into the rubber tube. The tube must fit tightly and no air must be let in. Then close the tap.

As water is lost from the leaves by transpiration, more water goes up the stem. This water is taken from the glass tubes. Air goes into the capillary tube at one end as water is taken from the other end.

The movement of water in the capillary tube shows how fast water is absorbed by the shoot. You can time the speed of this movement over a fixed distance on the scale. When there is no water left in the capillary tube the potometer can be re-set. Do this by opening the tap again.

To show how the speed of transpiration changes you can use the potometer in different conditions.

Transpiration is fastest in *hot, dry, windy* conditions. It is slowest in *cold, still* conditions or when the air has a lot of water vapour in it. Transpiration is faster in bright light than in dim light. This is because the stomata open and let more water out of the leaves in bright light.

Most but not all of the water taken in by plants is lost in transpiration. (See figure 6.7.)

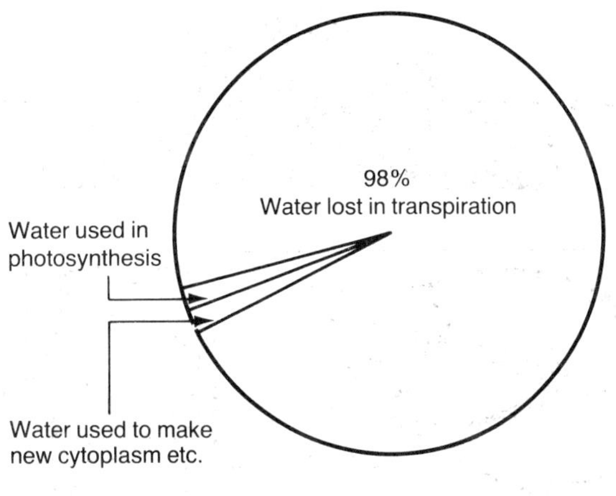

Figure 6.7
What happens to the water taken in by a plant

Summary

Roots absorb a solution of water and mineral salts from soil. The water moves across roots by *osmosis* to the *xylem* tubes. Mineral salts may move across the root by *diffusion*.

Xylem tubes take the solution to all parts of the plant. Sugar is made in leaves and is taken away in *phloem* tubes. Xylem and phloem tubes are the *transport system* of plants.

The flow of water and mineral salts from roots to leaves is called the *transpiration stream*. Some of the water absorbed by roots is used to keep cells *turgid*. Turgidity is important for support in some plants.

A *potometer* is used to compare the speed of transpiration of a plant under different conditions.

Fancy that!
A big tree can lose as much as one tonne of water in transpiration on a hot day!

Important words

Transport system	the xylem and phloem tubes.
Transpiration	loss of water vapour by plants.
Transpiration stream	the upward flow of water through plants.
Osmosis	the movement of water from a less concentrated solution to a more concentrated solution through a selectively permeable membrane.
Diffusion	the movement of substances from a high concentration to a lower concentration.
Turgid	stiff.
Turgor pressure	a force pushing outwards on a cell wall making it turgid.
Plasmolysis	when the cytoplasm of a cell shrinks away from the cell wall; this happens when the cell is put into a solution stronger than the cytoplasm.
Potometer	an apparatus used for finding the speed of transpiration of plants.
Wilting	this happens when plant cells are short of water: they become less turgid and the plant cannot stay upright.

Things to do

1. Cut a short length of stem from a leafy plant. Stand the stem in water containing a dye such as neutral red. Leave for about 20 minutes. Then cut the stem through in different places. Use a lens to look at the cut ends of the stem. What part of the stem has the dye stained? How far has the dye moved up the stem?

2. Collect three privet leaves. Put a thin layer of grease on both sides of the first leaf, on the top of the second leaf and on the bottom of the third. Weigh each leaf and write the weight down. Hang the leaves up in the same place with cotton fixed to their stalks. After 24 hours weigh the leaves again. What do the results tell you about the importance of the two sides of the leaf in transpiration?

Questions

A.
Write out each sentence in your book. Fill in the missing words from those in the box. Some words may be used more than once.

> turgid — phloem — transpiration — transpiration stream — osmosis — vapour — stomata — potometer — turgor pressure — xylem — wilt — plasmolysed — proteins

1. The transport system of a plant is made of ...... and ....
2. Water is lost from leaves as water ...... which is an invisible gas.
3. ...... is the loss of water from leaves.
4. Water and mineral salts move up the stem in ...... tubes.
5. Water moves across roots by ....
6. Sugar moves up and down a stem in ...... tubes.
7. The movement of water from roots to leaves is called the ....
8. Leaves use mineral salts to make ...... and other substances.
9. When plants are short of water they ....
10. Water moves into cells by osmosis and increases the ....
11. ...... pushes outwards on cell walls and makes the cells ....
12. Cells in a strong solution are ...... by it.
13. A ...... compares the speeds of transpiration of a plant in different conditions.
14. In bright light the ...... open and transpiration increases.

B.
Put each of these parts of sentences into the correct order.

1. when more water moves into the solution inside / the cell gets weaker / a cell by osmosis
2. the solution in root hair cells the solution of / is much weaker than / mineral salts and water in soil
3. more water is lost / the stomata open wide and / in bright light / by transpiration
4. most of the water taken in by a plant / is used for photosynthesis / is lost in transpiration and only a little

C.
These sentences describe how to set up a potometer and what happens when it is working. Put the sentences into their correct order. Work with a partner and each write some of the sentences on strips of paper. Swap the pieces of paper round to find the best order. Copy this into your book.

1. The speed at which the water moves along the capillary tube can be measured using the scale and a clock.
2. The tap is closed and a leafy shoot is pushed into the rubber tube.
3. The tap is closed and the funnel is filled with water.
4. The tap is then opened to fill the glass tubes with water.
5. As water is lost by the leaves more water moves out of the glass tubes.
6. The potometer is put into bright sunshine.

D.
The speed at which a leafy shoot absorbed water when placed in certain conditions (A) was measured with a potometer. This was repeated in different conditions (B). The results are given in the table below. They show the distance moved by the water in the capillary tube each time a measurement was made.

1. Draw a graph of the results as shown in figure 6.8.
2. On the same graph draw the results for B.
3. If a distance of 1 mm on the capillary tube equals 1 mm^3, what was the total amount of water taken in by the plant in A?
4. What was the total amount of water taken in by the plant in B?
5. When did the plant lose most water in A?
6. What sort of conditions do you think A and B were?

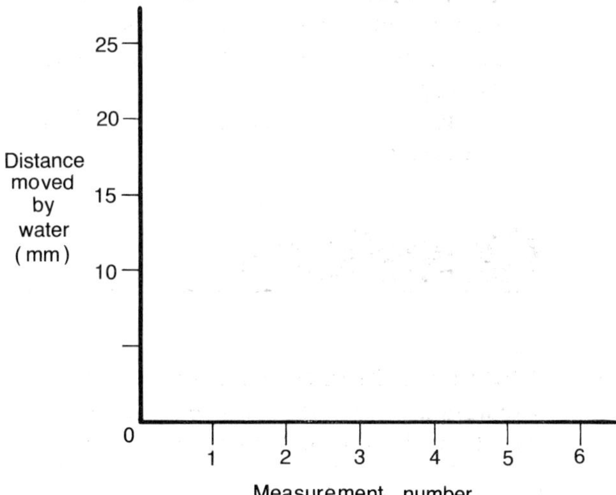

Figure 6.8

Measurement number	1	2	3	4	5	6
A	3mm	5mm	8mm	12mm	17mm	24mm
B	1mm	3mm	4mm	3mm	3mm	3mm

TOPIC 7

VEGETATIVE REPRODUCTION

LIFE CYCLES

Different plants have different kinds of life cycle. Some are *annuals*, some are *biennials* and others are *perennials*.

An annual plant dies after it has made seeds. Only the seeds live through the winter. The whole life cycle takes one year. A poppy is an annual plant. (See figure 7.1.)

Biennials don't make flowers or seeds in their first year. They make large food storage organs which contain a lot of food. This food is used up to make flowers and seeds in the second year. Then the plant dies. The whole life cycle takes two years. A carrot is a biennial plant but we usually eat it after the first year! (See figure 7.2.)

Plants which live for many years are called perennials. In trees and bushes, parts of the branches and trunk grow every year. These plants are woody perennials. You can always see them because they do not die in winter.

The horse chestnut tree is a woody perennial. It is *deciduous* because all its leaves fall off in autumn.

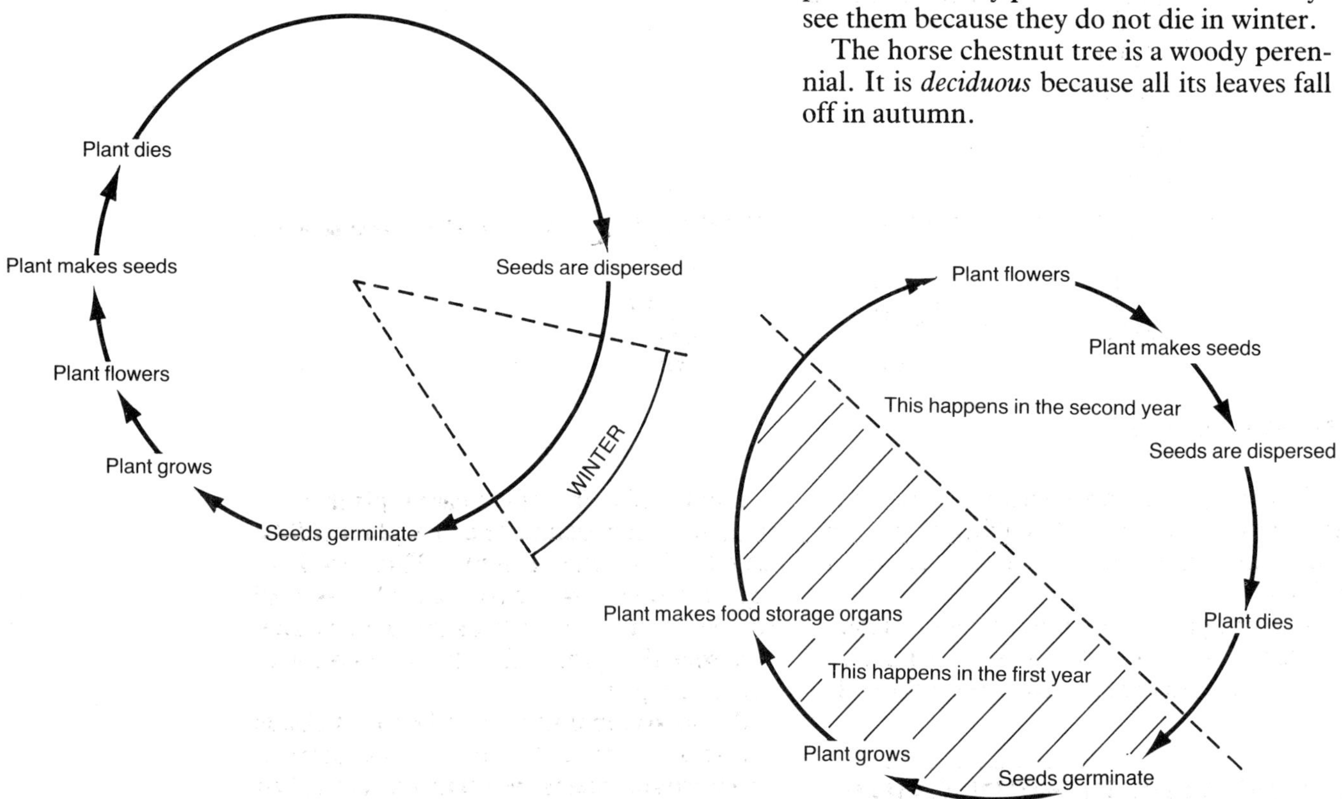

Figure 7.1 Annuals

Figure 7.2 Biennials

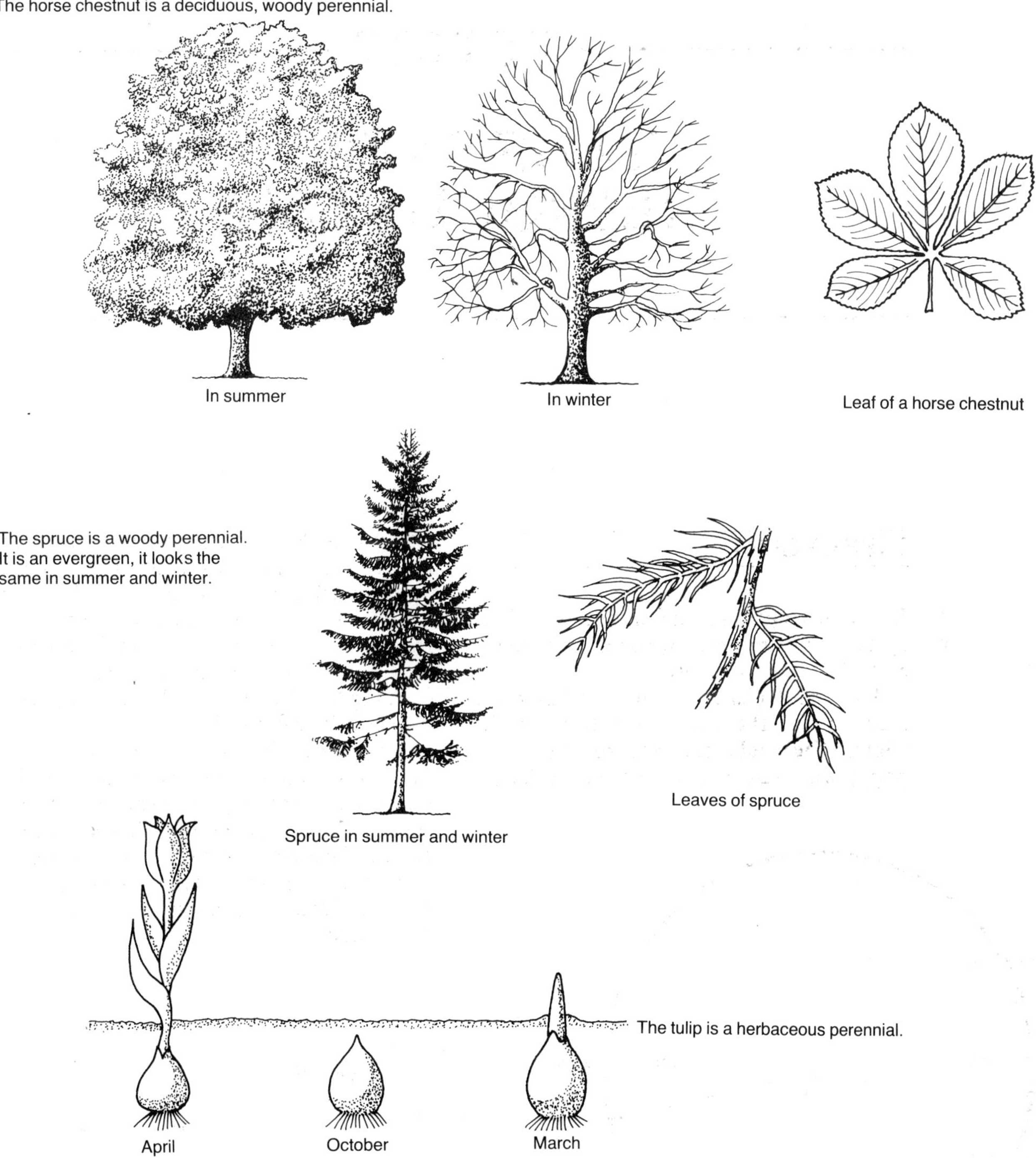

Figure 7.3 Perennials

The spruce tree is a woody perennial but it is *evergreen*. The leaves fall off a few at a time throughout the year instead of all at once in winter.

In some plants the leaves and shoots die in winter. They are *herbaceous* perennials. Some may keep a few leaves above the soil.

VEGETATIVE REPRODUCTION

Some flowering plants make new plants by *vegetative reproduction*. This is reproduction without seeds. Part of the parent plant grows to make a new plant. The new plant will be exactly like the parent. This kind of reproduction is also called asexual reproduction. Many plants use both asexual and sexual reproduction (with flowers) to make new plants.

A potato is an underground *stem* with buds and small leaves called scale leaves. Swollen underground stems like potatoes are called tubers. Two kinds of shoots grow from potato tubers. Some shoots grow above the soil and make flowers and leaves. Other

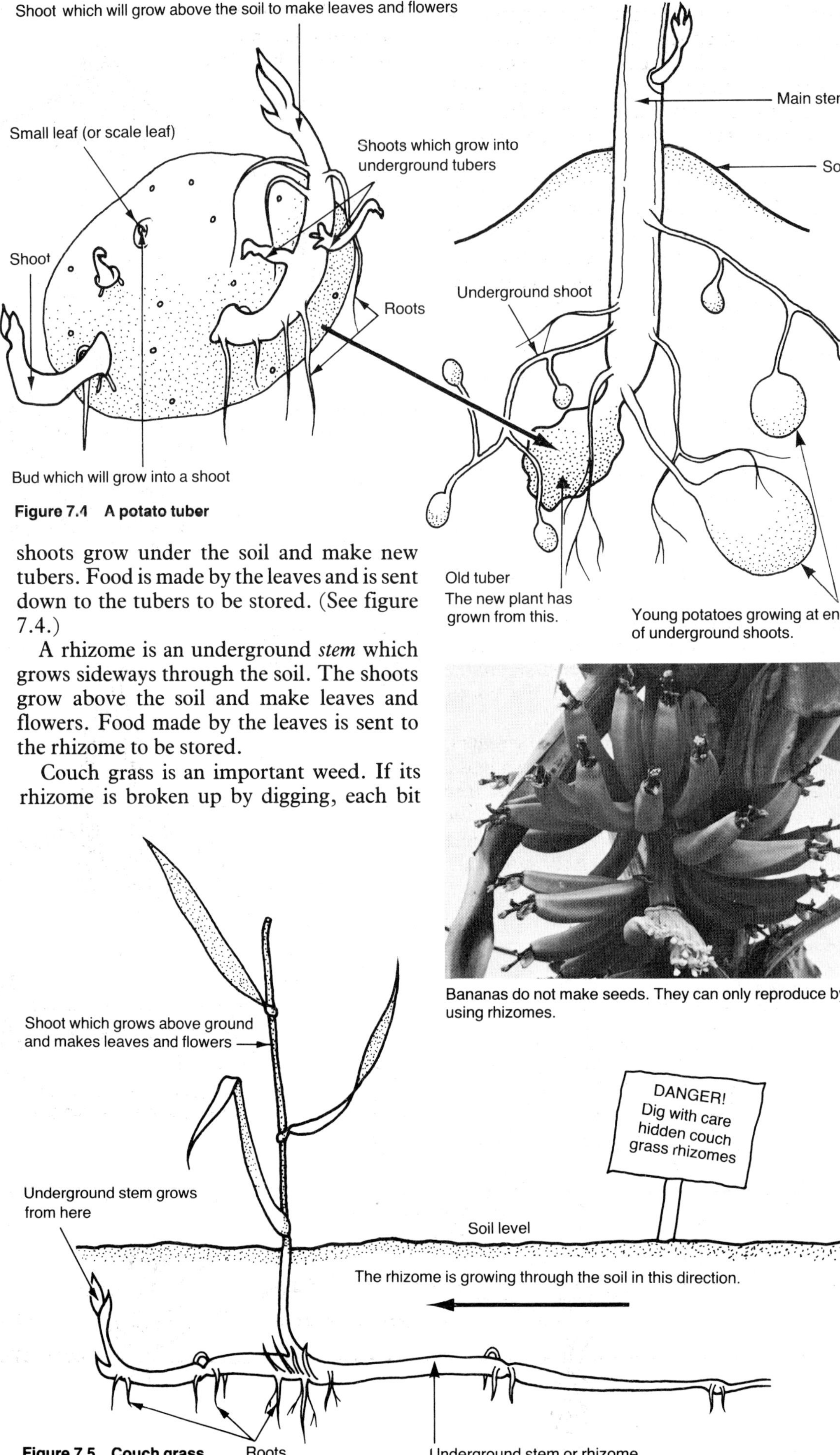

Figure 7.4 A potato tuber

shoots grow under the soil and make new tubers. Food is made by the leaves and is sent down to the tubers to be stored. (See figure 7.4.)

A rhizome is an underground *stem* which grows sideways through the soil. The shoots grow above the soil and make leaves and flowers. Food made by the leaves is sent to the rhizome to be stored.

Couch grass is an important weed. If its rhizome is broken up by digging, each bit

Bananas do not make seeds. They can only reproduce by using rhizomes.

Figure 7.5 Couch grass

grows into a new rhizome! Couch grass is a herbaceous perennial. (See figure 7.5.)

Bulbs are underground shoots. The stem is very short and never grows above the soil. White, swollen scale leaves grow from the stem. These leaves store food and also never grow above the soil.

In spring, a shoot grows from a bud in the bulb using food from the store in the scale leaves. The shoot has flowers and green leaves. Food is made by the green leaves and sent down to the bulb. Some of this food goes into a small bud on the stem. The bud swells and makes next year's bulb. This is how new bulbs are made by vegetative reproduction.

Plants which have bulbs are herbaceous perennials. (See figure 7.6.)

Corms are like tubers but they have more scale leaves. Food is stored in a short swollen stem covered with these dry scale leaves. The stem stays below the soil.

In spring, green leaves grow from the corm using food from the stem. Food is made by the green leaves and sent down into the corm. This food goes into a new stem growing on top of the old one. This new stem will make next year's corm. As one corm is made on top of another, they push out of the ground. Contractile roots pull the corms down into the soil. (See figure 7.7.)

Some plants reproduce using runners. These are shoots which grow out from buds. The runners grow over the soil and new plants grow from them. Food from the parent plant moves along the runner to help the new plant to grow. When the new plant can make its own food the runner rots away. (See figure 7.8.)

Figure 7.6 An onion bulb

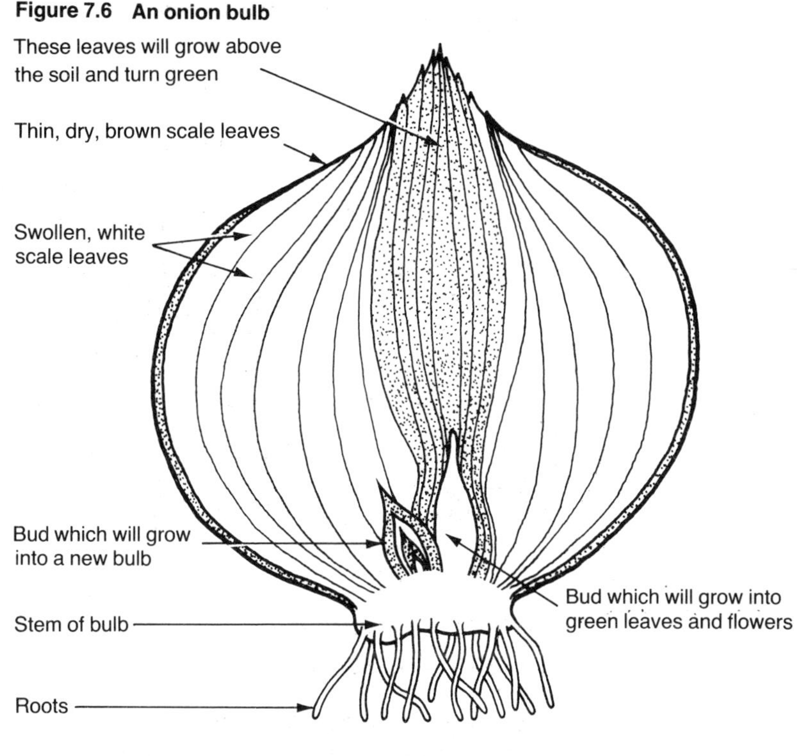

Figure 7.7 A crocus corm

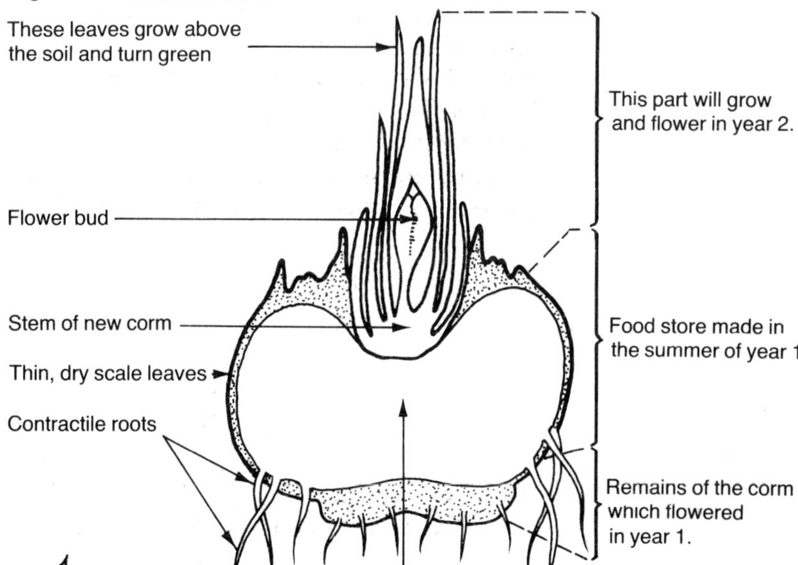

Figure 7.8 A strawberry runner

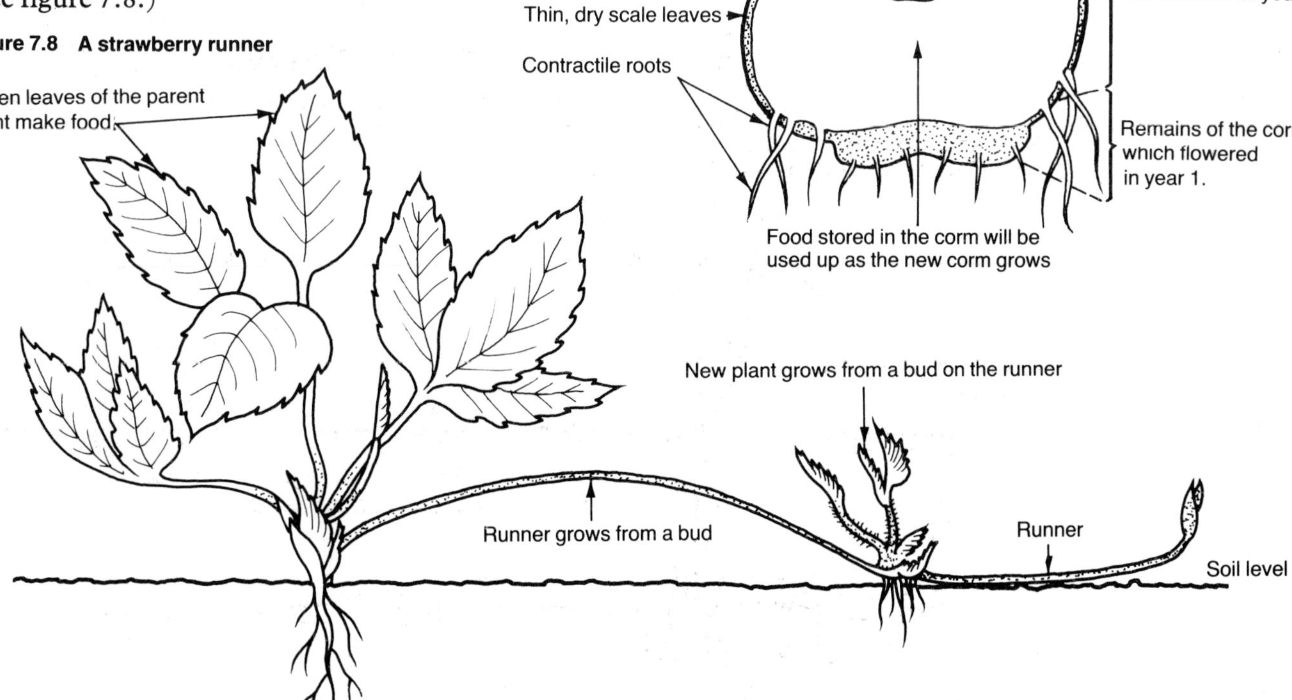

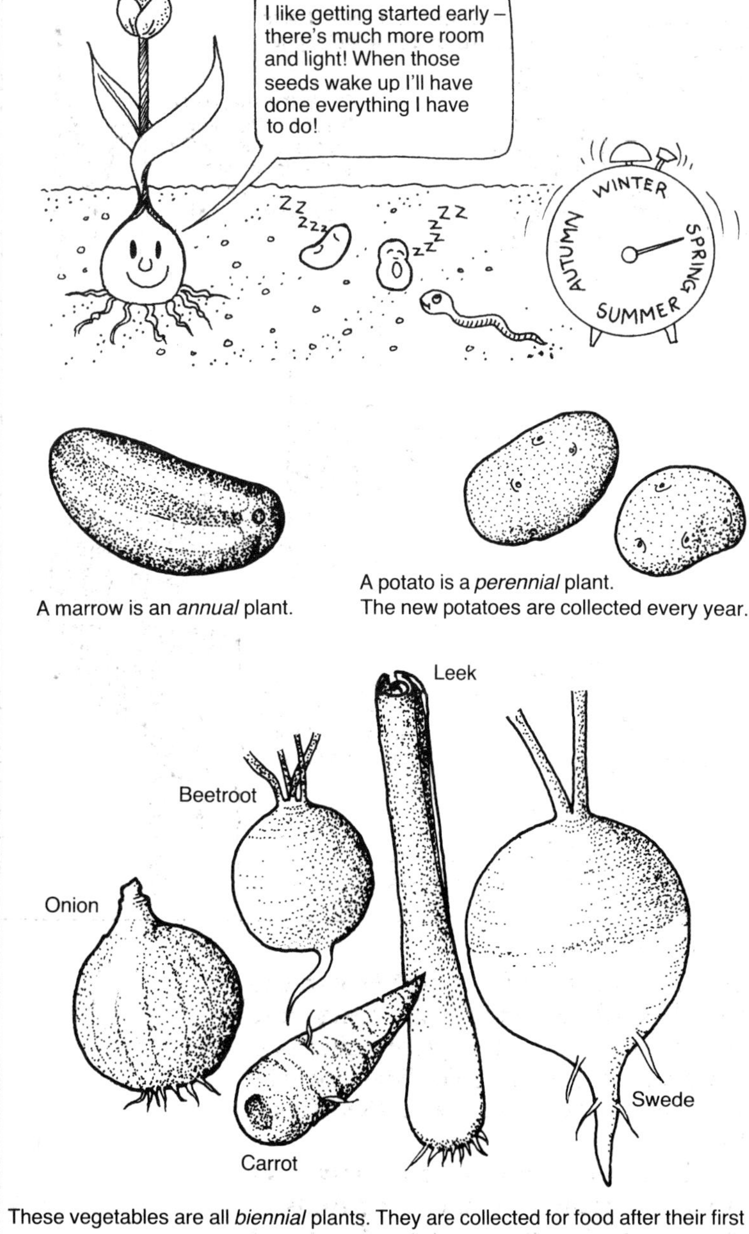

A marrow is an *annual* plant.

A potato is a *perennial* plant. The new potatoes are collected every year.

These vegetables are all *biennial* plants. They are collected for food after their first growing season. If they were left to grow they would make seeds in the second growing season. They would use up their stored food if this happened.

Figure 7.9

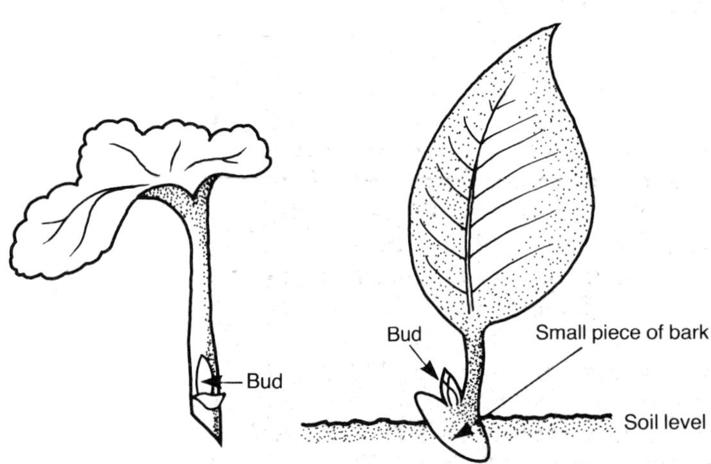

Figure 7.10 A stem cutting

Figure 7.11 A bud cutting

WHY PLANTS STORE FOOD

There are two main reasons why plants store food.

1. They can use the food to start growing very early in spring. Many plants which grow in spring have bulbs, corms, tubers or rhizomes. Daffodils, crocuses snowdrops and bluebells are examples. Seeds can only store a little food. They must wait for warmer weather before they can start growing. By growing early in spring, plants can get plenty of light, water and minerals. They do not have to compete for these with many other plants later in spring.
2. Stored food can be used for vegetative reproduction. The parent plant uses its food to start the young plant growing. This is less wasteful than making seeds. A lot of seeds die because they never find the right place to grow.

   We use plants which have food storage organs for food. (See figure 7.9.)

MAN-MADE PLANTS

Young plants can be made by taking *cuttings* or by making *grafts*.

To make a stem cutting, put the cut end of a stem into damp soil or water. Roots will grow from the bottom of the stem. The stem must be cut just below a bud as shown in figure 7.10. You can grow geraniums and carnations like this.

To make a bud cutting, cut a small piece of bark from a twig. The bark should have a bud and leaf fixed to it. Push the cutting into the soil as shown. (See figure 7.11.) Roots will grow from the bud.

To make a cleft graft, cut a small twig from the plant which you want to grow. This is cal-

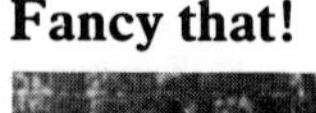

Fancy that!

"Heavy weight champions"; three growers of record-breaking vegetables with their produce: a 69lb (31.05 kg) marrow, a 211lb 8½oz (96.15 kg) pumpkin and a 6lb 7½oz (2.94 kg) onion.

led the scion. Push the scion into a cut made in a twig of another closely-related plant. This is called the stock. The stock has roots.

Hold the graft together with tape and cover it with wax. This keeps out rain, bacteria and fungi. The cambium layer of the stock should touch the cambium layer of the scion for best results. This method can be used with apple trees. (See figure 7.12.)

A variety of apple may have a good flavour but its seeds might grow into plants with small, sour apples. Grafting makes sure that the right sort of apples are made by the tree. A fruit grower cuts the scion from the sort of apple tree he wants to grow. He grafts this onto a wild apple stock. The apples will always have a good flavour.

Rose growers use bud grafting. Roses may have a beautiful colour or scent but their seeds may grow into plants with poor flowers. Grafting makes sure that the right kind of flowers are made. A rose grower cuts

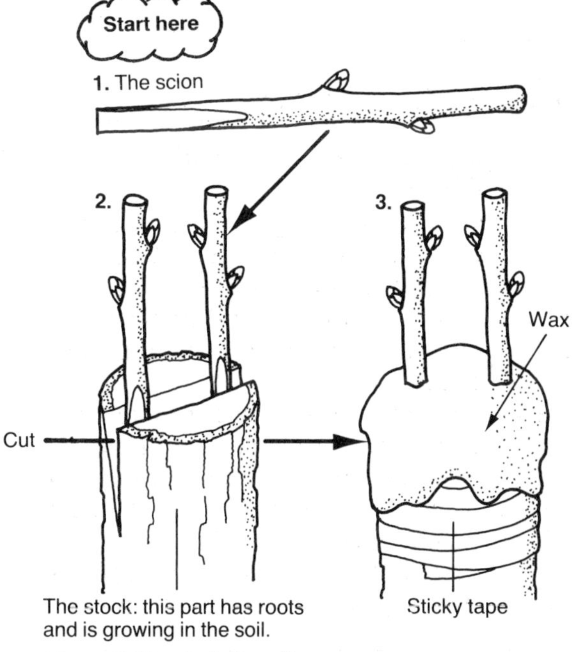

Figure 7.12 A cleft graft

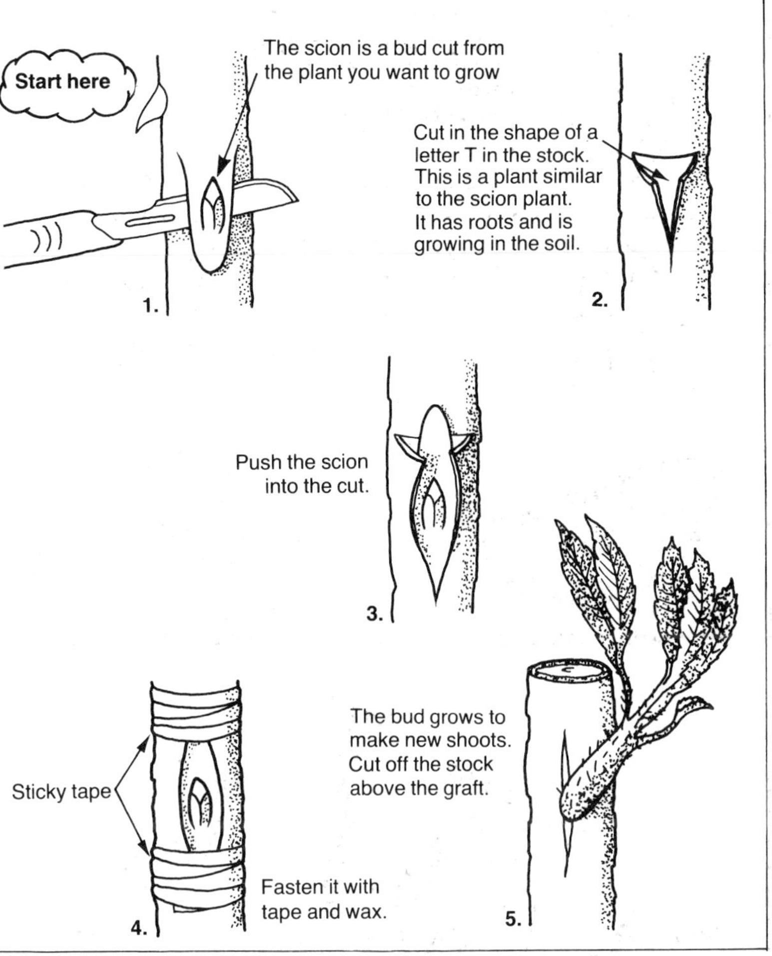

Figure 7.13 A bud graft

a scion from the sort of rose bush he wants to grow. He grafts this onto a wild hedge rose grown from seed. The bud grows using food and water from the stock. The flowers will be like those of the scion plant. (See figure 7.13.)

Cuttings and grafts are ways of reproducing plants that have good fruits or flowers. It makes sure that the fruits and flowers are always the same. Sexual reproduction cannot be used for this because it causes variation in seeds.

Summary

Plants have different kinds of *life cycles*. *Annuals* like poppies live for one year. *Biennials* like carrots live for two years. Biennials make their seeds in the second year. *Perennials* live for many years. Trees and bushes are *woody perennials* because their stems do not die in winter. Some woody perennials are *deciduous* and drop their leaves in winter. *Evergreen* woody perennials never lose their leaves all at once.

Many plants reproduce by *vegetative reproduction* when part of the plant grows to make a new plant. These new plants are exactly like the parent plant. *Tubers, bulbs, corms* and *rhizomes* are underground food storage organs. Many food storage organs are important human foods.

Cuttings and *grafts* are ways of getting young plants exactly the same as the parent. Plants grown from seeds are not exactly the same as the parents.

Important words

Annual	a plant which lives for one year.
Biennial	a plant which lives for two years.
Perennial	a plant which lives for many years.
Herbaceous	plants in which the shoots die in winter.
Vegetative reproduction	the growth of a new plant from a part of the old plant without using seeds; it is a kind of asexual reproduction.
Grafting	making new plants by joining together a piece of stem or a bud from one plant with the stem of another plant.
Cutting	making new plants by pushing a piece of stem into soil.
Deciduous	a plant which sometimes has no leaves because all its old leaves fall off at one time of year.
Evergreen	a plant which always has leaves because the old leaves do not all fall off at once.

Questions

A.

Put each of these parts of sentences into the correct order.

1. marrows are annuals / biennials and make — seeds in their second year but / onions and carrots are

2. vegetative reproduction helps / but does not help — their dispersal / young plants to grow well

B.

1. Why do you think many plants use vegetative reproduction as well as sexual reproduction?

2. Why do plants store food?

3. Think of four different ways in which you can cook potatoes and write them down. Which of these different methods is (a) quickest, (b) most nutritious, and (c) most expensive?

4. Keep a record of how many times each week you eat (a) stem tubers, (b) bulbs, and (c) root tubers. What kinds of food substance are in each one(see Topic 20)?

C.

Use the key to identify each of the storage organs shown in figure 7.14. Write down the name of each type of storage organ when you have identified it.

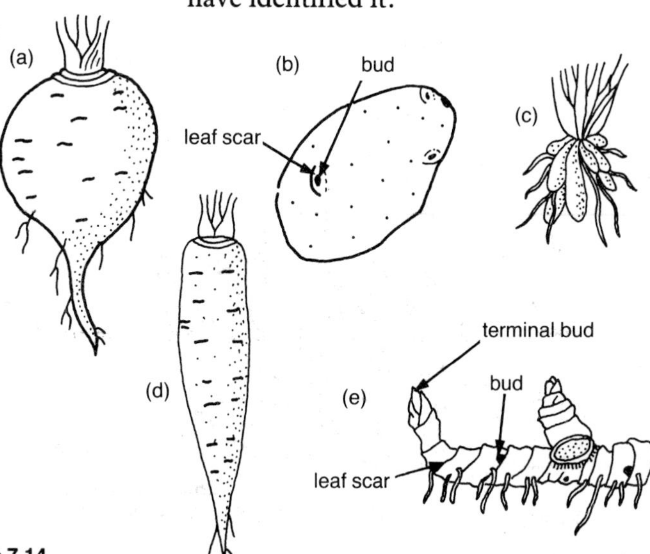

Figure 7.14

Key

1. Mainly made up of a number of fleshy leaves .... Bulb
Does not consist mainly of fleshy leaves .... go to 2

2. Buds and scars both present ... go to 3
Buds and scars not both present .... go to 5

3. An elongated horizontal stem .... Rhizome
A short swollen stem .... go to 4

4. A vertical swollen stem with some roots clearly visible .... Corm
A swollen stem possessing 'eyes' .... Stem tuber

5. A single, large swollen root with a few thin secondary roots .... Tap root
Several swollen roots with a number of thinner roots ..... Root tuber

(EAEB)

TOPIC 8

THE FLOWER

Plants which have flowers use them to make *seeds*. The seeds are made by sexual reproduction and will grow into new plants.

The female sex organs are the *carpels*. Each carpel is made of an *ovary*, a *style* and a *stigma*. (See figure 8.1a.) Inside the ovary are one or more *ovules*. Each ovule has a female sex cell inside.

The male sex organs are the *stamens*. Each stamen is made of a filament and an *anther*. (See figure 8.1b.) The filament (or stalk) holds up the anther. The anther makes *pollen* grains. Each pollen grain has a male sex cell inside.

Most flowers have both male and female sex organs and are called *hermaphrodite*. Some flowers have *either* male or female sex organs. (See figure 8.2.)

Some flowers have only one carpel, while others have many carpels. (See figure 8.3.) The buttercup flower has many carpels.

Flowers often have coloured and scented *petals* which may be protected by *sepals*. The sepals are often green and look like small petals. (See figure 8.4.)

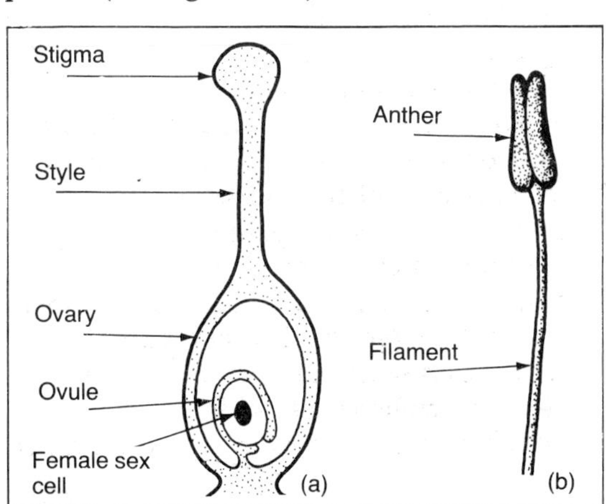

Figure 8.1

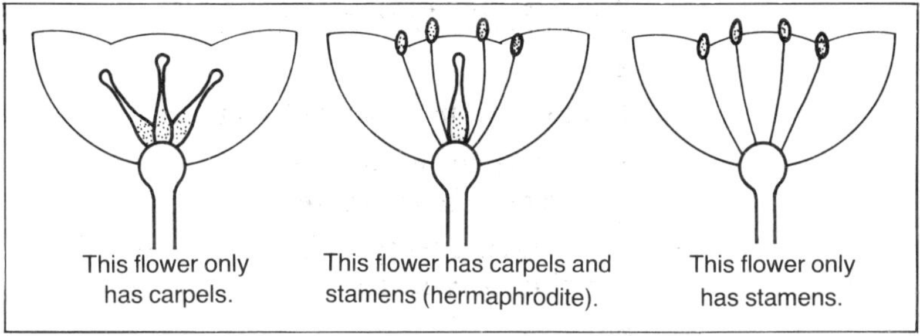

Figure 8.2

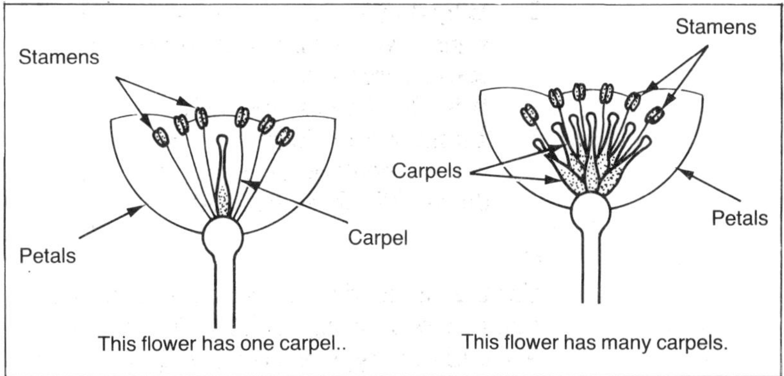

Figure 8.3

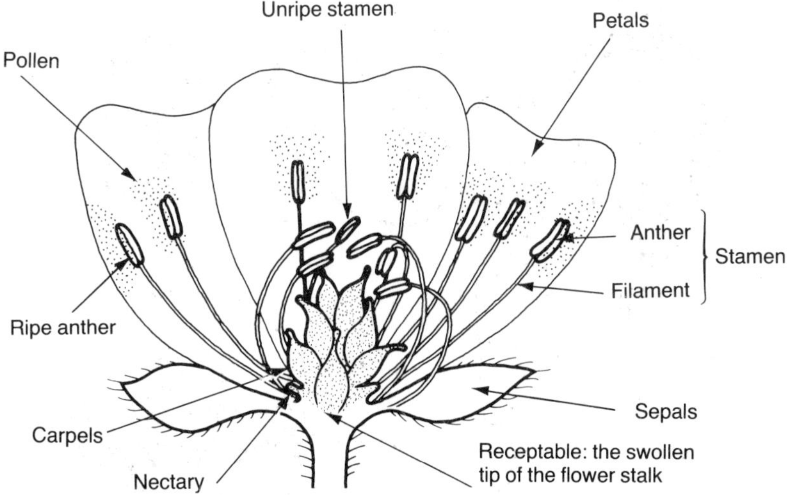

Figure 8.4 Section through a buttercup flower

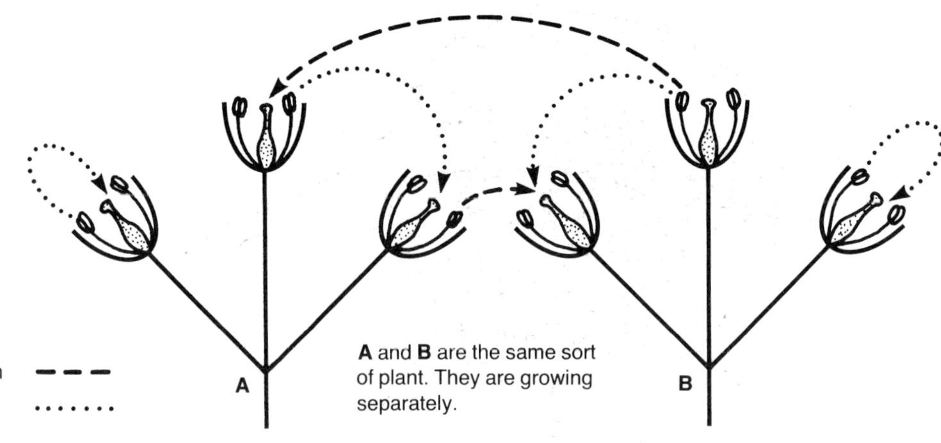

Figure 8.5

POLLINATION

Pollination happens when pollen is carried from anthers to stigmas.

Cross-pollination happens between two flowers on separate plants of the same sort. Pollen goes from the anthers of one flower to the stigmas of the other flower.

In self-pollination, pollen goes either from anthers to stigmas of the same flower, or from anthers to stigmas of another flower on the same plant. (See figure 8.5.)

Cross-pollination makes seeds which grow into stronger, more disease-free plants. Many flowers have ways of helping cross-pollination to happen. Holly and willow have male flowers on one plant and female flowers on another plant and so only cross-pollination can happen. Buttercup flowers (see figure 8.4) have stamens *and* carpels (hermaphrodite) but these ripen at different times. Because of this, cross-pollination is more likely than self-pollination in buttercups. If cross-pollination does not happen, some plants use self-pollination as a last chance. Any pollination is better than none at all!

HOW POLLINATION HAPPENS

Pollen can be carried from flower to flower by insects or wind. Pollination is very important and most flowers are adapted to use either wind or insect pollination. This gives them a better chance of being pollinated.

Wind pollinated flowers

The false oat has wind pollinated flowers. (See figure 8.6.) Wind pollinated flowers like the false oat often have:

1. small flowers which are not brightly coloured or easy to see,
2. no scent or nectar to attract insects,
3. feathery stigmas which hang outside the flowers (the stigmas can catch more pollen like this),
4. anthers which hang outside the flowers so that all the pollen is blown away,
5. flowers which open before the leaves (leaves might stop pollen getting to the flowers),
6. a lot of pollen (most of the pollen will be wasted so a lot has to be made),
7. pollen grains which are smooth and light (the wind can carry these long distances as they stay in the air longer).

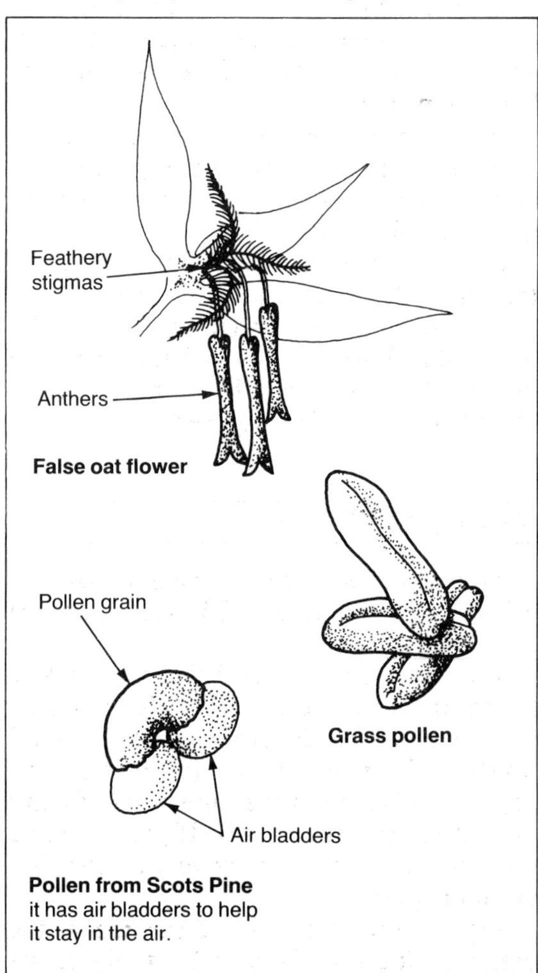

Figure 8.6

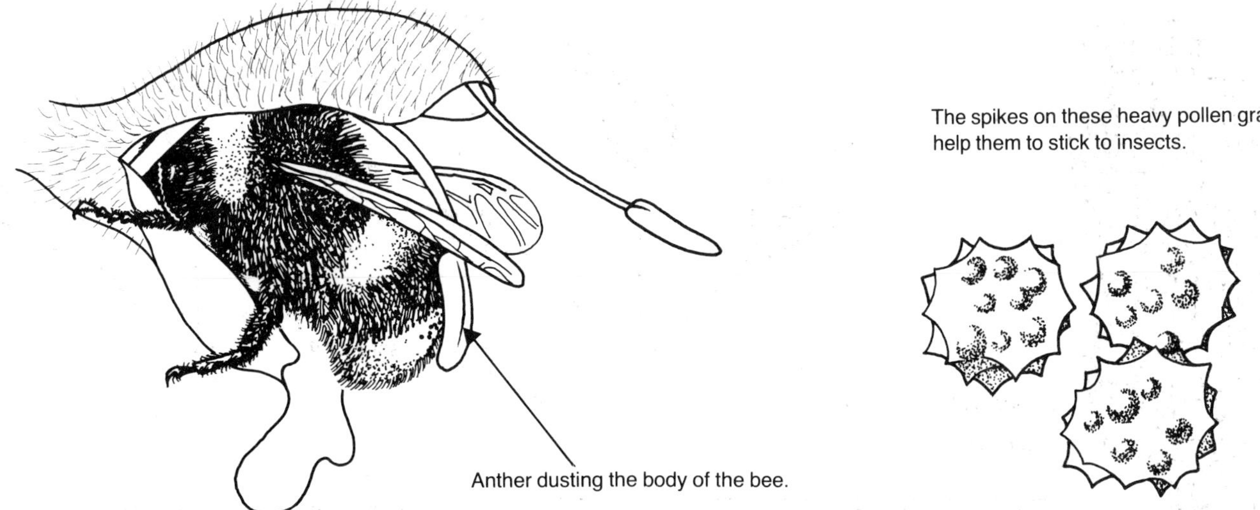

Figure 8.7 Insect pollination in the meadow sage flower

Insect pollinated flowers

The meadow sage has insect pollinated flowers. In figure 8.7, the bee is pushing into the flower to get nectar. An anther has moved down to drop pollen onto the hairy body of the bee. The bee might carry this pollen to another meadow sage flower on another plant. Cross pollination will then have happened.

Insects are attracted to some flowers because of their bright colours, scent and nectar. Nectar is a sweet liquid which some insects use for food.

Insect pollinated flowers are big so that they can hold up big insects like bees.

The stamens and stigmas are usually inside the flowers. This is because pollen need not be set free into the air, as the insects come to collect it! (See figure 8.8.)

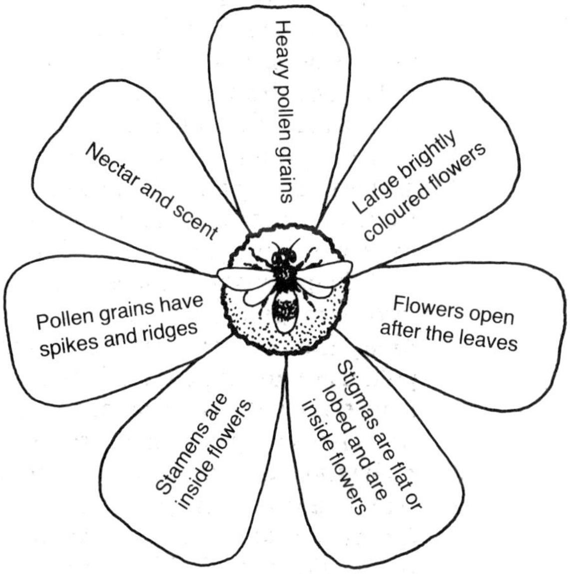

Heavy pollen grains
Large brightly coloured flowers
Flowers open after the leaves
Stigmas are flat or lobed and are inside flowers
Stamens are inside flowers
Pollen grains have spikes and ridges
Nectar and scent

Figure 8.8 An insect pollinated flower

FERTILISATION

Fertilisation means the joining of a male sex cell and a female sex cell. These sex cells are also called *gametes*.

The male gamete (sex cell) is a tiny nucleus found in each pollen grain. The female gamete is a slightly larger nucleus found inside each ovule. Before fertilisation can happen, pollen from the same kind of plant must drop onto the stigma. If pollen from a different kind of plant arrives, fertilisation cannot happen.

Sugary liquid from the stigma makes the pollen on it grow. Each pollen grain bursts and a pollen tube grows out. (See figure 8.9.)

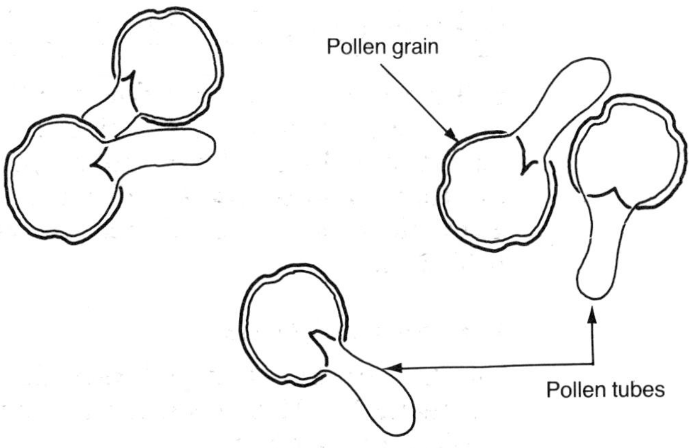

Figure 8.9 Pollen grains growing in sugar solution

The pollen tube pushes down through the style to the ovary. It finds an ovule and gets inside through a tiny hole called the *micropyle*. Then the male gamete goes down the pollen tube. The tip of the pollen tube bursts and the male gamete goes into the ovule. Fertilisation happens when male and female gametes join together. The joined gametes are called a *zygote*. The zygote develops into an *embryo* (or young plant) inside a seed. A seed is made of an embryo, a seed coat (or *testa*) and a food store. (See figure 8.10.)

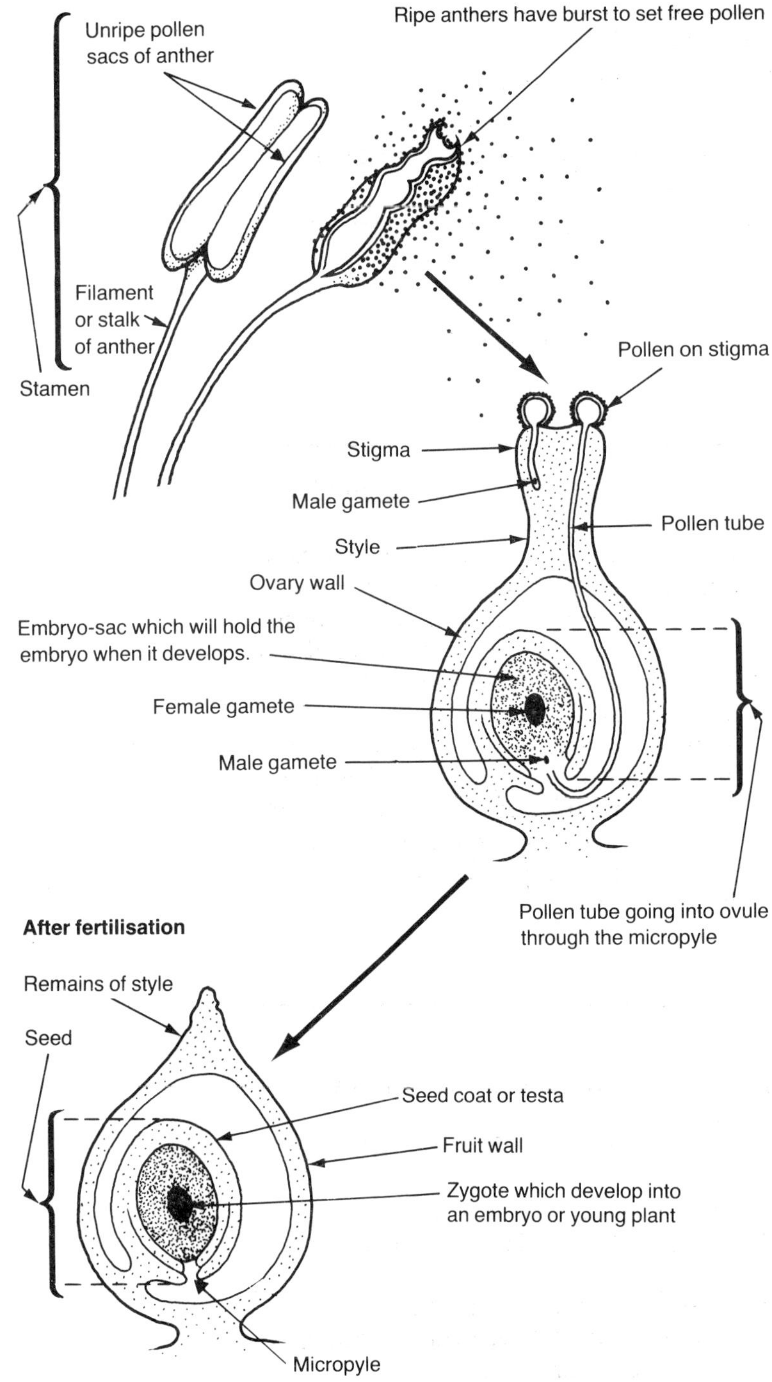

Figure 8.10

An ovule which is not fertilised cannot make a seed. An ovary with 60 ovules inside needs 60 pollen grains to fertilise all its ovules.

A seed is made from a fertilised ovule. The testa is made from the wall of the ovule. The embryo is made from the zygote. The fruit is made from the ovary.

Summary

Flowers make *seeds* by sexual reproduction. Many flowers have both male and female sex organs in them and are *hermaphrodite*. Other flowers have only male or female sex organs. Male sex organs are *stamens* which make *pollen* inside their *anthers*. Pollen contains male sex cells. Female sex organs are *carpels* which contain the female sex cells inside *ovules*. Male and female sex cells are sometimes called *gametes*.

Pollination is when pollen is carried from anthers to stigmas. *Cross-pollination* happens between two flowers on separate plants of the same sort. *Self-pollination* happens in the same flower or between different flowers on the same plant. Pollination is done by wind or insects.

Fertilisation happens when a male and a female sex cell join. This happens inside an ovule and a *zygote* is made. The zygote develops into a young plant or *embryo*. The ovule develops into a *seed* which has the embryo inside.

Fancy that!

A single hazel catkin makes about 4 million pollen grains each year!

Hayfever is caused by pollen affecting the eyes and noses of people who are sensitive to it. Grass pollen is the main cause of hayfever.

Butterflies and moths can feed only on liquids. Nectar is their main food.

Some tropical flowers are pollinated by birds such as the hummingbird.

Some greenhouse plants, such as tomatoes, need pollinating by hand. Gardeners use a small brush for this!

Important words

Seed — a small structure, made by sexual reproduction in flowering plants, which grows into a young plant.
Carpel — the female part of a flower.
Ovary — part of a carpel which contains the ovules.
Ovule — a structure inside an ovary containing a female gamete.
Gamete — a male or female sex cell.
Zygote — a fertilised female gamete.
Stigma — the part of a carpel that pollen lands on in pollination.
Style — the part of a carpel that holds up the stigma.
Stamen — the male part of a flower.
Anther — part of a stamen which makes pollen.
Pollination — the process by which pollen is carried from an anther to a stigma.
Petal — part of a flower which is usually coloured and often scented; in insect pollinated flowers, it helps to attract insects.
Sepal — part of a flower which helps to support and protect the petals.
Pollen — small grains made by anthers; pollen grains contain male gametes.
Fertilisation — the joining together of a male and a female gamete.

Things to do

Grow your own pollen grains!
You will need:

a microscope slide
7% sucrose solution (this is a solution of sugar)
some Visking sheet
a petri dish
some ripe stamens from a flower
a pair of forceps
a piece of filter paper

1. Cut a piece of Visking sheet to fit onto a microscope slide.
2. Put a few drops of the sucrose solution onto the Visking sheet.
3. Use your forceps to pull off a ripe stamen.
4. Shake the anther over the Visking sheet.
5. Put the slide with the Visking sheet on top into a petri dish which has a piece of wet filter paper in the bottom. Put the lid on the petri dish.
6. After 24 hours take the slide out of the dish. Put a cover slip over the Visking sheet. Look at it under the high power of a microscope. You should be able to see pollen tubes coming from some of the pollen grains.

Questions

A.
Write out each sentence in your book. Fill in the missing words from those in the box. Some words may be used more than once.

anthers — gamete — pollination — pollen grains — ovules — seed — big — filaments — fertilisation — carpel — zygote — wind — small — nectar — insect — hermaphrodite — micropyle

1. A …… is the female sex organ of a flower.
2. A style, stigma and ovary make a …… .
3. Pollen is made by …… .
4. Stamens are made of …… and …… .
5. An ovary contains one or more …… .
6. Flowers which have male and female sex organs are …… .
7. Some flowers make a sweet liquid called …… .

8. ...... is when pollen is carried from stamens to stigmas
9. ...... is when a male and female sex cell join.
10. Wind pollinated flowers are usually ....
11. Flowers which open before leaves are usually ...... pollinated.
12. Insect pollinated flowers are usually ....
13. The stigmas of ...... pollinated flowers are usually feathery.
14. Pollen from ...... pollinated flowers usually has spikes.
15. A ...... is a male or female sex cell.
16. The male sex cells are inside ....
17. The female sex cells are inside ....
18. A ...... is made when male and female sex cells join.
19. The ...... is where a pollen tube goes into an ovule.
20. After fertilisation an ovule is called a ......

B.

Figures 8.11 and 8.12 are two drawings of the same grass flower at different stages of development.

1. Name the parts labelled W and X on the two grass flowers.
2. Which of the two grass flowers is the younger? Give one reason which is visible for your answer.
3. Figure 8.13 is of a foxglove flower cut in half. Draw the structures that are the same as W and X on the grass flower diagrams.

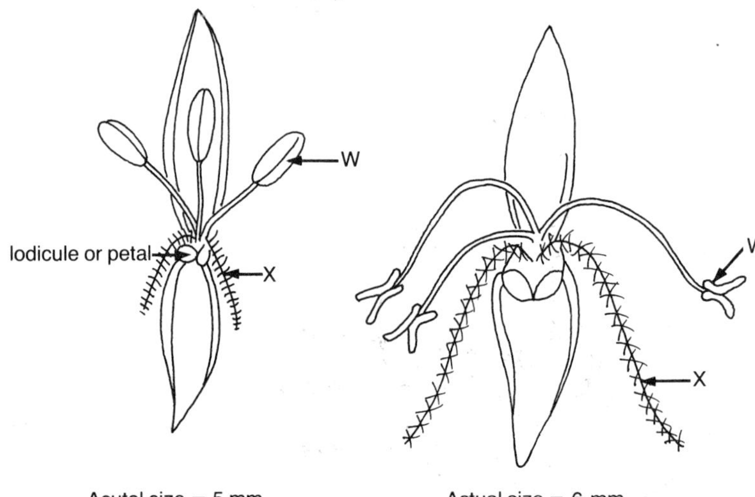

Figure 8.11 **Figure 8.12**

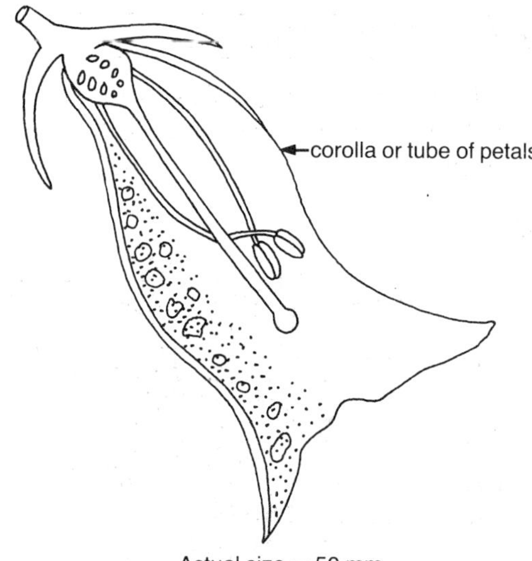

Figure 8.13

4. State four differences between the two flowers.
5. Figure 8.14 shows the distribution of plants of bulbous buttercup and the creeping buttercup two years after a field has been ploughed into ridges and furrows to improve the drainage.
(a) Which buttercup is more common on the ridges of the field?
(b) How many bulbous buttercups and creeping buttercup per square metre are found in the furrow 30 metres from the edge of the field?
(c) Suggest a factor which could be responsible for the different distribution of these two forms of buttercups.

(SREB)

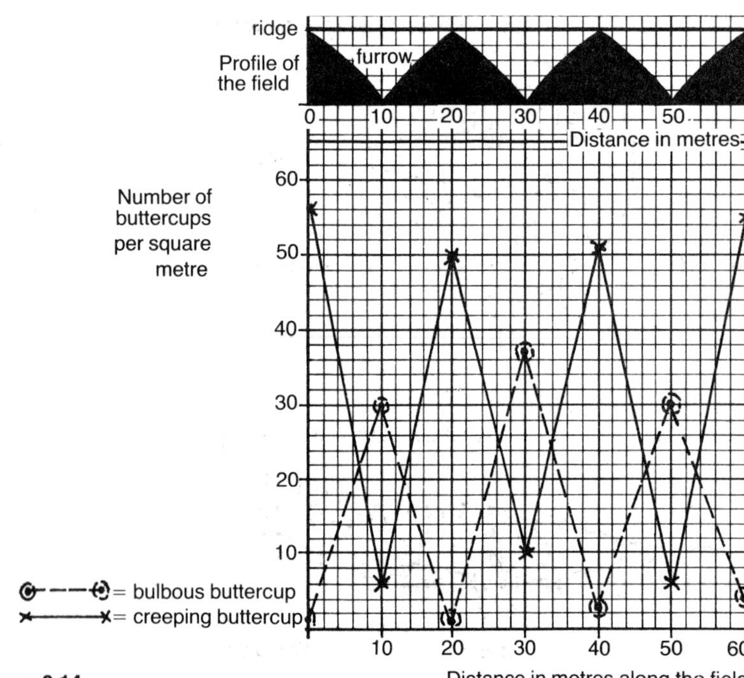

Figure 8.14

TOPIC 9

DISPERSAL OF SEEDS AND FRUITS

HOW FRUITS ARE MADE

A seed is made from a fertilised ovule. A fruit is made from the ovary after fertilisation. (See figure 9.1.)

Figure 9.1

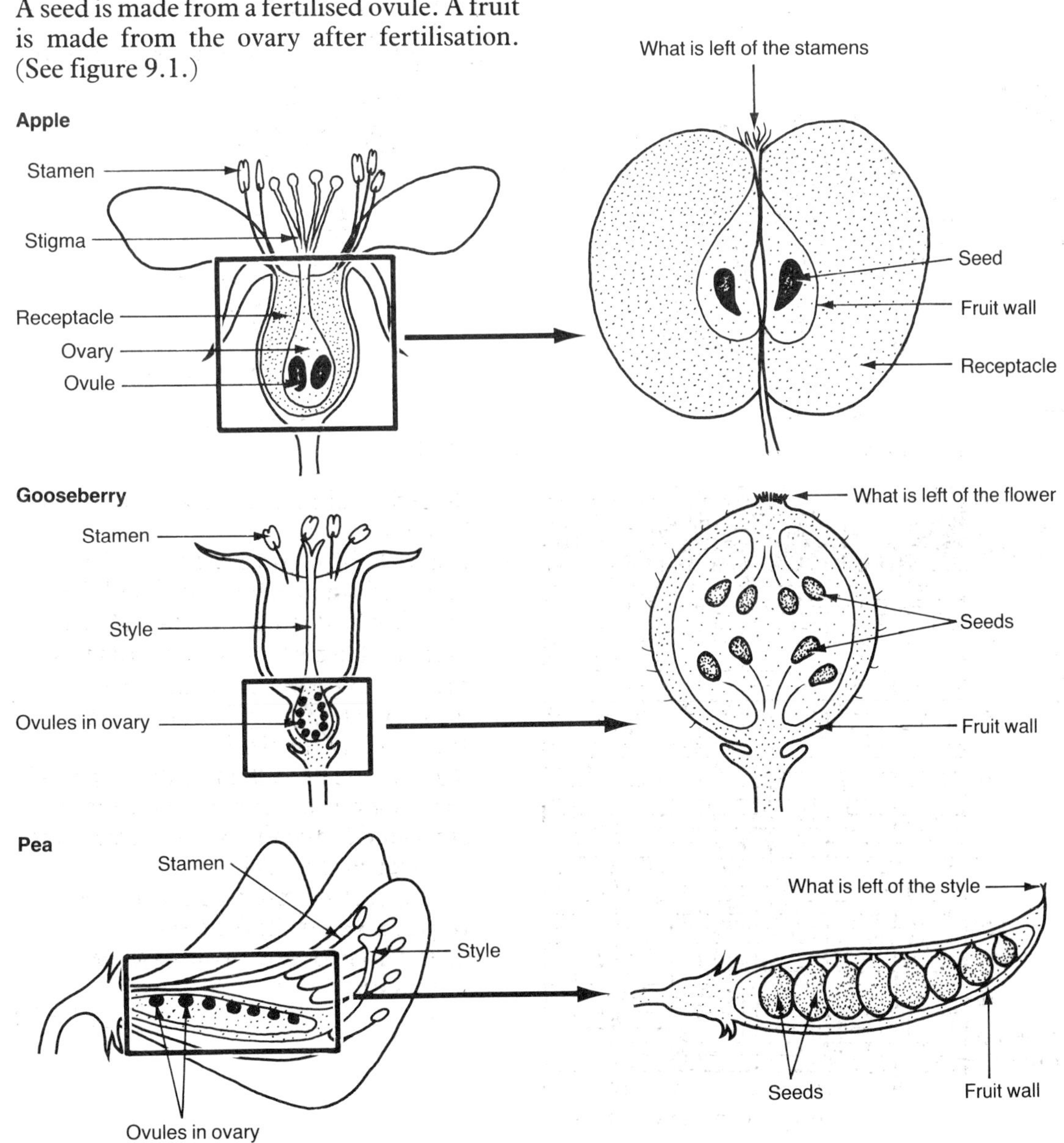

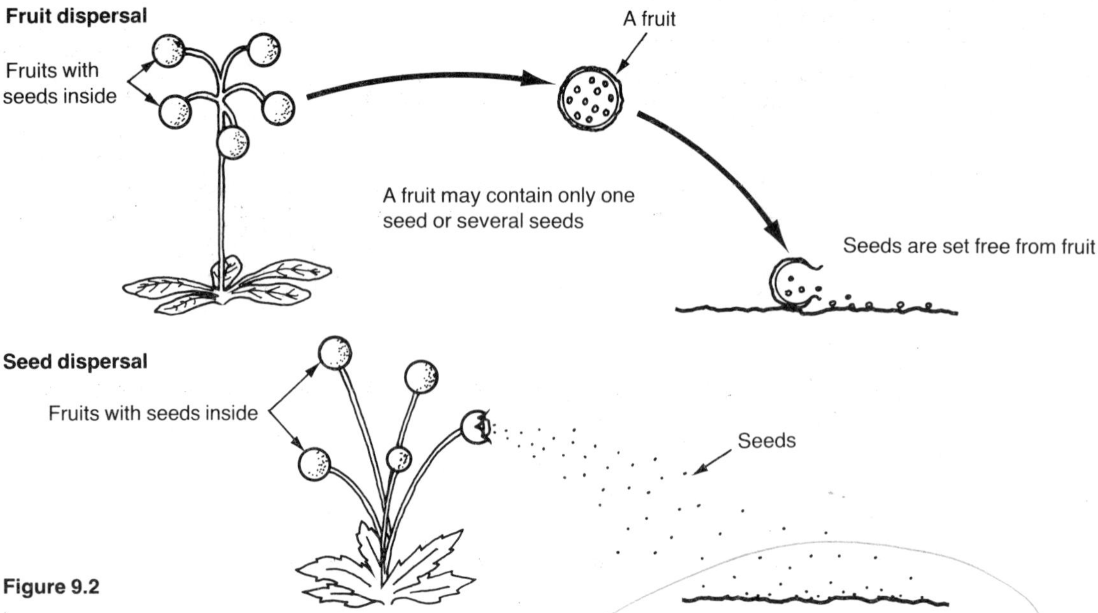

Fruit dispersal

Fruits with seeds inside

A fruit

A fruit may contain only one seed or several seeds

Seeds are set free from fruit

Seed dispersal

Fruits with seeds inside

Seeds

Figure 9.2

DISPERSAL OF FRUITS AND SEEDS

Fruits protect seeds and help to disperse them. Dispersal happens when fruits and seeds are carried away from the plant that made them. Dispersal is needed so that the seeds will not be overcrowded when they grow. Seeds need plenty of space to grow properly. In some plants the whole fruit is dispersed. In other plants, the seeds are dispersed from the fruit. (See figure 9.2)

Fruits and seeds are usually dispersed by:

- wind, or
- animals, or
- the plant itself.

Most dispersal happens by wind or animals.

WIND DISPERSAL

Fruits and seeds dispersed by wind have some of these characteristics (see figure 9.3):

- small size,
- a wing,
- a 'parachute' of hairs.

Dandelion

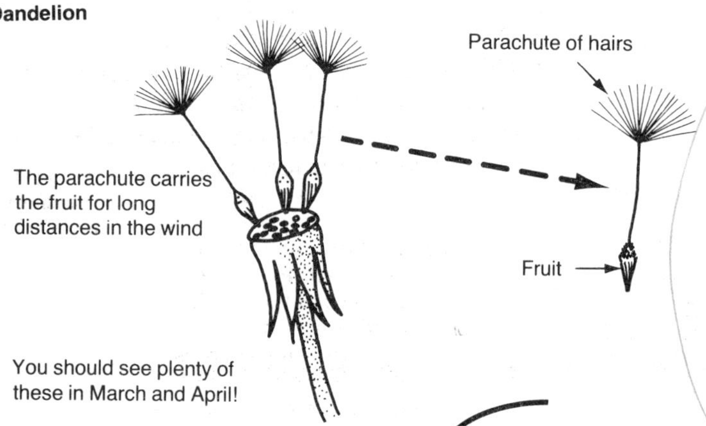

Parachute of hairs

The parachute carries the fruit for long distances in the wind

Fruit

You should see plenty of these in March and April!

Poppy

A poppy fruit; look closely and think how the seeds are dispersed from the fruit.

Sycamore

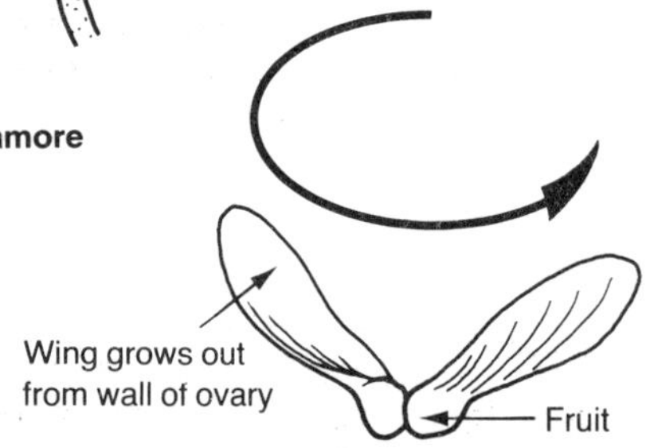

Wing grows out from wall of ovary

Fruit

The wing makes the fruit spin as it falls. It takes longer to drop because it spins and is carried further away from the tree. Look for sycamore trees in gardens, hedges, woods and roadsides

Thistle

Look for thistles on waste ground

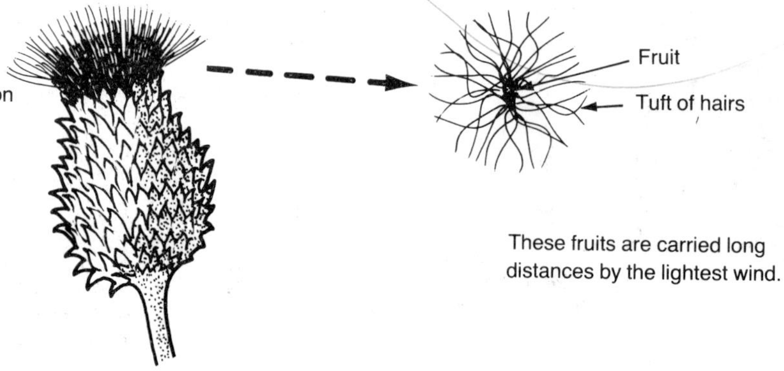

Fruit

Tuft of hairs

These fruits are carried long distances by the lightest wind.

Figure 9.3

ANIMAL DISPERSAL

Fruits and seeds dispersed by animals often have these characteristics (see figure 9.4):
- hooks,
- juicy flesh,
- bright colour.

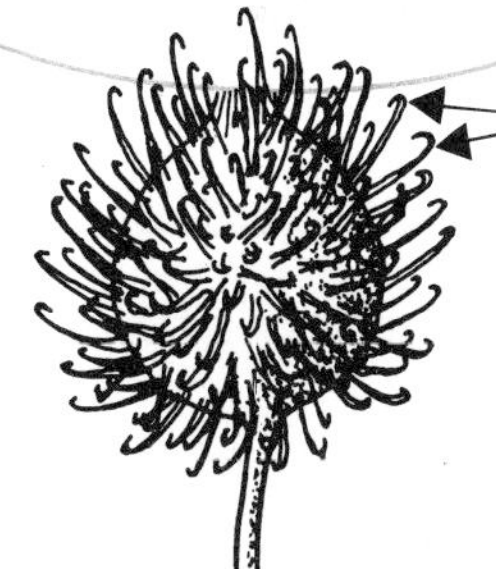

Hooks

The hooks catch in the fur of animals Later the fruits fall off when the animal is some distance away from the plant that made them.

Burdock grows in woods and hedges. The hooks also catch in clothing!

A burdock fruit

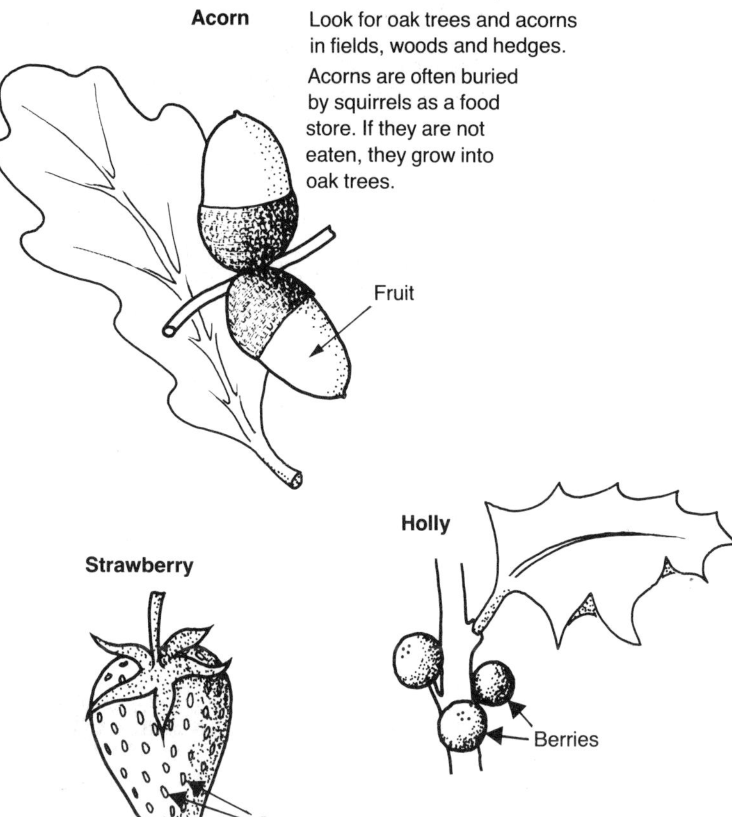

Look for oak trees and acorns in fields, woods and hedges. Acorns are often buried by squirrels as a food store. If they are not eaten, they grow into oak trees.

These 3 fruits are shiny and juicy. They are very attractive to birds. Blackberries are the favourite food of many birds: thrushes, robins, crows and blackbirds. The seeds are not digested and pass out with the droppings. When they reach the ground they have some ready fertiliser to help them grow!

Figure 9.4

SELF-DISPERSAL

Seeds dispersed by the plant itself are usually thrown out. A sudden strong twisting movement of the fruit wall does this. (See figure 9.5)

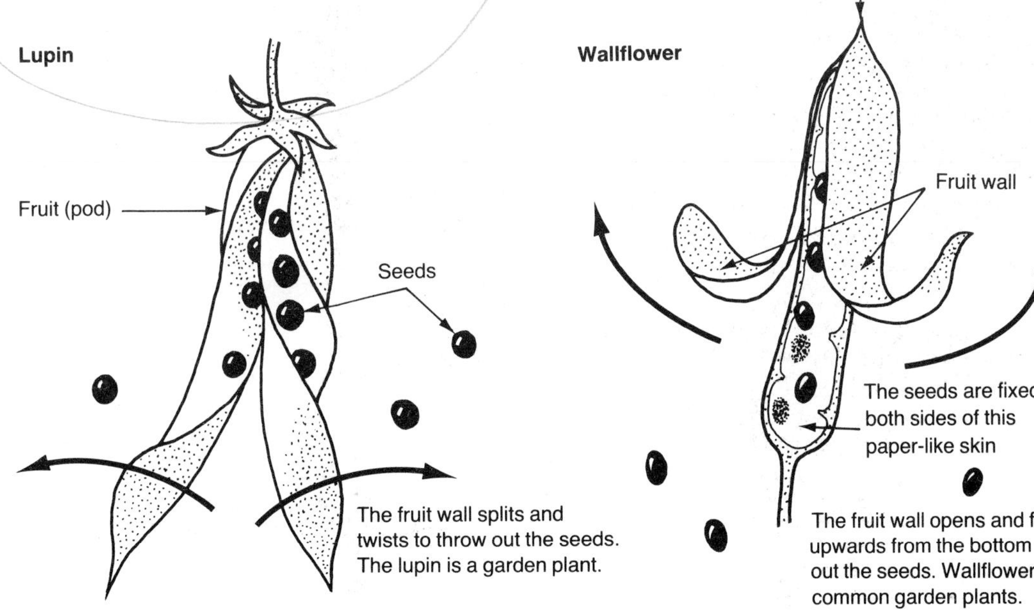

Figure 9.5

Fancy that!

Orchids have seeds as small as dust! They are blown for great distances by the wind.

The fruit of the peanut plant develops underground! After fertilisation, the flower stalk turns downwards and pushes into the soil.

Summary

A seed is made from a fertilised *ovule*. Seeds are protected by a *fruit* which develops from an *ovary*.

Seeds or fruits are *dispersed* by *wind*, *animals* or the *plant itself*. Wind dispersed fruits and seeds are small. Animal dispersed fruits and seeds are bigger and may have bright colours, juicy flesh or hooks.

Important words

Ovule	contains a female sex cell which can be fertilised by a male sex cell.
Seed	a fertilised ovule which grows into a young plant.
Fruit	develops from the ovary after fertilisation.
Ovary	contains the ovules.
Dispersal	the spreading of seeds or fruits from plants.

Things to do

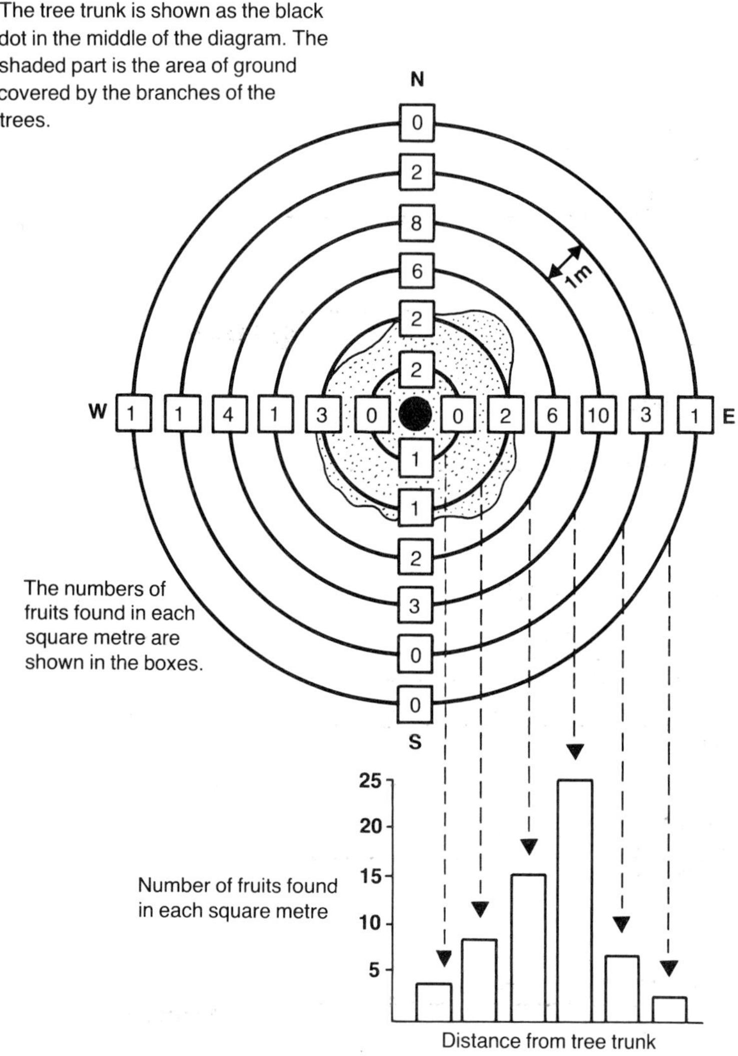

Figure 9.6 **The graph shows how far most fruits are dispersed**

1. You will need:
   a magnetic compass
   a piece of rope or string several metres long, marked off in metres.

   Find a sycamore or ash tree with plenty of fruits. The best time to do this is in September and October. Try to find a tree with a lot of space around it.

   Find north with your magnetic compass. Lay the rope out along this line from the bottom of the tree trunk. Count the number of fruits in an area one metre square at distances of one metre along the rope. Do this until you can find no more fruits. Write down the number of fruits you find at each square meter.

   Do this again along the south, west and east lines from the tree.

   Along which line did you find most fruits? What could have caused this to happen?

   Make a graph of how far the fruits dispersed from the tree. Do this by adding up the numbers in the four boxes of each circle. Figure 9.6 shows you how to make the graph.

   How far did most of the fruits disperse from the tree?
2. Fasten a hair dryer to a retort stand. Hold some wind dispersed seeds above and in front of it. Turn the hair dryer on. Drop the seeds and measure how far they are blown. Compare different seeds to find out which is blown the furthest.

Questions

A.

Write out each sentence into your book. Fill in the missing words from those in the box. Some words may be used more than once.

pod — self-dispersal — fruit — dispersal — animals — wind — seed

1. A fertilised ovule develops into a ....
2. The ovary develops into a ...... after fertilisation.
3. The fruit often helps the ...... of seeds.
4. In some plants the whole ...... containing the seed is dispersed.
5. Seeds are contained inside the ...... which may help to disperse them.
6. Overcrowding of young plants is stopped by the ...... of seeds and fruits.
7. Dandelion fruits are dispersed by .... .
8. Blackberry and holly fruits are dispersed by ....
9. Lupins and wallflowers spread their seeds by ....
10. The fruit of a lupin is called a ....

B.

1. Why must seeds and fruits be dispersed?
2. Which kind of dispersal do you think carries the seeds furthest? Give a reason for your answer.
3. Why are fruits dispersed by animals often juicy and brightly coloured?
4. Why do you think many seeds cannot be digested by birds?

C.

Copy the following figures into your book, labelling them where indicated, and then answer the questions.

1. (a) Name the plant bearing this fruit.
   (b) State the method of dispersal.
   (c) What is the advantage of this method?

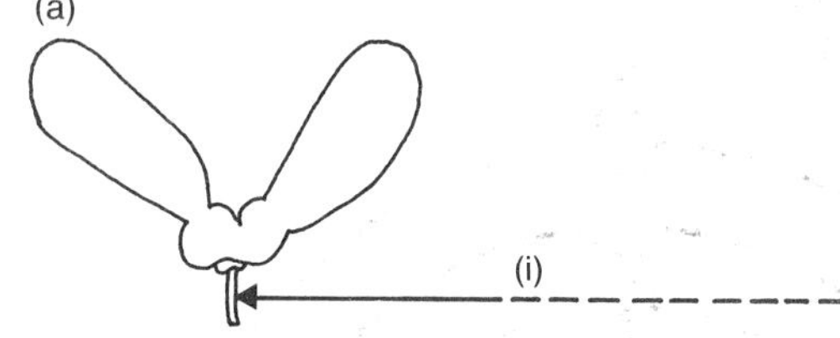

2. (a) Name the plant bearing this fruit.
   (b) State the method of dispersal.
   (c) How is the fruit adapted to this method?

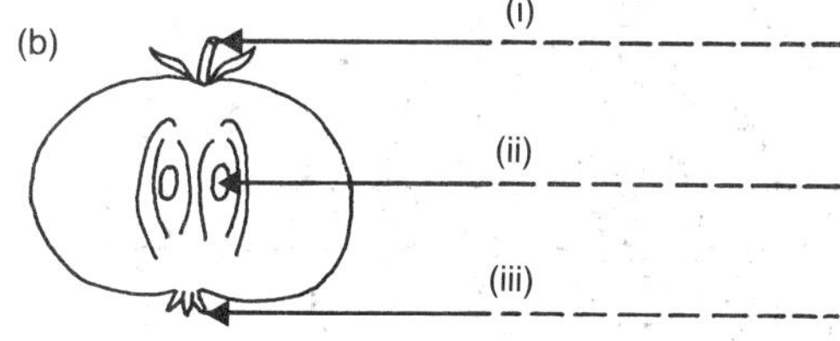

3. (a) Name the plant bearing this fruit.
   (b) State the method of dispersal.
   (c) What is the disadvantage of this method?

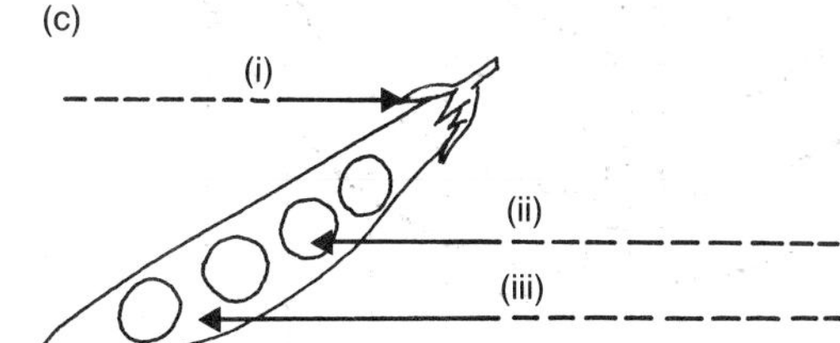

4. (a) Name the plant bearing this fruit.
   (b) State the method of dispersal.
   (c) Name two other plants bearing similar fruits.

(SEREB)

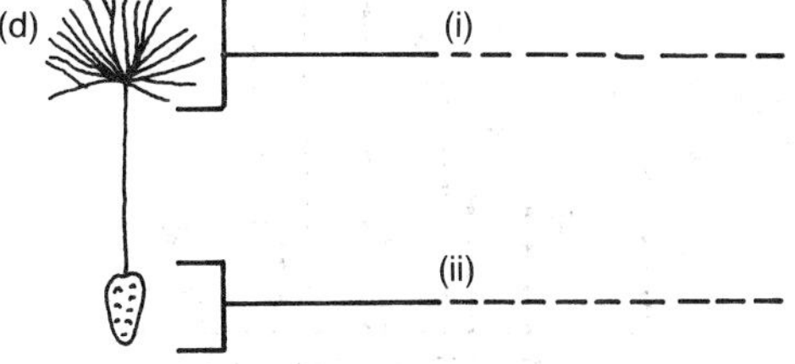

Figure 9.7

TOPIC 10

SEEDS AND GERMINATION

Seeds grow from fertilised ovules and are then dispersed (or spread out) from thc plant that made them. If they drop in the right sort of place, seeds grow into seedlings or young plants. (See figure 10.1.)

Figure 10.1

1. Seed dispersed by wind. It contains an embryo-plant and a store of food.

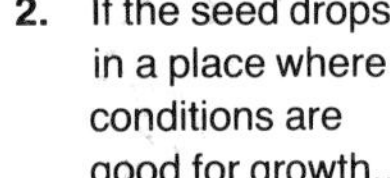

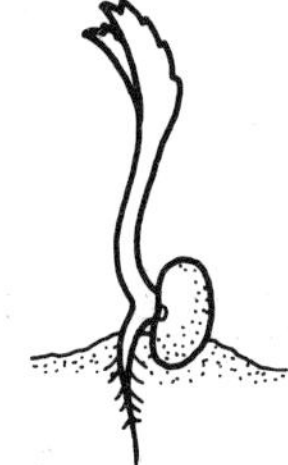

3. ...it germinates and a young plant grows out.

A seed has a tough coat or *testa* around it. Thc tcsta is madc from thc laycrs which protect the ovule.

The *micropyle* is a tiny hole in the testa. The pollen tube went into the ovule through the micropyle at fertilisation.

The *hilum* is the place where a seed was fixed to the ovary.

The *embryo* is a tiny plant inside the testa. It has a small root or *radicle*, and a shoot or *plumule*.

The *cotyledons* are the seed leaves. They often have a food store which is used by the seed when it starts to grow. The cotyledons are fixed to the embryo with short stalks. Plants with narrow leaves, such as wheat, maize and grasses, have seeds with one cotyledon. These plants are called *monocotyledons*. Other flowering plants have seeds with two cotyledons and are called *dicotyledons*.

Figure 10.2
A cross-section of a fertilised ovule showing where the parts of the seed come from.

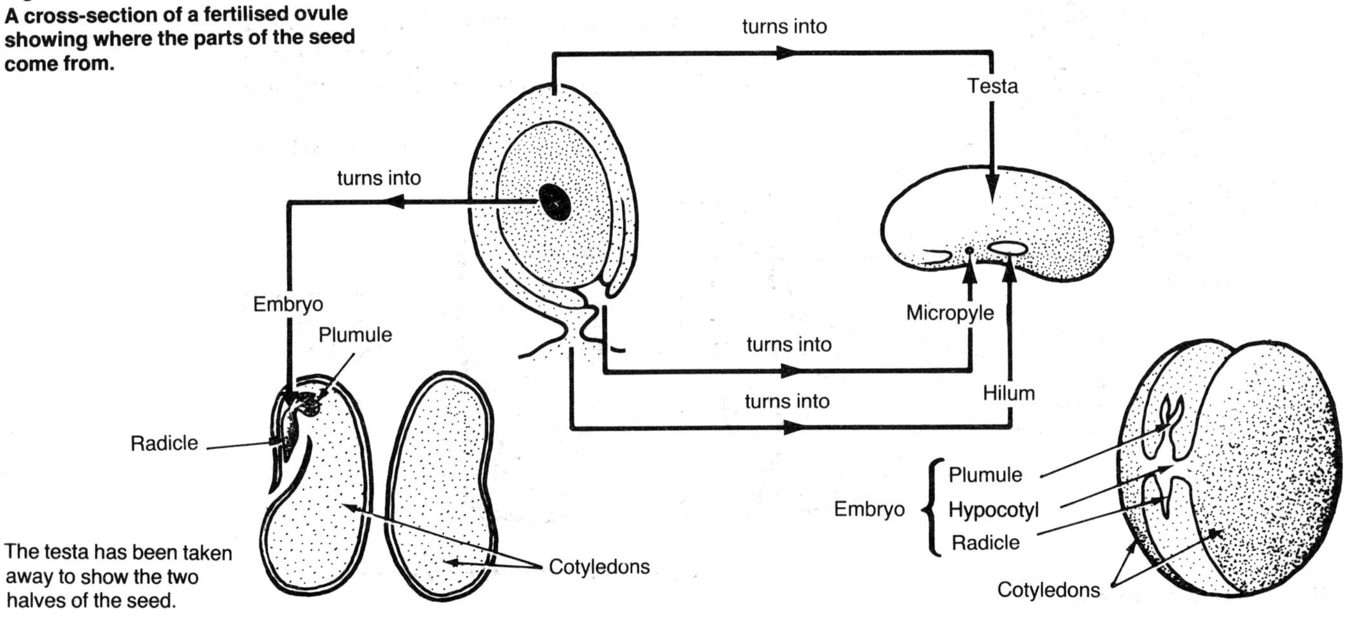

turns into
Testa
turns into
Embryo
Plumule
Micropyle
turns into
turns into
Hilum
Radicle
Embryo { Plumule, Hypocotyl, Radicle
Cotyledons
Cotyledons

The testa has been taken away to show the two halves of the seed.

GERMINATION...

Seeds start to grow (or germinate) in warm, wet soil. Water goes through the micropyle and makes the seed swell. This makes the testa split open and the radicle grows out. Root hairs grow from the radicle and begin to absorb water and minerals from the soil. Side roots grow from the main root and fix the seed firmly in the soil.

...IN THE FRENCH BEAN SEED

The hypocotyl starts to grow and pulls the cotyledons out of the testa. The cotyledons protect the plumule as the hypocotyl pushes up through the soil. When they are above the soil, the cotyledons fold back and the plumule grows out. The cotyledons get smaller as the food in them is used up by the growing seedling. The leaves made by the plumule begin to make food for the plant by photosynthesis.

The French bean has *epigeal germination* because the cotyledons grow up above the soil. (See figure 10.3.)

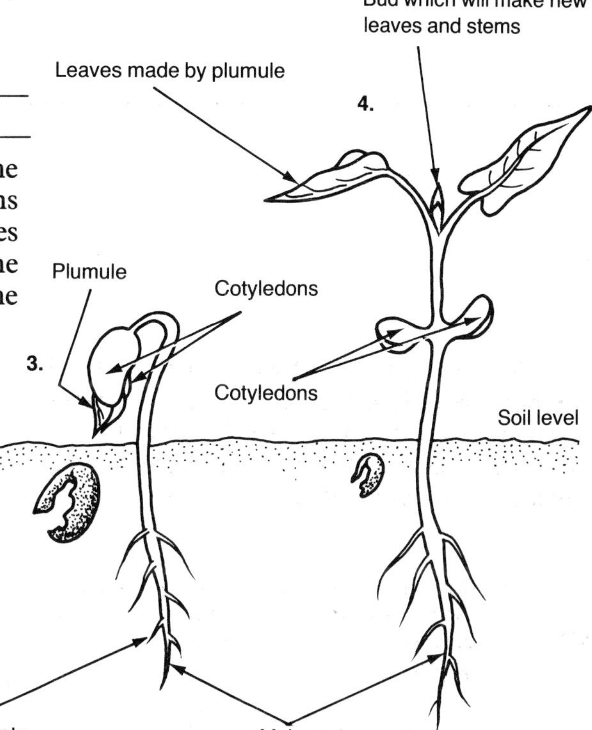

Figure 10.3 Germination of the French been seed

...AND IN THE MAIZE FRUIT

Maize fruits are packed closely together on a 'cob'. They are sometimes called 'corn-on-the-cob.' Each fruit has one cotyledon inside. When the fruit grows, the cotyledon stays below the ground. This is called *hypogeal germination*. The cotyledon absorbs food from the food store (or endosperm) and

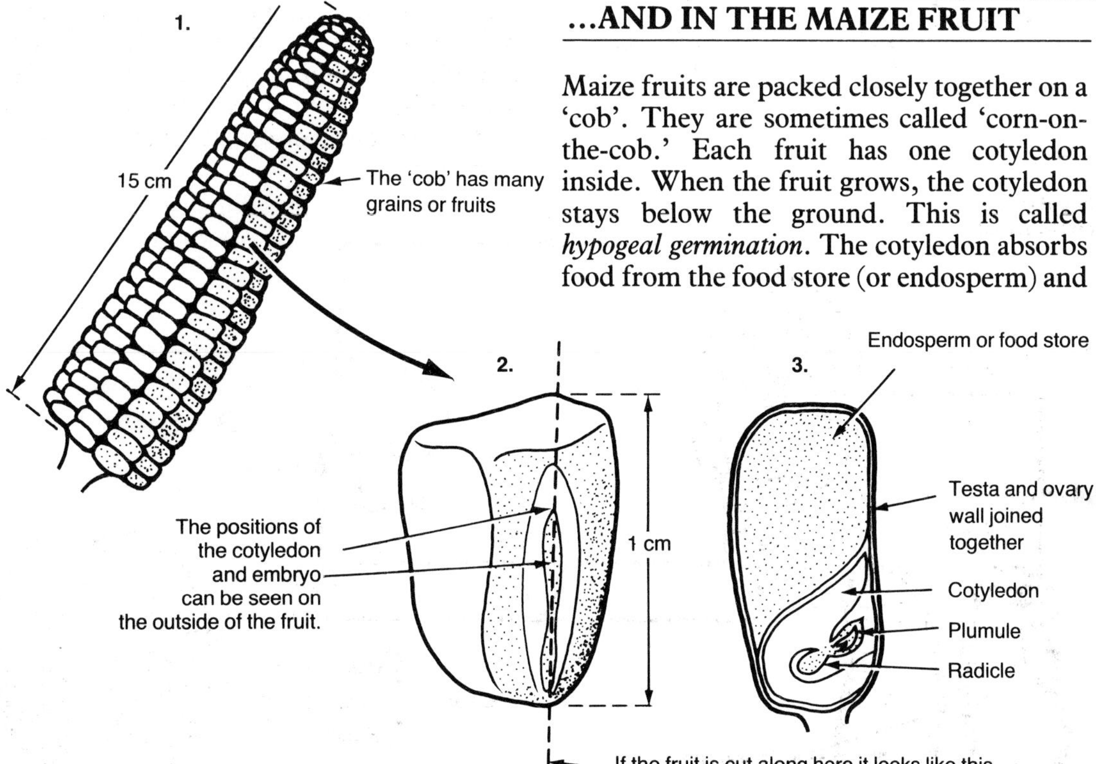

Figure 10.4 A maize fruit

passes it on to the root and shoot. The plumule is protected by a sheath or *coleoptile* as it pushes through the soil. When it is above the soil, the plumule bursts out of the coleoptile. The leaves made by the plumule then start to make food by photosynthesis. (See figures 10.4 and 10.5.)

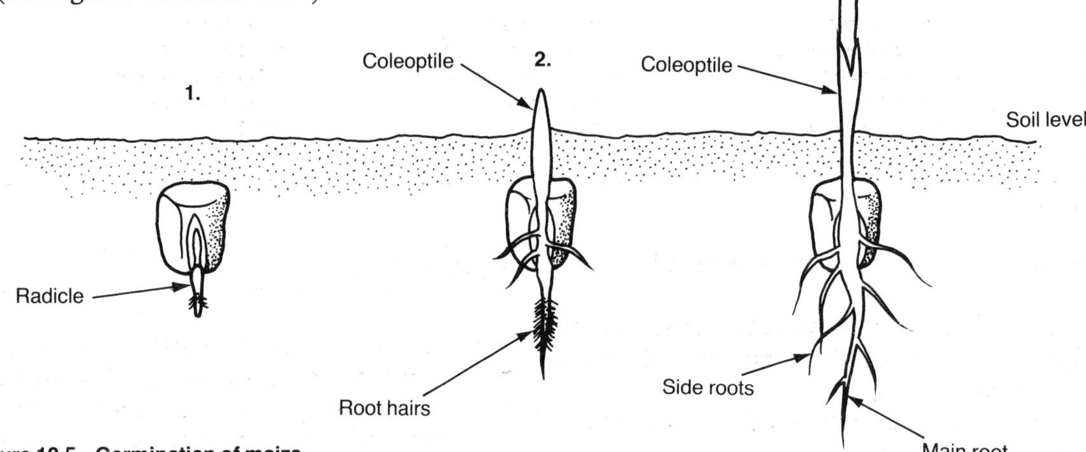

Figure 10.5 Germination of maize

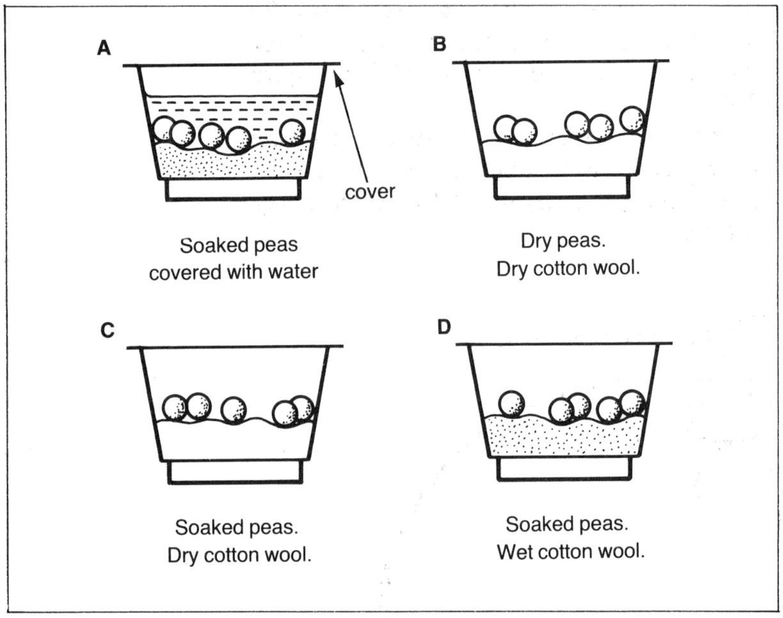

A
cover
Soaked peas covered with water

B
Dry peas. Dry cotton wool.

C
Soaked peas. Dry cotton wool.

D
Soaked peas. Wet cotton wool.

Figure 10.6

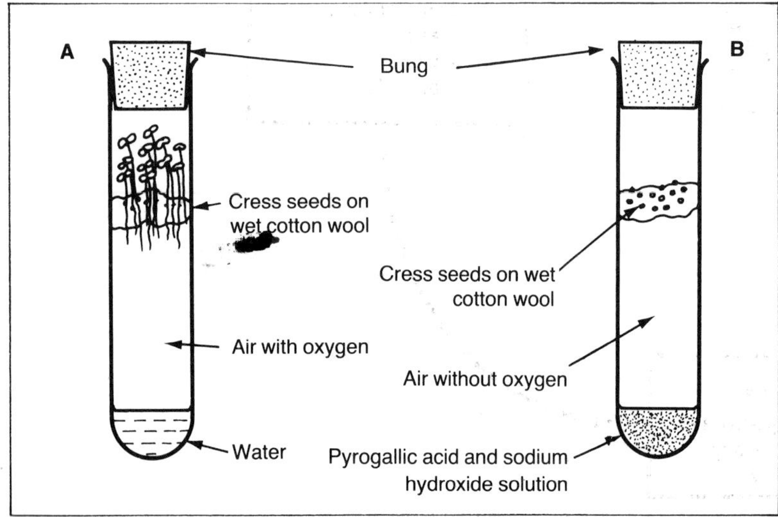

Figure 10.7

WHAT IS NEEDED TO MAKE SEEDS GERMINATE?

Is water needed for germination?

Set up four margarine tubs, as shown in figure 10.6. Soak the seeds for 24 hours before you use them.

Put all four tubs in the same warm place and leave for a few days.

Result

Only the seeds in **D** will grow well.

Is oxygen needed for germination?

Set up two test tubes, as shown in figure 10.7.

A solution of pyrogallic acid and sodium hydroxide absorbs oxygen from the air. The cotton wool must not touch this solution.

Take great care with the pyrogallic acid solution. It attacks clothing and skin. Wash off any spills at once with plenty of water.

Put both tubes in the same warm, light place. **A** is a control experiment. You use it to show that the seeds will only germinate if oxygen is present.

Result

Only the seeds in tube **A** will grow well.

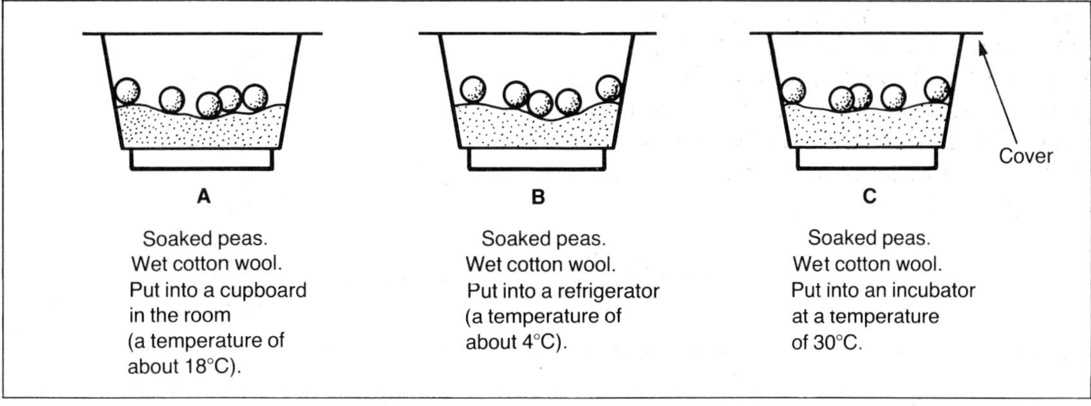

Figure 10.8

Is warmth needed for germination?

Set up three margarine tubs, as shown in figure 10.8. Soak the seeds for 24 hours before you use them.

Leave the seeds for a few days. Look at the temperature every day.

Result

Only the seeds in **A** will grow well. The seeds in **B** will not germinate at all. The seeds in **C** will germinate but they may have fungi on them.

Seeds need water, oxygen and warmth to germinate. They cannot germinate properly if the temperature is too high or too low.

DORMANCY

Seeds do not always germinate as soon as they are dispersed. They may lie *dormant* in the soil, especially in autumn and winter. Dormant seeds are alive but there are not many chemical reactions happening inside them. Can you think why seeds may lie dormant? Some seeds can be dormant for many years and still germinate! (See figure 10.9.)

Seeds are very dry when they are dispersed. Because water is needed to start germination, this dryness helps seeds to stay dormant.

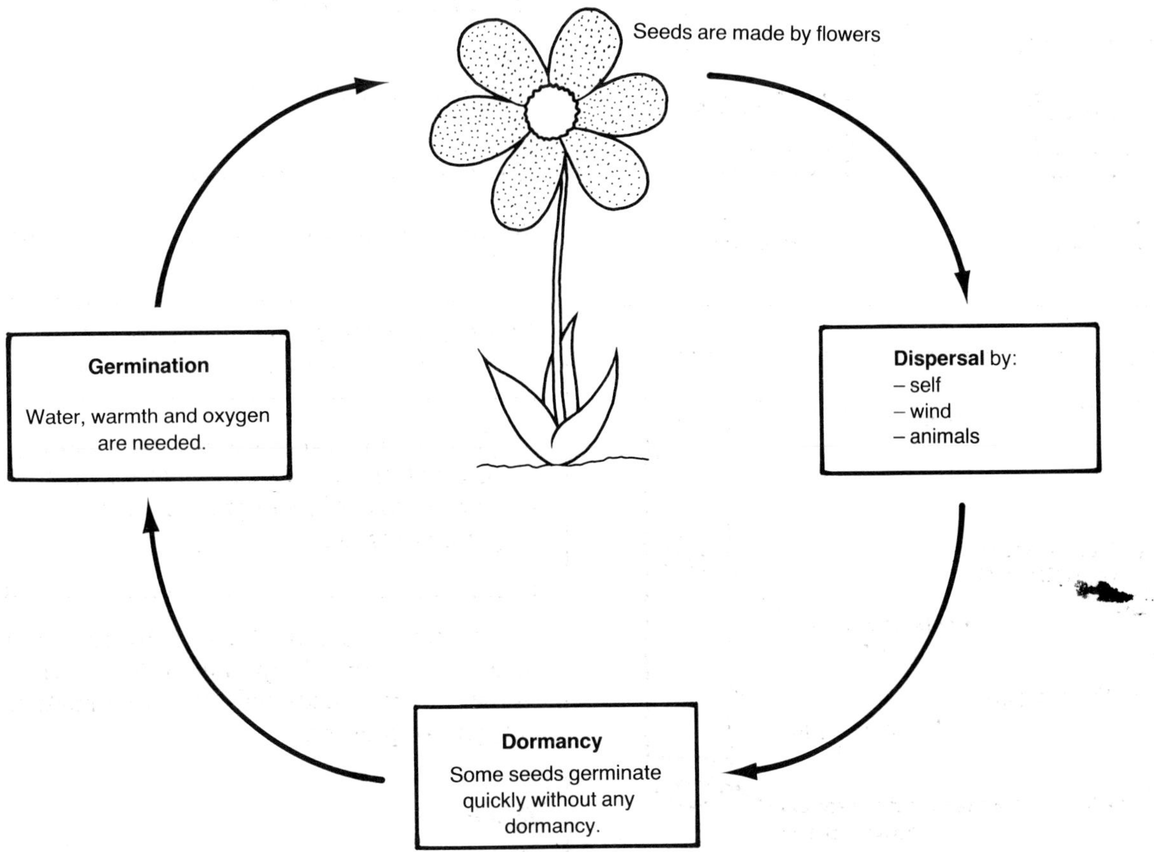

Figure 10.9 What happens to a seed

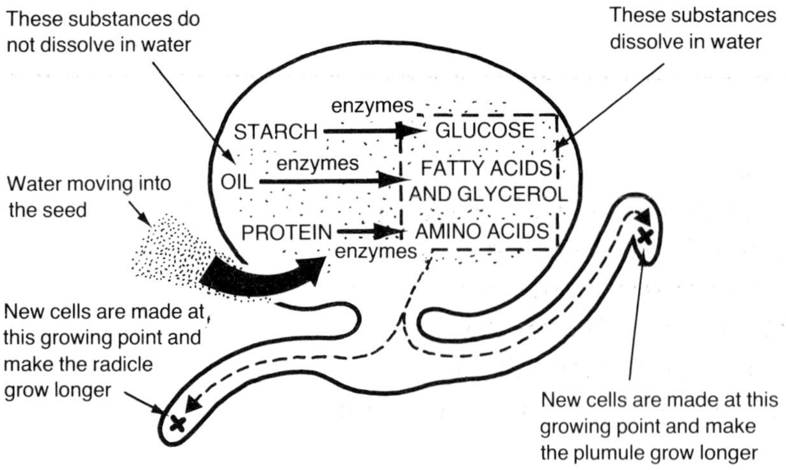

These substances do not dissolve in water

These substances dissolve in water

STARCH → enzymes → GLUCOSE
OIL → enzymes → FATTY ACIDS AND GLYCEROL
PROTEIN → enzymes → AMINO ACIDS

Water moving into the seed

New cells are made at this growing point and make the radicle grow longer

New cells are made at this growing point and make the plumule grow longer

Figure 10.10

WHAT HAPPENS INSIDE GERMINATING SEEDS

Food stored inside seeds is dry and hard. In germination this food has to be digested and dissolved. Then it can be taken to the growing points of a seed. Chemicals called enzymes digest the stored food and dissolve it. Enzymes can only work in water. Water gets into a seed through the micropyle.

Plants use some digested food to make new cells and some to set free energy. Most of this energy is used in chemical reactions happening at the growing points. (See figure 10.10.)

SEEDS AS FOOD

Different seeds and fruits have different food stores. Sunflower and peanut fruits store oil. Pea and bean seeds store starch and protein. Soya bean seeds store oil and protein.

Many seeds are important as food for ourselves and for animals. (See figure 10.11.) Seeds can be stored easily without going bad because they are so dry.

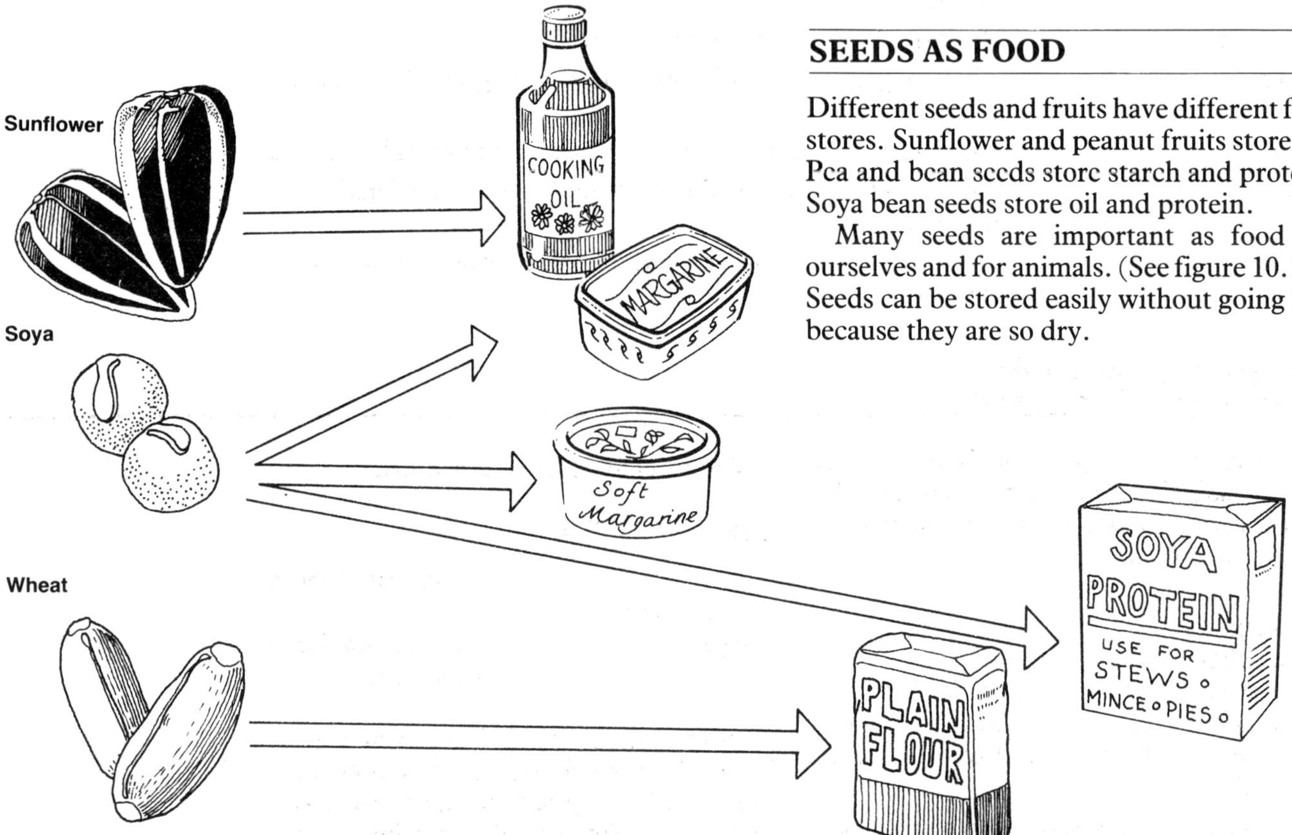

Sunflower

Soya

Wheat

COOKING OIL

MARGARINE

Soft Margarine

SOYA PROTEIN
USE FOR STEWS MINCE PIES

PLAIN FLOUR

Figure 10.11 Some important seeds and fruits

Summary

A fertilised *ovule* grows into a *seed* which is then *dispersed* from the plant. A seed has an *embryo* and a *food store* inside it. When a seed *germinates* the embryo grows using the stored food. In some seeds, such as peas and beans, the food is stored inside the seed leaves or *cotyledons*.

In maize the food is stored in a different part of the fruit called the *endosperm*. Wheat and maize have one cotyledon and are called *monocotyledons*. Most seeds have two cotyledons and are *dicotyledons*. Seeds such as French bean have *epigeal* germination. Fruits such as maize have *hypogeal* germination.

Seeds need *oxygen*, *water* and *warmth* to germinate. Many seeds do not germinate when dispersed but stay *dormant* for a time. During germination the stored food is *digested* by *enzymes* and used for growth.

Important words

Testa	the tough seed coat.
Micropyle	a small hole in the testa.
Hilum	a scar on the testa where the seed was fixed to the ovary.
Embryo	part of a seed which grows into a young plant.
Radicle	part of an embryo which grows to form the root.
Plumule	part of an embryo which grows to form the shoot.
Cotyledon	a simple leaf forming part of the embryo of a plant.
Monocotyledons	a group of flowering plants which have one cotyledon in their seeds.
Dicotyledons	a group of flowering plants which have two cotyledons in their seeds.
Germination	the start of growth in seeds and spores.
Epigeal	a kind of germination where the cotyledons grow above the soil and turn green.
Hypogeal	a kind of germination where the cotyledons stay inside the seed.
Coleoptile	a sheath which protects the plumule of monocotyledons in germination.
Dormant	a word used to describe organisms which are resting and not growing.

Things to do

Seeds can easily be grown without planting them in soil. The ones given here are also good to eat! **Do not eat any seed unless you are sure it is safe.**

What you need:

- a jam jar
- a rubber band
- a piece of muslin or some old tights
- alfalfa, mung bean, fenugreek or lentil seeds. (Buy these from a garden shop.)

Put ¾ cup of the seeds into the jam jar. Fasten the piece of cloth over the mouth of the jar with the rubber band. pour some barely warm water into the jar and shake the seeds in the water. It is important that the water is not too hot or too cold. Pour the water away. Do this twice more. Put the jar on its side in a warm place, not on top of a radiator. Twice a day pour slightly warm water over the seeds and drain it out again.

The seeds will be ready to eat in 2–3 days. Use them in salads or sandwiches.

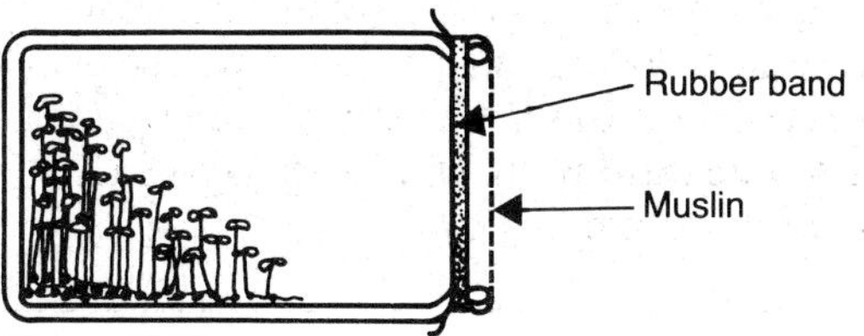

Figure 10.12

Try this recipe for alfalfa seeds.

Baked Alfalfa Cheese

4 slices bread	¾ cup grated cheese
2 slices bacon	2 eggs
margarine	¾ cup alfalfa shoots (4 mm long)

Heat the oven to 350°F. Fry or grill the bacon. Beat the cheese, alfalfa shoots and eggs together. Spread the mixture on to the bread slices. Put a dab of margarine on top of the mixture. Bake for about 15 minutes until the mixture goes puffy. Crumble the bacon over each slice. Serves 4 people. Delicious!

Questions

A.

Write out each sentence into your book. Fill in the missing words from those in the box. Some words may be used more than once.

enzymes — warmth — radicle — plumule — embryo — endosperm — cotyledons — monocotyledons — germination — hypogeal — epigeal — ovules — testa — coleoptile — photosynthesis

1. Seeds develop from fertilised ....
2. The ...... is a protective coat around a seed.
3. The tiny plant inside a seed is the ....
4. The young root is called a ....
5. Food is often stored in the ...... of a seed.
6. The young shoot is called a ....
7. Plants which have two ...... in their seeds are called dicotyledons.
8. Grasses and plants with narrow leaves are called ....
9. ...... is when seeds start to grow.
10. Seeds in which the cotyledons stay below ground during growth have ...... germination.
11. The French bean seed has ...... germination. In epigeal germination the cotyledons protect the ...... as it pushes through the soil.
12. The maize fruit has ...... germination. In monocotyledons the plumule is protected by the ...... as it pushes through the soil.
13. The food in a maize fruit is stored in the .... The cotyledon of maize absorbs food from the food store and passes it to the ....
14. Leaves made by the plumule turn green and make food by ....
15. Water, oxygen and ...... are needed for germination. Food stored in seeds is digested by ....
16. Water is needed in germination so that the ...... can begin to work.

B.

1. Explain the difference (apart from colour) between (a) white flour and wholemeal flour (b) white rice and brown rice.
2. In which parts of the world are rice and bread important in peoples' diet?
3. From which kinds of plants do we get rice and flour (see Topic 44)?

C.

Equal numbers of pea seeds were placed in each of five beakers. The pea seeds in each beaker were treated as shown in figure 10.13. Figure 10.13 also shows the results of this experiment after the pea seeds had been left to germinate for several days.

1. (a) State the meaning of the term *germination*.
   (b) In which of the beakers did the peas germinate?
   (c) For each beaker in which the seeds did *not* germinate, give an explanation why germination did not occur.
2. According to these results what external conditions are required for the germination of pea seeds?
3. Describe briefly the development of a broad bean seed from the moment it is planted until the emergence of the shoot (plumule) above ground.

(EAEB)

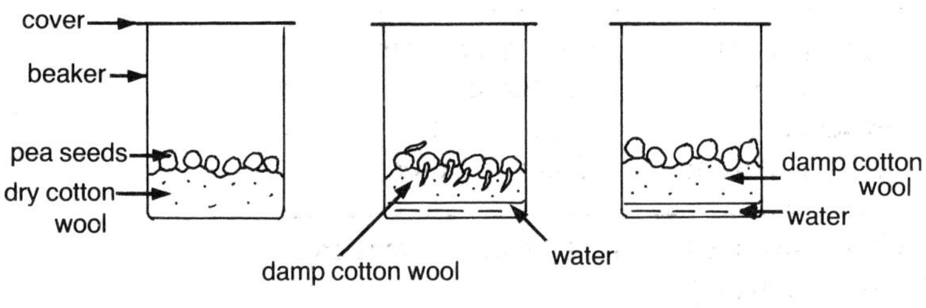

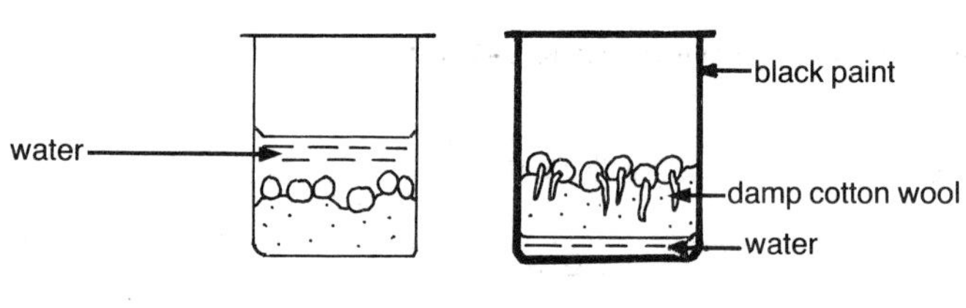

Figure 10.13

TOPIC 11

PLANT MOVEMENTS

All living things must know what changes are happening in their surroundings. The organisms must *respond* to these changes which are sometimes called *stimuli*.

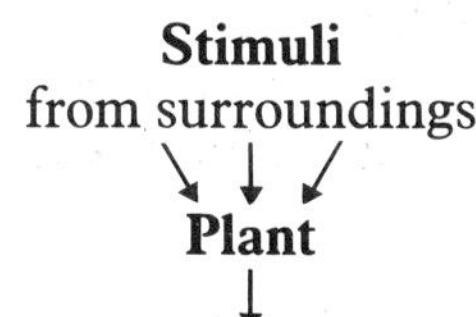

If an organism does not respond to an important stimulus it might die. Plants usually respond to a stimulus by growing towards it or away from it. These responses are called *tropisms*.

Light, water and gravity are important stimuli for plants.

PHOTOTROPISM

The response a plant makes to the stimulus of light is called *phototropism*. The stems and leaves of plants grow *towards* light and are *positively* phototropic. The roots of a few plants are *negatively* phototropic and they grow *away* from light.

Figure 11.1 shows an experiment where some cress seedlings were grown in light coming from only one side. After a few days, these seedlings were all growing towards the light. In a *control* experiment, where seedlings were grown in light coming from all directions, the cress grew normally.

The two sets of cress seedlings look different after this experiment.

Seedlings grown in light coming from one side	Seedlings grown in normal light – the **control**
Tall thin stems Small leaves Few leaves Yellow in colour	Short thick stems Big leaves Many leaves Green in colour

This shows us that, as well as causing phototropism, light:

1. slows the growth of stems,
2. is needed to make the green substance, chlorophyll.

Figure 11.1 Phototropism in leaves and stems

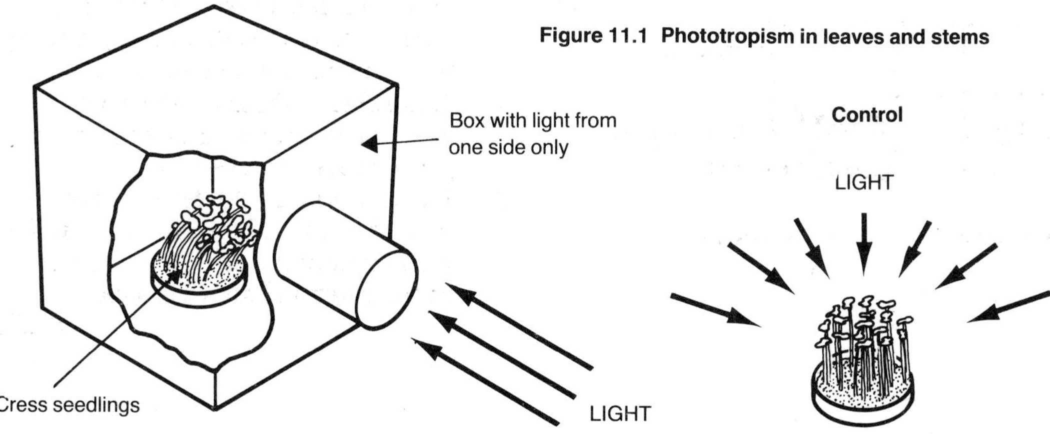

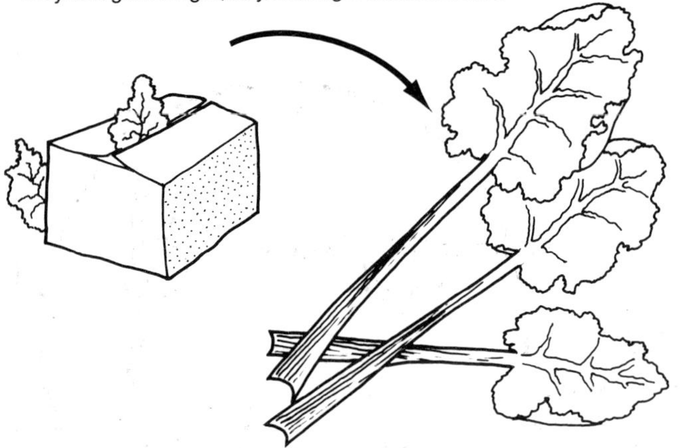

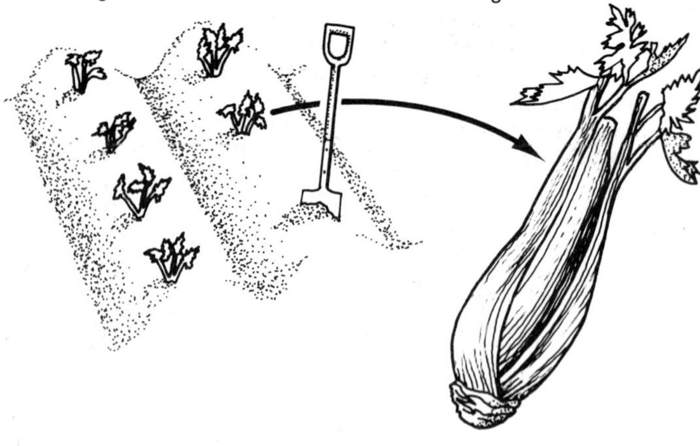

Figure 11.2

Seedlings which look like those grown in the box are said to be *etiolated*. Etiolation is sometimes used by gardeners to get tastier crops (figure 11.2).

GEOTROPISM

Gravity is a force that pulls downwards on everything which is near to or on the surface of the earth. Gravity is a stimulus acting on plants. Plants respond to this stimulus with a growth movement called *geotropism*. Stems usually grow *upwards* against the pull of gravity and are *negatively* geotropic. Roots grow *downwards* with the pull of gravity and are *positively* geotropic.

A *klinostat* (see figure 11.3) is useful for showing geotropism. A klinostat has an electric motor which slowly turns a small disc. If you fix a plant on the disc it will turn about four times an hour. This means that gravity will pull equally on all parts of the plant.

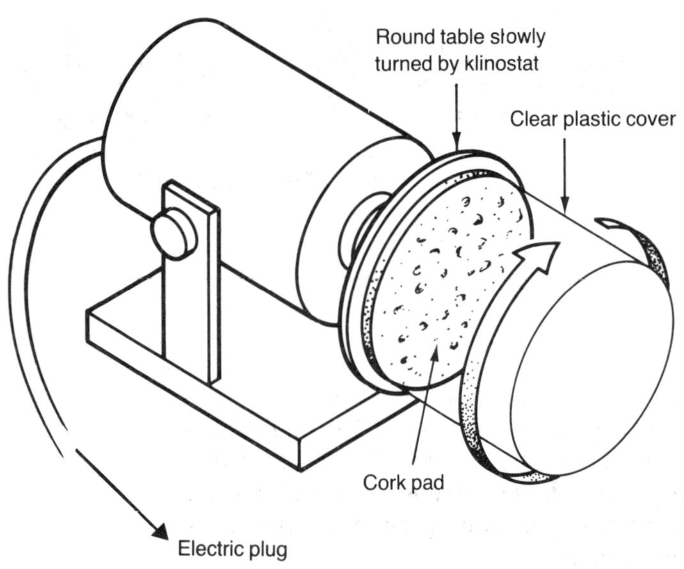

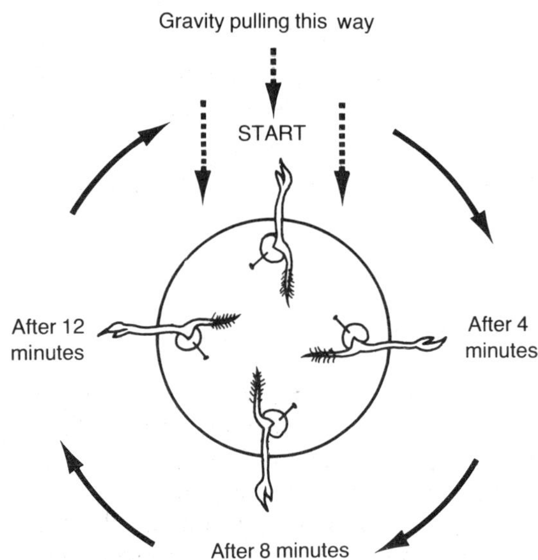

Figure 11.3 A klinostat

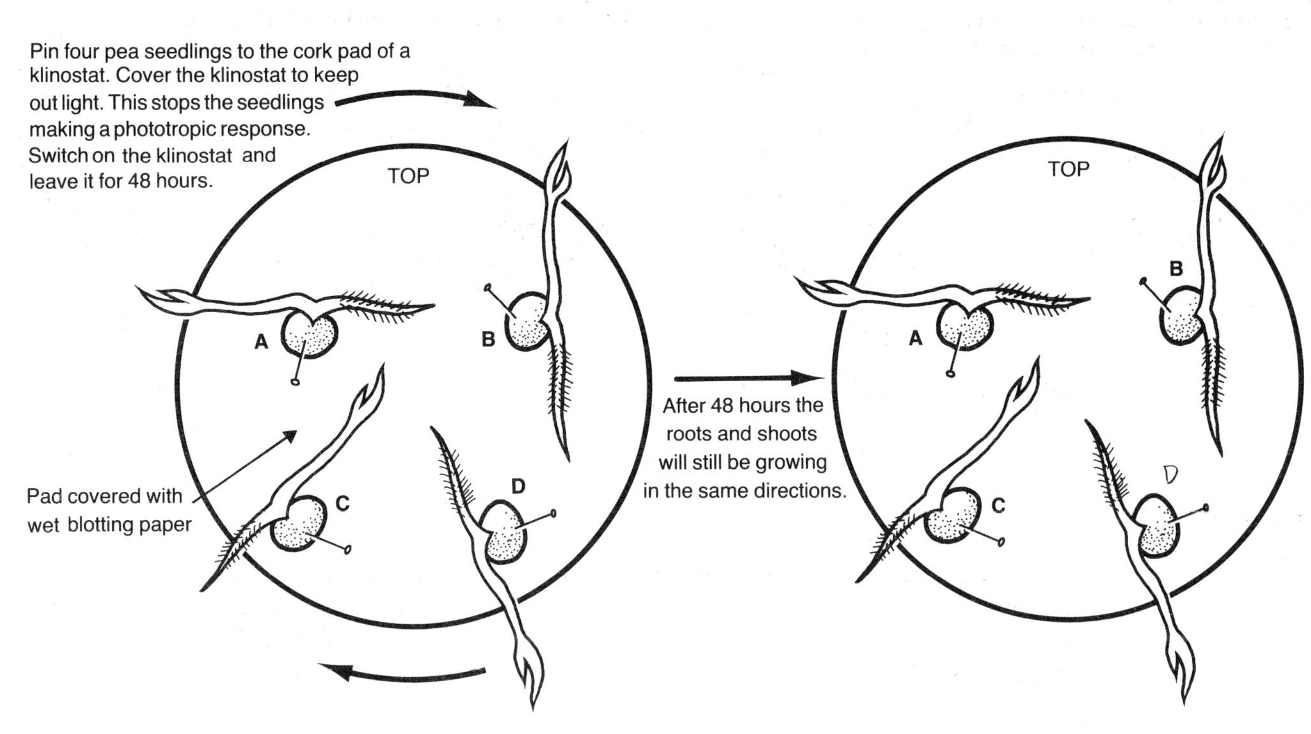

The control experiment

Pin some seedlings in the same positions as above. Cover the klinostat but do *not* switch it on

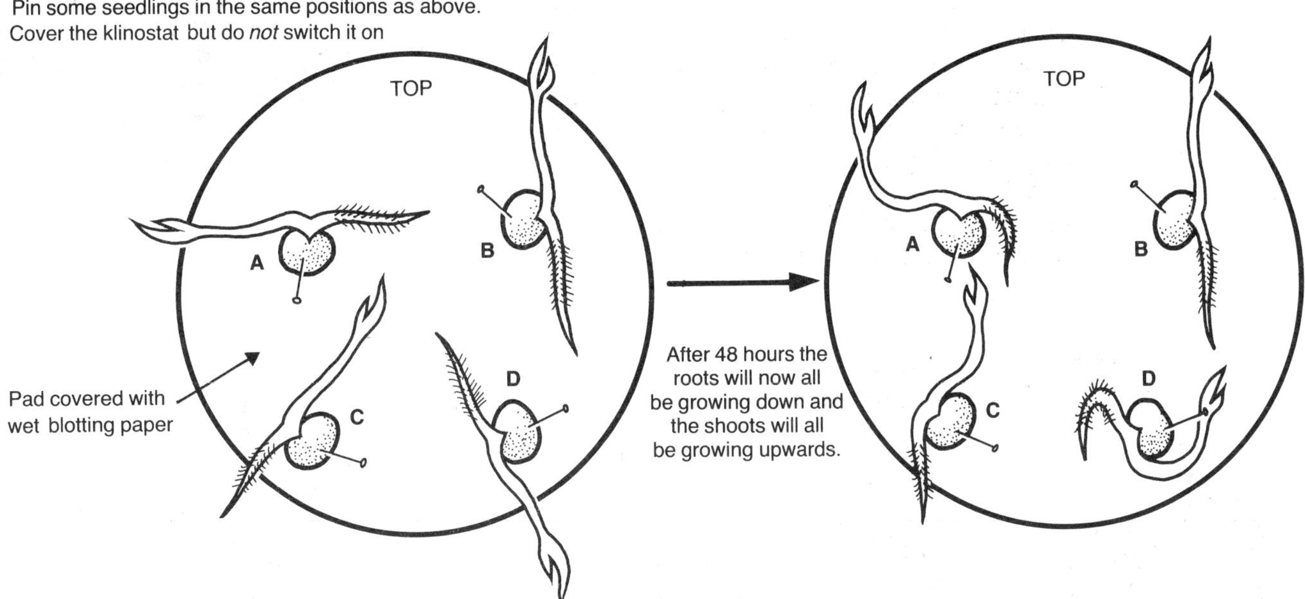

Geotropism in stems and roots

On the klinostat, gravity pulls equally on all sides of the roots and shoots. Gravity is 'shared out' by the klinostat and the plant makes no geotropic response.

In the control experiment, the klinostat does not turn. Gravity pulls on all parts of the plants in the same direction all the time. The roots respond to this 'one-sided pull' with a positively geotropic growth movement – they turn down. Shoots respond with a negatively geotropic growth movement – they turn up.

Figure 11.4 Geotropism in stems and roots

WHAT CAUSES TROPISMS

Tropisms are caused by *hormones* called *auxins*. Plants make auxins near the tips of roots and shoots.

Auxins make the cells of plant *shoots* grow faster. If there is less auxin the cells do not grow as quickly. (See figures 11.5 and 11.6.)

Auxins make the cells of plant *roots* grow more slowly. If there is less auxin the cells will grow more quickly. (See figure 11.7.)

Both tracks move and the tractor goes straight on

One track stops and the tractor turns towards it.

A 'tractortropic' response!

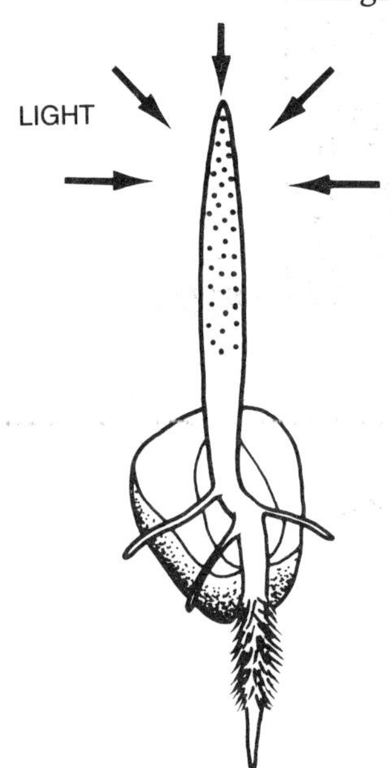

1 When light comes from all directions, auxins are evenly spread in the tip of the shoot. The shoot grows upwards.

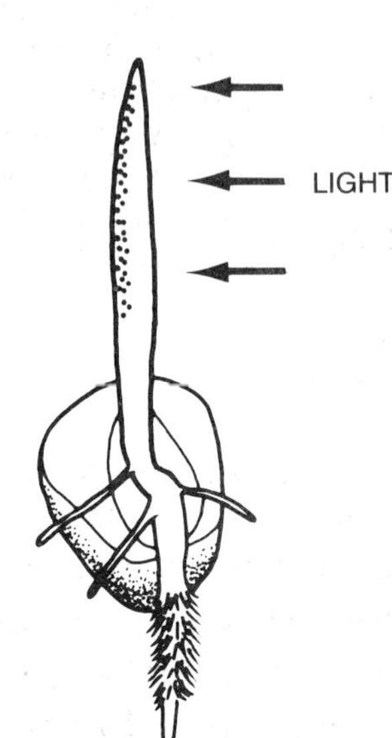

2 When light comes from one side, auxin collects on the darker side of the shoot. This makes the cells grow faster on the darker side and...

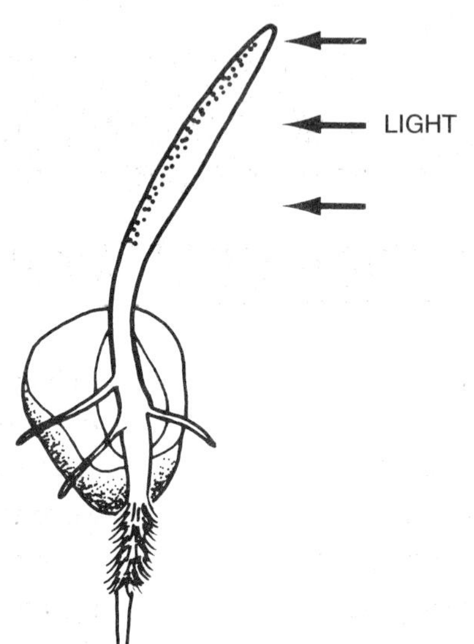

3 ...the shoot bends over towards the light

Figure 11.5 Auxins in the shoot in phototropism

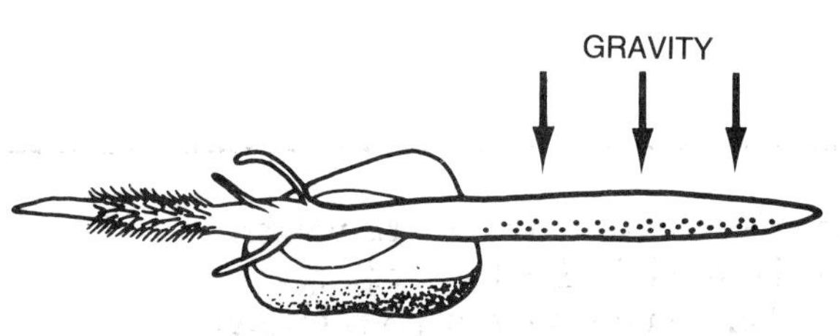

1 This shoot is growing sideways and auxin has collected on the lower side.

2 The cells on the lower side grow faster and the shoot turns upwards. This will happen in the dark or the light. It is a geotropic response which has nothing to do with light.

Figure 11.6 Auxins in the shoot in geotropism

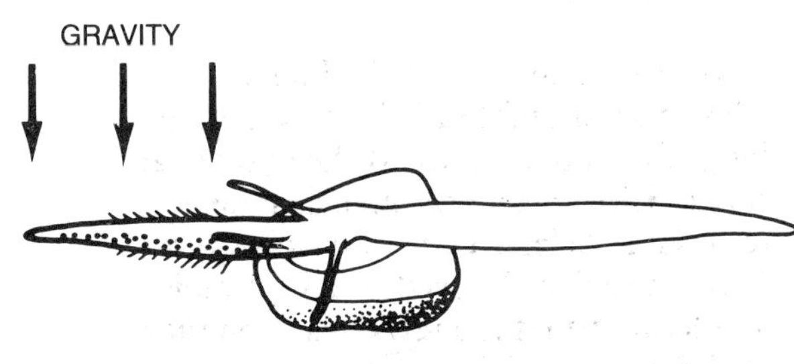

1 This root is growing sideways and auxin has collected on the lower side.

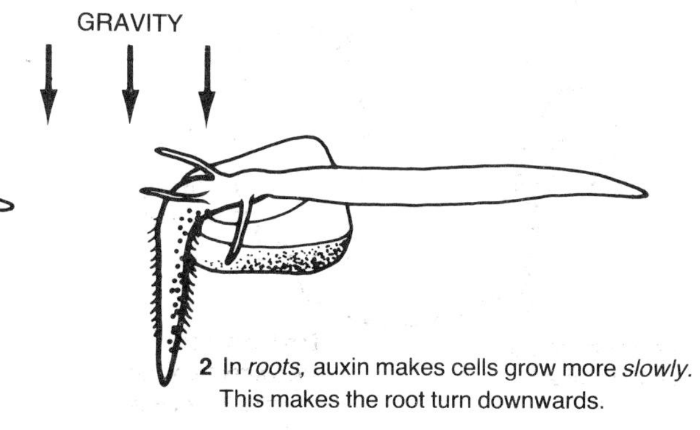

2 In *roots,* auxin makes cells grow more *slowly.* This makes the root turn downwards.

Figure 11.7 Auxins in the root in geotropism

HORMONE WEED KILLERS

Auxins are used in some weed killers. When they are sprayed onto grass with weeds in (such as daisies) the auxin kills the weeds but not the grass. This happens because more auxin is absorbed by the bigger leaves of the weeds.

Summary

Changes in a plant's surroundings are called *stimuli*. Plants *respond* to these stimuli by growth movements or *tropisms*. *Phototropism* is the response to light. *Geotropism* is the response to gravity. Shoots are *positively* phototropic but *negatively* geotropic. Roots are *positively* geotropic.

Growth movements are caused by *auxins*. Large amounts of auxins cause *faster* growth in *shoots* but *slower* growth in *roots*. Stems which are grown in darkness are *etiolated*.

Important words

Stimulus	a change in an organism's surroundings which causes a response in the organism. (Plural: stimuli)
Response	the change in an organism caused by a stimulus.
Tropism	a growth movement caused by a stimulus.
Phototropism	a growth movement caused by light.
Geotropism	a growth movement caused by gravity.
Etiolation	the effect of growing plants in too little light.
Klinostat	apparatus used for showing geotropic growth movements.
Hormones	chemicals made in one part of an organism and carried to another part where they have an important effect.
Auxins	hormones which affect the growth of plants.

Things to do

1. Germinate a few pea seeds. When the radicles are about 2 cm long, use waterproof ink to put marks on them about 2 mm apart. Choose seedlings with straight radicles and mark them carefully. Use a wire loop with a piece of cotton stretched across it to make the marks. (See figure 11.8.) Fix the seedlings with their radicles pointing downwards and leave them to grow for a few days. The part of the root which grows most quickly will now have more widely spaced marks. Which part of the root grows most quickly?

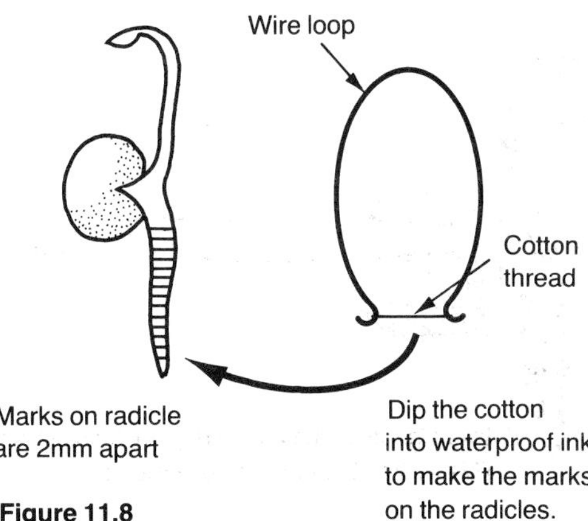

Figure 11.8

2. Germinate some pea seeds. Pick out a few with straight radicles about 2 cm long. Cut about 1 mm off the tips of half the radicles. Fix all the seedlings so that the radicles are growing sideways. Make sure that the seeds are kept moist and leave them for a few days. You may find that the radicles with tips turn downwards but those without tips do not. What does this tell you about the root tip?

Questions

A.

Write out each sentence in your book. Fill in the missing words from those in the box. Some words may be used more than once.

> klinostat — tropisms — auxins — positively phototropic — positively geotropic — etiolated — respond — phototropism — gravity — tips — growth movement.

1. Plants ...... to stimuli from their surroundings.
2. A tropism is another name for a ....
3. The response to light is called a ......
4. Stems grow towards light and are ....
5. Geotropism is the response to ....
6. Seedlings grown in darkness are ....
7. Stems grow upwards against ...... and are negatively geotropic.
8. Roots grow towards gravity and are ....
9. A ...... is an instrument which is useful for showing ....
10. Tropisms are caused by hormones called ....
11. Growth hormones are made at the ...... of roots and shoots.

B.

Figurc 11.9 shows two oat shoots (coleoptiles) each being treated differently. It also shows the results after each coleoptile had been allowed to grow in the dark for three hours.

Result after 3 hours in dark

lanolin

Coleoptile P

Result after 3 hours in dark

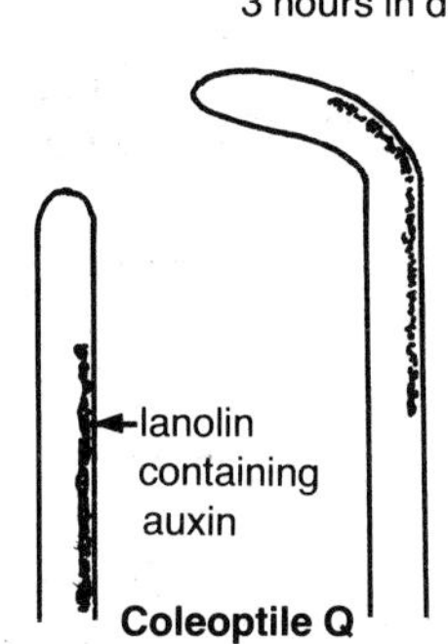

Figure 11.9

Coleoptile P was smeared with lanolin (a neutral substance) along its right-hand side and then placed in the dark for three hours. Coleoptile Q was smeared with lanolin containing an auxin (plant hormone) along its right-hand side and then placed in the dark for three hours.

1. Coleoptile P acts as a control. Explain the reason for its inclusion in the experiment.
2. Which side of coleoptile Q must have grown quicker in order to bring about the curvature?
3. Give a detailed explanation of the results obtained.

(EAEB)

C.

Figure 11.10 shows the effect of a plant hormone (auxin) on the growth of roots and stems. Which concentration of auxin will produce maximum growth in a stem, but stop growth in a root: (a) 0; (b) 3; (c) 4.5; (d) 6; or (e) 8.5?

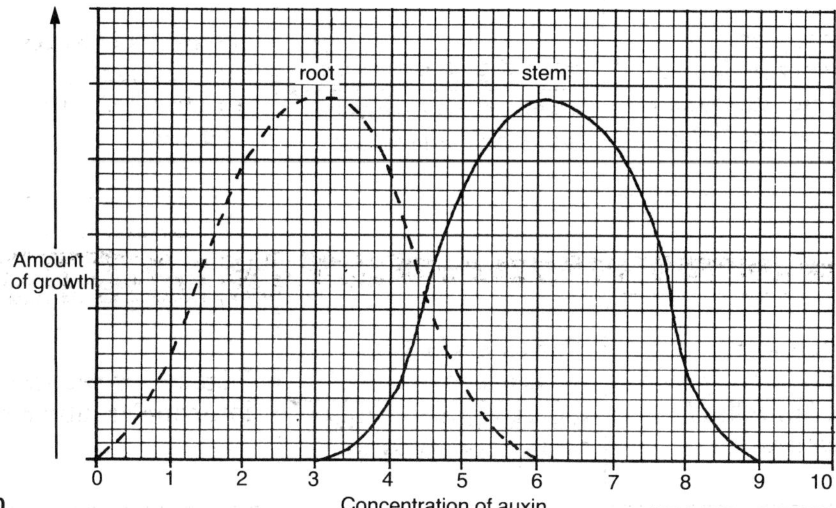

Figure 11.10

(EAEB, LREB,ULESEC)

TOPIC 12

HOW GREEN PLANTS FEED

DIFFERENT SORTS OF FEEDING OR NUTRITION

Different organisms feed in different ways.
The main ways in which organisms get their food are shown below.

1. *Holophytic nutrition:* all green plants feed like this.

Carbon dioxide Water Mineral salts	are absorbed → into plant	Made into carbohydrates, proteins and fats

2. *Holozoic nutrition:* animals feed like this.

Proteins, carbohydrates, fats and minerals in plants and other animals	Food killed and → eaten by animals	Digested inside animal into simpler substances	► Made into carbohydrates, fats and proteins

3. *Saprophytic nutrition:* fungi and some bacteria feed like this.

Proteins, fats and carbohydrates in dead and decaying substances such as wood and flesh	Food digested outside → organism by digestive juices poured on to it	Simpler substances made by digestion are absorbed into organism	► Made into carbohydrates fats and proteins

4. *Parasites:* tapeworms, lice, fleas and some plants feed like this.

Proteins, fats and carbohydrates in digested food, blood or cells of living organisms	Food absorbed or sucked into → parasite without always killing the organism	Digested, if necessary, into simpler substances	► Made into carbohydrates, fats and proteins

WHAT HAPPENS IN PHOTOSYNTHESIS

Green plants make their own food by photosynthesis. To do this they need only two chemicals: *carbon dioxide* and *water*. These two chemicals are changed into *sugar* and *oxygen* by a chemical reaction in the plant. A lot of energy is needed to make this reaction work. The energy comes from *sunlight* which is trapped by a green substance in leaves called *chlorophyll*.

The word equation for photosynthesis

$$\text{CARBON DIOXIDE} + \text{WATER} \xrightarrow[\text{sunlight}]{\text{chlorophyll}} \text{SUGAR} + \text{OXYGEN}$$

The chemical equation for photosynthesis

$6CO_2$	+	$6H_2O$	→	$C_6H_{12}O_6$	+	$6O_2$
Six molecules of carbon dioxide		Six molecules of water		One molecule of sugar		Six molecules of oxygen

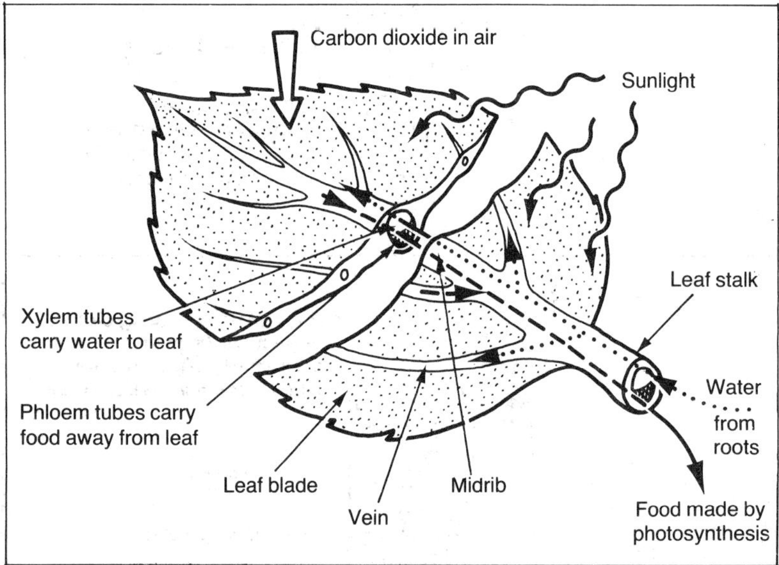

Figure 12.1 A leaf – the food factory of green plants

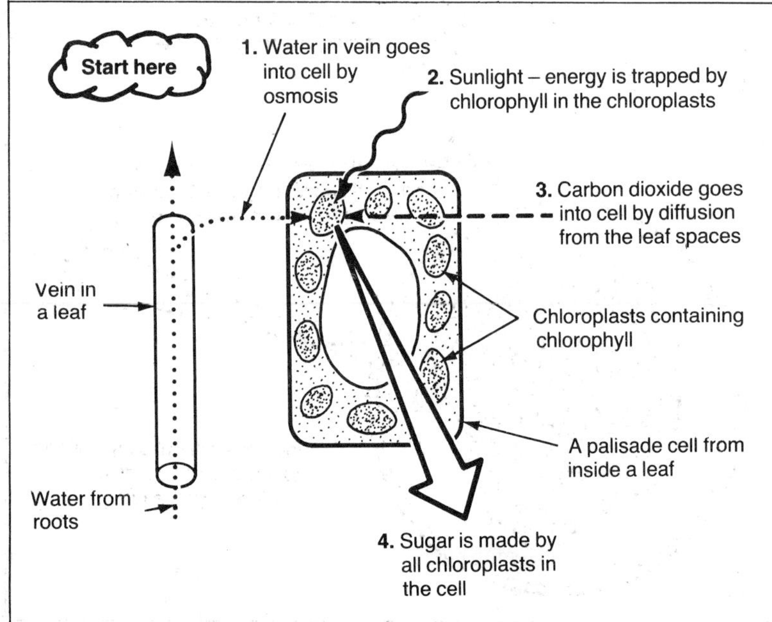

Figure 12.2 Photosynthesis in a leaf cell

Some of the sugar made by plants in photosynthesis is used in respiration to set free energy.

Plants need *mineral salts* as well as carbon dioxide and water. The mineral salts are used to make new cells and they are absorbed from the soil by plant roots.

Photosynthesis happens mostly in leaves but any green part of a plant can photosynthesise. (See figures 12.1 and 12.2.)

Leaves are useful for photosynthesis because:

1. they are wide and flat and catch a lot of sunlight,
2. they have a lot of chlorophyll in their palisade cells,
3. they have many breathing pores (or stomata) to let carbon dioxide in,
4. water can move into every part of a leaf from the veins,
5. there are many spaces between the leaf cells. This lets carbon dioxide get to every cell.

The oxygen set free in photosynthesis diffuses out of the cells into the leaf spaces. From here it goes out of the leaf through the stomata.

WHAT HAPPENS TO THE SUGAR

Most plants quickly change the sugar made in photosynthesis into starch.

$$\text{SUGAR} \xrightarrow{\text{can be changed into}} \text{STARCH}$$

Starch is insoluble but sugar is soluble.

Insoluble substances are better for storing in leaves. When there has been a lot of photosynthesis, starch collects in the leaves and is changed back into sugar. The sugar goes into the phloem tubes and is taken to different parts of the plant. (See figure 12.3.)

STARCH —can be changed into→ SUGAR

Iodine solution can be used as a chemical test for starch. If iodine solution is put onto any substance with starch in it, a blue-black colour appears.

This test can be used to show that photosynthesis is happening in a leaf. (See figure 12.4.)

DE-STARCHING LEAVES

In most of the experiments on page 80 you have to test leaves for starch. This is to find out if leaves kept in different conditions make starch. The leaves must have no starch in them before the experiment starts. If you want to de-starch leaves, keep them in water in the dark for two days. Pot plants can be put in a dark cupboard to de-starch them.

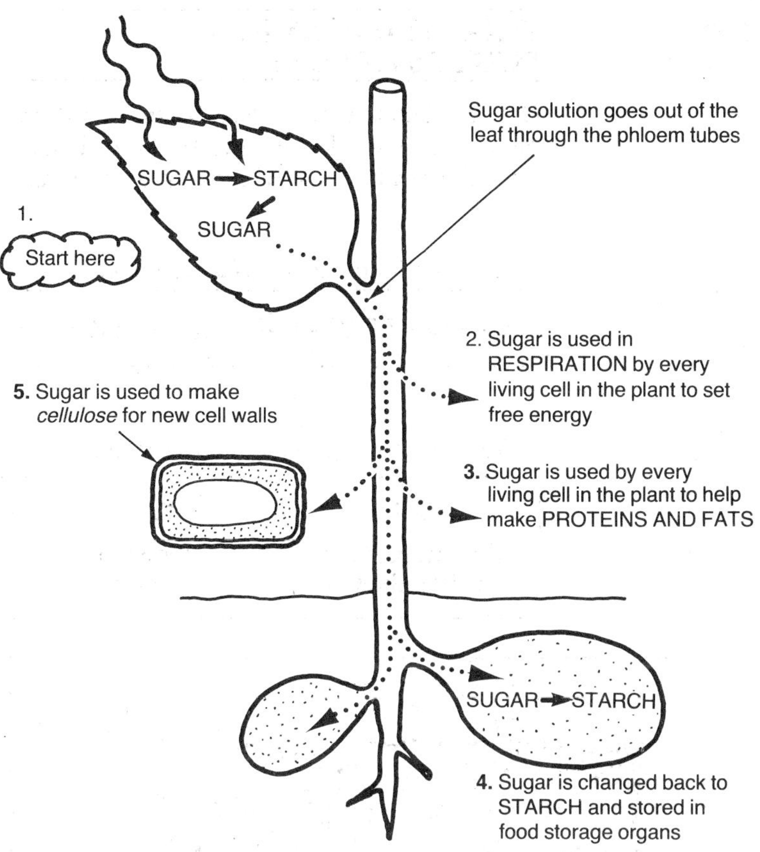

Figure 12.3

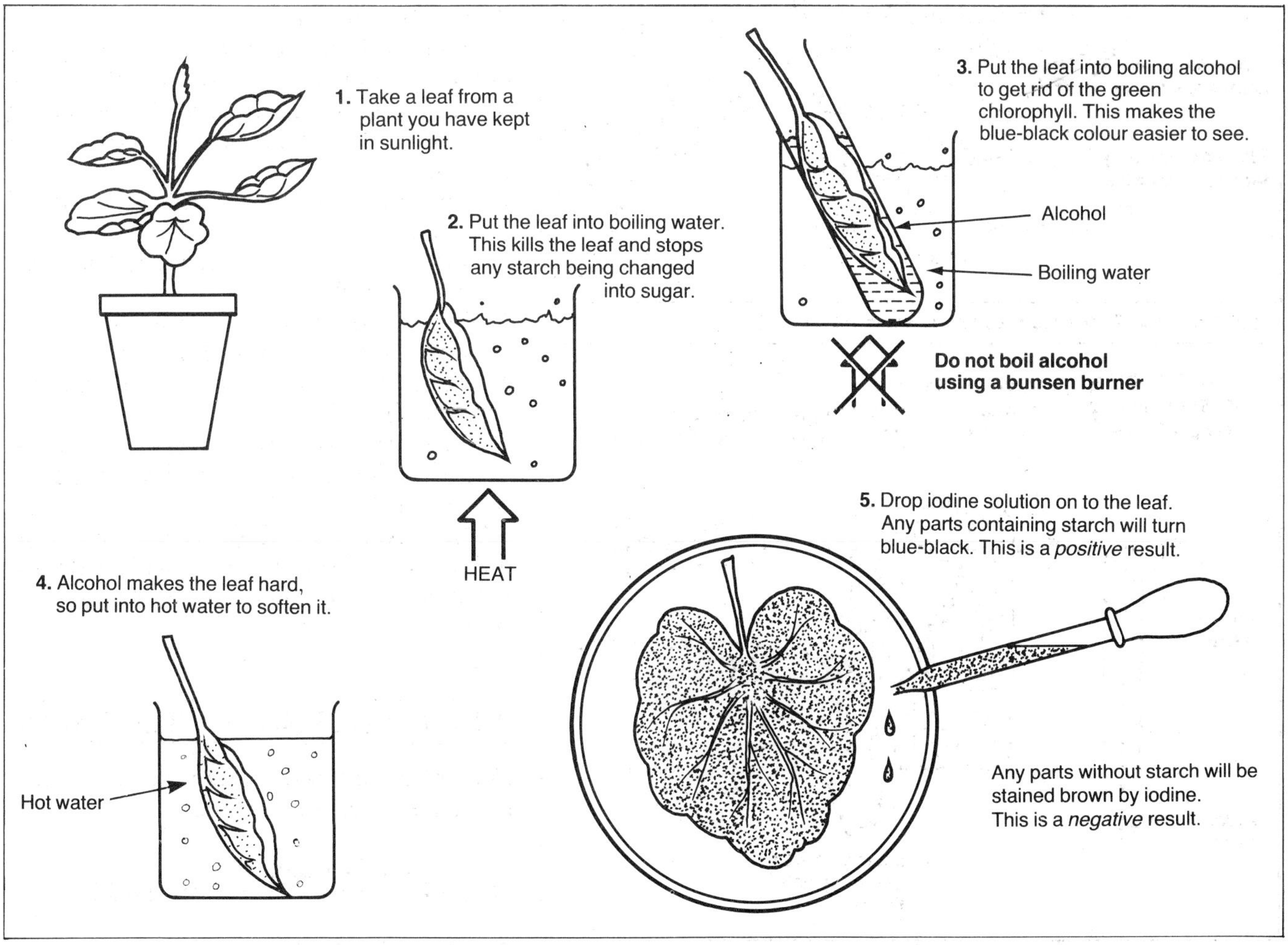

1. Take a leaf from a plant you have kept in sunlight.

2. Put the leaf into boiling water. This kills the leaf and stops any starch being changed into sugar.

HEAT

3. Put the leaf into boiling alcohol to get rid of the green chlorophyll. This makes the blue-black colour easier to see.

Alcohol

Boiling water

Do not boil alcohol using a bunsen burner

4. Alcohol makes the leaf hard, so put into hot water to soften it.

Hot water

5. Drop iodine solution on to the leaf. Any parts containing starch will turn blue-black. This is a *positive* result.

Any parts without starch will be stained brown by iodine. This is a *negative* result.

Figure 12.4 Testing a leaf for starch

Is CHLOROPHYLL needed for photosynthesis?

What to do
Use a variegated leaf.
These only have chlorophyll in parts.

De-starch the leaf and then put it into sunlight for a few hours.

Then take the leaf off the plant and test it for starch.

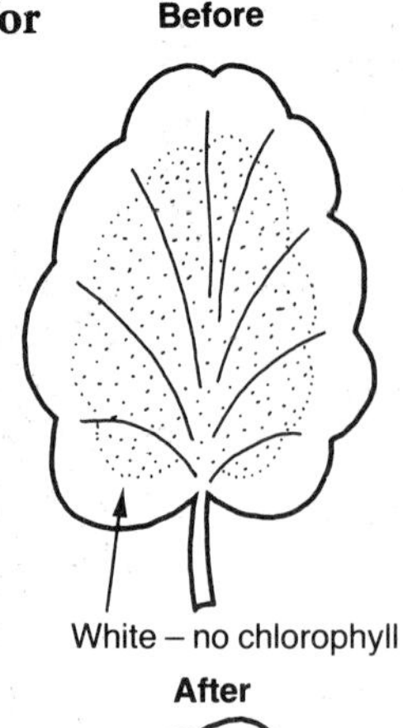

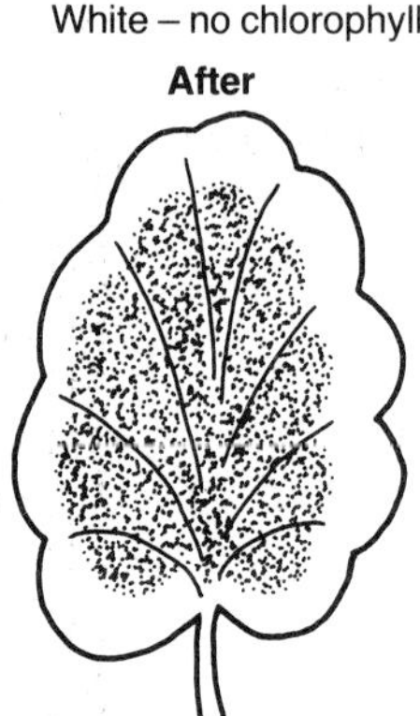

What happens
The parts of the leaf with chlorophyll will be coloured blue-black by the iodine. This shows that there is starch in those parts of the leaf.

This means photosynthesis can only happen where there is chlorophyll.

Is LIGHT needed for photosynthesis?

What to do
Cut out a shape from a piece of card and fix it to a de-starched leaf which is still growing on the plant. Cover the back of the leaf.

Put the leaf into sunlight for a few hours.

Then take the leaf off the plant and test it for starch.

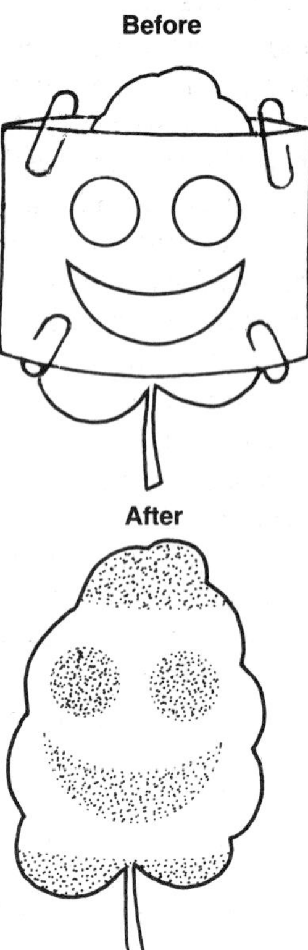

What happens
The parts of the leaf hit by light will be coloured blue-black by iodine. This shows that there is starch in those parts of the leaf.

This means photosynthesis only happens in light.

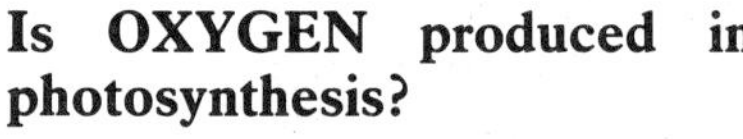

Is CARBON DIOXIDE needed for photosynthesis?

What to do
Fasten a plastic bag over a de-starched potted plant. Put soda-lime inside the bag. Soda-lime absorbs carbon dioxide from the air inside the bag.

Cover another de-starched potted plant with a plastic bag but use no soda-lime. This is the control experiment.

Leave both plants in sunlight for a few hours. Test a leaf from each plant for starch.

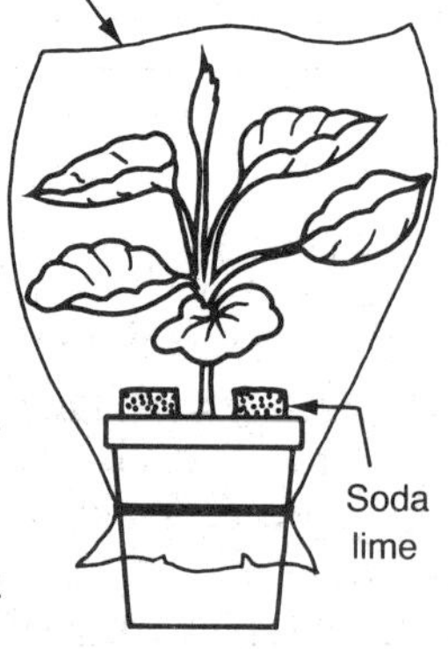

What happens
The leaf without carbon dioxide will not be coloured blue-black by iodine. The leaf with carbon dioxide will be coloured blue-black. This shows that no starch is made if the leaf can't get carbon dioxide.

This means photosynthesis can only happen where there is carbon dioxide.

Is OXYGEN produced in photosynthesis?

What to do
Make two sets of apparatus as shown in the diagram. Put one set into sunlight for a few hours. Put the other set into a dark cupboard where photosynthesis cannot happen. This is the control experiment.

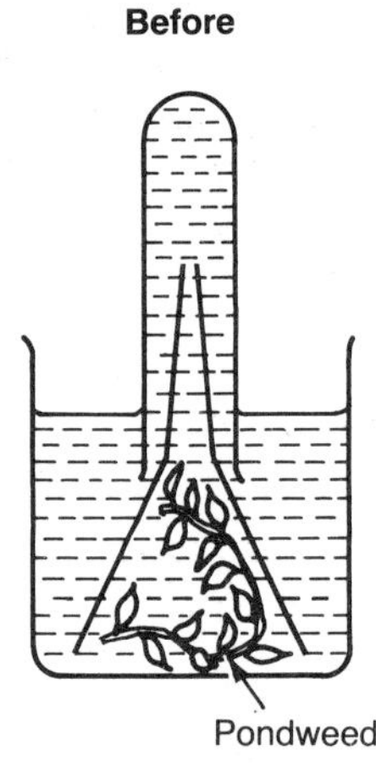

What happens
A gas will collect in the tube of the apparatus in sunlight. If you put a glowing match into this gas it will burst into flames. This is a test for oxygen. No gas will collect in the control tube. This shows that the plant only gives off oxygen in sunlight.

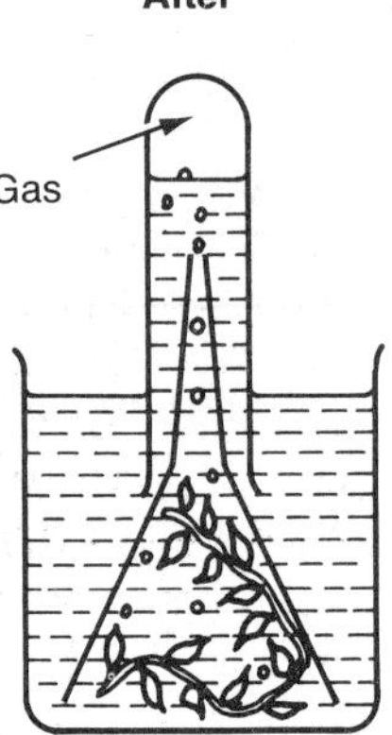

This means oxygen is given off in photosynthesis.

MINERALS

Sugar made in photosynthesis can be changed into cellulose, starch, fat or oil by plants. Plants need other substances to grow properly and stay healthy. These substances are minerals and plants get them from the soil. The minerals dissolve in water and are absorbed by a plant's roots. Plants use the minerals for making proteins. To do this they need a lot of some minerals but only a little of others.

Plants can be grown in *culture solutions* to show what happens when some minerals are missing. (See figure 12.5.) You can make culture solutions by adding the right amount of minerals to pure water. Culture solutions can be made without nitrogen, without magnesium etc.

The culture solution in figure 12.5 has all the minerals the plant needs in the right amounts. The plant is strong and healthy.

The plant in figure 12.6 has been growing in a culture solution without any calcium in it. The leaves are yellow and the plant is very small compared with the one in figure 12.5. The plant has a mineral deficiency (or shortage).

Nitrogen and phosphorus are important minerals. Farmers need to add them to the soil to stop mineral deficiencies. Some plants take more minerals from the soil than others. Plants such as clover put nitrogen back into the soil.

Fancy that!

About 100,000,000,000 tonnes of substances are made by photosynthesis every year!

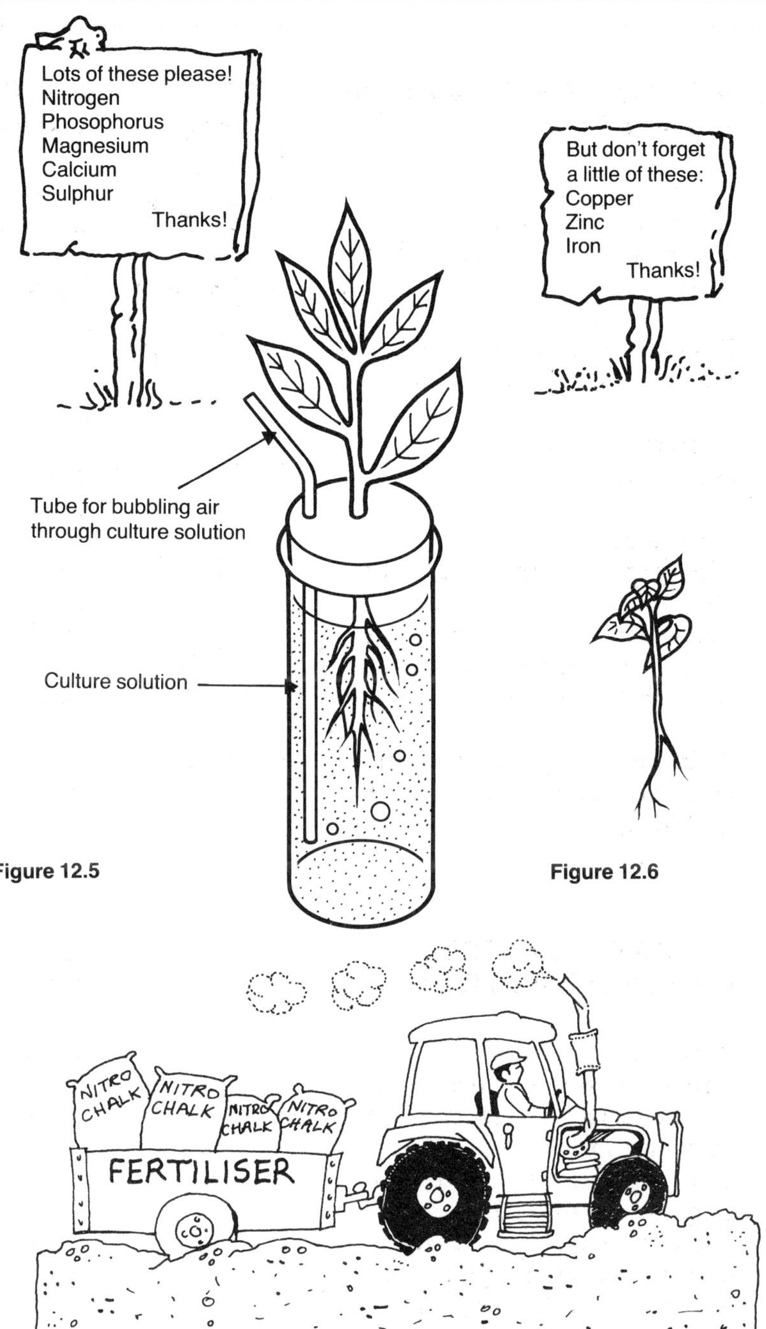

Figure 12.5

Figure 12.6

Summary

Different organisms feed in different ways. In *holozoic nutrition* animals kill and eat other organisms. In *saprophytic nutrition* (used by fungi and some bacteria) dead and decaying substances are digested by juices poured onto them. The simpler substances made by this digestion are absorbed by the organisms. *Parasites* feed on digested food inside other organisms or on the cells of living organisms without always killing them.

Green plants feed by *holophytic nutrition* using *photosynthesis*. This is a chemical reaction which plants use to make their own food. In photosynthesis, energy in *sunlight* helps to make *sugar* from *carbon dioxide* and *water*.

The green substance *chlorophyll* traps the sunlight to make this chemical reaction work. The sugar is taken to all parts of the plant. It is stored as *starch*, used to make other substances or used in respiration to set free energy.

Important words

Holophytic nutrition	feeding like green plants using carbon dioxide, water and minerals.
Photosynthesis	feeding like green plants using carbon dioxide and water to make starch; light and chlorophyll are needed.
Holozoic nutrition	feeding like animals by eating living plants or other living animals.
Saprophytic nutrition	feeding on dead or decaying organisms.
Parasites	organisms that feed on the inside or outside of another living organism, from which they get all their food.
Chlorophyll	a green substance which gives leaves their colour and which traps the energy in sunlight.
Mineral salts	chemical substances of which there are a lot found in soil.
Culture solution	a solution containing minerals needed for plant growth.

Questions

A.

Write out each sentence in your book. Fill in the missing words from those in the box. Some words may be used more than once.

oxygen — mineral salts — saprophytic — chemical — holozoic — carbon dioxide — holophytic — chlorophyll

1. ...... is a gas in the air used in photosynthesis.
2. Photosynthesis is a ...... reaction.
3. The green substance in leaves is called ....
4. ...... is used to trap the energy in sunlight.
5. The gas made in photosynthesis is ....
6. Plants need carbon dioxide, water and ...... to make starch.
7. Plants feed using ...... nutrition.
8. Fungi and some bacteria use ...... nutrition.
9. Organisms which feed using ...... nutrition eat other living organisms.
10. In ...... and ...... nutrition, food usually has to be digested.

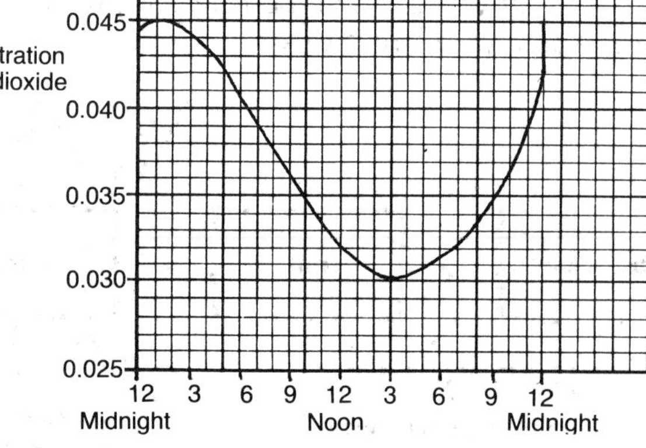

Figure 12.7

B.

Figure 12.7 shows the different concentrations of carbon dioxide in a field of corn during one day.

1. At what time of the day is the percentage of carbon dioxide the least?
2. Which biological process caused the sudden drop in the concentration of carbon dioxide?
3. What happened to the carbon dioxide which disappeared from the air?
4. Between which three hours did the % carbon dioxide in the air rise the most?
5. Which biological process caused the increase in the amount of carbon dioxide in the air?

(EMREB)

TOPIC 13

RESPIRATION

Every living organism needs energy to keep itself alive. Movement, growth, reproduction, feeding and excretion all need energy. Organisms get this energy from their food. The energy in the food has to be set free by chemical reactions which happen in all living cells. This is called respiration. It is one of the most important chemical reactions that happens in cells.

There are two kinds of respiration: aerobic and anaerobic. In most cells both can happen at the same time.

Aerobic respiration uses oxygen to set energy free.

Anaerobic respiration does not use oxygen to set energy free.

AEROBIC RESPIRATION

Energy is usually set free from fat or sugar in respiration.

> 'to respire' means 'to do respiration'

Figure 13.1 shows that when organisms respire aerobically they:

USE UP	oxygen and sugar (or fat),
GIVE OFF	carbon dioxide gas and water vapour,
SET FREE	energy.

To find out if oxygen is used up in aerobic respiration

Put a few small animals such as woodlice into a syringe. A piece of sponge should separate the woodlice from some lumps of soda lime. Soda lime absorbs carbon dioxide. Any carbon dioxide given off by the woodlice will go through the sponge and be absorbed by the soda lime. The syringe must be kept at the same temperature all the time. If there is even a small change in temperature, the air inside the syringe will make the coloured water move and give a wrong result. To keep the syringe at the same temperature put it into water. (See figure 13.2.)

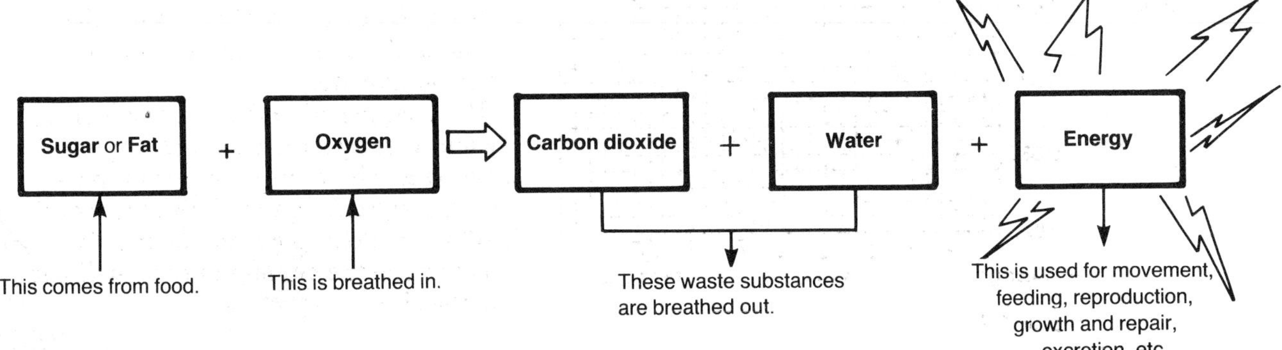

Figure 13.1

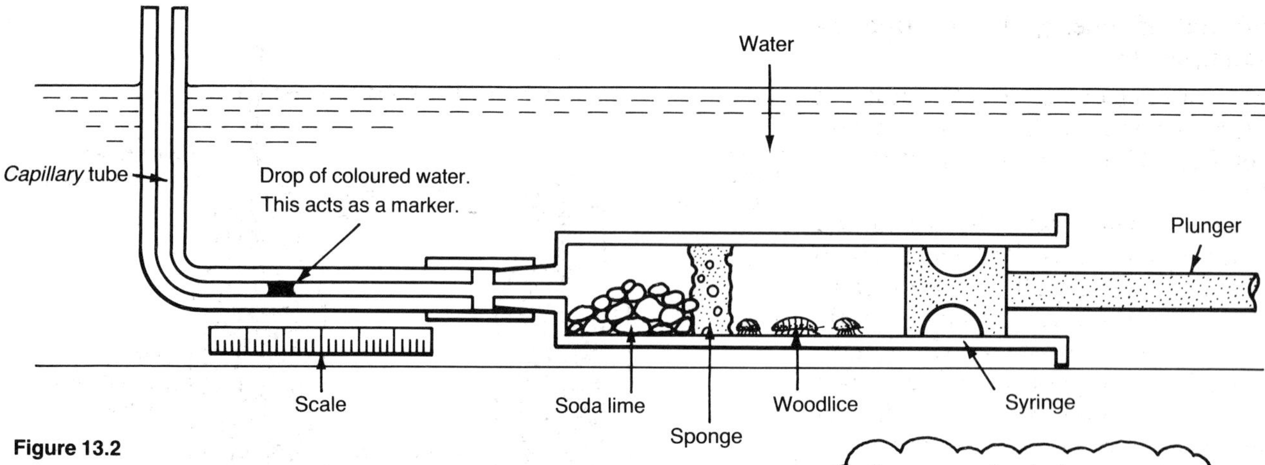

Figure 13.2

As the woodlice respire they use up oxygen. The carbon dioxide they give off is absorbed by the soda lime. The amount of air in the syringe therefore gets less. This makes the coloured water move towards the syringe and shows that oxygen has been used up.

You should use a second syringe without any woodlice. This is the control. The coloured water will probably not move in the control. This shows that in the experiment oxygen has been used up by something which happens in *living* things (the woodlice).

This is what happens

Don't forget the control!

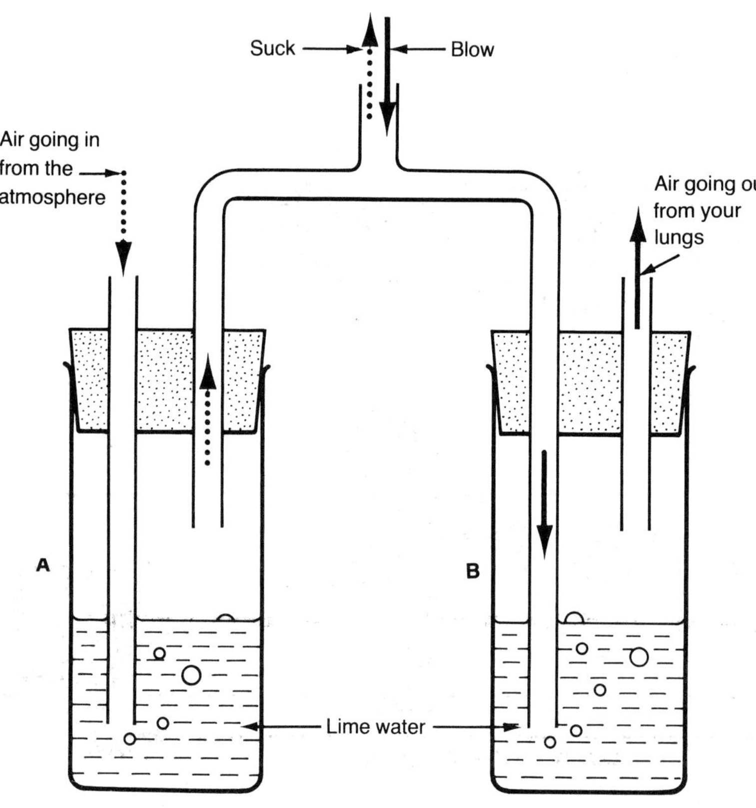

Figure 13.3

To find out if carbon dioxide is given off during breathing

Use the 'huff 'n puff' machine (see figure 13.3) to find out if carbon dioxide is given off during breathing.

Limewater goes milky when carbon dioxide is bubbled through it.

Gently suck air through the 'huff 'n puff' machine. This air from the atmosphere bubbles through the limewater in tube **A**. Now gently breathe out through the 'huff 'n puff' machine. This air bubbles through the limewater in tube **B**.

Do this sucking and blowing a few more times.

Result

The limewater in tube **B** will go milky. The limewater in tube **A** will not change (or it may go slightly milky if you suck a lot of air through it).

Why this happens

There is not enough carbon dioxide in the atmosphere to turn the limewater in tube **A** milky. You breathe out the carbon dioxide given off by your cells in respiration and this turns the limewater in tube **B** milky.

To find out if energy is set free by germinating seeds

If living organisms give off heat in respiration this means that energy is also being set free. This is because heat is one kind of energy.

Soak some wheat grains for 24 hours. Divide them into two lots. Boil one lot for 10 minutes to kill the grains. These dead grains are used as a control. Soak both lots of grain in a weak solution of bleach for 10 minutes. This kills off any fungi on the wheat which might make it go bad. Wash both lots of wheat grains with water. Put the dead wheat into a vacuum flask and the living wheat into another flask. Put a thermometer into each flask and plug the flasks with cotton wool. Leave both flasks for several days. (See figure 13.4.)

Thermometer
Temperature at start *and* finish of experiment
Temperature at end of experiment
Cotton wool
Living, germinating wheat
Dead wheat
Control Flask
Experiment Flask

Figure 13.4

What happens

The temperature in the experiment flask will be much higher than in the control flask. The temperature in the control flask should not change. This shows that the temperature rise is due to something happening in *living* organisms. (It does not really show that it is caused by *respiration* however. It could be caused by another chemical reaction.) If the temperature of the control flask changes, the change in temperature of both flasks must be compared.

Aerobic respiration can only happen when oxygen is present. The oxygen comes from the air or water around the organism.

ANAEROBIC RESPIRATION

In *anaerobic* respiration the energy in food is set free without using oxygen to do it.

When you walk, your muscles are working slowly. They can get plenty of oxygen and their respiration is *aerobic*.

When you sprint, your muscles work hard and need a lot of oxygen. When they cannot get oxygen quickly enough for aerobic respiration, they change to *anaerobic* respiration.

For the first few metres of a sprint your muscles use aerobic respiration. Anaerobic respiration is used for the rest of the race. (See figure 13.5.) Your muscles can work hard without oxygen for about 15 seconds.

Figure 13.5

Sugar — Without oxygen → Lactic acid + Energy

This comes from food.

This collects in muscles and stops them working.

This is used for movement, feeding, growth and repair, excretion, etc.

Figure 13.6

Figure 13.6 shows that when cells respire anaerobically you:

USE UP	sugar,
MAKE	lactic acid,
SET FREE	energy.

More energy is set free in aerobic respiration than in anaerobic respiration.

Too much lactic acid will soon stop muscle cells working: the sprinter cannot carry on sprinting! At the end of the race a lot of oxygen must be breathed in. The oxygen breaks down the lactic acid to carbon dioxide and water. More energy is set free when this happens.

Bacteria and fungi

Yeast and some bacteria get most of their energy from *fermentation*. This is a kind of anaerobic respiration in which alcohol is made instead of lactic acid.

Figure 13.7 shows that in fermentation, organisms:

USE UP	sugar,
GIVE OFF	carbon dioxide gas,
MAKE	alcohol,
SET FREE	energy.

We use yeast to make bread and alcoholic drinks such as wine and beer. (See figures 13.8 and 13.9.)

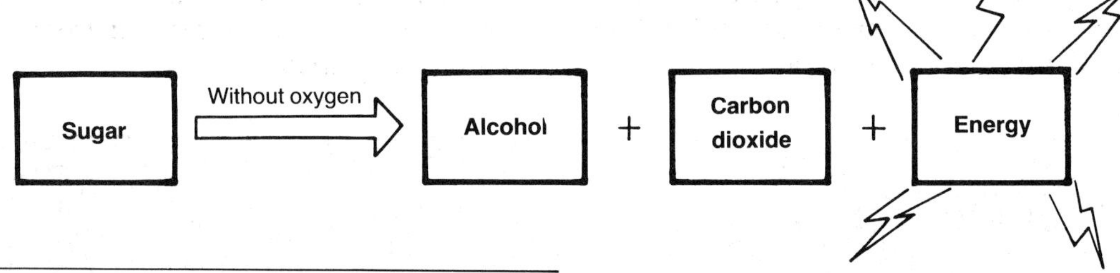

Figure 13.7

HOW WINE IS MADE

1. Grapes contain a lot of sugar.

2. The grapes are crushed.

3. Then they are pressed and filtered.

Grape juice

Carbon dioxide is given off here

4. Grape juice is fermented by yeast to alcohol and carbon dioxide.

5. Fermented grape juice is put into barrels and kept.

6. The wine is put into bottles.

Figure 13.8

HOW BREAD IS MADE

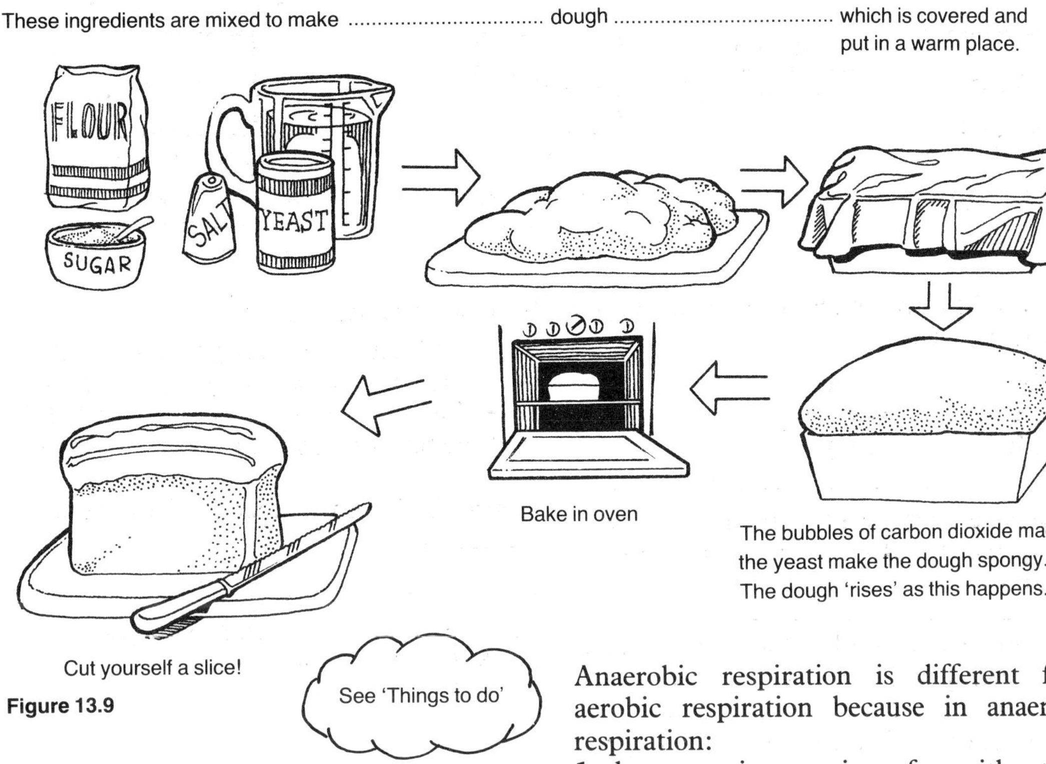

Figure 13.9

See 'Things to do'

Yeast ferments the sugar and other carbohydrates in the dough. The alcohol made by the yeast is destroyed by baking. The carbon dioxide given off makes the dough lighter and better to eat.

Anaerobic respiration is different from aerobic respiration because in anaerobic respiration:

1. the energy in sugar is set free without using oxygen to do it,
2. sugar is not completely broken down to carbon dioxide and water,
3. much less energy is set free than from aerobic respiration.

Summary

Every organism needs *energy* to keep itself alive. This energy comes from a chemical reaction called *respiration*. Respiration happens in every living cell.

In *aerobic* respiration, *oxygen* is used to set free the energy in food. In *anaerobic* respiration this energy is set free without oxygen. Aerobic respiration sets free more energy than anaerobic respiration. Most cells can use both sorts of respiration. Other cells can use only anaerobic respiration.

In anaerobic respiration in animals *lactic acid* is made. Lactic acid stops cells working but it is changed into carbon dioxide and water when oxygen gets to the cells again.

Fermentation is a sort of anaerobic respiration used by yeast and some bacteria. *Alcohol* is made in fermentation and carbon dioxide is given off. Fermentation is used to make wine, beer and bread.

Important words

Respiration	the setting free of the energy in food by chemical reactions in cells.
Aerobic respiration	setting free the energy in food by using oxygen.
Anaerobic respiration	setting free the energy in food without using oxygen to do it.
Fermentation	a kind of anaerobic respiration which makes alcohol.

Things to do

Bread is quick and easy to make, so bake yourself a loaf (in a kitchen, not the laboratory!).

You will need:

- 0.5kg plain white flour
- 14g yeast
- 1 teaspoon salt
- 1 teaspoon sugar
- some lard
- 0.25 litres warm water
- a mixing bowl and an oven
- some clean clay flower pots

What to do

Put the yeast into the warm water to dissolve it. The water should feel just warm to your hand. If it is too hot it will kill the yeast. Add the sugar to the yeast mixture and stir.

Put the flour and salt into the mixing bowl. Mix well. Pour the yeast mixture into the flour. Mix the flour and yeast to a dough and 'knead' the dough for 10 minutes. Do this on a flat surface covered with flour. 'Kneading' means folding the dough over and pushing it with your fist. This mixes the yeast evenly in the dough. If you do not do the kneading properly the dough will not rise.

Wash the clay pots well. Dry them and grease inside with lard. Half fill the pots with the dough. Cover them with a cloth and stand them in a warm place – near a radiator will do. If the dough gets too hot the yeast will be killed.

When the dough has risen to the top of the pots put it in the oven. Bake for 30 minutes at 450°F (or mark 8 gas). Then turn the heat down to 350°F (or mark 4 gas) and bake for another 15 minutes.

Questions

A.

Write out each sentence in your book. Fill in the missing words from those in the box. Some words may be used more than once.

> lime water — oxygen — soda lime — aerobic — cell — fermentation — food — chemical reaction — heat — carbon dioxide — anaerobic — yeast

1. Respiration happens in every living ....
2. Respiration is a ...... in which energy is set free.
3. Respiration sets free the energy in ....
4. In ...... respiration carbon dioxide, water and energy are set free.
5. Carbon dioxide is absorbed by ...... which goes milky.
6. Carbon dioxide is absorbed by ...... which is a solid.
7. ...... is one sort of energy.
8. Germinating seeds set free ....
9. In ...... respiration lactic acid and energy are set free.
10. ...... respiration sets free more energy than ...... respiration.
11. Lactic acid is broken down by ...... to carbon dioxide and water.
12. In ...... , alcohol, carbon dioxide and energy are set free.
13. Fermentation is a kind of ...... respiration.
14. Bread is spongy because of bubbles of ...... made by ....

B.

The apparatus shown in figure 13.10 was used to show the effects of living yeast cells on glucose in the *absence of oxygen*. It was left in a warm place and after a few hours the lime water turned *milky*.

1. What gas was given off from the mixture in the boiling tube?
2. What process was taking place in the mixture?
3. What other substance, not tested here, would also be found in the boiling tube at the end of the experiment?
4. Name two different industrial processes which use this reaction between yeast and sugar to make their products.

(NREB)

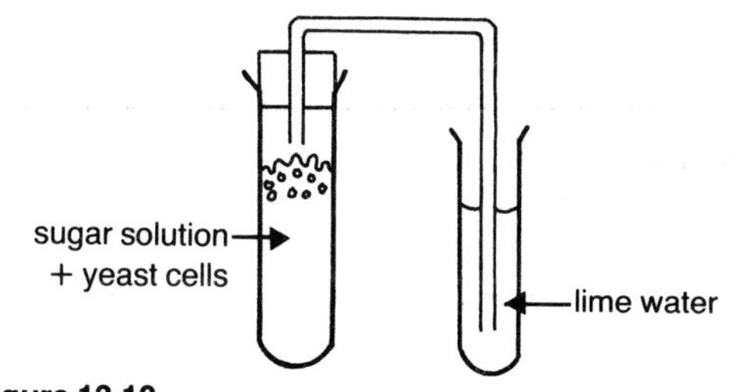

Figure 13.10

C.

Figure 13.11 shows apparatus used to demonstrate that an active mouse produces carbon dioxide during respiration.

Figure 13.12 shows similar apparatus to demonstrate that a potted flowering plant produces carbon dioxide during respiration.

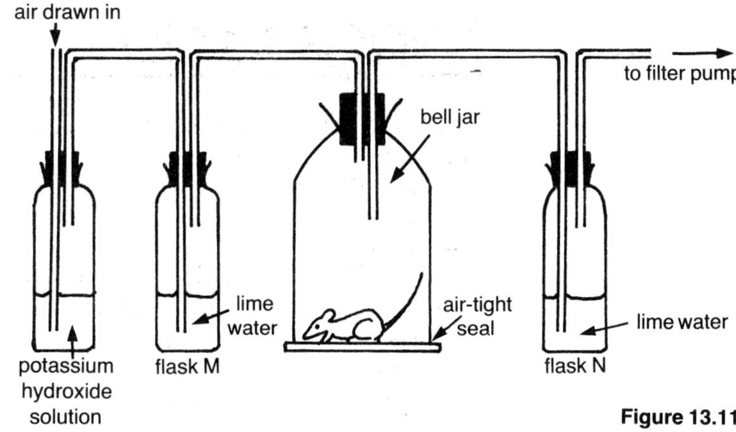

Figure 13.11

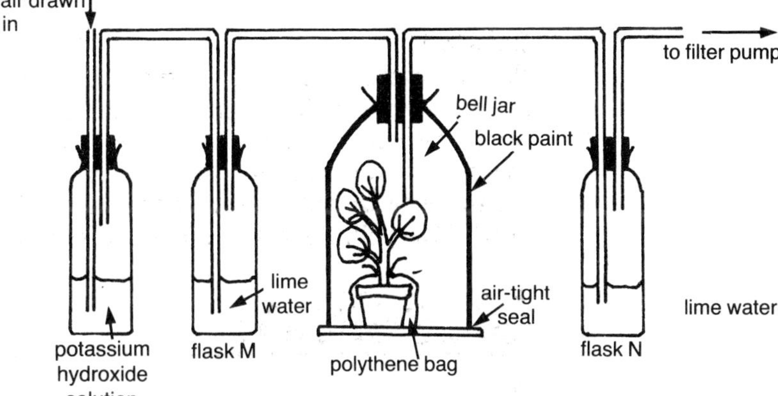

Figure 13.12

1. Name the gas absorbed by the potassium hydroxide solution.
2. What is the purpose of the limewater in flask M?
3. (a) What change would be expected, after a few minutes, in flask N?
   (b) This change would be quicker in flask N attached to the bell jar holding the mouse, than in flask N attached to the bell jar holding the plant. Suggest one reason for this fact.
4. Name the gas which both the mouse and plant use in respiration.
5. (a) Why is the plant pot covered in polythene?
   (b) Explain why the bell jar containing the plant is painted black.

(EAEB)

D.

Study the pieces of apparatus shown in figure 13.13 then answer the following questions.

1. Draw a *well-labelled* diagram to show how you would set up this apparatus to show that the air we breathe in contains less carbon dioxide than the air we breathe out. *Clearly show* the direction taken by the air breathed *out*.
2. Briefly state how you would use this apparatus once you had set it up.
3. What results would you expect?

(EMREB)

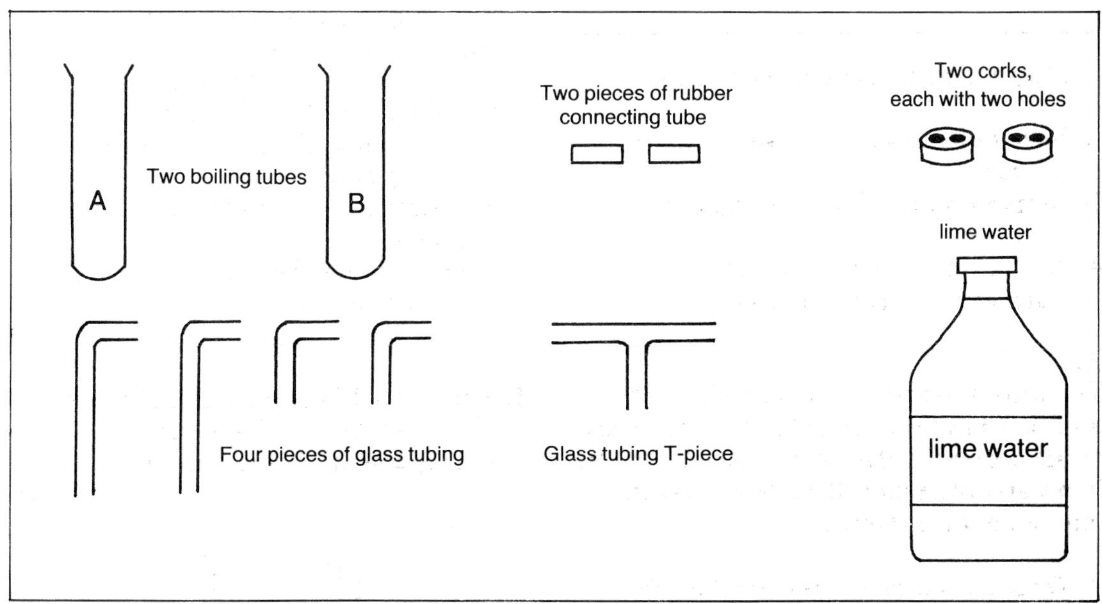

Figure 13.13

TOPIC 14

THE CARBON CYCLE

WHY CARBON IS IMPORTANT

Carbon is an important chemical for all living things. Living things set free energy from carbon *compounds* in their food, by respiration, because they need energy to stay alive. The main energy-giving foods which contain carbon compounds are carbohydrates and fats. Living things also use carbon compounds to make new cells for growth. The main 'body-building foods' which contain carbon compounds are proteins.

Carbon itself is an *element*: a substance which cannot be broken down into a simpler substance.

Living things use a lot of carbon but there is always plenty to go round. This is because carbon circulates: it is used again and again by different organisms.

Living organisms 'borrow' carbon from their surroundings. When the organisms die, bacteria and fungi make their dead bodies rot and the carbon compounds in their bodies go back into the surroundings. Other organisms can use these carbon compounds to build *their* bodies. You may have carbon in your body which once belonged to a dinosaur!

The carbon compounds which are used to build cells can't circulate while the cells are alive. They are 'locked away' for the life of the cell. The carbon in compounds in food used to set free energy circulates more quickly. This happens during respiration when carbon leaves the organism, as carbon dioxide gas, and energy is set free.

HOW ANIMALS USE CARBON

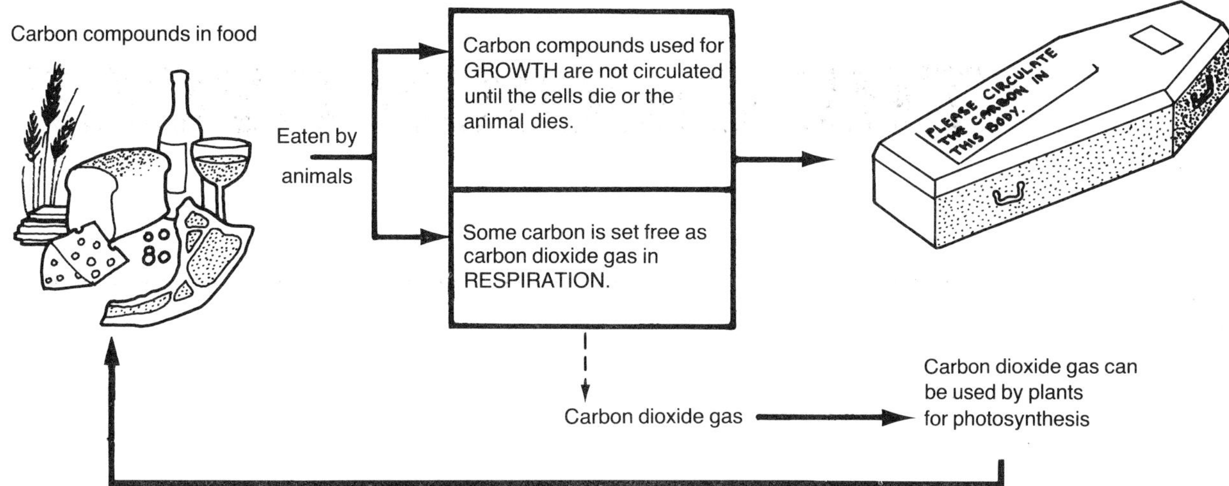

Figure 14.1

HOW GREEN PLANTS USE CARBON

Green plants make food by photosynthesis. They take carbon dioxide gas out of the air and join it with water to make sugar and other carbon compounds.

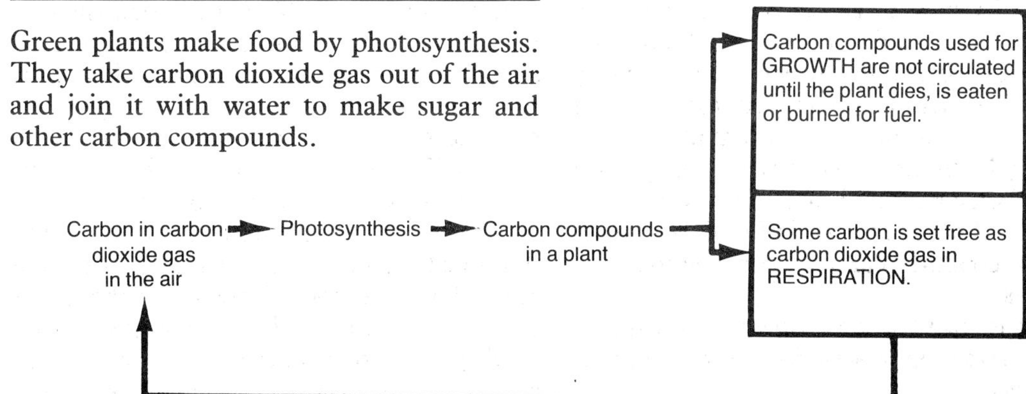

Figure 14.2

CARBON AND FUEL

Coal, oil, natural gas and peat have a lot of carbon in them. They are called *fossil fuels* because they were made millions of years ago from the bodies of dead organisms. Oil and natural gas were made from the bodies of small animals which lived in the sea. Coal and peat were made from the bodies of plants. The animals and plants did not rot properly because of the conditions where they died. Their dead bodies were heated and pressed by rocks. When we burn fossil fuels they set free a lot of energy and carbon dioxide gas. The carbon in this gas has been out of circulation for a very long time!

What happens when fuel is burned

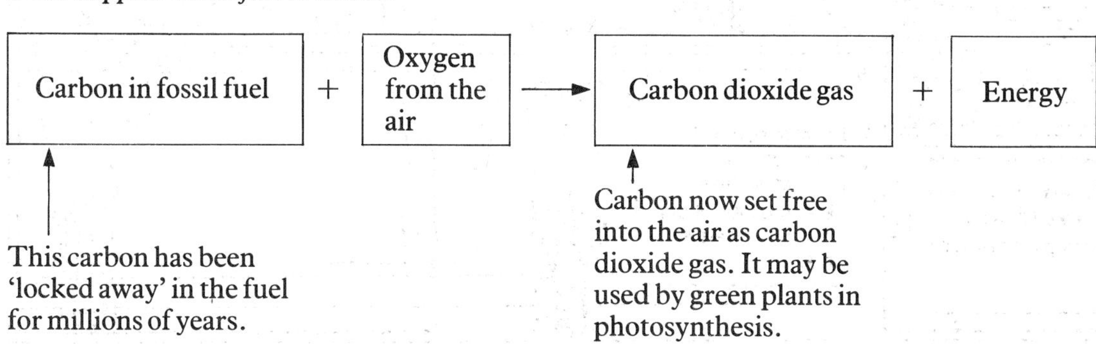

THE CARBON CYCLE

Fancy that!
Pure carbon is found as diamond – the hardest natural substance known!

The world is running out of fossil fuels and new forms of energy must be found.

It is now possible to make food from oil and natural gas!

CARBON DIOXIDE IN AIR
Photosynthesis
CARBON COMPOUNDS IN PLANTS
Respiration
Eaten
Death and decay
Burning
Death and decay
Respiration
Death – no decay – heat and pressure
OIL AND NATURAL GAS
CARBON COMPOUNDS IN ANIMALS
Death – no decay – heat and pressure (small sea animals)
COAL

Figure 14.3

Modern coal-cutting 'shearer' in operation at Nottinghamshire Bentinck Colliery.

Summary

Food containing carbon compounds is used to set free energy in *respiration* and to make new cells for growth. *Carbohydrates* and *fats* are important energy-giving foods. *Proteins* are important growth foods.

Carbon *circulates* and is used again and again by different organisms. *Bacteria* and *fungi* make dead organisms rot and circulate their carbon. Carbon circulates in the air as *carbon dioxide* gas. This can be used by green plants in *photosynthesis*. Fossil *fuels* contain carbon and set free energy and carbon dioxide when *burned*.

Important words

Compound — a chemical made of fixed amounts of different elements: carbon dioxide is a compound.

Element — a chemical substance which cannot be broken down by chemical reactions into a simpler substance: carbon, nitrogen and oxygen are elements.

Fossil — the remains of an organism that lived millions of years ago.

Fuel — a substance that can be burned to give out heat or chemical energy: most fuels are carbon compounds.

Things to do

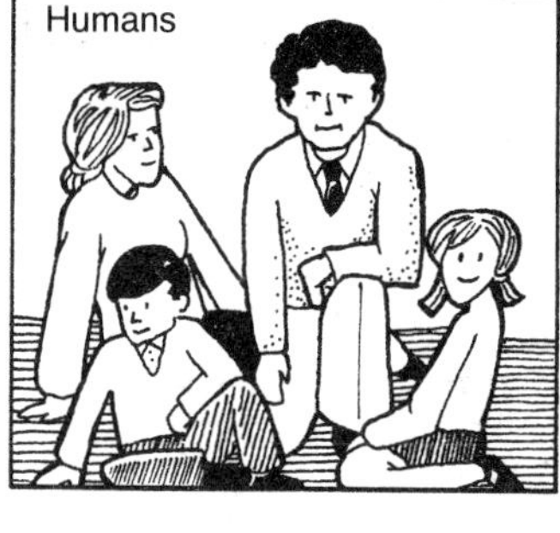

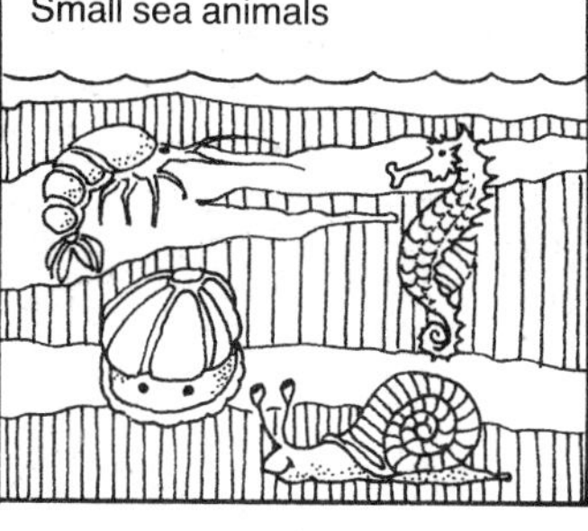

Carbon dioxide

Trace or draw these pictures. Cut out your drawings and lay them in front of you. Put the carbon dioxide picture down on the table. Then put all the other pictures down one at a time in the right order. Now stick them into your book and join them up with arrows. To finish your carbon cycle, over each arrow write the word to describe what is happening. Use the words given below. You may have to use some of the words more than once.

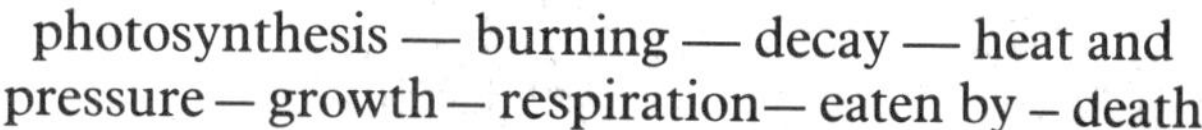
photosynthesis — burning — decay — heat and pressure – growth – respiration – eaten by – death

Figure 14.4

Questions

A.

Copy this into your book using another word (or words) for those in italics. Do not change the meaning of the sentences.

1. Carbon and other chemicals *are used again and again* in living organisms.
2. Living organisms get energy by *joining oxygen with substances containing carbon.*
3. The energy in fuel can be set free by *heating it in oxygen.*

B.

1. Why is carbon important to living things?
2. What would happen if there were no bacteria and fungi?
3. Why can no more fossil fuels be made?
4. Imagine you are a molecule of carbon. Describe what might happen to you as you circulate among different organisms.
5. What kinds of fuels are used to heat (a) your home and (b) your school? What kinds of heating appliances are used (a) in your home and (b) in your school?

   The table shows fuel costs in 1983. In 1983, which were the cheapest and which were the most expensive heating appliances to run?

Fuel	Price per unit	Type of appliance	Cost per useful unit of heat energy
gas	29.3p	convector	1.6p
oil	10.2p	central heating	3.2p
electricity	5.1p	convector	5.1p

TOPIC 15

THE NITROGEN CYCLE

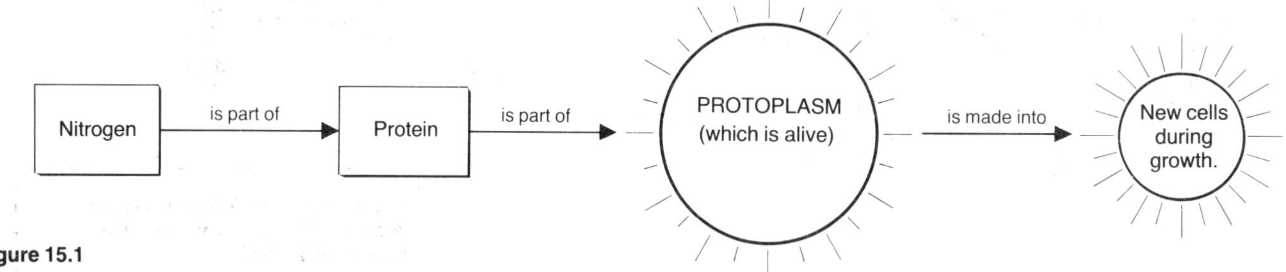

Figure 15.1

WHY NITROGEN IS IMPORTANT

Nitrogen is an important chemical for living organisms. Without nitrogen there would be no life. This is because living things use nitrogen to make proteins. Proteins are an important part of *protoplasm* which is used to make new cells.(See figure 15.1.) Protoplasm is alive!

HOW PLANTS AND ANIMALS GET NITROGEN

Most of the air is made of nitrogen but most organisms can't use this nitrogen to make proteins. They can only use nitrogen when it is joined onto some other chemicals. Substances containing nitrogen are called nitrogen compounds.

Plants get their nitrogen from nitrogen compounds in the soil called nitrates. In a nitrate, nitrogen is joined onto oxygen. Potassium nitrate is a nitrogen compound found in soil. It is made of nitrogen, oxygen and potassium. Animals get their nitrogen from proteins in the plants and other animals which they eat.

Figure 15.2 shows how nitrogen passes (or circulates) from one organism to another. This also happens when organisms die. Proteins in dead bodies are broken down or *decayed* by *bacteria* and *fungi*. The breakdown and build-up of protein and the circulation of nitrogen happens in many small steps. A car is made on an assembly line in a factory in a similar way. (See figures 15.3. and 15.5.)

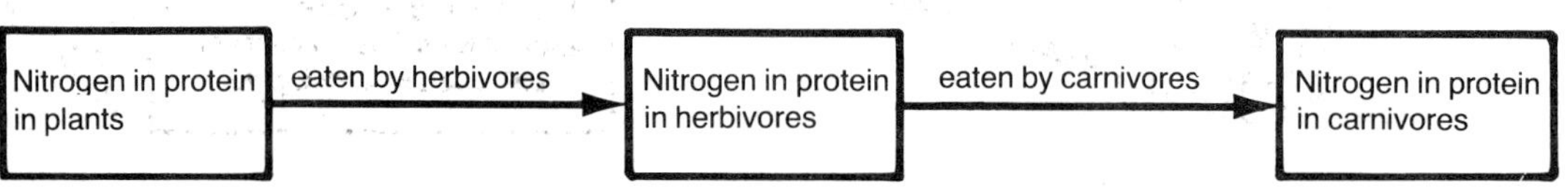

Figure 15.2

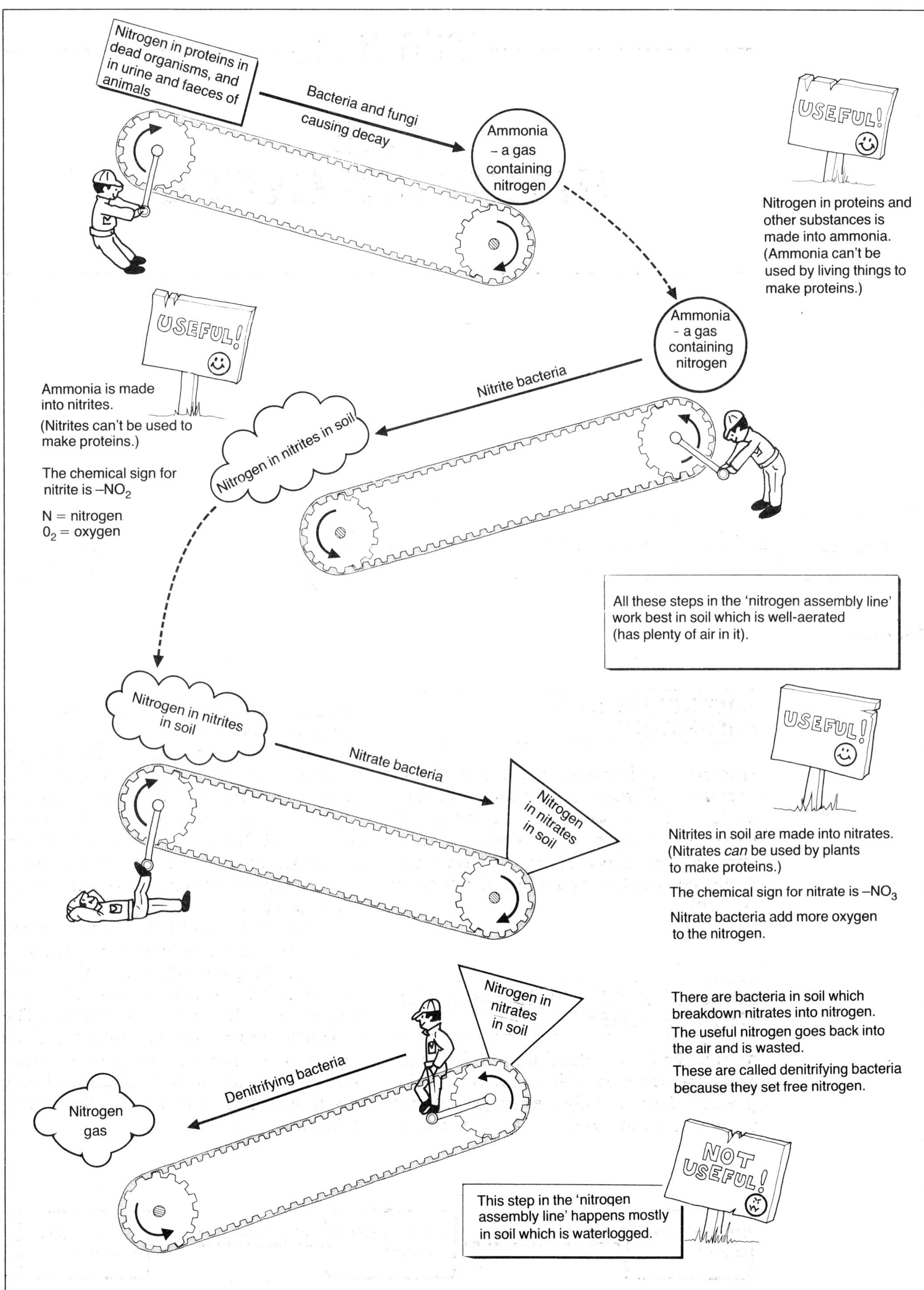

Figure 15.3 The nitrogen assembly line

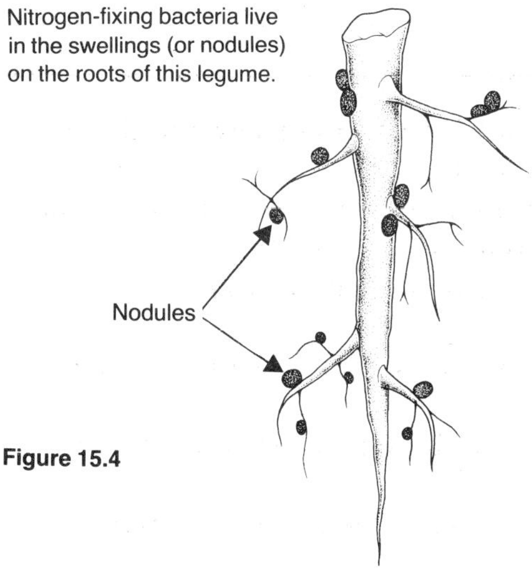

Nitrogen-fixing bacteria live in the swellings (or nodules) on the roots of this legume.

Figure 15.4

Some bacteria can change nitrogen gas into nitrates. This is called 'fixing' nitrogen. Some of these bacteria live in soil but others live in the roots of plants called *legumes*. (See figure 15.4.) Peas, beans and clover are legumes.

Nitrogen can also be fixed by lightning. A lightning flash is hot enough to make nitrogen join with oxygen.

Bacteria do not do all this because they want to be helpful! Each step in the 'assembly line' sets free energy which the bacteria use to keep themselves alive.

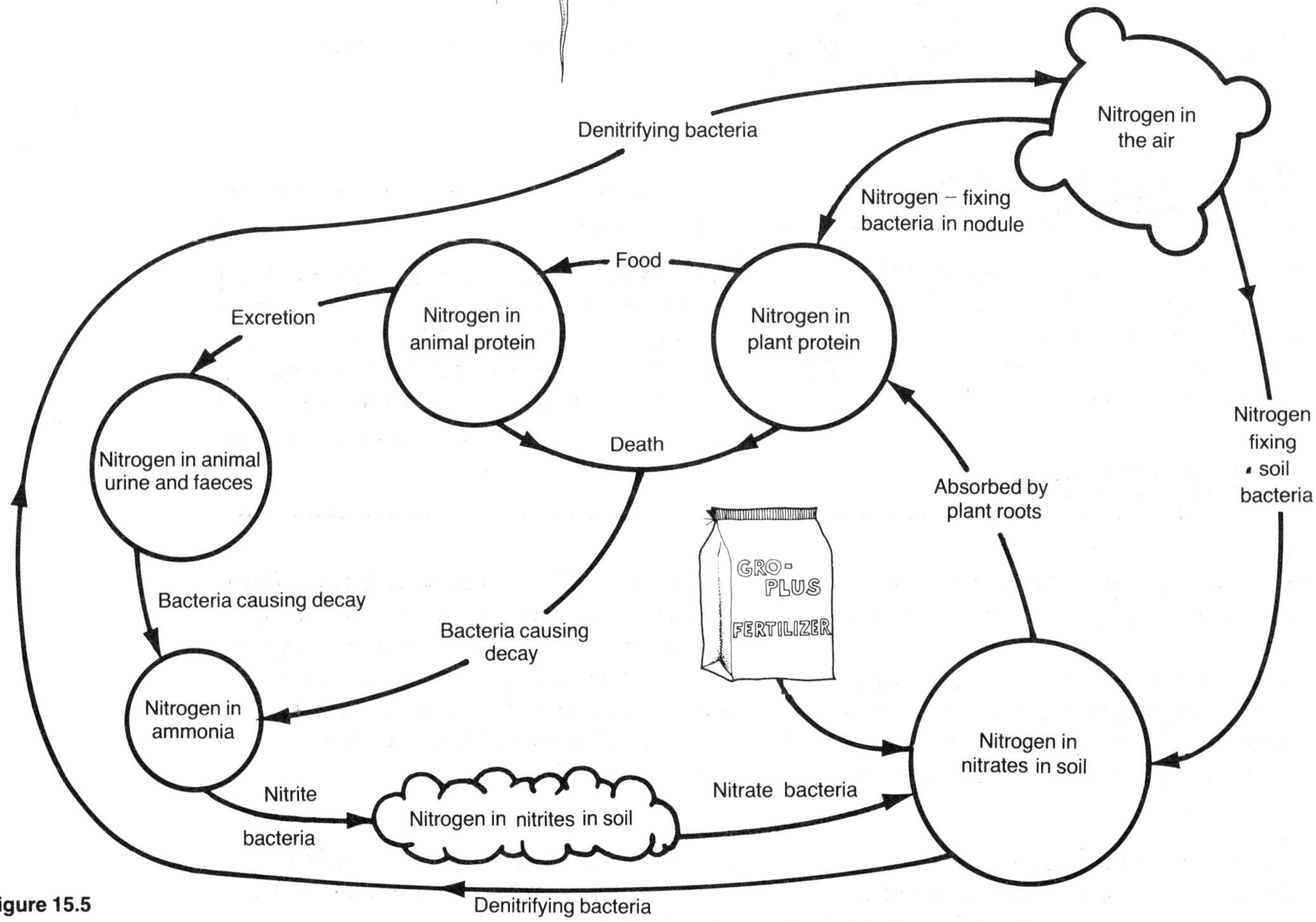

Figure 15.5

Summary

Nitrogen is needed to make *proteins* which are part of living *protoplasm*. Most organisms can't use the nitrogen gas in air to make proteins. *Plants* get their nitrogen from *nitrates* in soil. *Animals* get nitrogen from proteins in plants and animals which they eat.

Nitrogen gas can be *fixed* by:
1. *bacteria* in the root nodules of *legumes*, **2.** some *soil bacteria*, **3.** lightning.

Denitrifying bacteria are not useful because they set free nitrogen from nitrates. Nitrogen in the proteins of dead animals and plants is set free in a gas called *ammonia*. This happens when the dead bodies of these organisms decay. Ammonia is also made from the breakdown of urine and faeces.

Nitrates are added to soil as *fertilisers* to make plants grow better.

Important words

Protoplasm — a jelly-like substance which is found in every living cell; it is made up of a nucleus and cytoplasm.

Bacteria — organisms made of one cell and which are neither animals nor plants; some cause decay of dead organisms.

Decay — the chemical processes that break down substances in dead organisms.

Legumes — a group of plants which have nitrogen-fixing bacteria in their roots.

Fertilisers — chemical substances that can be added to soil to make crops grow better.

Fungi — a group of plants many of which cause decay. They cannot photosynthesise.

Things to do

Dig up a clover plant. Wash the roots carefully to get all the soil off. Are the nodules on the biggest roots or the smallest roots? What colour are the nodules? What do the nodules have inside them?

Fancy that!

Legume crops can add as much as 392 kg per hectare (350 lb per acre) of nitrogen to the soil as nitrate. About 95 kg (15 cwt) of fertiliser would have to be spread to add this much nitrogen to the soil!

Questions

A.

Copy this into your book choosing the correct word from inside the brackets.

A good soil has a lot of (nitrates/nitrites) which (animals/plants) absorb (to/too) make (protein/ammonia). (Fertilisers/Fertelisers) are used (to/too) increase the (nitrates/proteins) in soil. (Denitrifying/Denitryfing) bacteria set free (ammonia/nitrogen) from (nitrates/protein) in soil. Some bacteria can fix (ammonia/nitrogen) so that (plants/animals) can use it. Animals can only get (there/their) nitrogen from (nitrates/proteins).

B.

All plants need nitrogen. Although four fifths of the air is nitrogen, most plants cannot use it directly. Instead, they get their nitrogen in the form of nitrates, which they absorb from the soil. If these soil nitrates were not replaced, they would eventually run out. There are several natural ways in which these nitrates are replaced, which are discussed in the chapter. However, farmers often find it necessary to help this natural replacement along. They may spread manure from their farm livestock on the fields. They may use crop rotation. A four-year example of crop rotation would be to plant a field with turnips in the first year, barley in the second year, clover in the third year and wheat in the final year. Or they may use chemical fertilisers. However, the long term use of chemical fertilisers is expensive and destroys the crumb structure of the soil; this means that the soil is more likely to become dry and powdery and to be blown away by the wind.

1. Why is nitrogen needed by all living things?
2. If four fifths of the air is nitrogen, what other gas occupies most of the remaining fifth?
3. In what natural ways are soil nitrates replaced?
4. Explain how the three different methods used by farmers to help replace soil nitrates work.
5. Why is crop rotation no longer suitable for most farmers?
6. Outline three problems with using chemical fertilisers.
7. Imagine you are a molecule of nitrogen. Use figure 15.5 to help you write about what might happen to you.

TOPIC 16

BACTERIA AND VIRUSES

Bacteria are tiny, single-celled organisms. They are the smallest, simplest living things which can live freely on their own. (*Viruses* are smaller, but they have to live inside other living cells.) You can only see bacteria under the highest magnification of a microscope. Even then, you can only see them as dots or rods. (See figures 16.1 and 16.2.)

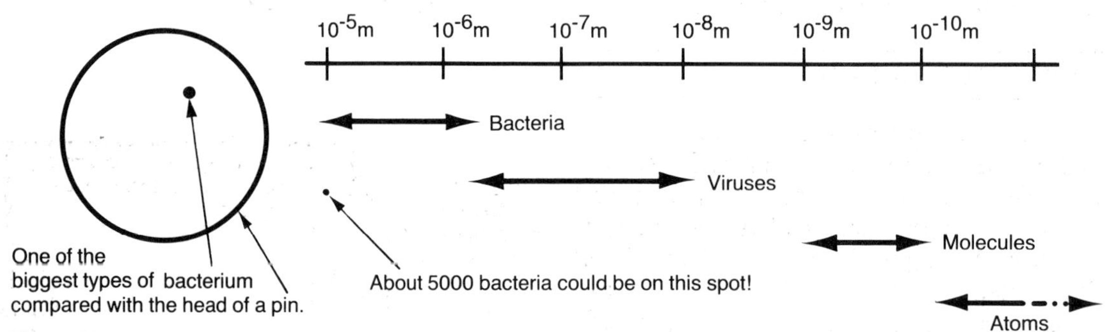

Figure 16.1 Bacteria are very small!

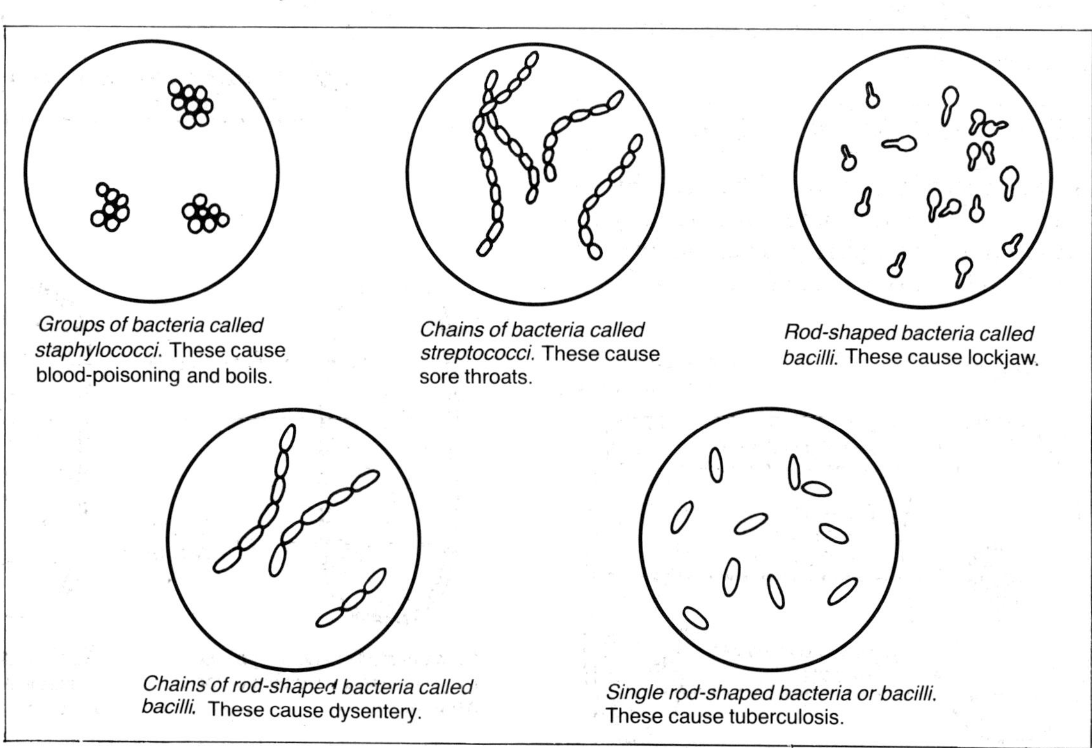

Figure 16.2 What bacteria look like

HOW BACTERIA REPRODUCE

Bacteria can reproduce and grow so fast that they make clumps called colonies. Colonies are big enough to see without a microscope or lens. Bacteria reproduce by asexual reproduction. They just divide into two. This can happen every 30 minutes. In one day, one bacterium could make 280 billion new bacteria! This never happens, as before that the bacteria are either poisoned by their own wastes or they use up all their food.

Some bacteria can make spores which have a thick wall around the cytoplasm. (See figure 16.3.) Inside a spore a bacterium just rests. Bacterial spores are everywhere — in soil, dust, air and on the surface of everything. Spores are easily blown about in air or carried by other organisms and this is how bacteria are spread. Spores are very tough – some are not affected by boiling water! In the right conditions the spores open and the bacteria start to grow again. Warmth, moisture and a good food supply give the best conditions for growth.

HOW BACTERIA FEED

Unlike green plants most bacteria cannot make their own food. Some bacteria get their food from the *dead* bodies of plants and animals. These are called saprophytic bacteria. (See figure 16.4.) Other bacteria get their food from the bodies of *living* organisms. These are called parasitic bacteria. (See figure 16.5.)

Parasitic bacteria may cause disease in animals and plants.

HOW BACTERIA RESPIRE

A few bacteria can be either aerobic or anaerobic, depending upon whether they can get oxygen. Some purely anaerobic bacteria are killed by oxygen. (See figure 16.6.)

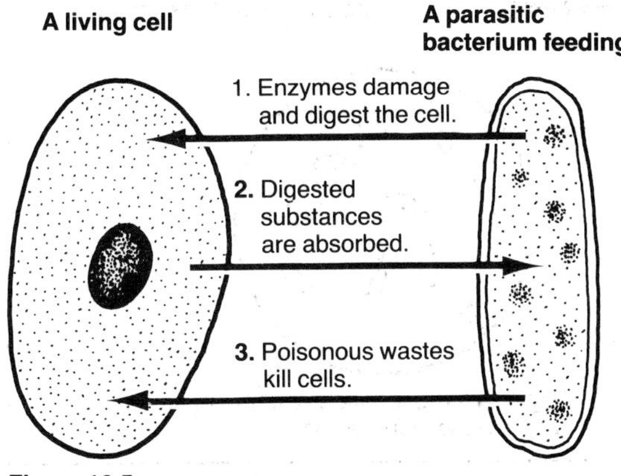

Figure 16.5

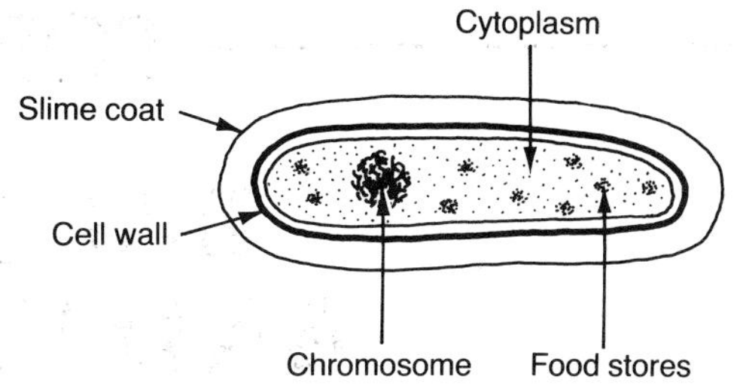

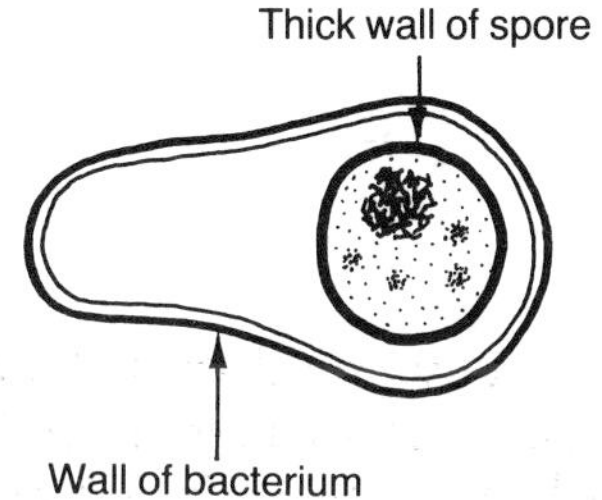

Spores are usually made when conditions for growth are not good.

Figure 16.3

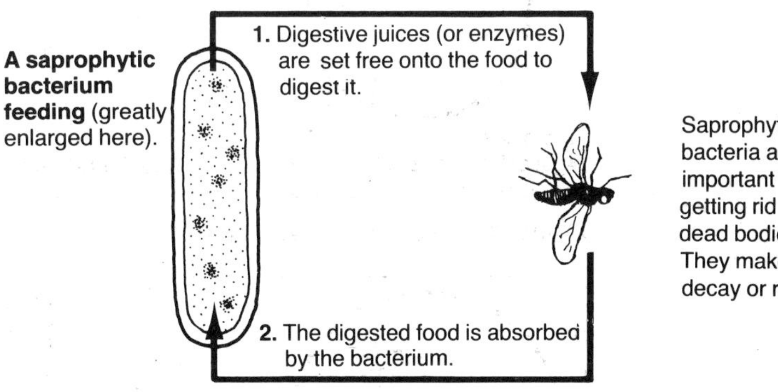

Figure 16.4

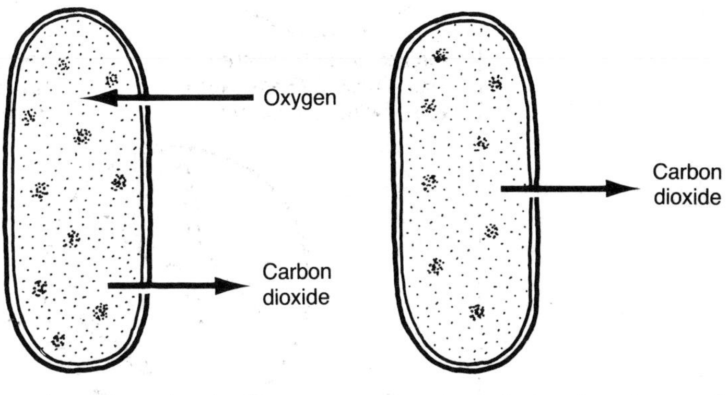

Some bacteria need oxygen for respiration and are called aerobic bacteria.

Some bacteria do not need oxygen for respiration and are called anaerobic bacteria.

Figure 16.6.

IMPORTANCE OF BACTERIA

Some bacteria are useful to us, others are harmful. Without bacteria our lives would be very different.

Harmful bacteria

Bacteria that live as parasites damage the cells of animals and plants. They make poisonous wastes (or toxins) and cause disease. Diseases caused by bacteria can spread to other organisms very quickly.

Figure 16.7 Bacteria like these little habits of ours because they all help to spread disease!

Some diseases caused by bacteria

Disease	How disease is spread	What disease causes
Diptheria	Sneezing, coughing, spitting, touching infected objects (e.g. sucking infected pencils).	Sore throat, difficult breathing; toxins attack heart and nervous system.
Lockjaw	Caused by bacteria which get into your body through deep cuts – like those caused by nails and thorns.	Toxins attack muscles which cannot then work properly. This starts with the jaw muscles.
Tonsillitis	Sneezing, coughing and spitting.	Raised temperature; headache; sore throat; difficult to swallow.
Whooping cough	Sneezing, coughing, spitting, touching infected objects.	Raised temperature; bad cough with a loud 'whoop'.

Making frozen peas. The peas are stored at –20°C. Bacteria cannot grow at this low temperature.

People can be protected against many diseases caused by bacteria. This is done by giving the person a weak dose of a disease. The person's blood then makes *antibodies* against that disease. The antibodies give protection against further attacks and the person is said to be immune to the disease. (See Topic 25.)

Keeping food fresh

Bacteria which cause decay (saprophytic bacteria) attack human food and make it go bad. Fungi also do this. We need to preserve our food from these organisms. There are many ways of preserving food (see p.101).

HOW TO BE NASTY TO BACTERIA AND FUNGI (and preserve your food)

What to do	What happens	Useful for
Make them very hot!	High temperatures kill bacteria and fungi. After treatment the food is put into a sterile container.	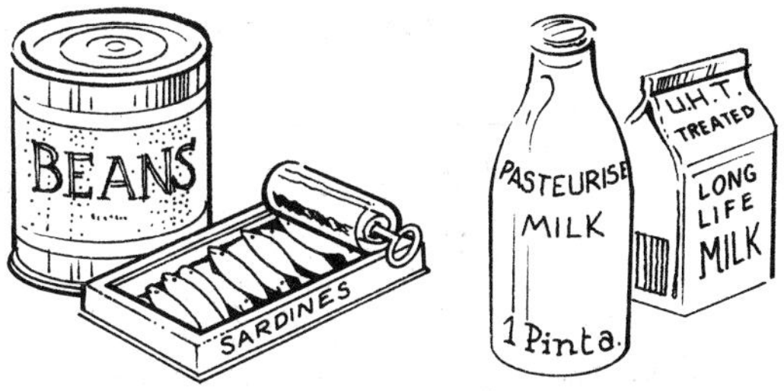
Make them very cold!	Bacteria stop growing at 5°C. A refrigerator reaches this temperature. A freezer reaches -20°C and will keep food for many weeks.	Cooked and uncooked meats; butter; milk; cheese; fruit juice; eggs; fish; pastry; cream. 
Sweeten them up!	Bacteria cannot live in a strong sugar solution. The fluid in their cells is drawn out by osmosis into the sugar solution and they die.	
Salt them down!	Bacteria cannot live in a strong solution of salt because of osmosis (see above).	
Dry them out!	Bacteria need water to keep alive. If water is removed from food, bacteria and fungi cannot grow on it.	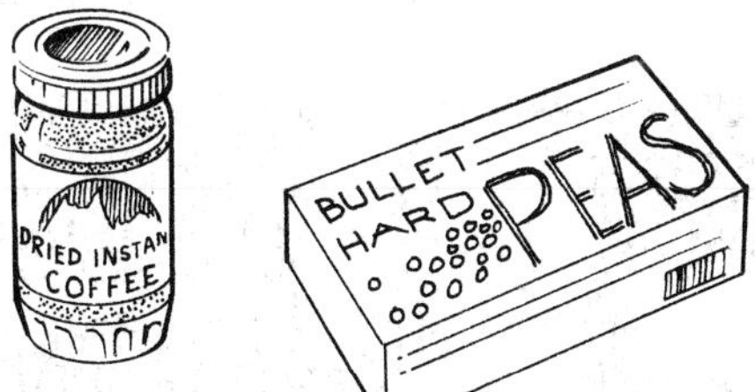
Drop them in acid!	Bacteria cannot grow very well in acid solutions. The most commonly used acid is vinegar.	

USEFUL
USEFUL
DEPARTMENT OF BACTERIAL DECAY
Dead animals,
Excreta and urine,
Dead plants,
Paper,
Wool and cotton,
Hair,
Waste food
Are all broken down by saprophytic bacteria.
Simpler substances
Absorbed by plants
Living plants
Eaten by animals
Living animals
Animal dies or is used by humans
Plant dies or is used by humans

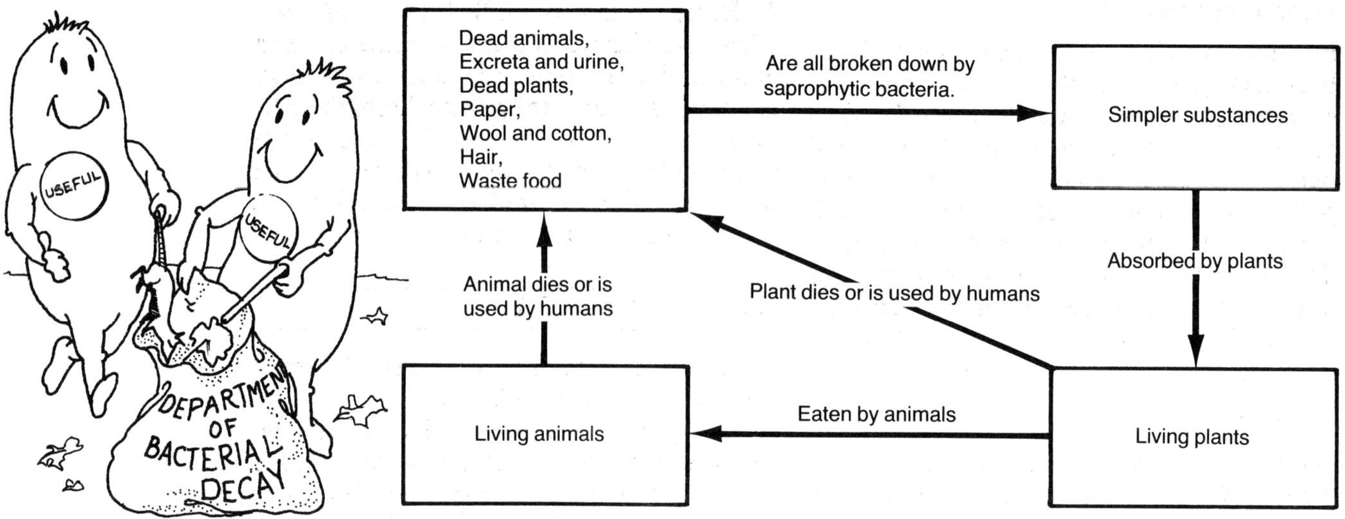

Figure 16.8 How saprophytic bacteria keep things going round!

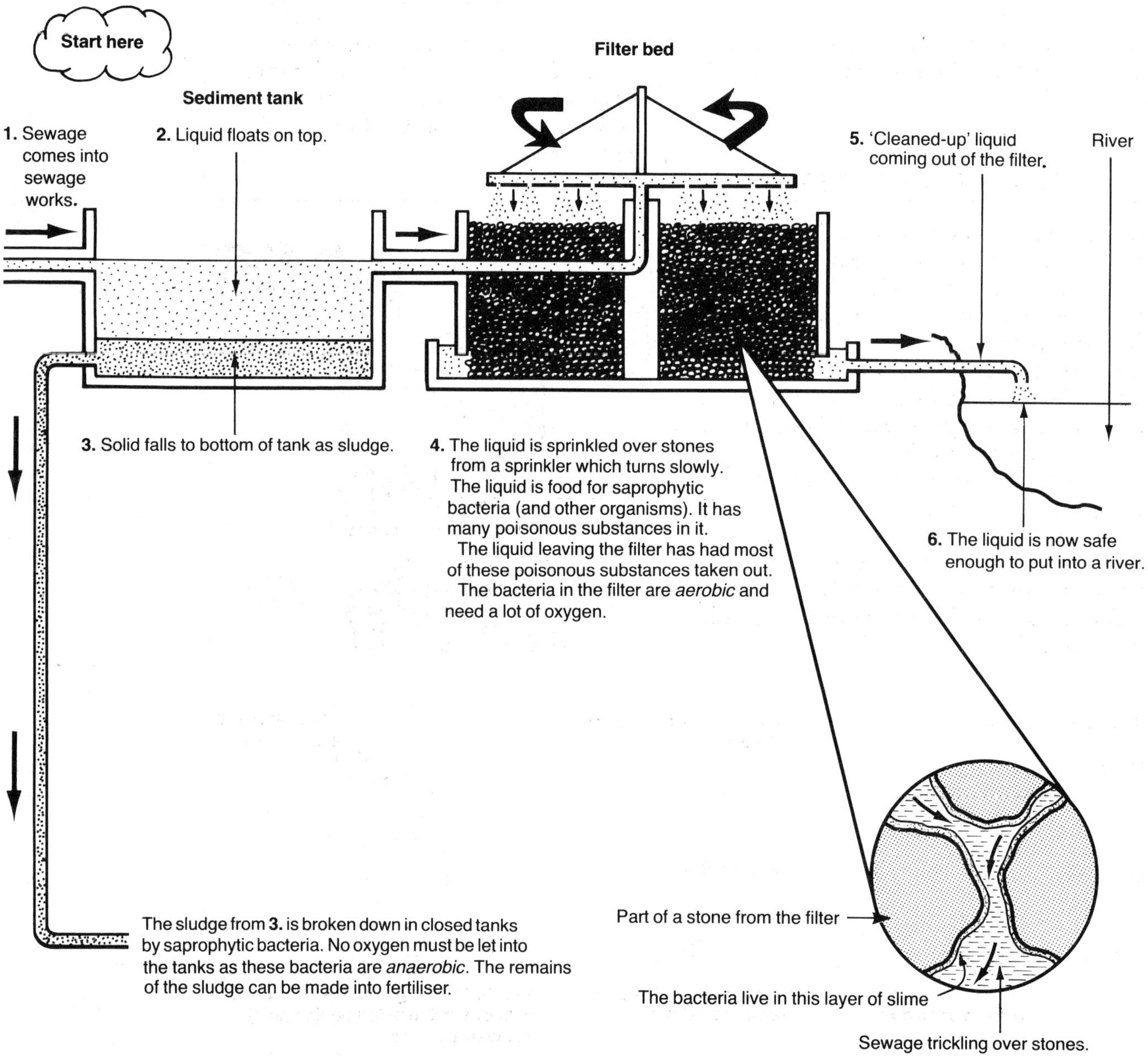

Start here
Filter bed
Sediment tank
1. Sewage comes into sewage works.
2. Liquid floats on top.
5. 'Cleaned-up' liquid coming out of the filter.
River
3. Solid falls to bottom of tank as sludge.
4. The liquid is sprinkled over stones from a sprinkler which turns slowly. The liquid is food for saprophytic bacteria (and other organisms). It has many poisonous substances in it.
The liquid leaving the filter has had most of these poisonous substances taken out.
The bacteria in the filter are *aerobic* and need a lot of oxygen.
6. The liquid is now safe enough to put into a river.
The sludge from **3.** is broken down in closed tanks by saprophytic bacteria. No oxygen must be let into the tanks as these bacteria are *anaerobic*. The remains of the sludge can be made into fertiliser.
Part of a stone from the filter
The bacteria live in this layer of slime
Sewage trickling over stones.

Figure 16.9 How saprophytic bacteria clean-up sewage

Useful bacteria

Bacteria which cause decay (saprophytic bacteria) are useful for clearing up everybody's mess! Some of these bacteria break down substances like leather and paper which are made from animals and plants. Some saprophytic bacteria also break down the dead bodies of animals and plants. The chemicals in their bodies are set free for other organisms to use. Saprophytic bacteria recycle these chemicals. (See figure 16.8.)

Useful guests!

Many animals that eat plants, like rabbits, sheep and cows, can't digest the cellulose in plants by themselves. Cellulose is digested for them by bacteria which live in their digestive systems.

Tasty bacteria!

We use bacteria to make some sorts of food. Yoghurt and soft cheeses are made from milk by bacteria.

HOW TO KILL BACTERIA

Because some bacteria can be dangerous we need to know how to kill them.

1. Bacteria can be killed by steam. A machine called an autoclave is used for this. An autoclave looks and works like a big pressure cooker. Autoclaves are used for killing bacteria on instruments needed for operations in hospital. Something without any bacteria on it is called *sterile*.

2. Bacteria can be killed by chemicals called *disinfectants*. 'Dettol' is a common disinfectant.

3. Chemicals used to stop the growth of bacteria which make wounds go bad are called *antiseptics*. These are put onto boils, pimples and cuts.

4. Bacteria can be killed by *antibiotics*. These are chemicals made by some bacteria and fungi. Antibiotics are more useful than antiseptics because they do not harm the cells of your body and they can be used inside your body. Usually you swallow a tablet made of the antibiotic. Penicillin and Terramycin are antibiotics.

KEEP IT CLEAN!

Your skin always has bacteria on it. A cut lets these bacteria get under your skin, where they may start an infection. Bacteria can get into your sweat glands. If dirt has collected in your sweat glands, a pimple or boil may grow. (See figure 16.10.) If you have a lot of infected sweat glands, you have acne. This is common on the faces of teenagers.

Regular washing with soap and water is needed to stop skin infections. Washing your hands is very important when handling food to stop infection spreading.

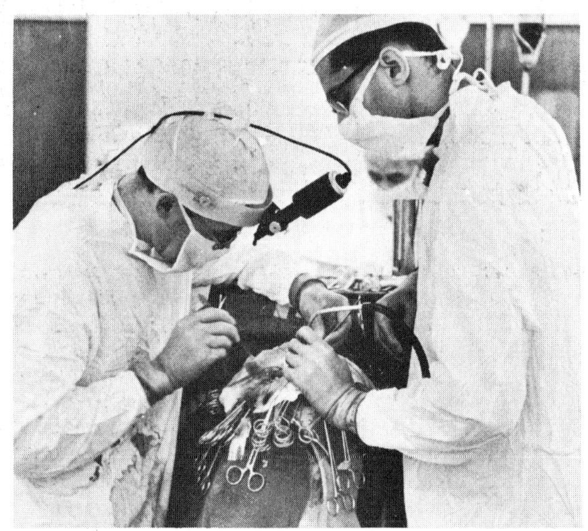

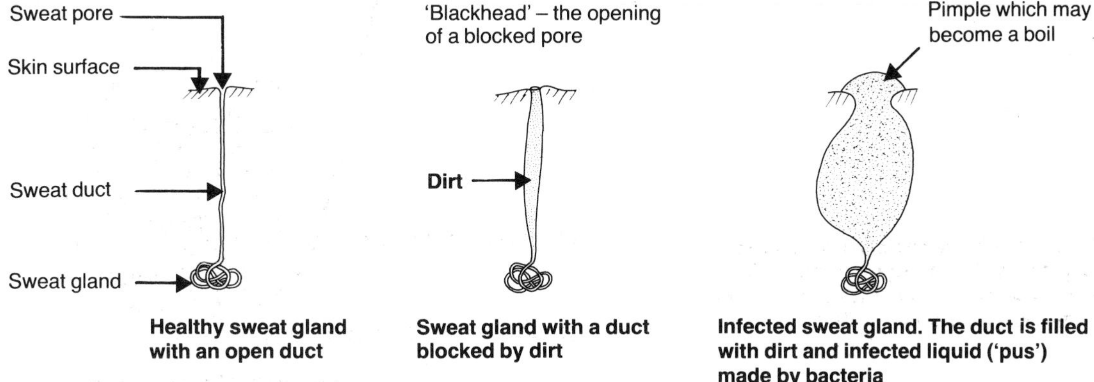

Healthy sweat gland with an open duct

Sweat gland with a duct blocked by dirt

Infected sweat gland. The duct is filled with dirt and infected liquid ('pus') made by bacteria

Figure 16.10

VIRUSES

Viruses are much smaller than bacteria. Viruses cannot grow or reproduce by themselves. They can only grow and reproduce inside other living cells. They are all parasites and cause disease in the organisms in which they live. Diseases such as poliomyelitis (polio), influenza, chicken pox and rabies are all caused by viruses. These diseases are spread in much the same way as bacterial diseases. Because viruses can only live inside other cells they cannot be killed by antibiotics. (See figure 16.11.)

Fancy that!

The oldest can of beef known to exist can still be seen in the Liverpool Museum of Public Health. It was canned in 1824!

A poison made by a bacterium called *Clostridium botulinum* (found in soil) is so deadly that 0.00001 mg will kill a man!

Cows have been fed with chopped paper and cardboard! As this is made of cellulose, the bacteria in their digestive systems can break it down.

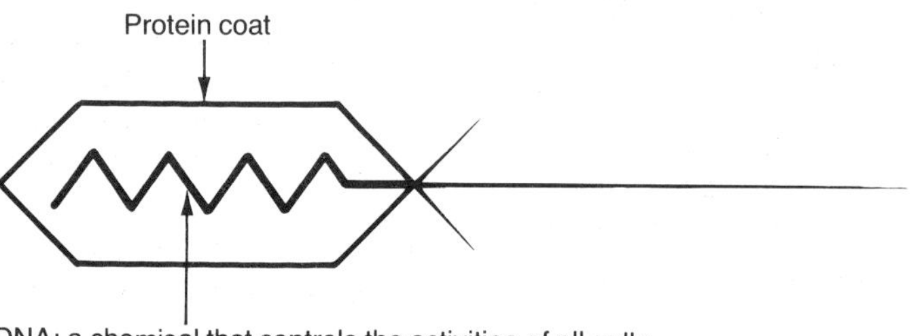

Figure 16.11 A virus

Summary

Bacteria are everywhere but are too small to be seen. They reproduce by *asexual reproduction*. *Aerobic* bacteria need oxygen for respiration but *anaerobic* bacteria do not.

Some bacteria are harmful, others are useful. *Parasitic* bacteria are harmful and feed on *living* cells, causing disease. Some harmful *saprophytic* bacteria feed on human food and make it go bad. There are different ways of *preserving* food to stop this happening. Some useful saprophytic bacteria *recycle* the chemicals of which *dead* organisms are made. They do this by feeding on their bodies and making them *decay*. Other useful bacteria digest cellulose, clean up sewage or are used to make some kinds of food.

Bacteria can be killed by *steam*, *disinfectants* or *antibiotics*. *Antiseptics* stop the growth of bacteria which make wounds go bad.

Viruses are smaller than bacteria and are all parasites. They can only live inside other cells.

Important words

Bacteria	organisms made of one cell; they are neither animals nor plants (singular: bacterium).
Viruses	disease-causing bodies smaller than bacteria; they can only grow inside a living cell.
Sterile	describes something that has no viruses, bacteria or other simple organisms in or on it.
Disinfectant	something that can kill disease-causing bacteria; heat, sunlight and some chemicals are disinfectants.
Antiseptic	a substance that stops the growth of disease-causing organisms in wounds.
Antibiotic	a substance that stops certain bacteria from reproducing.

Things to do

1. *Making low-fat yoghurt*

Make this in a kitchen at school or at home – NOT in the science laboratory!

You will need:
0.5 litres of milk
a jug (big enough to hold 0.5 litres)
a saucepan
a carton of yoghurt

Boil 0.5 litres of milk and let it cool. When just still warm, take the skin from the surface. Pour the milk into a jug. Mix in 2 tablespoons of yoghurt from your carton. Eat the rest! Cover the jug and stand it in a warm place for 12–18 hours. A cupboard used for airing clothes is good for this. Carefully pour off any liquid and you have a jug of yoghurt. Add fruit or sugar if you wish.

You can use this yoghurt to make more. Just use the last 2 tablespoons of it in the same way.

2. *To find out where bacteria live*

We can grow bacteria in the laboratory on 'soup' made-up in a jelly. The 'soup' can be made from Oxo. The jelly is called agar and is made from seaweed! Soup and agar are mixed together and sterilised by heating. This kills any bacteria already in the soup or agar. The mixture sets when it is poured into sterile petri dishes.

a. *Do not take the lid off your petri dish.* Write your name on the lid.

b. Each member of your class can test different objects for bacteria. Try the window ledge; window glass; the end of a pencil; the floor; the bench surface; the skin of an apple or orange; the bottom of your shoe; your finger tips.
Collect the bacteria like this: cut a piece of Sellotape about 10 cm long. Fold back about 3 cm of it to hold. Press the sticky surface of the tape onto the object.

c. Lift the lid of the petri dish. *Gently* press the tape onto the surface of the jelly. There is no need to use Sellotape when you are collecting bacteria from your fingers. Just rest your finger tips on the jelly.

d. *Quickly* put back the lid of your petri dish. Write on the lid where you collected the bacteria.

e. Sellotape the lid of the dish to the base. Place the dish in a warm place for two days.

f. One dish prepared by the class should be labelled 'Control'. The lid must not be lifted at all. No bacteria should be placed on the jelly in this dish.

g. Look to see if any colonies of bacteria have grown in your dish. What colour are the colonies? How big are they? Do your results show that bacteria are found everywhere?

Do not lift the lid of the petri dish. Some of the bacteria may be dangerous.

Questions

A.

Join these sentences together using either the word 'and' or the word 'because', whichever is correct.

1. Some bacteria in a sewage works are anaerobic. They break down sludge.
2. Sewage sludge is digested in closed tanks. The bacteria which do this are anaerobic.
3. Bacteria in a sewage filter are aerobic. They breakdown substances in the sewage.
4. Harmful substances in sewage are made harmless. Organisms in the filters feed on them.

B.

1. Why don't substances such as plastic and rubber rot?
2. Why do you think that meat from a freezer should be thawed out properly before you cook it?
3. What do you think would happen if there were no saprophytic bacteria?
4. Make a list of the ways in which bacteria can spread from one person to another.
5. Make a list of all the food you eat and drink in a week which has been made by micro-organisms. In what way has the food been changed by the micro-organisms? Has the food been made by bacteria or by fungi?

TOPIC 17

SOIL

WHY SOIL IS IMPORTANT

Soil is the top few centimetres of the Earth's surface. It is 'home' for many different organisms like bacteria, fungi, insects and worms. These live in spaces between the soil particles or 'crumbs'.

The lives of other living things depend on these soil organisms. This is because they set free mineral salts from the bodies of dead organisms. Plants can absorb these mineral salts and use them for growth. The plants will then be eaten by herbivorous animals which in turn will be eaten by carnivores.

Mineral salts are also dissolved from small pieces of rock in soil.

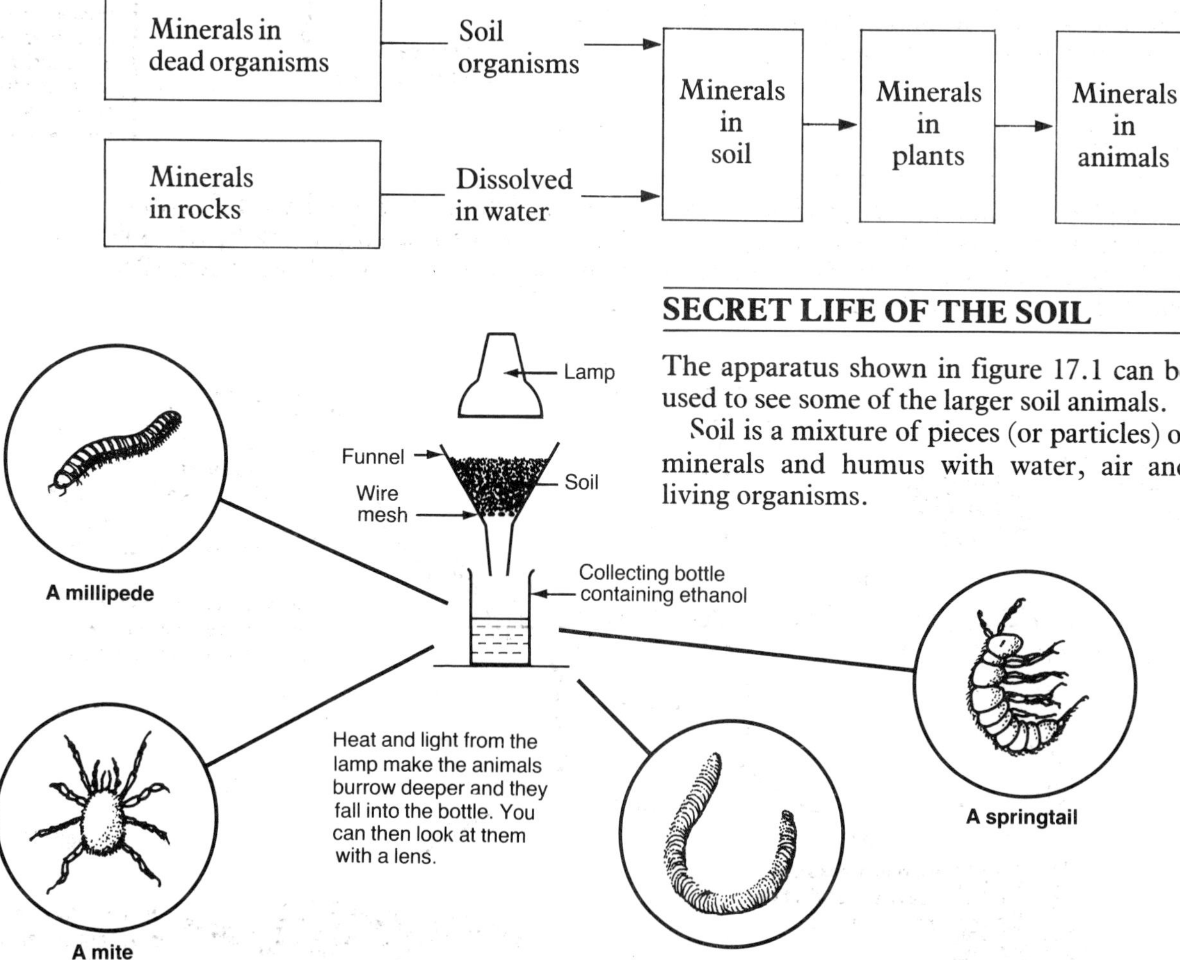

Figure 17.1

SECRET LIFE OF THE SOIL

The apparatus shown in figure 17.1 can be used to see some of the larger soil animals.

Soil is a mixture of pieces (or particles) of minerals and humus with water, air and living organisms.

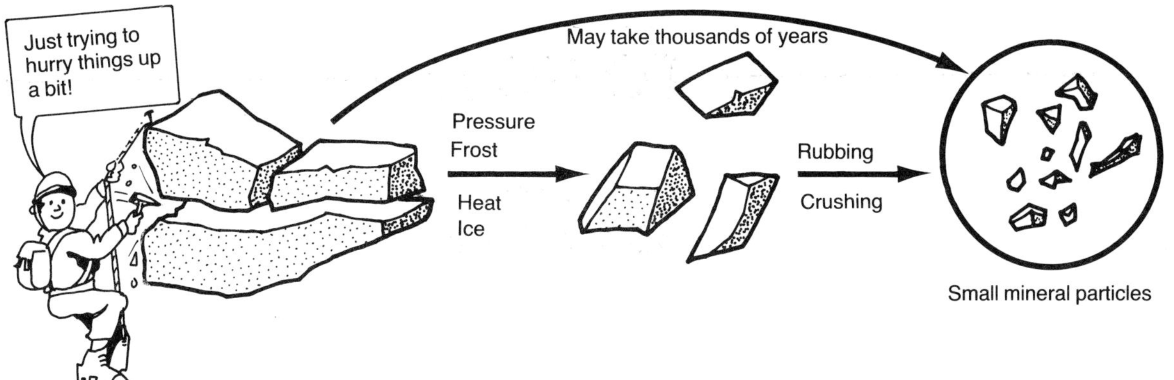

Figure 17.2

MINERALS

Mineral particles are tiny pieces of rock. They are made by the break-up or weathering of rocks. Frost, ice, heat, crushing and rubbing change lumps of rock into tiny pieces of sand, clay and silt – the mineral particles. (See figure 17.2.)

Rocks are also broken up by chemicals. Carbon dioxide in air dissolves in rain to make carbonic acid. This weak acid slowly dissolves rocks, especially limestone rock.

Mineral particles make the soil 'framework' and help to support plant roots. Mineral particles *slowly* set free mineral salts into the soil. The size of mineral particle affects how much air there is in the soil and how well it drains. (See figure 17.3.)

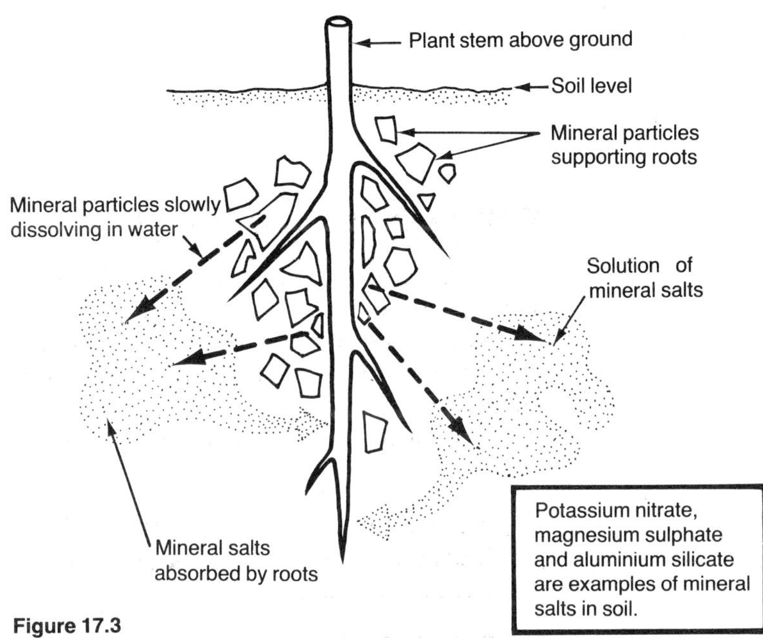

Figure 17.3

HUMUS

When plants and animals die, soil organisms make their dead bodies rot or decay. The black substance made from the remains is called humus. Plant humus is 'stringy' because of the cellulose and woody bits in it. Animal humus is a soft, sticky liquid. Soil with a lot of humus in it looks black. (See figure 17.4.)

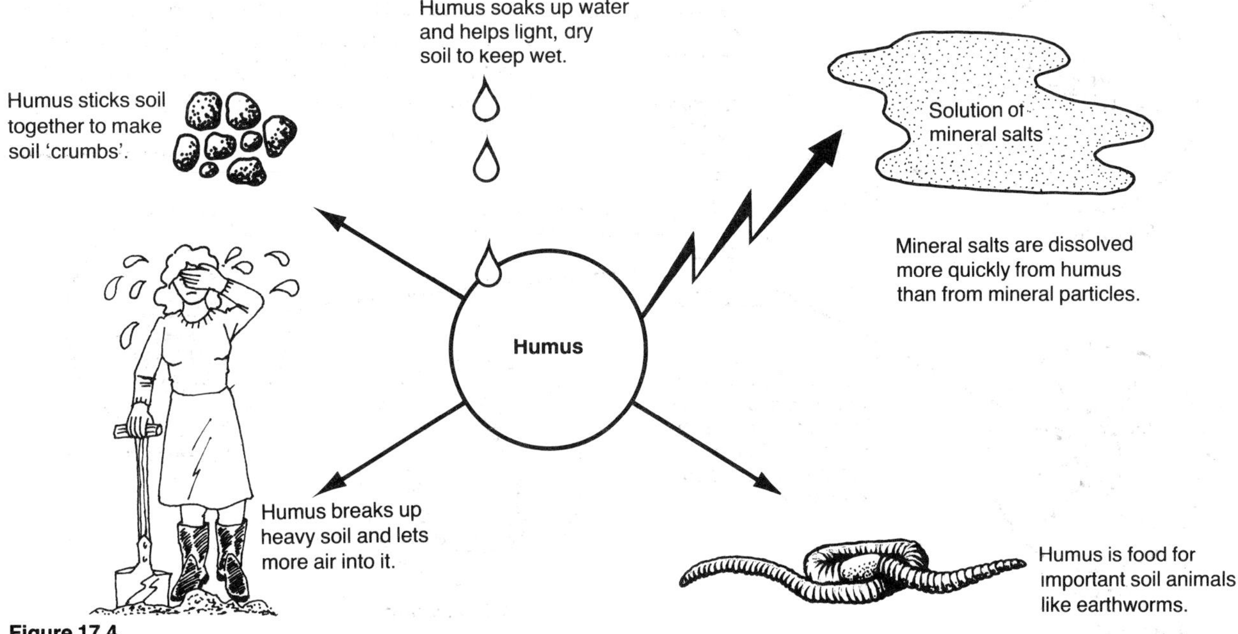

Figure 17.4

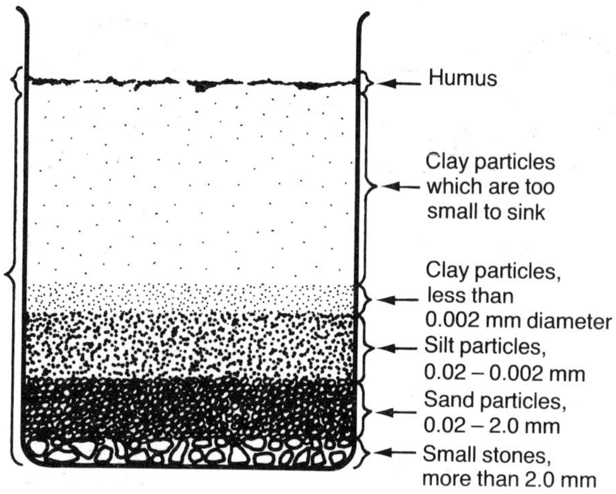

This part is made from plant and animal remains

This part is made from weathered rocks

Humus

Clay particles which are too small to sink

Clay particles, less than 0.002 mm diameter

Silt particles, 0.02 – 0.002 mm

Sand particles, 0.02 – 2.0 mm

Small stones, more than 2.0 mm

Figure 17.5

WHAT SOIL HAS IN IT

If you shake some soil with water and leave it to stand it will look like figure 17.5.

The heavy particles sink quickly and lighter particles sink slowly. Very light substances like humus float.

AIR AND WATER

Plants and soil organisms need both the air and water in soil to live. (See figure 17.6.)

Water in soil usually comes from rain but it is also drawn up from water deeper in the soil.

The sizes of air space in soil depends on the sizes of the soil particles. (See figure 17.7.) Big soil particles have big air spaces. Small soil particles have small air spaces. The size of air space affects:

1. drainage – how water moves *down* through soil,
2. evaporation – how water is *lost* from soil to the air,
3. capillarity – how water is *drawn up* from deeper in the soil.

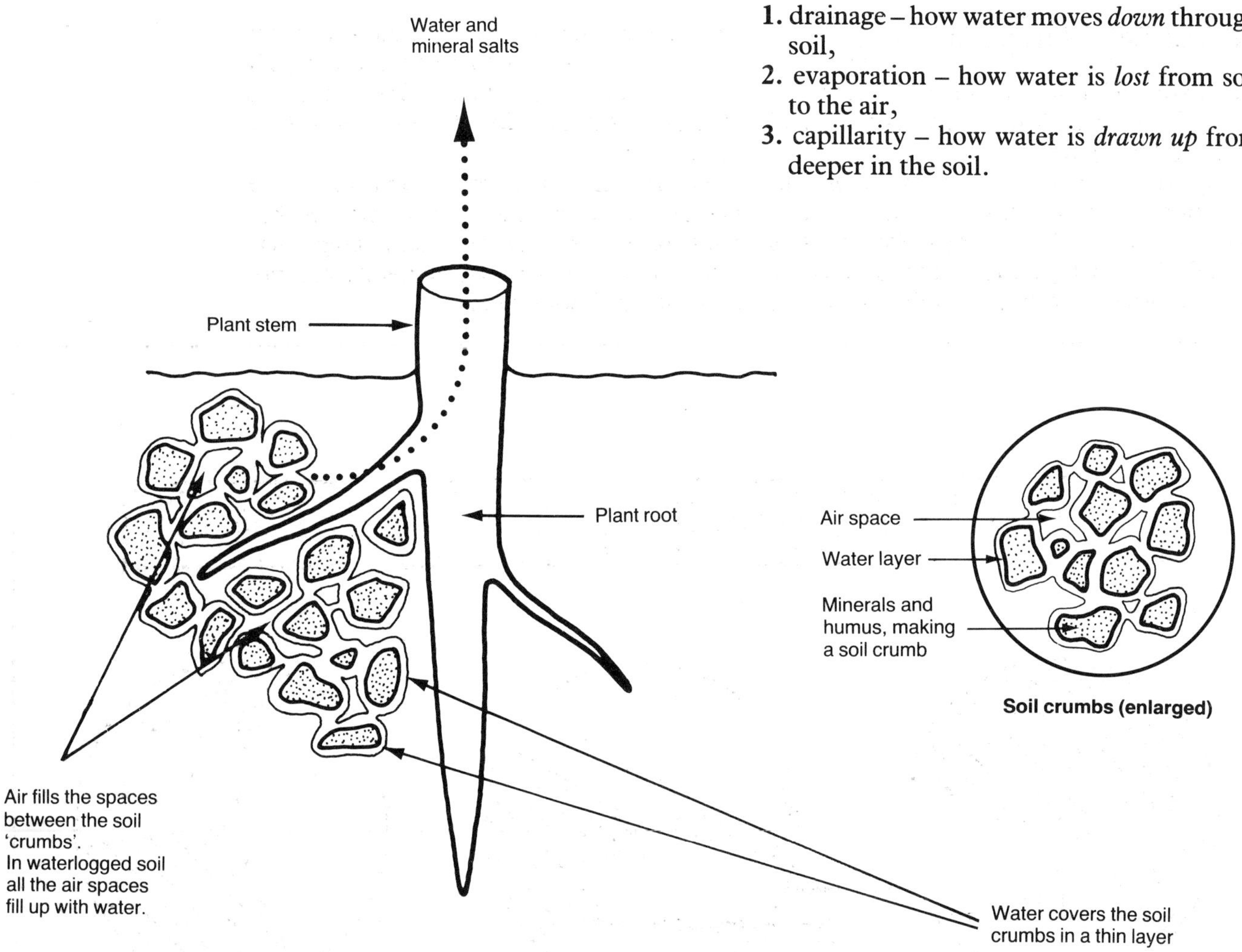

Water and mineral salts

Plant stem

Plant root

Air space

Water layer

Minerals and humus, making a soil crumb

Soil crumbs (enlarged)

Air fills the spaces between the soil 'crumbs'.
In waterlogged soil all the air spaces fill up with water.

Water covers the soil crumbs in a thin layer

Soil organisms and plant roots use the air for respiration.

Water is absorbed by plant roots and keeps the plant cells firm. This is how small plants keep upright. Water is used in photosynthesis. It is also needed to dissolve mineral salts.

Figure 17.6

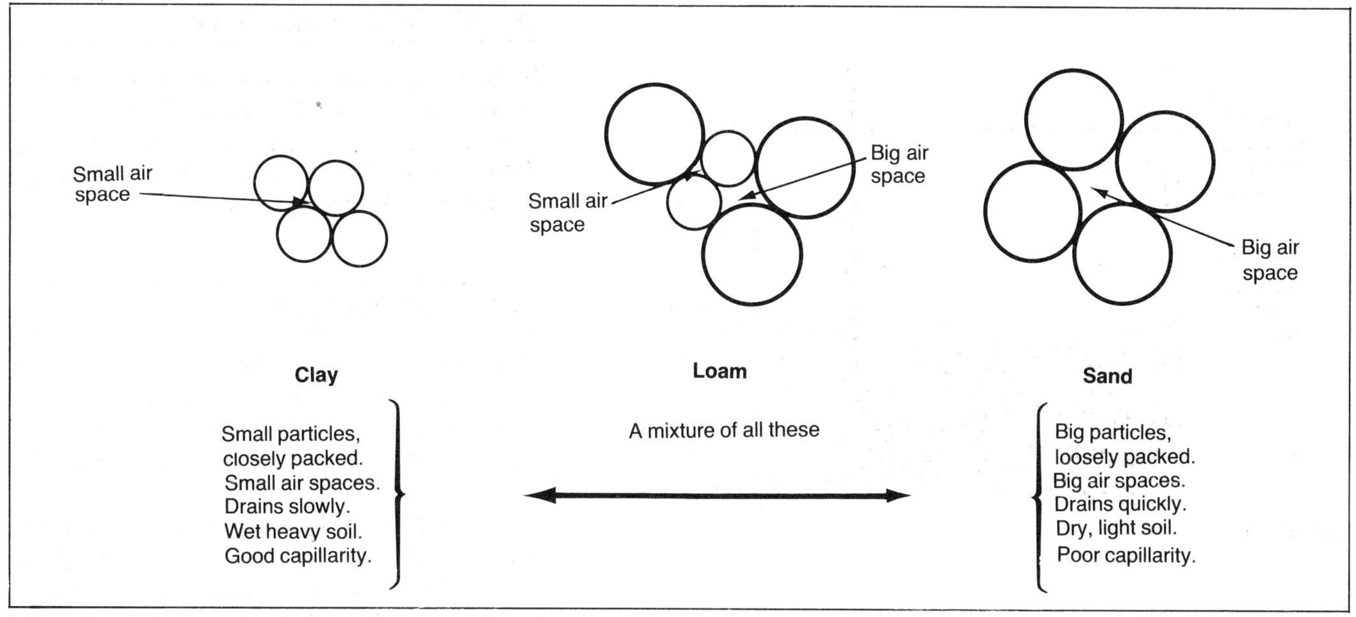

Figure 17.7 How size of particle affects the size of air space.

DIFFERENT KINDS OF SOIL

The main kinds of soil are: *sand*, *clay* and *loam*. These are made of different sizes of soil particle. (See figure 17.7.)

Clay soil is heavy, slow to drain and difficult to dig. It does not have much humus and dries out into hard lumps. Sandy soil is light, drains quickly and is easy to dig. Sandy soil is not very *fertile* because rain washes out the minerals very quickly. Loam is the most fertile soil. It is a mixture of sand, clay, silt and humus. There can be different amounts of these substances in different loams. (See figure 17.8.)

Loam warms up quickly, is easy to dig and has plenty of air spaces. It drains well but holds back some water so that it keeps wet. Loam is fertile because minerals are not easily washed out by rain.

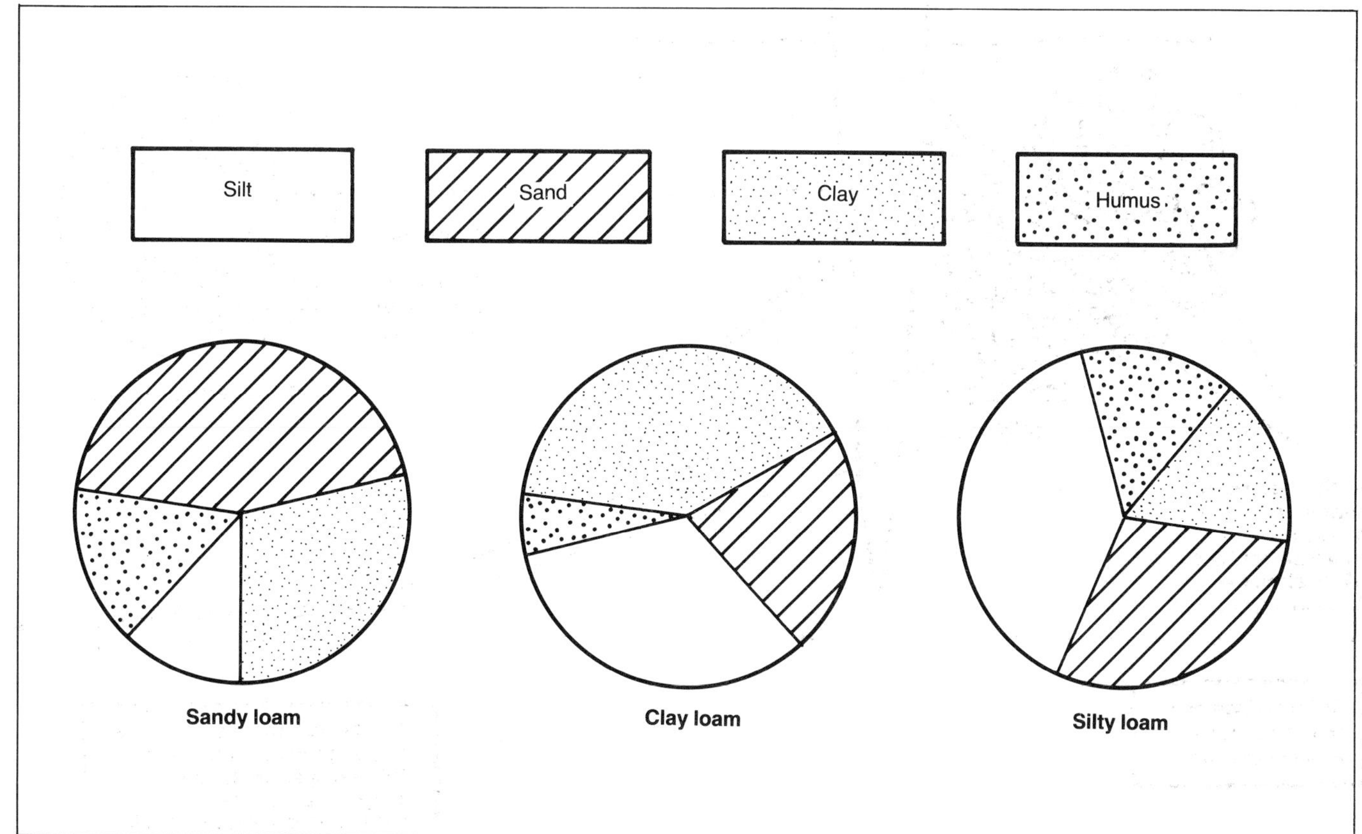

Figure 17.8

Mr Greenbud's Gardening Column

This week:
HOW TO IMPROVE YOUR SOIL

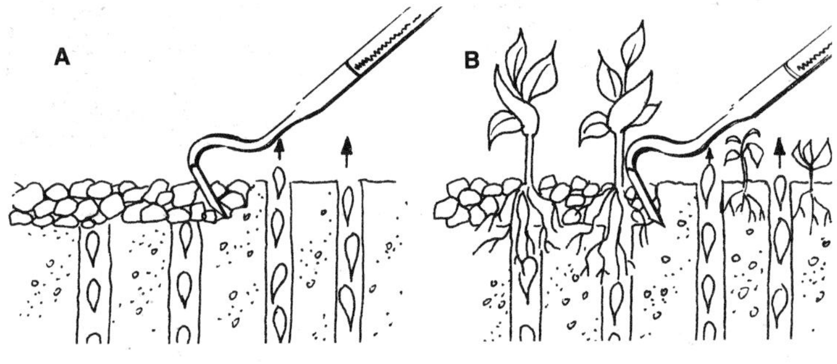

1. Hoeing

A. If you hoe the soil in dry weather you will stop water evaporating from it quite so fast. This happens because hoeing blocks the air spaces through which the water gets out.

B. Hoeing also traps water around plant roots, making the plants grow bigger.

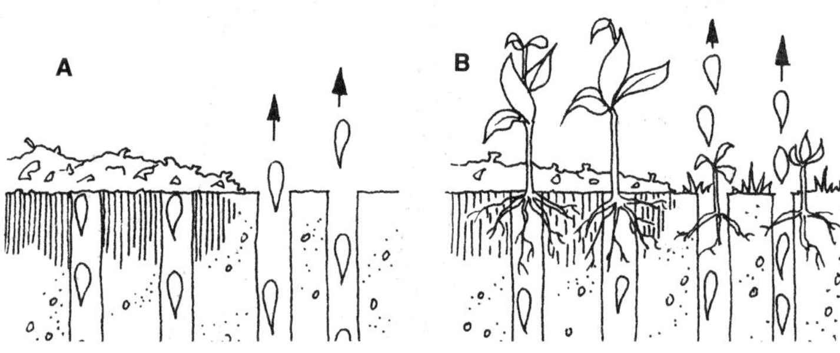

2. Mulching

A. A mulch is a layer of dead leaves, grass or compost which you can spread on the soil. It stops water evaporating from the soil and stops weeds from growing.

B. Plants grow better in hot weather on a mulched soil because they can get more water.

3. Spreading compost and manure

If you mix manure and compost with your soil it will keep the soil crumbs stuck together and the air spaces open. This helps it to drain and improves capillarity. Also minerals in compost and manure make soil more fertile.

Manure is a mixture of straw and excreta of horses or cows. Compost is made from waste plant substances like grass cuttings, dead leaves, potato peelings etc. You should pile these up and leave them to rot before you dig them into your soil. Manure is a good way of adding nitrates to soil.

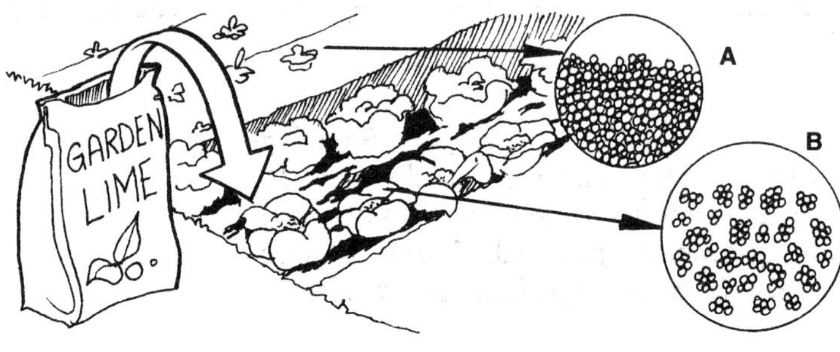

4. Spreading lime

A. Clay soil has small air spaces and drains slowly.

B. You can spread garden lime on clay soil. Lime makes clay particles stick together into bigger particles. This helps it to drain and lets air into the soil. Lime also makes soil less acid.

5. Spreading fertilisers

A. Fertilisers put more minerals into soil and so make plants grow better.

B. If you always grow food crops on the same soil, you must add fertiliser. Without fertilisers, crops get smaller. Common fertilisers are ammonium sulphate and 'super-phosphates'. Fertilisers do not last long in soil because they are soon washed out. Fertilisers do not improve the soil crumbs.

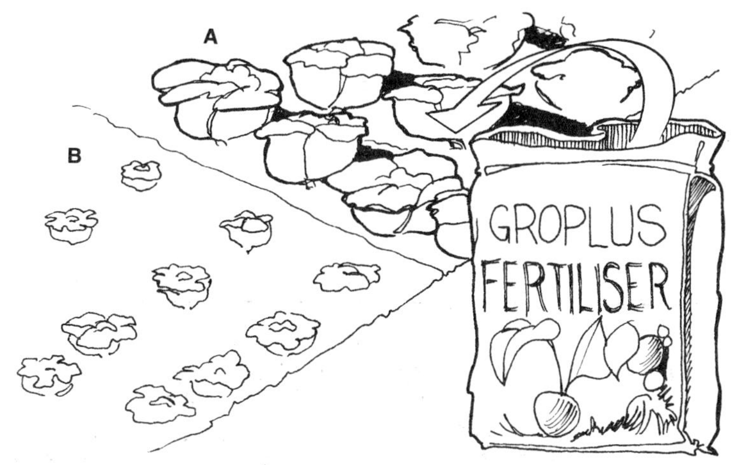

6. Earthworms

A. Earthworms eat soil when they burrow in it. Worm casts are made of waste substances and undigested food passed out by the worm. Worm casts make soil more fertile.

B. Worms pull dead leaves into their burrows to eat. This puts more humus into the soil.

C. Air and water get into soil through earthworm tunnels. Worms help to mix up the different layers of soil.

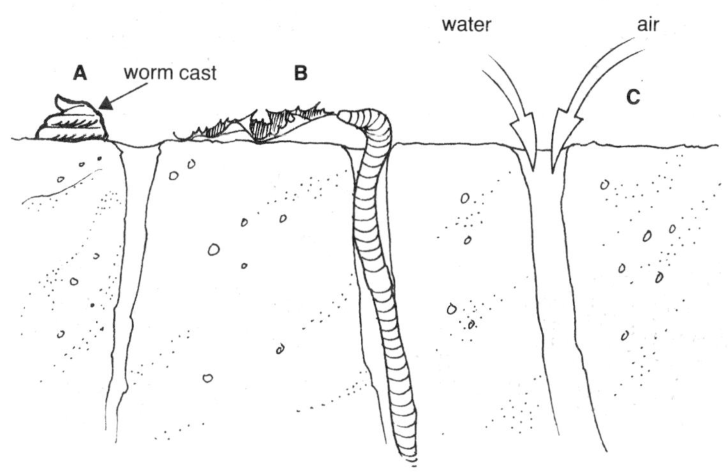

7. Crop rotation

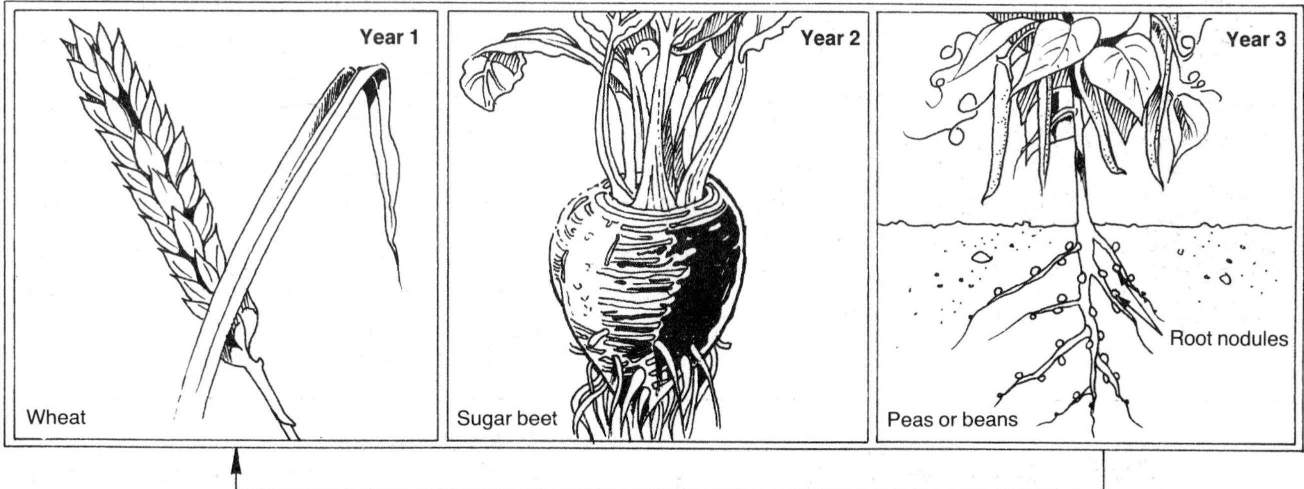

Some plants, such as wheat and sugar beet, take more minerals from the soil than other plants. Nitrates taken from soil by plants can be put back by legumes such as peas, beans and clover. These plants have root nodules with bacteria in them (see page 96). The bacteria change nitrogen in the air into nitrates. Growing a crop of legumes after growing other crops is called crop rotation. This also helps to stop plant diseases.

Summary

Soil is made of *mineral particles* and *humus* mixed with *air* and *water*. It also has living organisms in it. Mineral particles are made from rocks by *weathering* and by *chemicals* which dissolve rocks. Humus is made from the dead bodies of animals and plants. Organisms in soil make these dead bodies rot or decay. *Mineral salts* are dissolved from mineral particles and humus. Humus is an important food for soil organisms and for making *soil crumbs*.

The size of the mineral particles affects the size of the *air spaces* in the soil. The size of the air spaces affects the *drainage*, *evaporation* and *capillarity* of the soil. *Sand*, *clay* and *loam* are the main kinds of soil. They have different sizes of particles.

Soil can be improved by adding *lime*, *manure* and *fertiliser*. *Hoeing* and *mulching* slow water loss in hot weather. *Earthworms* are important soil animals. *Crop rotation* is used to keep soil *fertile*.

Important words

Humus	a part of the soil. It comes from dead, decaying plants and animals.
Mineral	a substance such as aluminium silicate found in soil; some minerals dissolve in water to make mineral salts.
Clay	soil with particles less than 0.002 mm in diameter.
Silt	soil made from very small pieces of rock; the particles are smaller than sand particles but bigger than those of clay.
Loam	soil made of clay and sand (and some humus); the best soil for growing plants.
Capillarity	the rise of water up small tubes (capillary tubes) and spaces.
Evaporation	the change of a liquid such as water to a gas such as water vapour.
Fertile soil	a soil that can grow good crops.
Manure	the waste products of animals put onto soil.
Lime	a chemical we can put onto soil to cure acidity and help improve drainage of clay soil.
Fertiliser	a substance put onto soil by gardeners and farmers to help plants grow better.

Things to do

1. Put a small lump of clay in some water in a measuring cylinder. Shake it well until the water is coloured by the clay. Stand the cylinder in front of a lamp and look at the water. Can you see any particles of clay? Now pour in some limewater. Leave it for a few minutes. What can you see now? What do you think has happened? How is this important in gardening?

Fancy that!

Soil takes thousands of years to make! Each year enormous areas of soil are lost. They are covered with concrete or tarmac during building and road making.

The mass of soil organisms in a field is much greater than the mass of cows grazing in the field!

2. Fix up the apparatus shown in figure 17.9. Stand the lower edge in about 2 cm depth of water in a dish. Put some ink into the water. What happens? Is this what happens in capillarity in sand and clay?

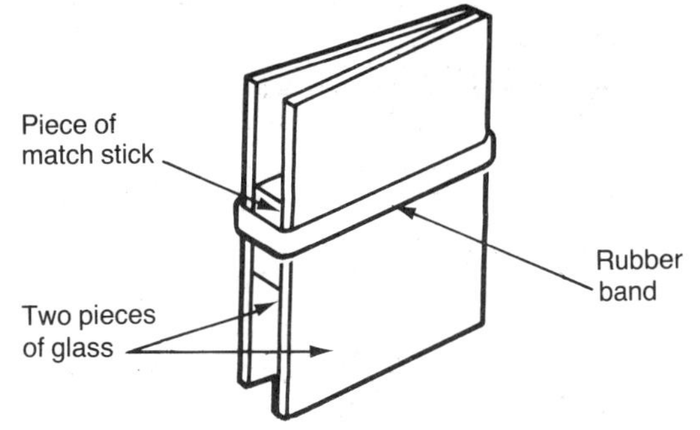

Figure 17.9

3. Which kind of soil holds most water?

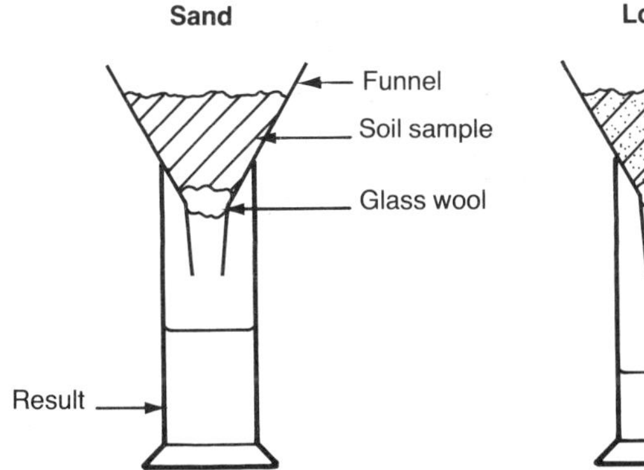

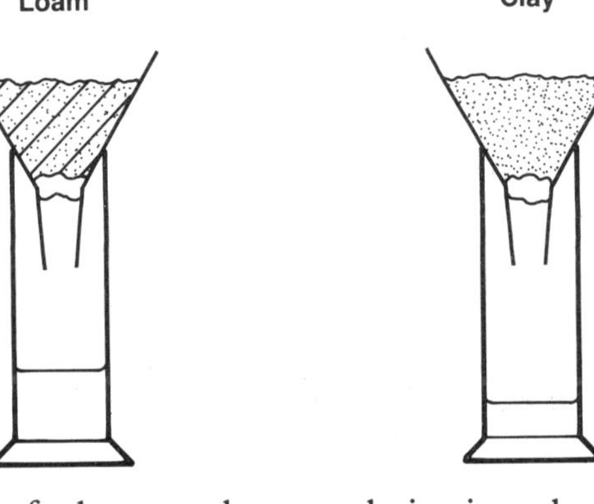

Figure 17.10

Half-fill the funnels with equal volumes of dry soil. Take out all the lumps and stones. Pack the soil equally firmly in each funnel. Pour 50 ml water into each funnel. Find out how much water drains into the measuring cylinders.

Which kind of soil holds back most water?

4. Which kind of soil drains fastest?

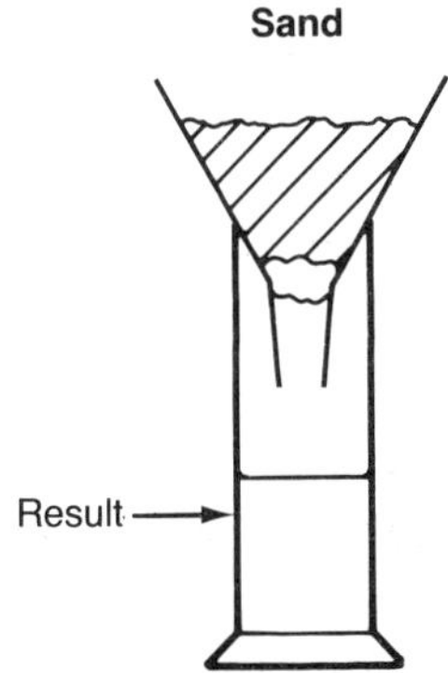

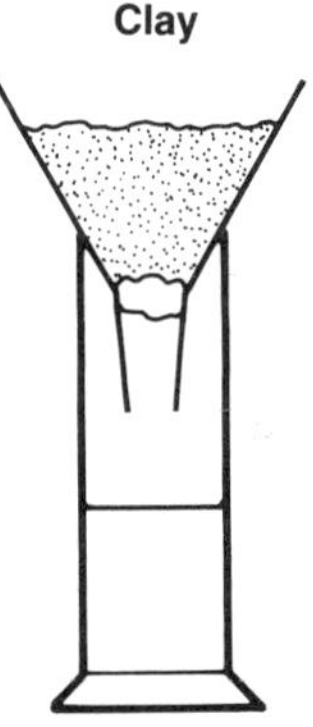

Figure 17.11

Use the funnels of wet soil from **3.** above. Pour another 50 ml of water into each funnel of wet soil at the same time.

In which soil does water drain through (i) fastest (ii) slowest?

5. How water rises up different soils.
Carefully fill three glass tubes with equal volumes of dry soil. Fill one with clay, one with loam and one with sand. Take out all the large lumps and stones. Pack the tubes equally firmly. Stand the tubes in a dish of water and leave for three weeks.

Result
At first the water rises higher in the sand than in the clay. This is because the water moves quickly into the big air spaces in the sand. After three weeks the water level is higher in the clay than in the sand. This is because the smaller air spaces in clay are like narrow 'tubes'. The water can creep up these tubes by capillarity. Water cannot creep up the bigger 'tubes' in sand so easily.

Dry clay
Water level after a few days
Cotton wool plug

Figure 17.12

Questions

A.

You may know of areas near your school or home where waste substances from homes and factories are dumped on the soil.

1. Give two ways in which the waste substances might affect the soil under and near the dump.
2. Give three reasons why you should avoid these dumps.
3. What would have to be done to restore the dump to allow trees to grow on it?

B.

Four glass capillary tubes of different widths were stood in a shallow trough of red ink as shown in figure 17.13. The ink ran up inside the tubes.

1. Copy figure 17.13 into your book and complete it by showing the levels to which you think the ink rose in each tube. This has been done for you in the second tube.
2. What name is given to this force which causes liquid to rise in narrow spaces against gravity?
3. In which *tissue* of a tree is this important?
4. Samples of dry clay, dry loam and dry sand were placed in identical tall glass cylinders plugged at the base with cotton-wool. The cylinders were supported upright in a trough of water and left for two weeks. The level of water as it rose in each type of soil was recorded and the results are shown in figure 17.14. Refer to figure 17.14 to answer the following questions.
(a) In which soil did water rise to the greatest height?
(b) What does this result tell us about the spaces between the particles of this soil?
(c) On day 3, what was the height of the water in each of the soils?
(d) In which soil did the water rise most rapidly?
(e) In which soil would plants survive best in a drought? Explain your answer.
(f) Why are the results for loam intermediate between those for sand and clay?
(NREB)

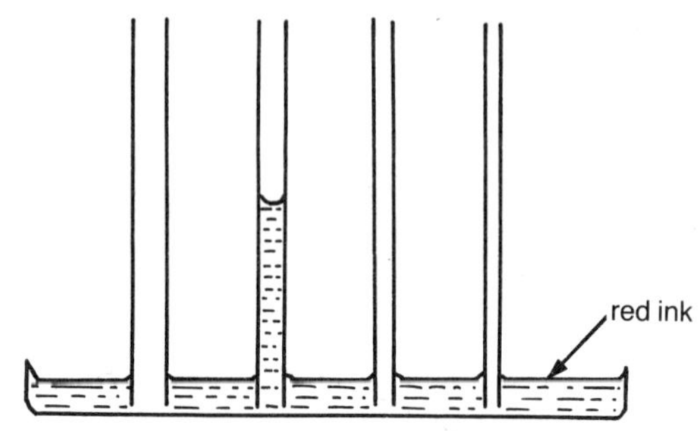

Figure 17.13

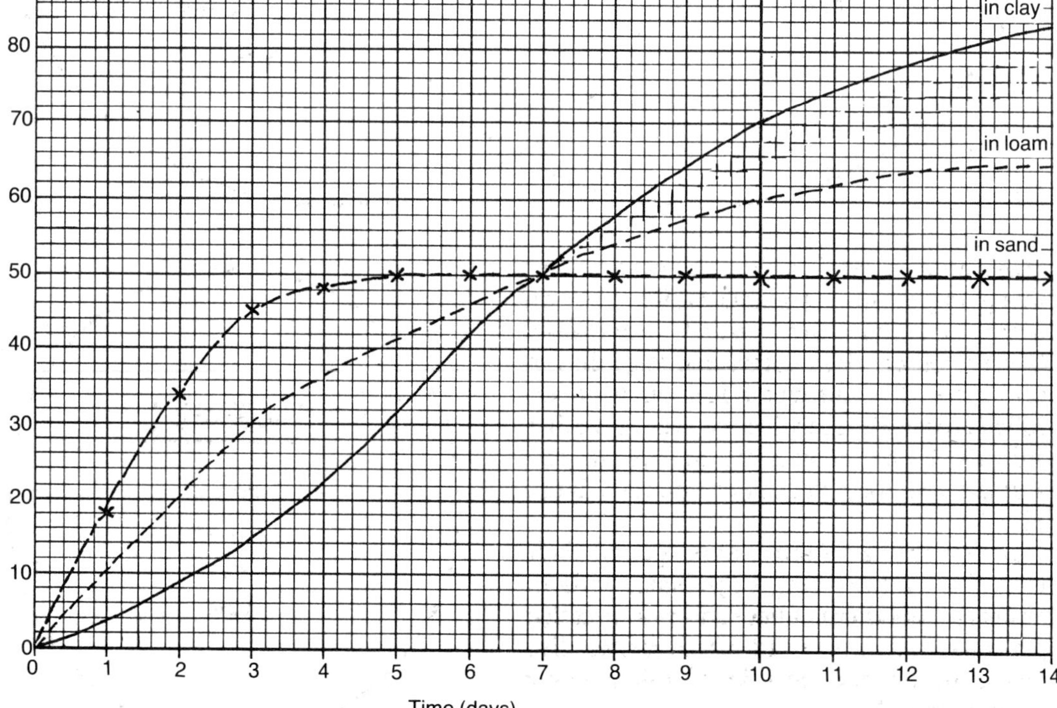

Figure 17.14

TOPIC 18

HOW ANIMALS FEED

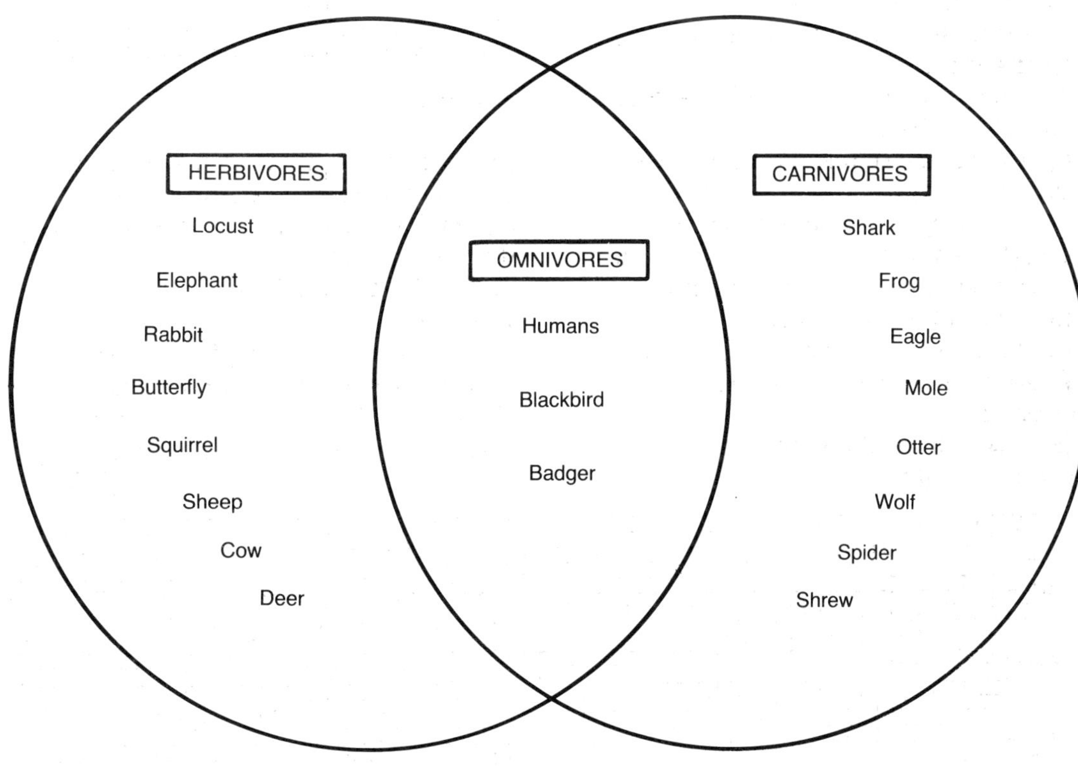

Figure 18.1
Animals which eat living organisms

Most animals get their food by eating other living organisms. Animals which feed on other *animals* are called *carnivores*. Carnivores are flesh-eaters and they do not eat plants. Animals which feed on *plants* are called *herbivores*. Herbivores do not eat other animals. Some animals eat both plants and animals and are called *omnivores*. (See figure 18.1.)

A few animals (and plants) get all their food from other living organisms, without always killing them. These animals are called *parasites*.(See figure 18.2.) Parasites live inside or on the outside of other living animals and plants.

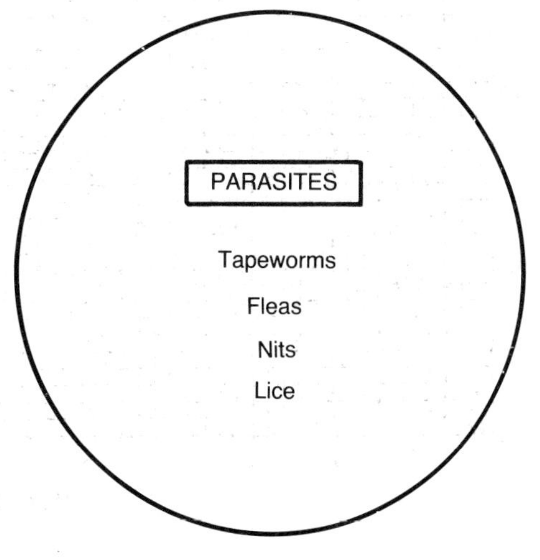

Figure 18.2
Animals that feed on other living organisms without always killing them

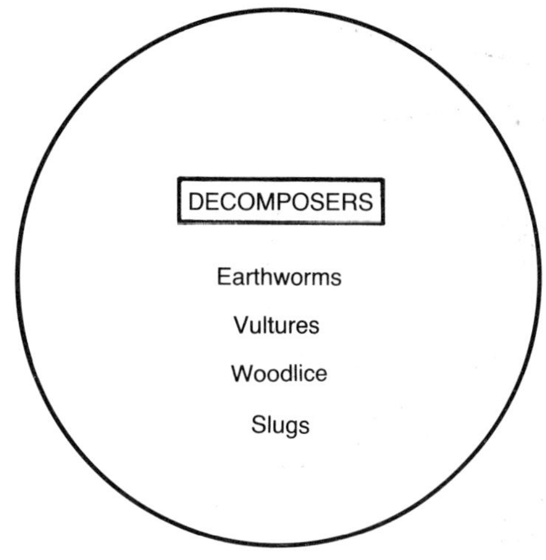

Figure 18.3 **Animals that eat dead organisms**

Some animals get their food by eating dead organisms. (See figure 18.3.)These animals are called *decomposers* and many of them live in soil. The dead organisms which they eat may have been killed or have died from disease or old age.

> **Fancy that!**
>
> Humming birds feed on nectar which they get by pushing their long beaks into flowers!
>
> Spiders catch their food by killing it with a poisonous bite. The bite of some spiders is so poisonous that they can kill birds and hurt humans!

Herbivores have to eat a lot of food and they spend most of their time eating. This is because their food does not contain much nourishment. Carnivores have to catch their food and kill it. They must be quick and strong. Feeding is very important to animals so they must be able to do it well. Animals feed in many different ways but most are adapted to feeding on one kind of food. This may be:

- solid food of large size,
- solid food of small size,
- liquid food.

ANIMALS THAT EAT SOLID FOOD OF LARGE SIZE

These animals often have some way of chopping up their food into smaller pieces.

A locust feeds on plants of almost any sort by using its mouth parts. These smell, taste, hold and chop the food. (See figure 18.4.) In countries like Africa, locusts do a lot of damage to crops. Huge clouds of locusts, called swarms, often eat every plant over large areas.

A frog is a carnivorous animal feeding mainly on insects and worms. Insects are caught by its sticky tongue which is fixed at the *front* of its mouth. (See figure 18.5.) A frog's tongue can be flicked out to trap insects which are then swallowed whole. Small, backward-pointing teeth stop the food from escaping.

Figure 18.5 **A frog catching a small insect**

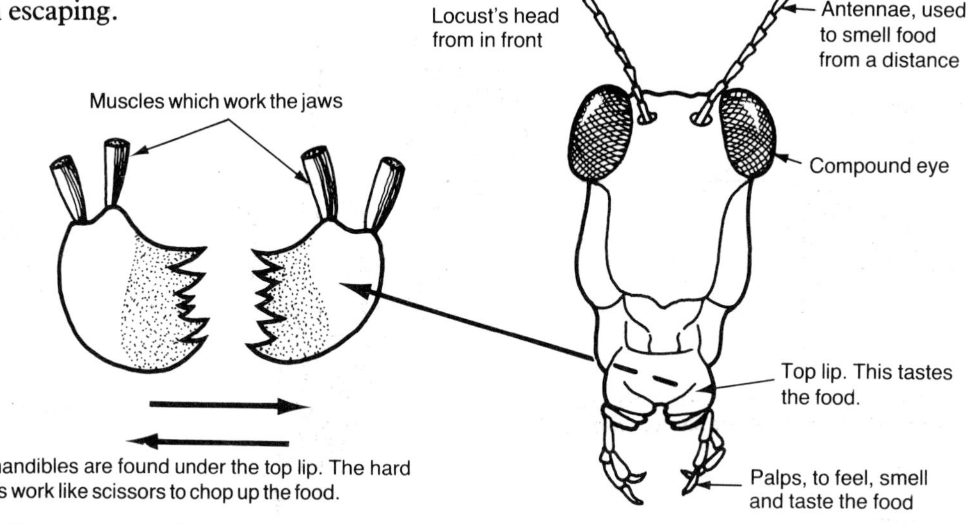

Figure 18.4 **The mouth parts of a locust**

A pike is a *predator*.
It feeds by hunting smaller animals.
The smaller fish
is its *prey*.

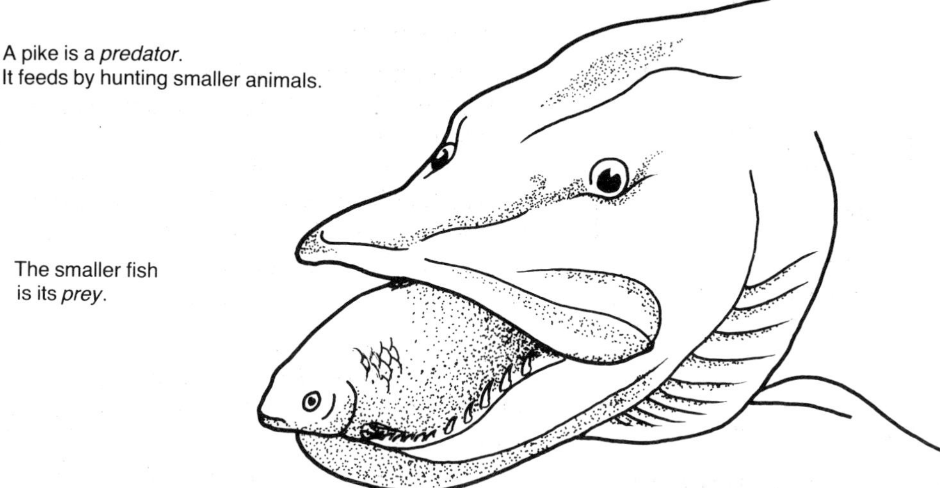

Figure 18.6 A pike eating a small fish

A pike is a carnivorous fish which lives in lakes and rivers. It can grow up to 100 cm long. A pike catches food by using its mouth. (See figure 18.6.) Its teeth point backwards and stop the food from escaping. The food is swallowed whole because the teeth are not used for chewing.

Birds use their beaks for feeding. The shape and size of the beak is suited to the sort of food the bird eats. (See figure 18.7.) Birds which eat seeds have strong, short beaks which are thick at the base. Carnivorous birds have strong curved beaks which they use to tear flesh. Birds have no teeth.

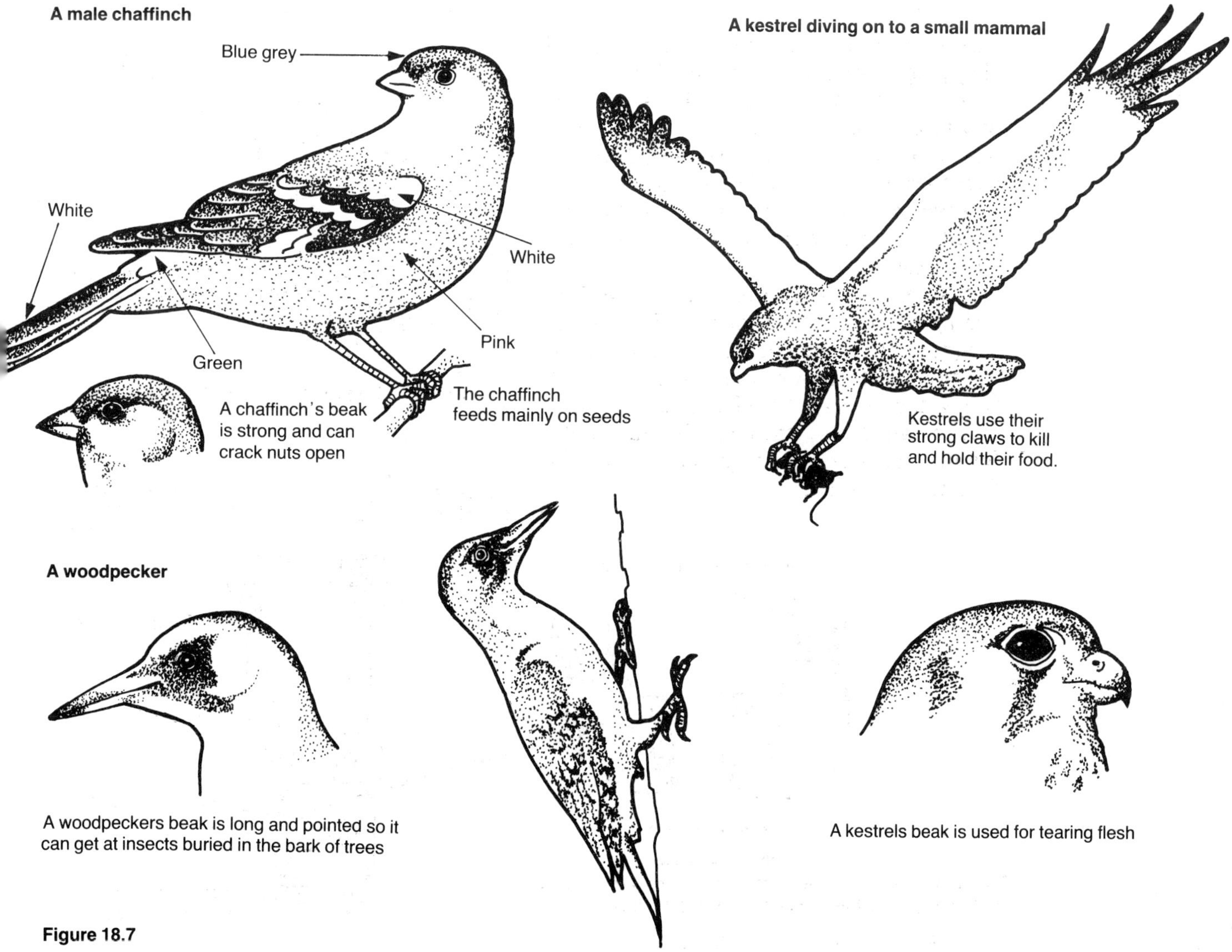

A male chaffinch
Blue grey
White
White
Pink
Green
A chaffinch's beak
is strong and can
crack nuts open
The chaffinch
feeds mainly on seeds
A kestrel diving on to a small mammal
Kestrels use their
strong claws to kill
and hold their food.
A woodpecker
A woodpeckers beak is long and pointed so it
can get at insects buried in the bark of trees
A kestrels beak is used for tearing flesh

Figure 18.7

ANIMALS THAT EAT SOLID FOOD OF SMALL SIZE

Many animals feed on small animals and plants which live in water. These small animals and plants are filtered off from the water by a bigger animal and eaten. Animals which feed like this are called *filter-feeders*.

Mussels are molluscs which live on rocks along the sea shore. When the animals are covered with water by the tide the shell opens and they start to feed. Water is drawn in and the small organisms in it are filtered off by the gills; these are also used for breathing. The water is then forced out. (See figure 18.8.)

A blue whale feeds on small animals and plants which it filters from sea water. It does this by using a filter inside its mouth. The blue whale is one of the largest animals known. It is a mammal not a fish and weighs about 150 tonnes! (See figure 18.9.)

A duck feeds on small animals and plants in water. It filters these off using bristles along the edges of its beak. Mallards are common ducks. You may see them on ponds in pairs. (Scc figure 18.10.)

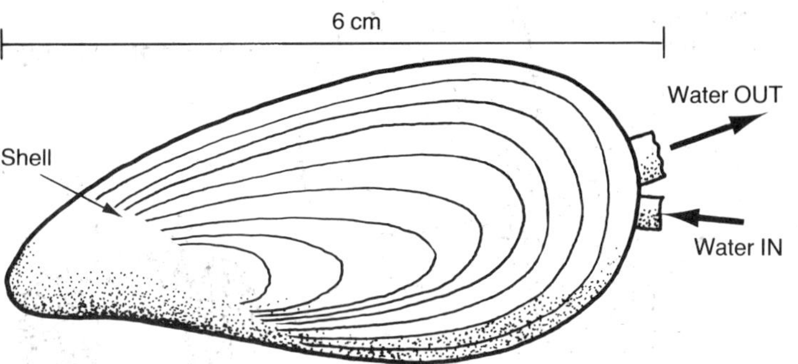

Figure 18.8 **A mussel**

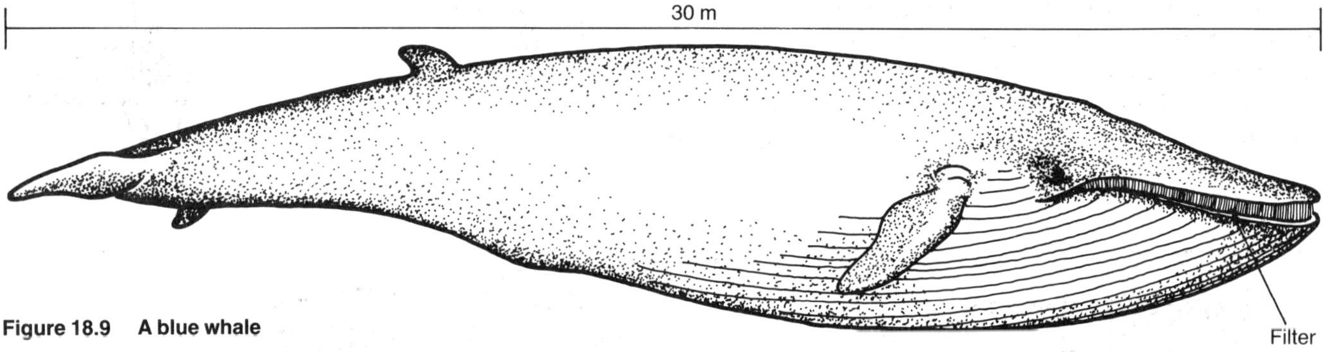

30 m

Filter

Figure 18.9 **A blue whale**

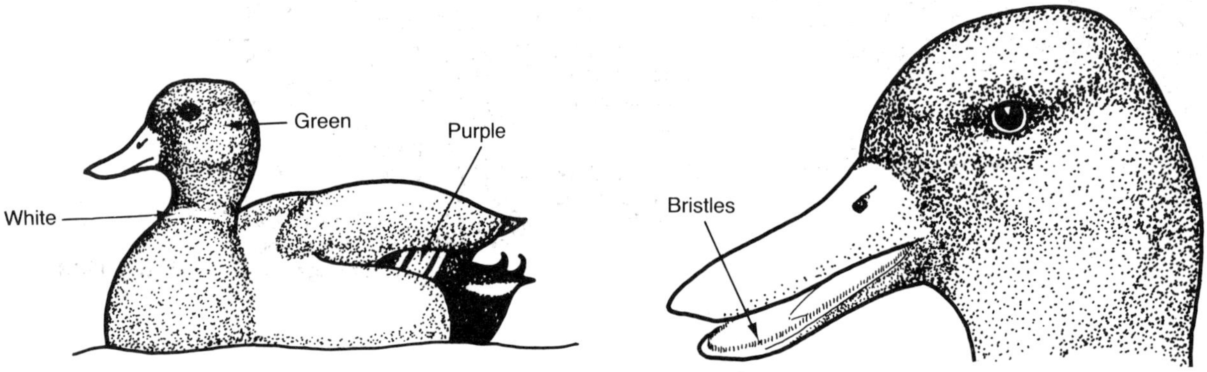

Green

Purple

White

Bristles

Figure 18.10 **A drake (male mallard)**

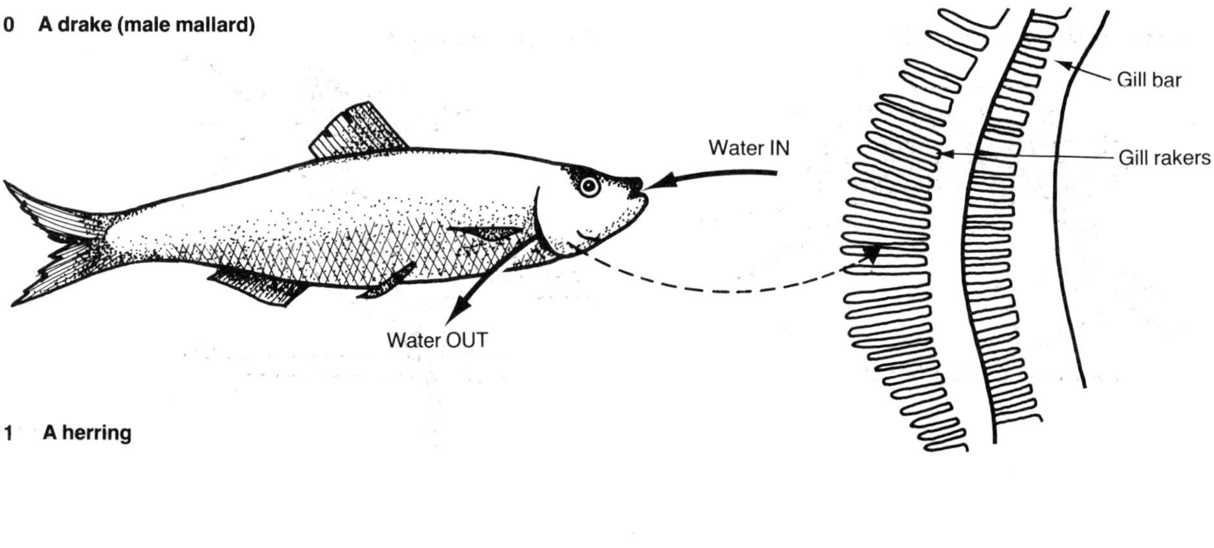

Water IN

Gill bar

Gill rakers

Water OUT

Figure 18.11 **A herring**

Fish breathe using gills. Herrings and some other fish also use their gills to catch small organisms in the water. The rakers comb through the gills to remove the organisms which the fish then swallows. (See figure 18.11.)

ANIMALS THAT EAT LIQUID FOOD

Many animals can only eat liquid food. They often get this food by sucking it up through special mouth parts.

Butterflies feed on liquid sugar (or nectar) made by flowers. They use a long tube or proboscis. When a butterfly feeds it pushes its proboscis down into a flower and sucks up the nectar. The proboscis is coiled up like a spring when the butterfly is not feeding. (See figure 18.12.)

Flies feed on dead and decaying substances such as dead animals, faeces, sewage etc. They also feed on human food. They spread disease when they move from their dirty food to our food. Flies spread diseases such as typhoid, diarrhoea and cholera. (See figure 18.13.)

Some mosquitoes feed on human blood which they get by stabbing the skin with sharp mouth parts. The mosquito pours saliva into the cut to stop the blood from clotting. Mosquitoes spread disease such as malaria and yellow fever. (See figure 18.14.)

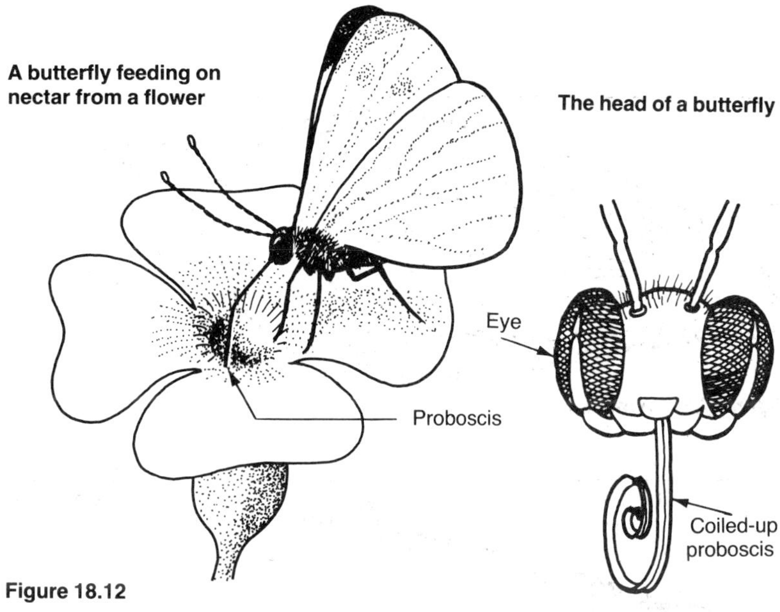

Figure 18.12

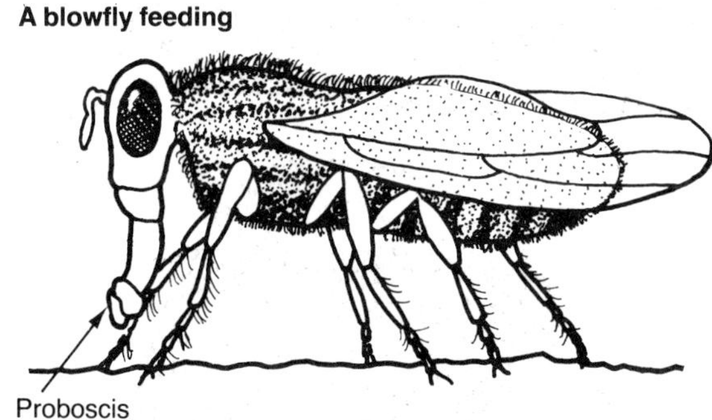

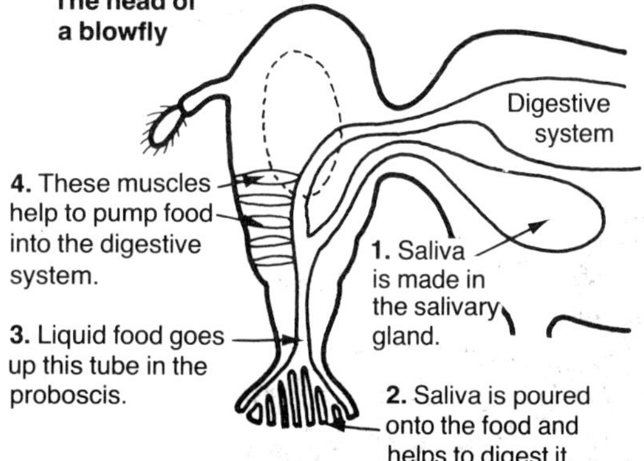

Figure 18.13

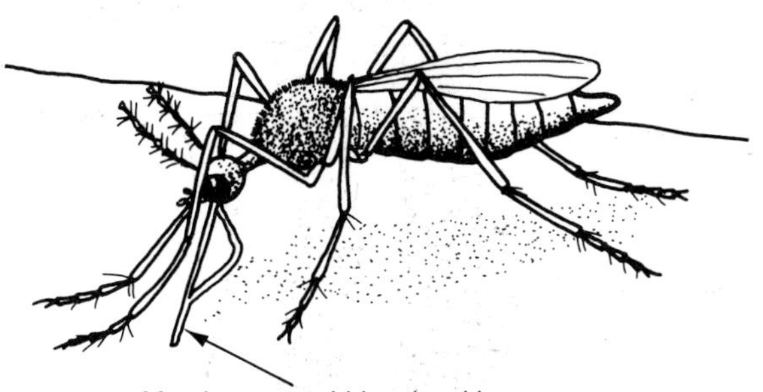

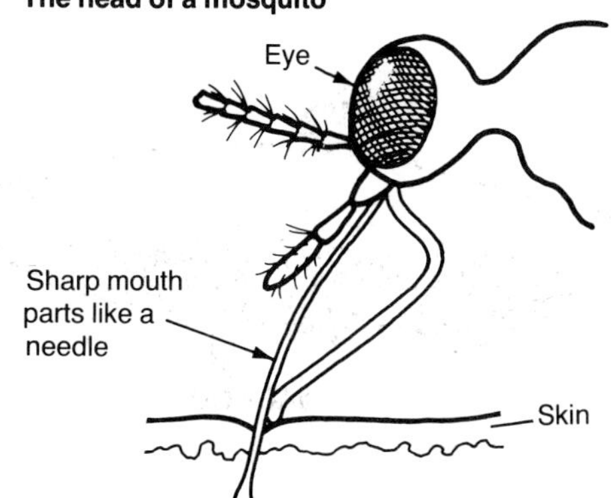

Figure 18.14

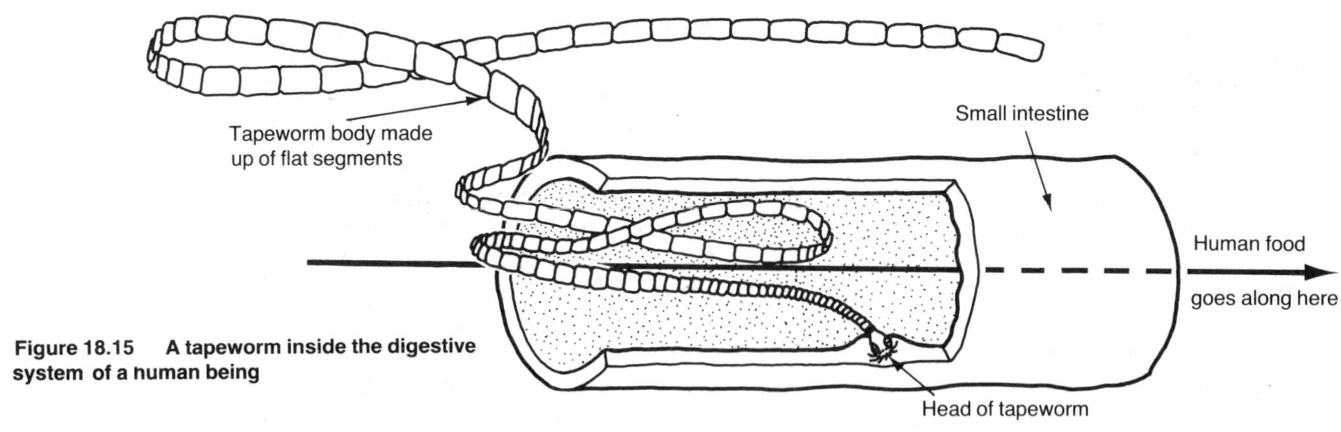

Figure 18.15 A tapeworm inside the digestive system of a human being

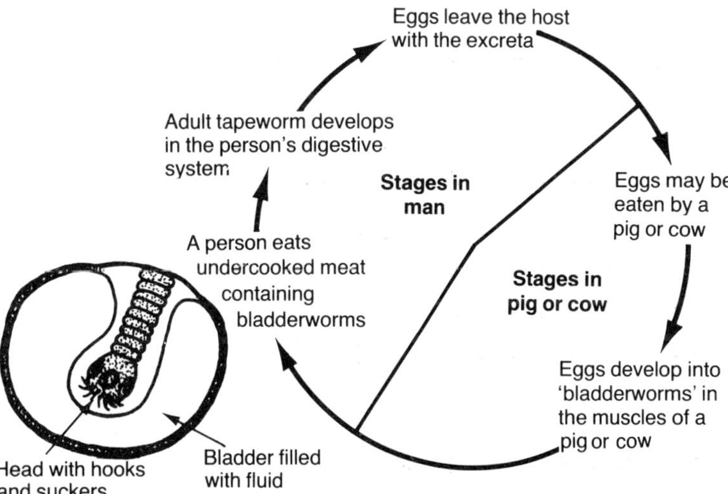

Figure 18.16 A bladderworm

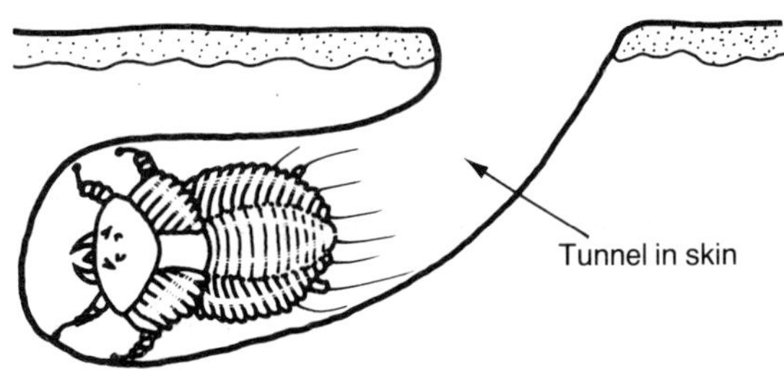

Figure 18.17 A mite underneath human skin

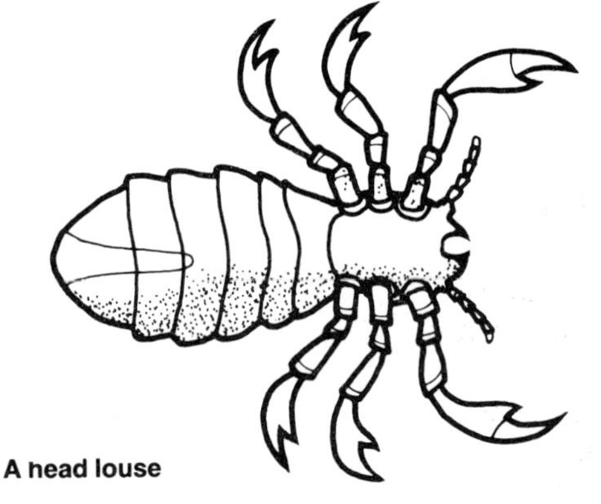

Figure 18.18 A head louse

PARASITES

Parasites feed on other living organisms called 'hosts'. Parasites get all their food from their hosts. Some live inside their hosts and are surrounded by food. Other parasites live on the outside of their hosts.

Tapeworms live in the digestive system of humans and other animals. They are fixed to the wall of the digestive system with hooks and suckers. A tapeworm absorbs food all over its body.(See figure 18.15.)

Figure 18.16 shows the life cycle of a tapeworm. The adult tapeworm is found in humans but pigs or cattle are needed to complete its life cycle. The spread of tapeworms is stopped by:

1. proper sewage treatment (this stops the eggs from reaching pigs and cattle and breaks the life cycle);
2. eating properly cooked meat (bladder-worms are killed by heat;
3. careful examination of meat for bladder-worms (this happens at the slaughter-house).

Mites dig small tunnels into the skin. (See figure 18.17.) They feed and lay their eggs in these tunnels. Mites suck blood for food. They cause a disease called scabies.

The head louse is a light grey insect found in hair. (See figure 18.18) It clings on using claws on its legs and feeds by biting the skin and sucking blood. Its white eggs are called 'nits' and are large enough to be seen. Schoolchildren often have their hair looked at for nits during visits by the school nurse. Head lice can be caught from people already infected with the parasite. This may happen if you borrow an infected comb.

Adult head louse → About 60 eggs or 'nits' are laid each month and stuck to hairs → Eggs hatch in seven days into small lice or *nymphs* → Adult lice

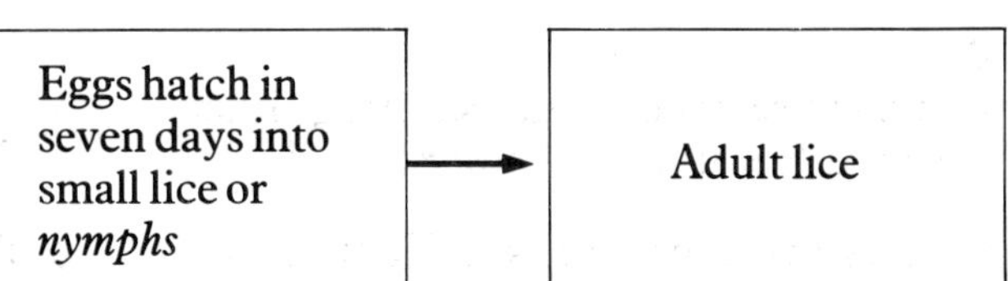

Summary

Carnivores eat only animals and *herbivores* eat only plants. *Omnivores* eat animals and plants. *Parasites* are animals (or plants) that live inside or on the outside of other living organisms. Parasites do not always kill these organisms. *Decomposers* eat dead organisms.

Locusts, pike, frogs and birds eat solid food which is swallowed whole or chewed. Blue whales, ducks and herrings are large animals which feed on much smaller organisms. Butterflies, blowflies and mosquitoes can eat only liquid food. Mites, nits and lice are parasites which live on the outside of humans and other animals. Tapeworms are parasites which live inside other animals.

Important words

Carnivore	an animal that gets all its food by eating other animals.
Herbivore	an animal that gets all its food by eating plants.
Omnivore	an animal that feeds on both plants and animals.
Parasite	an organism that lives in or on its host, from which it gets all its food.
Host	an organism that has parasites living in or on it.
Decomposers	organisms that feed on dead and decaying organisms.
Predator	an animal that catches its food by hunting for it.
Prey	an animal that is caught and eaten by a predator.
Filter feeder	an animal that feeds by filtering off small organisms from the water in which it lives.

Questions

A.
Put each of these parts of sentences into the correct order.

1. but their caterpillars
feed on nectar

adult butterflies only
eat solid food

2. herrings and mussels
and for catching food

for gas exchange
use their gills

3. decaying substances and then
blowflies spread disease

by landing on
visiting human food

4. malaria is caused by
disease into a cut

in our skin when they feed
mosquitoes which put the

5. to catch their food
because they are

tapeworms do not have
surrounded by it

B.
Join these sentences together using either the word 'because' or the word 'and'.

1. Mites live under the skin. They cause scabies.

2. Tapeworms have no digestive system. They are surrounded by digested food.

3. Flies spread disease. They carry harmful bacteria.

TOPIC 19

CONNECTIONS

Owls are *carnivores* that catch small mammals such as field-mice and shrews for food. Field-mice are *herbivores* that feed on wheat, small fruits and berries. Humans are *omnivores* and feed on both animals and plants.

FOOD CHAINS AND WEBS

Figure 19.1 shows the links between animals and their food. The organisms and the links between them make up a *food chain*. Most food chains have the same pattern: a plant is

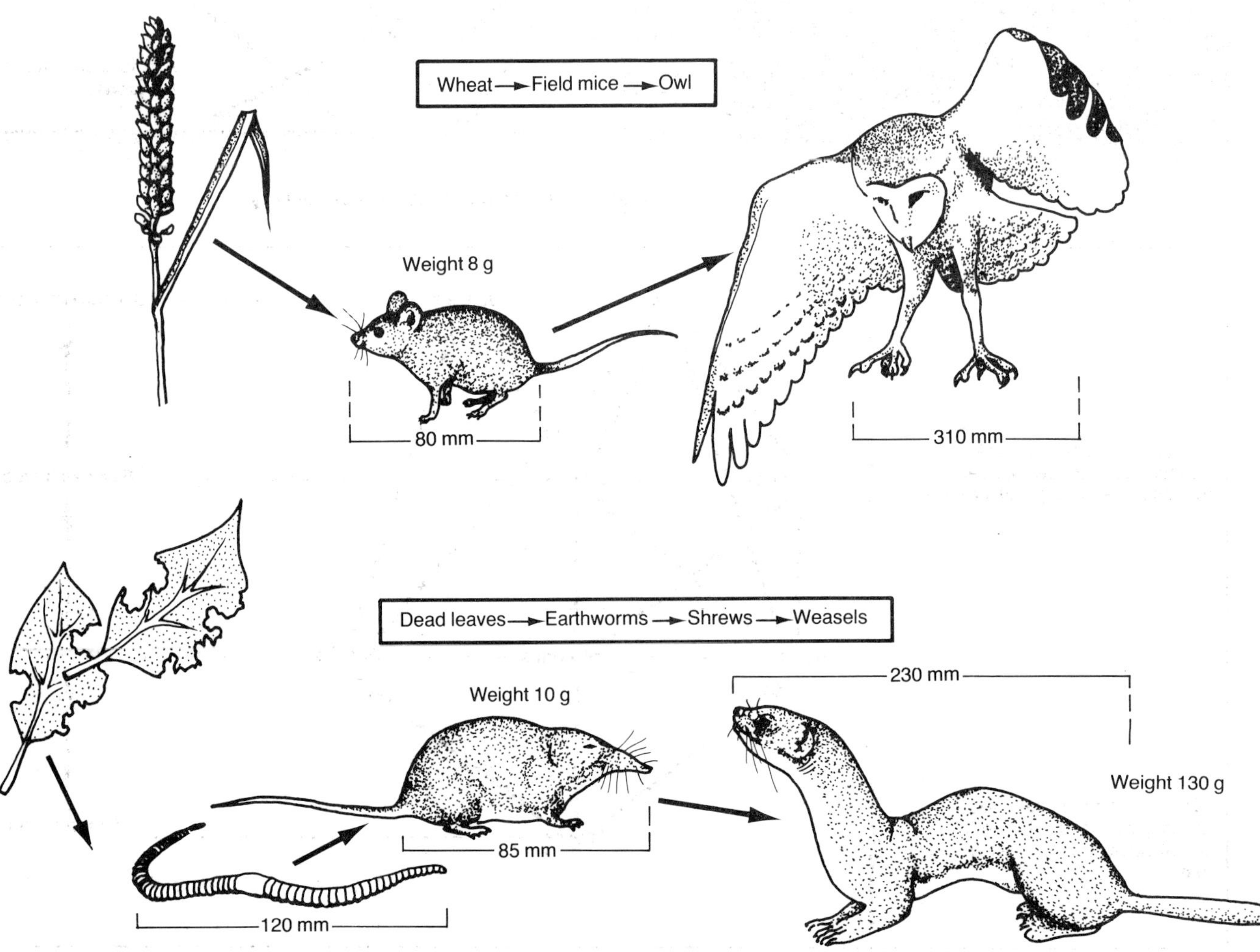

Figure 19.1

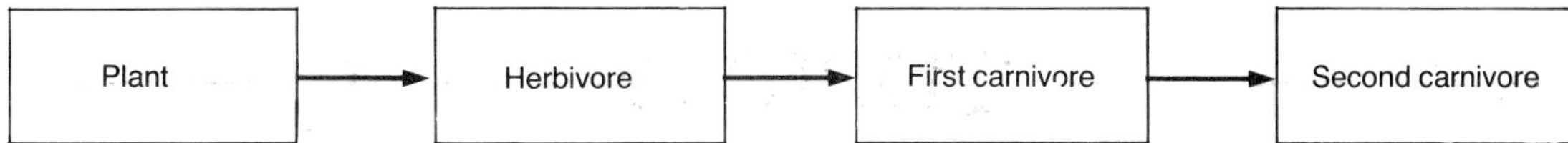

eaten by a herbivore which is then eaten by a carnivore. This carnivore may even be eaten by a bigger, stronger carnivore.

Most food chains start with plants because plants can make their own food. They do this by trapping the sun's energy in photosynthesis. Animals cannot make food; they must eat the food made by plants. So all living things depend on the sun to keep them alive. Most of the sun's energy that reaches the earth is wasted! (See figure 19.2.)

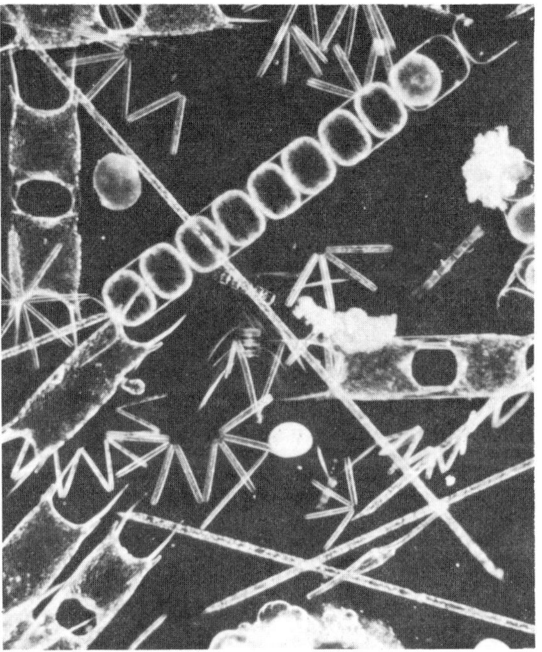

Various types of diatom, tiny plants which float at the surface of water.

Food chains in water begin with the tiny plants shown in the photograph on this page. They float at the surface of the water where light can reach them.

The food chains in Figure 19.1 are very simple. Owls, for example, eat insects and small birds as well as shrews and mice. These animals are 'shared out' between more than one food chain.

Figure 19.3 is a *food web*, which shows the sharing-out of herbivores between different carnivores. Food webs show more clearly than food chains what really happens.

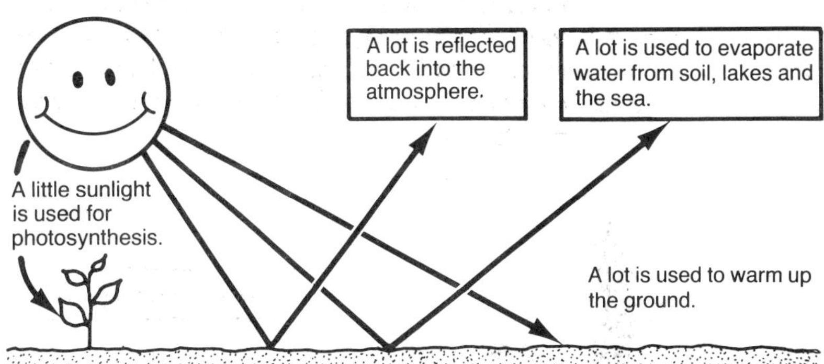

Figure 19.2 **What happens to the sun's energy**

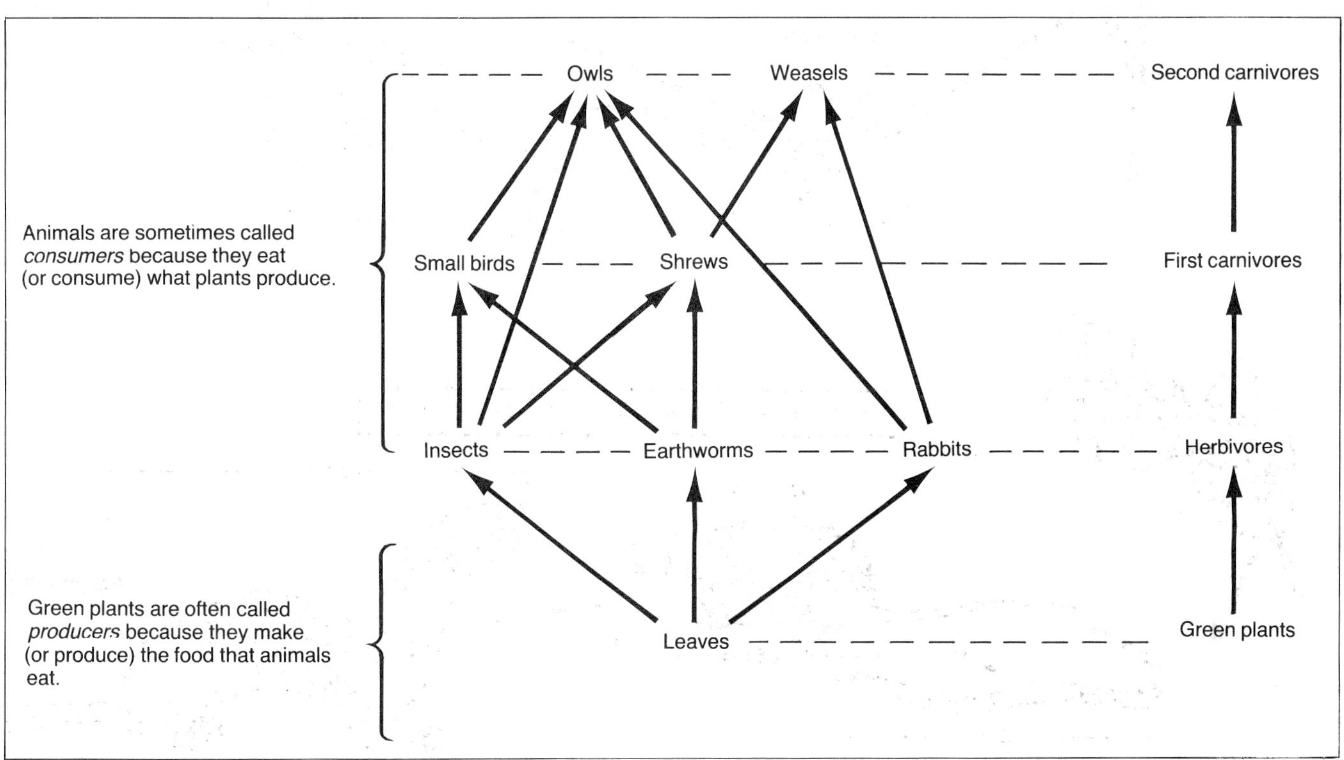

Figure 19.3

Remember:
FOOD IS
ENERGY!

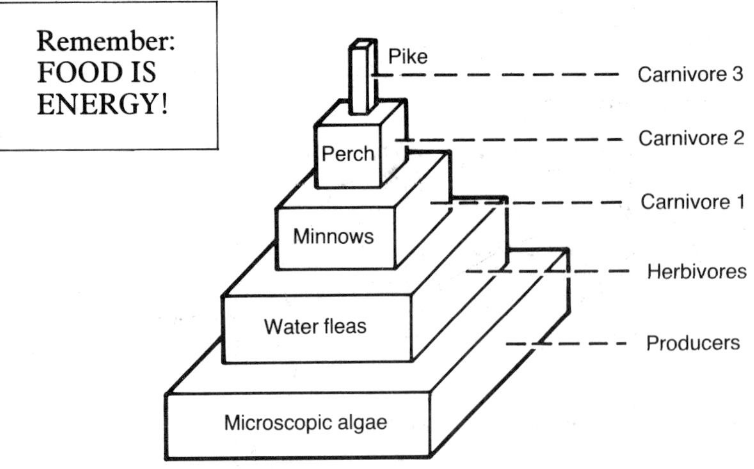

Figure 19.4 A pyramid of numbers

A common butterwort, which is a carnivorous plant. You can see that some insects have become stuck to the leaves.

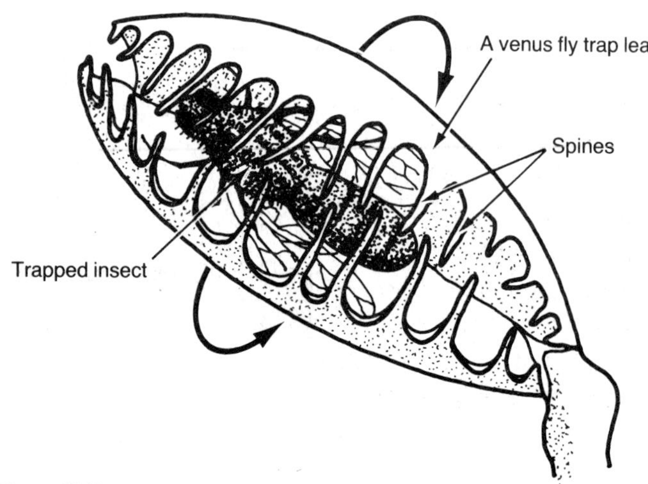

Figure 19.5

BALANCE OF NATURE

There are usually *more* organisms at the start of food chains than at the end. Organisms at the ends of food chains are usually *larger* than those at the start. (See figures 19.1 and 19.4.)

The pyramid shows that:

– there are more water fleas than minnows (water fleas are smaller than minnows),

– there are more minnows than perch (minnows are smaller than perch),

– there are very few pike (pike are bigger than perch or minnows),

– there are plenty of small algae for the water fleas to eat.

The whole pyramid looks well balanced. If this 'balance of nature' is kept, all the organisms in the food chain will get enough food to eat. The algae use the sun's energy to help to make their food. This food is eaten by the water fleas, and so on up to the pike.

CARNIVOROUS PLANTS

The food chains in Figures 19.1, 19.3 and 19.4 all show plants as food for animals. However there are some plants that eat animals! *Carnivorous plants* catch and digest small insects. These plants grow in places where it is difficult to get enough nitrogen for their needs. In acid soils, for example, the important nitrifying bacteria cannot work properly. Carnivorous plants get extra supplies of nitrogen by digesting insect proteins.

The common butterwort grows on moors and bogs in Britain. It has sticky leaves and looks like a green starfish. The edges of its leaves slowly roll over to cover insects caught on their sticky surfaces. Digestion of the insect then starts.

The Venus fly trap is an American carnivorous plant. Its leaves snap shut when an insect lands on them! The insect cannot escape because of the spines on the leaves.

Figure 19.5 shows a leaf that has caught a fly. The fly will be digested.

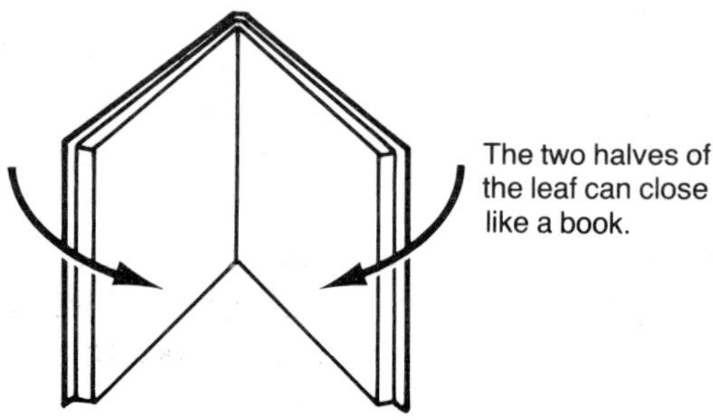

SYMBIOSIS

Some plants and animals live closely together to help each other to survive better. This is called *symbiosis*. Lichens are organisms which grow on rocks, walls and trees. These are difficult places to live because the wind dries them and water quickly drains away. Lichens are made of two plants: an alga and a fungus. The two plants are so closely mixed together that they cannot be separated. The fungus gets mineral salts and water from the surface the lichen grows on. The fungus shares these substances with the alga. The alga photosynthesises to make starch, which it shares with the fungus. Alga and fungus together survive better than either growing by themselves.

The nitrogen-fixing bacteria which live in the roots of legumes are another example of symbiosis (see page 96).

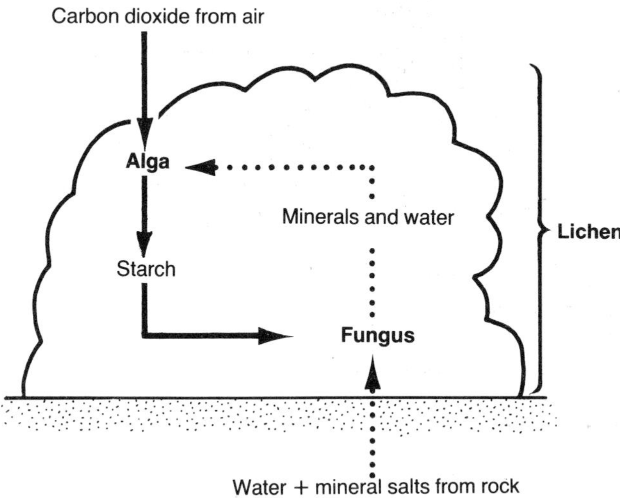

Figure 19.6 How the alga and fungus in a lichen help each other to live

Summary

Most organisms depend on energy from the sun to keep them alive. *Green plants* use this energy to help them make food in *photosynethsis*. *Herbivores* eat only plants and *carnivores* eat only other animals, while *omnivores* eat both animals and plants.

Food chains show how energy in food passes from one organism to another. *Food webs* show how one kind of organism can be eaten by many different herbivores, carnivores or omnivores.

A *pyramid of numbers* shows that there are usually more organisms at the start of food chains than at the end.

Some plants eat small insects to get extra nitrogen.

Some organisms live closely together to help each other survive. This is called *symbiosis*.

Important words

Carnivore	an animal which gets all its food by eating other animals.
Herbivore	an animal which gets all its food by eating plants.
Omnivore	an animal which gets its food by eating both animals and plants.
Food chain	a group of three or four organisms arranged in a way which shows how they get their food from each other.
Food web	a group of food chains arranged to show how the feeding of the organisms in the food chains is connected.
Carnivorous plants	plants which catch and digest small insects.
Symbiosis	organisms which live closely together to help each other to survive better.

Things to do

See if you can buy a Venus fly trap from a local garden centre. Stand the pot in a saucer of water in the most sunny part of a room. Now watch the plant catching flies!

Fancy that!

Shrews have enormous appetites. They can eat their own weight in fresh meat in 24 hours!

There are about 1400 species of lichens in Britain (compared to about 1800 species of flowering plants). Dyes and antibiotics are made from some species of lichens!

Questions

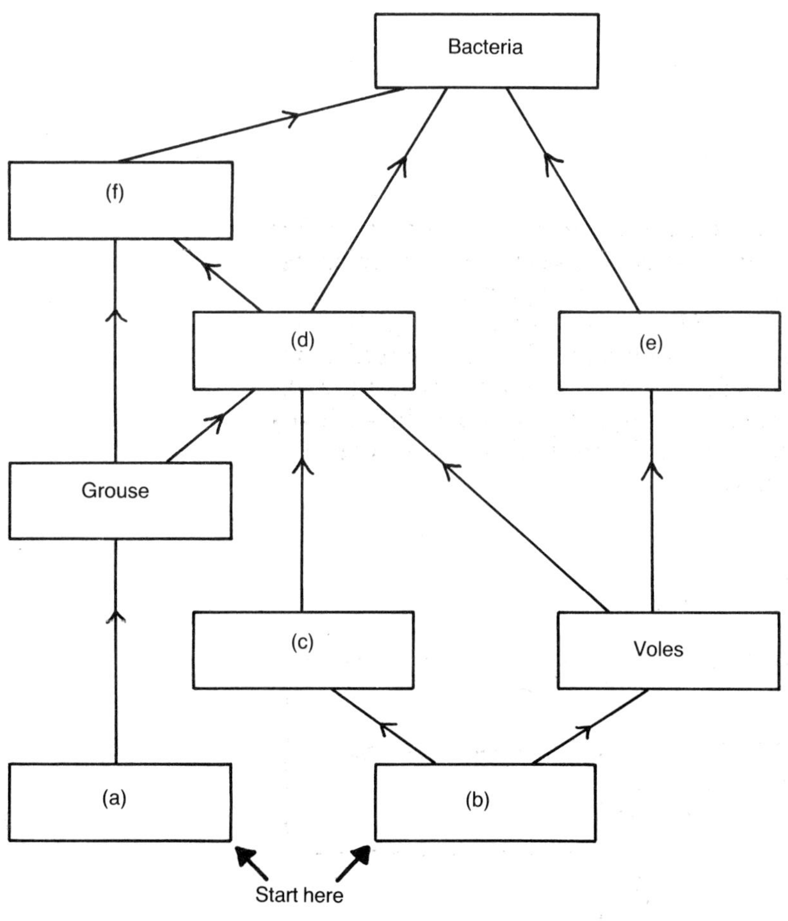

Figure 19.7

A.

Study the following statements about the ways in which some moorland organisms feed.

Heather is eaten by grouse (game birds).
Grass is eaten by voles and beetles.
Grouse, beetles and voles are eaten by foxes.
Voles are eaten by stoats.
Grouse and foxes have fleas.
Bacteria obtain energy by decaying the dead bodies of animals.

1. *Using this information* complete the food web shown in figure 19.7 by writing the name of *different* organisms for each letter in the boxes. (→– means 'eaten by')
2. Use this food web to answer the following questions.
   (a) Name *all* the producers.
   (b) Name *all* the herbivores.
   (c) Name *two* predators.
   (d) Which organisms are parasites?
   (e) Which organisms are saprophytes?
   (f) Give *two* ways in which the bacteria benefit this community of organisms?
   (g) If more grouse than usual are shot on this moor, what do you think will happen to the populations of voles and beetles? Explain your answer.

(NREB)

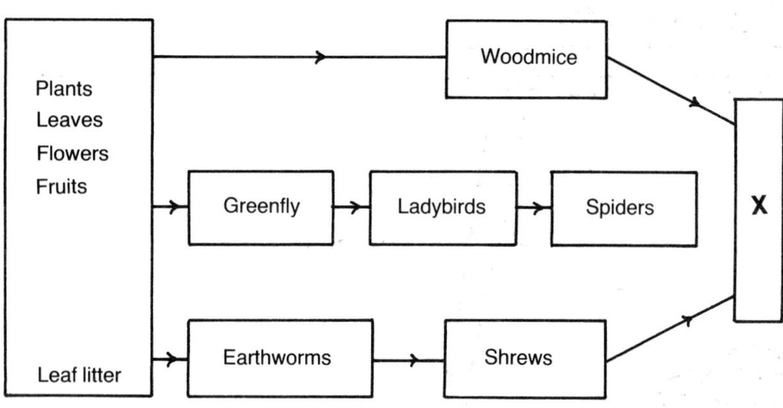

Figure 19.8

B.

Figure 19.8 is a food web found in a deciduous wood.

1. Name an example of each of the following found in the above food web.
   (a) A primary consumer
   (b) A secondary consumer
   (c) A scavenger
2. Copy box X into your notebook and write the name of a possible tertiary consumer in it.
3. Describe the possible effects on the food web if the number of woodmice decreased.

(EAEB, LREB, ULESEC)

TOPIC 20

FOOD

WHAT FOOD DOES IN THE BODY

Food has three main jobs to do in your body (see figure 20.1). These jobs are done by different kinds of food.

Carbohydrates are sugary and starchy foods which give your body fuel for energy.

Fats and oils contain a lot of energy! One gram of fat or oil gives twice as much energy as one gram of carbohydrate.

Proteins are used to make new cells. They are body-building foods, important for growth. Proteins are also used to make enzymes. Enzymes are found in all living cells and help their chemical reactions to work.

Figure 20.1 What food does in your body

Figure 20.2 Do you know what you're eating? Find out from this diagram!

Mineral	These foods contain a lot of the mineral	What the mineral does in your body
Iron	Meat, liver, eggs, peas and beans	You need it to make haemoglobin, the red substance in blood. Too little iron in your diet causes *anaemia*.
Calcium and phosphorus	Milk, cheese and fish	You need these for the growth of bones and teeth.
Sodium chloride (or common salt)	Table salt, bread, cheese, bacon and biscuits	You need it to make blood plasma (the liquid part of blood) and to help your nerves to work properly.
Iodine	Sea food such as winkles, whelks, mussels and fish; watercress	You need it to make the hormone thyroxine. This is made by the thyroid gland in your neck.

MINERALS AND VITAMINS

Minerals are substances which do many different jobs in your body (see the table above). You need only small amounts of most minerals each day. You need quite a lot of a mineral called calcium however. A pint of milk will give you nearly all you need for one day!

Vitamins are substances which help you to keep healthy. You need small amounts of vitamins each day. If these are missing from your diet you may get a *deficiency disease*. These disease are described in the last column of the table on page 130.

FIBRE

Although you *cannot* digest fibre it is an important part of your diet! It is made up mostly of cellulose from plants. The muscles of your digestive system need to grip food to squeeze it along. Fibre is easier to grip than soft, squashy food. Nowadays, many people eat too little fibre. Doctors think that this is what causes constipation and other diseases of our digestive system.

The need to squeeze!

Vitamin	These foods contain a lot of the vitamin	What the vitamin does in your body
A	Liver, cod-liver oil, green vegetables, carrots, milk, butter and margarine	It helps cells to grow and keeps the surface of your body healthy, for example the skin and lining of your nose, throat and the cornea of your eyes. It helps your eyes to see in poor light. If you have too little of the vitamin you get skin infections and you cannot see well at night.
B This is a group of several different vitamins.	Liver, meat, eggs, yeast, green vegetables, milk and fish	You need these vitamins to help your cells to grow and to keep your nerves and skin healthy. Too little of these vitamins causes dry skin, nervous troubles, poor growth and a deficiency disease called *beri-beri*. This disease affects the leg muscles which cannot then grow properly.
C This vitamin is destroyed by cooking, mincing or grating.	Green vegetables, potatoes, oranges, lemons, tomatoes, blackcurrants ('Ribena')	You need this to keep your skin, teeth and gums healthy. It also keeps the linings of your blood vessels healthy. Too little of the vitamin causes a disease called *scurvy* in which gums go soft and your teeth become loose. Any wounds do not heal properly and your skin bleeds easily.
D This vitamin can be made in your body by sunlight acting on a substance in your skin.	Butter, cheese, eggs, fish, liver	You need this to grow healthy bones and teeth. Too little of the vitamin causes a disease called *rickets* in which your bones go soft. Your leg bones cannot support the weight of your body and they bend.

The best drink of all?

WATER

Water is not a food but we cannot live for long without it. Water is needed for:

– all the chemical reactions in your body. (these reactions can only work in solution)

– digestion and transport of digested food substances around your body,

– making new protoplasm.

We lose about 1 litre of water each day in urine and sweat. This water must be replaced by drinking and by eating food which has water in it. A good supply of clean water is important for a healthy life.

Death by water

At least 13 million children will die in developing countries this year because of dirty water, the head of the World Health Organisation said yesterday. Dr Halfdan Mahler said the responsibility for this lay with governments which had done too little to provide their people with clean drinking water and adequate sanitation. A UN Decade for Clean Water, will be launched by the General Assembly on November 10 this year. – UPI 1980

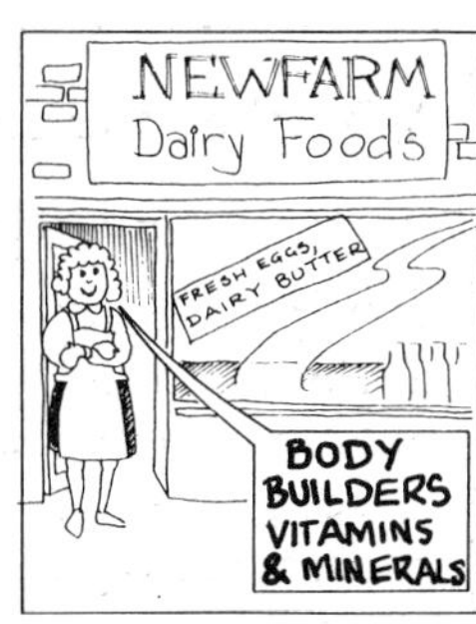

A BALANCED DIET

Your diet must have in it the right kinds of food in the right amounts. There must be enough carbohydrate, fat, protein, minerals and vitamins for your body's needs. This is called a *balanced diet*. A diet which is balanced for one person may not be balanced for another. Your age, sex, health, the size of your body and your job all affect your food needs. A balanced *meal* should have about 5 parts carbohydrate, 1 part protein and 1 part of fat. (See figures 20.3 and 20.4.)

Pregnant women, nursing mothers and teenagers all need plenty of protein. This is because their tissues are growing quickly.

The daily pinta

Milk is a special food and is almost a balanced diet on its own. It has carbohydrates, fats, proteins, vitamins, and calcium and phosphorus. Very young mammals are fed only on milk.

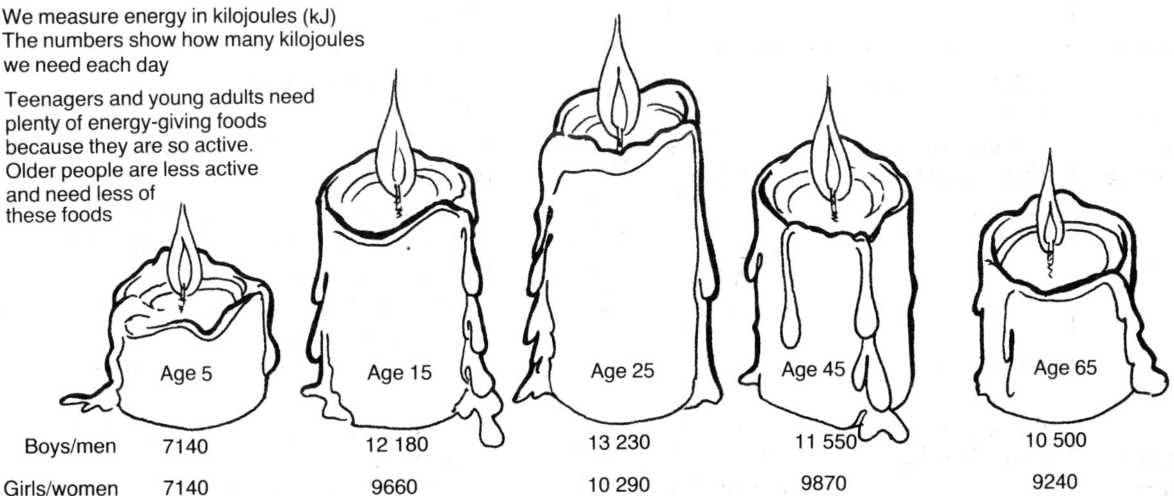

Figure 20.3 Our energy needs at different ages

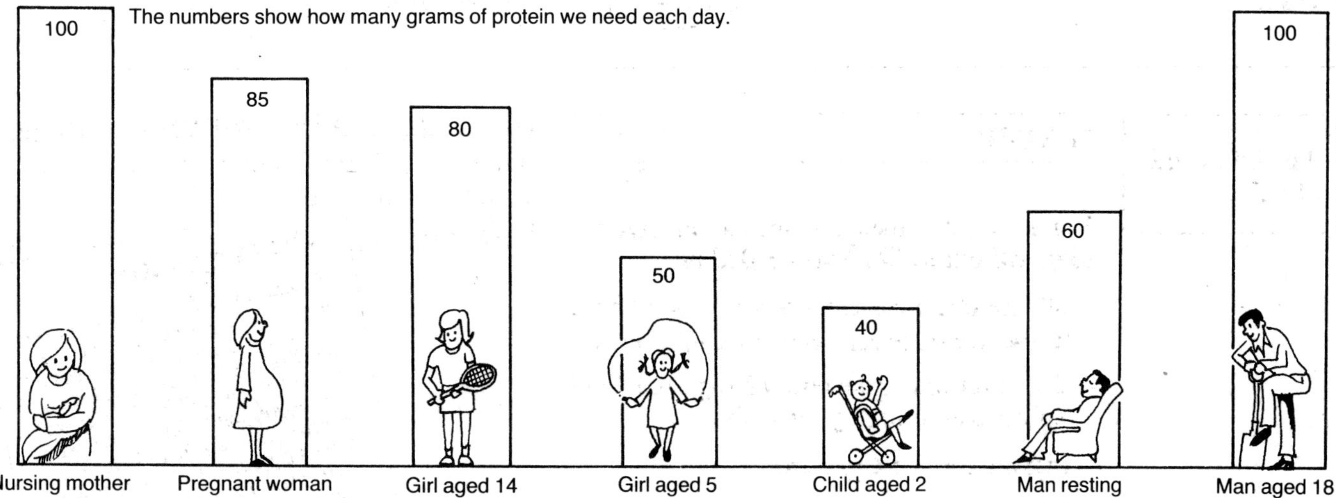

Figure 20.4 Our protein needs

SCHOOL MEALS

Write down what you eat for lunch at school each day.

State schoolchildren are being encouraged to guzzle junk food

Expensive and nasty

What did your child have for dinner at school today? Chances are he is at a school where the old complaints about meat, lumpy mash and watery cabbage are becoming a folk memory. They are being replaced by parental wails about hamburgers, doughnuts and puppy fat or the equally genuine, and perhaps even more horrific option of sausage roll with sauté potatoes and canned spaghetti.

A new school of thought on meals

By John Fairhall, Education Editor

The pessimistic view of school dinners – if you give children what is good for them it will end in the waste bin, and if you give them what they like it will be chips and junk food and a nutritional disaster – was firmly rejected yesterday by an expert on the subject, Dr Robin Osner.

Do you think this is right?

Chips win and nutrition loses as schools abandon meat and two veg

by Peter Wilby, Education Correspondent

The traditional school meal – meat, two veg and a stodgy pudding – is facing extinction. Schools throughout the country are switching to cafeterias, where the choice of beefburgers, sausages, fish fingers, chips, ice cream and doughnuts rivals motorway service areas in quantity and quality.

Horrified nutritionists are worried that the virtual disappearance of vegetables from the diets of thousands of children will lead to constipation and even scurvy.

Do you eat vegetables every day?

'Prison food healthier than schools'

by David Lister

Convicts in a county's prisons are eating healthier food than children in local schools.

In Lancashire where prisoners grow their own avocado pears and, in common with convicts throughout the country, have four meals a day, three of them cooked and a considerable amount of home grown vegetables, schoolchildren have been given a lunch menu condemned by a nutritionist this week as 'horrifying'.

But you can eat the right food without going to prison!

What sort of food are the children below eating? Is it a balanced meal?

School dinners should contain 32 g fat and 29 g protein, with carbohydrate making up the rest. The meal should have an energy value of 8700 kJ. In 1980, many schools changed from serving this balanced meal of meat, vegetables and pudding. Café-type snacks started. Some people think that children cannot get a balanced meal at school now. There is a worry that children will not eat enough fruit and vegetables.

HOW AND WHAT TO EAT

Eat fewer sweets, especially between meals.
Eat some fresh fruit every day.
Eat more vegetables, especially peas and beans.
Eat slowly and taste each mouthful.
Don't eat too many 'junk' foods such as sausages, beefburgers, chips, tinned spaghetti, ice cream and squash.
Eat less fat.

Think slim

Remember: Bad eating habits can be hard to change when you get older!

A lot of teenagers get fat *after* they have stopped growing. This is often because it is hard to change bad eating habits. Many people in poor countries cannot get enough food to eat. They die slowly from starvation and disease.

FINDING OUT WHAT FOOD HAS IN IT

The substances in food can be found using chemical tests.

Testing for carbohydrates

(a) *Testing for starch*

1. Pour about 2 cm depth of starch solution into a test tube.
2. Add a few drops of iodine solution. The solution will go blue-black. This is a test for starch.
3. Now add a few drops of iodine solution to:
   - the cut surface of a potato
   - the cut surface of a bean
   - a small piece of bread.

Do these foods have starch in them?

(b) *Testing for glucose*

1. Pour about 2 cm depth of glucose solution into a test tube.
2. Add about 2 cm depth of Benedict's solution.
3. Boil the solution **but point the mouth of the test-tube away from people.** The blue solution will go red. This is a test for glucose.
4. Now do the Benedict's test with:
   - some mashed-up carrot
   - some mashed-up onion
   - a sweet.

Do these foods have glucose in them?
Try both of these tests on sugar and egg. Do they contain carbohydrate?

Testing for oil and fat

1. Pour about 2 cm depth of ethanol into a test tube.
2. Add 2 drops of cooking oil and shake the tube.
3. Pour the solution into about 2 cm depth of water in a test tube. The solution goes milky. This is a test for oil and fat.
4. Now do the fat and oil test on:
   - a squashed peanut
   - some small bits of cheese.

Do these foods have oil or fat in them?
Try this test on sugar and egg white. Do they contain oil or fat?

Testing for protein

1. Pour about 2 cm depth of 1% albumen solution into a test tube. Albumen comes from egg white.
2. Add to it about 2 cm depth of dilute sodium hydroxide solution (**take care not to spill this on your skin or clothes**) and about 2 cm depth of 1% copper sulphate. The solution goes purple. This is called the Biuret test and is a test for protein.
3. Now do the Biuret test on:
   - milk
   - a squashed peanut
   - a broad bean.

   Add a little water to the squashed seeds, and then add the sodium hydroxide and copper sulphate solutions to the seed-and-water solution.

Do these foods have protein in them?
Try this test on sugar and cooking oil. Do they contain protein?

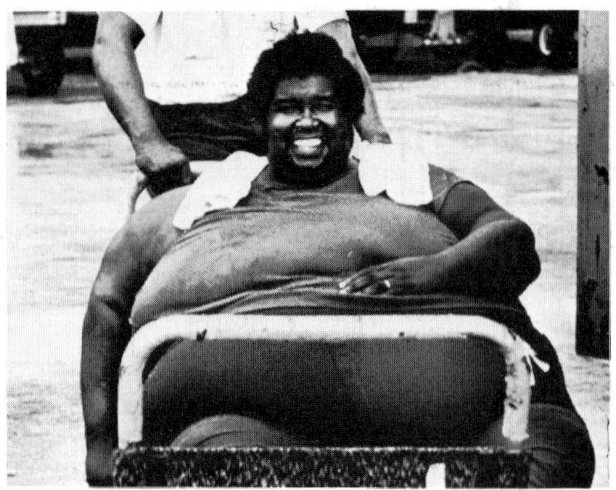

In this photograph, T.J. Albert Jackson from Florida weighed 62 stone (394 kg). How many of your class put together would it take to weigh this much? (See 'Fancy that'.)

Summary

A *balanced diet* contains the right sort of food in the right amounts. *Carbohydrates* and *fats* give you energy. *Proteins* are needed to help you grow and *vitamins* keep you healthy. *Minerals* make blood, bones, hormones, etc. Your diet must also have *fibre* in it.

Your *age, sex, health* and *job* all affect the sort of food you need. Bad eating habits are hard to change and may cause disease when you grow up.

Important words

Carbohydrates	substances such as starch, cellulose or sugar; energy-giving foods.
Fats	energy-giving substances which contain more energy than the same amount of carbohydrate.
Proteins	substances used for the growth and repair of cells.
Minerals	substances used to make bone, teeth, blood, hormones, etc.
Vitamins	substances needed in small amounts to keep you healthy.
Deficiency disease	disease caused by not enough vitamins or minerals in a person's diet.
Anaemia	a deficiency disease caused by not enough iron in a person's diet; not enough red blood cells are made.
Rickets	a deficiency disease caused by not enough vitamin D in a person's diet; the bones bend because they are too soft.
Beri-beri	a deficiency disease caused by not enough vitamin B in a person's diet; the nerves are painful and the skin swells.
Scurvy	a deficiency disease caused by not enough vitamin C in a person's diet; the joints swell and are painful and the gums bleed easily.
Fibre	plant cellulose; important in a person's diet.
Balanced diet	a diet which contains the right sorts of food in the right amounts for a particular person.

Things to do

Collect some labels from food tins and boxes. Many labels say what is in the food. Breakfast cereal packets are good for this. Cut out the labels and group them into: 'Energy foods', 'Protein foods' and 'Vitamin foods'. Stick each group onto a large sheet of paper. This should help you to think about your diet.

Fancy that!

The world's heaviest man was Francis Lang, born in 1934 in the USA. He weighed 538 kg!

Two slices of bread and butter give 1000 kJ of energy. This would be used up by walking on flat ground for 45 minutes!

Questions

A.

In 16th and 17th century England, people had a very different diet compared with today. The menu shows the food eaten at one meal by rich people!

1. Why is this not a balanced meal?
2. How would you improve it?
3. Which of the foods shown are not usually eaten today?
4. Which of the foods contain fat?
5. Is there a dinner followed by a pudding like we have today?

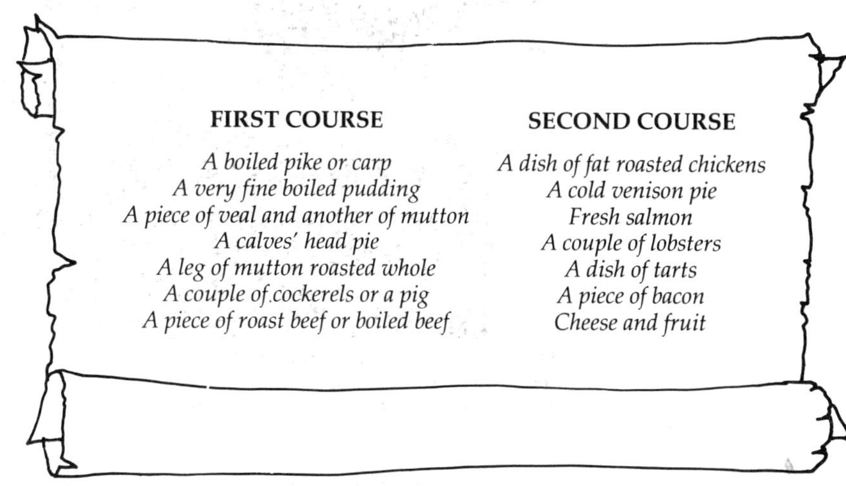

B.

Figure 20.5 shows an experiment to find the energy content of food. Stored energy is converted into heat and the heat output measured. The table below contains the results for a peanut and bread.

1. Calculate the temperature rise of the water obtained with the peanut and with the bread.
2. The amount of heat absorbed by the water can be found by using the following formula.

   Heat absorbed (joules) =
   4.2 x amount of water x temperature rise

   Calculate the amount of heat absorbed by the water for each of the two foods.
3. From the results:
   (a) Which food contains the most energy?
   (b) What evidence have you for your answer to 3(a)?
4. Give *one* reason for stirring water in the test tube before taking the temperature.
5. Why is it essential to measure the amount of water ($20 cm^3$) in each experiment?
6. Why was the temperature of the water taken before burning either food?
7. Why was the test tube clamped at an angle?

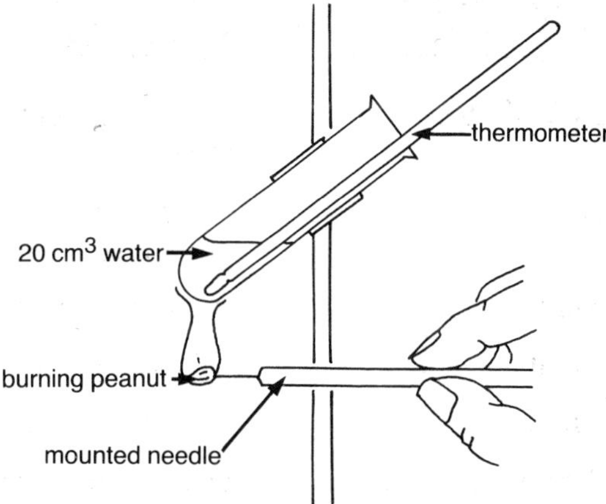

Figure 20.5

8. The results were slightly inaccurate because not all the heat given off was used to heat the water. Give *two* ways in which some of the heat given out will be lost.
9. Name a substance present in the peanut that makes it burn easily.
10. Name the element left behind after both the peanut and the bread have stopped burning.
11. Both the foods tested were solids. Design a simple modification to the experiment that would allow you to test a liquid food such as cooking oil.

Name of food	Mass of food (g)	Temperature of water before heating (°C)	Temperature of water after heating (°C)
Peanut	1.0g	17°C	95°C
Bread	1.0g	19°C	40°C

(ALSEB)

TOPIC 21

THE DIGESTIVE SYSTEM

Your digestive system is made of your *alimentary canal*, your *pancreas* and your *liver*.

Your alimentary canal is a long tube which goes from your mouth to your *anus*. Inside your alimentary canal, food is broken-up (or digested) into smaller molecules.

Your liver is a big, red-brown organ which is found under your diaphragm. Your liver does many important jobs in your body.

Your pancreas is a cream-coloured organ found below your *stomach*. Your pancreas makes some of the *enzymes* used to digest food. Enzymes are chemicals made inside cells. The enzymes are set free from these cells and go into your alimentary canal. Different enzymes are made in different parts of your alimentary canal.

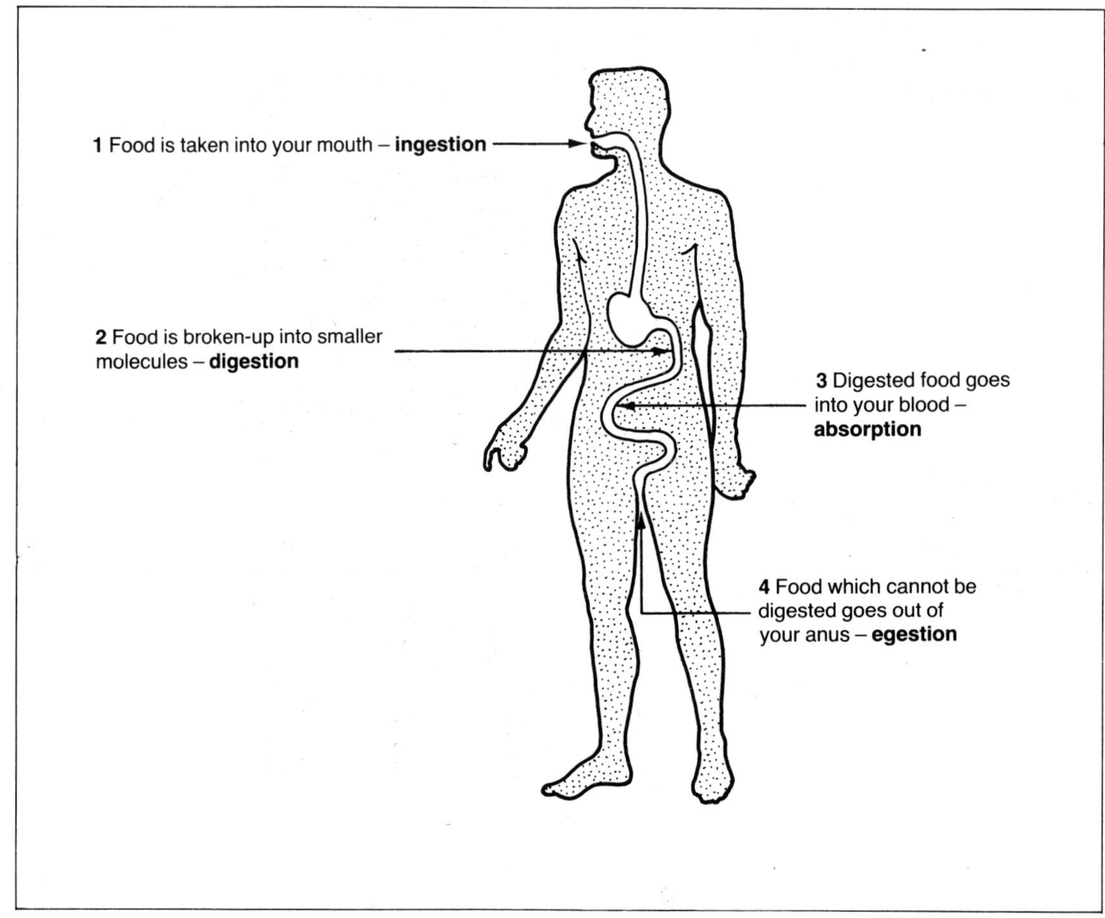

Figure 21.1 What happens in your alimentary canal

In adults the *small intestine* is 6 metres long and the *large intestine* is 1.5 metres long. Your small intestine is narrower than your large intestine.

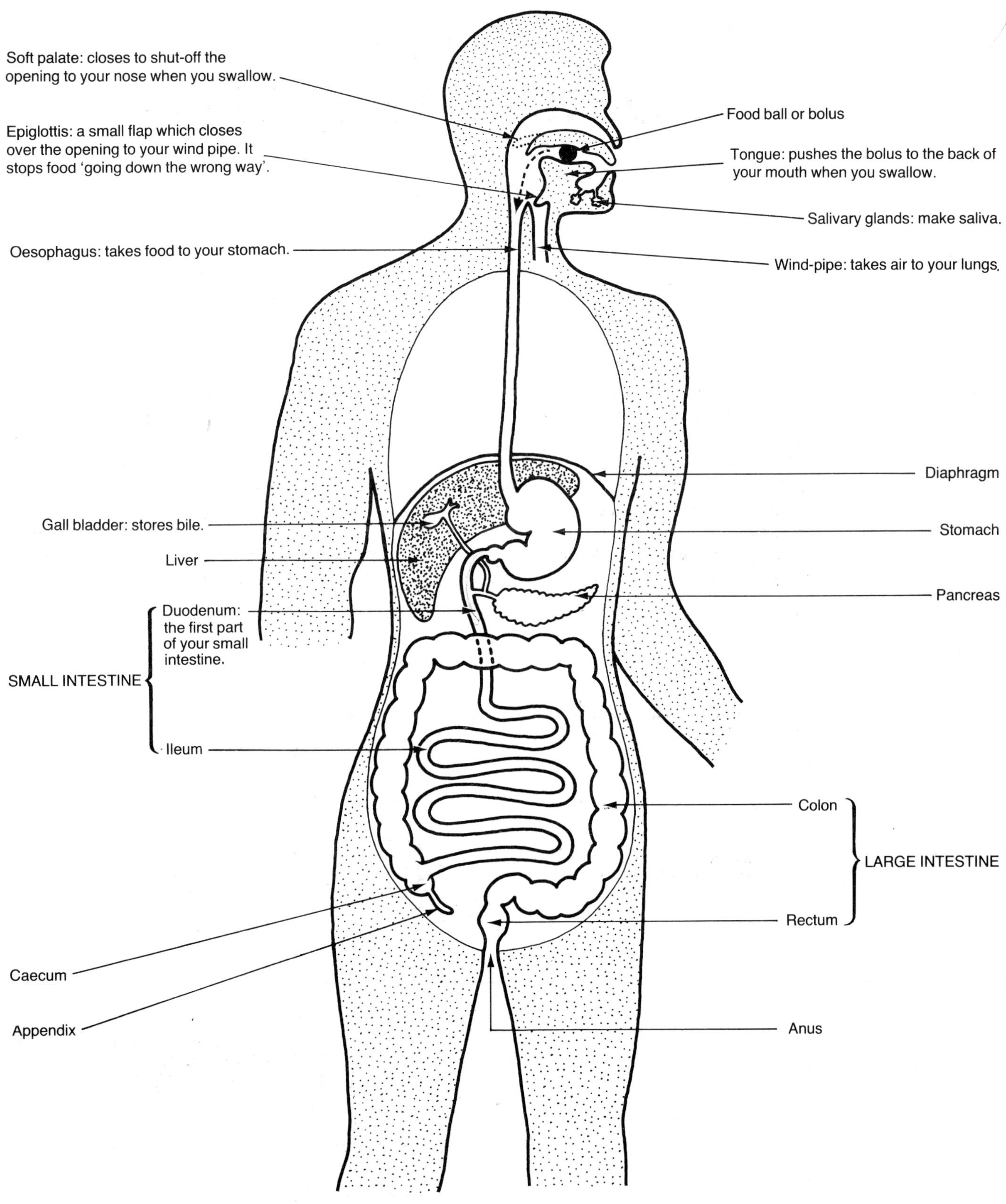

Figure 21.2 The human digestive system

WHAT HAPPENS IN YOUR: MOUTH

Food is chopped and crushed into smaller pieces by your teeth. It is mixed with saliva made by your *salivary glands*. Saliva makes food easier to swallow and has enzymes in it which digest starch. The food is rolled into a ball (or bolus) by your tongue and then it is swallowed.

OESOPHAGUS

The food bolus is gripped by your *oesophagus* and squeezed down to your stomach. This is called *peristalsis* and is why you can swallow when you are upside-down (figure 21.3)!

You can copy peristalsis by squeezing a dried pea along a soft rubber tube.

STOMACH

Inside your stomach food is squeezed into a substance like rice pudding! It is mixed with gastric juice made by cells in your stomach wall. Gastric juice is very acid and has enzymes in it which digest protein. Food stays in your stomach for different lengths of time. A meal with a lot of fat and protein in it may stay in your stomach for two or three hours. A meal with a lot of carbohydrate in it may stay there for only one hour.

DUODENUM

The first part of your small intestine is called the duodenum. Pancreatic juice and bile are mixed with food in your *duodenum*. Pancreatic juice is made in your pancreas. It has enzymes in it which digest proteins, starch and fat. Bile is a green liquid made in your liver and it is stored in your *gall bladder*. (See figure 21.4.)

ILEUM

The rest of your small intestine (everything except the duodenum) is called the ileum. Digestion is finished off in your *ileum*, by enzymes in the intestinal juice. This juice is made by cells in the wall of your ileum. An important job done by your ileum is to absorb digested food into your blood.

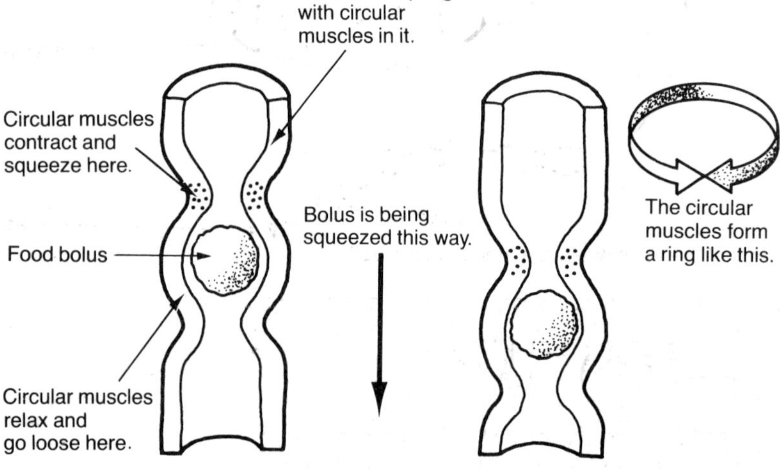

Figure 21.3 Peristalsis

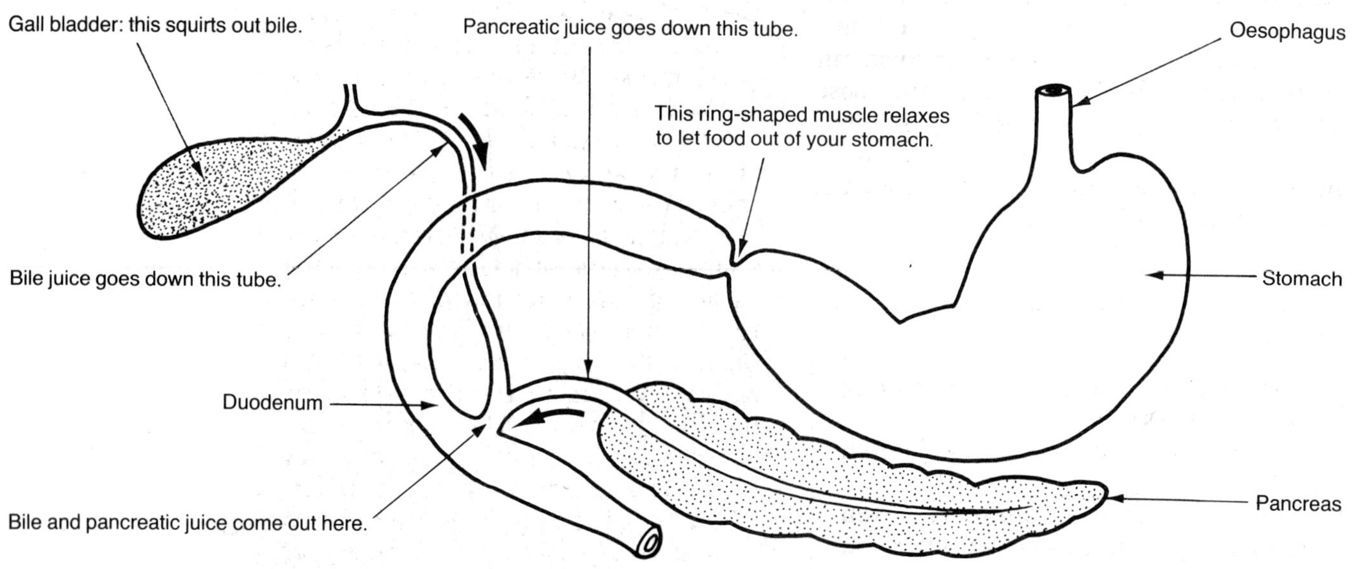

Figure 21.4

LARGE INTESTINE

Colon

The food which goes into your large intestine cannot be digested. It has had all the useful substances taken out of it. The food has a lot of water and fibre in it. An important job done by your *colon* is to absorb water from this waste food. The waste food, or *faeces*, goes into your *rectum* where it is stored. About once or twice a day the faeces leave your body through your anus. This is called defecation.

Caecum and appendix

Your *caecum* and *appendix* do not seem to be important for digestion. This is one way in which human digestion is different from digestion in other animals. In herbivores such as rabbits and horses, the caecum and appendix are more important than in humans. Bacteria which live inside the caecum and appendix of herbivores digest cellulose in the food. Although herbivores like rabbits only eat plants, they cannot digest cellulose! The bacteria in their caecum and appendix do this for them. This is a good example of symbiosis.

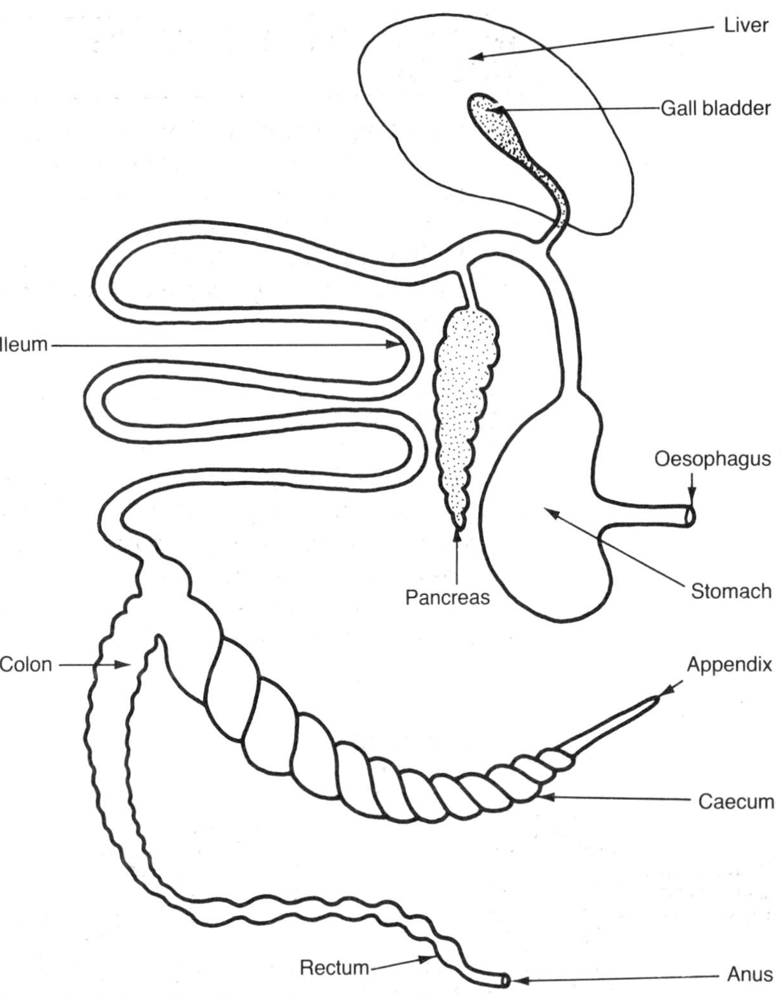

Figure 21.5 The digestive system of a rabbit

HEALTH AND YOUR DIGESTIVE SYSTEM

Food which cannot be digested should leave your rectum every 12–24 hours. Constipation is when this does not happen. It is often caused by not eating enough fruit and vegetables. Your faeces are then hard and dry and difficult to move out of your rectum.

Bad diet or an infection of your colon can cause diarrhoea. In this, your faeces are loose and watery. Being sick or vomiting is caused by an upset stomach. The direction of peristalsis changes and food is brought back up into your mouth.

Fancy that!

Cows swallow their food and then bring it back up to chew!

Humans make up to 1 litre of bile each day!

Your stomach is J-shaped when you are standing up and U-shaped when you lie down!

Summary

Food is digested in your *alimentary canal* which is the main part of your *digestive system*. Your alimentary canal has four main parts: the *oesophagus*, the *stomach*, the *small intestine* and the *large intestine*.

Your oesophagus takes food from your mouth to your stomach. Your stomach stores the food as it is swallowed and starts to digest protein. The first part of your small intestine, or *ilueum*, is the *duodenum*. Enzymes from your *pancreas* and bile from your *gall bladder* go into your duodenum. The rest of your ileum finishes off digestion and starts to absorb the digested food. Your large intestine is made of the *colon*, *caecum*, *appendix* and *rectum*. Your colon absorbs water from the waste food. The caecum and appendix are more important for digestion in herbivores than in ourselves. Waste food is called *faeces* and is stored in your *rectum*. It is removed from your body through your *anus*.

Important words

Alimentary canal	a long tube forming most of your digestive system.
Oesophagus	a tube which takes food from your mouth to your stomach.
Stomach	a large organ which stores food as it is swallowed and which starts digestion.
Small intestine	the part of your alimentary canal between your stomach and your large intestine.
Large intestine	a wide tube connected to the end of your small intestine.
Duodenum	the first part of your small intestine joined to your stomach.
Ileum	the rest of your small intestine after your duodenum.
Caecum	part of the large intestine important for digestion of cellulose in herbivores.
Colon	part of your large intestine important for absorbing water from your food.
Rectum	the last part of your large intestine where faeces are stored.
Faeces	waste food which cannot be digested and which is passed out of your body.
Anus	the end of the alimentary canal through which faeces leave your body.
Appendix	a finger-like structure leading from your caecum.
Gall bladder	a bag-like structure which stores bile.
Pancreas	an organ which makes pancreatic digestive juice.
Salivary glands	organs which make saliva.
Liver	a large organ which does many important jobs such as making bile juice.
Peristalsis	the way in which food is squeezed along your alimentary canal.
Digestive enzymes	chemicals made by cells that cause food to be digested.

Questions

A.

Write out each sentence in your book. Fill in the missing words from those in the box. Some words may be used more than once.

gall bladder — appendix — faeces — digestion — digested food — acid — saliva — bolus — ingestion — water — ileum — caecum — small intestine — liver — duodenum — gastric juice — oesophagus — peristalsis — enzymes — alimentary canal — large intestine

1. Your ...... is the main part of your digestive system.
2. Taking food into your digestive system is called ....
3. Food is digested by ....
4. Digested food is absorbed from your ....
5. Your tongue and cheek muscles roll the food into a ....
6. Your ...... takes food from your mouth to your stomach.
7. Food in your mouth is mixed with ....
8. Food is moved along your alimentary canal by ....
9. Your stomach mixes food with ....
10. ...... is what happens to food in your alimentary canal.
11. In your ...... bile and pancreatic juice are mixed with the food.
12. Gastric juice is ...... and has ...... in it.
13. Bile is made in your ....
14. ...... is absorbed in your ileum.

15. Your ileum and duodenum are called your ....
16. ...... is absorbed from your colon.
17. Digestion is finished off in your ....
18. Your rectum contains ....
19. Herbivores digest cellulose in their ...... and ....
20. Bile is stored in your ....
21. Your rectum and colon are part of your ....

B.
Copy this into your book using another word (or words) for those in *italics*. Do not change the meaning of the sentences.

Food is *ingested* into your mouth and made into a *food ball* by your tongue and cheeks. The food is swallowed and goes down the *tube joining your mouth and stomach*. After being *digested* the food is *absorbed* into your blood. Waste food which contains a lot of *cellulose* goes into your *colon and caecum*. It is stored in your rectum and is *passed out of* your body through your anus.

C.
1. Write down three ways in which the alimentary canals of humans and rabbits are different. Give a reason for *one* of these differences.
2. Why is fibre important?
3. Why is your ileum such a long tube?
4. Write these down in the order in which they happen: defecation; absorption; digestion; ingestion.
5. What do these words mean: (a) molecules (b) contract (c) infection?

D.
Figure 21.6 is of the human digestive system.
1. Name the parts labelled (a) to (j).
2. Select from the diagram the letter which fits each of the parts described below.
   (i) The part where faeces are stored.
   (ii) The part where most water is absorbed.
   (iii) The part which has acid conditions.
   (iv) The part that can produce enzymes and a hormone.
   (v) The part where most absorption takes place.
   Figure 21.7 shows a villus partly cut open.
3. *Name* the part of the gut that contains villi.
4. Give *one* reason why villi need a good blood supply.

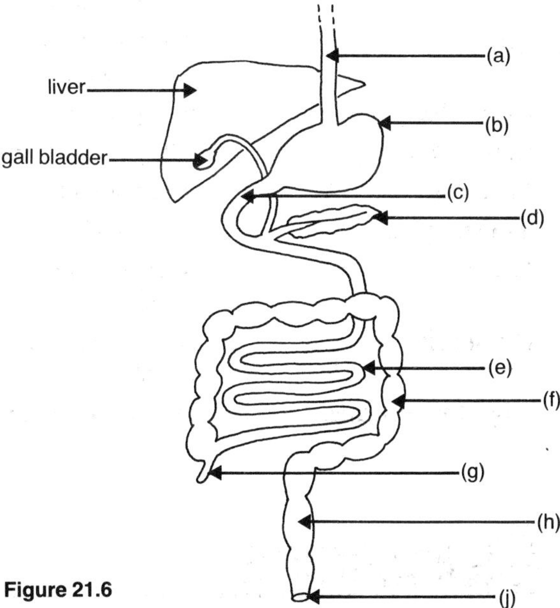

Figure 21.6

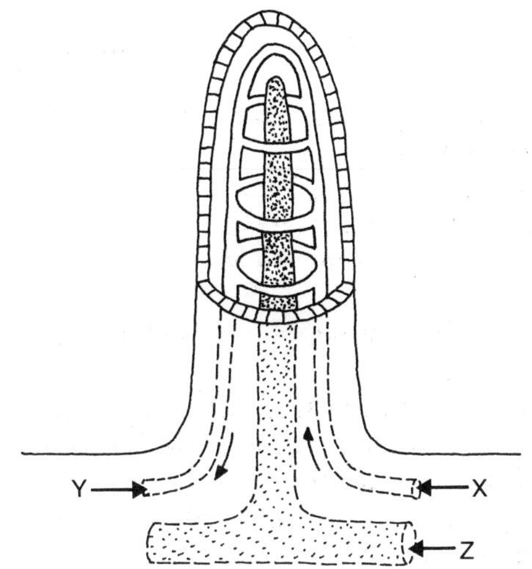

Figure 21.7

5. (i) Name *two* substances that will have increased in concentration between the parts labelled X and Y.
   (ii) Why will the substances have increased in concentration?
6. Name *one* substance absorbed from the gut into the part labelled Z.
7. Copy figure 21.8 into your book and complete it to show what the region of the gut containing villi would look like when cut across.
8. Give *one* reason why villi are important in the gut.

(ALSEB)

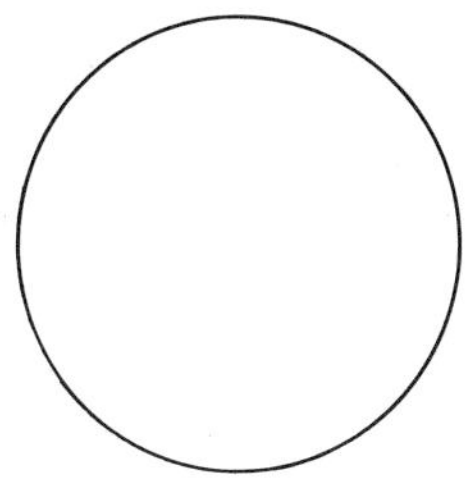
Figure 21.8

TOPIC 22

DIGESTION

DIGESTION

Most of our food is made of big molecules which cannot be used by our bodies. Breaking up these big molecules into smaller ones is called *digestion*. Small molecules can be used by our bodies for growth and to give energy.

Digestion happens in the digestive system or alimentary canal. It is done by chemicals called *enzymes*.

amylases	are enzymes which digest	**starch**
lipases	are enzymes which digest	**fats**
proteases	are enzymes which digest	**proteins**

This starch molecule is made of a lot of glucose molecules joined together.

Digestion by amylases and other enzymes.

These smaller glucose molecules can be used by cells.

Figure 22.2

CARBOHYDRATE DIGESTION

Carbohydrates like starch have very big molecules. In digestion starch molecules are broken up into glucose molecules. (See figure 22.2.)

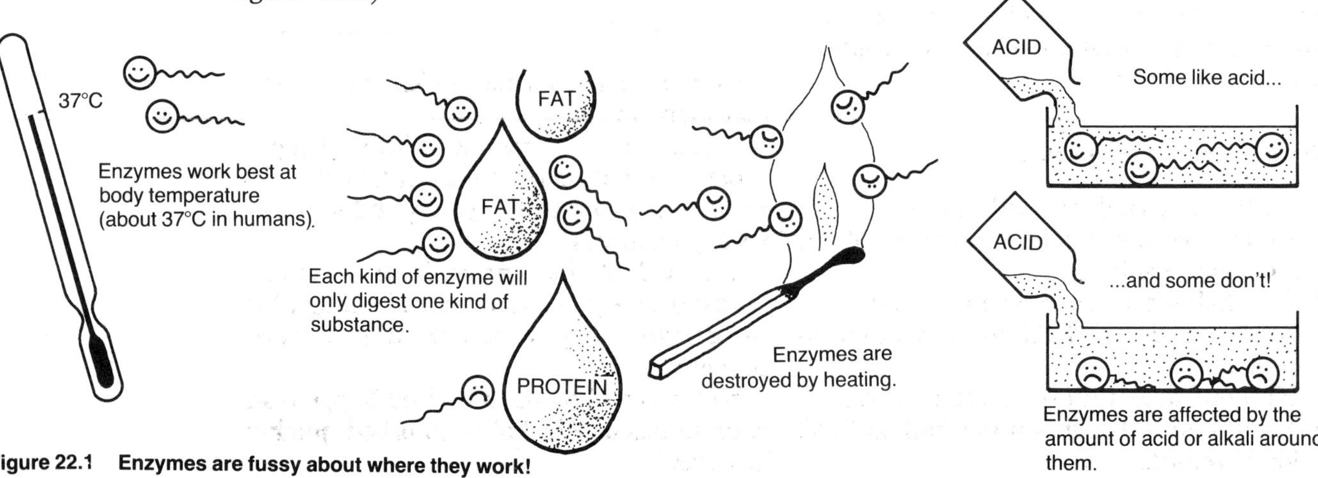

Figure 22.1 Enzymes are fussy about where they work!

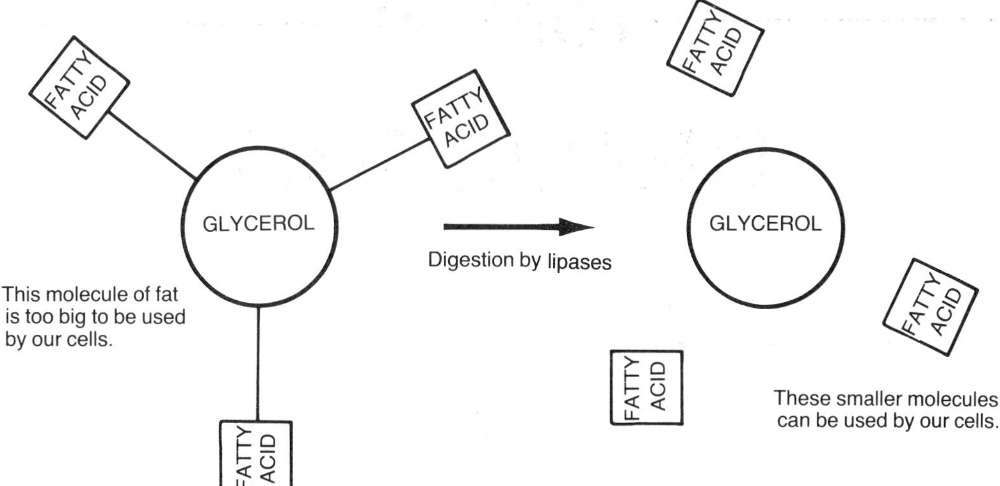

Figure 22.3

FAT DIGESTION

Fats are made of glycerol and fatty acids. Glycerol is a thick sweet liquid. Vinegar is a fatty acid. In digestion, fats are broken up into these smaller molecules. (See figure 22.3.)

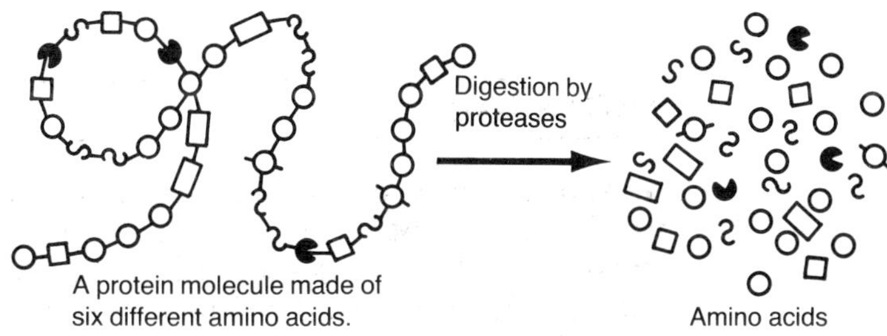

Figure 22.4

PROTEIN DIGESTION

Proteins are made of amino acids. Different proteins are made of different amino acids. Only the amino acids, not the proteins, can be used by our cells. In digestion, proteins are broken up into amino acids. (See figure 22.4.)

DIGESTION IN YOUR MOUTH

Saliva has an amylase in it which starts the digestion of starch. It changes some of the starch to sugar. That is why if you chew a piece of bread it slowly gets sweeter. Amylase works best in neutral or slightly acid surroundings.

Does saliva digest starch?

1. Swill your mouth out with water.
2. Collect some saliva in a test tube: about 2 cm depth will do.
3. Pour half the saliva into another test tube.
4. Add 2 cm depth of 1% starch solution to each tube.
5. Heat one tube until the solution boils.
6. Stand both tubes in a water bath at 37°C for 20 minutes.
7. Add a few drops of iodine solution to both tubes.

The boiled solution should go blue-black. The unboiled solution should not go blue-black. Can you explain the results?

DIGESTION IN YOUR STOMACH

Your stomach makes gastric juice which has in it:

pepsin **rennin** **acid**

Pepsin is an enzyme which starts the digestion of protein.

Rennin is an enzyme which changes protein in milk into a solid – it 'clots' milk. Rennin is only made in young children and young mammals.

The acid kills bacteria on the food you eat. It also makes your stomach acid enough for the enzymes in your gastric juices to work properly.

Not much absorption of food happens in your stomach. Alcohol is absorbed quickly however.

DIGESTION IN YOUR SMALL INTESTINE

In your duodenum food is mixed with pancreatic juice and bile.

> Pancreatic juice has in it:
>
> **lipase** **amylase** **protease**

Lipase breaks up fat into fatty acids and glycerol. Amylase breaks up starch into sugar. Protease breaks up proteins into amino acids.

Bile makes food alkaline so that the pancreatic enzymes can work properly. It also changes big drops of fat into smaller drops. This helps lipase to break up fat into fatty acids and glycerol more easily. (See figure 22.5)

In your ileum, intestinal juice is mixed with the food. Intestinal juice has lipase, protease and other enzymes in it. Any fat, protein or carbohydate still left is digested by these enzymes.

The small molecules of food made in digestion have to get from your alimentary canal into your blood. This is called *absorption*.

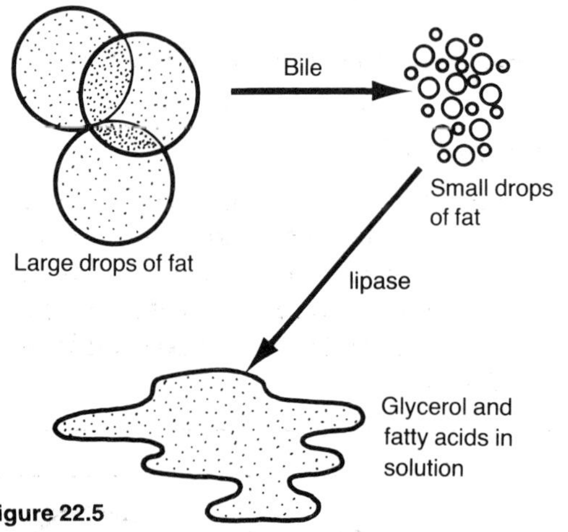

Large drops of fat
Bile
Small drops of fat
lipase
Glycerol and fatty acids in solution

Figure 22.5

ABSORPTION OF DIGESTED FOOD

Absorption of food happens in your ileum. Glucose, glycerol, fatty acids and amino acids are absorbed here.

Absorption is helped by:

1. the long length of the ileum
2. the **villi** (singular: **villus**)

Villi are like tiny fingers sticking out from the inside wall of your ileum. Each villus is about 1mm high. (See figure 22.6.)

The villi make a very big surface through which food can be absorbed. Without villi,

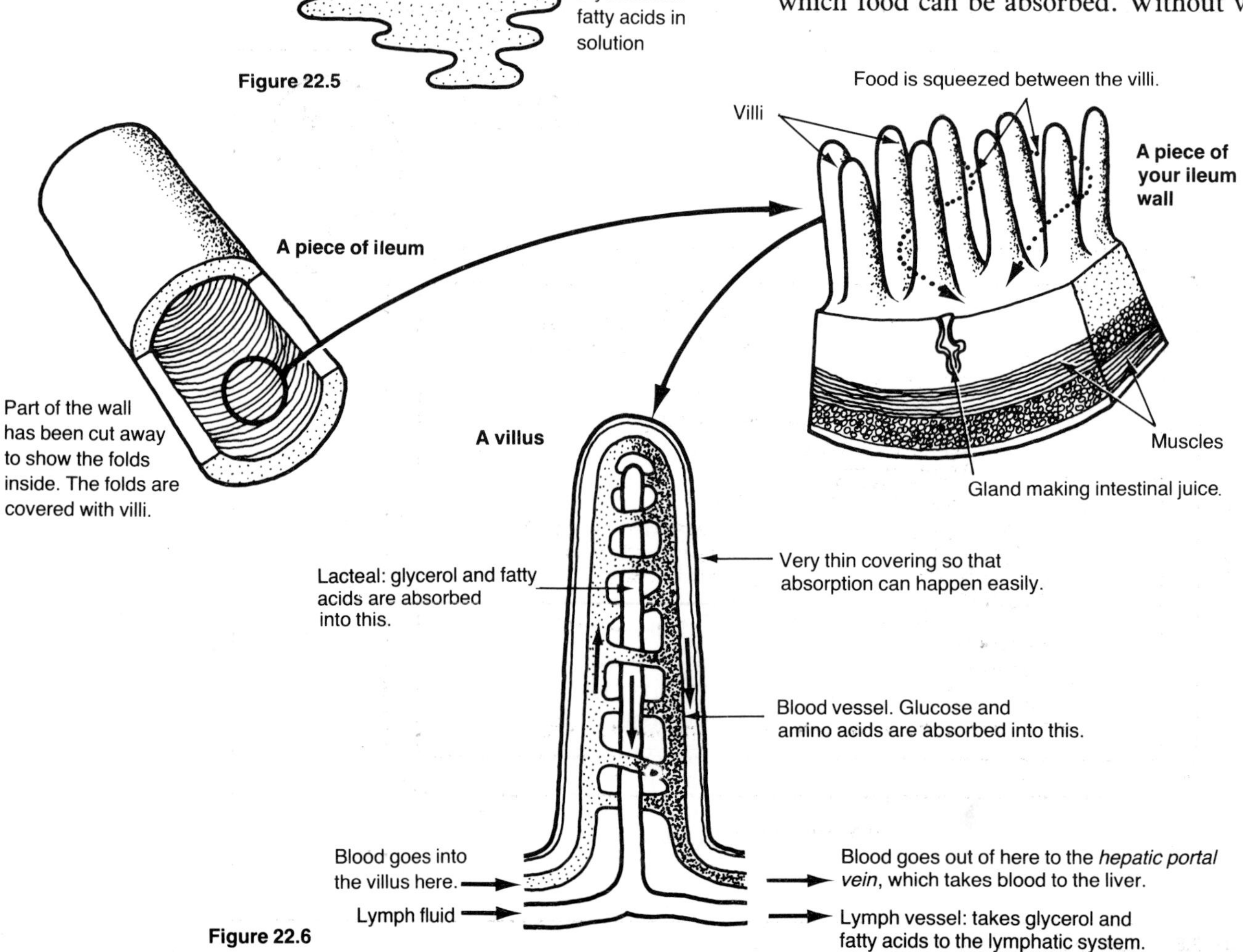

Figure 22.6

the surface would be much smaller and absorption not as good. (See figure 22.7.)

No enzymes are made in your large intestine. Your colon absorbs water from the food which is left and prepares the food for defecation (leaving your body). Your large intestine has many useful bacteria, some of which make vitamin B.

WHAT HAPPENS TO DIGESTED FOOD

Glucose and amino acids from your digestive system go into your hepatic portal vein. This takes them to your liver. (See figures 22.8 and 22.9.)

Glycerol and fatty acids from your digestive system go into your lymph system. Your lymph system empties into a vein in your neck (see p.153). From here the food is taken to your cells by your blood system. (See figure 22.10.)

Glucose is used by your cells:

1. in respiration to set free energy,
2. to store energy as glycogen.

Glycogen stored in your liver and muscles can be changed back to glucose. This happens when your body needs extra energy.

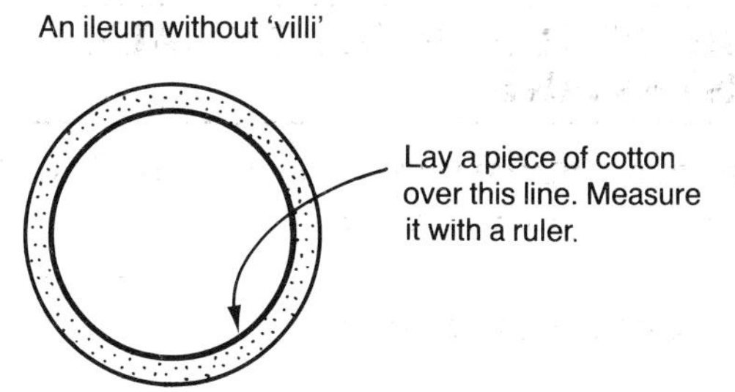

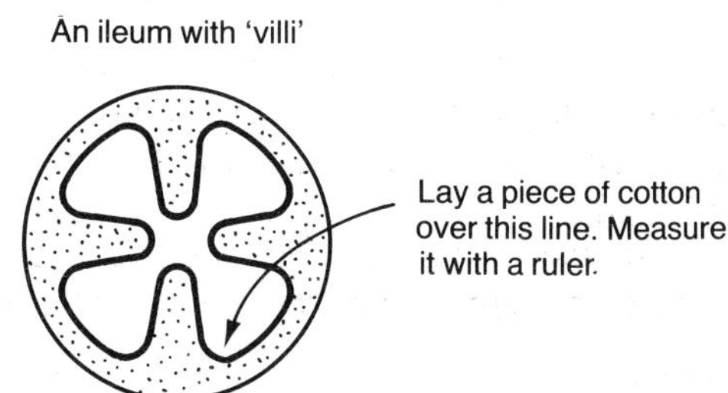

Figure 22.7 What difference do the 'villi' make?

> **Fancy that!**
>
> There are about 5 million villi in your intestine! They make an area of about 30 square metres for absorption of food.
>
> If bile salts were not made about a quarter of the fat in your food would not be digested!

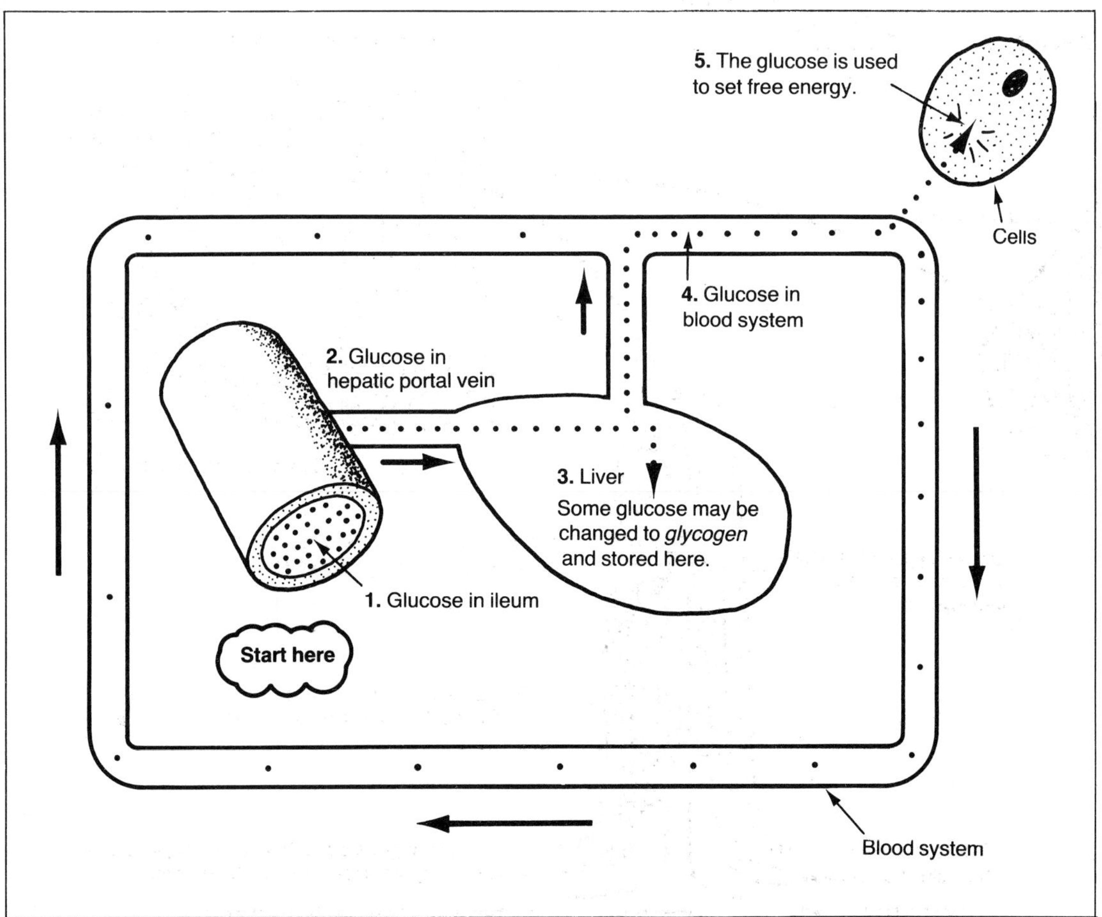

Figure 22.8 Absorption of glucose

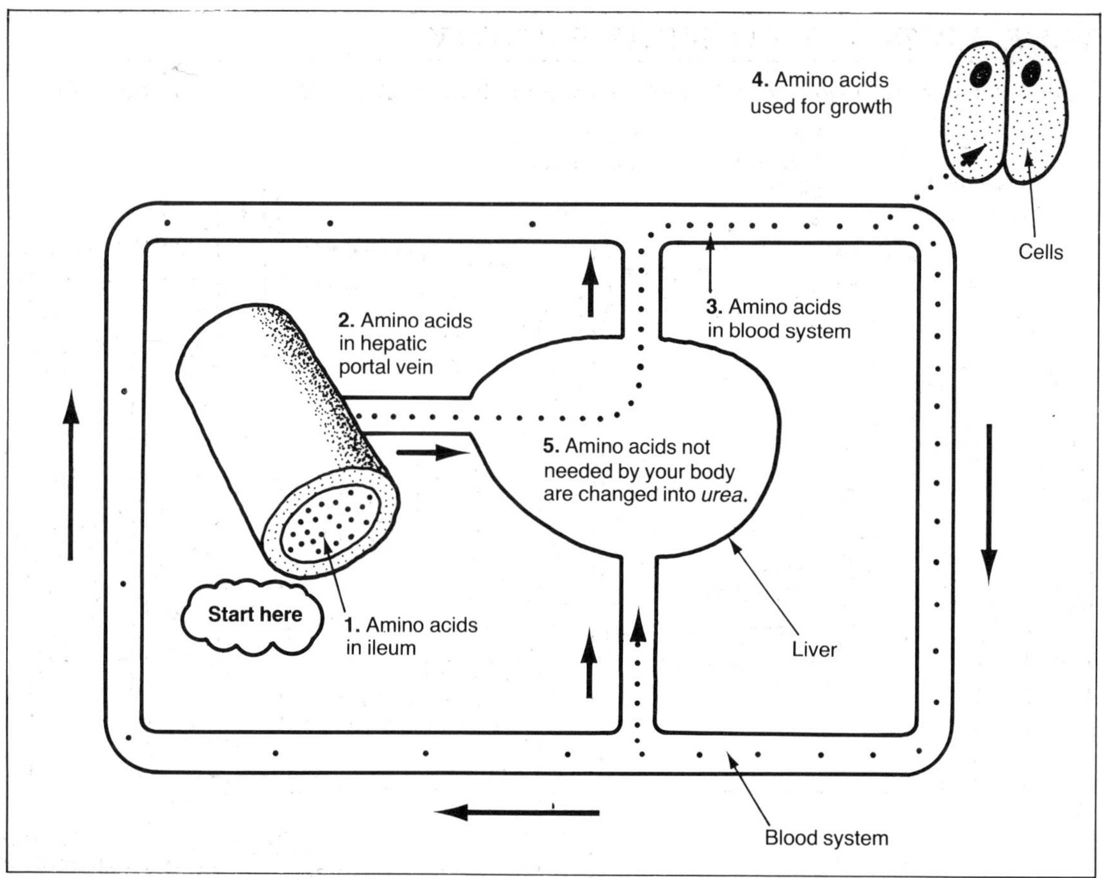

Figure 22.9 Absorption of amino acids

Amino acids are used by your cells to make protein. Protein is needed for growth of new cells and repair of old ones.

Fats are used by your cells:

1. in respiration to set free energy,
2. to store energy. Much more fat can be stored in your body than glycogen.

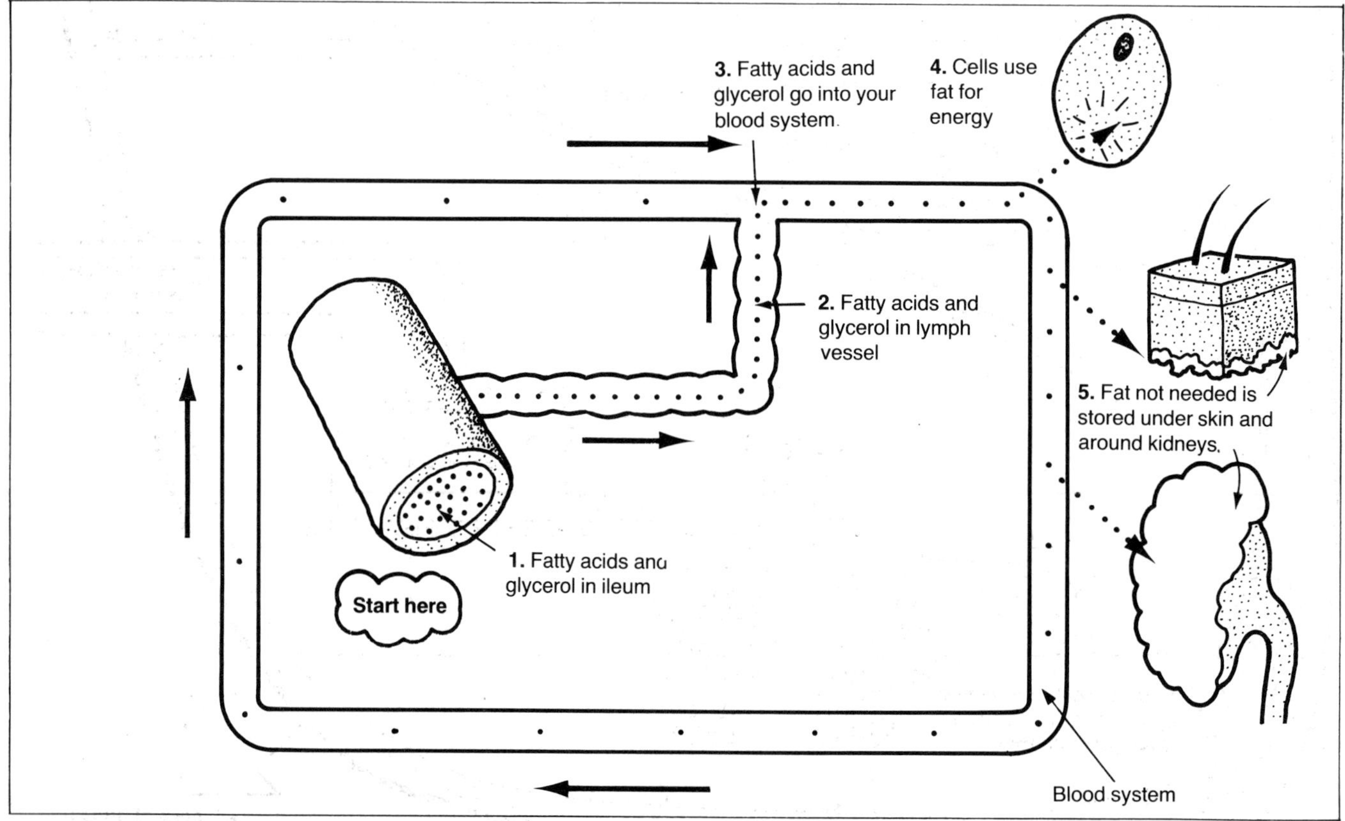

Figure 22.10 Absorption of fatty acids and glycerol

YOUR LIVER – A CHEMICAL FACTORY

Your liver is a big organ which does many jobs.

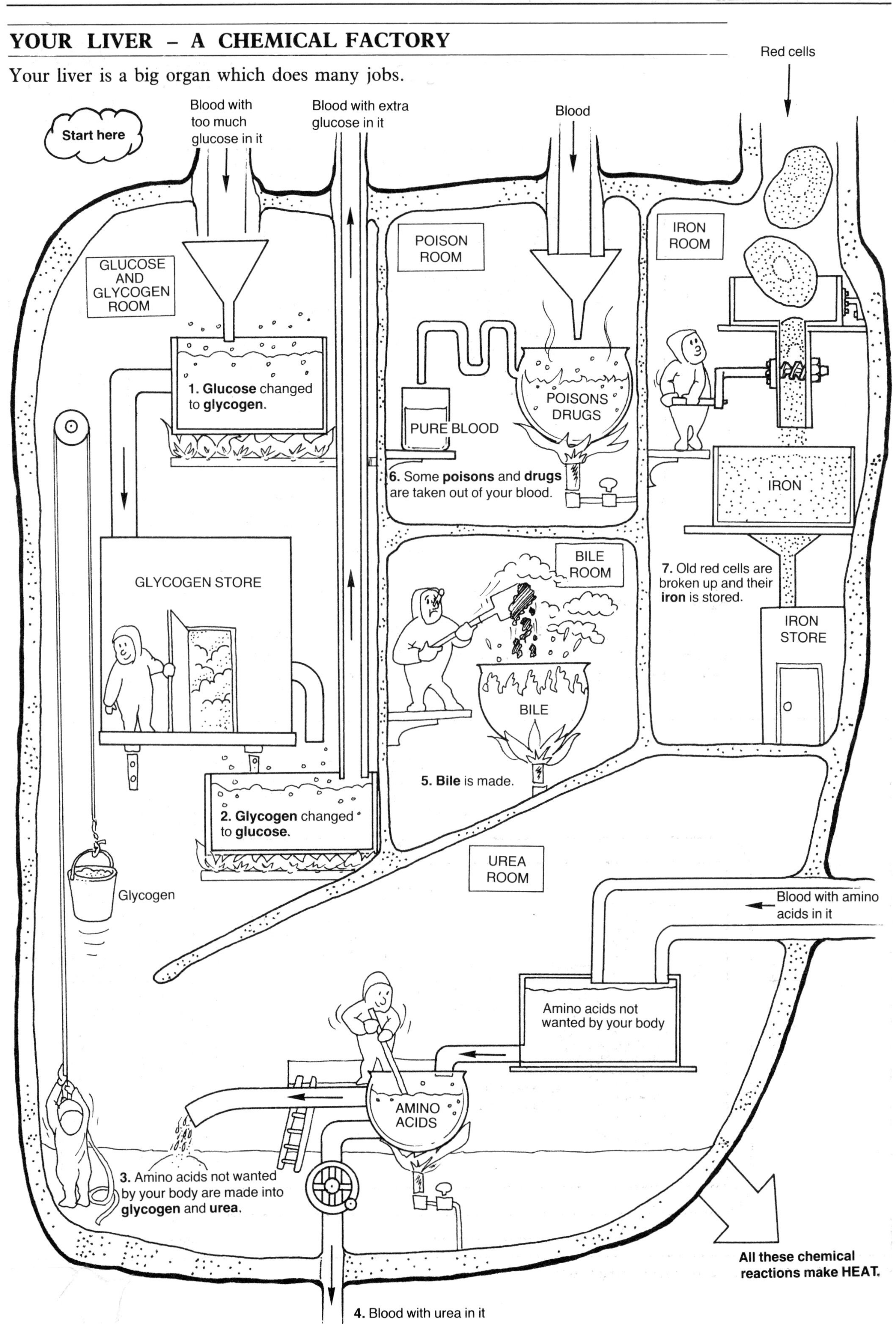

Summary

Food is made of molecules that are too big to go into your blood. *Digestion* makes these molecules smaller. The small molecules can go into your blood.

Digestion is done by *enzymes*. Different enzymes digest different sorts of food. *Amylases* digest starch; *lipases* digest fats; *proteases* digest proteins. These different enzymes work in different conditions.

Digested food is absorbed by *villi*. Digested *fat* goes into *lacteals* inside the villi and then into your blood system. Digested carbohydrate and protein go to your *liver* and then into your blood system.

Carbohydrate and fat are used to give you *energy*. Fat is used to *store* a lot of energy. Protein is used to make new cells for *growth*.

Important words

Digestion	the break-up of food by enzymes into substances which your body can absorb.
Enzymes	chemicals made by all living cells which speed up the rate at which chemical reactions happen.
Amylases	enzymes which digest starch into sugar.
Lipases	enzymes which digest fat into glycerol and fatty acids.
Proteases	enzymes which digest proteins into amino acids.
Pepsin	an enzyme which starts the digestion of protein in your stomach.
Bile	a juice made by your liver.
Absorption	the movement of digested food from your digestive system into your blood or lymph system.
Villi	small finger-like structures in your ileum which absorb digested food (singular: villus).
Hepatic portal vein	the vein which carries digested food from your digestive system to your liver.
Lacteal	the tubes of your lymph system found in villi.
Urea	a chemical substance made in your liver from unwanted amino acids.

Questions

A.

Put each of these parts of sentences into the correct order.

1. carbohydrates like starch into simpler substances like glucose	which break up amylases are enzymes
2. simpler substances called glycerol and fatty acids are made	when fats are digested by enzymes called lipases
3. many different kinds of and are digested by proteases	proteins are made of amino acids
4. bile does not have any to break up	big drops of fat enzymes but helps

B.

1. Describe in your own words what is happening in figures 22.9 and 22.10.
2. How does your liver help to control the sugar in your blood?
3. Proteins are digested into amino acids. Cells then use the amino acids to make proteins! Why does this happen?

C.

Here is a table of results showing the time taken for any enzyme controlled reaction to occur at different temperatures.

1. Present these results in the form of a graph. Join your plotted points with a curve *not* straight lines.
2. From your graph, at which temperature does this reaction take place in the shortest time?
3. In your opinion, what does this graph suggest about the time which it would probably take for the reaction to occur at 60°C and 10°C?

(EMREB)

Time taken for reaction to occur in mins.	Temperature of reaction in °C.
7.8	20
3.2	30
1.2	35
1.8	40
5.2	45
7.0	50

D.

Figure 22.12 shows a model gut made of Visking (cellulose) tubing containing a mixture of saliva and starch in water.

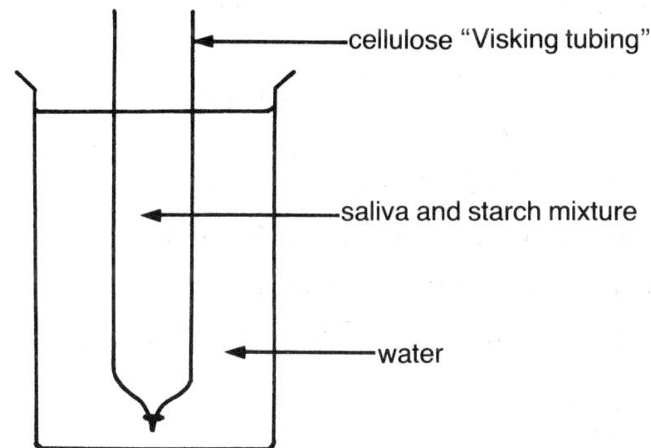

Figure 22.12

1. (a) At what temperature should this experiment be kept?
   (b) Give *one* reason for your answer.
2. In the body, what is represented by the water?
3. Give *one* reason why starch cannot pass through the Visking tube?
4. (a) Name a substance you would find in the water after one hour.
   (b) Describe the test you would carry out to identify this substance and the result.
5. Saliva contains an enzyme, salivary amylase. What is an enzyme?

(ALSEB)

E.

Figure 22.13 shows a very small portion of the inner lining of the human small intestine. Two villi are shown surrounded by the products of digestion. The transport system within a villus is shown in detail in one of the villi.

1. Explain how each of the following helps to ensure rapid absorption of food materials.
   (a) The single-layered epithelium.
   (b) The surface area of each villus.
2. (a) Name three products of digestion which are present in the small intestine.
   (b) State which of these products will pass into the vessel labelled X.
3. Which one of the vessels P,Q,R carried lymph?
   (a) Name the main carbohydrate storage material in the human body.
   (b) Name the organ in which this material is stored.

(EAEB)

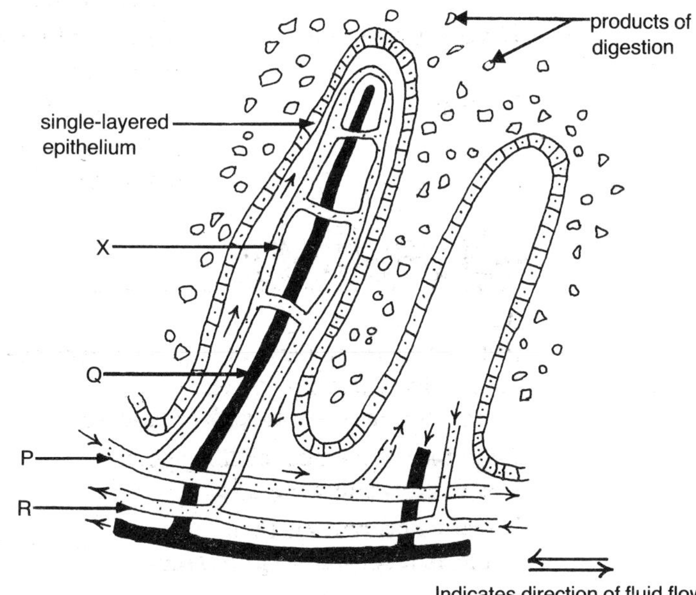

Figure 22.13

TOPIC 23

CIRCULATION

Blood moves round your body in small tubes called *blood vessels*. (See figure 23.1.) There are three kinds of blood vessel:

arteries	**veins**	**capillaries**

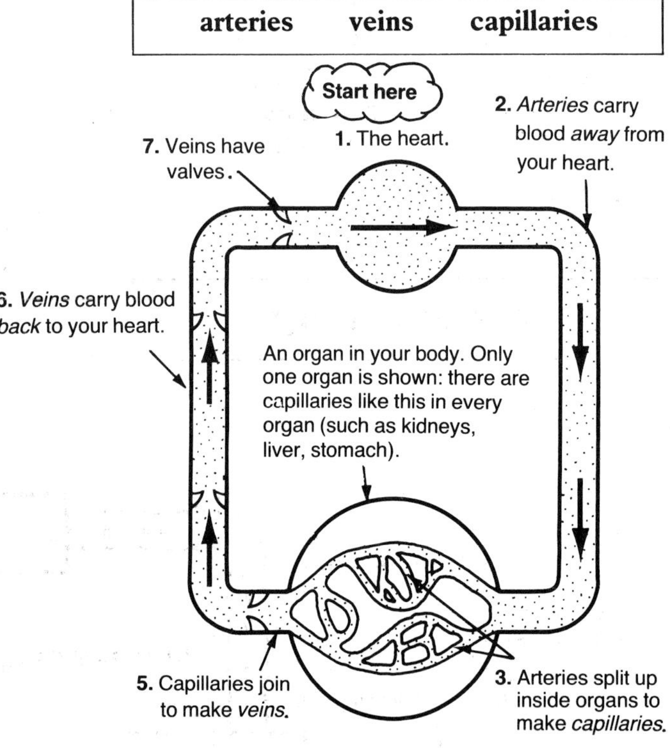

Figure 23.1

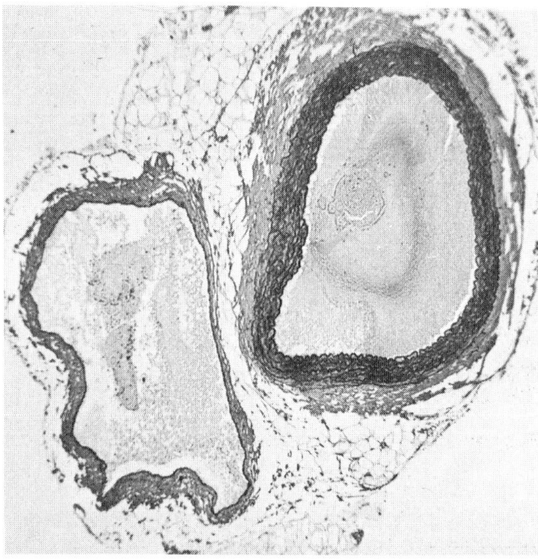
A cross section through an artery (right) and a vein (left).

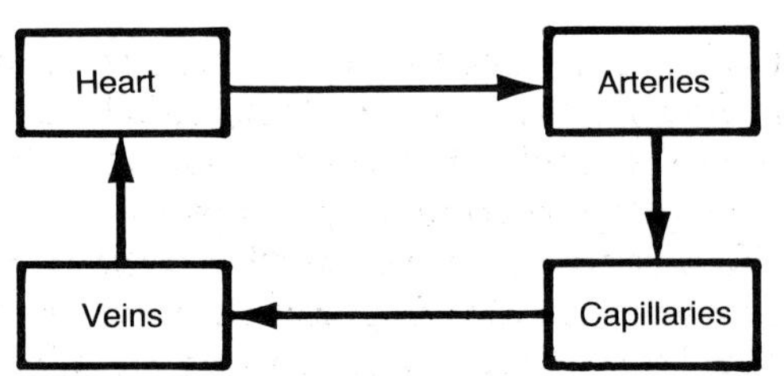

Figure 23.2

Blood moves in one direction through your blood vessels. (See figure 23.2.)

Blood is pumped into arteries by your heart. This stretches the muscles in the walls of your arteries. (See figure 23.3.) As your blood moves on, the muscles 'bounce back' again. This squeezes the blood and pushes it towards the capillaries. This stretching and bounce-back causes a beat or *pulse* in your arteries. A pulse can be felt at your wrist.

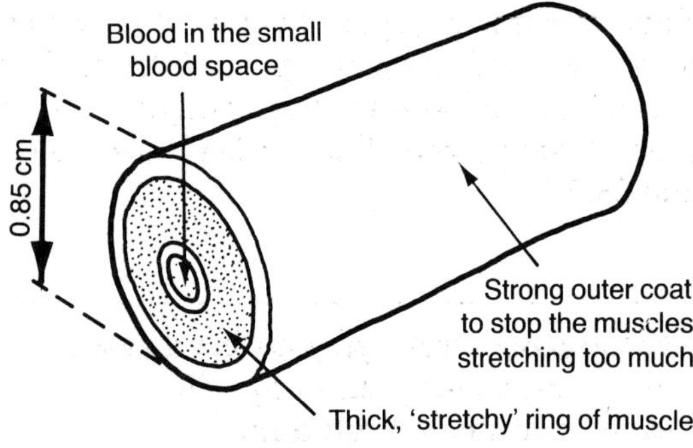

Figure 23.3 Part of an artery

Blood in your veins is not pushed as hard as in your arteries. This is because:

1. your veins are a long way from your heart,
2. the blood space in your veins is bigger than in your arteries,
3. there is less muscle to squeeze the blood in your veins than in your arteries.

Veins have valves to stop blood flowing the wrong way. (See figure 23.4.)

Capillaries are tiny blood vessels. Red blood cells can move along the smallest capillaries only in single file!

Capillaries have very thin walls. Substances in the blood can easily get through these walls. (See figure 23.5.)

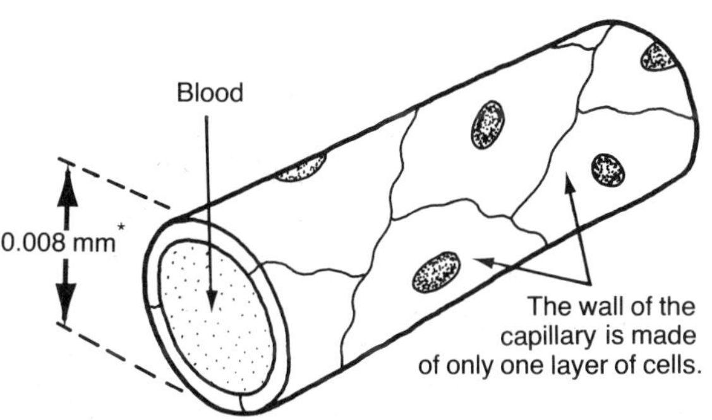

* Notice that this is mm (millimetres), not cm (centimetres); this means that capillaries are 1000 times smaller than arteries!

Figure 23.5 Part of a capillary

Part of a vein

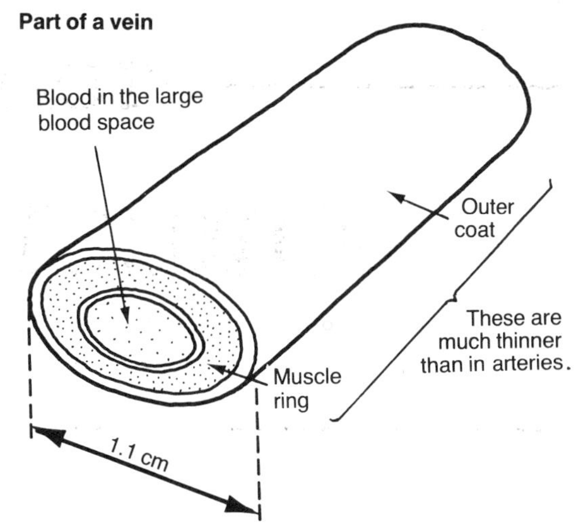

The valves are like doors which only open one way

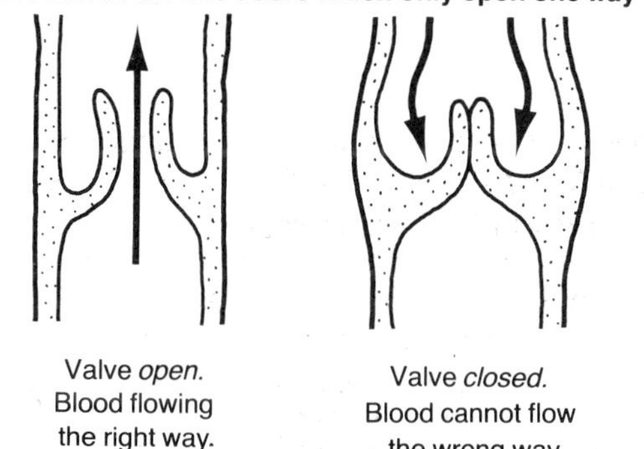

Figure 23.4

Capillaries are leaky!

YOUR CIRCULATORY SYSTEM

Blood moves round your body in your *circulatory system*. To do this, blood keeps passing through your heart. Your heart has to pump the blood to keep it moving.

Your capillaries are so small that they slow down your blood as it passes through them. Your lungs have many capillaries. Blood coming back from your lungs in your *pulmonary vein* has been slowed down a lot. This blood must go back to your heart so that it can be speeded up again. Your heart then pumps the blood out with enough force to push it round your body. (See figures 23.6 and 23.7.)

Blood passes through your heart **twice** on its way round your body. This is called a **double circulation.**

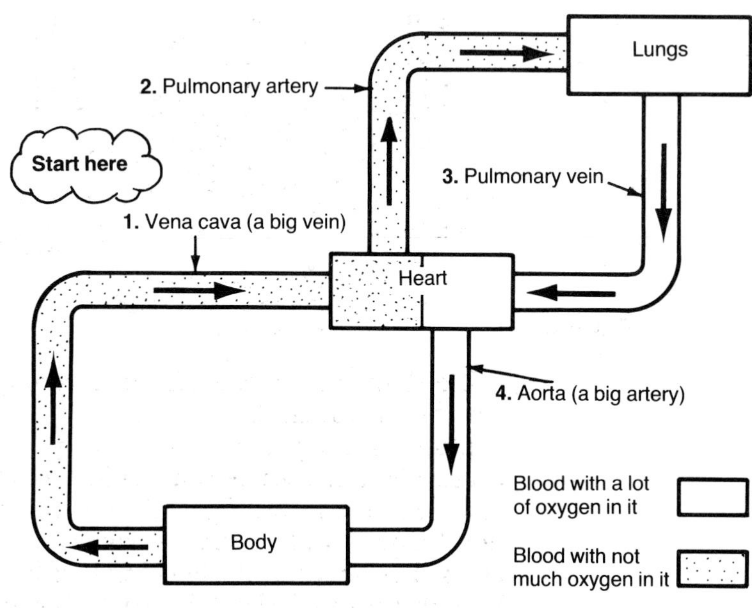

Figure 23.6 A double circulation

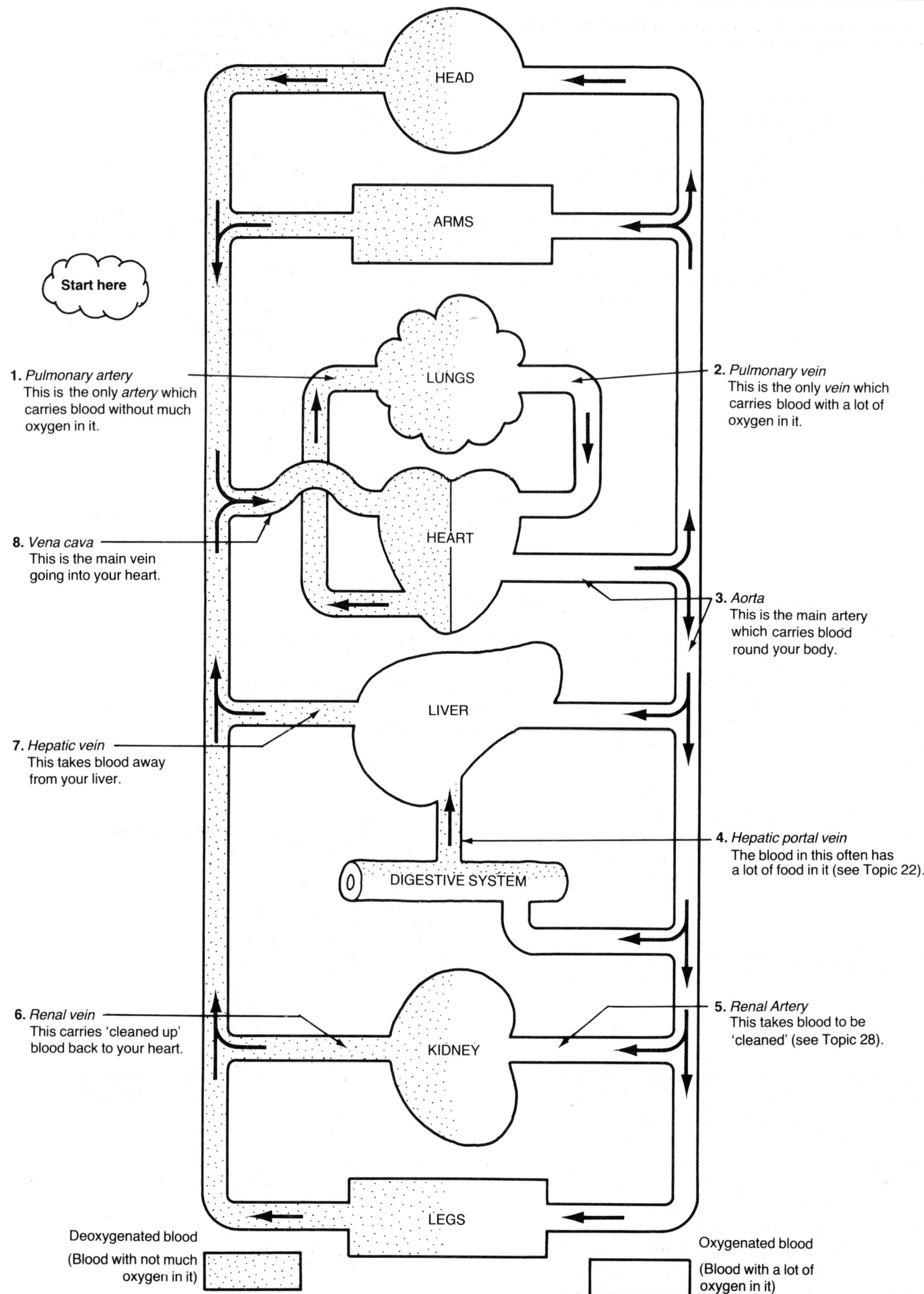

Figure 23.7 This diagram shows the main blood vessels

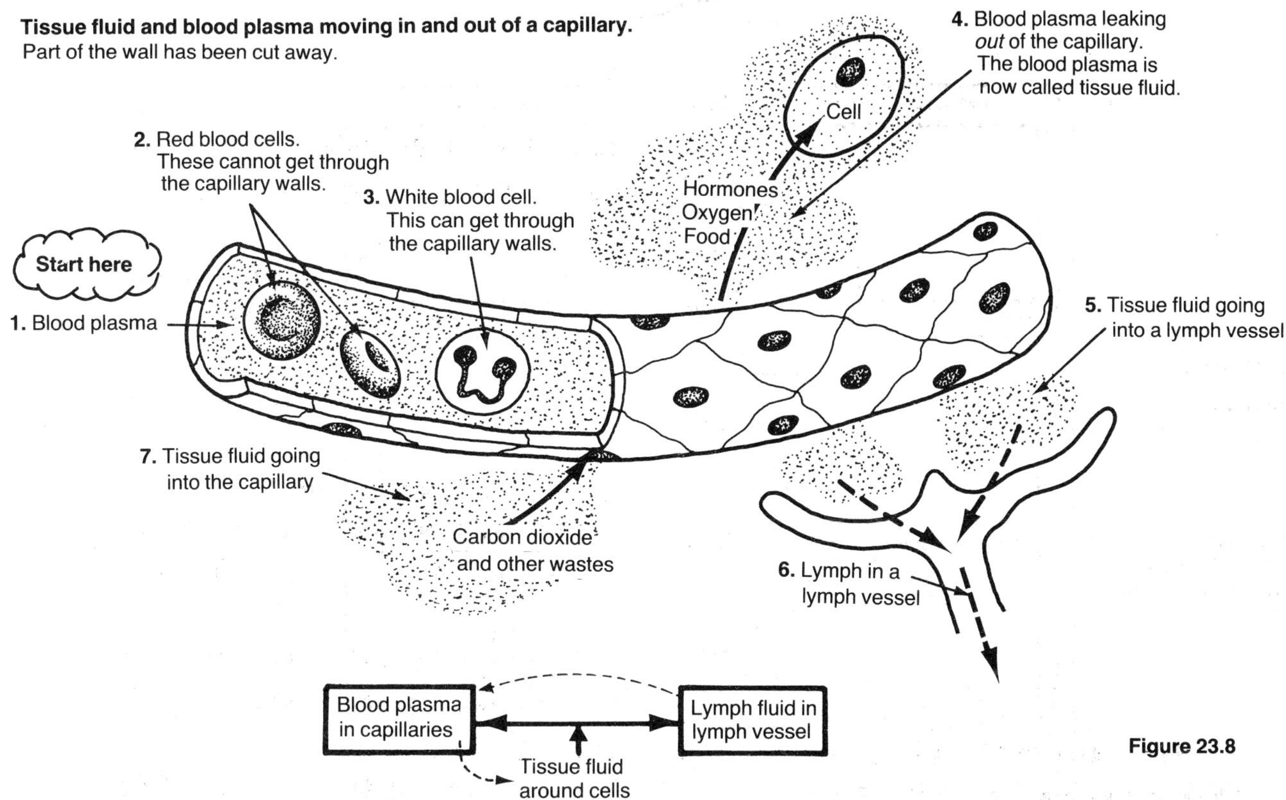

Figure 23.8

HOW YOUR CELLS ARE FED, WASHED AND CLEANED!

Fluid or *plasma* from your blood can pass through the walls of your capillaries. When it does this it fills up the spaces between cells and is then called *tissue fluid*. This tissue fluid carries with it useful substances needed by cells. The cells excrete their wastes into the tissue fluid. Some of the 'used' tissue fluid goes back into the capillaries and becomes blood plasma again. The rest is collected by your *lymphatic system* and is called *lymph*. (See figure 23.8.)

YOUR LYMPHATIC SYSTEM

Your lymphatic system is a kind of drain! It collects tissue fluid and returns it to your blood system. Lymph vessels are like veins: they have valves and thin walls. Lymph vessels are found all over your body. They have swellings called lymph glands along them. White cells are made in your lymph glands. Bacteria and other disease-causing organisms in the body are killed by these cells. Your tonsils are lymph glands. When you have an infection, your lymph glands are often painful. Your main lymph vessels empty the lymph from your lymphatic system into a vein in your neck. (See figure 23.9.)

Your lymphatic system:

1. helps to collect tissue fluid with wastes in it,
2. collects digested fat from your digestive system,
3. helps to fight disease.

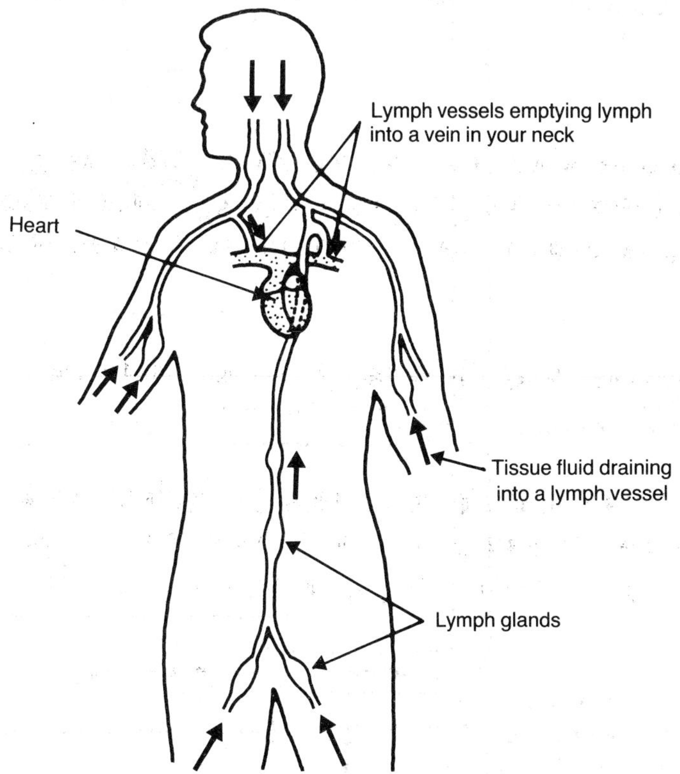

Figure 23.9 The main lymph vessels in your body

HEALTH AND CIRCULATION

As you get older the space inside your arteries may get smaller. This happens because a fatty substance blocks the arteries. This can start in children but the effects usually show up when people are over 40 years old. Narrow arteries may cut off the blood supply to part of your brain and cause a stroke. A heart attack can be caused by not enough blood getting to the heart because of narrow arteries. These diseases of the circulation may be caused by eating too much animal fat.

Standing still for a long time can make people faint. This is because blood collects in the veins of the legs and not enough reaches the brain.

Summary

Your *heart* pumps blood around your body. Blood moves in tubes called *blood vessels*. *Arteries* are blood vessels which take blood *away* from your heart. *Veins* are blood vessels which *return* blood to your heart. *Capillaries* are blood vessels which connect arteries and veins together.

Cells are cleaned and fed by *tissue fluid*. This is *blood plasma* which goes through the walls of your capillaries. The *lymphatic system* helps to collect up tissue fluid and return it to your blood system.

Important words

Blood vessels	arteries, veins and capillaries.
Artery	a blood vessel that takes blood away from your heart.
Vein	a blood vessel that takes blood back to your heart.
Capillary	a small blood vessel that joins an artery and a vein.
Circulatory system	your heart and blood vessels.
Pulmonary vein	a vein that carries oxygenated blood from your lungs to your heart.
Pulmonary artery	an artery that carries deoxygenated blood from your heart to your lungs.
Double circulation	a circulation in which blood goes through your heart twice before going round your body.
Aorta	the main artery that carries blood from your heart to your body.
Vena cava	the main vein that brings blood back to your heart from your body.
Hepatic portal vein	the vein that carries digested food from your digestive system to your liver.
Tissue fluid	liquid which surrounds your cells.
Blood plasma	the liquid part of the blood.
Lymphatic system	small tubes which carry away tissue fluid.
Lymph	a colourless liquid made of tissue fluid and white blood cells.

Things to do

Let your arm hang down by your side. Open and close your hand 250 times. Have a short rest. Now hold your hand above your head and open and close it agian. How many hand movements can you make now? What do you think has happened?

Fancy that!

"There are 48,274 kilometres of blood vessels in your body!

There are about 25 million million cells in a human body. Each one is very close to a capillary!"

Questions

A.

Put each of these parts of sentences into the correct order.

1.	round your body through your heart	twice before it is sent blood goes
2.	the artery which carries your aorta is	to your body blood from your heart
3.	from your digestive system your hepatic portal vein	carries digested food to your liver
4.	your renal vein your renal artery takes blood to	your kidney from where it is collected by

B.

Copy this into your book using another word (or words) for those in *italics*. Do not change the meaning of the sentences.

The *liquid part of your blood* passes out through your *smallest blood vessels* into your tissues and is then called tissue fluid. This takes food and *a gas needed for respiration* to your tissues. It collects waste substances such as *the gas produced in respiration*. The tissue fluid may then go into *vessels like veins* and is then called lymph fluid. The tissue fluid may go back into the *smallest blood vessels again* and is then called *the liquid part of the blood*.

C.

Figure 23.10 shows a capillary bed, together with some of the body cells it supplies.

1. In which direction is the blood flowing inside?
   (a) What name is given to the liquid which bathes all the cells?
   (b) Where has this liquid come from?
2. Give *two* ways in which this liquid is different from blood.
3. X is not a blood vessel. It helps to drain the liquid away from amongst the cells. What is X called?
4. Where does X take this liquid?

(NREB)

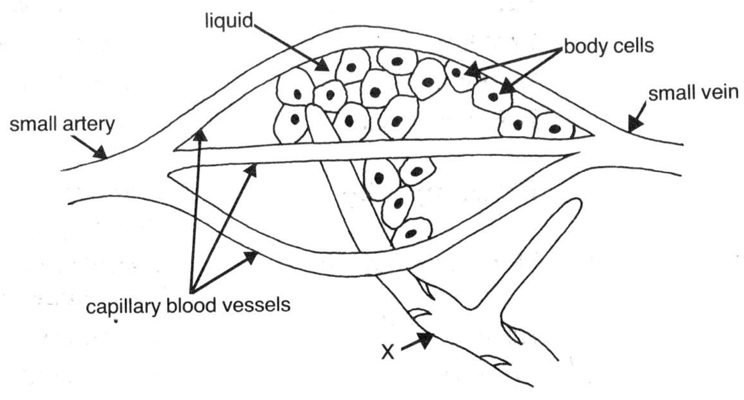

Figure 23.10

D.

Examine figure 23.11, which shows two cross-sections through mammalian blood vessels.

1. Which vessel is the artery? Give *two* reason for your choice.
2. Which vessel carries blood at high pressure? Give *one* reason for your choice from the figure.
3. How is backflow of blood prevented in veins?
4. Give *one* way in which an artery can help the movement of blood.

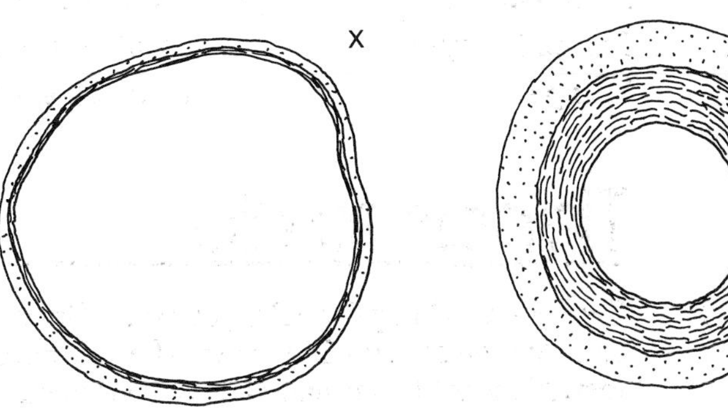

Figure 23.11

TOPIC 24

THE HEART

Blood is pumped round your body by your heart. This is a bag of thick muscle about the size of your fist. It has four 'rooms' or chambers inside. The top chambers are called *atria* (singular: *atrium*) and the bottom chambers are called *ventricles*.

The right side of your heart is drawn on *your* left as you look at figure 24.1. This is because the person is drawn lying on his or her back. Your heart is in the centre of your chest, but you feel your heart beat on the left side of your chest.

THE STRUCTURE OF YOUR HEART

Your right atrium and right ventricle are connected to each other. Your left atrium and left ventricle are also connected. There is no connection between the left and right sides *inside* your heart. The right and left sides are connected by the blood vessels of your circulatory system. Figure 24.3 shows you how.

Your atria are smaller than your ventricles and they have thinner walls. The left ventricle has the thickest wall. This is because it has to push blood all the way round your body. Your right ventricle only has to push blood a short distance to your lungs.

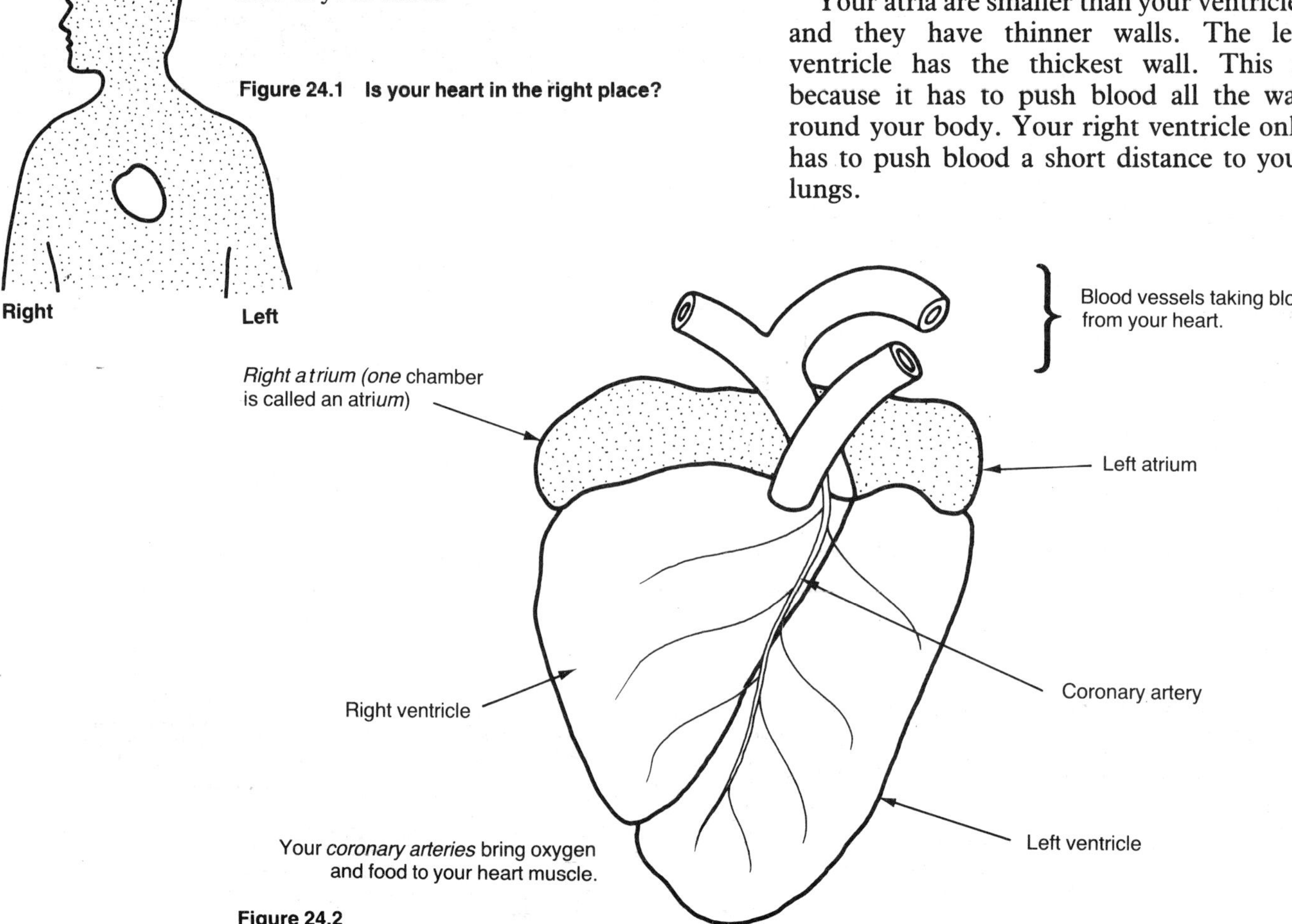

Figure 24.1 Is your heart in the right place?

Figure 24.2

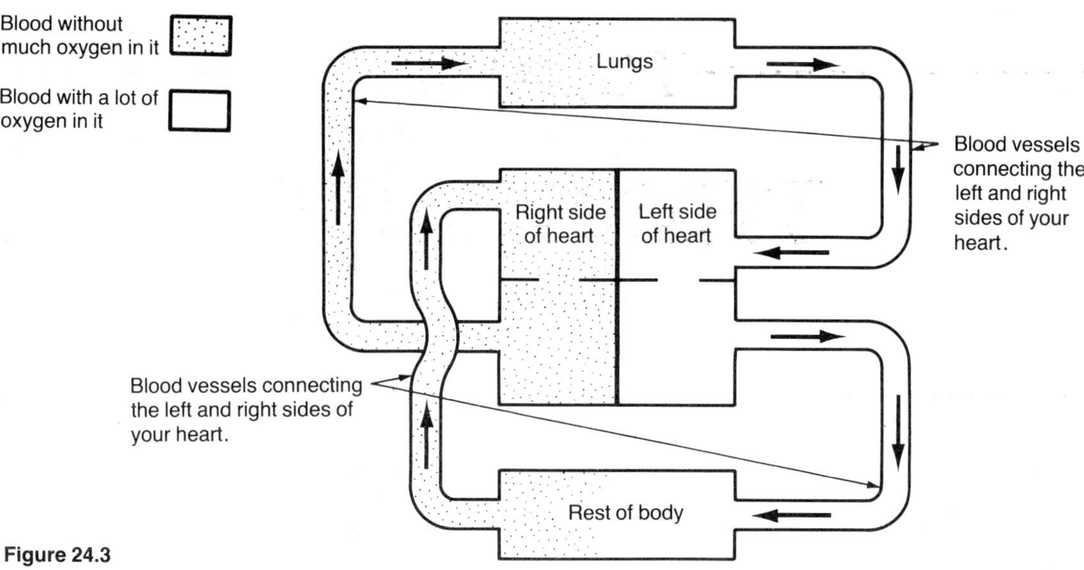

Figure 24.3

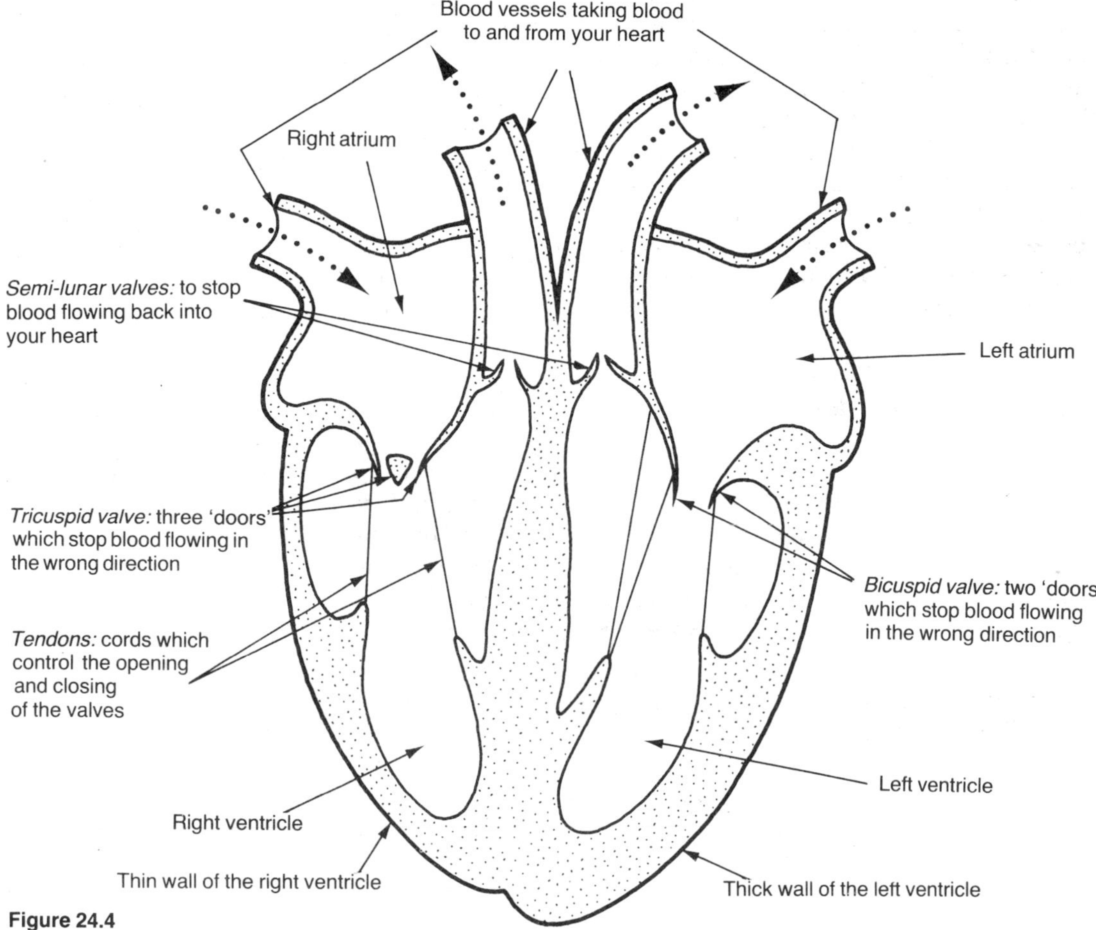

Figure 24.4

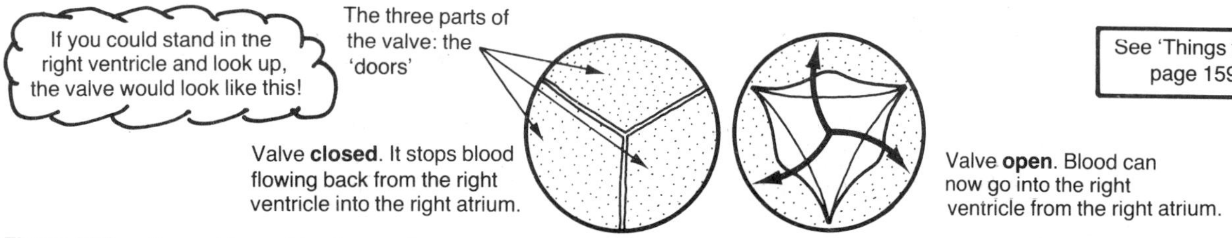

If you could stand in the right ventricle and look up, the valve would look like this!

The three parts of the valve: the 'doors'

Valve **closed**. It stops blood flowing back from the right ventricle into the right atrium.

Valve **open**. Blood can now go into the right ventricle from the right atrium.

See 'Things to do' page 159

Figure 24.5 How a tricuspid valve works

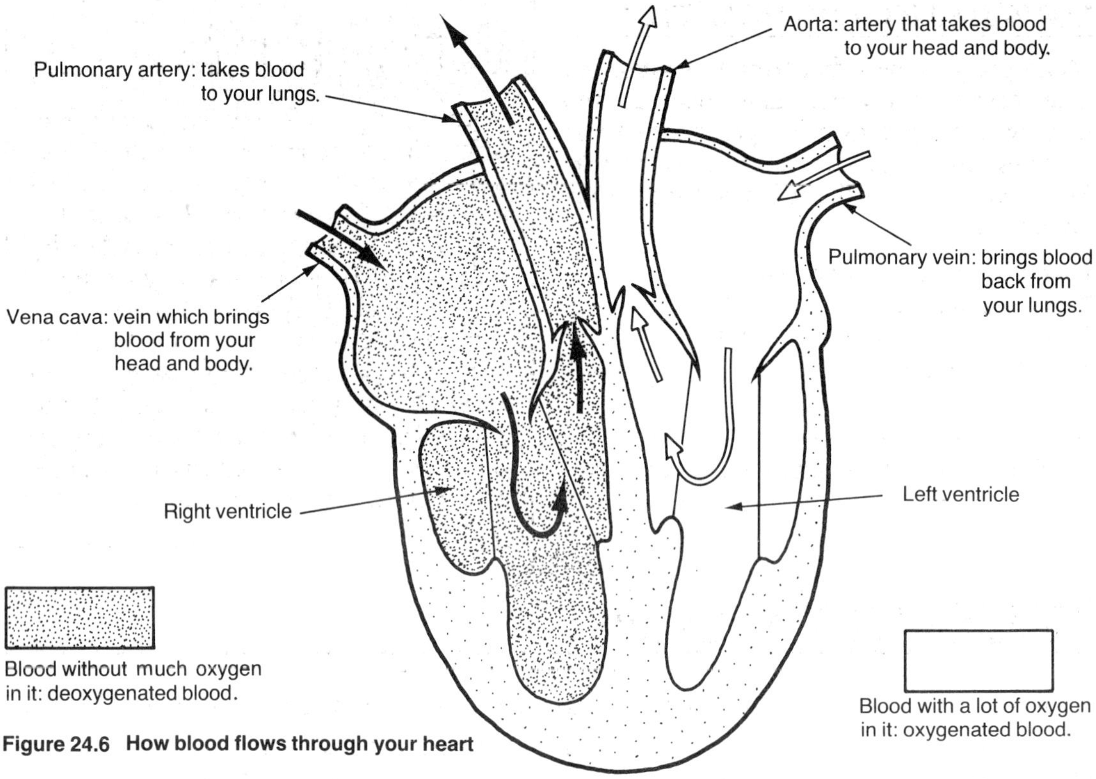

Pulmonary artery: takes blood to your lungs.

Aorta: artery that takes blood to your head and body.

Vena cava: vein which brings blood from your head and body.

Pulmonary vein: brings blood back from your lungs.

Right ventricle

Left ventricle

Blood without much oxygen in it: deoxygenated blood.

Blood with a lot of oxygen in it: oxygenated blood.

Figure 24.6 How blood flows through your heart

> **Fancy that!**
> Smaller animals have faster heart rates than large animals. Mice have heart rates of 740 a minute and elephants 25 a minute!

YOUR HEART AT WORK

Blood flows through your heart like this:

- deoxygenated blood from your head and body goes into your *right* atrium,
- then into your *right* ventricle,
- then to your lungs;

oxygenated blood comes back from your lungs and goes into

- your *left* atrium,
- then your *left* ventricle,
- then to your head and body.

Both atria fill and empty together and both ventricles fill and empty together. When the atria and ventricles *relax* they get bigger and *fill* with blood. When the atria and ventricles *contract* they get smaller and force blood *out*. Both your atria and ventricles hold a similar *volume* of blood.

The heart of an adult beats about 70 times a minute. During exercise or excitement this may increase to 150 times a minute.

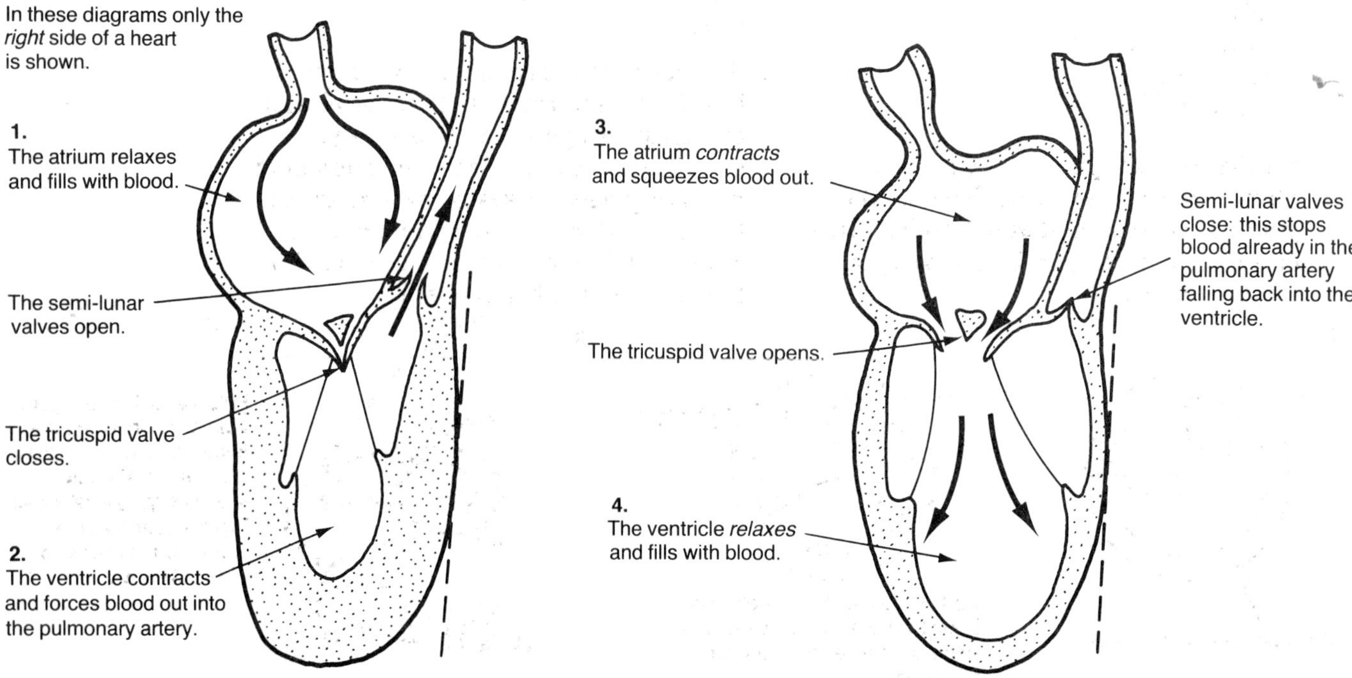

Figure 24.7 How a heart pumps

YOUR HEART AND HEALTH

Many people now suffer from heart disease. The coronary arteries may become too narrow. Not enough blood gets to the heart muscles and this causes a heart attack. People can decrease the risk of getting a heart attack by:

1. getting plenty of exercise,
2. not smoking,
3. eating less fat and more fruit,
4. not getting too fat.

Don't leave it too late – start now!!

Summary

Your heart has four chambers inside. The top two chambers are called *atria*. The two bottom chambers are called *ventricles*. The atria connect with the ventricles through holes controlled by *valves*. Blood goes through your heart *twice* on each journey round your body. The *right* atrium and ventricle pump *deoxygenated* blood; the *left* atrium and ventricle pump *oxygenated* blood. When an atrium or ventricle *contracts* it *empties* blood out; when an atrium or ventricle *relaxes* it *fills* with blood.

Important words

Atrium	one of the two top chambers in the heart (plural: atria).
Ventricle	one of the two lower chambers in the heart.
Coronary arteries	small arteries that bring blood (containing food and oxygen) to the heart muscle.
Semi-lunar valves	small valves that stop blood flowing back into the heart from the aorta and pulmonary artery.
Triscuspid valve	a valve between the right atrium and right ventricle.
Bicuspid valve	a valve between the left atrium and left ventricle.

Things to do

1. Make a model of a tricuspid valve.

   You will need:
   scissors
   a drawing compass
   white card
   a craft knife.

   Set the compass points 2.5 cm apart Draw a circle on the card. Now set the points 2 cm apart and draw another circle inside the first. Figure 24.8 shows you what to do next.

2. Buy a sheep's heart from the butchers. Open it up and try to find all the main parts (use figure 24.2 and 24.4 to help you).

3. As your ventricles contract they force blood into your arteries. These swell and this is called a pulse. The pulse at your wrist is easy to find. Count the number of beats your pulse makes in one minute. Do this sitting down and then after exercise. How long does your pulse take to return to the lower number of beats?

1.

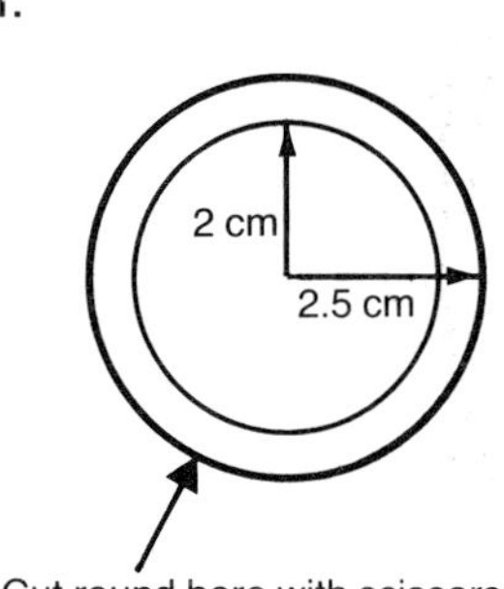

2.

DO NOT CUT HERE

Mark 3 lines like this; carefully cut along the lines marked by arrows with a craft knife; don't cut the 3 'hinges'.

3.

Hold the rim between your thumb and finger. Push a finger through the middle of the flaps: they move apart easily; try to take your finger out and the flaps grip it. How is this like a tricuspid valve?

Figure 24.8

Questions

A.

Write out each sentence in your book. Fill in the missing words from those in the box. Some words may bc uscd morc than once.

left — right — ventricle — tricuspid — heart rate — pulmonary artery — coronary arteries — oxygenated — atrium — semi-lunar — vena cava — deoxygenated — thinner — relax

1. Your heart beat is felt on the ...... side of your chest.
2. Each of the top two chambers in your heart is called an ....
3. Your ...... take oxygen and food to your heart muscle.
4. Your right atrium and right ventricle connect through the ...... valve.
5. The ...... side of your heart contains deoxygenated blood.
6. Your left ...... has the thickest wall of the four chambers.
7. Your ...... valve has three flaps.
8. Blood does not flow back into your heart because of the ...... valves.
9. Your atria have ...... walls than your ventricles.
10. Blood is taken from your heart to your lungs by the ....
11. Your ...... brings blood to your heart from your head and body.
12. Blood without oxygen is called ....
13. Your aorta contains ...... blood.
14. When your atria and ventricles ...... they fill with blood.
15. During exercise your ...... increases.

B.

Read the following passage carefully and then copy it into your book correcting the mistakes.

Your atrium is bigger than your ventricles and have thicker walls. Your left atria has the thickest wall because it has to push blood to your lungs. Your right ventricle only has to push blood to your body.

C.

Figure 24.8 is a diagram of a mammalian heart.

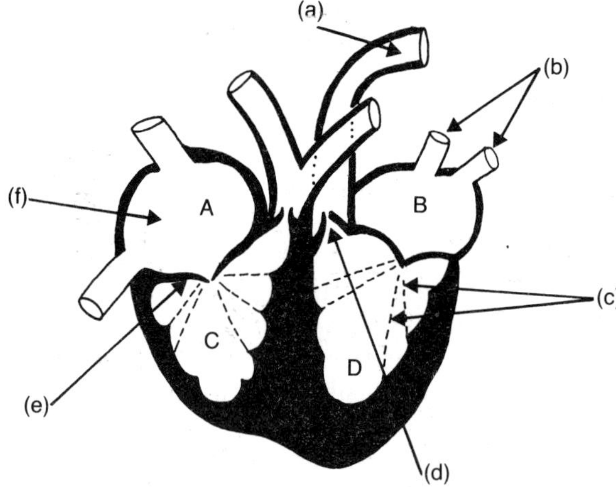

Figure 24.8

1. Label the parts (a) to (f).
2. Which chamber of the heart (A,B,C or D) first receives blood from the lungs?
3. Why is the wall of chamber D thicker than the wall of chamber C?
4. Why does the heart contain valves?
5. The heart is made of a unique type of muscle. What is this muscle called and how is it different from any other type of muscle?
6. In the developing embryo most of the blood by-passes the lungs through a connection between the right and left auricles. This connection closes at birth. Why do the embryonic lungs not require much blood supply?

(SREB)

D.

Figure 24.9 shows the rate of a human heart beat.

1. What was (a) the slowest rate and (b) the fastest rate?
2. What might have caused the change from the normal heart beat?
3. How long did it take before the heart beat returned from the maximum rate to normal?

(SEREB)

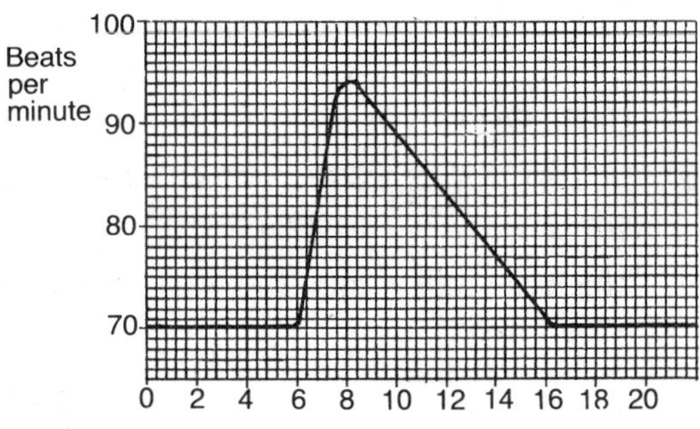

Figure 24.9

TOPIC 25

BLOOD

Blood is a liquid which carries food, oxygen and waste substances quickly round your body. All the cells in your body must have a supply of blood or they will die.

Blood is pushed round your blood system by your heart. Unless something goes wrong, blood never leaves your blood system.

Blood is made up of the parts shown in figure 25.1

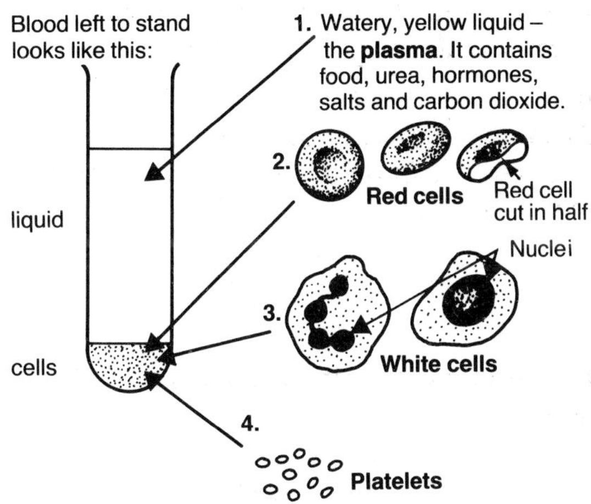

Figure 25.1

RED CELLS

Red cells have *haemoglobin* in them. This is a red substance which easily picks up oxygen. The oxygen is then carried by your red cells to all parts of your body. Red blood cells have no nucleus. They are made in your bone marrow and they live for about four months. Your liver destroys the old red cells. Figure 25.2 shows how haemoglobin works.

1. Haemoglobin in your red blood cells picks up oxygen from the air in your lungs. The haemoglobin is now called *oxyhaemoglobin*. Haemoglobin is dark red and oxyhaemoglobin is bright red.
2. Oxyhaemoglobin gives up its oxygen to cells which don't have much oxygen in them. The cells use the oxygen for respiration.
3. As it gives up its oxygen, oxyhaemoglobin changes back to haemoglobin.
4. Haemoglobin picks up more oxygen in your lungs.

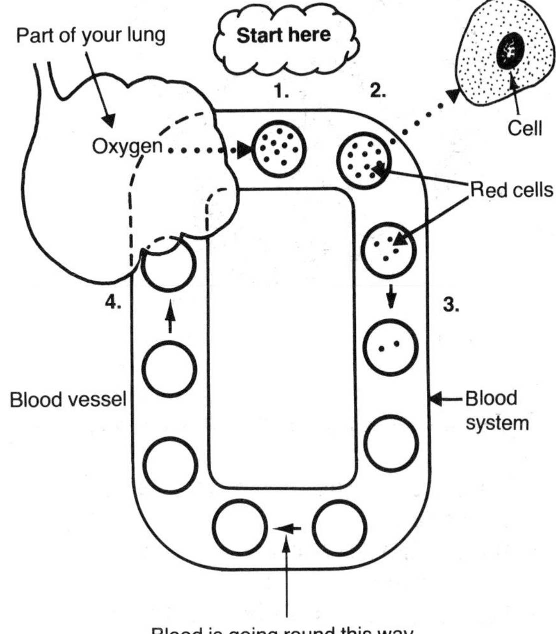

Figure 25.2

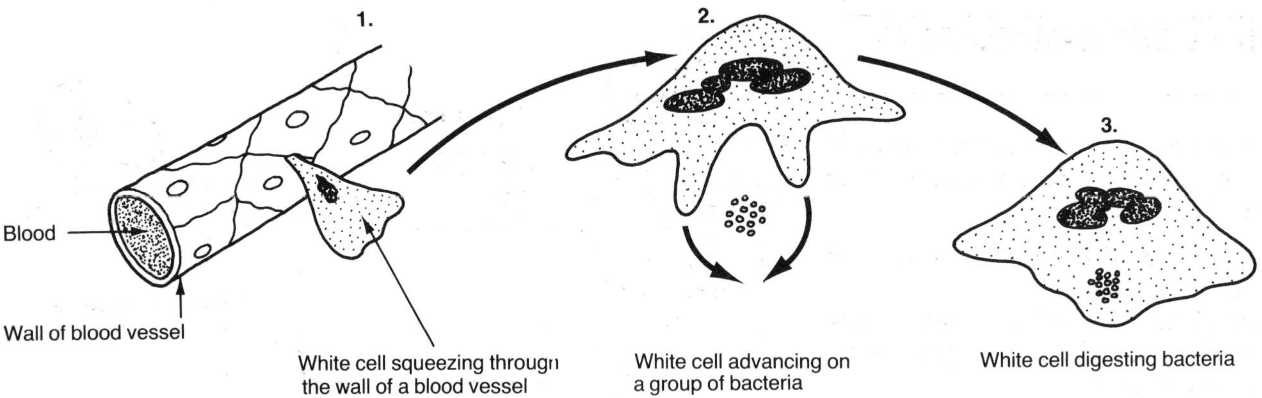

Figure 25.3 How white cells kill bacteria

WHITE CELLS

White blood cells have a nucleus and are made in your bone marrow and lymphatic system. There are different kinds of white cells. Some can change their shape like Amoeba. They can squeeze through the walls of your blood vessels and move between your cells. They digest bacteria and damaged cells. There are about 600 red cells to every white cell. (See figure 25.3.)

GRAND MATCH!
BACTERIA
V
WHITE CELLS

Bertie Bacterium, a germ of great charm,
Was deep in a cut in Anthony's arm.
Bertie's poisons and wastes were made
with great skill
And made our poor Anthony feel quite ill.
But young Anthony knew that all would
be well
When off to the rescue he sent BIG
WHITE CELL.
Now Bertie and friends have all
disappeared,
For, thanks to BIG WHITE, all
infection has cleared!

PLATELETS

When a blood vessel is cut your *platelets* set free a chemical. This chemical changes a protein in your blood into fibrin. Fibrin quickly makes a sticky net which stops any more blood getting out of the blood vessel. The sticky net makes a blood clot which dries and turns into a scab. (See figure 25.4.)

As well as:

1. carrying oxygen,
2. killing bacteria and
3. clotting,

blood has other important jobs. (See figure 25.5. to 25.8 opposite.)

Fancy that!
There are about 5.5 litres of blood in an adult man!

Scientists are trying to make artificial blood!

A red blood cell takes about 45 seconds to make one journey round your body!

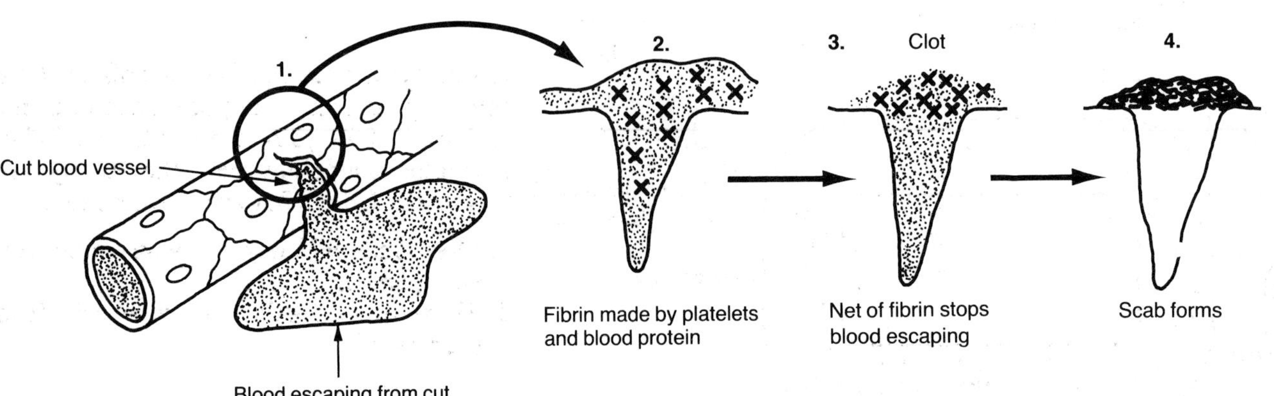

Figure 25.4 How blood clots

BLOOD'S OTHER IMPORTANT JOBS

Carbon dioxide is a waste substance made in all cells and must be removed from your body. (See figure 25.5.)

1. Carbon dioxide diffuses from your cells into your blood.
2. Carbon dioxide is carried to your lungs.
3. Carbon dioxide diffuses into your lungs and you breathe it out.
4. 'Cleaned-up' blood returns to your blood system.

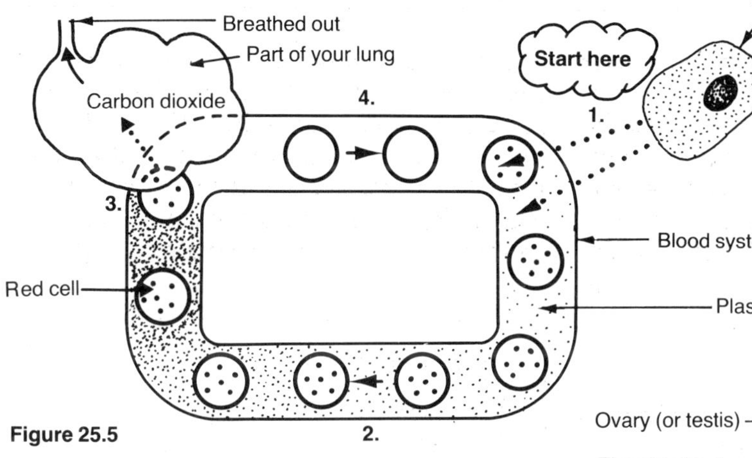

Figure 25.5

Liver cells make a substance called urea from unwanted amino acids. Urea must be removed from your body. (See figure 25.6.)

1. Urea diffuses from your liver cells into your blood.
2. Urea is carried by your blood to your kidneys.
3. Urea is taken out of your blood by your kidneys.
4. 'Cleaned-up' blood returns to your blood system.
5. Wastes (now called urine) leave your kidneys and go to your bladder.

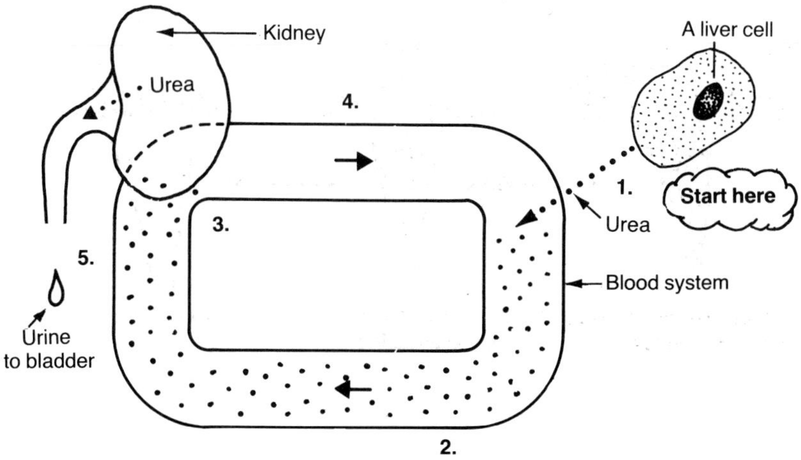

Figure 25.6

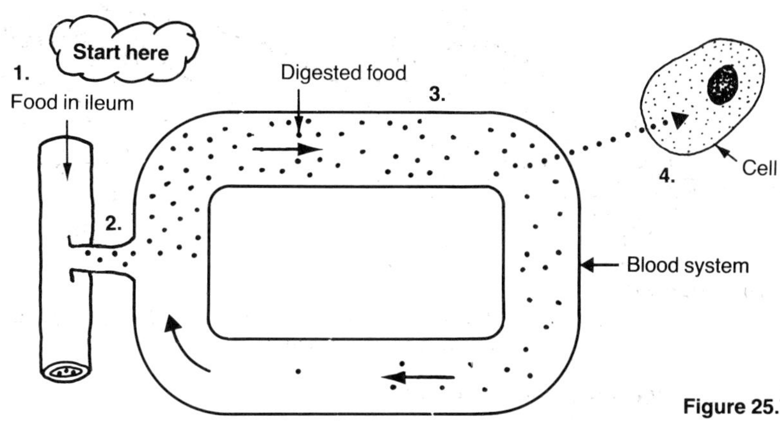

Figure 25.7

Your cells need food to keep them alive. This food is carried to your cells in your blood plasma. (See figure 25.7.)

1. Digested food in your digestive system.
2. Digested food is absorbed from your digestive system and goes into your blood.
3. Food is carried to your cells by your blood.
4. Food diffuses into your cells and they use it for growth, respiration etc.

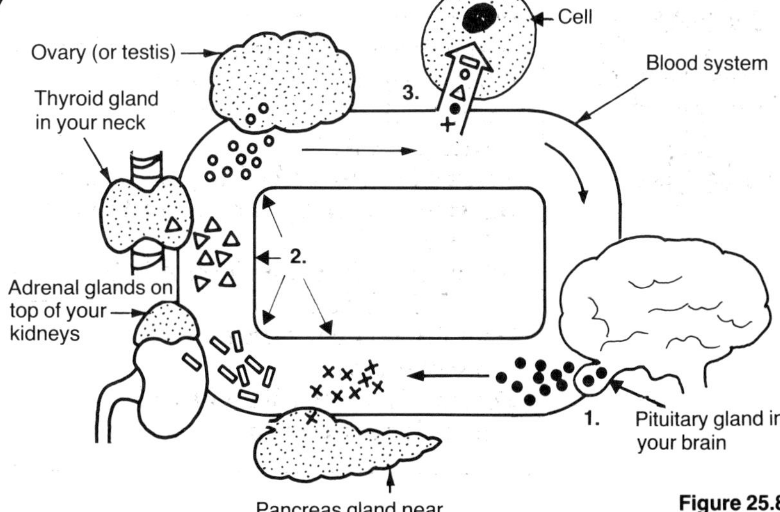

Figure 25.8

Hormones are chemicals which affect all the cells in your body. They are made in glands and carried in your blood plasma. When hormones reach your cells they change the way in which the cells work. (See figure 25.8.)

1. Hormones diffusing into your blood from your glands.
2. Hormones diffusing into your cells from your blood.

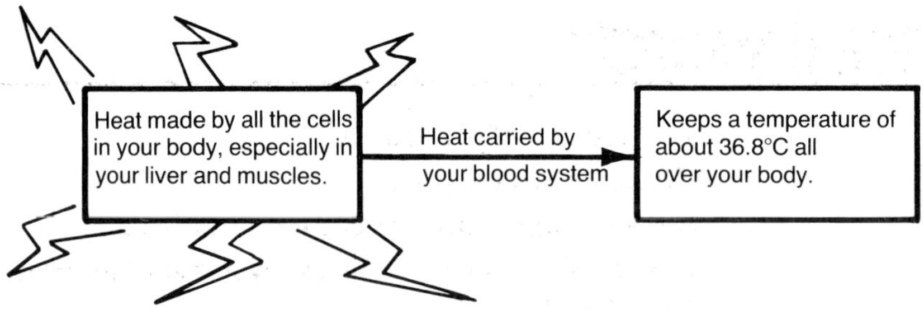

Heat made by all the cells in your body, especially in your liver and muscles.

Heat carried by your blood system

Keeps a temperature of about 36.8°C all over your body.

Figure 25.9 Blood carries heat around your body

PROTECTION FROM DISEASE

Some white cells make chemicals called *antibodies* when they kill bacteria. These antibodies can also kill bacteria (and viruses). Your body 'remembers' how to make antibodies which is useful if a disease attacks again. The second time this happens the disease will probably be quickly overcome. Antibodies you make against, say, measles can only attack measles viruses: they cannot kill other viruses or bacteria.

People who have some antibodies against a disease, or can make them, are *immune* from that disease. This means that they do not catch it (see figure 25.10).

Antibodies can not always stop you from getting a disease but they often make it less serious. People can be *given* immunity with a *vaccine* made from weakened or dead disease-causing bacteria or viruses. This can be injected into your body. Your body can then 'learn' how to make antibodies against the disease injected. Immunity you are given can last for a few months or several years and is called artifical immunity.

BLOOD DONORS

Blood often has to be given to people who bleed after accidents or operations. People who give blood are called blood donors. If you are a blood donor about 500 cm^3 of blood is taken from a vein in your arm. The blood is stored in a 'blood bank' in a hospital. Some of it is used to make antibodies for vaccines.

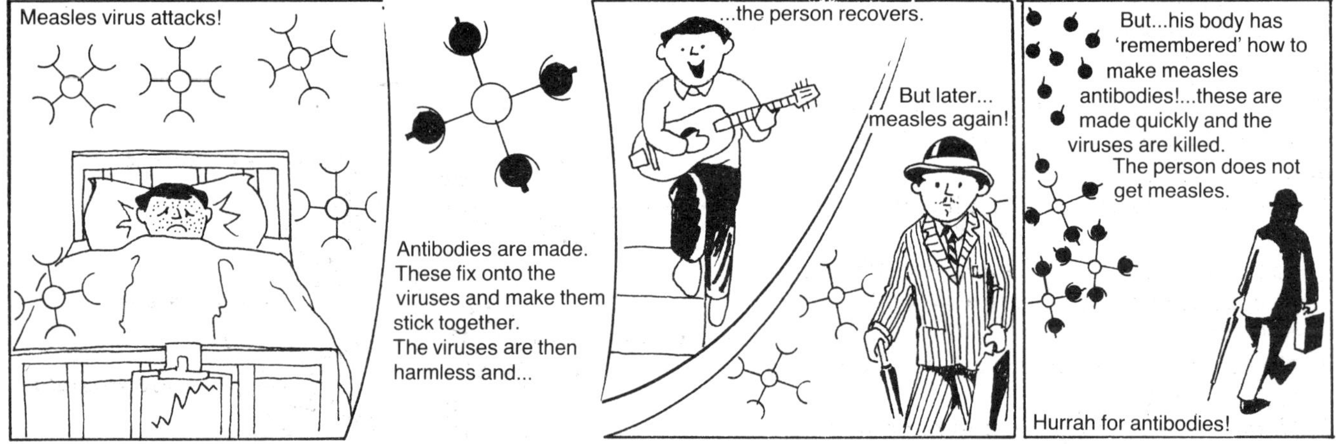

Figure 25.10

Summary

Blood is pushed round your blood system by your heart. Blood takes *food*, *oxygen* and *hormones* to your cells and carries away waste substances such as *carbon dioxide*. It also carries away the waste substance *urea* from your liver.

Red blood cells contain *haemoglobin*. When this picks up oxygen it is called *oxyhaemoglobin* which is bright red. When oxyhaemoglobin loses its oxygen it changes back to haemoglobin which is dark red.

White blood cells attack bacteria in your body and also help to make *antibodies*.

Blood *platelets* make blood *clot* if it escapes from your blood system.

Blood carries *heat* made by chemical reactions inside cells to all parts of your body.

Important words

Plasma	the liquid part of your blood.
Red cells	cells which carry oxygen.
White cells	cells which digest bacteria and make antibodies.
Platelets	parts of cells (from bone marrow) which start the process of blood clotting.
Antibodies	chemical substances made by some white cells.
Vaccine	a liquid made from dead or weakened disease-causing bacteria or viruses and used to give artificial immunity against disease.
Immunity	the ability to overcome an attack of a disease.
Haemoglobin	the chemical inside red cells which picks up oxygen. Some animals such as earthworms also have haemoglobin.
Oxyhaemoglobin	haemoglobin which has picked up oxygen.

Questions

A.
Put each of these parts of sentences into the correct order.

1.	some white blood cells make chemicals called antibodies	attacking your cells which kill bacteria
2.	the walls of blood vessels and digest bacteria	which may be attacking your cells some white cells get through
3.	if the disease returns be made again quickly	a disease can antibodies made against
4.	vaccines which stop certain diseases	antibodies can be given as people getting

B
Figure 25.11 represents human blood as seen through a microscope using high power magnification.

1. Which of the structures labelled in figure 25.11 are responsible for: (a) the transport of oxygen; (b) making antibodies (c) engulfing bacteria; and (d) blood clotting?
2. Name *four* substances transported in the blood plasma.
3. Name the pigment present in red blood cells. Which mineral element is required in the diet for the formation of this pigment?
4. Name the body condition which is caused by a shortage of red blood cells. State *one* symptom of this body condition.

(EAEB)

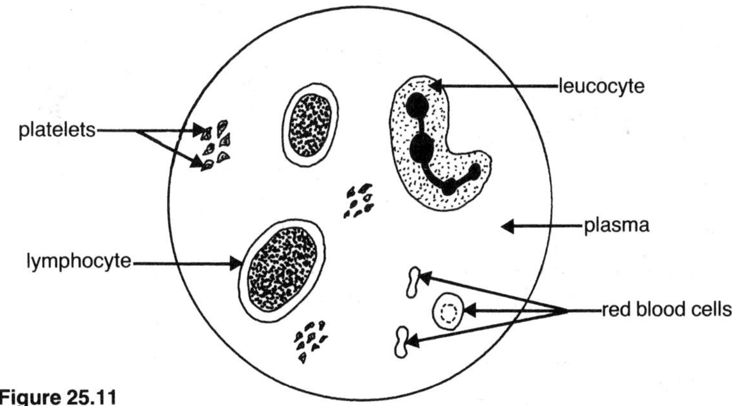

Figure 25.11

C.
Write about what you think figure 25.12 shows.

D.
1. Write about what is happening in figure 25.8
2. Write about what happens when you cut your finger.

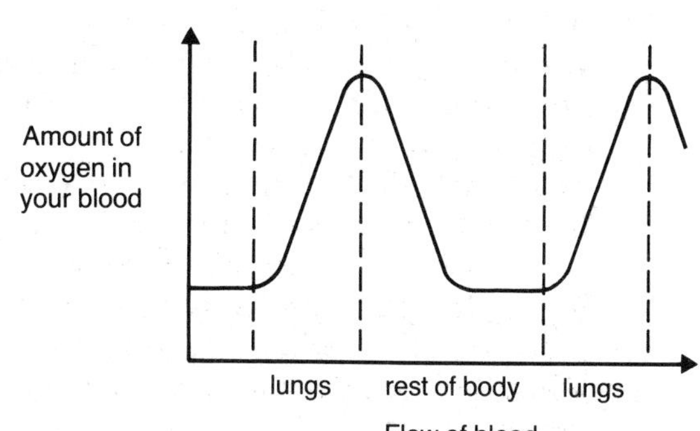

Figure 25.12

TOPIC 26

HUMAN BREATHING

You breathe when air is moved in and out of your lungs. Your lungs are part of your respiratory system and are inside your chest or thorax. They are protected by your ribs.

INSIDE YOUR CHEST

Your lungs are two pink stretchy bags with very thin walls. They connect with the air outside your body through your windpipe and your two bronchi (each one is called a bronchus). Your bronchi divide into smaller tubes or bronchioles which have air sacs at the ends. Your chest cavity is separated from your abdominal cavity by your diaphragm. (See figures 26.1, 26.2 and 26.3.)

As you look at figures 26.1 and 26.2, the left side of the chest is on YOUR right. This is because they have been drawn as if the person was lying on his or her back.

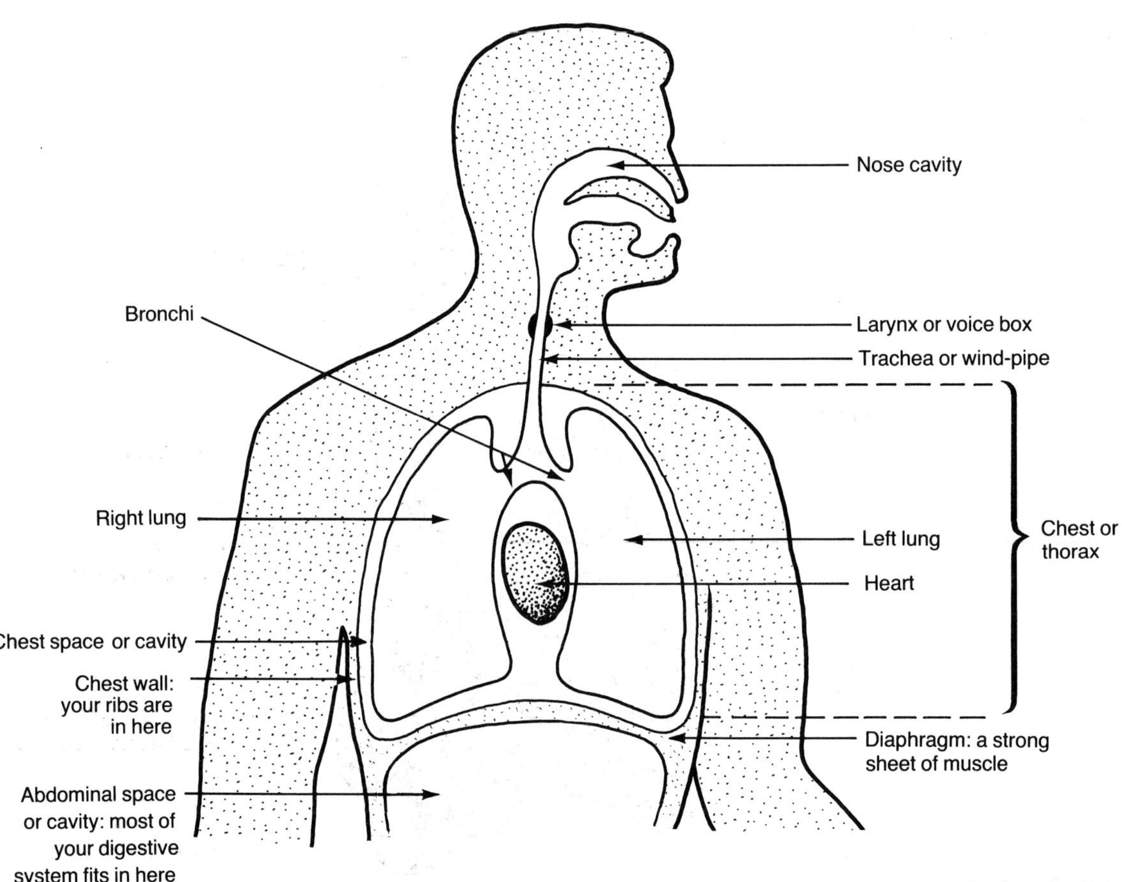

Figure 26.1

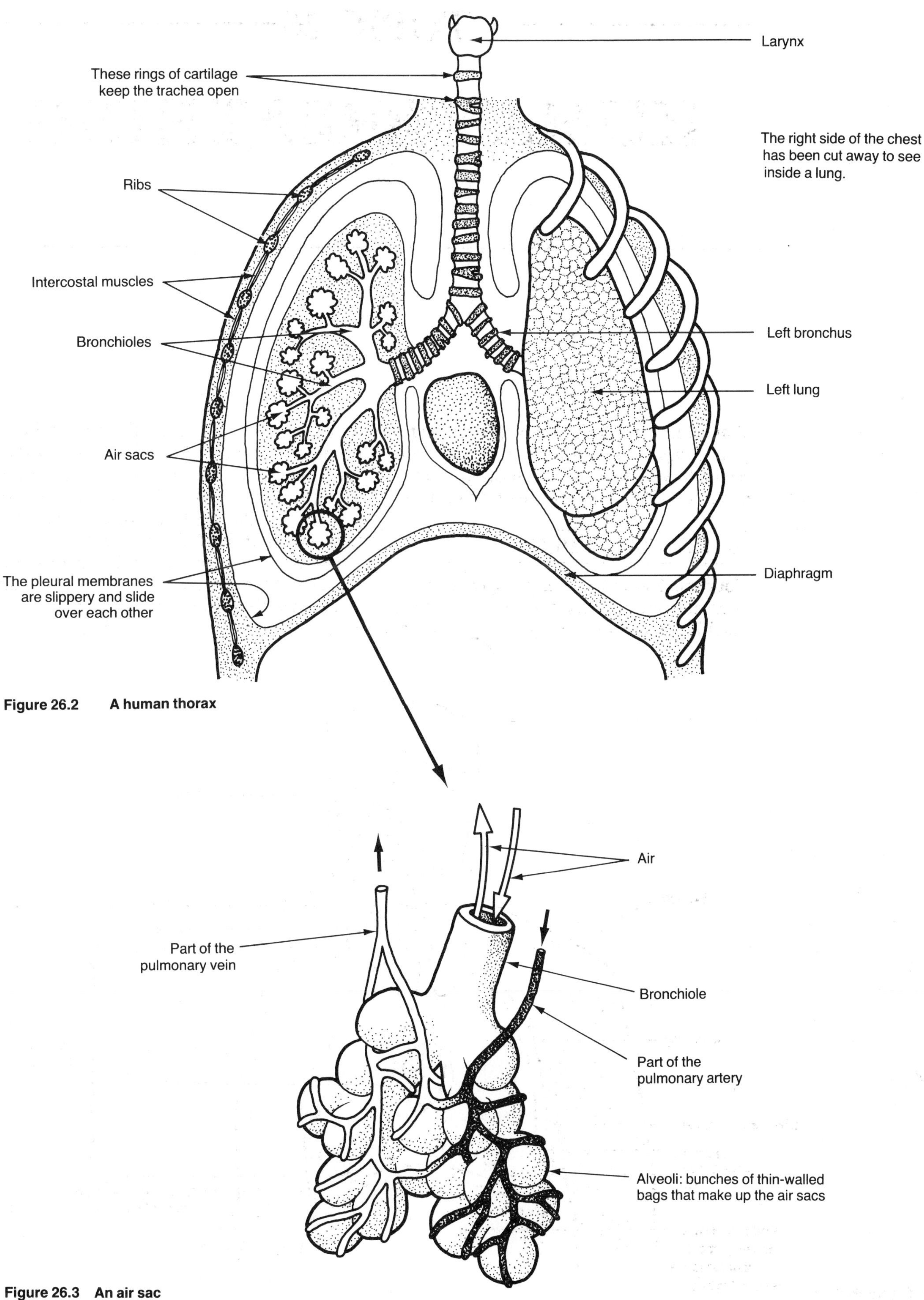

Figure 26.2 **A human thorax**

Figure 26.3 **An air sac**

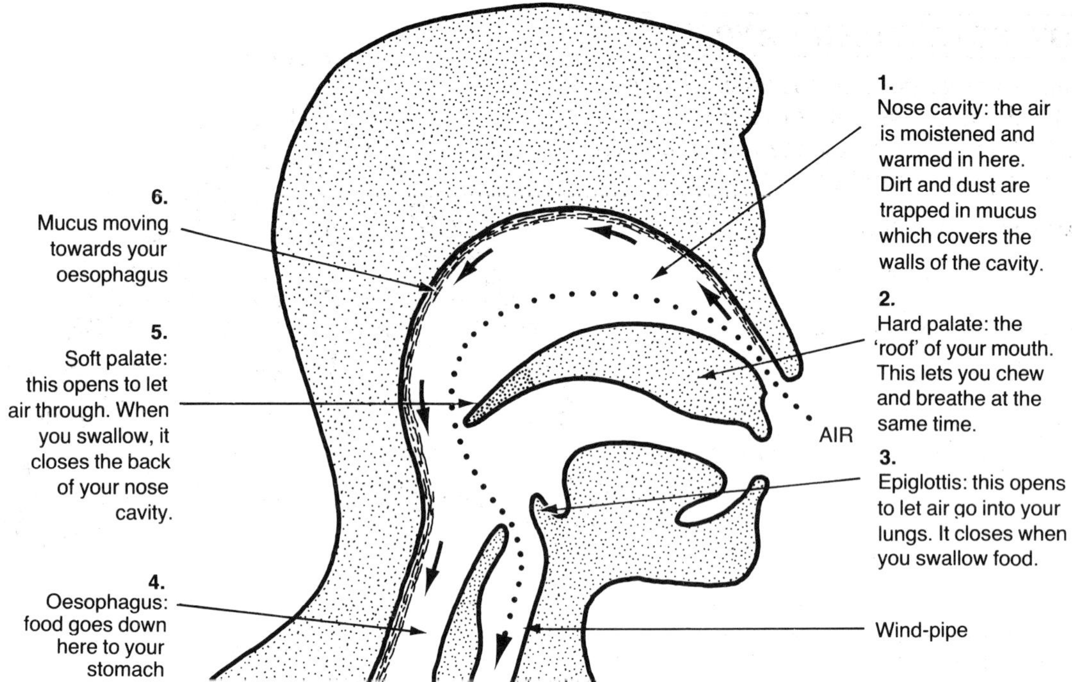

Figure 26.4 What happens in your nose

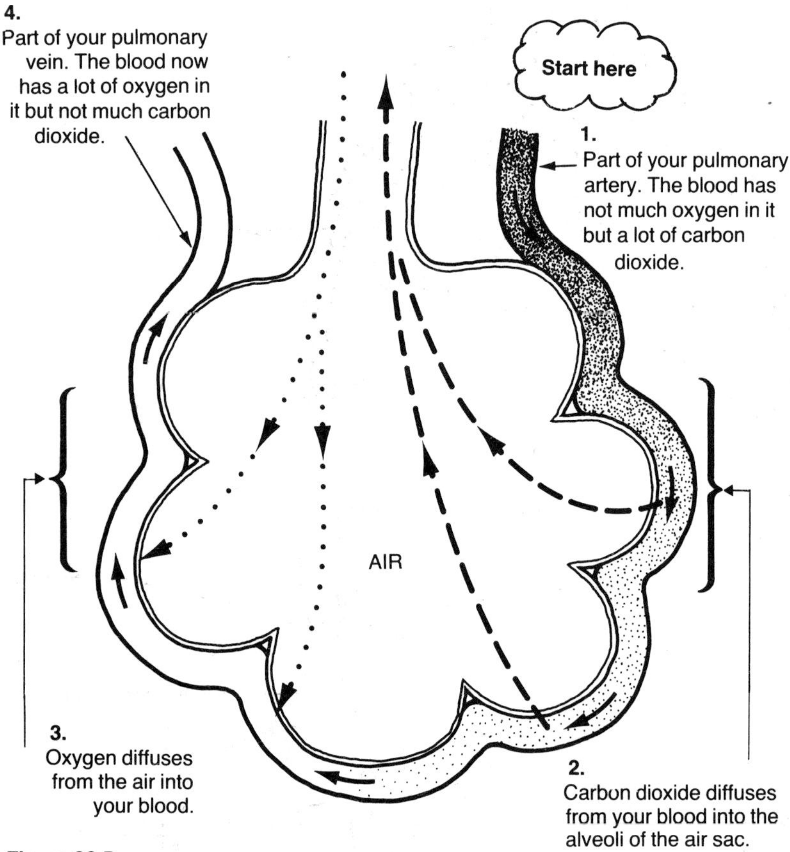

Figure 26.5

Mucus is made by cells which line your nose cavity. The mucus is moved towards your oesophagus and takes dust and dirt with it. In a dog, the mucus is moved towards its nose which is why it is always wet.

WHAT HAPPENS IN YOUR ALVEOLI

Carbon dioxide diffuses from your blood into the air in your alveoli (singular: alveolus). Oxygen diffuses from the air in your alveoli into your blood. This 'swopping' of oxygen and carbon dioxide is called gaseous exchange. (See figure 26.5.)

Diffusion of oxygen and carbon dioxide in gaseous exchange is helped by:

1. the thin walls of your alveoli,
2. the layer of moisture in your alveoli.

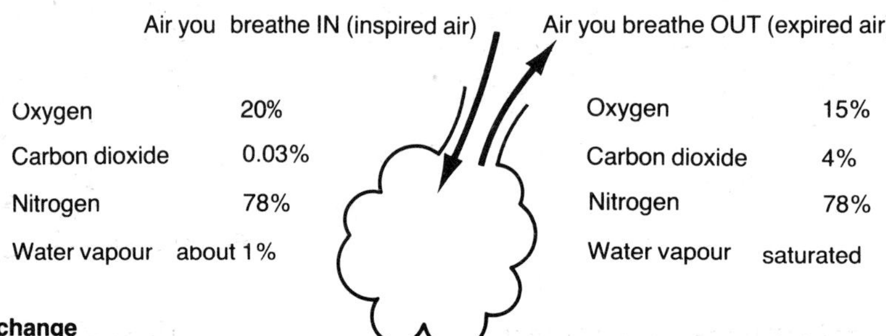

Figure 26.6 What happens in gaseous exchange

HOW BREATHING HAPPENS

Your diaphragm and intercostal muscles make air go into and out of your lungs. Air is pushed in and out by making your chest cavity bigger or smaller.

Breathing in (inspiration)

Your chest cavity is made *bigger* when:

1. Your ribs move up and out. This happens when your intercostal muscles contract.

2. Your diaphragm flattens out from its usual dome shape. This happens when your diaphragm muscles contract.

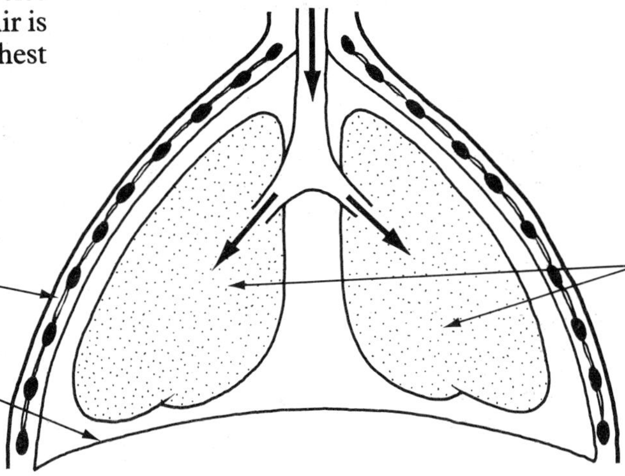

Air is pushed into your lungs to fill up the bigger space in your chest cavity.

Breathing out (expiration)

Your chest cavity is made *smaller* when:

1. Your ribs move down and in. This happens when your intercostal muscles relax.

2. Your diaphragm goes back to its usual dome shape. This happens when your diaphragm muscles relax.

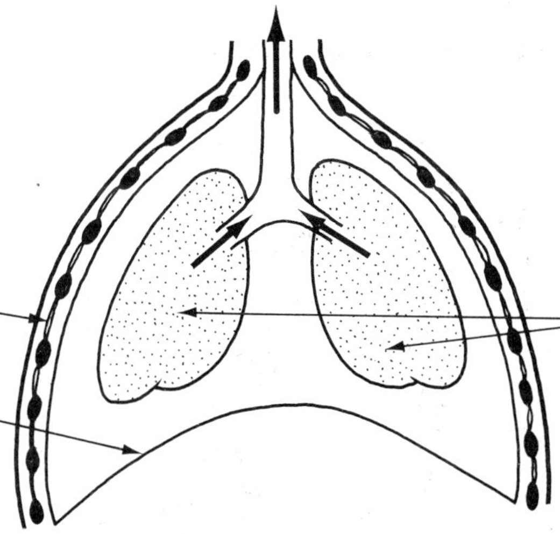

Air is pushed out of your lungs as the space in your chest cavity gets smaller.

Figure 26.7

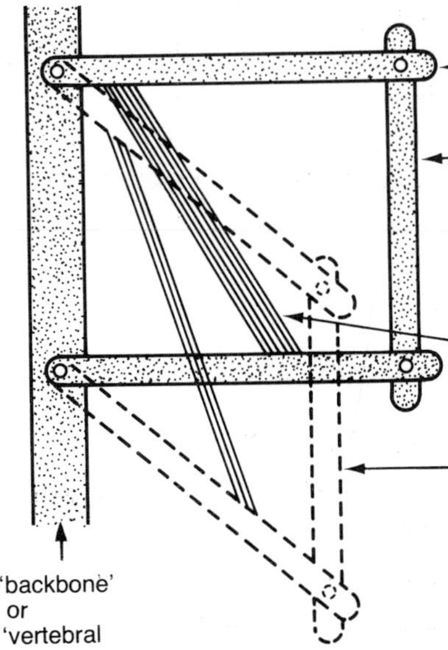

Figure 26.8 This model shows how your ribs work

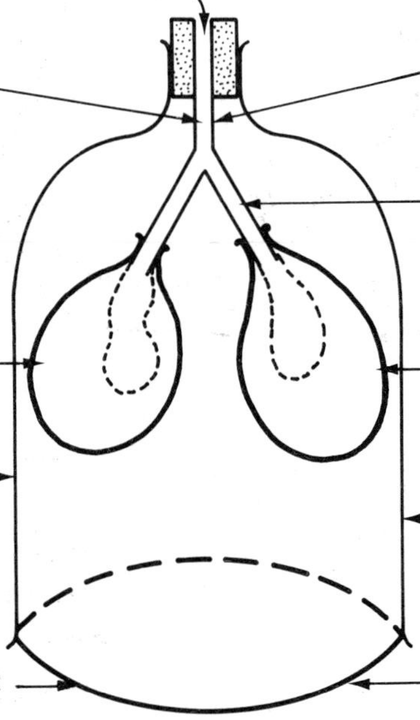

Figure 26.9 This model shows how your diaphragm works

SMOKING AND HEALTH

Figure 26.10 shows how many thousands of men died in Britain in 1978 from diseases caused by smoking. The men were aged 35–64.

Smoking is a dangerous habit. More than one in ten cigarette smokers will get lung cancer, heart disease or bronchitis. Cancer is a disease in which cells keep growing out of control and damage other cells. In bronchitis, breathing becomes difficult because a person's bronchioles and air sacs fill with mucus. Heart disease affects arteries which bring blood to the heart. Some people get these diseases even if they have never smoked. They are much more likely to get them if they smoke however. Smoking is a habit which is hard to give up. Half the people who smoke want to stop but cannot do so.

85 out of every 100 teenagers who start smoking can't stop.

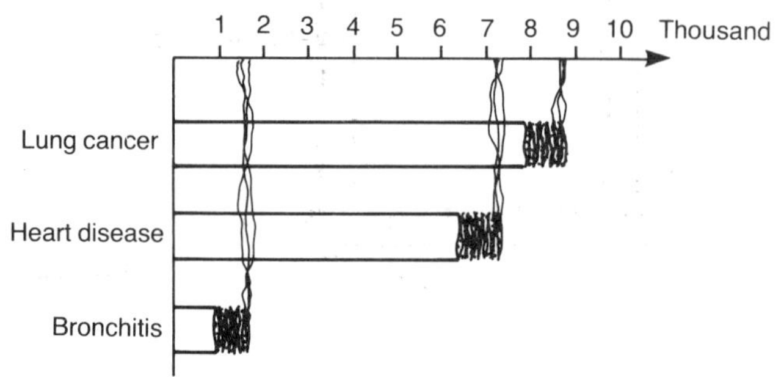

Figure 26.10

Fancy that!

There are about 300 million alveoli in your lungs! If you spread them out flat they would cover an area the size of a tennis court!

Smokers lose about 5½ minutes of their lives for every cigarette they smoke!

An adult's lungs hold about 5 litres of air!

Pauline Kite of the Lower Third
Was nowhere to be seen or heard.
She should have been with Mrs Palmer
Learning dance and doing drama
But Pauline felt she'd had enough.
At least two lessons without a puff!
Smoking made her feel quite grand,
She didn't really understand:
Cancer? Bronchitis? – what a joke
NOTHING'S more important than a smoke!

Summary

Air moves in and out of your lungs when you breathe. Air is pushed into your lungs when your diaphragm *lowers* and your ribs move *upwards*. This is called *inspiration*. Air is pushed out of your lungs when your diaphragm lifts *upwards* and your ribs move *downwards*. This is called *expiration*. In your *alveoli* oxygen from the air diffuses into your blood. Carbon dioxide in your blood diffuses into your alveoli. This is called *gaseous exchange*. Smoking may cause lung cancer, heart disease and bronchitis.

Important words

Trachea	the tube taking air from your nose and mouth into your chest.
Bronchus	a tube taking air from your trachea into each lung (plural: bronchi).
Bronchioles	small tubes made by branches of the bronchi.
Alveolus	a small bag with thin walls at the end of a bronchiole (plural: alveoli)
Gaseous exchange	the exchange of carbon dioxide and oxygen by diffusion through the alveoli.
Diaphragm	a sheet of muscle between your thorax and abdomen.
Intercostal muscles	muscles between your ribs.

Things to do

Make a working model of the ribs.
You will need:
- some strong cardboard (corrugated cardboard from a box will do)
- 4 brass paper fasteners
- an elastic band about 12 cm long
- a sharp craft knife.

Cut 4 strips of card 20 cm long by 2 cm wide. Make a hole with the craft knife at each end of the strips. Fix the strips into a square using the paper fasteners.

Make a hole at A and at B (see figure 26.11). Cut the elastic band open. Thread one end through A and knot it. Thread the other end through B and knot it. Hold the 'backbone' upright in your left hand and pull the 'breast-bone' down. Is the rubber band, or 'intercostal muscle', contracted or relaxed?

Now let the 'breastbone' go and see what happens.

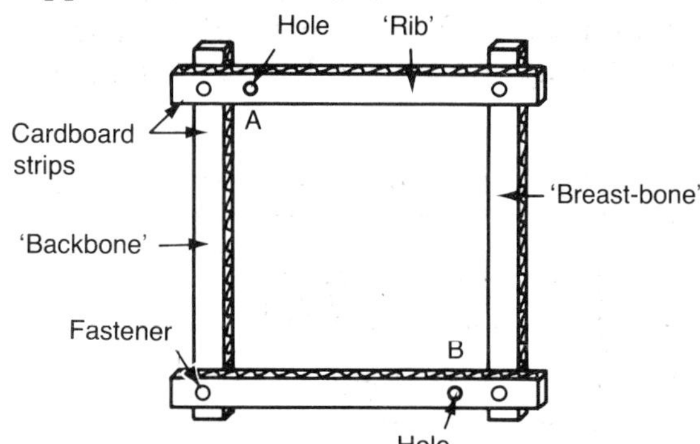

Figure 26.11

Questions

A.
Copy this into your book and correct the mistakes.

Your pulmonary artery takes blood away from your lungs. The blood in it contains a lot of oxygen but not much carbon dioxide. Oxygen diffuses from the blood in your pulmonary artery into your bronchioles. Your pulmonary vein carries blood to your lungs. The blood in your pulmonary vein contains a lot of oxygen but not much carbon dioxide. Gaseous exchange is the exchange of carbon dioxide in the alveoli. Expired air contains more oxygen and carbon dioxide than inspired air.

B.
Join these sentences together using either the word 'because' or the word 'and' whichever is correct.
1. Air is pushed into your lungs. Your intercostal and diaphragm muscles contract.
2. During inspiration your chest cavity is made bigger. Air is pushed into your lungs.
3. During expiration your chest cavity is made smaller. Your intercostal and diaphragm muscles relax.
4. During expiration your chest cavity is made smaller. Air is pushed out of your lungs.

C.
1. Why is there more water vapour in expired air than in inspired air?
2. Explain why the balloons empty and fill with air in figure 26.9.
3. How many thousands of men died in 1978 because of diseases caused by smoking?
4. Explain what happens in gaseous exchange.

D.
Figure 26.12 shows some of the bones and muscles from the chest region of a man.
1. Name the structures A, B, C and D.
2. What is the function of structure X? Explain how a physical property of structure X assists its function.
3. What happens to structure C when structure D contracts?

(NEA)

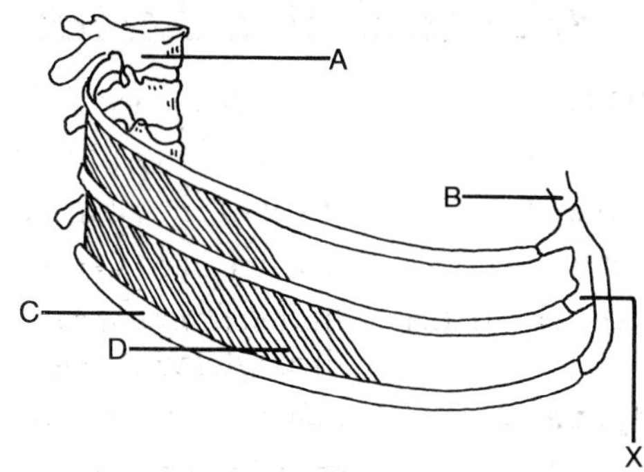

Figure 26.12

TOPIC 27

BREATHING IN ANIMALS

WHAT BREATHING ORGANS DO

The breathing organs of animals exchange oxygen and carbon dioxide with air or water in the surroundings. Oxygen diffuses through their breathing organs into their blood. Carbon dioxide in their blood diffuses through their breathing organs into the air or water. (See figure 27.1.)

The breathing organs of all animals are thin and moist. This helps the exchange of oxygen and carbon dioxide to happen quickly.

The surfaces of breathing organs are usually folded to make them bigger. A big surface can exchange more oxygen and carbon dioxide than a smaller surface.

Breathing surfaces usually have a lot of blood vessels so that plenty of gas exchange can happen.

DIFFERENT SORTS OF BREATHING ORGANS

Animals which live in different places have different sorts of breathing organs (see figure 27.2). Animals made of one cell live in water and use the whole cell for gas exchange.

Fish, crabs, tadpoles and many other animals which live in water use *gills* as breathing organs. Gills are thin pieces of skin which exchange oxygen and carbon dioxide with the water.

Insects use breathing tubes or *tracheae* as breathing organs. Tracheae are small tubes which carry air to all parts of the body.

Mammals, birds, reptiles and amphibians use lungs as breathing organs.

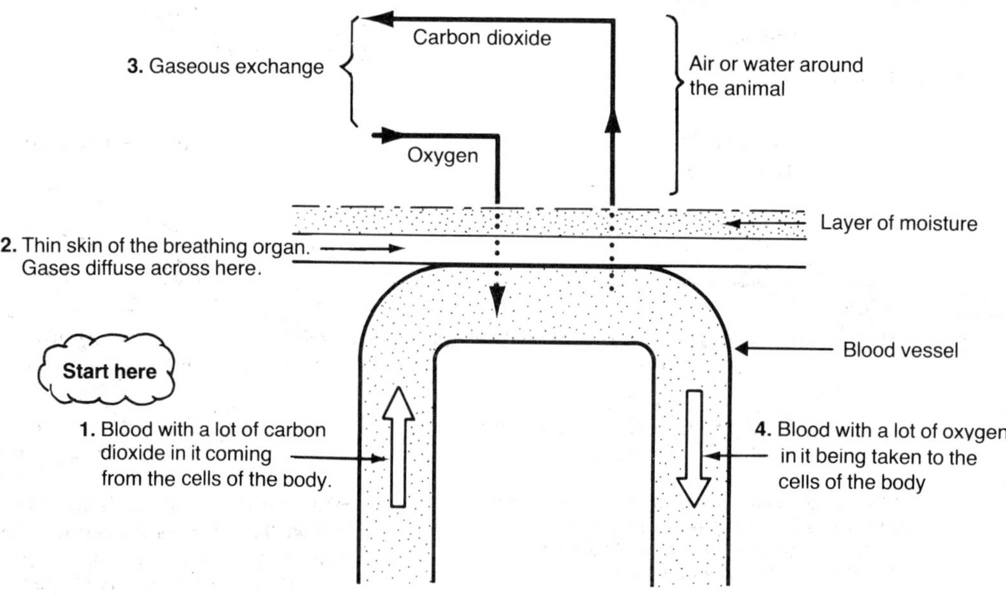

Figure 27.1 What happens at a breathing organ

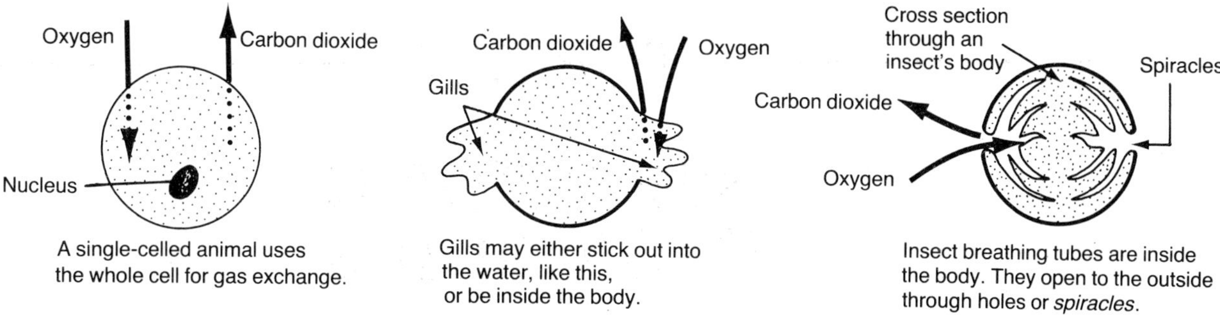

Figure 27.2

BREATHING IN FISH

The gills of fish are protected by a cover called the operculum. (See figure 27.3.)

Each gill is made of many filaments which have blood vessels inside. Oxygen diffuses into the blood from the water which flows over the gill filaments.

Because there are a lot of gill filaments there is a very big surface for gas exchange.

Water is pumped over the gills so that gas exchange can happen quickly. The floor of the fish's mouth pumps the water over its gills. (See figure 27.4.)

See 'Things to do' (page 176)

Fancy that!

Some fish can breathe air and move on land! Some lungfishes drown if they are held under water for too long!

When active, trout pump 40 litres of water an hour over their gills!

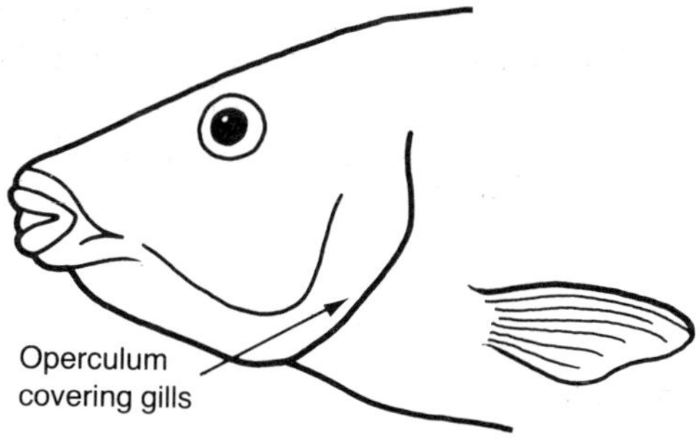

The filaments are a bit like the pages of a book.

Water flows between the gill filaments like this

Operculum covering gills

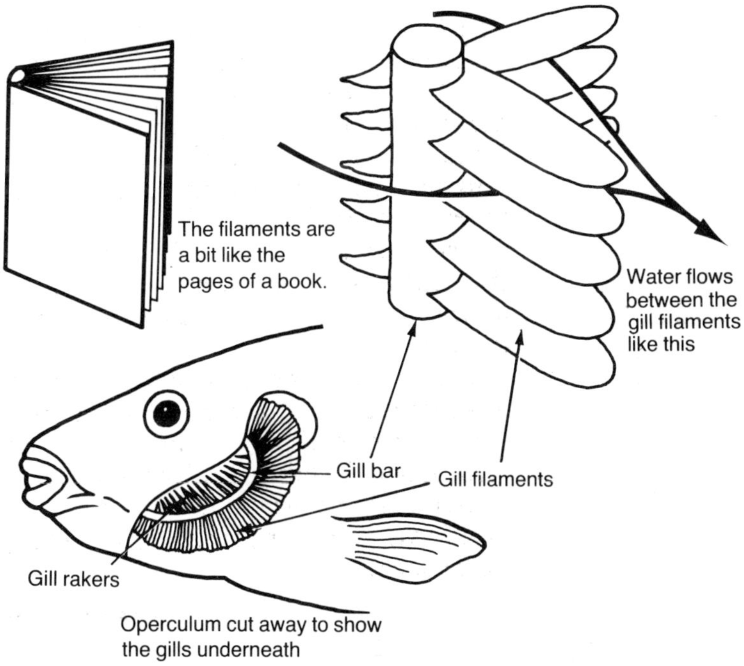

Gill bar

Gill filaments

Gill rakers

Operculum cut away to show the gills underneath

Figure 27.3 The gills of a herring

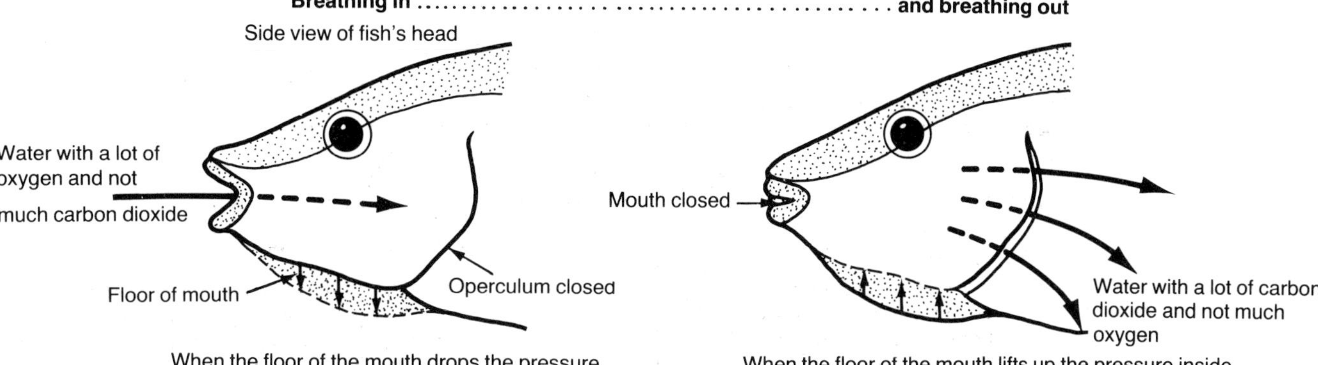

When the floor of the mouth drops the pressure inside is less than the pressure outside. Water is then pushed or drawn into the mouth. The operculum closes when this happens.

When the floor of the mouth lifts up the pressure inside is more than the pressure outside. Water is forced over the gills and out from the operculum. The mouth closes when this happens.

Figure 27.4

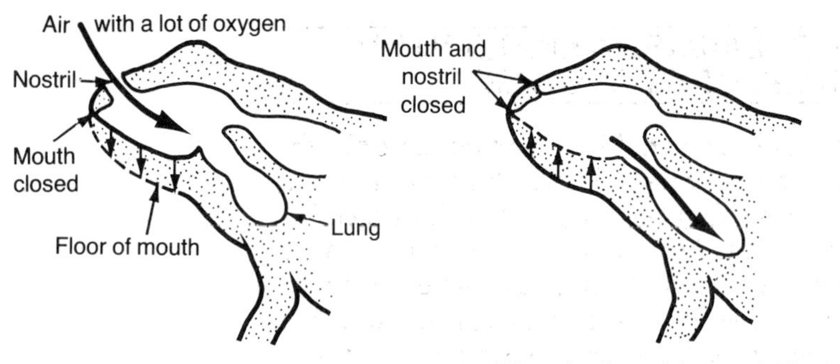

When the floor of the mouth drops the pressure inside is less than the pressure outside. Air is then pushed or drawn into the mouth through the nostrils.

When the floor of the mouth lifts the pressure inside is more than the pressure outside. Air is forced into the lungs because the nostrils and mouth close.

Figure 27.5 How a frog breathes in

HOW FROGS BREATHE

When a frog is active it uses its lungs for breathing. You can see strong movements of its throat when this happens. When a frog is not active, enough oxygen for its needs can diffuse through its skin. This is very thin and is always kept wet even when the frog is out of water. The lining of a frog's mouth can be used for breathing when it is not active. To do this it moves its throat gently up and down to pump air in and out. (See figures 27.5 and 27.6.)

GAS EXCHANGE IN INSECTS

An insect uses small tubes (tracheal tubes or tracheae) to carry air to all parts of its body. The tracheae branch into smaller tubes so that every cell is close to an air tube. The air tubes open to the outside through small holes or *spiracles*. When the insect is not active it closes these to control loss of water from its body. (See figure 27.7.) An insect's method of breathing is quite different from that most other animals use (see figure 27.8).

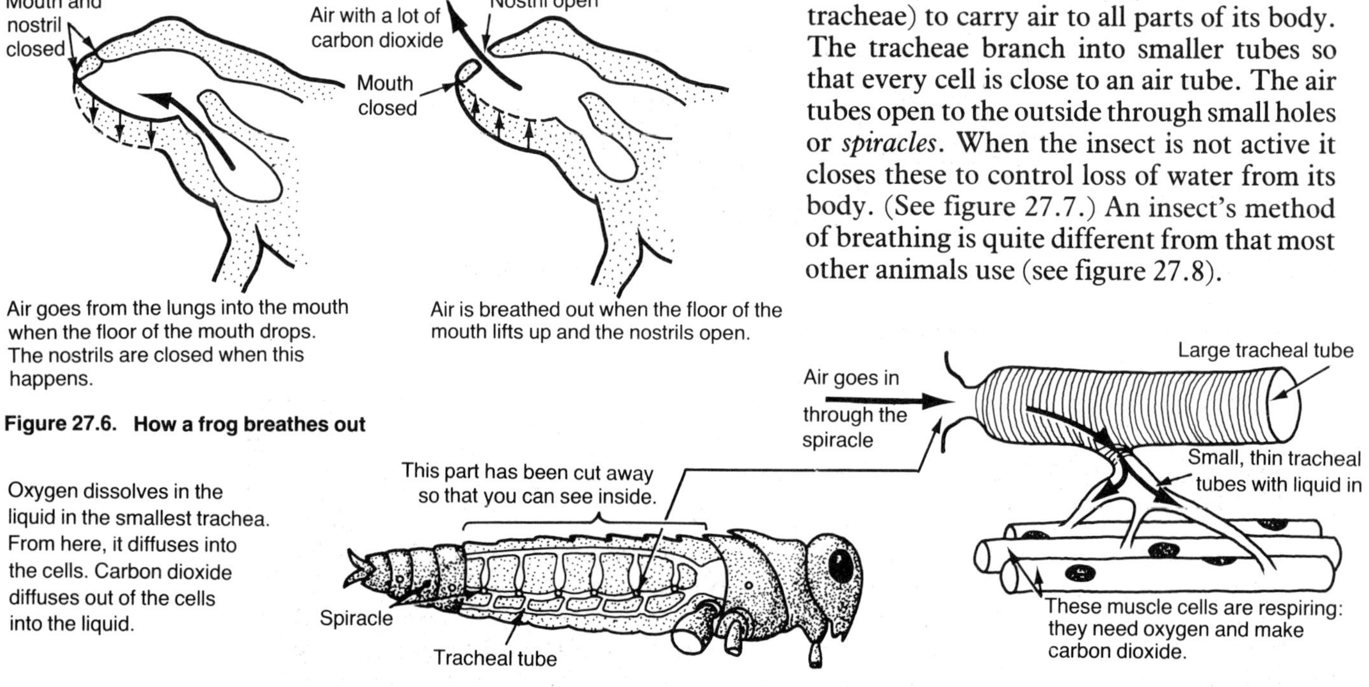

Air goes from the lungs into the mouth when the floor of the mouth drops. The nostrils are closed when this happens.

Air is breathed out when the floor of the mouth lifts up and the nostrils open.

Figure 27.6. How a frog breathes out

Oxygen dissolves in the liquid in the smallest trachea. From here, it diffuses into the cells. Carbon dioxide diffuses out of the cells into the liquid.

Figure 27.7

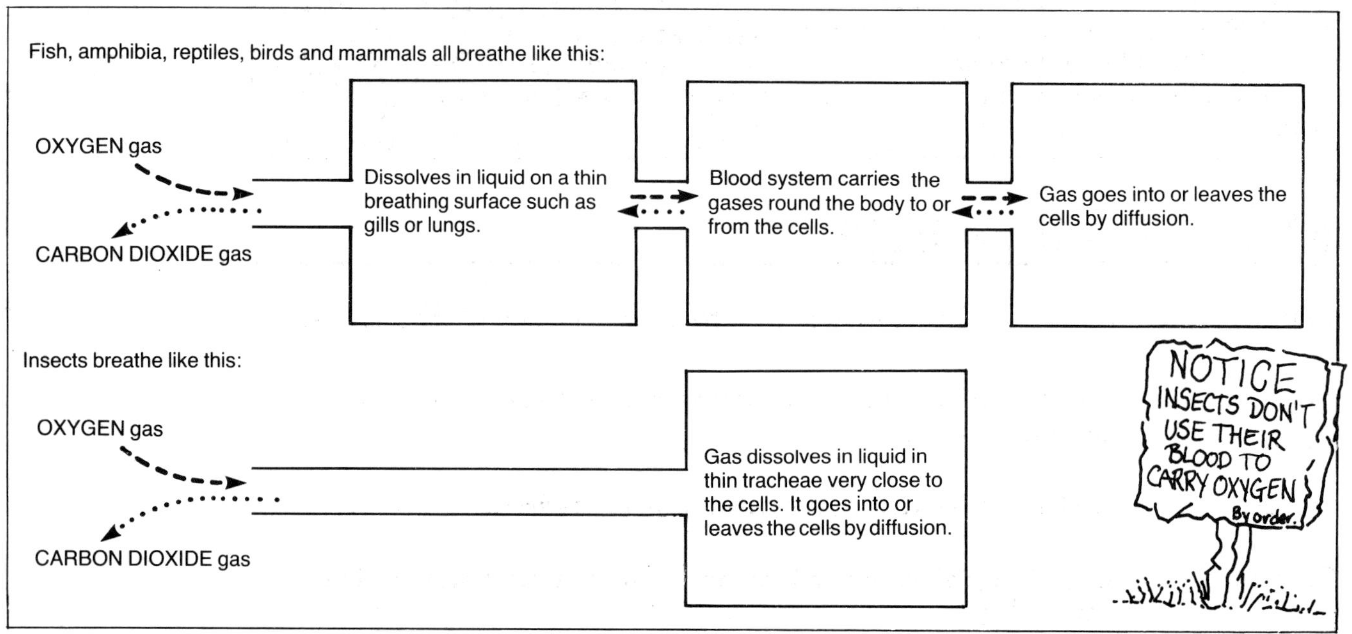

Figure 27.8

HOW EARTHWORMS BREATHE

An earthworm uses its skin for breathing. Oxygen and carbon dioxide dissolve in a thin layer of liquid on its skin. Oxygen diffuses into its blood and carbon dioxide diffuses out. The blood is red because it contains haemoglobin, the same substance as in our blood. An earthworm's blood can hold a lot of oxygen because of the haemoglobin. (See figure 27.9.)

WHY LARGE ANIMALS NEED BREATHING ORGANS

In water, oxygen diffuses much more slowly than in air. Small animals which live in water (like Amoeba) can still get enough oxygen for their needs by diffusion. They are so small that oxygen can diffuse fast enough to every part of their bodies. Diffusion is too slow for larger animals. These have large breathing organs and well-developed blood systems to carry oxygen to their cells quickly.

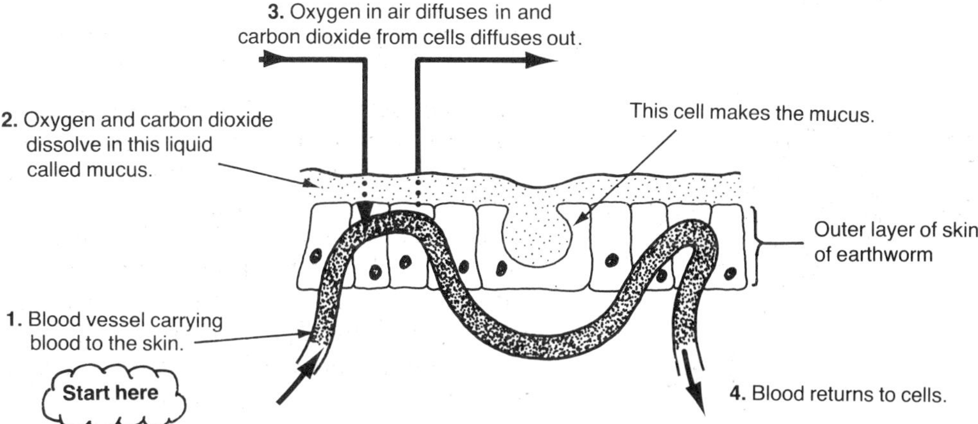

Figure 27.9 Cross section through an earthworm's skin

Summary

Oxygen and carbon dioxide are exchanged by the *breathing organs* of animals. Different animals use different kinds of breathing organs. Fish use *gills* and mammals, birds, reptiles and amphibians use *lungs*. Insects use *tracheae* and earthworms use their *skin*.

A *fish* breathes by pumping water into its mouth and over its gills. A *frog* can breathe using its skin and the lining of its mouth as well as with its lungs.

Fish, *amphibia*, *birds*, *reptiles* and *mammals* use their blood systems to carry oxygen and carbon dioxide. *Insects* do not use their blood systems to carry oxygen and carbon dioxide.

All breathing organs are thin and moist and have a large surface area.

Important words

Gills	thin pieces of skin used for gas exchange by many animals living in water.
Tracheae	a network of air tubes in insects that reaches all parts of the body. (Singular: trachae.)
Spiracles	small holes which let air pass in and out of the tracheae.
Gas exchange	the exchange of oxygen and carbon dioxide between animals and their surroundings.

Things to do

Find out how a fish breathes using this simple model.
You will need:
an empty washing-up liquid bottle
a sharp, pointed knife: **CARE!**

Squeeze most of the air out of the bottle. Hold it under water and stop squeezing. Water will slowly go into the bottle. Find out why from page 173.

Take the bottle out of the water and close it with the cap. Make one slit on each side, about 2 cm long, near the top of the bottle. These slits are the 'gills' of the fish. Now squeeze the bottle. What happens and why?

Questions

A.

Copy this into your book using another word (or words) for those in *italics*. Do not change the meaning of the sentences.

During *breathing* oxygen goes into an animal and carbon dioxide comes out. These two gases dissolve in water on the breathing surface and then *diffuse* in different directions. A fish pumps water into its body by *changing* the pressure inside its mouth. Air goes in and out of an insect's body through *spiracles*. It then goes to every cell inside *small air tubes*.

B.

1. How is the breathing system of a mammal different from that of an insect?
2. Why do small animals not have breathing organs?
3. The figures show how much oxygen is used by each gram of tissue in breathing for one hour:

Earthworm	60 mm^3
Frog	150 mm^3
Mouse (at rest)	2500 mm^3
Mouse (running)	20000 mm^3
Butterfly (at rest)	600 mm^3
Butterfly (flying)	1000000 mm^3

(a) Which are the two most active animals?
(b) Which are the two least active animals?
(c) Why do you think that a butterfly, when flying, needs more oxygen than a mouse when running?
(d) How can a butterfly's breathing system bring so much oxygen to its muscles?

4. Name *four* characteristics of surfaces used for breathing.
5. Write a few sentences about breathing using all the following words: diffusion; oxygen; carbon dioxide; air; water; gas exchange.

C.

Figure 27.9 shows a small part of the tracheal system in an insect.

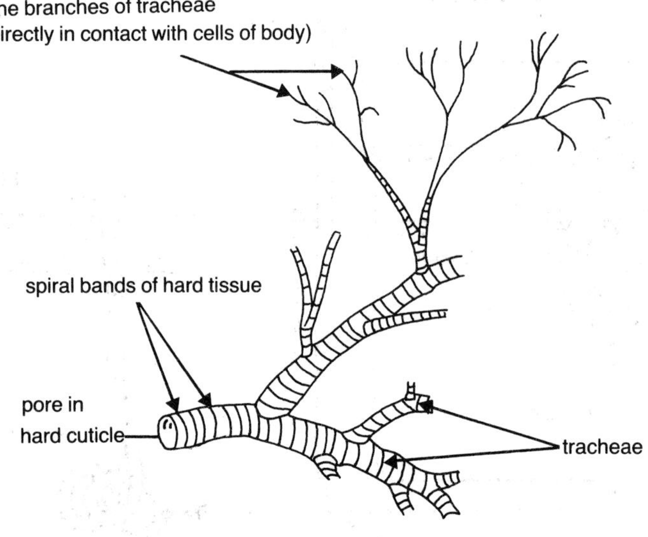

Figure 27.9

1. Name the pore which opens onto the body surface of the insect.
2. Oxygen moves from a high concentration in the air to the finer branches of the system where there is a much lower concentration of oxygen. Name the process responsible for the movement of this gas.
3. Explain why there is a high concentration of carbon dioxide within the finer branches of the system.
4. Suggest a reason for the spiral bands of tissue around the tracheal tubes.
5. Name the respiratory surfaces through which gases are exchanged in the following animals: (a) mammal; (b) fish; and (c) amoeba.
6. State *two* similarities between the surfaces through which gases are exchanged in a mammal and a fish.

(EAEB)

TOPIC 28

EXCRETION

Every living cell produces waste substances. They are made when chemical reactions take place inside the cells. The chemical reactions keep the cells alive. Some of the waste substances are poisonous and must be taken away quickly. Getting rid of these waste substances from your body is called excretion. (See figure 28.1.)

In animals the main substances to be excreted are:

1. carbon dioxide,
2. water,
3. urea.

Figure 28.1 What goes into and comes out of your cells

A cell
Food
Oxygen
Water
Chemical reactions
Carbon dioxide
Water
Wastes → Excretion

WHAT HAPPENS TO WATER AND CARBON DIOXIDE

The main excretory organs (figure 28.2.) are:

1. your kidneys,
2. your lungs,
3. your skin.

Figure 28.2

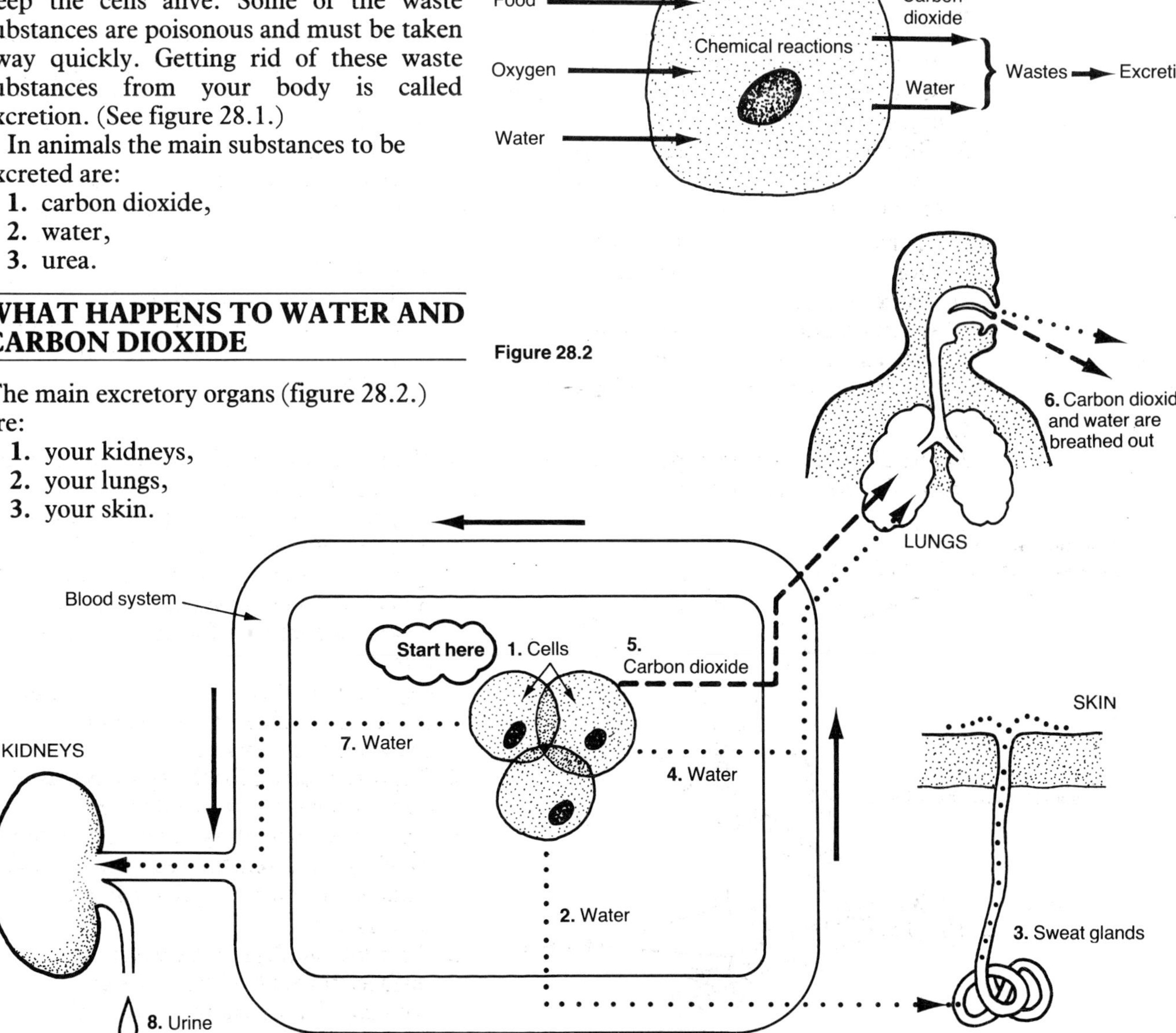

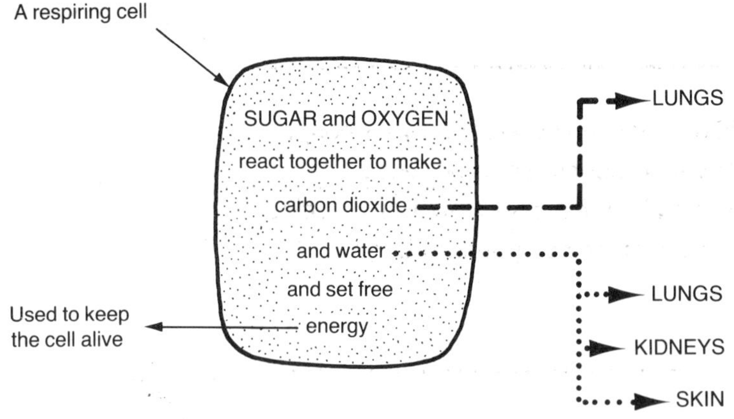

Figure 28.3 **How waste carbon dioxide and water are made**

Water and carbon dioxide are waste substances made by cells during respiration. This is the main chemical reaction which happens in cells.

HOW UREA IS MADE

Protein in food is digested in your digestive system to amino acids. The amino acids are used to build the proteins which are needed for new cells. Any spare amino acids are made into urea in your liver. The urea is excreted by your kidneys in a liquid called urine. Urine also contains other substances such as salts and hormones. Your skin also excretes a small amount of urea.

WHAT HAPPENS TO WASTE FOOD

Waste food which has not been absorbed from your digestive system goes out through your anus. This is called defecation. This waste has *not* been made by your cells and is *not* an excretion.

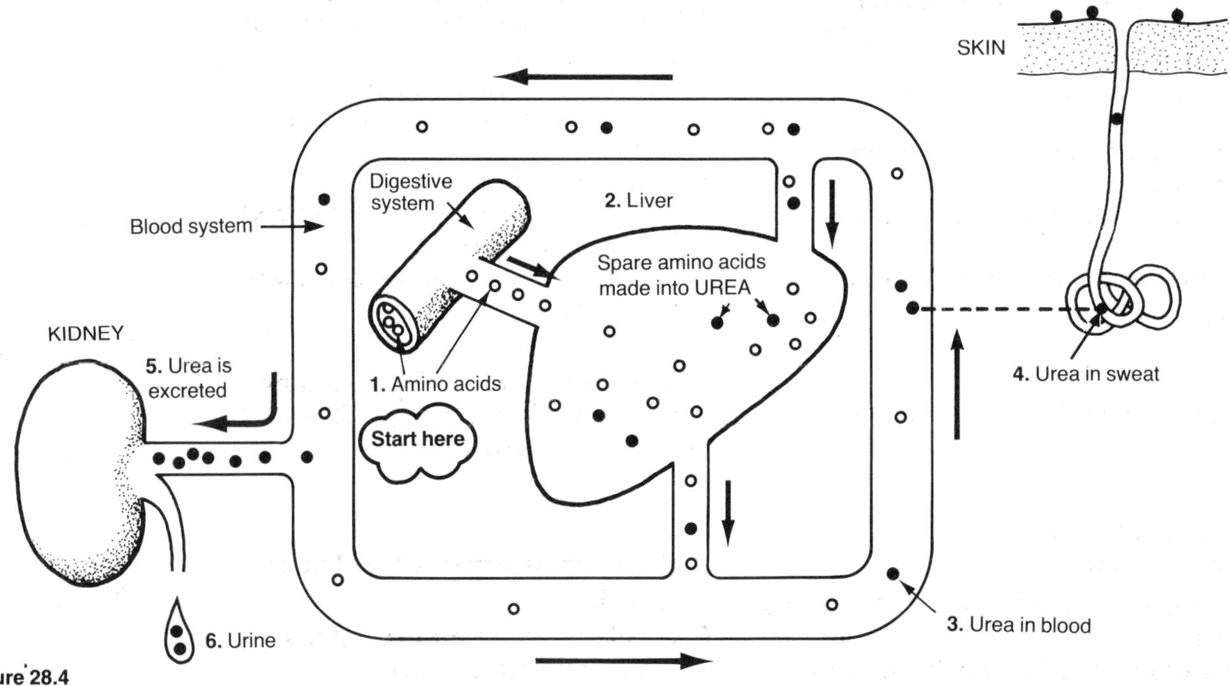

Figure 28.4

Summary

All cells make waste substances. Some of these substances are poisonous and must be quickly removed from your body. This is called *excretion*. Excretory organs such as your *kidneys, lungs* and *skin* get rid of these waste substances.

Carbon dioxide and *water* are waste substances made by all cells in respiration. They are breathed out by your lungs.

Urea is made from unwanted amino acids by liver cells. It is excreted mainly by your kidneys as urine. Urine contains urea, salts, hormones and other substances.

Waste food is not an excretion as it is not a chemical waste made by cells. Waste food leaves your body through your anus. This is called defecation.

Important words

Excretion	the process of getting rid of waste substances from your body.
Excretory organ	an organ that gets rid of waste products from your body.
Urea	a waste product made by your liver from unwanted amino acids.
Urine	a liquid containing urea that is excreted by your kidneys.

Questions

A.
Write out each sentence in your book. Fill in the missing words from those in the box. Some words may be used more than once.

> lungs — liver — urine — chemical reactions — defecation — poison — water — respiration — amino acids — excretion — proteins — blood system

1. Wastes are made by ...... happening inside cells.
2. ...... is a chemical reaction carried out by all cells.
3. Carbon dioxide is excreted by your ....
4. Wastes are carried to your excretory organs by your ....
5. Your lungs, skin and kidneys all excrete ....
6. ...... produces carbon dioxide and water as wastes.
7. Wastes must be removed from your body because they can ...... cells.
8. Urea is a waste substance made from unwanted ....
9. ...... are made from amino acids.
10. ...... contains urea, hormones and salts.
11. Urea is made in your ....
12. ...... is the removal of unwanted food from your digestive system.
13. ...... is the removal of wastes made by your cells.

B.
1. Explain what is happening in figure 28.2.
2. Figure 28.4 shows six different things happening. What are they? (Start with the digestive system.)

C. *Experiment Corner*
Think about these facts.
1. Ammonia is an alkaline gas that dissolves in water.
2. An enzyme called urease digests urea to ammonia.
3. Alkaline gases turn moist red litmus paper blue.

How could you do an experiment to show that urea is present in urine?

D.
Think about these facts.
1. Clinitest tablets change colour when added to glucose solution.
2. With a Clinitest tablet:
   a 2% glucose solution gives an orange colour,
   a 0.75% glucose solution gives a green-brown colour,
   a 0.25% glucose solution gives a dark green colour,
   a solution with no glucose in gives a blue colour.
3. Diabetes is a disease in which glucose is excreted in the urine.
4. Diabetes can be treated to reduce the amount of glucose in the urine.
   How could you show that:
   (a) a person is *not* suffering from diabetes,
   (b) a person is suffering from diabetes and is not being treated,
   (c) a person is suffering from diabetes and is being treated.

TOPIC 29

THE KIDNEY

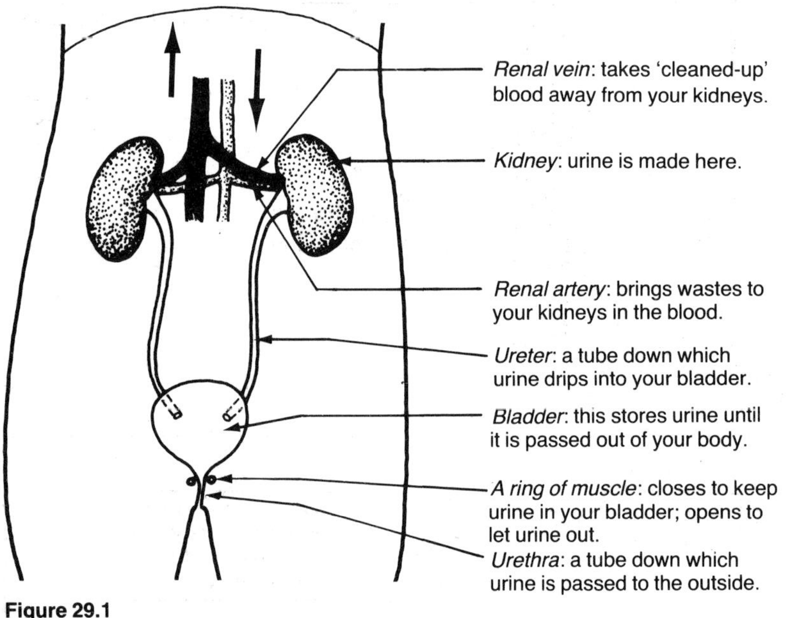

Figure 29.1

Your two kidneys remove a lot of waste substances from your body in urine. These waste substances are left by the chemical reactions that keep your cells alive. Urine contains urea, salts, hormones and water.

Close your fists. Push them into the middle of your back on each side of your backbone. This is where your kidneys are found. They are red-brown in colour. (See figure 29.1.)

A CLOSER LOOK AT A KIDNEY

Look at figures 29.2 and 29.3 and find all the parts of a kidney. The tubules (see figure 29.4) are very small: each kidney contains about one million! A model tubule (figure 29.5) may help you to understand what they look like.

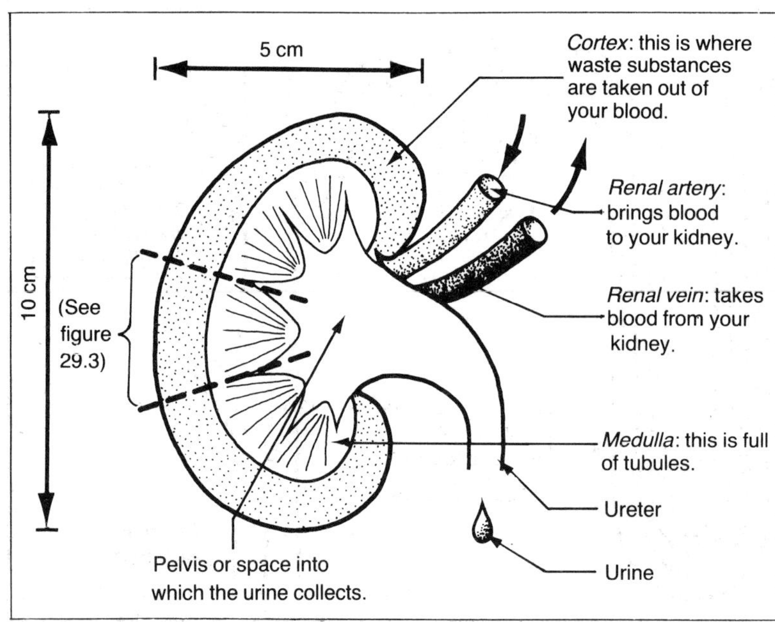

Figure 29.2 Section cut through a kidney

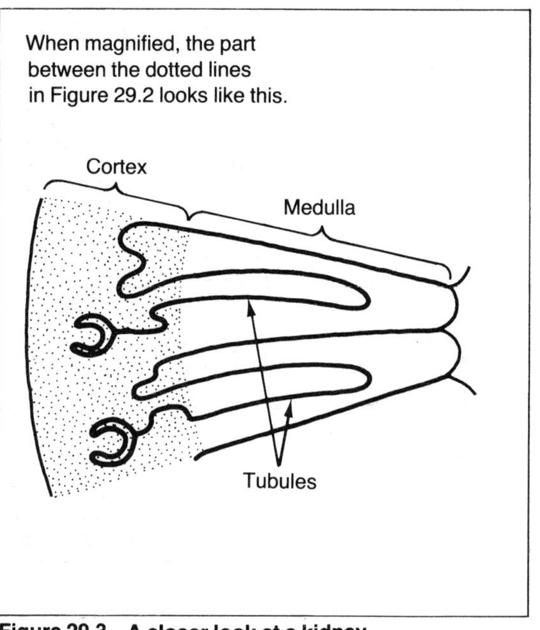

Figure 29.3 A closer look at a kidney

WHAT TUBULES DO AND HOW THEY DO IT

Kidney tubules separate waste substances from your blood and excrete them.

Blood goes into your kidneys at high pressure. This pressure forces many substances out of the blood capillaries into the Bowman's capsules. Your kidneys will not work without this high pressure which helps to filter off the waste substances. The liquid forced into the Bowman's capsules is blood plasma without some of its larger molecules. Most of the *useful* substances in this liquid must return to your blood. (See figure 29.6.)

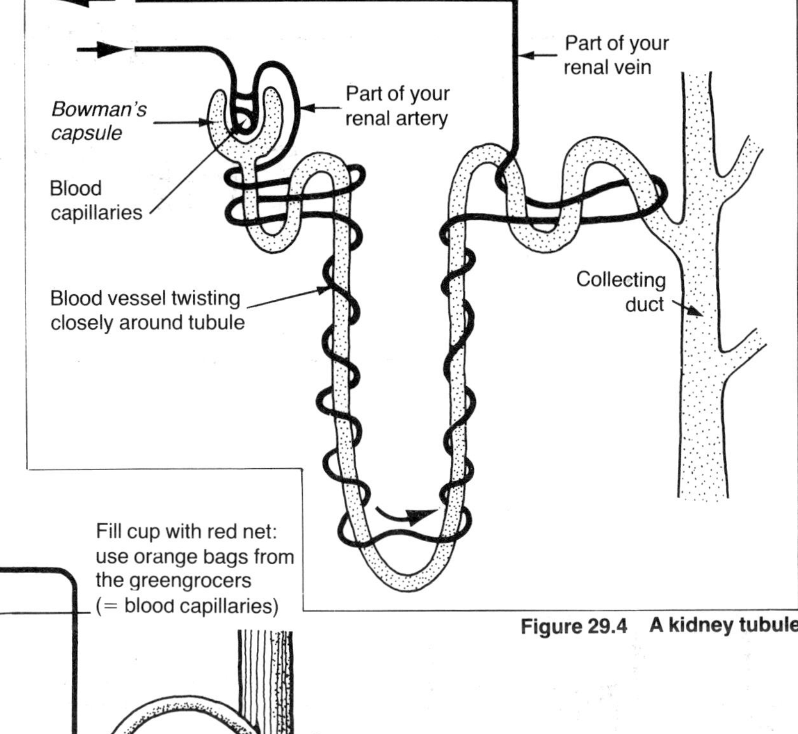

Figure 29.4 A kidney tubule

Wire with blue plastic cover (= renal vein)
Wire with red plastic cover (= renal artery)
Fill cup with red net: use orange bags from the greengrocers (= blood capillaries)
Plastic yoghurt carton (= Bowman's capsule)
Hosepipe with rubber tubing pushed into slits (= collecting tubule)
Rubber tube pushed into small hole made in yoghurt carton (= tubule)
Red net wrapped around tube (= blood vessel)
Rubber tubing

Figure 29.5

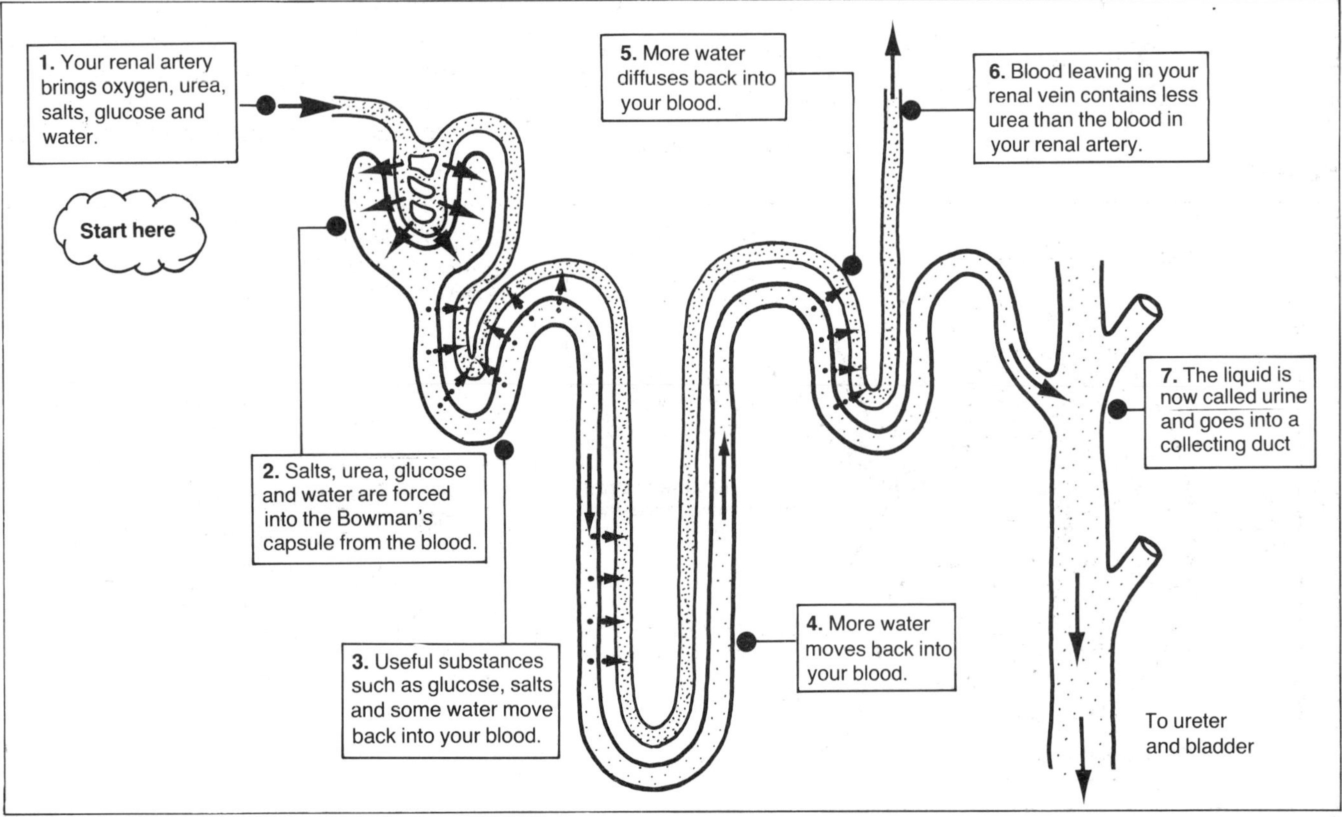

Figure 29.6

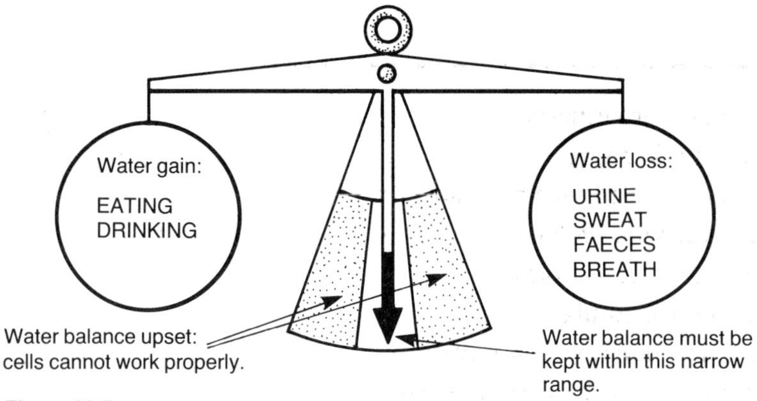

Water gain:
EATING
DRINKING

Water loss:
URINE
SWEAT
FAECES
BREATH

Water balance upset: cells cannot work properly.

Water balance must be kept within this narrow range.

Figure 29.7

WATER BALANCE

Your kidneys are important for controlling the amount of water in your body. Cells can only work properly when the right amount of water is present. (See figure 29.7.)

When your body does not have enough water your kidneys make:
- stronger urine (*less* water in it),
- less urine.

When your body has too much water your kidneys make:
- weaker urine (*more* water in it),
- more urine.

Controlling the water in this way is called *osmoregulation*.

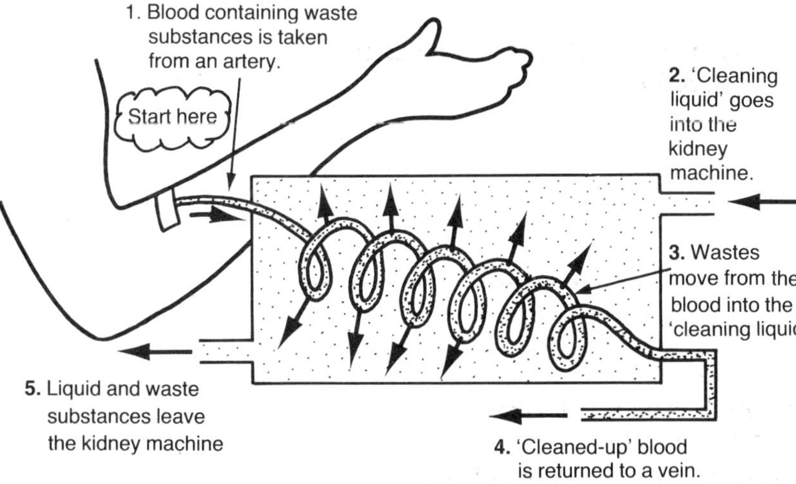

Figure 29.8

REPLACEMENT KIDNEYS

Some diseases which affect kidneys stop them from working properly. People with these diseases will die unless their blood is cleared of waste substances. Kidney machines do this job for them. The machines are large and expensive and there are not enough for people to use. (See figure 29.8.)

Diseased kidneys can be replaced by healthy ones from other people. This is called a kidney transplant. People who want to give their kidneys often carry a donor card. If they die or are killed in an accident their kidneys can then be removed quickly and put into the people needing them.

Summary

Your kidneys help to get rid of waste substances made by your cells. They do this by using blood pressure to filter off the waste substances from your blood. This happens in the *Bowman's capsules* in the *cortex*.

The wastes then travel down *tubules* where useful substances such as glucose, mineral salts and some water are absorbed back into your blood. This happens in the *medulla*.

The wastes are now called *urine* and contain mainly *urea* and water. The urine leaves your kidneys in the *ureter* and goes to your *bladder*. From the bladder it passes out of your body down the *urethra*.

Your kidneys also control the amount of water in your body. This is called *osmoregulation*.

Fancy that!

About 170 litres of liquid go into the Bowman's capsules each day! Only 2–3 litres of this leave your body each day as urine!

Babies cannot control the muscle which closes the urethra and have to wear nappies!

Important words

Renal artery	carries blood (with urea) to your kidneys.
Renal vein	carries blood away from your kidneys.
Cortex	part of your kidney containing the Bowman's capsules.
Bowman's capsules	filters waste substances from your blood.
Medulla	part of your kidney containing the tubules.
Kidney tubules	loop-shaped structures in the medulla.
Ureter	tube carrying urine from your kidney to your bladder.
Urethra	tube carrying urine from your bladder to the outside.
Osmoregulation	the control of the amount of water in your body.

Things to do

1. Buy a lamb's kidney from the butchers. It will probably have a lot of white fat around it. Take away the fat and cut the kidney in half as in figure 29.2. Try to find all the parts.

2. Make the model kidney tubule shown in figure 29.5.

Questions

A.
Put each of these parts of sentences into the correct order.

1. waste substances / your blood / in your Bowman's capsules / are taken out of

2. waste substances / and then into your ureter / go into the pelvis of your kidneys / taken from your blood

B.

1. Why are your kidneys important organs?

2. How much liquid passes back into your blood from the tubules each day? (See *Fancy that!*)

3. Why do so many substances leave your blood in the Bowman's capsules?

4. What substances, other than urea, are excreted by your body and what organs excrete them?

C.
Figure 29.9 shows part of a kidney tubule. The table shows the percentages of water, protein, glucose and urea in three different fluids.

1. Explain why no protein is found in the filtrate even though it is present in the plasma.

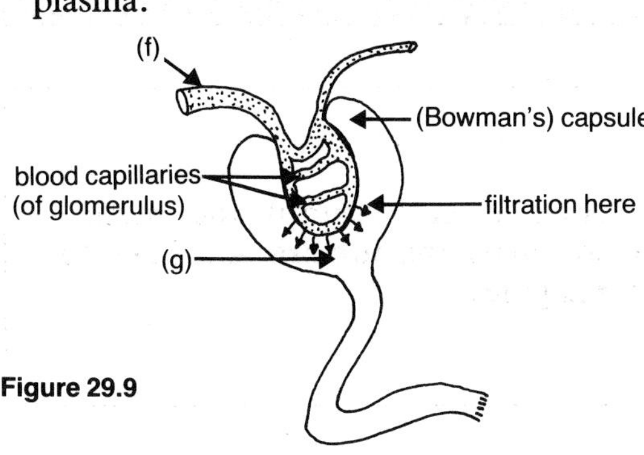

Figure 29.9

Substance	% in plasma in artery (f)	% in filtrate in capsule (g)	% in urine
Water	90 – 93	90 – 93	95
Protein	7.0	0	0
Glucose	0.1	0.1	0
Urea	0.03	0.03	2.0

2. (a) State *one* source of the glucose present in the plasma.
(b) Explain why glucose is not present in the urine even though it is filtered into the tubule.

3. (a) Name the organ from which the blood gains most urea.
(b) Explain why urea is more concentrated in the urine than in the filtrate.

(EAEB)

TOPIC 30

SKIN

Skin covers the whole surface of your body and does many important jobs. (See figures 30.1 and 30.2.)

STRUCTURE OF YOUR SKIN

The *epidermis* is the protective layer of your skin. Cells are slowly worn away from the surface of the epidermis. New skin replaces it from below. Hairs stick through the epidermis and sweat pores open onto its surface.

The *dermis* contains several structures. *Sebaceous glands* oil your hair and skin to keep them soft. *Sweat glands* produce a watery solution of urea and salts called sweat. This helps to cool your body. Blood vessels bring oxygen, food and heat to your skin. Hairs only grow from their 'roots'. Cutting off a hair at the surface does not stop it growing. Hair muscles raise or lower each hair. This is useful in hairy mammals for controlling their body temperature. Sense organs send messages about pain, touch and temperature to your nervous system. A dark coloured pigment (coloured chemical) called *melanin* helps to give colour to your skin and keeps out harmful rays from the sun.

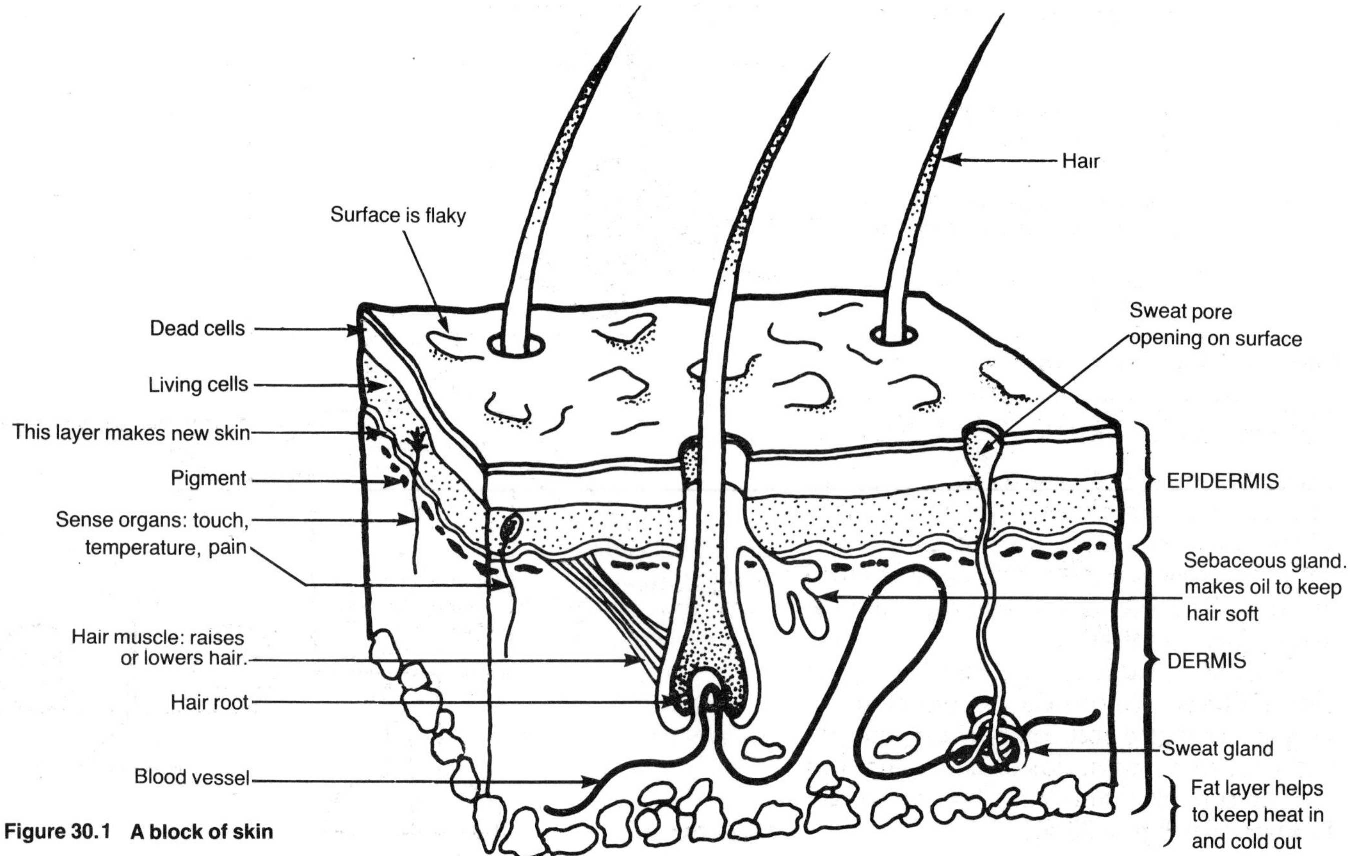

Figure 30.1 A block of skin

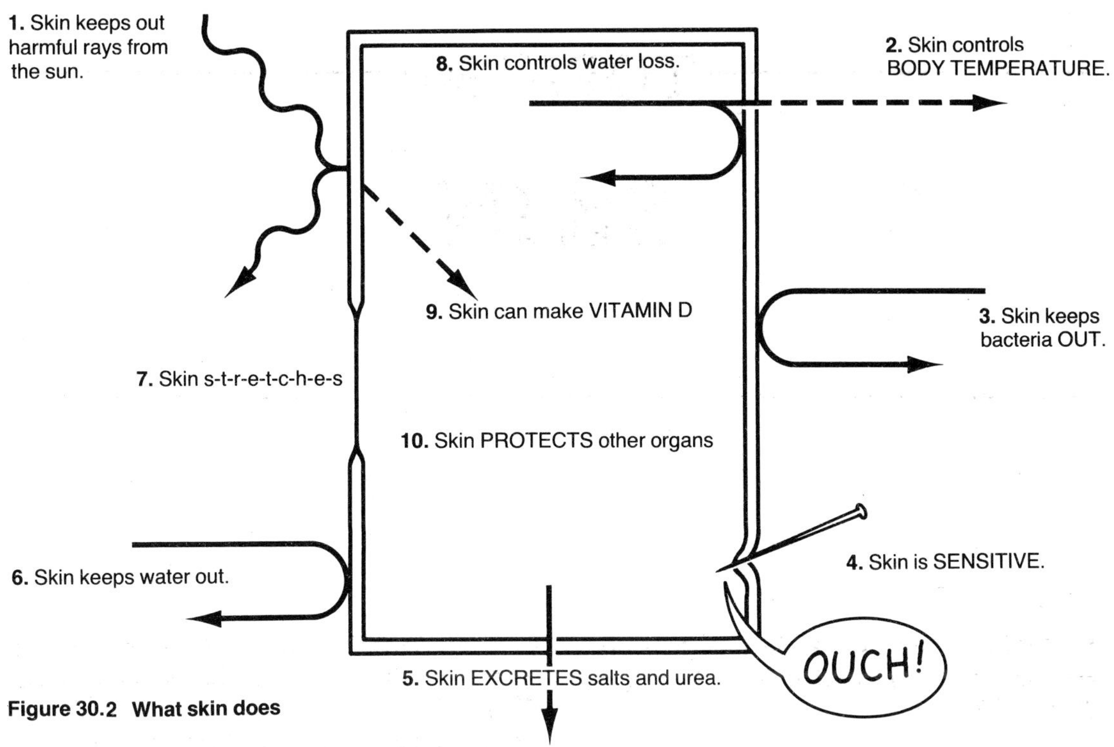

Figure 30.2 What skin does

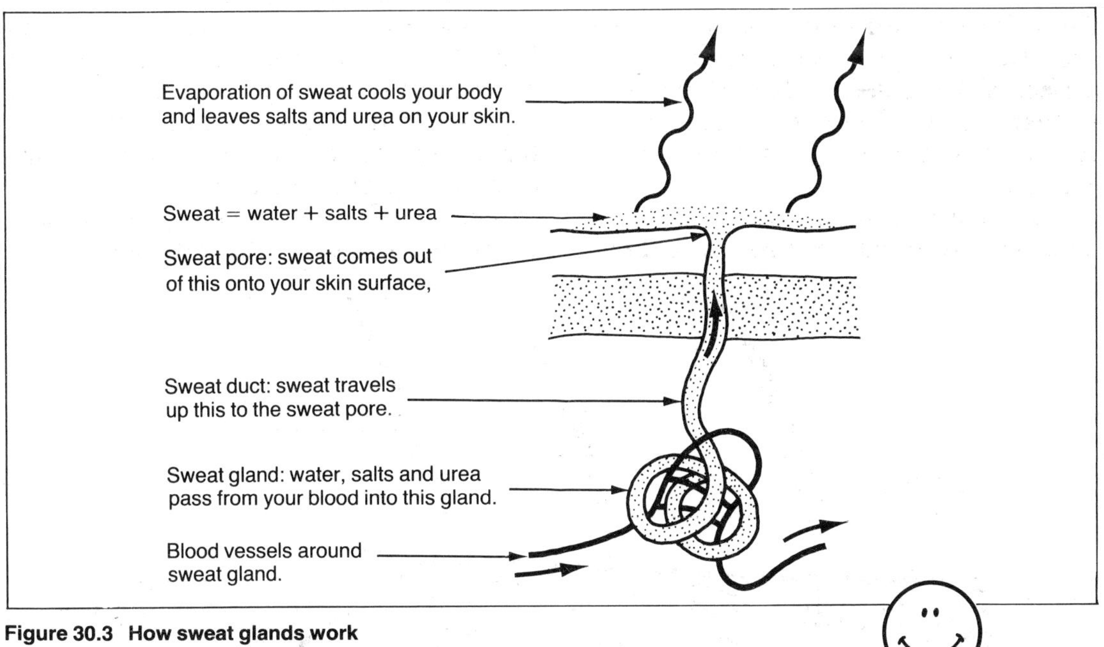

Figure 30.3 How sweat glands work

YOUR BODY TEMPERATURE

Mammals and birds make heat from the chemical reactions that happen in their cells. Most heat is produced in liver and muscle cells. The heat is carried away by their blood systems. Heat may be lost by evaporation of sweat. (See figure 30.3.)

Heat can sometimes be *gained* from your surroundings. Your skin is important in keeping a balance between the heat you gain and lose. In humans, this balance keeps our temperature at about 36.8°C when we are healthy. (See figure 30.4.)

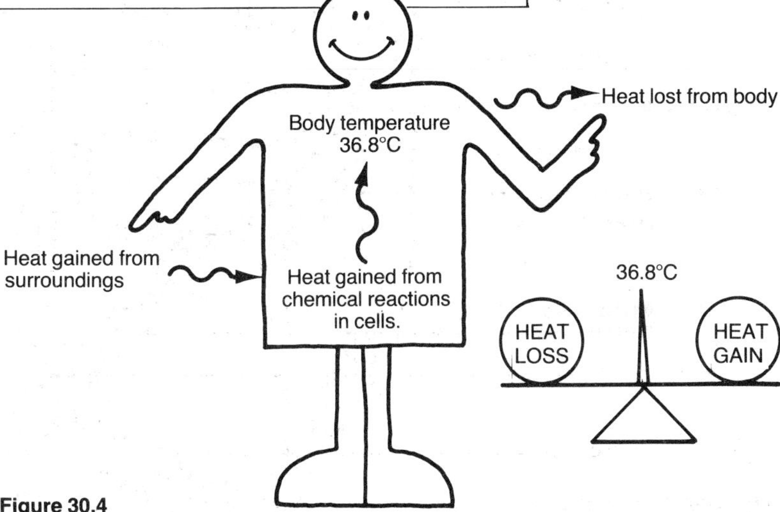

Figure 30.4

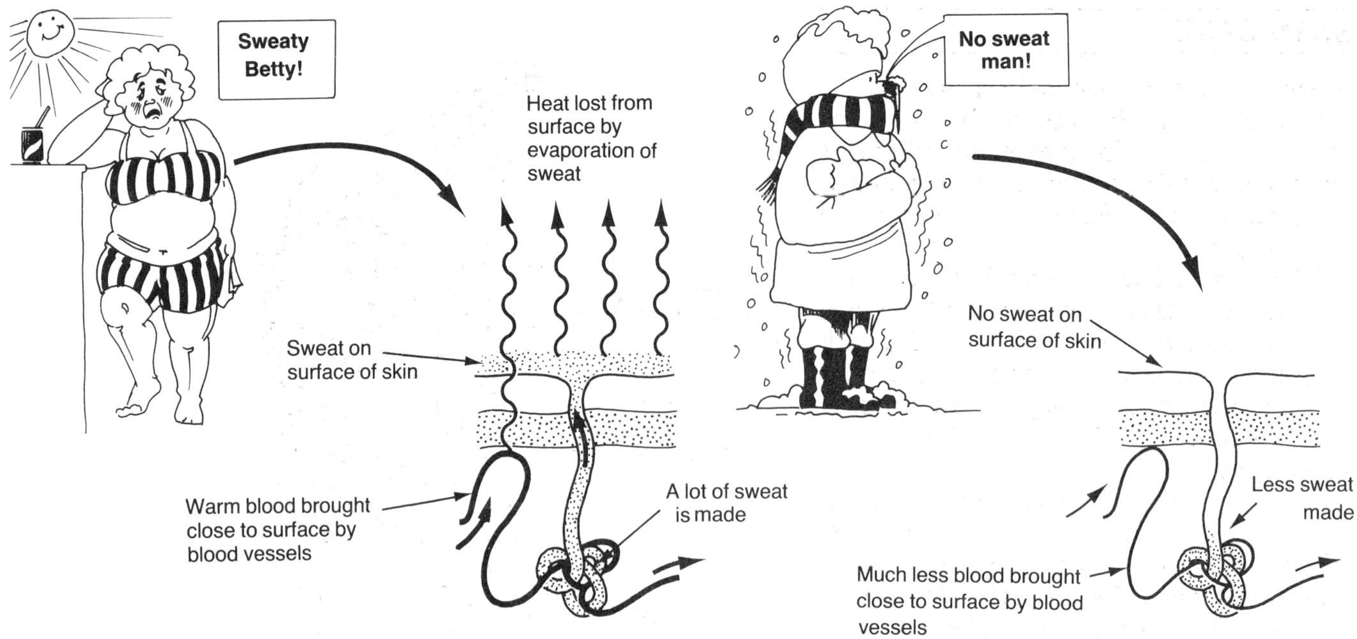

Figure 30.5

Figure 30.6

Your body may sometimes get too hot. Exercise, disease or too much sun can make this happen. Blood vessels in your skin will then get larger. (In white people this makes their skin look red.) More blood now comes near the surface and can be cooled. More sweat is poured out onto the surface of your skin and this also helps to cool your body. (See figure 30.5.)

Your body can also get too cold. Too little clothing, not enough food, or cooling too quickly can make this happen. It is quite common in old people in winter. Blood vessels in your skin will then get narrow and less blood comes near the surface. This makes your skin look pale but you lose less heat and stop sweating. You may start to shiver if your muscles contract very quickly. Shivering makes heat which warms you up a little! (See figure 30.6.)

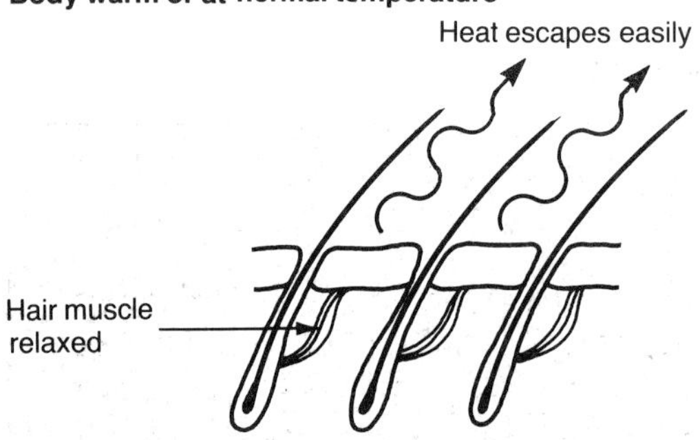

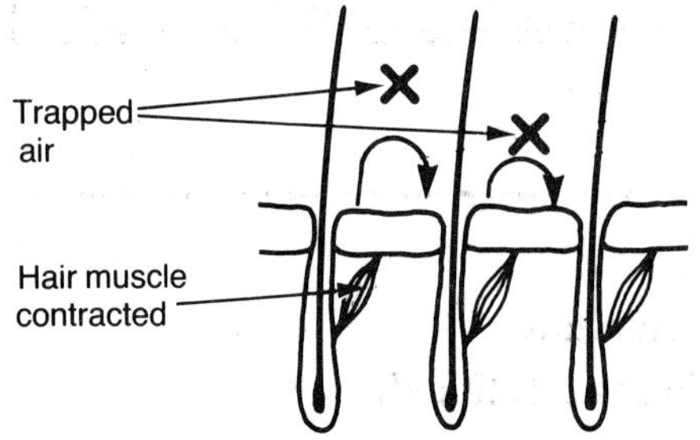

Figure 30.7

Your hair muscles contract to make your body hairs stand up when you are cold. The air trapped between the hairs and your skin helps your body to keep warm. This does not work well in humans because we do not have much hair on our bodies. 'Goose pimples' appear! (See figure 30.7.)

Mammals with fur can fluff it out to keep warm. Birds do the same with their feathers.

HUMANS COME IN SEVERAL COLOURS!

People from different parts of the world often have different colours of skin. This is caused by:

1. the amount of melanin present. Dark skin has a lot of melanin. Freckles or moles are big patches of melanin. The number of melanin cells in a certain area of skin is the same for all races, but in coloured races more melanin is made. People who have no melanin at all are called albinos.
2. the thickness of the epidermis. Blood cannot be seen through a thick epidermis. This makes a person's skin look yellow.

SKIN CARE

Teenagers often have skin problems. A greasy skin can be caused by oil from sebaceous glands. The grease can collect dirt and bacteria and this often causes infection of the glands. The infection may then cause acne or spots.

When sweat dries on your skin urea is left behind. Bacteria act on the urea and grease to make substances which smell! Washing with soap and warm water is the best way to keep your skin clean. A teenager with a greasy skin may need to wash his or her face several times a day.

When washing, give close attention to the parts of your body shown in figure 30.8. Wash your feet daily. Change your underwear and socks regularly. Wash your hair at least twice a week. Don't borrow someone else's comb. They may have head lice!

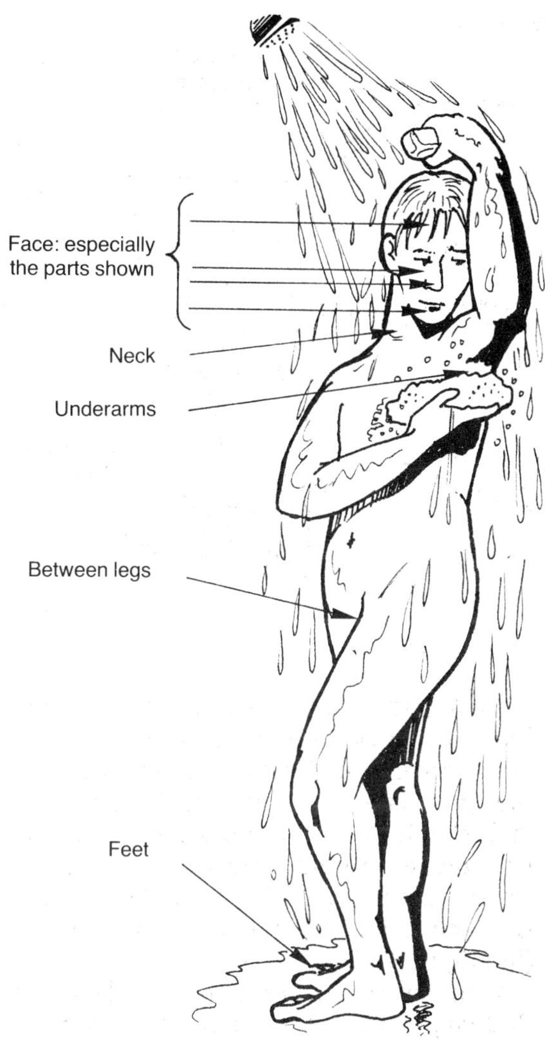

Figure 30.8

Fancy that!

There are about 3 million sweat glands in the body!

Dogs have no sweat glands. They lose heat from their wet noses and by panting.

A suntan is the skin's way of protecting itself against harmful rays!

If you could collect all the melanin from a person with brown skin it would fit onto a 1p coin! A white person has even less than that!

Summary

Your skin controls your *body temperature* and helps to *excrete* waste substances. It is *sensitive* to touch, temperature and pain and helps to keep out harmful bacteria.

Your body temperature is controlled by the amount of blood brought to your skin. In *hot* weather a lot of blood is brought to your skin capillaries and more *sweat* is poured onto your skin. Your body is *cooled* as the sweat *evaporates*. In *cold* weather much less blood is brought to your skin and no sweat is made.

Important words

Epidermis	the outside layer of the skin.
Dermis	the layer of skin below the epidermis.
Sebaceous gland	a gland in the dermis; it makes an oily liquid.
Sweat gland	a gland in the dermis; it makes a weak solution of mineral salts called sweat.
Melanin	a coloured chemical or pigment which is found in the dermis.

Things to do

No-one in the world has finger prints like yours! Find out what yours look like. Paint the end of your thumb (not the nail) with black drawing ink. Don't spread it too thickly. Roll your thumb gently from side-to-side onto a piece of paper. With practice you should be able to make a good print. Now try a print of your first finger. Collect thumb and finger prints from a few of your friends. Can you group the prints into similar sets?

Questions

A.

Write out each sentence in your book. Fill in the missing words from those in the box. Some words may be used more than once.

more — less — bigger — contracts — evaporates — oil — fat — salts — urea — bacteria — water — epidermis

1. The protective layer of your skin is the ....
2. Sebaceous glands make ...... to keep your hair and skin soft.
3. Sweat is made of ...... and ....
4. A layer of ...... in your dermis helps to keep your body warm.
5. When sweat ...... your body is cooled. When your body is hot your sweat glands make ...... sweat.
6. When a hair muscle ...... the hair stands up.
7. When your body is cold ...... blood is brought to the surface of your skin.
8. Body odour (B.O.) is caused by ...... acting on substances on your skin.

B.

Join these sentences together using either the word 'and' or 'because', whichever is correct.

1. Heat is lost from your body. Sweat evaporates from your skin.
2. In hot weather your skin gets hotter. More blood is brought to it in your blood vessels.
3. In cold weather not much blood is brought to your skin. Not much sweat is made.

C.

Each pupil in a class took his/her temperature by putting a clinical thermometer in his mouth. The pupils wrote their results in °C on the blackboard. The results for the whole class are listed below:

37.0	36.6	36.7	37.2	38.1
36.5	36.8	36.9	37.7	37.1
36.4	37.0	37.0	37.1	37.6
37.0	37.3	37.8	37.0	37.9
36.2	36.6	37.7	37.1	37.4
37.2	37.0	37.6	37.4	37.5

Copy the table below into your book.

1. Using the list of results, count how many pupils have temperatures with each of the ranges indicated in the table.

Temperature range of pupils		Total number of pupils in each temperature range
A	36.2 — 36.5°C	
B	36.6 — 36.9°C	
C	37.0 — 37.3°C	
D	37.4 — 37.7°C	
E	37.8 — 38.1°C	

Record the total number of pupils in each temperature range in your table.

2. Using the results you obtained in part (1), plot a bar chart (histogram) of these results to show the range of body temperature in the class.
3. From your graph, answer the following questions.
(a) What is the range of temperature within the class?
(b) What is the most common temperature range in °C within the class? What evidence have you for this from your graph?
(c) Give *one* reason why some healthy pupils may have a body temperature above or below the temperature given in (b).
4. During hot conditions or periods of heavy exercise your body temperature may rise above 37°C. Give *two* ways by which your body can bring about a quick return to normal temperature.
5. Why is high body temperature dangerous?

(ALSEB)

TOPIC 31

THE SKELETON

WHAT USE ARE SKELETONS?

Skeletons are important because they:

1. help animals to move,
2. support an animal's body,
3. protect some soft organs of an animal's body.

There are two main kinds of skeletons: *endoskeletons* and *exoskeletons*. There is more about exoskeletons on page 200.

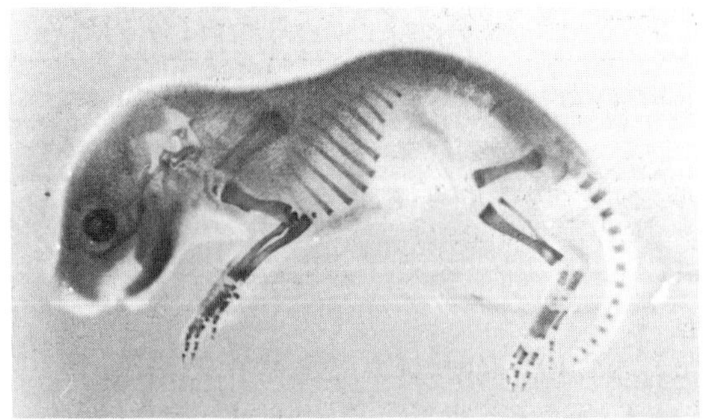

The skeleton of a baby rat

THE ENDOSKELETON

All vertebrates – fish, amphibia, reptiles, birds and mammals – have an endoskeleton. This is usually made of bone and is **inside** their bodies. Bone contains a lot of minerals such as calcium and phosphorus. These make bones very hard and strong.

Softer spongy bone helps to absorb knocks that might damage your skeleton while hard bone gives strength. (See figure 31.1.)

Your bone marrow makes red blood cells and some white blood cells. Slippery cartilage on the ends of bones helps to make your joints work smoothly.

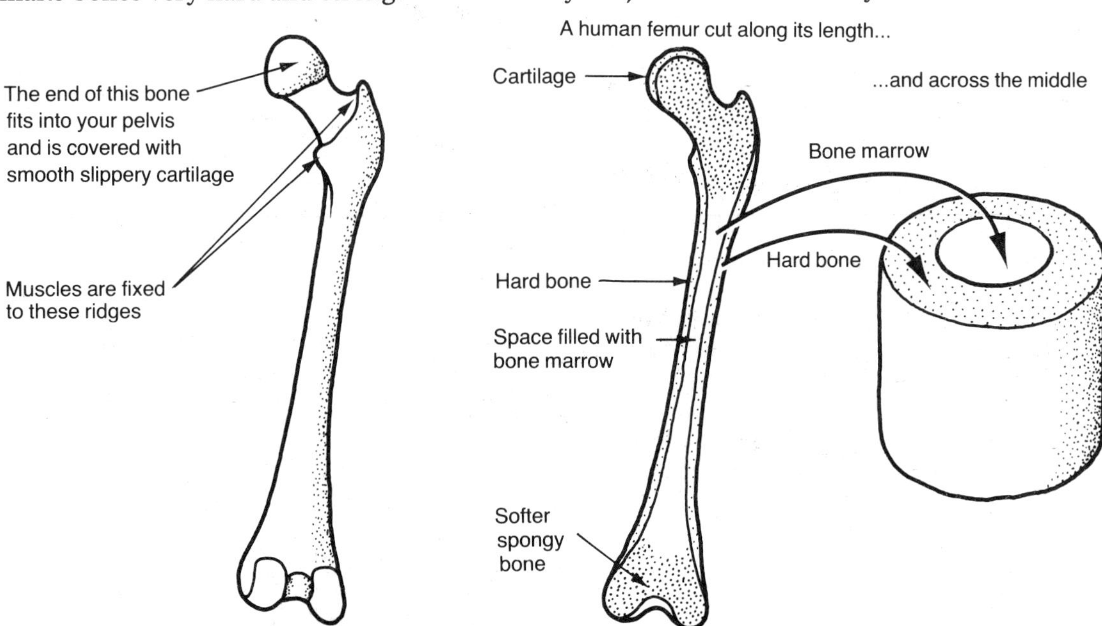

Figure 31.1 A human femur (the big bone in your thigh)

Humans, dogs and chimpanzees are all mammals. Each has a skeleton which is adapted for a different way of life. (See figure 31.2.) A human skeleton is adapted for walking and running. The hands are used for holding things. A dog's skeleton is adapted for walking and fast running. A chimpanzee's skeleton is adapted for swinging from branches in trees. It has long arms and can grip with its hands and feet.

A mammal's skull protects its brain. Its rib cage protects its heart and lungs and its backbone protects its spinal cord.

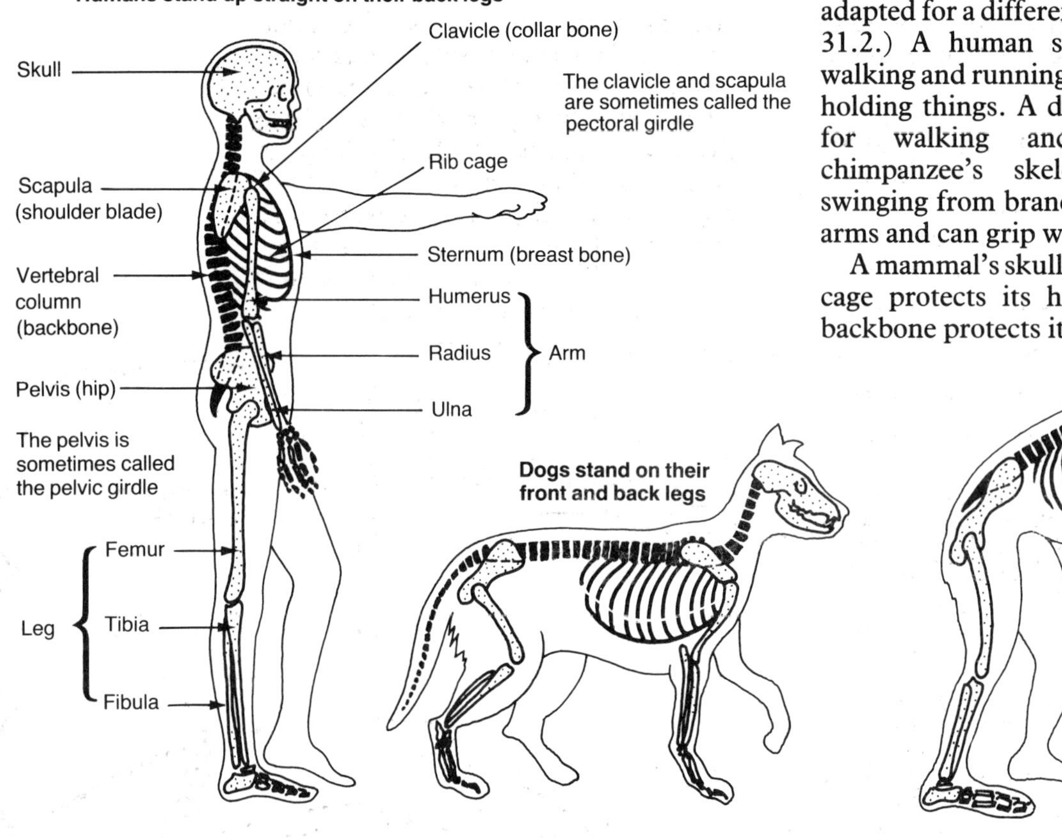

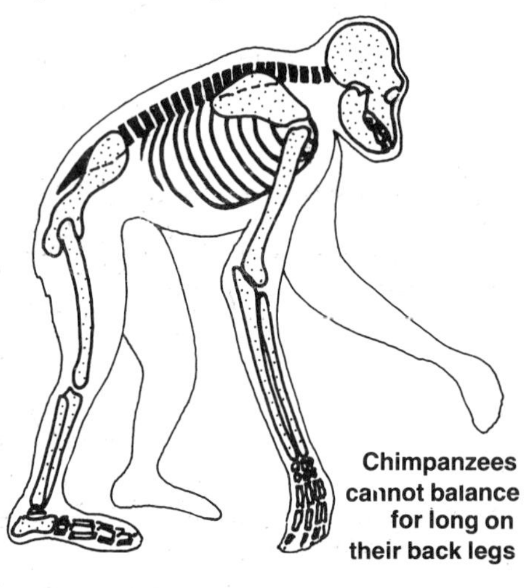

Figure 31.2 Some different sorts of endoskeletons

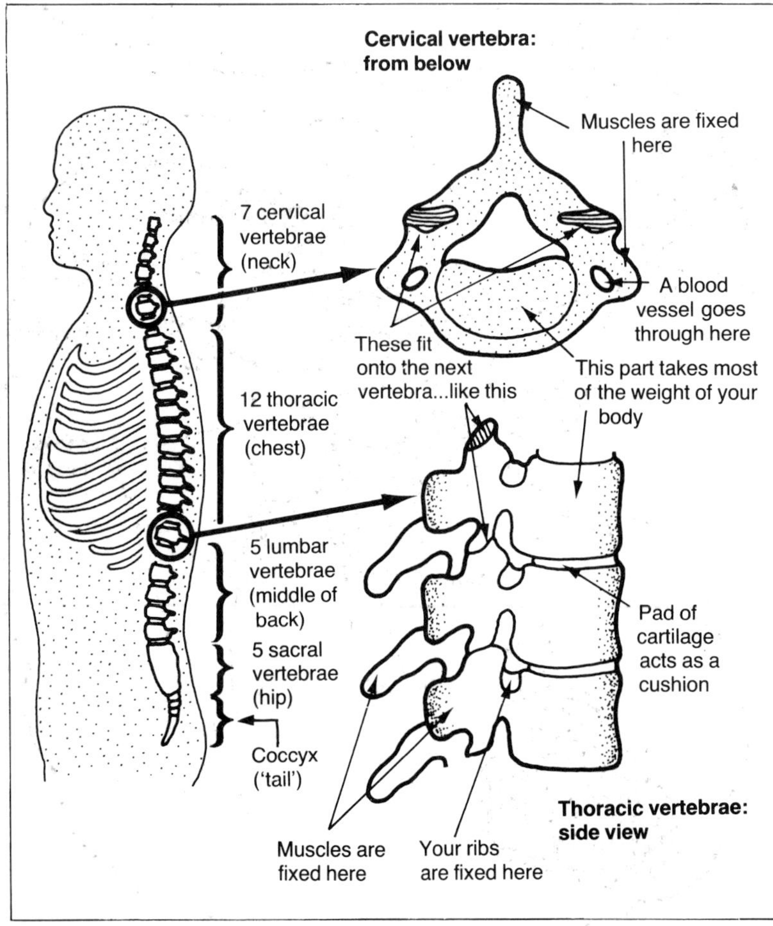

Figure 31.3 How your backbone works

Vertebrae fit here

Your sacrum is fixed to your pelvis here

Nerves from your spinal cord come through these holes

Figure 31.4 The Sacrum

THE BACKBONE

An important part of a mammal's skeleton is its backbone or *vertebral column*. (See figure 31.3.) This is made of many small bones called *vertebrae* (singular: *vertebra*). Joints between the vertebrae let your backbone bend forward, backward, side-to-side and round in a circle. There is a pad of cartilage between each vertebra. This pad stops bumps and shocks from damaging your backbone. The pads are called discs. Your pelvis is firmly fixed to your *sacrum*. The sacrum is made of five vertebrae all joined together. (See figure 31.4.)

JOINTS

Joints are found where two or more bones meet. There are several kinds of joints in your body. (See figure 31.5.)

1. Joints which do not move, or *sutures*. These fixed joints are found in your skull, sacrum and pelvis.
2. Joints where only a little movement happens. These joints are found in your backbone. A small sliding movement can happen between each vertebra. There is a special pivot joint between your atlas and axis vertebrae. Your skull can nod and turn from side-to-side on this pivot.
3. Joints where a lot of movement happens. These are called *synovial joints* and are filled with synovial fluid. This helps to cushion and 'oil' the joint. The ends of bones in synovial joints are covered with cartilage. This is a smooth slippery substance. Strong fibres called *ligaments* hold your bones in place at joints.

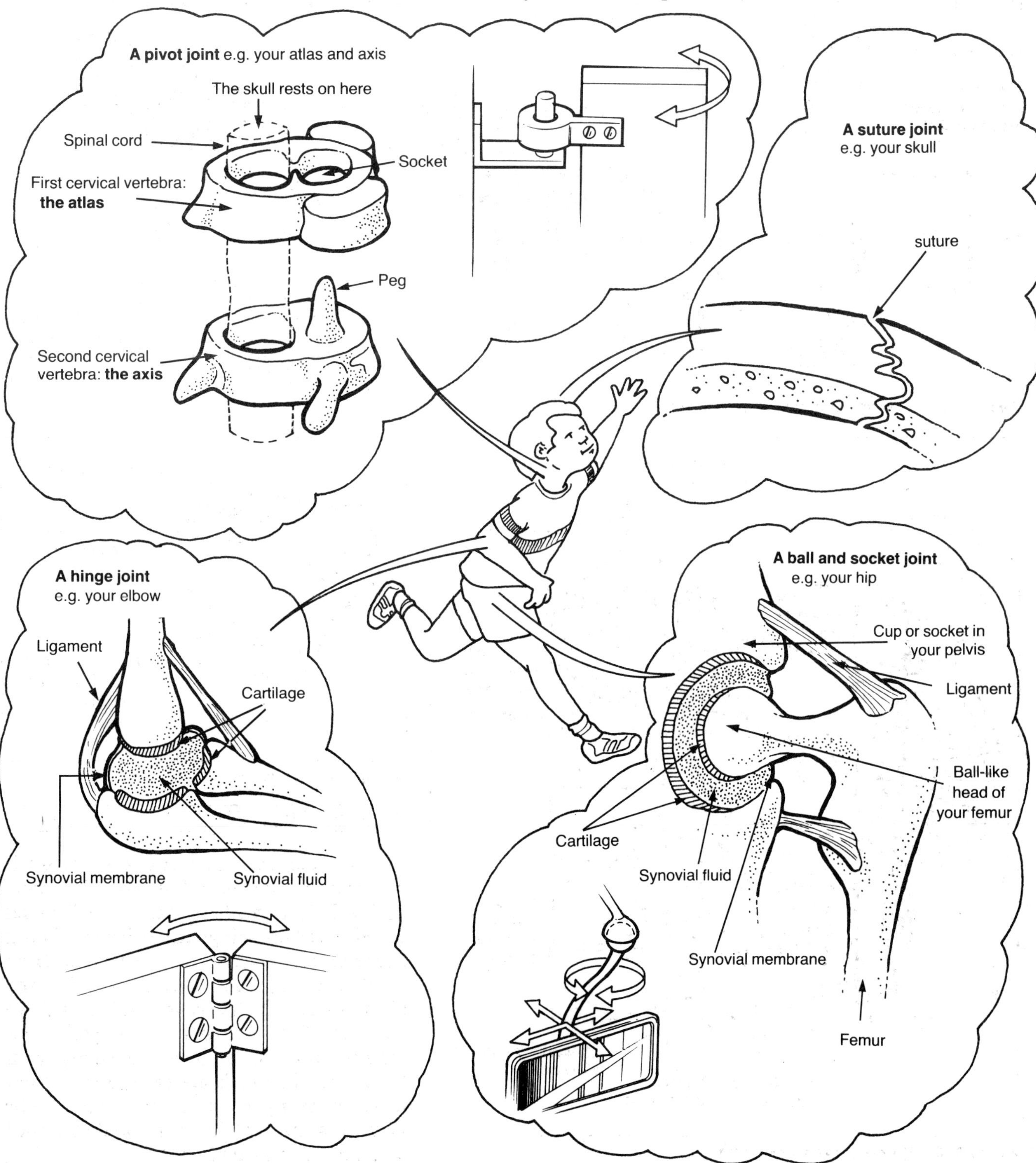

Figure 31.5 Joints

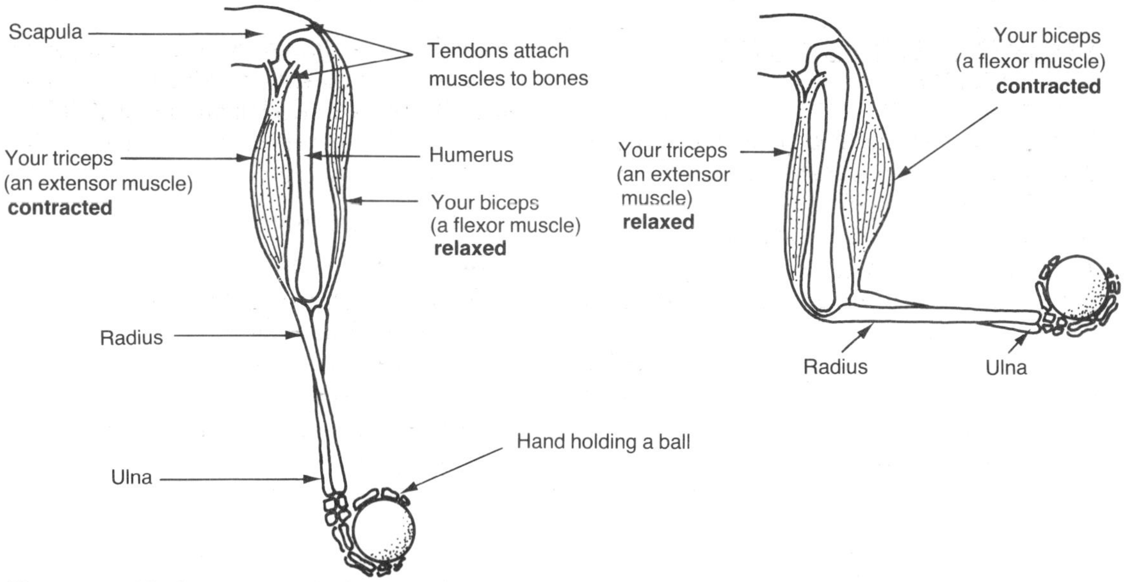

Figure 31.6 Flexing your muscles!

MUSCLES

Muscles cause movement by pulling on bones. Muscles are fixed to bones by *tendons*. These are very strong cords which do not stretch when they are pulled.

Muscles work by contracting and relaxing. A muscle gets shorter and fatter when it contracts and pulls on a bone. When this happens, the muscle cannot return to its first position by itself. It has to be pulled back by another muscle. Because of this most muscles work in pairs.

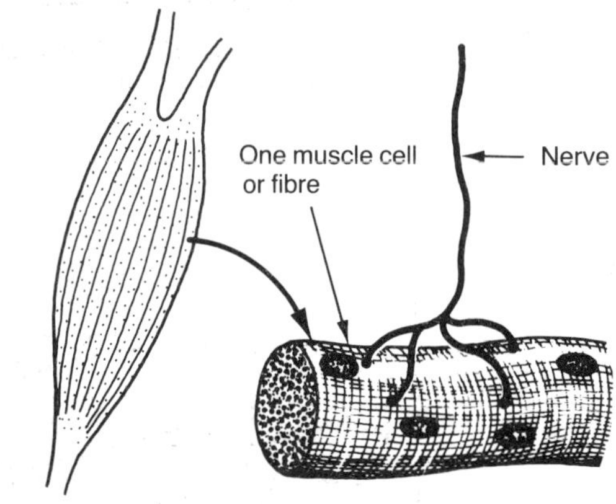

Figure 31.7 Voluntary muscle

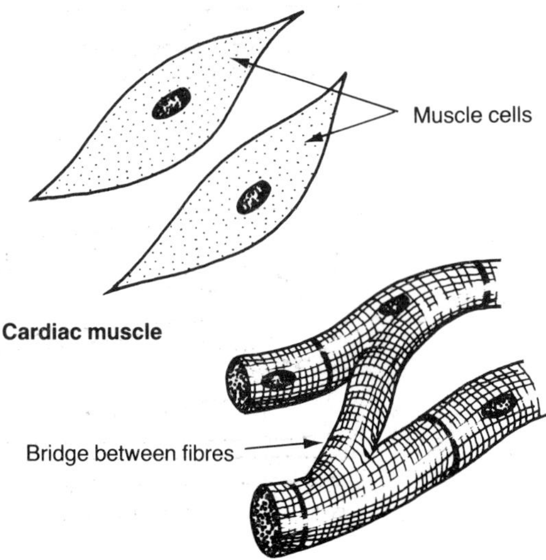

Figure 31.8 Involuntary muscle

Muscles which work in pairs at hinge joints are called *flexor* and *extensor* muscles. Your arm is straightened by an extensor muscle called the triceps muscle. It is bent by a flexor muscle called the biceps muscle. (See figure 31.6.)

Extensor muscles and flexor muscles pull in opposite directions to each other and are called *antagonistic*. Your body is held in position by antagonistic muscles pulling against each other. This happens whether you are moving or keeping still. Muscles which move your skeleton are called *voluntary muscles*. This is because you can control their movements. Muscles which cannot be controlled like this are called *involuntary muscles*.

Voluntary muscle is made up of striped muscle fibres. If you look at them through a microscope, the fibres seem to be striped. The fibres only contract when stimulated by a nerve. These muscles contract powerfully and quickly but soon get tired. (See figure 31.7.)

Involuntary or *smooth* muscle is found in your bladder, digestive system and uterus. It contracts slowly but not very powerfully. It is called 'smooth' because it does not have any stripes when looked at through a microscope. (See figure 31.8.)

Cardiac muscle is only found in the wall of your heart. The fibres have bridges between them. Cardiac muscle contracts quickly and rhythmically about 70 times a minute as long as you live. Cardiac muscle does not need nerves to stimulate it and make it contract. (See figure 31.8.)

LOOKING AFTER YOUR SKELETON

One and a half million people go to their doctors every year because of pain in their backs. The causes of this may often start in young people. Back pain can be caused by: **1.** lifting heavy weights, **2.** slipped discs, **3.** bad posture (wrong habits of standing and sitting), **4.** arthritis.

Slipped discs are caused when the cartilage disc between two of your vertebrae moves out of place. You feel pain if the slipped disc presses on a nerve.

Arthritis is a disease of a person's joints and is quite common in older people. The joints affected are swollen and painful. They cannot work properly. The cause of the disease is not understood.

Bad posture can be caused by:

1. disease and poor diet,
2. bad habits such as standing and sitting with slumped shoulders,
3. poor lighting and ventilation,
4. clothing that is too tight,
5. furniture that does not support your body properly.

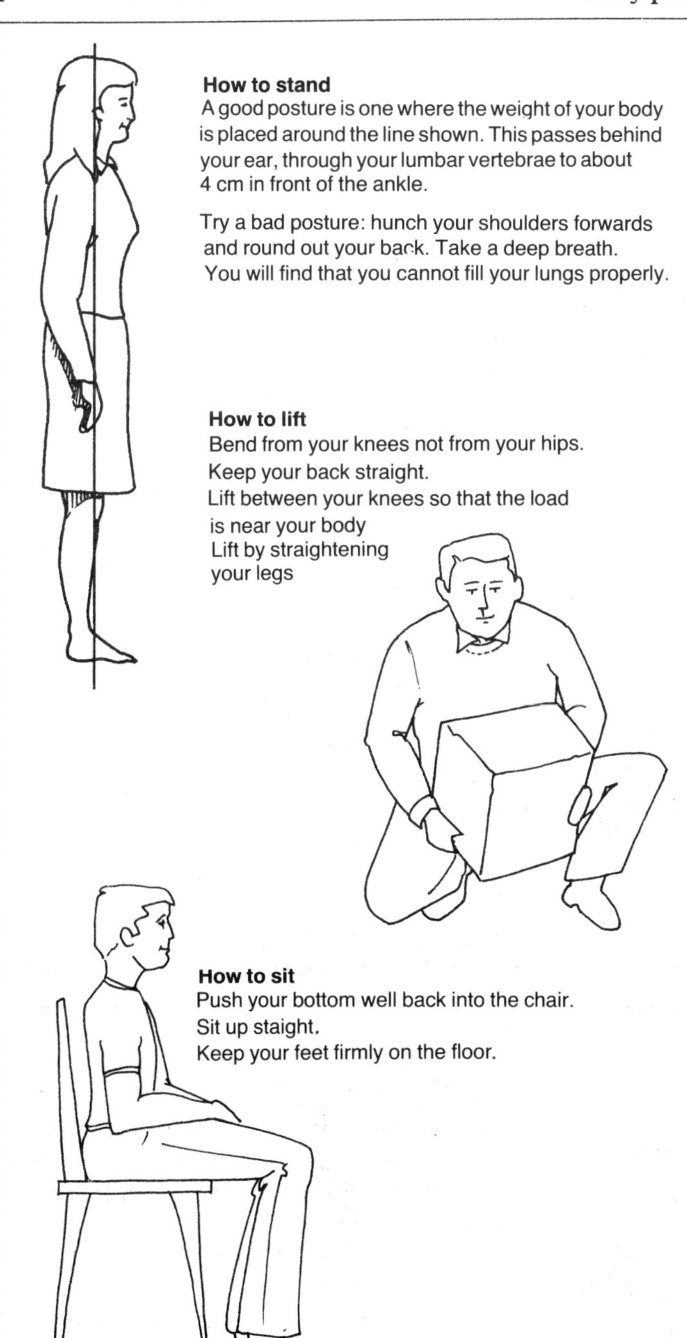

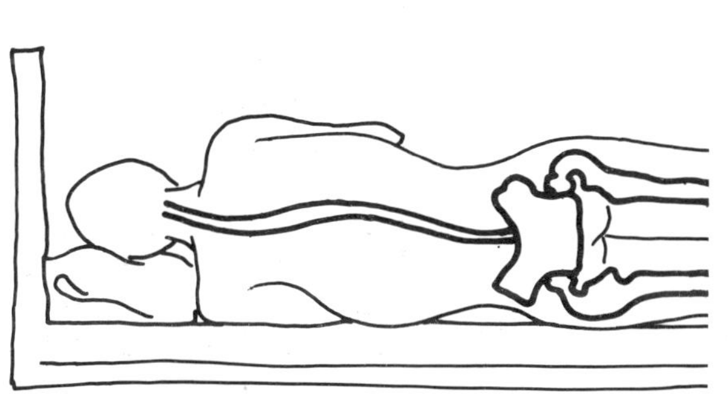

This mattress is too hard. The person's backbone is pushed out of its normal position

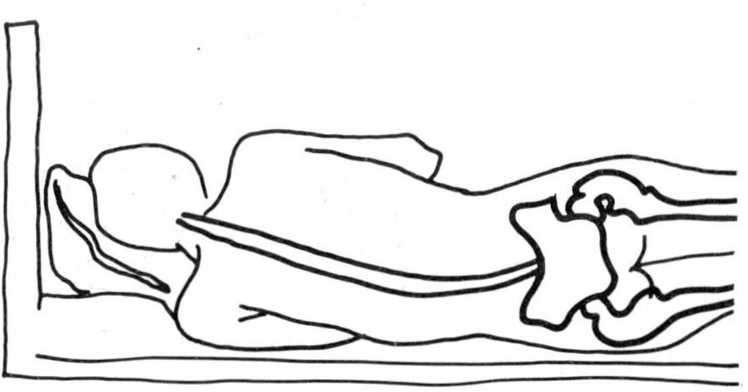

This mattress to too soft and the person's backbone is not supported properly

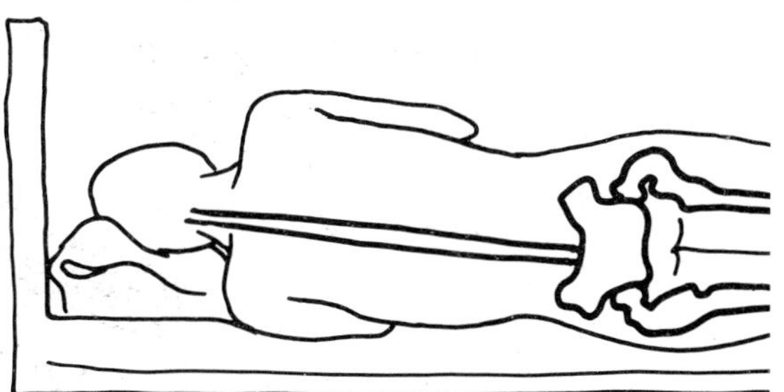

This mattress is just right. The person's backbone is supported in its normal position

Figure 31.9

Fancy that!

About 40-50% of the weight of mammals is made up of muscles!

There are about 70 synovial joints in your skeleton!

Your skeleton is made up of about 200 bones!

Summary

Some animals have an *exoskeleton* round the outside of their bodies.

Vertebrates have an *endoskeleton* inside their bodies. Skeletons *support* animals, help them to *move*, and *protect* soft organs. An endoskeleton is made of many bones which are moved by *muscles* and *joints*.

Muscles work by *contracting* and *relaxing*. A muscle gets *shorter* when it contracts. Many muscles work in pairs: as one muscle contracts, the other relaxes. Different sorts of muscles do different jobs. *Cardiac* muscle is only found in your heart; *voluntary* muscles move your bones; *smooth* muscle is found in your digestive system, bladder and uterus.

Important words

Endoskeleton	a hard skeleton inside an animal.
Exoskeleton	a hard skeleton round the outside of an animal.
Vertebrae	small bones making up the backbone (singular: vertebra).
Vertebral column	a jointed rod, or backbone, forming an important part of the skeleton of vertebrates.
Sutures	joints that do not move.
Synovial joints	joints that have synovial fluid in them.
Ligaments	strong elastic cords that hold joints in position.
Tendons	strong cords that fix muscles to bones.
Flexor muscle	a muscle that bends a hinge joint.
Extensor muscle	a muscle that straightens a hinge joint.

Things to do

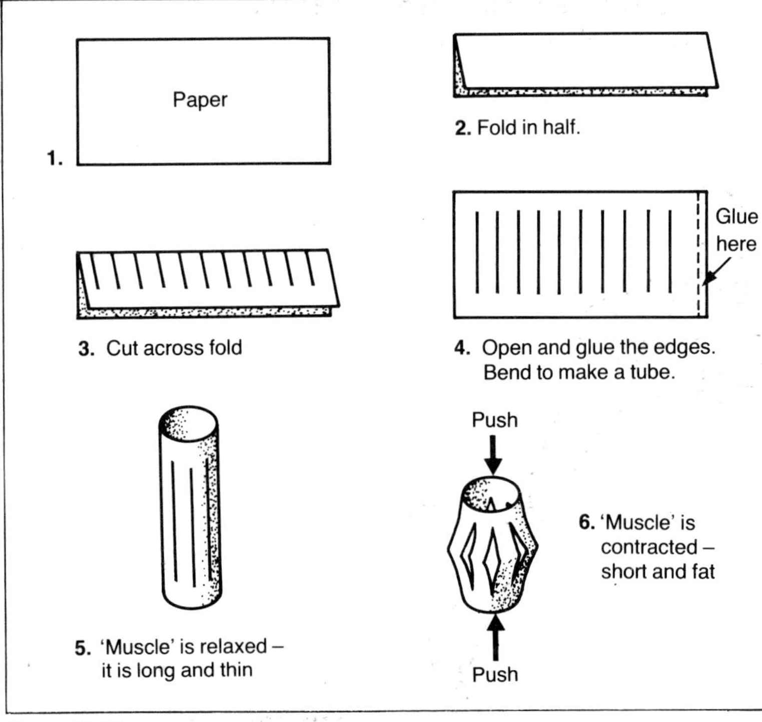

Figure 31.10

1. Make a model muscle as shown in figure 31.10.
   You will need:
   a piece of paper (about 20 cm x 30 cm will do)
   scissors
   glue or Sellotape

2. Draw this simple skeleton (figure 31.11) in your book.

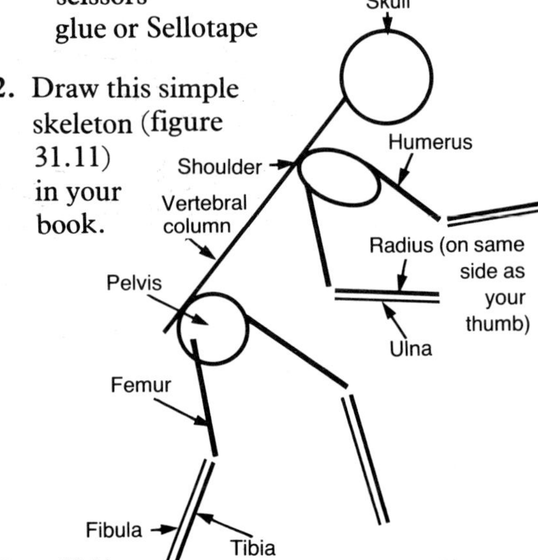

Figure 31.11

Questions

A.

Put each of these parts of sentences into the correct order.

1.	ball and socket joints in all directions	which give movement your hips and shoulders have
2.	your atlas vertebra your head can move because	has a peg which fits inside because your axis vertebra
3.	the joints at your elbows and knees	have synovial fluid inside them and are hinge joints
4.	ligaments are strong fibres which but tendons	fix muscles to bones hold your bones in place
5.	when a muscle contracts and because of this	it may pull on a bone it gets shorter

B.

Look carefully at figure 31.2 on page 190.

1. How many ribs can you see?

2. How many vertebrae are there in the tail?

3. Does the elbow joint point forwards or backwards?

4. Does the knee joint point forwards or backwards?

5. How many bones are there in the lower forearm?

C.

Figure 31.10 shows some of the muscles and bones of the human leg.

1. Choose words from the list to name the bones A to C:

> femur – humerus – ulna – radius – tibia – pelvic-girdle

2. Which muscle must contract to straighten the leg at the knee?

3. What must happen in the other muscle to allow this?

4. What structure connects muscle X to bone C, to move it?

5. What tissue, over the ends of bone B, prevents it from wearing at the joints?

6. What holds the bones together at the knee joint?

7. What lubricates the joint?

8. What type of synovial joint is found at (a) the knee and (b) the hip?

9. Give *one* advantage of having main limb bones which are hollow.

10. Give *one* function, other than support and locomotion, performed by B.

11. Name *two* substances which must be brought by the blood to muscles to enable them to contract.

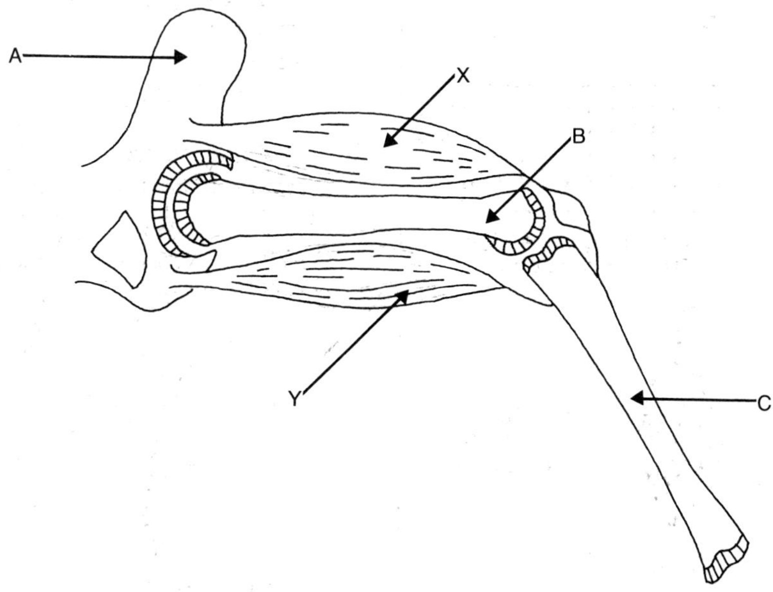

Figure 31.12

(*NREB*)

TOPIC 32

ANIMAL MOVEMENT

Most animals have some kind of skeleton which helps them to move. The central part of the skeleton of vertebrates is the backbone or vertebral column.

HOW FISH MOVE

Perch (figure 32.1) are fish which live in lakes, ponds and rivers. You can catch them with a hook baited with worms or insects. They are good to eat.

Fish have a streamlined shape which lets water flow over their bodies easily. (See figure 32.3.) Streamlined shapes can move much faster through the water than non-streamlined shapes.

The fins help a fish to steer and to balance itself. (See figure 32.3.) The pectoral fins are used to make the fish swim up or down. They do this by tilting in different directions.

The tail fin helps to push a fish forwards by pressing on the water. This happens when the tail swings from side-to-side. The whole body helps this movement because fish use the muscles on each side of their backbones. The backbone is a long rod made up of small bones called vertebrae. When a fish contracts the muscles on one side of its backbone, it bends the tail towards that side. Then it relaxes those muscles and contracts the muscles on the other side of its backbone. This swings its tail to the other side. (See figure 32.4.)

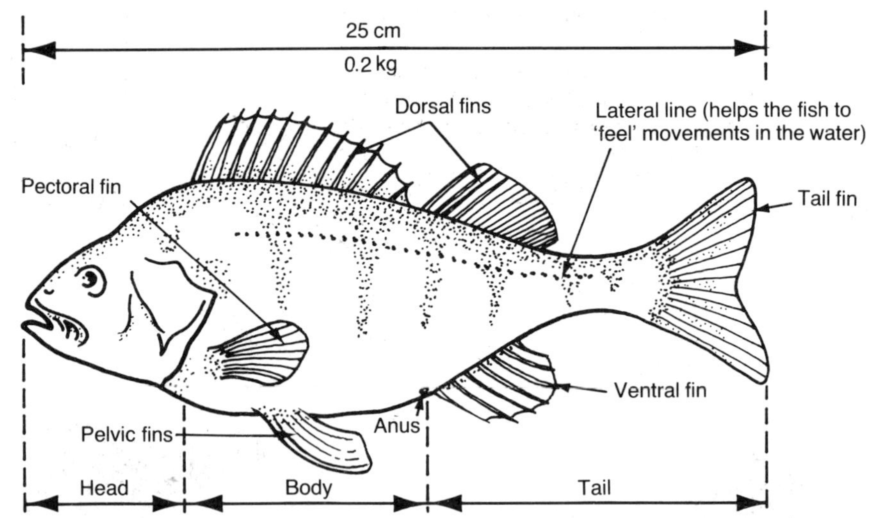

Figure 32.1 A perch

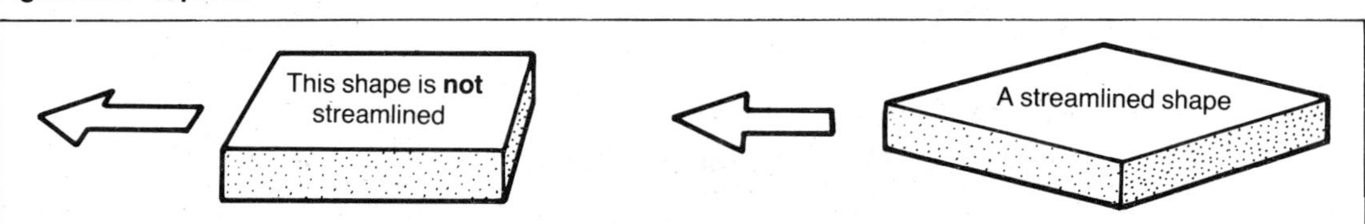

Figure 32.2

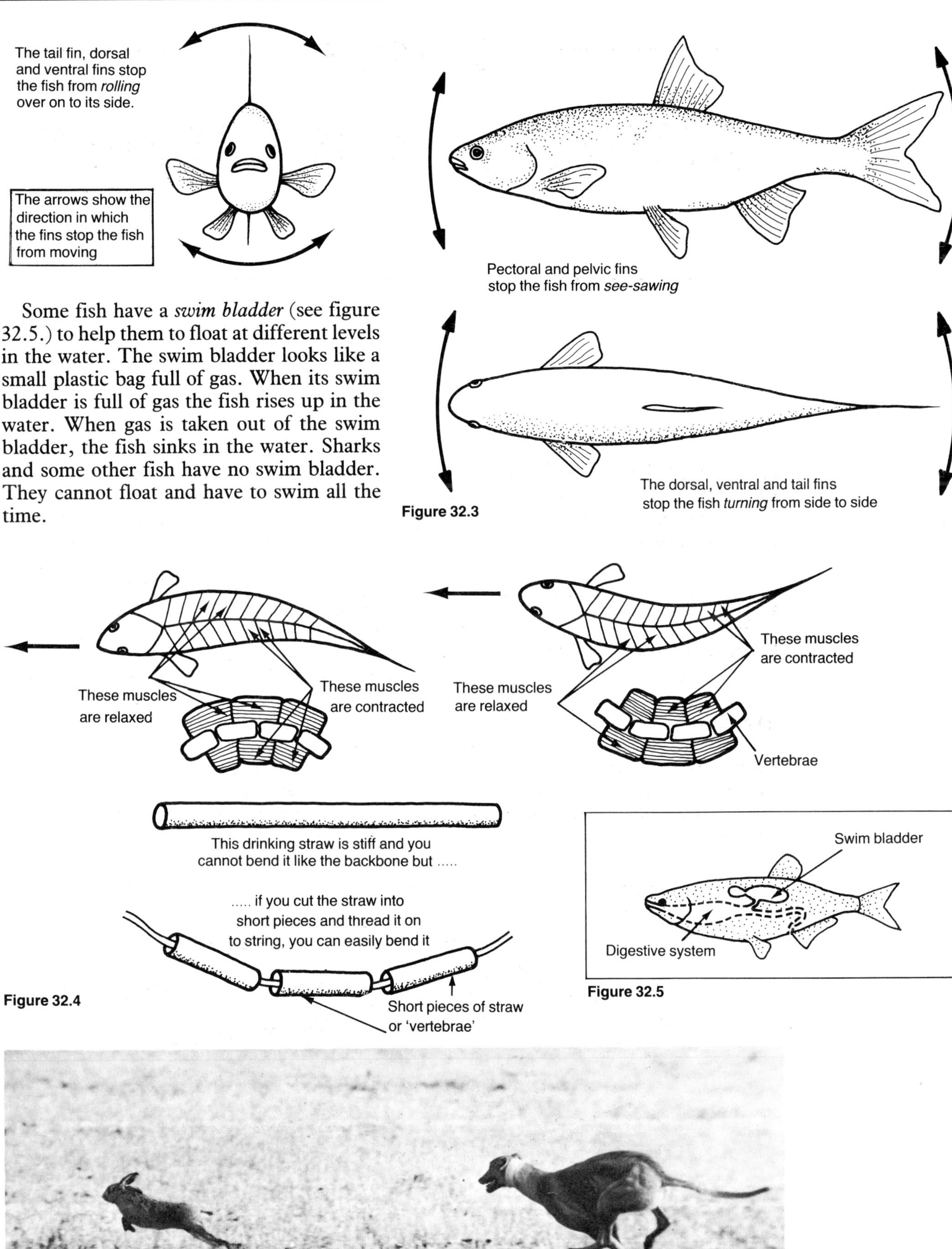

Some fish have a *swim bladder* (see figure 32.5.) to help them to float at different levels in the water. The swim bladder looks like a small plastic bag full of gas. When its swim bladder is full of gas the fish rises up in the water. When gas is taken out of the swim bladder, the fish sinks in the water. Sharks and some other fish have no swim bladder. They cannot float and have to swim all the time.

Figure 32.3

Figure 32.4

Figure 32.5

A greyhound chasing a hare. (See Question B on page 204.)

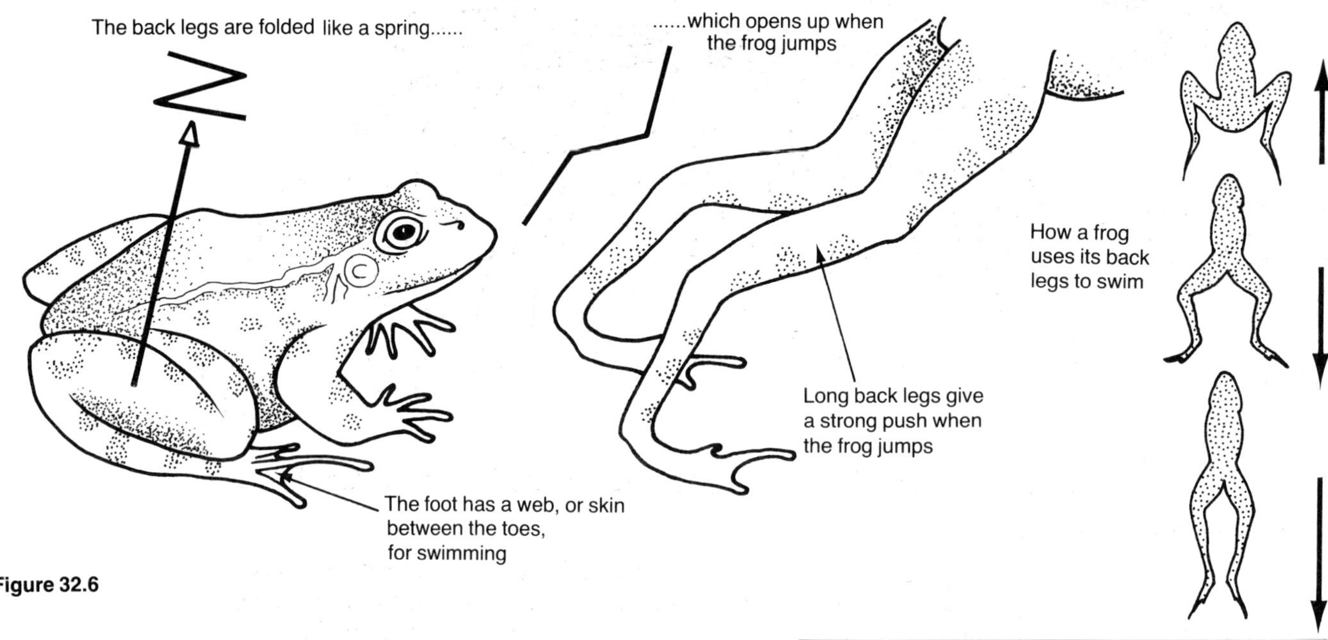

Figure 32.6

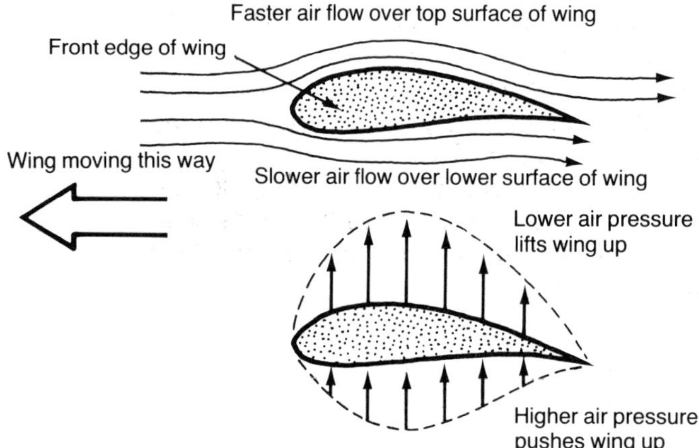

Figure 32.7

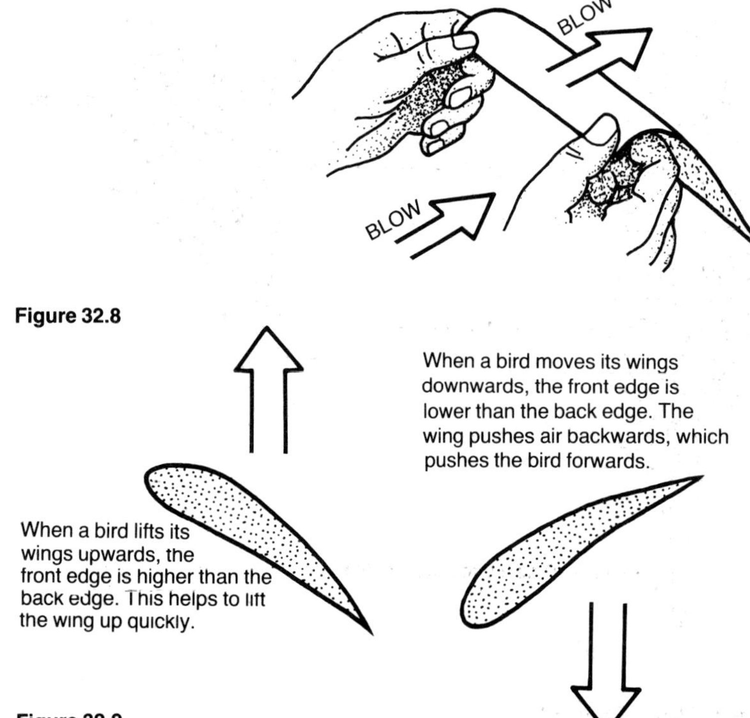

Figure 32.8

Figure 32.9

HOW FROGS MOVE

Frogs swim in water and jump when on land. (See figure 32.6.) They use their back legs for swimming and jumping. Their back feet are webbed to give a bigger surface to press against the water. A frog cannot bend its backbone from side-to-side like a fish.

HOW BIRDS MOVE

A cross section of a bird's wing has a curved shape called an *aerofoil*. When this kind of shape moves through air, it makes the wing lift up. This happens because of the different speed of air flowing over the top and bottom of the wing. Air moves faster over the top surface of the wing than over the bottom surface. Fast moving air has a lower pressure than slow moving air. This means that the wing is lifted up by low pressure above it. At the same time it is pushed up by high pressure from underneath. (See figure 32.7.)

You can make a simple copy of the way an aerofoil works. Hold a piece of paper between the thumb and first finger of both your hands as shown in figure 32.8. The paper now has the shape of an aerofoil. Blow gently and steadily underneath the paper. What happens? Now blow across the top of the paper. What happens this time?

As well as the *lift* from the aerofoil shape, the wings *push* the bird forwards. (See figure 32.9.)

The secondary feathers (see figure 32.10) are the main aerofoil part of the wing that give it lift. The primary feathers give both lift and a forward push during flight.

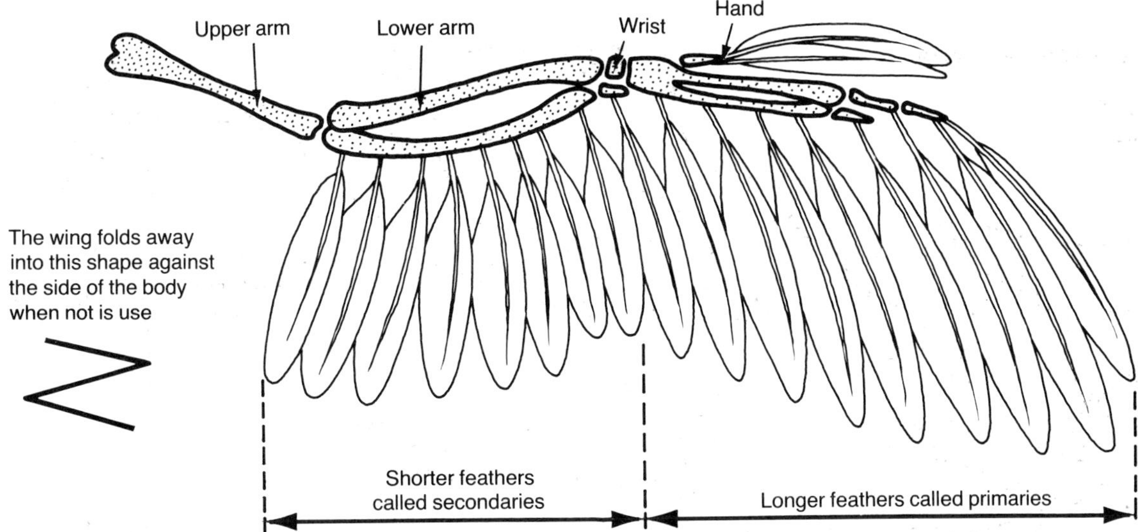

Figure 32.10 A bird's wing

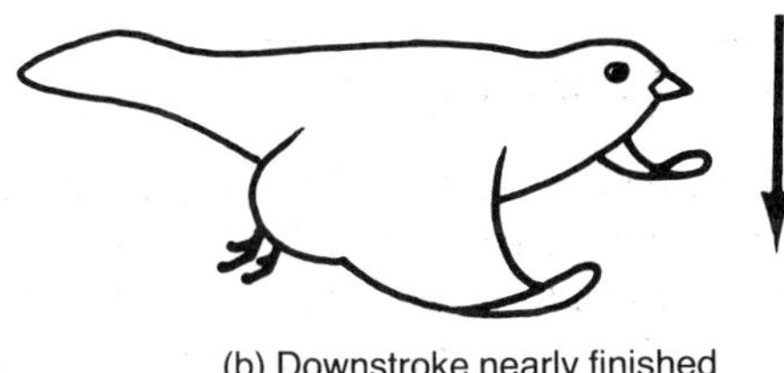

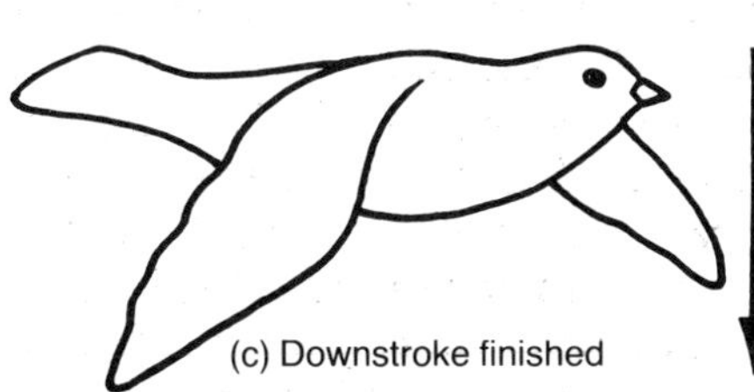

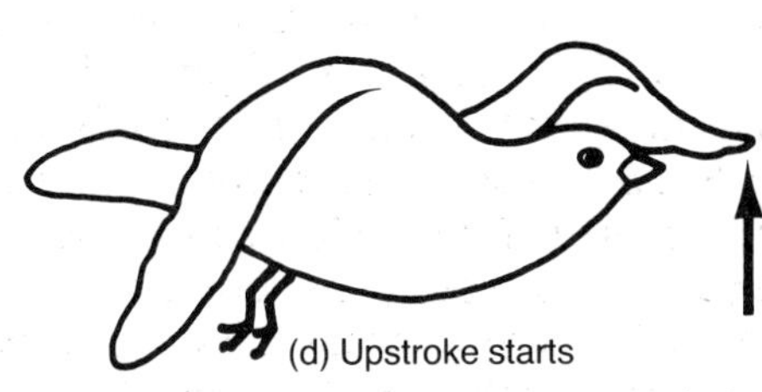

Figure 32.11 How the wings move when a bird flies

The muscles fixed to the quills can make the feathers lift up. Birds use these muscles in cold weather to 'fluff' out their feathers and keep warm. The *vane* is held together by small hooks which stop it opening when it is pressed down on the air. A bird can repair damaged feathers by preening them with its beak. (See figure 32.12.)

Fast-flying birds have small wings so that they can move them quickly. Birds with slow, gliding flight have big wings. (See figure 32.13.)

Barbules
Shaft
Vane
Barb
Quill: fixes the feather into the skin

Figure 32.12 A feather

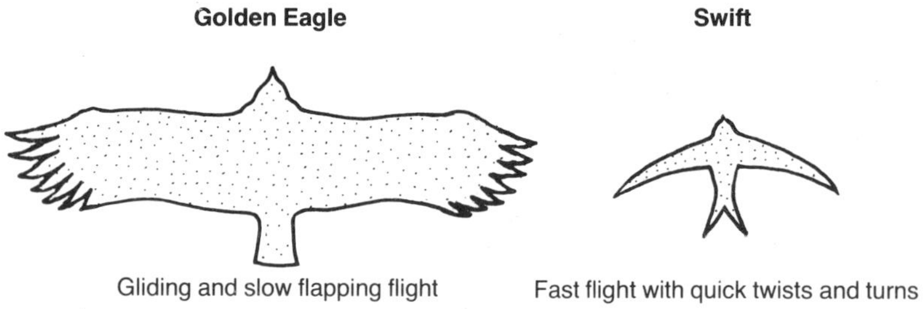

Golden Eagle

Gliding and slow flapping flight

Swift

Fast flight with quick twists and turns

Figure 32.13

As well as wings and feathers, birds have other characteristics which help them to fly.

1. The bones of their skeletons are hollow. This makes them light and strong.
2. They have a streamlined shape.
3. They have strong breast muscles to move their wings. (See figure 32.14.)

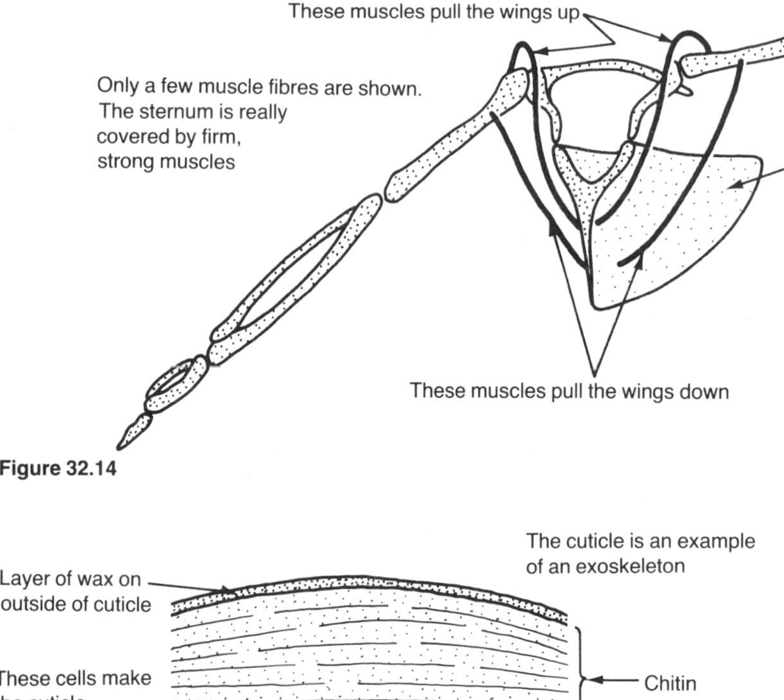

Figure 32.14

THE EXOSKELETON

Some invertebrates such as crabs, lobsters and insects have a skeleton around the *outside* of the body. We call this an exoskeleton. Insects have an exoskeleton called a cuticle. It is made of a light, strong substance called *chitin*.

The cuticle has a thin layer of wax on the outside. (See figure 32.15.) This stops the insect from losing water and drying up.

Insects' bodies are made of segments. Each segment is covered with stiff sheets of chitin. The cuticle between the segments is softer to let them move in different directions. (See figure 32.16.)

The cuticle is an example of an exoskeleton

Layer of wax on outside of cuticle

These cells make the cuticle

Chitin

Figure 32.15

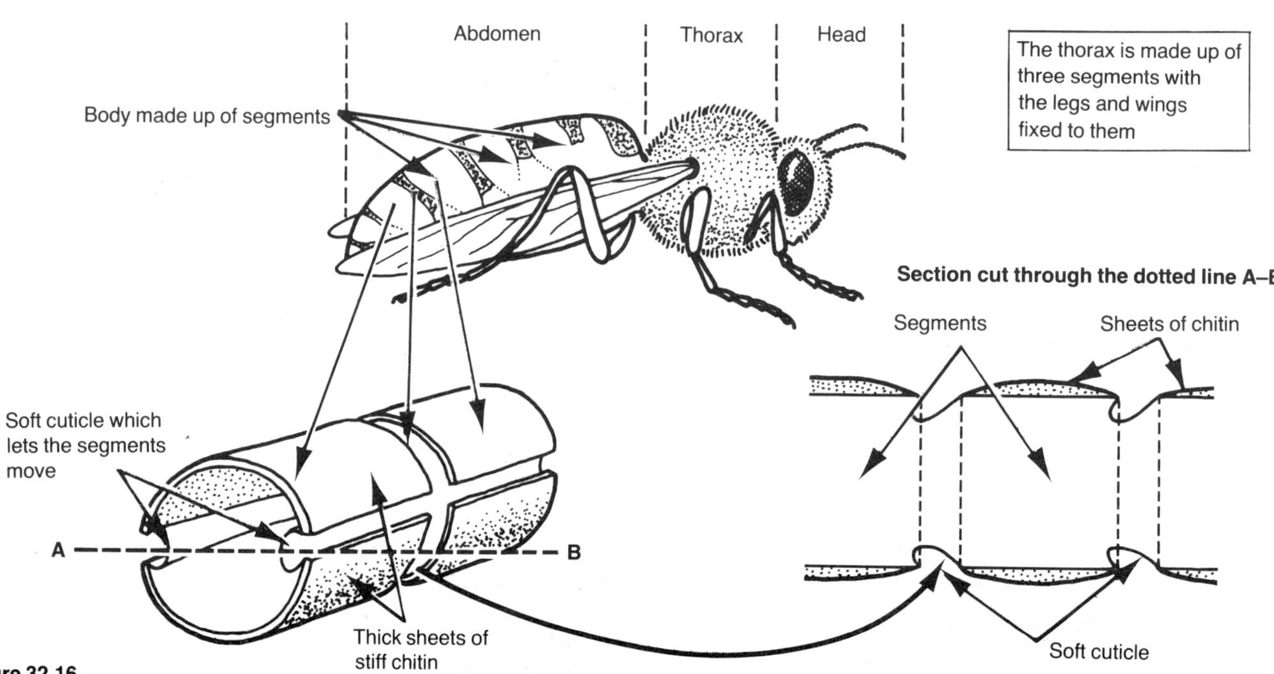

Figure 32.16

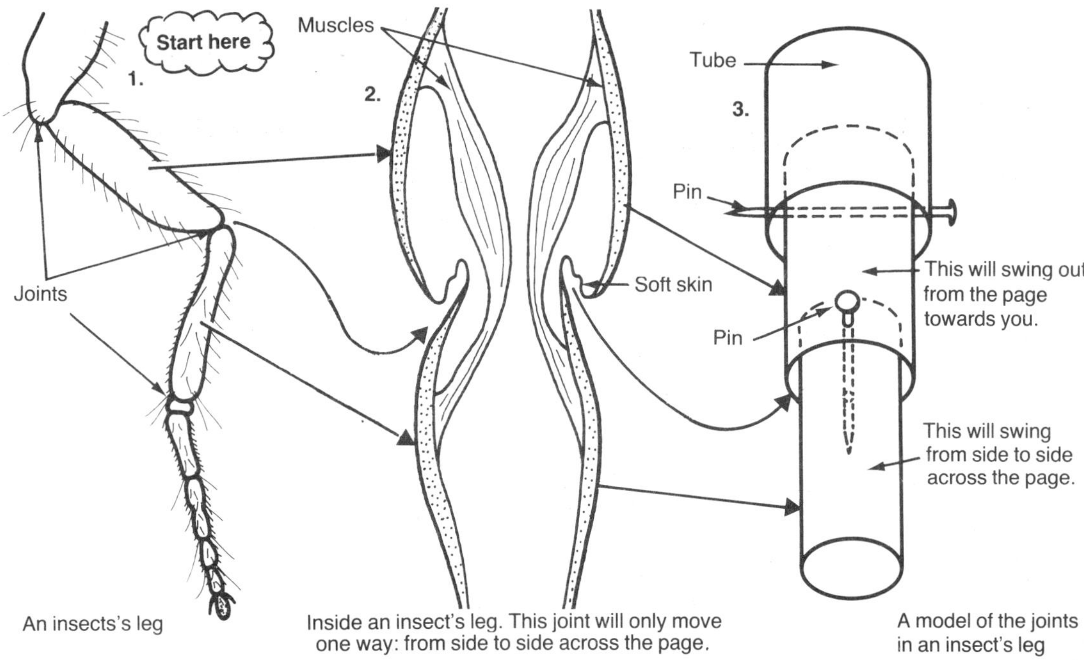

Figure 32.17

HOW INSECTS MOVE

Figure 32.17 shows how the muscles which move the segments are fixed to the inside of the cuticle.

The muscles pull across the joints in the legs to bend or straighten them. Each leg has several joints. The insect can move each joint in one direction only but different joints move in different directions. This lets the insect move its whole leg in any direction.

An insect's thorax is like a box. When they fly, wasps, bees and flies change the shape of this box with their flight muscles. This makes their wings move up and down. (See figure 32.18.)

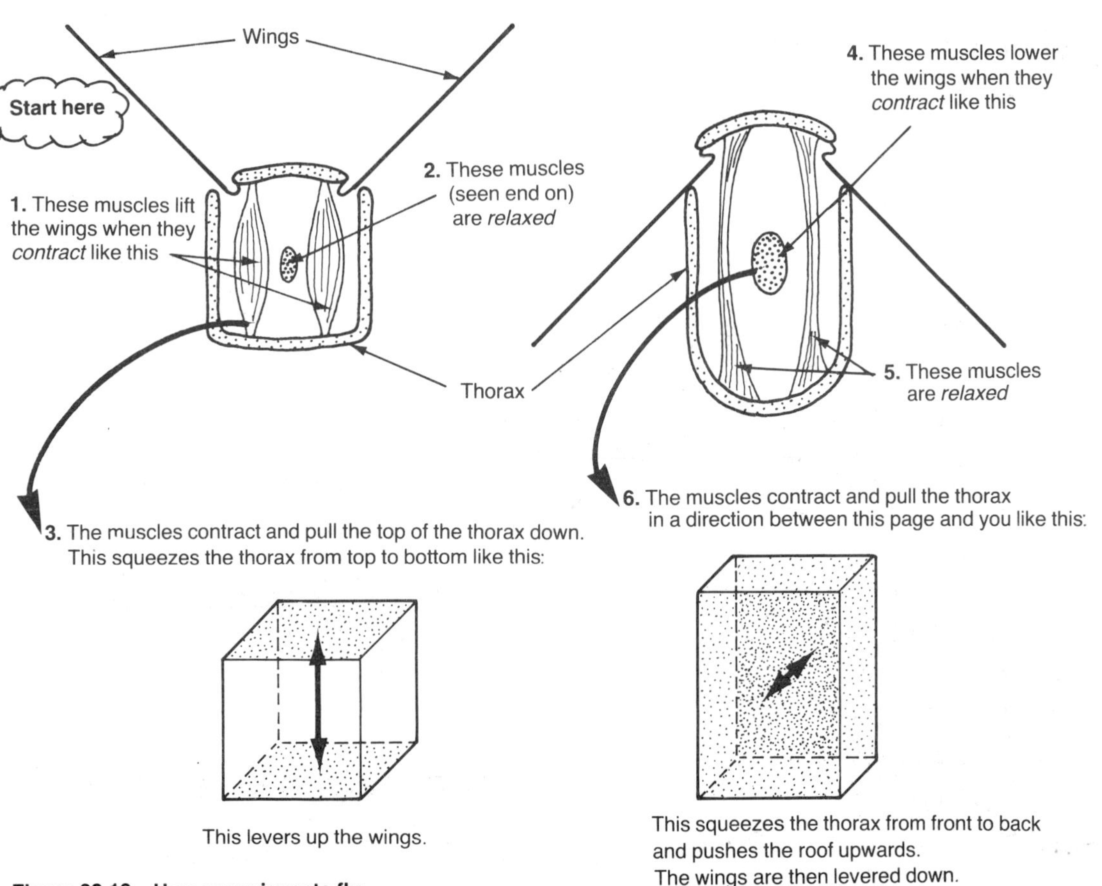

Figure 32.18 How some insects fly

HOW AN EARTHWORM MOVES

Earthworms have no hard skeleton at all. They are supported by a fluid inside their cells and body spaces. They move by squeezing this fluid with muscles and changing their shape. Worms move by *pushing* and *pulling* against the soil. (See figure 32.21.)

Fancy that!

The albatross is the largest of all flying birds. Its wings measure 3.8 metres from tip to tip across its body!

The wings of humming birds beat 200 times a second! The birds can hover and fly backwards!

In a competition held in 1973 a frog called 'Wet Bet' jumped 5.29 metres in one jump!

The fastest insects can fly at a speed of 58 km/hour!

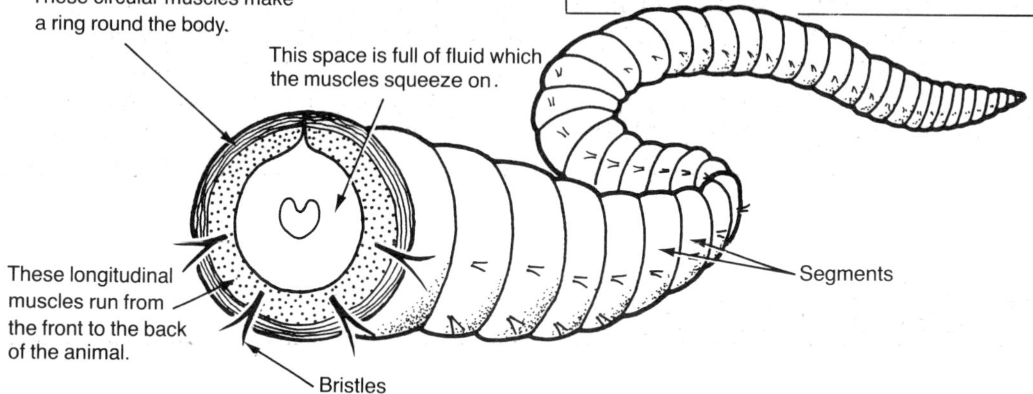

Figure 32.19 An earthworm's muscles

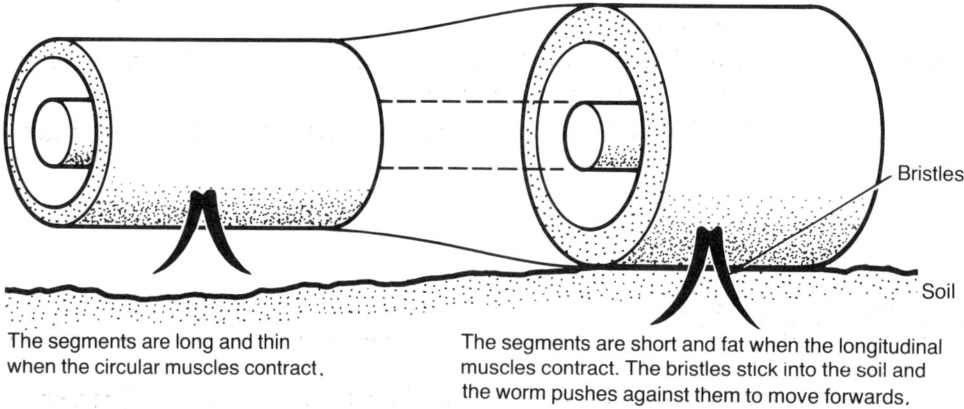

Figure 32.20 Diagram of an earthworm's body, from the side

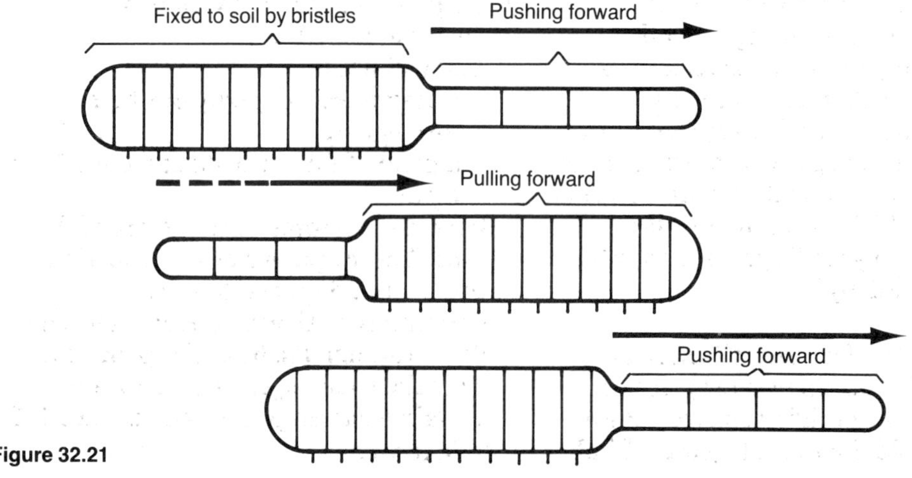

Figure 32.21

Summary

Fish, amphibia, reptiles, birds and mammals are *vertebrates* and have an *endoskeleton*. The *vertebral column* is an important part of the endoskeleton.

A *fish* moves by bending its vertebral column from side to side. Its fins are used for balancing and steering. Some fish have a *swim bladder* which helps them to float at different depths.

Frogs swim in water but jump on land. Their back legs have *webbed feet* and are used for swimming and jumping.

Most *birds* use their *wings* for flying. When air flows over wings they are lifted up from above and pushed up from underneath. *Feathers* make the wings light and strong and keep birds warm.

Some *invertebrates* such as *crabs* and *insects* have an *exoskeleton*. Their bodies are made of segments covered by pieces of exoskeleton. The segments are moved by muscles pulling across joints between the segments. The wings of some insects are moved by muscles which change the shape of the thorax.

Earthworms have no hard skeleton. They move using muscles which squeeze on fluid inside a space in their bodies.

Important words

Aerofoil	a shape, such as the wing of an aeroplane or of a bird, which helps to keep an object in the air.
Chitin	a substance which gives the exoskeleton of insects strength but is quite light.
Swim bladder	a gas-filled bag which helps some fish to float at different levels in water without having to swim.
Vane	the wide, flat part of a feather which is held together by barbules.

Things to do

1. Make a 'flicker book' to show how birds move their wings. Trace the outline of *each* of the birds in figure 32.11 *four* times. Cut round each of the drawings in a square. Stick one drawing of figure 32.11a into the bottom right hand corner of a page in your exercise book or a note book. Ask your teacher first! Stick the other three drawings of figure 32.11a in the same place on the three pages in front. Follow on with figure 32.11b, c and d. Now flick the corners of the pages between your finger and thumb. Watch the bird fly!

2. Make a model of an insect's leg as in figure 32.17. Use three short pieces of cardboard tube of different sizes. Push pins in to hold the tubes together. Find out how the parts move in different directions.
3. Look at a bird's feather under a lens. Find out how the vane is held together.
4. Surprise your friends with this 'impossible trick'.
   You will need:
   a cotton reel with only one hole through it,
   a piece of thin card about 6 cm x 6 cm
   a pin.
   Push the pin through the centre of the card. Put the pin inside the hole of the cotton reel. Support the card underneath with your finger. Blow hard down through the hole. Keep blowing and take your finger away. Can you explain what happens? Look at page 198 to help you.

Questions

A.

Join these sentences using the word 'and' or the word 'because', whichever is correct.

1. The fins of a fish help it to balance. They press on the water.
2. Gas may leave a fish's swim bladder. The fish sinks in the water.
3. Air moves faster over the top of a wing. The wing lifts up.
4. An insect's wings lift up. The thorax is squeezed from top to bottom.
5. An earthworm's circular muscles contract. The earthworm gets longer.
6. An earthworm gets shorter. Its longitudinal muscles contract.

B.

Look carefully at the photograph on page 197.

1. Draw a simple diagram to show the shape of the backbone and positions of the legs in the greyhound and the hare. Use one line for the front legs, one for the back legs, and one for the backbone.
2. Draw two other diagrams to show the next position of the backbone and legs of the hare and greyhound.
3. How does the backbone help these animals to run quickly?

C.

Figure 32.22 shows a dorsal view of a fish illustrating the muscle arrangement.

1. Name X.
2. If muscle block 8 is contracted, state the condition of muscle block H.
3. Name the fins used for braking when the fish stops swimming.
4. State how the backwardly pointing scales of a fish help in movement.

(WJEC)

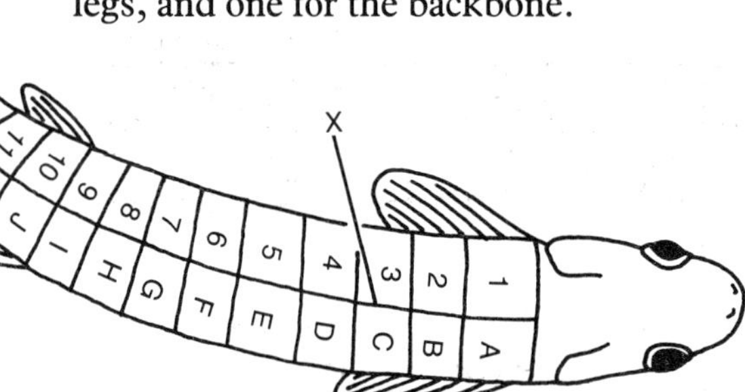

Figure 32.22

D.

1. Figure 32.23 shows the positions taken by an earthworm as it moves long the ground.
   (a) Measure the distance travelled by the earthworm in 15 seconds.
   (b) How does the earthworm grip the ground as it moves along?
   (c) Why does the skin in an earthworm produce mucus (slime)?
2. When you hold an earthworm up against the light you can see a black line which extends from mouth to anus. What is this line and why is it black?
3. How does the earthworm's behaviour benefit the farmer?

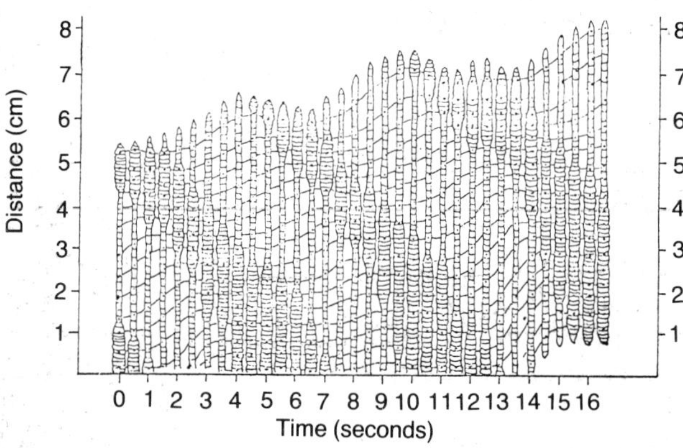

Figure 32.23

(SREB)

TOPIC 33

TEETH

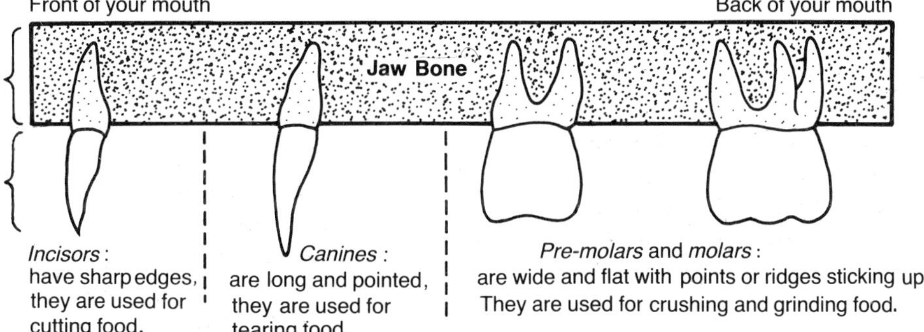

Figure 33.1

You can tell the sort of food mammals eat by the kind of teeth they have.

Carnivores use their teeth to kill other animals and tear the flesh or meat. Herbivores use their teeth to cut through plants and to grind them up. Omnivores use their teeth to eat both flesh and plants. All these jobs are done by four kinds of teeth. (See figure 33.1.)

Incisors and canines have one root but premolars and molars have more than one. Each root fits into a socket in your jawbone. (See figure 33.2.)

HOW TEETH GROW

Most mammals grow two sets of teeth during their lives. The first set are called *milk teeth* and are found only in young mammals. Milk teeth first appear in human babies when they are about 5 months old.

Between the ages of 5 and 17 years your milk teeth are replaced by *permanent teeth*. These should last you all your life! 'Wisdom' teeth are the last molars of the permanent teeth to grow.

In older carnivores and omnivores the hole in the root narrows. This slows down the blood supply to the teeth and they stop growing. In herbivores the hole in the root stays wide open and their teeth go on growing all their life. They need to do this because their teeth are worn away by grinding their food.

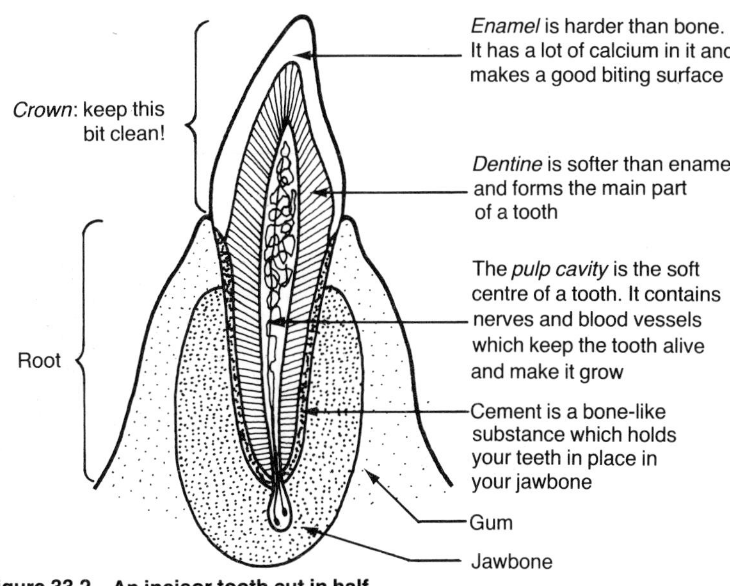

Figure 33.2 An incisor tooth cut in half

TEETH AT WORK

The lower jaw moves from side to side. This movement: (a) helps the incisors to slice through grass, (b) pulls the ridges of the pre-molars and molars across each other like this:

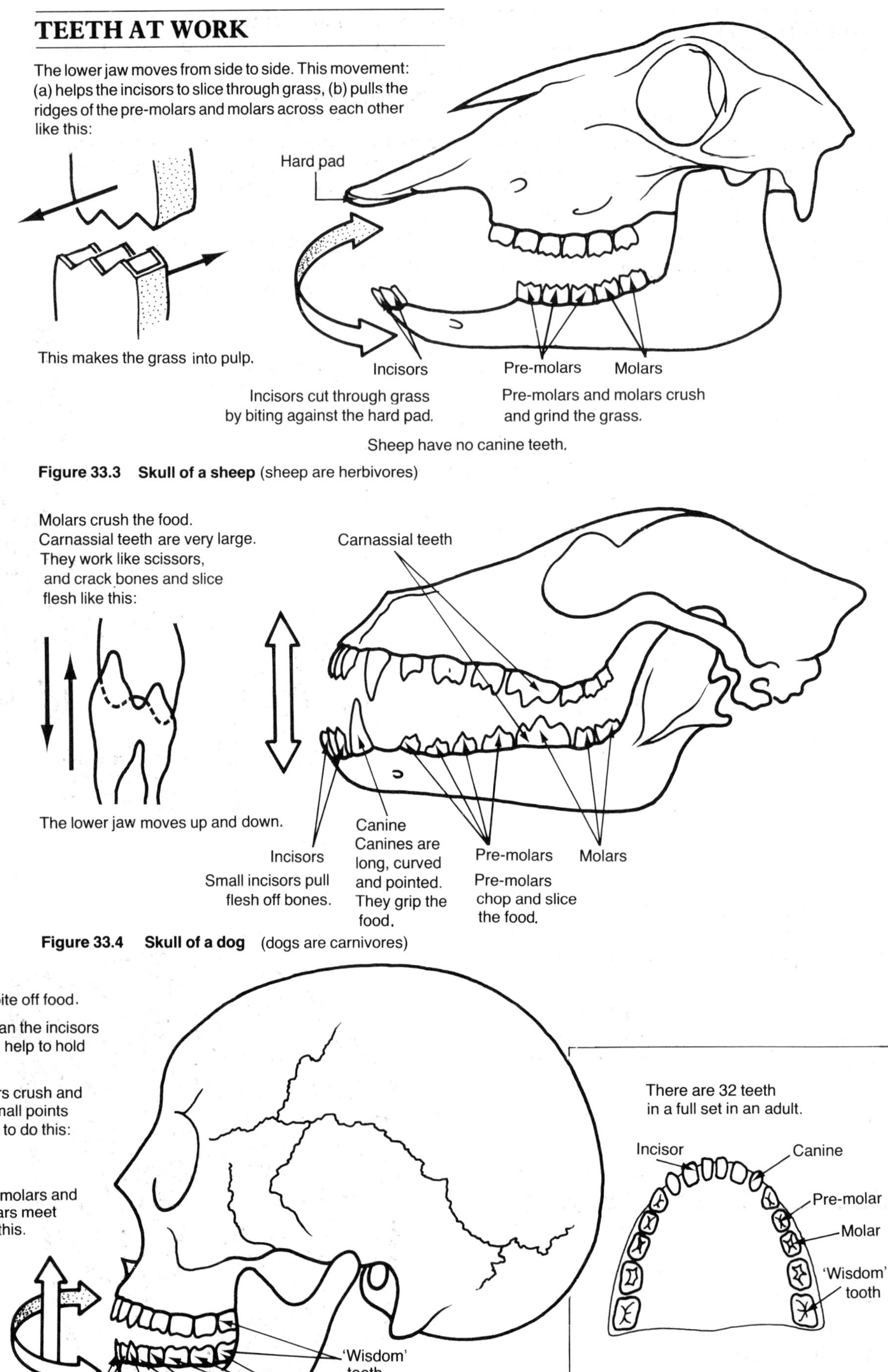

Figure 33.3 Skull of a sheep (sheep are herbivores)

Figure 33.4 Skull of a dog (dogs are carnivores)

Incisors are used to bite off food.

Canines are longer than the incisors and are curved. They help to hold and bite the food.

Pre-molars and molars crush and grind the food. The small points on their surfaces help to do this:

Pre-molars and molars meet like this.

The jaw moves up and down and slightly sideways when chewing.

Incisors 1 and 2 Canine Pre-molars 1 and 2 Molars 1 – 3

Figure 33.5 A human skull (humans are omnivores)

Figure 33.6 The teeth in the lower jaw of an adult

TOOTH DECAY

After a meal, small bits of food are left in your mouth. This food, with saliva and bacteria, makes a sticky, soft slime called *plaque*. This sticks to your teeth and it is hard to brush off. Bacteria change the sugar in plaque into acids which attack your tooth enamel. This is the start of tooth decay. In time, a hole develops in the enamel and you may need a filling. If the decay is bad your tooth may have to be taken out. (See figure 33.7.)

You may have plaque even on shiny white teeth as it is hard to see. Chemists sell 'disclosing solutions' to help to show-up plaque. You rinse the solution around your mouth and the plaque is stained so that you can see it.

Eating foods containing a lot of sugar is very bad for your teeth. Sugar helps to make more plaque as well as making acids.

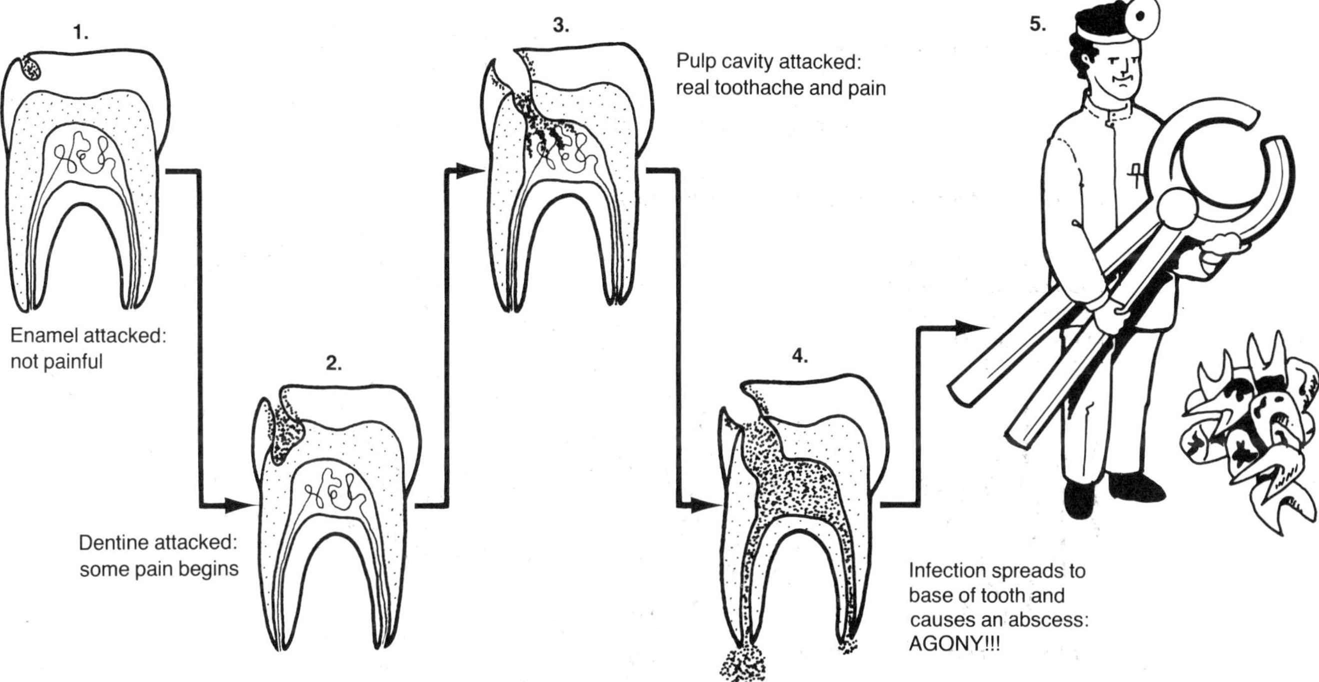

Figure 33.7 How the rot starts!

LOOKING AFTER YOUR TEETH

Your toothbrush should look like this:

Figure 33.8

If it looks like this, buy a new one!

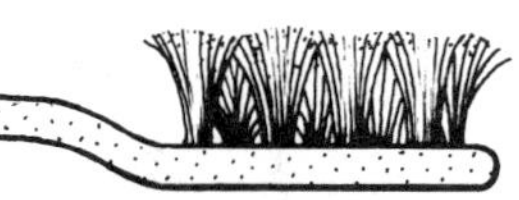

Figure 33.9

> **Fancy that:**
>
> Some babies are born with a few teeth already present!
>
> One in three people in Britain over 16 years-old have no natural teeth! They have all been taken out because they were decayed!

1. Difficult places for removing plaque

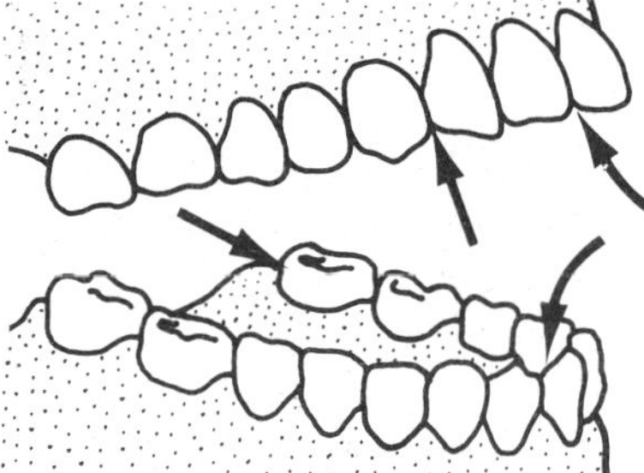

2. Use a disclosing solution to show plaque

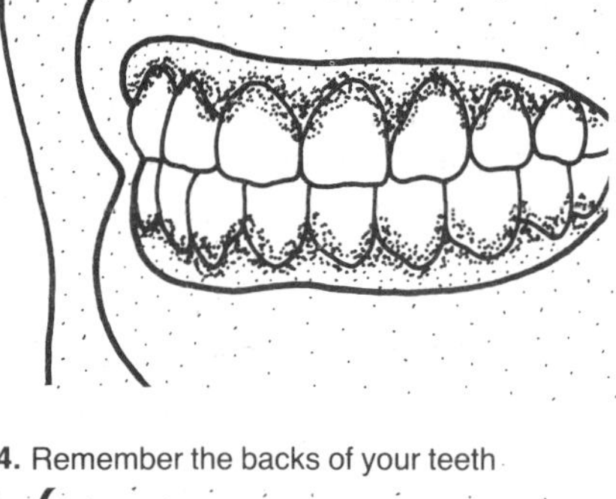

3. Brush with a 'circular' movement

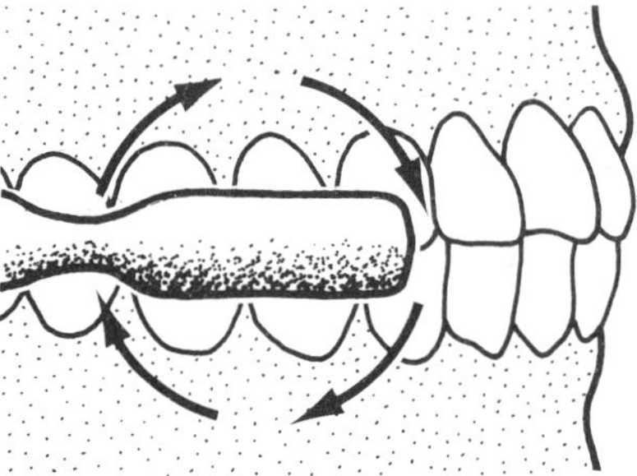

4. Remember the backs of your teeth

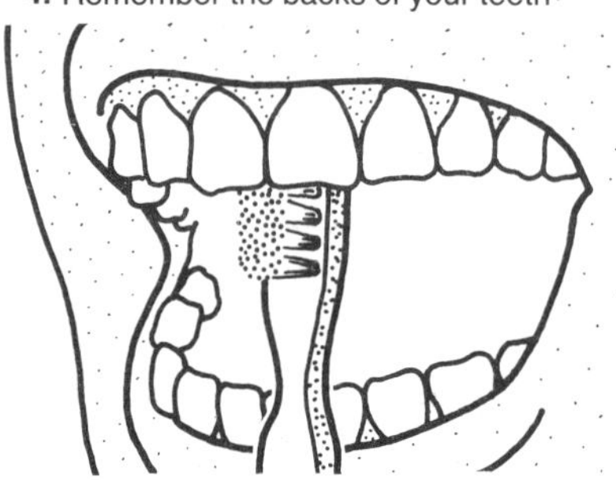

Figure 33.10 How to clean your teeth properly

In some places *fluoride* is put into the drinking water. (See figure 33.11.) Fluoride makes tooth enamel stronger so it is more difficult for acids to attack. It may also help to mend enamel after it has been attacked. Tooth decay is much reduced by fluoride. Brushing your teeth with a fluoride toothpaste is a good way of protecting them against decay. Some people think that fluoride should *not* be put into water. They think that you should not have to drink it if you don't want to.

Clean your teeth twice a day: *after* breakfast and *before* going to bed.

Don't have a sweet bedtime drink *after* you have cleaned your teeth.

Go to your dentist at least every six months. Any decay can then be stopped before it gets worse – and painful!

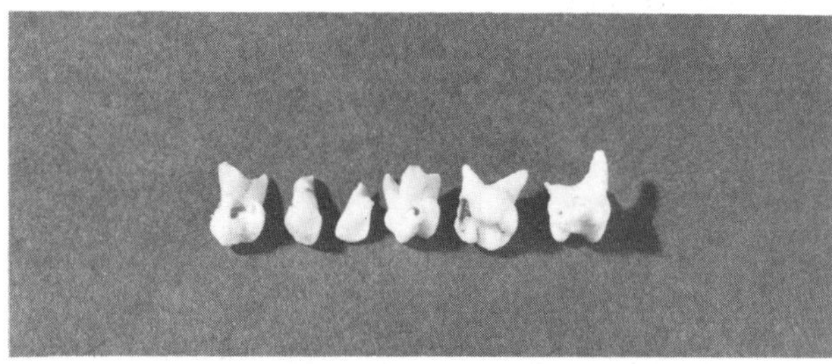

The teeth which had to be taken from 100 five-year old children in Droitwich (where fluoride is added to water).

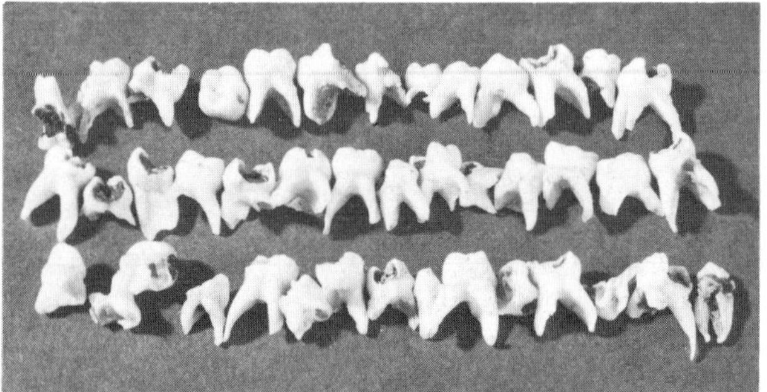

The teeth which had to be taken from 100 five-year old children in Worcester (where fluoride is *not* added to water). Over six times more teeth had to be taken from the Worcester children.

Figure 33.11 Where water has fluoride (1980)

Summary

Incisor teeth are used for cutting food; *canine* teeth are used for tearing and *premolars* and *molars* are for crushing and grinding.

Carnivores have long canine teeth for holding their food. *Herbivores* may have no canine teeth. Carnivores and herbivores may have different jaw movements because their teeth work in different ways. *Mammals* grow two sets of teeth. The *milk teeth* grow in young mammals and are replaced by the *permanent teeth*. The *crown* of a tooth is covered by hard *enamel*. Underneath there is softer *dentine*. The *pulp cavity* has *blood vessels* and *nerves* in it.

Sweet foods make *plaque* which sticks to your teeth. Bacteria in the plaque make acids which attack tooth enamel. Cleaning your teeth properly, eating the right foods and visiting your dentist often are all important for healthy teeth. *Fluoride* in drinking water or toothpaste helps to stop tooth decay.

Important words

Incisor	a tooth with a sharp cutting edge.
Canine	a pointed tooth used for biting.
Molar	a tooth with a flat surface used for grinding; it has two or three roots. There are no molars in the milk teeth.
Pre-molar	a tooth used for crushing and grinding; there are premolars in the milk teeth.
Milk teeth	the first set of teeth that grows in young mammals; there are no molars in the milk teeth.
Permanent teeth	the second set of teeth that mammals grow.
Enamel	a very hard substance that covers the crown of a tooth.
Dentine	forms the main part of a tooth.
Pulp cavity	a space inside the dentine. It contains nerves and blood vessels.
Plaque	a sticky substance on teeth made of food, saliva and bacteria.
Fluoride	a chemical substance added to some toothpaste and drinking water to help stop tooth decay.

Things to do

1. How much plaque have you got?

   You will need:
   some purple or blue food dye used to colour cake icing (**do not use any other sort of dye**)
   Vaseline
   cotton wool

   Rub some Vaseline on your lips to stop the dye from staining them. Soak a piece of cotton wool in the food dye and bite on it. Suck the dye out, rinse it round your mouth and spit it out. Look at your teeth in a mirror. The plaque will be stained. Clean your teeth with toothpaste and your toothbrush. Repeat the staining. Are you cleaning your teeth properly?

2. See if you can get a few teeth from your dentist. Stand them in disinfectant for an hour. Then, take them out, dry them and weigh them carefully on an accurate balance. Stand the teeth in a fizzy cola drink and leave them for a week. Then take them out, dry them and weigh them again. Is it true that cola drinks have something in them which attacks enamel?

Questions

A.

Study the table and answer the questions.

1. How much more fluoride is needed to reduce the number of decayed teeth from 6.3 to 3.3 and from 4.2 to 2.8?
2. By how much is tooth decay reduced when the fluoride content of the water is increased from 0.125 to 1.0 and from 0.5 to 2.5?
3. How can you provide fluoride protection for your teeth, apart from through the water supply.

Fluoride in water supply (ppm)	0.0	0.125	0.25	0.5	0.85	1.0	1.35	1.5	2.0	2.5
Number of decayed teeth per child	8.0	8.2	6.3	4.2	3.3	3.0	2.8	2.6	2.5	2.4

B.

Read the following passage carefully.

The teeth of vertebrates break food up into smaller particles and they vary in size and shape according to the diet of the animal.

The teeth grow in holes in the jaw bone called sockets, the part embedded in the socket is called the root and the part visible above the gum is called the *crown*. Each tooth is made up of several layers, in the centre is the pulp cavity which contains blood vessels and nerves and around this is the bone like tissue called dentine. The root of the tooth is covered with a substance called cementum, embedded in this are fibres which attach the tooth to the jaw bone and gum. Each tooth has its crown covered by enamel, this is the hardest tissue in the human body and its function is to protect the tooth. Calcium phosphate is needed in the diet to ensure healthy growth of both dentine and enamel.

In reptiles and amphibians all the teeth are simple and pointed in shape but in mammals the teeth are specialised to perform particular functions. In mammals the eight front teeth are called incisors, they are chisel shaped and are used for biting, these teeth are especially large in gnawing animals such as squirrels and beavers. The four pointed canine teeth, one in each corner of the mouth are used for tearing food. Flesh eating animals such as wolves and lions have very large canine teeth. Behind the canines are the premolars and molars these are adapted for cutting or grinding the food. Man has 8 premolars and 12 molars. In carnivores these back teeth include the very large carnassial teeth which can be used to crack bones and cut the flesh into pieces small enough to swallow. In herbivores the sideways jaw action moves the ridged back teeth over each other and so grinds the food between them this has the effect of wearing away the surface of the tooth but they never wear away completely because they continue to grow throughout the animal's life.

In man the first teeth start to appear at about six months after birth, the incisors appearing first. The complete set of 20 primary or milk teeth will ususally have appeared by the time a child is three-years-old. At the age of six the first molars will appear and gradually the primary incisors and canines will be replaced by permanent teeth. By the age of fourteen there are usually 28 permanent teeth present, fourteen in each jaw. The last 4 molar teeth to emerge are called *wisdom teeth* and they appear between the ages of fiteen and twenty-five, sometimes they fail to appear.

The two most common dental diseases are tooth decay or caries and *gingivitis* which is inflammation of the gums, both are related to the presence of plaque. *Plaque* consists of mucin from saliva and bacteria, it forms all over the tooth but builds up in the depressions between the cusps of premolar and molar teeth and also where the crown of the tooth meets the gum. As the plaque accumulates it may react with inorganic salts to form a hard scale like coating on the tooth, this is called tartar. Whenever sugar is present in the mouth the plaque becomes acid and this acid causes the breakdown of the enamel. Once the enamel is destroyed bacteria invade the tooth and cause inflammation of the pulp cavity which results in toothache, after the pulp has been destroyed by bacteria they move down the root and into the jaw itself and this causes a painful abcess.

1. Read the passage carefully and explain the meaning of the following, as they are used in the passage: crown (line 3); wisdom teeth (line 20); gingivitis (line 2); plaque (line 23).

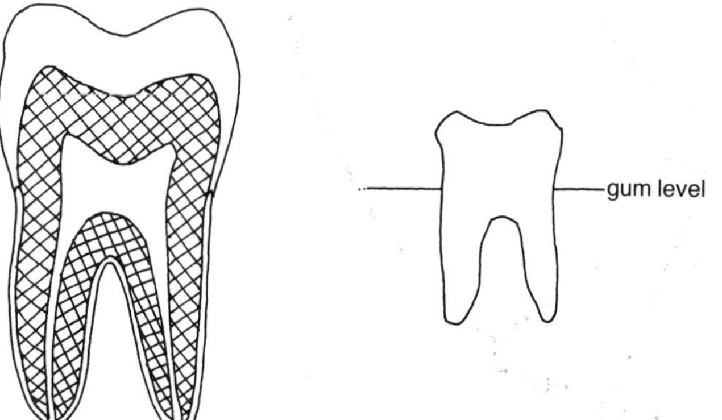

Figure 33.12

Figure 33.13

2. According to the passage what causes toothache?
3. Read the passage and then copy figure 33.12 into your book and label it; use only words mentioned in the passage.
4. If you chew a disclosing tablet it releases a dye which stains plaque red. Copy figure 33.13 and mark those parts of the tooth which are likely to stain a dark red colour because plaque has built up in these places. Why does plaque build up in these places?
5. Why should children be discouraged from eating sweets between meals?
6. Why do herbivores not have canine teeth?
7. How many teeth would you expect to find in the mouth of a twenty-five-year-old who had a complete set of teeth?

(SREB)

TOPIC 34

THE NERVOUS SYSTEM

WHAT YOUR NERVOUS SYSTEM DOES

Your nervous system controls all the other systems or parts of your body. It makes all these other parts work together. (See figure 34.1.)

Your nervous system is affected by changes or *stimuli* (singular: *stimulus*) outside or inside your body. It makes the other systems of your body 'reply' or *respond* to these stimuli. (See figure 34.2.)

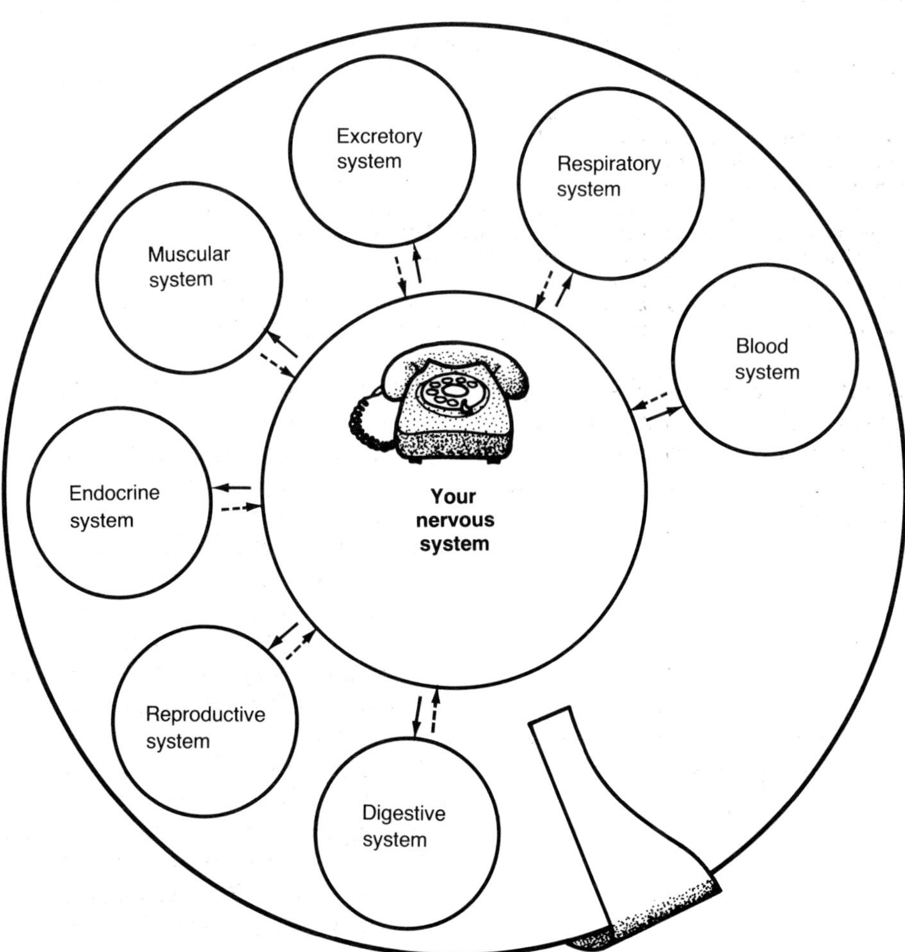

Figure 34.1 What your nervous system does

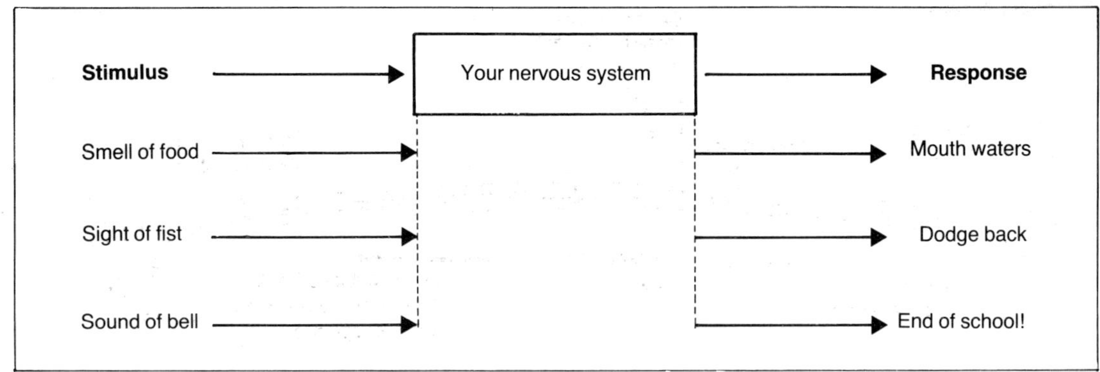

Figure 34.2

More than one system usually responds to the stimuli in figure 34.2, for example:

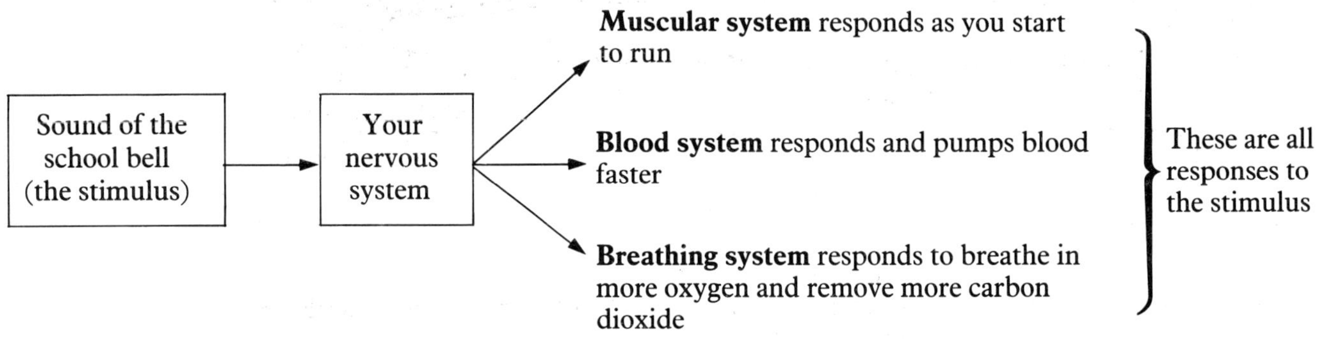

THE PARTS OF YOUR NERVOUS SYSTEM

The main parts of your nervous system are (see figure 34.3):

1. your brain and spinal cord (sometimes called your *central nervous system.*),
2. nerves which go from your brain and spinal cord to all parts of your body.

Your brain, spinal cord and nerves are all made up of nerve cells. There are two main kinds of nerve cells (see figure 34.4):

1. *sensory* nerve cells
2. *motor* nerve cells

'Messages' or *impulses* travel along nerve fibres. These impulses (messages) can only go in one direction. In a sensory nerve,

Brain (inside skull)
Spinal cord (inside vertebral column)
Central nervous system
Nerves going to and coming from all parts of your body

Figure 34.3

> **Fancy that!**
>
> Your brain weighs about 1.5 kg and contains about 50 thousand million nerve cells!
>
> Impulses travel along big nerves at about 100 metres a second!

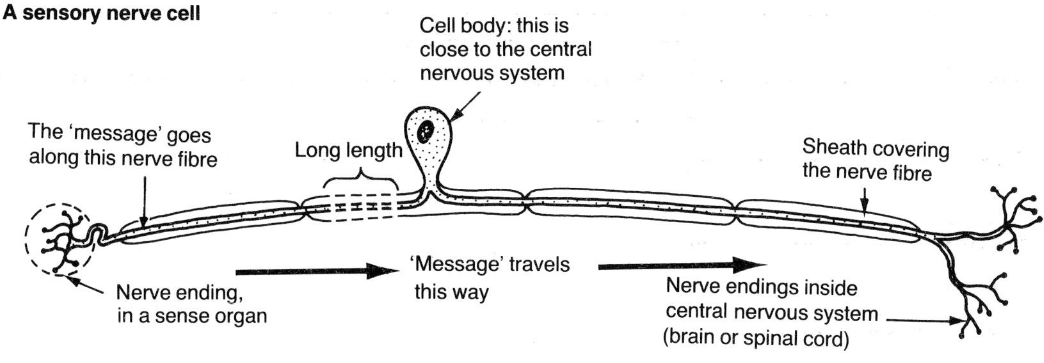

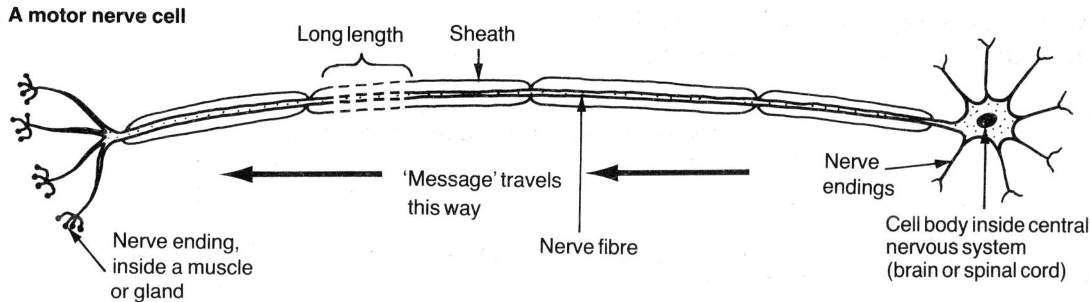

Figure 34.4

impulses go **from** *sense organs* to your central nervous system. From here they can go along other nerves which go to other parts of your body. In motor nerves, impulses go from your central nervous system **to** a muscle or a gland. The impulses make the muscle or gland work.

Nerve cells are grouped together in bundles to make nerves. The nerve in figure 34.5 is made of bundles of nerve cells.

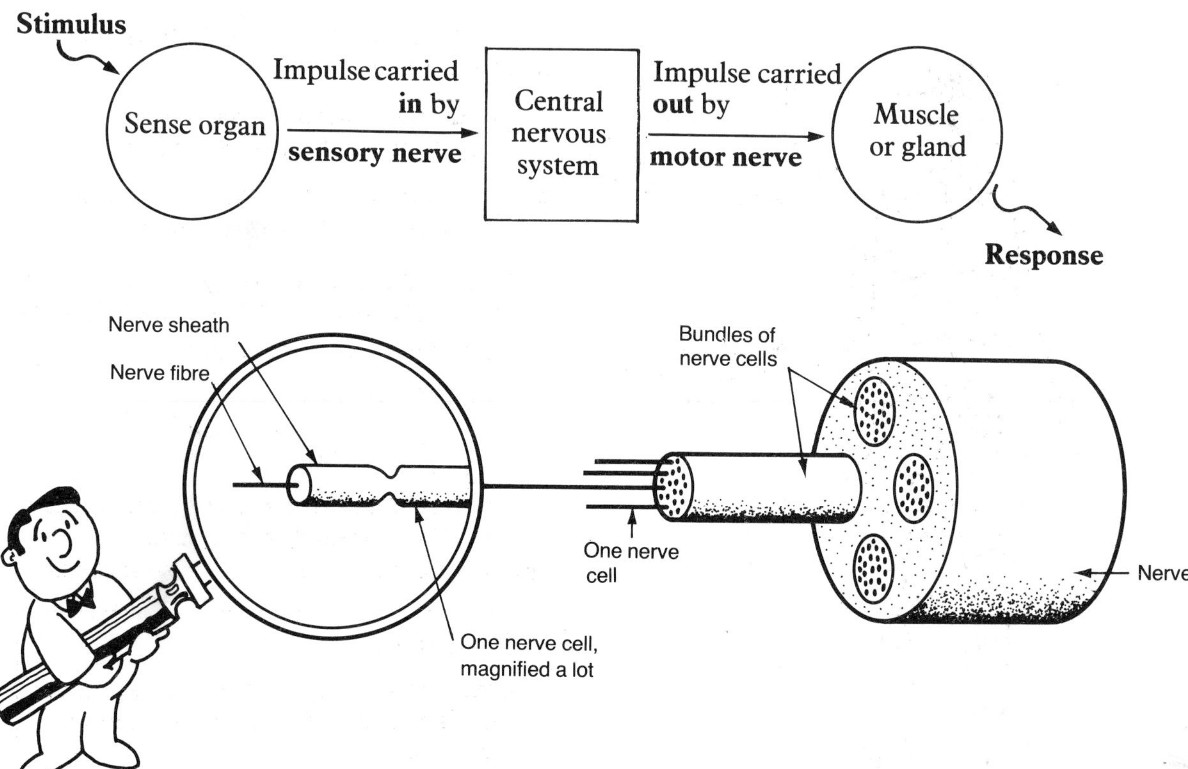

Figure 34.5

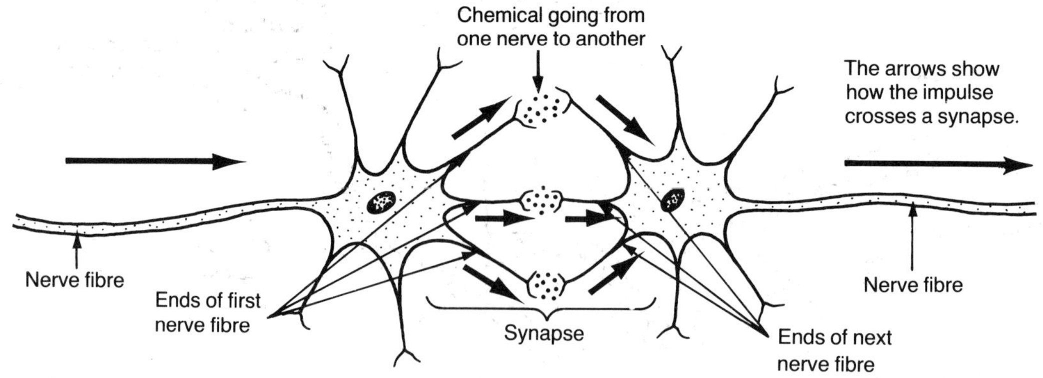

Figure 34.6

HOW YOUR NERVES WORK TOGETHER

Nerve impulses get from one nerve cell to another across a *synapse*. At a synapse the ends of nerve fibres are very close together but they do not touch. When an impulse arrives at a synapse, a chemical is set free by the end of the nerve. The chemical carries the impulse across the small gap. (See figure 34.6.)

Impulses from more than one nerve fibre may have to arrive at a synapse to cross it. When an impulse crosses a synapse it starts off an impulse in the next nerve fibre. A lot of nerve fibres sometimes meet at one synapse.

REFLEX ACTIONS

A *reflex action* happens when you respond very quickly to a stimulus. If you put your hand into hot water, you take it away very quickly! You do this without thinking. It is a reflex action and it is controlled by your spinal cord, not by your brain. (See figure 34.7.)

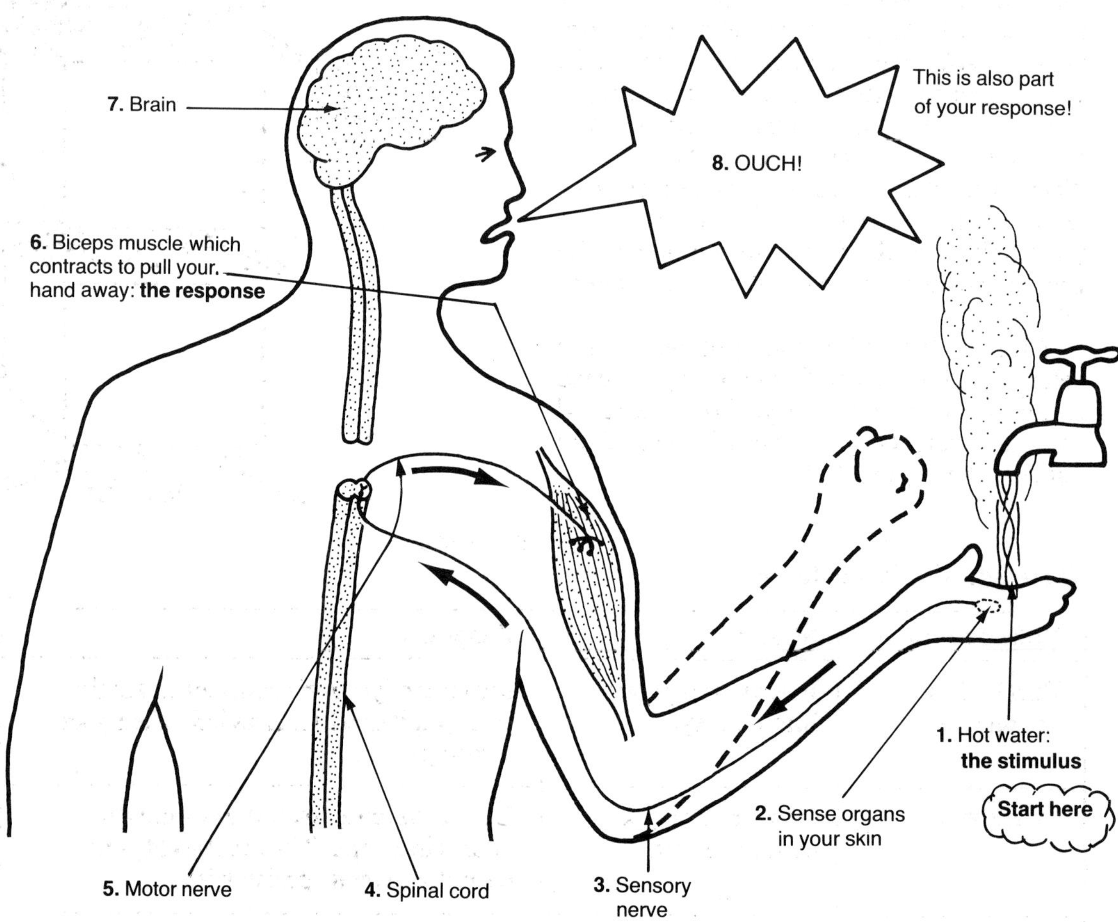

Figure 34.7

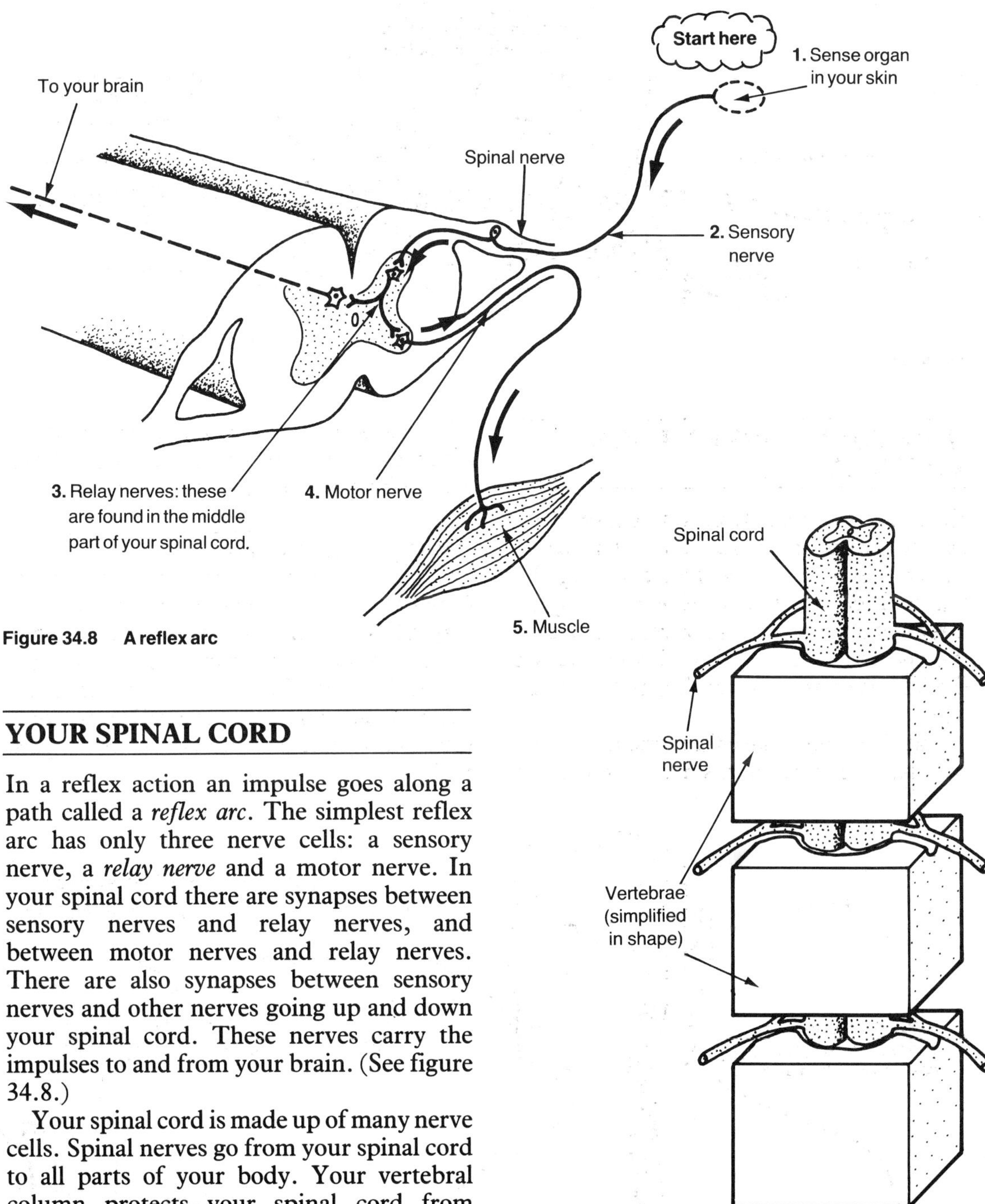

Figure 34.8 A reflex arc

Figure 34.9

YOUR SPINAL CORD

In a reflex action an impulse goes along a path called a *reflex arc*. The simplest reflex arc has only three nerve cells: a sensory nerve, a *relay nerve* and a motor nerve. In your spinal cord there are synapses between sensory nerves and relay nerves, and between motor nerves and relay nerves. There are also synapses between sensory nerves and other nerves going up and down your spinal cord. These nerves carry the impulses to and from your brain. (See figure 34.8.)

Your spinal cord is made up of many nerve cells. Spinal nerves go from your spinal cord to all parts of your body. Your vertebral column protects your spinal cord from damage.(See figure 34.9.)

Examples of reflex actions

Reflex action	Stimulus	Response
Pupil reflex in your eye	Bright light going into your eye	Muscles of your iris contract and make your pupil smaller. Less light then goes into your eye.
Swallowing	Food in the back of your mouth	Epiglottis closes over the entrance to your wind-pipe. The muscles of your oesophagus start peristalsis.
Blinking	Something moving near your eye	Muscles controlling your eyelids make them close to protect your eye.

YOUR BRAIN

Most reflexes are not simple ones such as those shown in the table. More complicated reflexes are controlled by your brain, which is the main control centre of your body. It is made up of millions of nerve cells and synapses which help it to do complicated activities. Different activities are controlled by the three main parts of your brain: the fore-brain, mid-brain and hind-brain.

The fore-brain receives impulses from your nose. The mid-brain receives impulses from your eyes. The hind-brain receives impulses from your ears and skin.

A large, important part of your brain called the *cerebrum* develops from the roof of the fore-brain. The cerebrum is made of two halves or *cerebral hemispheres*. Your left cerebral hemisphere controls the right side of your body. Your right cerebral hemisphere controls the left side of your body.

The roof of the hind-brain develops into the *cerebellum*. The floor of the hind-brain develops into the *medulla*. (See figures 34.10 and 34.11.)

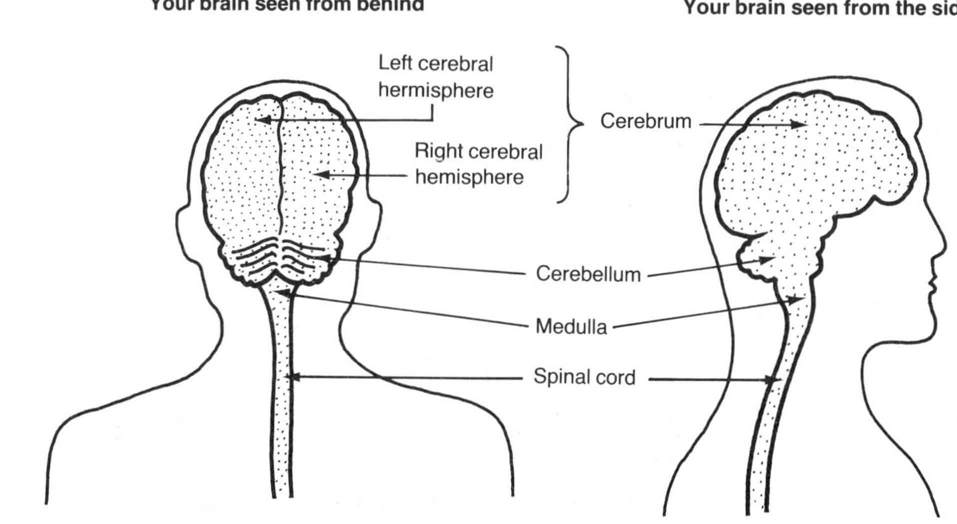

Figure 34.10

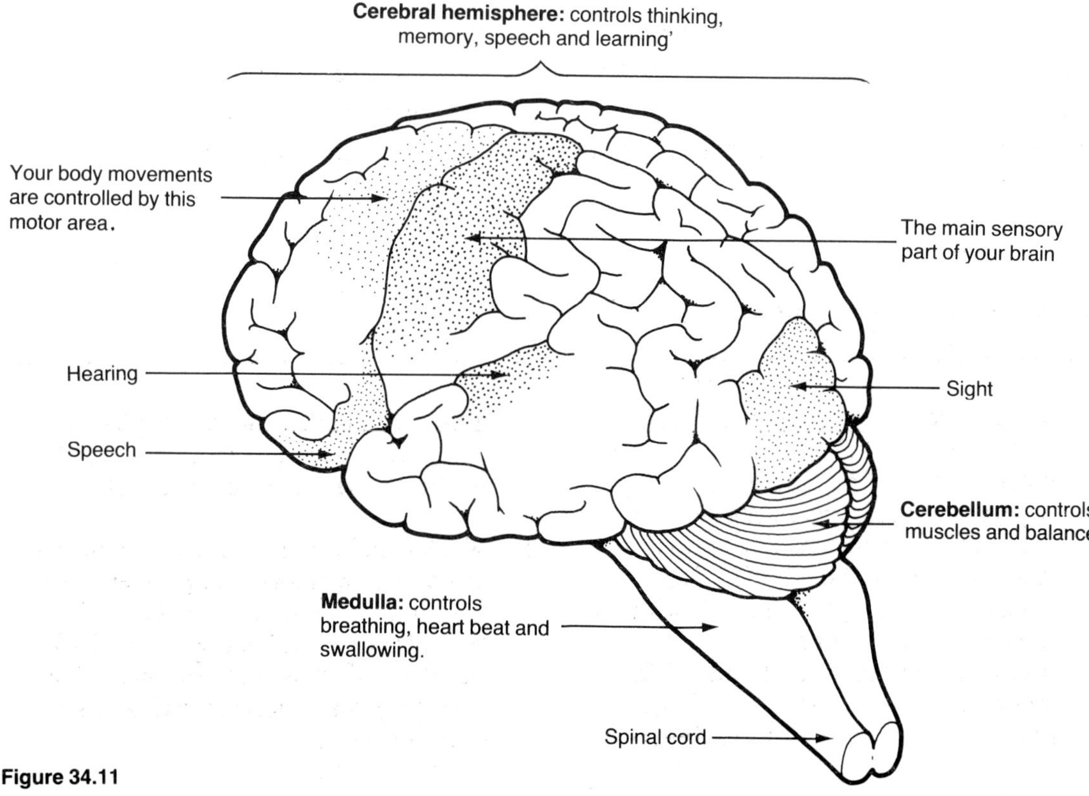

Figure 34.11

Summary

Your nervous system *controls* other parts of your body and makes them work together. It is affected by many different *stimuli* and makes your body *respond* to these stimuli. Your nervous system is made of *nerve cells*.

Your *brain* and *spinal cord* are called the *central nervous system*. This is made of a lot of nerve cells collected together.

Sensory nerves carry messages from *sense organs to* your central nervous system. *Motor nerves* carry messages *from* your central nervous system to muscles or glands. When you respond quickly to a stimulus this is called a *reflex action*. In a reflex action messages go along a path called a *reflex arc*.

Different parts of your brain control different activities.

Important words

Stimulus	a change in the conditions inside or outside an organism; the change causes an effect in the organism (plural: stimuli).
Response	the effect of a stimulus on an organism.
Central nervous system	the brain and spinal cord.
Sense organ	an organ that first senses a stimulus.
Impulse	a 'message' that goes along a nerve cell.
Sensory nerve	a nerve that carries impulses from sense organs to the central nervous system.
Motor nerve	a nerve that carries impulses away from the central nervous system to muscles or glands.
Relay nerve	a nerve in the spinal cord which connects sensory and motor nerves by synapses.
Synapse	a place where nerve fibres meet.
Reflex action	a simple, quick response to a particular stimulus.
Reflex arc	the path along which impulses go in a reflex action.
Cerebrum	part of the brain that controls speech, memory and learning.

Things to do

1. Work in pairs. One partner must hold a metre ruler at the 100 cm mark, so that it hangs down. The other must put a thumb and finger on each side of the ruler. Put them next to a mark on the ruler but not touching it. The first person should let go of the ruler without warning. The other has to catch it between their thumb and finger. The mark on the ruler next to their finger is the distance the ruler dropped before they responded. Now change places. The person who catches the ruler in the shortest distance responds fastest.

2. Work in pairs or use a mirror. Sit near a brightly-lit window. One partner must put a hand over one eye for about 15 seconds. Take the hand away and look out of the window. Your partner will be able to see your pupil reflex if he or she looks into your eye.

Questions

A.

Ten pupils decide to attempt to measure the velocity at which impulses travel along nerve fibres.

They formed a circle holding hands. Pupil number 1 started a stop-clock with his left hand and then, using his right hand, squeezed the left hand of pupil number 2. The stimulus was passed on round the circle until finally pupil number 10 had his left hand squeezed by pupil number 9. Pupil number 10 then stopped the clock with his right hand.

It is assumed that the nerve impulse passes from the fingertips of each person to the spinal cord, then up to the brain, from the brain to the spinal cord and finally out to the muscle in the right forearm which contracts to cause the squeeze.

These distances were measured on each person and the total distance for each person was obtained. (As shown below in the table).

1. Calculate the total distance travelled by the nerve impulse around the circle of pupils.

2. Imagine that the time taken for the impulse to travel around the circle of pupils was 2 seconds. Calculate the velocity of the nerve impulse in *metres per second*.
(Velocity = distance divided by time.)

3. Give one reason why this experiment is likely to give inaccurate results.

Pupil No.	1	2	3	4	5	6	7	8	9	10
Total distance nerve impulse assumed to travel in each pupil (cm)	200	218	178	186	210	187	167	168	180	206

(EAEB)

B.

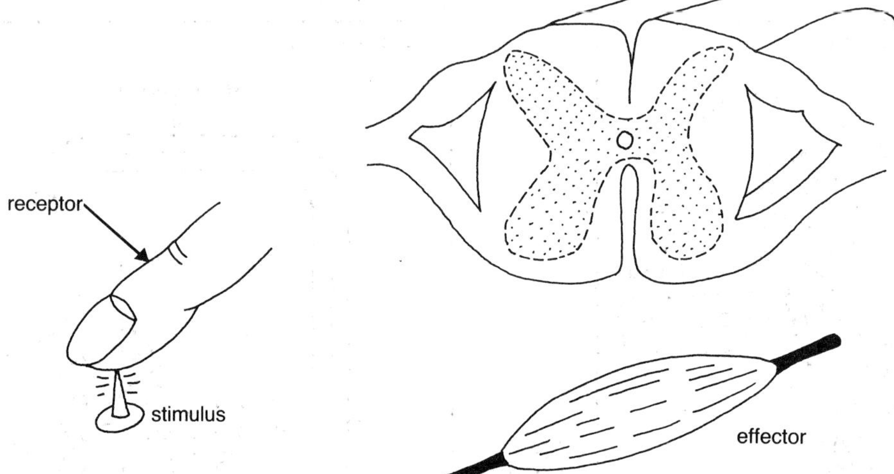

Figure 34.12

1. Copy figure 34.12 into your book and then complete it by drawing the pathway of the reflex arc in the following stages.
(a) Draw single lines to show the following nerve fibres: sensory (afferent); relay (intermediate); motor (efferent).
(b) Label the nerve fibres clearly.
(c) Draw arrows on the nerve fibres to show the direction of a nerve impulse.

2. List three differences between a reflex action and an action brought about by hormones.

3. When the impulse reaches the effector, it causes it to contract.
(a) Name two substances required to provide energy for contraction.
(b) State how these substances are carried to the effector.

(WJEC)

TOPIC 35

HORMONES

WHAT ARE HORMONES?

Hormones are chemicals which are made by glands (or groups of cells) in different parts of your body. These glands make up your *endocrine system* and they are called *endocrine glands*.

Hormones from these glands go into your blood, which carries them to all parts of your body. Hormones control the speed at which certain organs work, your heart for example. Some hormones act on every cell in your body.

Hormones and nerves both control the way your body works but they do it in different ways. (See figure 35.1.)

Messages sent by your brain travel along nerves straight to one special organ. This happens very quickly and the organ responds to the message in a very quick time.

Hormones travel more slowly in your blood system. Every part of your body gets some of the hormone but only certain parts can respond to it. The effects of hormones last longer than the effects of nerves. (See figure 35.2.)

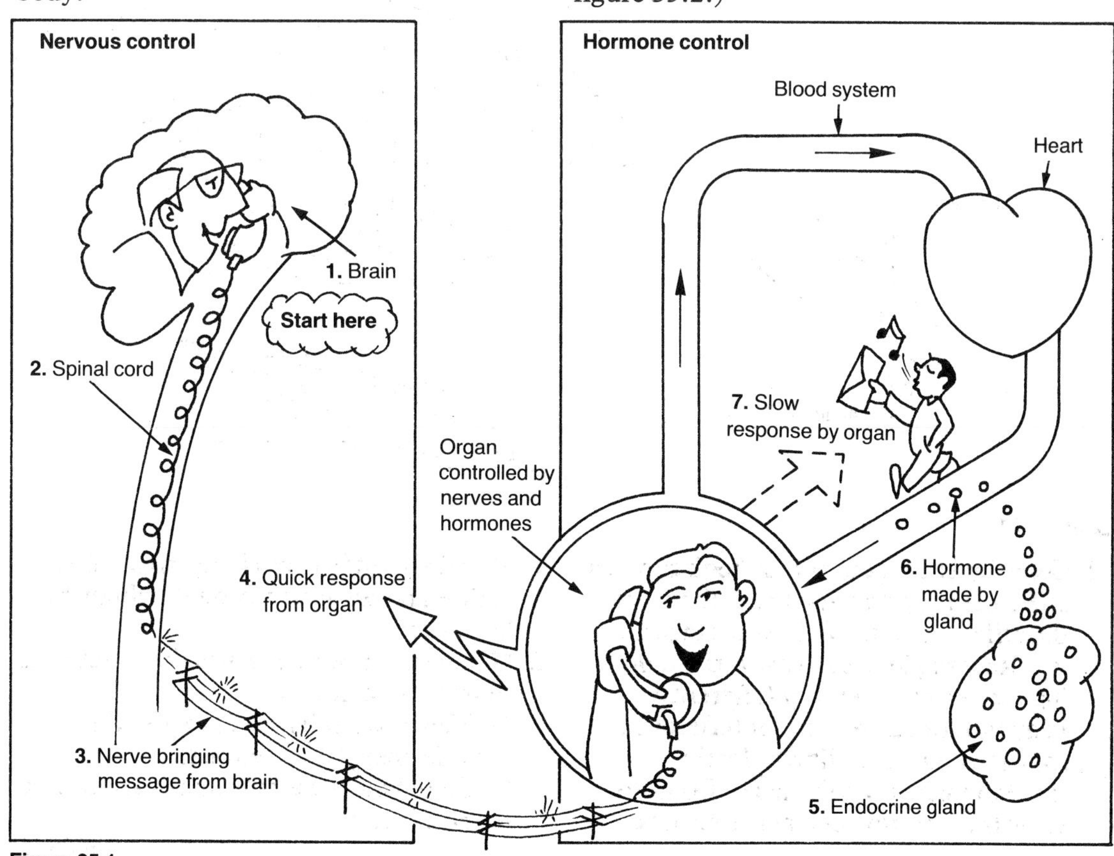

Figure 35.1

Name of endocrine gland	Hormone made by endocrine gland	What the hormone does
Pituitary	Growth hormone (and many others: see below)	Controls the growth of every cell in your body.
Thyroid	Thyroxine	Controls the speed at which chemical reactions happen in every cell. Controls growth and development.
Pancreas	Insulin	Controls the amount of glucose in your blood.
Adrenals	Adrenalin	An 'emergency' hormone: gets your body ready for action by speeding-up breathing and heart beat.
Ovaries (in FEMALES only)	Female sex hormones	Control *female secondary sex characteristics*: hips widen, breasts appear, etc.
Testes (in MALES only)	Male sex hormones	Control *male secondary sex characteristics*: voice deepens, hair grows on body, etc.

Figure 35.2 Endocrine glands and their hormones

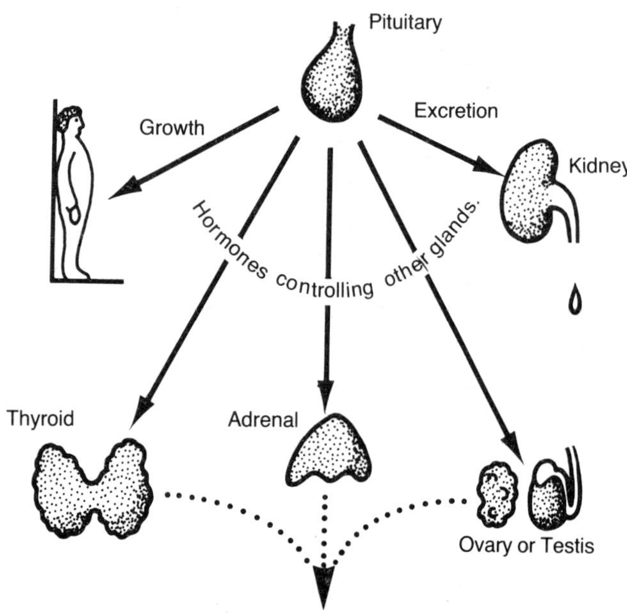

Figure 35.3

THE PITUITARY GLAND

Your *pituitary gland* makes many hormones. Some affect other endocrine glands and control how quickly these work. For example, your pituitary gland can make your thyroid produce less thyroxine. It can also increase the amount of male hormones made by a man's testis. (See figure 35.3.)

One hormone your pituitary makes controls the amount of water in your urine.

The pituitary gland is really the 'headteacher' of your endocrine system!

HOW INSULIN WORKS

Your pancreas makes digestive juices as well as insulin. The digestive juices are carried away by a tube into your digestive system. Insulin diffuses into your blood system and does not go through a tube. (See figure 35.4)

WHAT ADRENALIN DOES

A lot of adrenalin is made when you are frightened, angry or in danger. Your heart thumps, your skin goes pale and your mouth dries. These are signs that adrenalin is getting you ready for action. You may have to fight or run! (See figure 35.5.)

SEX HORMONES

Sex hormones control your *secondary sex characteristics*. (See pp.240 and 241.) They also cause the 'growth spurts' of boys and girls in *puberty*. This is the age at which the sex organs become active and is usually between the 12th and 17th year. Children who start puberty early will be taller than average for a while but their growth often soon stops. Children who start puberty later than usual will be shorter than average for a while. However they may carry on growing after others have stopped and become tall adults!

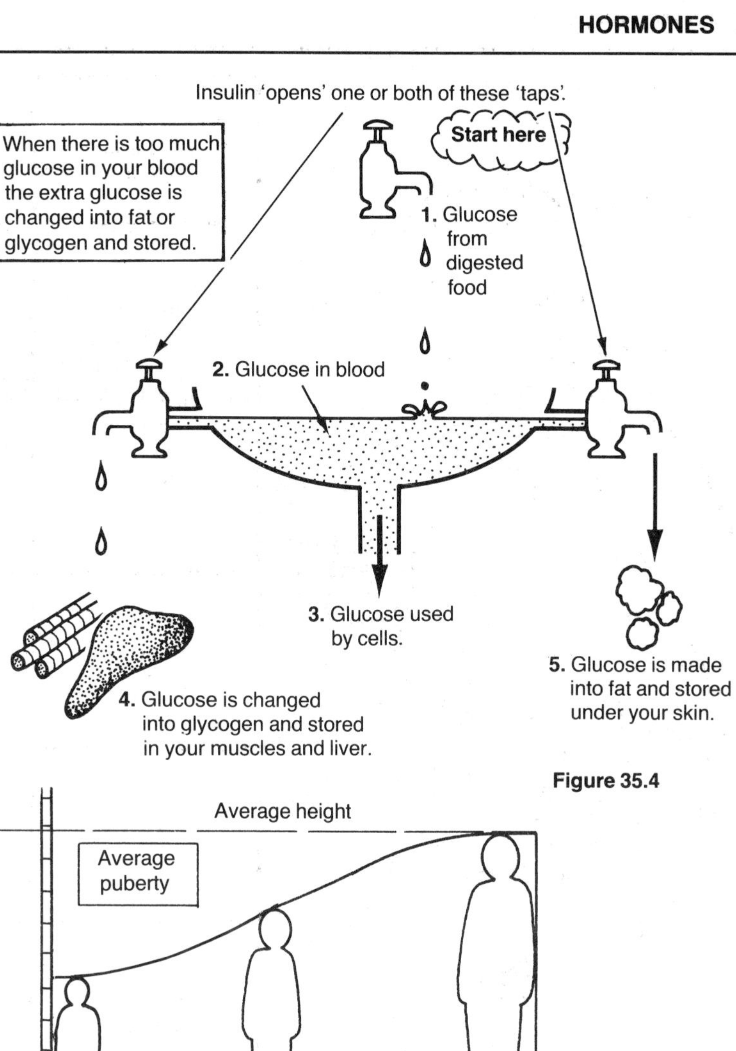

Figure 35.4

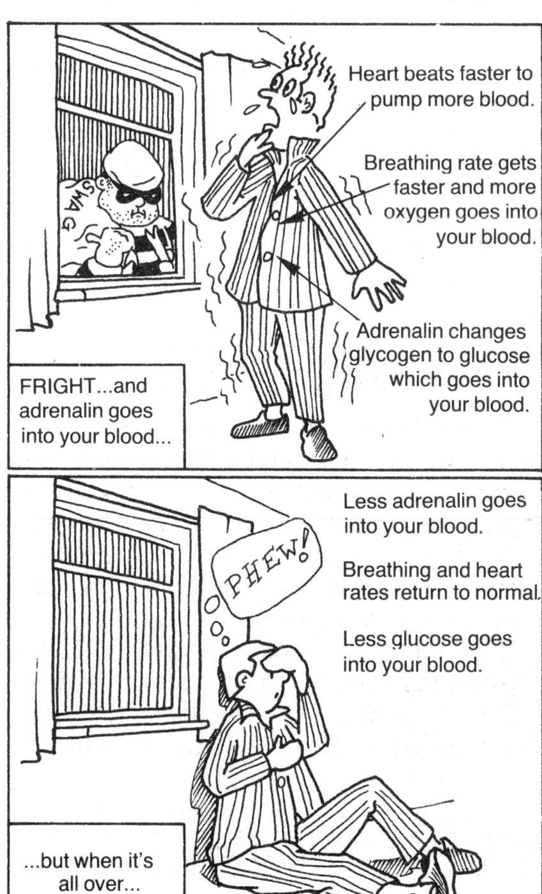

Figure 35.5

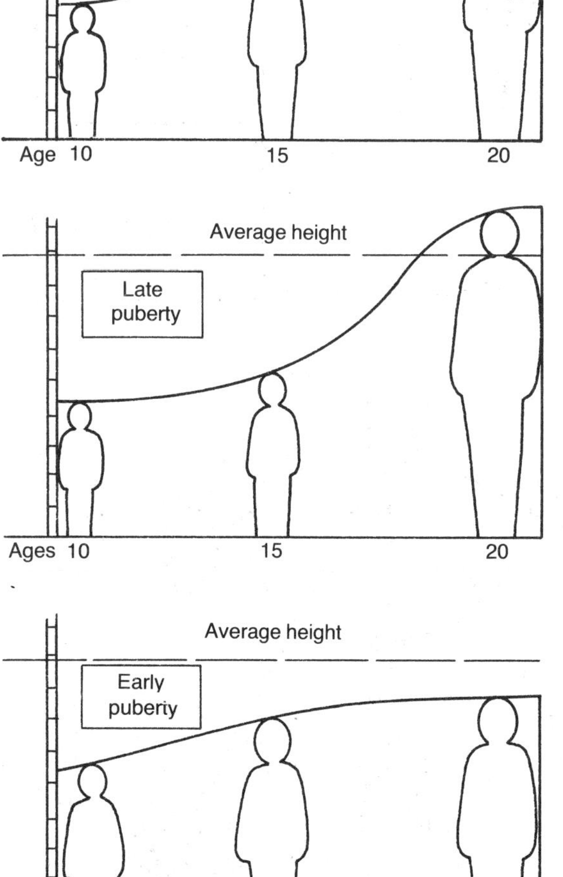

Figure 35.6 Sex hormones and growth

HORMONES AND HEALTH

The right amount of hormone must be made by each gland. Too much or two little hormone may cause poor health. If not enough insulin is made, for example, a person suffers from a disease called diabetes. (See figure 35.7.)

The extra sugar in a diabetic person's blood is excreted in their urine. The disease must be treated by careful diet or by giving the person more insulin. The amount of glucose in your blood is called your 'blood sugar'.

Your pituitary makes growth hormone. The amount of growth hormone affects your body size. (See figure 35.8.)

Figure 35.8

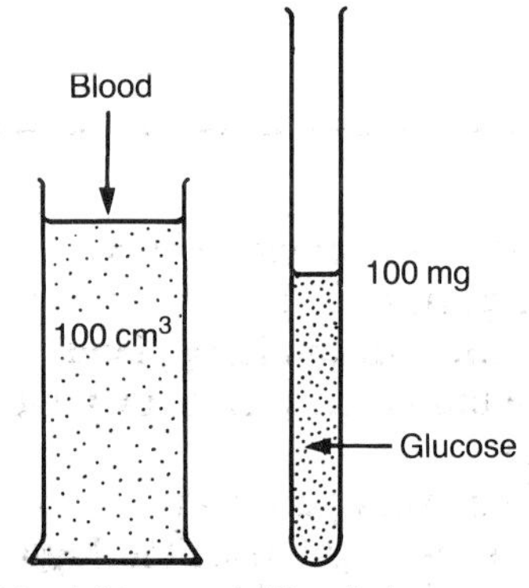

If the right amount of insulin is made it keeps the glucose in this amount of blood at 100 mg.

This person is healthy

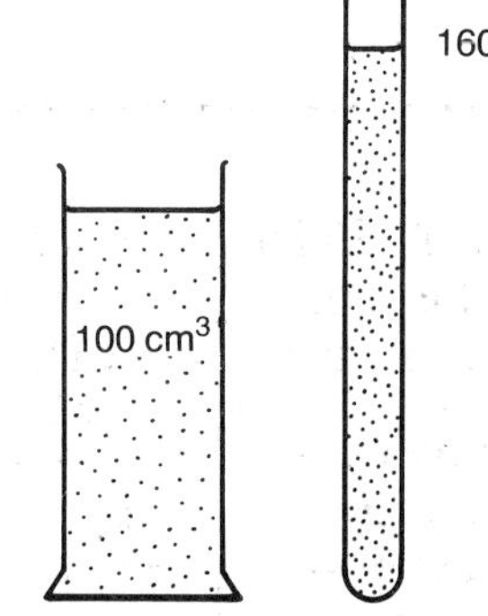

If not enough insulin is made, the glucose in this amount of blood may increase to 160 mg.

The person is diabetic

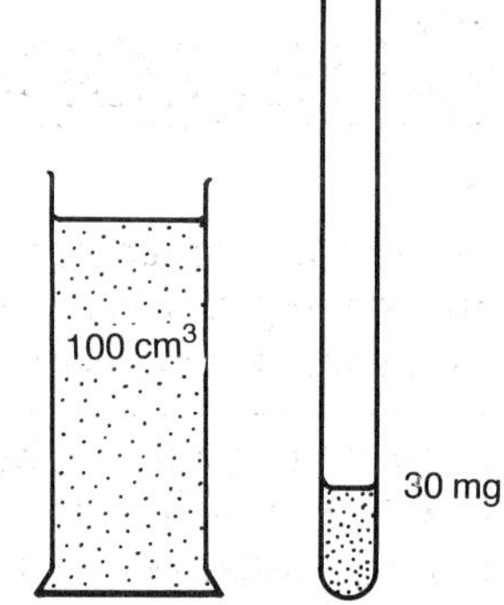

If too much insulin is made the glucose in this amount of blood may go down to 30 mg.

This person is also ill

Figure 35.7

A reminder!

Some hormones are set free all the time in small amounts: e.g. insulin, and the pituitary, thyroid and sex hormones.

Other hormones are set free in large amounts when needed: e.g. adrenalin.

Fancy that!

An American, Robert Wadlow, was probably the world's tallest man. When he died in 1918 aged 32, he measured 272 cm!

The shortest dwarf in the world was probably a Dutch woman, Pauline Musters. When she died in 1895 she measured 61 cm!

Summary

Hormones are *chemicals* made by groups of cells called endocrine glands. Hormones are carried to all parts of your body by your blood. Different glands make different hormones. Each hormone does a different job.

Pituitary hormones control your *growth* and *thyroid* hormones control the *chemical reactions* in your cells. *Pancreas* hormones control the *sugar* in your blood and *adrenal* hormones get your body ready for *action*. *Sex* hormones control the *secondary sex characteristics*.

Hormones help to control the way your body works.

Important words

Hormone	a chemical substance which is made in one part of an organism and has an effect on another part of the organism.
Endocrine system	all the glands in an animal that make hormones.
Endocrine gland	a gland that makes hormones.
Pituitary	an endocrine gland which makes hormones which control other endocrine glands.
Thyroxin	a hormone which contains iodine and controls growth and development.
Insulin	a hormone which controls the amount of sugar in your blood.
Adrenalin	a hormone which prepares you to deal with fear, anger or pain by fighting or by running away.
Puberty	the age at which a persons sex organs become active.
Secondary sex characteristics	changes that happen to your body at puberty.

Questions

A.

Write out each sentence in your book. Fill in the missing words from those in the box. Some words may be used more than once.

> nervous system — blood — adrenal — pituitary — insulin — digested food — fat — muscles — liver — hormones — faster — sugar — diabetes — puberty — thyroxine — glycogen

1. Your endocrine system includes all the glands which make ......
2. Hormones are set free into your ....
3. Your endocrine system and your ...... control your body.
4. ...... work more slowly than nerves but their effects last longer.
5. Your ...... glands are on top of your kidneys.
6. ...... controls the speed at which chemical reactions happen in your cells.
7. Your ...... makes hormones which control other glands.
8. Hormones from your pituitary gland affect the amount of ...... made by your thyroid gland.
9. ...... is made by your pancreas.
10. When your blood sugar rises too high, insulin changes the sugar into ...... or ....
11. Blood sugar comes from ....
12. When your blood sugar rises too high it is stored in your ...... and ....
13. When adrenalin is set free your heart beats ....
14. Adrenalin causes more ...... to go into your blood.
15. ...... is the time when a person's sex hormones get very active.
16. Diabetes is caused by not enough ....
17. In ...... , sugar is excreted in a person's urine.

B.

Figure 35.9 shows some endocrine glands in a woman. Study it carefully then answer the following questions.

1. What is the name of gland (a)?
2. What is the name of the hormone made by gland (a) and what is its use?
3. What is the name of gland (b)?
4. What is the name of the hormone made by gland (b) and what is its use?
5. What is the name of gland (c)?
6. State the name of the hormone made by gland (c) and one of its uses.

(EMREB)

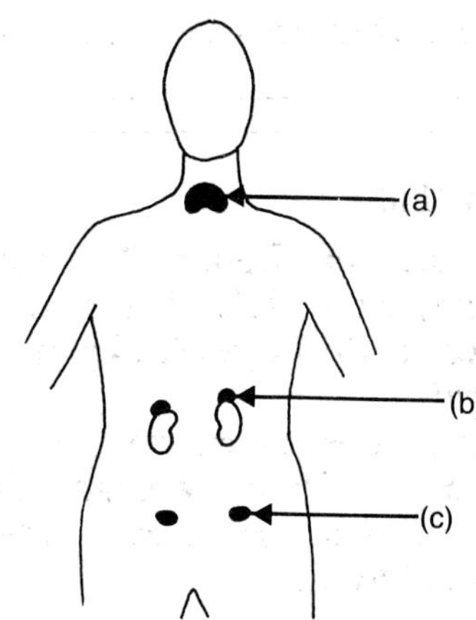

Figure 35.9

C.

Figure 35.10 shows the blood sugar level (amount of sugar in the blood) of a healthy man during a 12 hour period. Study it carefully before answering the following questions.

1. What is the level of blood sugar at 4 p.m.?
2. At what time of the day is the level of blood sugar the highest?
3. During which hour was the rate of increase in blood sugar level the greatest?
4. What occurred at points (a), (b) and (c) to cause the subsequent changes in blood sugar levels?
5. At points (i), (ii) and (iii) the concentration of blood sugar drops. Which hormone causes these drops in sugar level?
6. Where is this hormone made?
7. How does this hormone reduce the blood sugar level?
8. If the man were to be frightened at point (iv) what would you expect to happen to the blood sugar level?
9. What is the name of the hormone which causes this change after fright?
10. Why is this change associated with fright (as described in **8**) necessary to the human body?

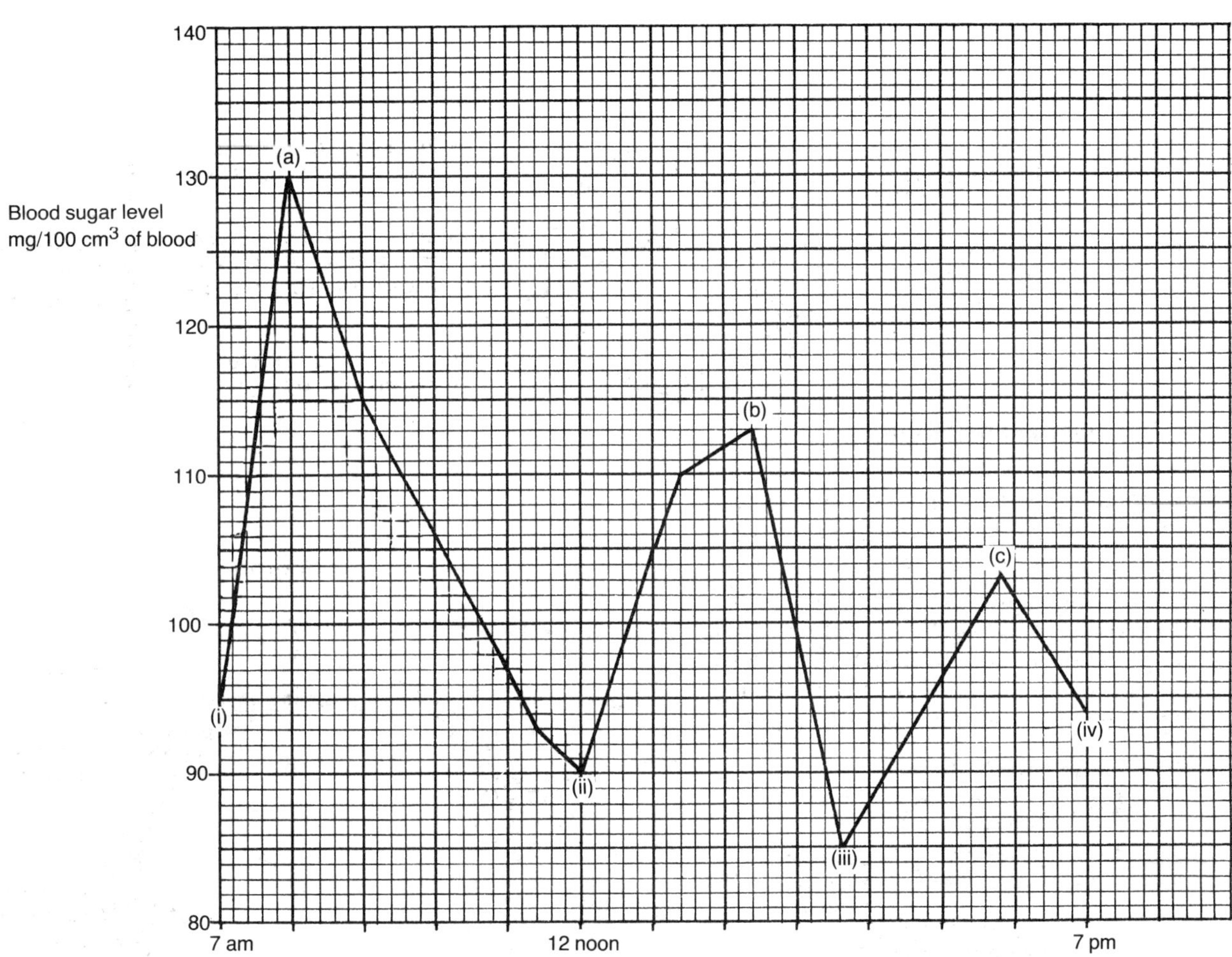

Figure 35.10

(EMREB)

TOPIC 36

THE EYE

Conjunctiva: a clear layer of skin.
Cornea: a clear layer through which light gets into your eyes.
Sclerotic layer: a tough skin forming the 'white' of your eye.
Choroid: this layer has many blood vessels which carry blood to the retina and other parts of your eye.
Retina: this layer has cells which are affected by light.
These are the 3 main layers of your eye.

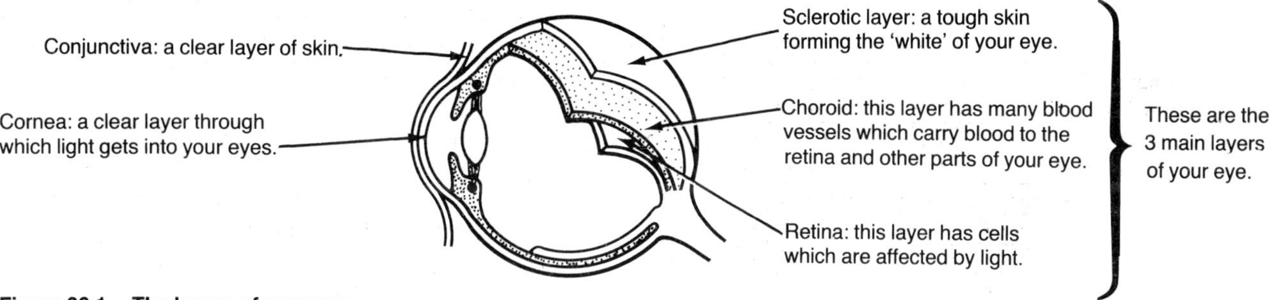

Figure 36.1 The layers of your eye

Your eyes have cells in them which are affected by light. These cells help your brain to make pictures of things in your surroundings. Your eyes are made up of 3 main layers. (See figure 36.1.) Liquids inside your eye help to keep its shape. (See figure 36.2.) Without these liquids your eye would collapse and you would not be able to see!

The liquids press outwards to keep the shape of your eye.
Vitreous humour: a liquid like a thin jelly.
Aqueous humour: a clear, thin liquid like water.

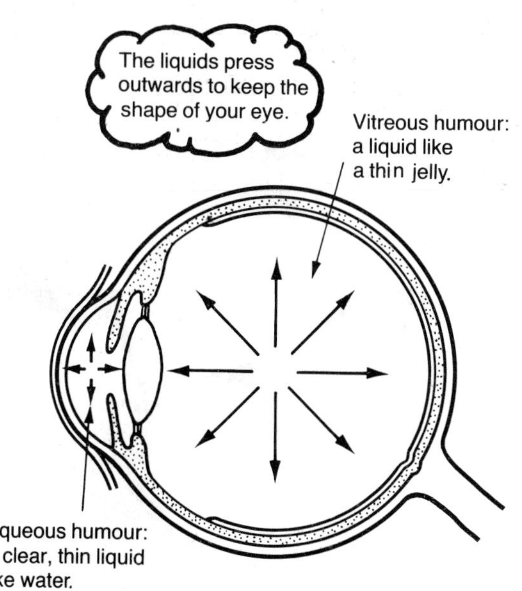

Figure 36.2

Sclerotic
Choroid
Conjunctiva
Retina
Ligaments: hold your lens in place.
Vitreous humour
Iris
Pupil
Yellow spot: the most sensitive part of your retina.
Aqueous humour
Lens
Ciliary body
Ciliary muscle
Blind spot
Optic nerve: takes messages from your retina to your brain.

Figure 36.3 Section through an eye

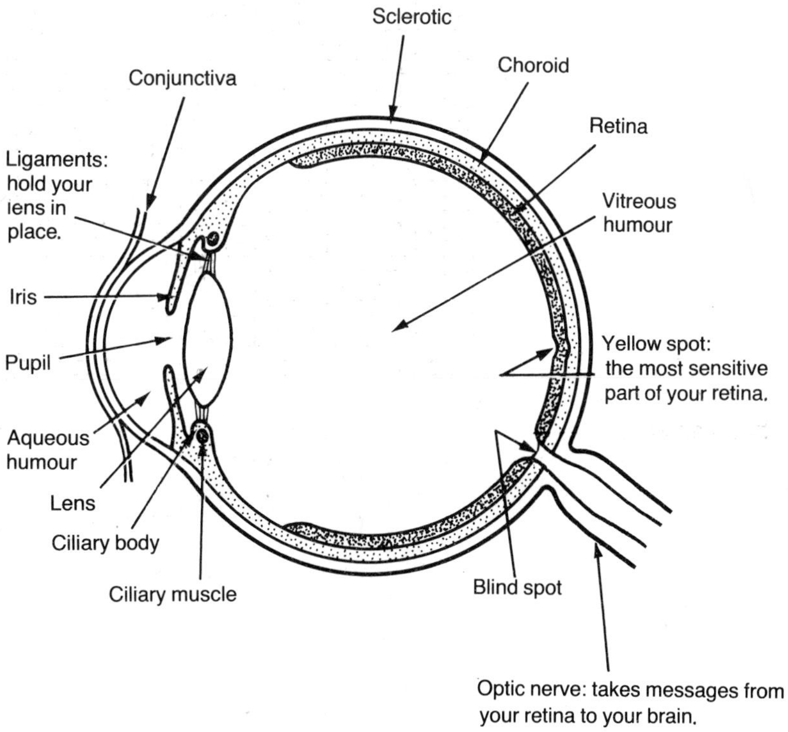

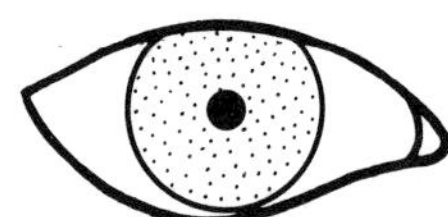

In bright light your pupil is small. This stops too much light getting into your eye. Your retina can be damaged by too much bright light.

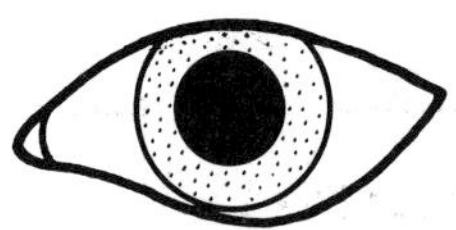

If there is not much light your pupil gets larger. This lets more light into your eye and helps your retina to make a good picture.

Figure 36.4

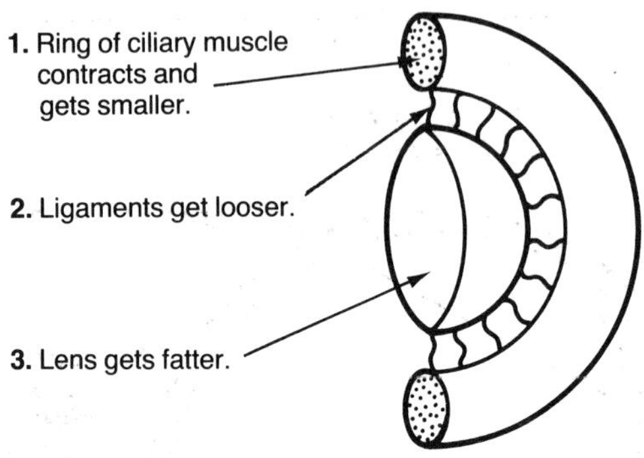

Figure 36.5 This happens when you look at near objects

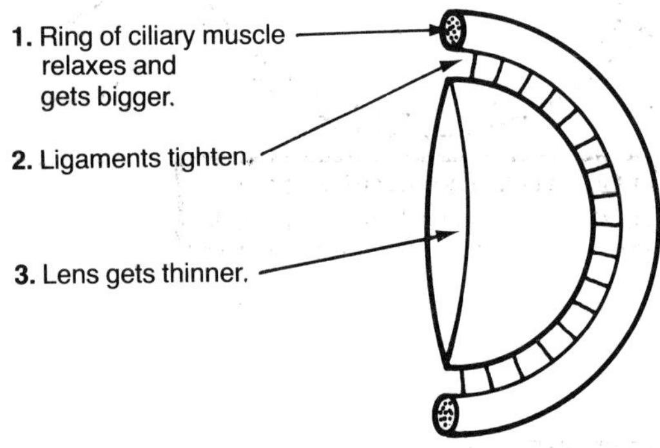

Figure 36.6 This happens when you look at distant objects

YOUR IRIS AND PUPIL

Your *iris* is the coloured part at the front of your eye. It is usually brown, black or blue. Your *pupil* is the small hole in your iris. Light goes through your pupil and hits your retina. (See figure 36.4.)

HOW YOUR LENS WORKS

The lens is held in place by ligaments. These are fastened all round a ciliary body which is ring shaped. The shape of your lens can be changed. Your *ciliary muscles* do this.

Your ciliary muscles are in the shape of a ring. When they *contract* the ring gets *smaller*. This makes the ligaments looser and they stop pulling on your lens. Your lens then gets fatter. A fat lens bends light more than a thin lens.

This happens when you are looking at near objects. (See figure 36.5.)

When your ring-shaped ciliary muscles *relax* the ring gets *bigger*. This makes the ligaments tight and they pull on your lens. Your lens then gets thinner. A thin lens bends light less than a fat lens.

This happens when you look at distant objects. (See figure 36.6.)

YOUR RETINA

As light goes through your lens it is bent and focused on your retina. In this way a clear picture is made on your retina. The cornea of your eye also helps to bend the light. (See figure 36.7.)

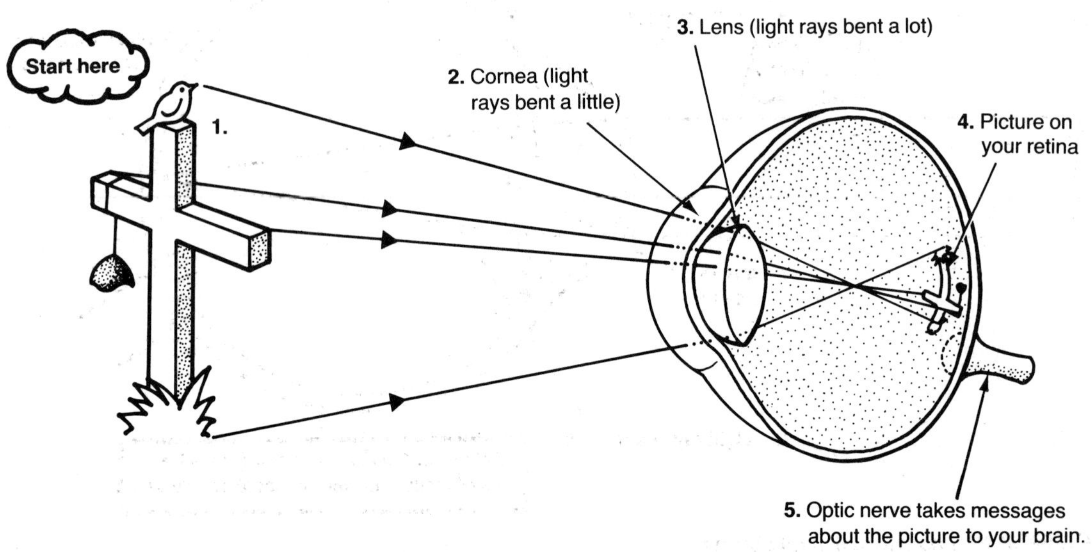

Figure 36.7

IT'S AN UPSIDE-DOWN WORLD!

The picture made on your retina is upside down but your brain turns it the right way up again. Your retina has two kinds of light-sensitive cells: *rods* and *cones*. Cones are sensitive to colour and only work in bright light. Rods are not sensitive to colour and can work in dim light. The clearest picture is made on the *yellow spot* (see figure 36.3) which has most of the cones in your retina. Nerves and blood vessels leave your eye at the *blind spot* which is not sensitive to light. Your eye cannot see a picture which falls onto the blind spot (see "Things to do").

Fancy that!

There are about 6 million cones in your eye!

Cats have a third eyelid! It can move across the eye to protect it.

Stereoscopic vision (see p.228) is only useful for guessing distances up to 50 metres away.

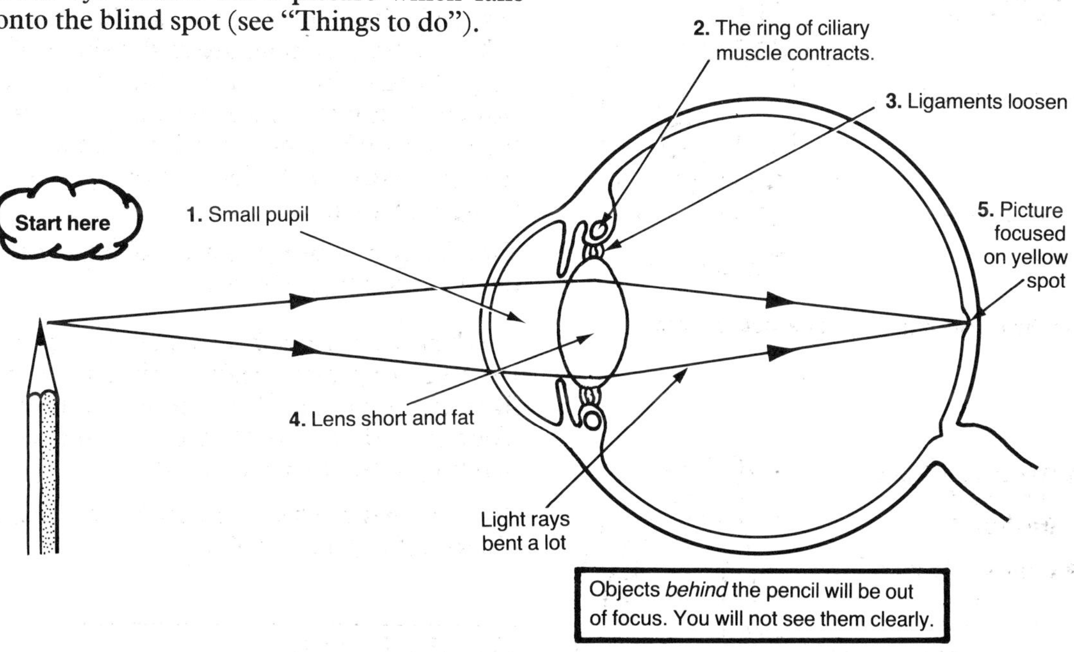

Figure 36.8 Looking at near objects

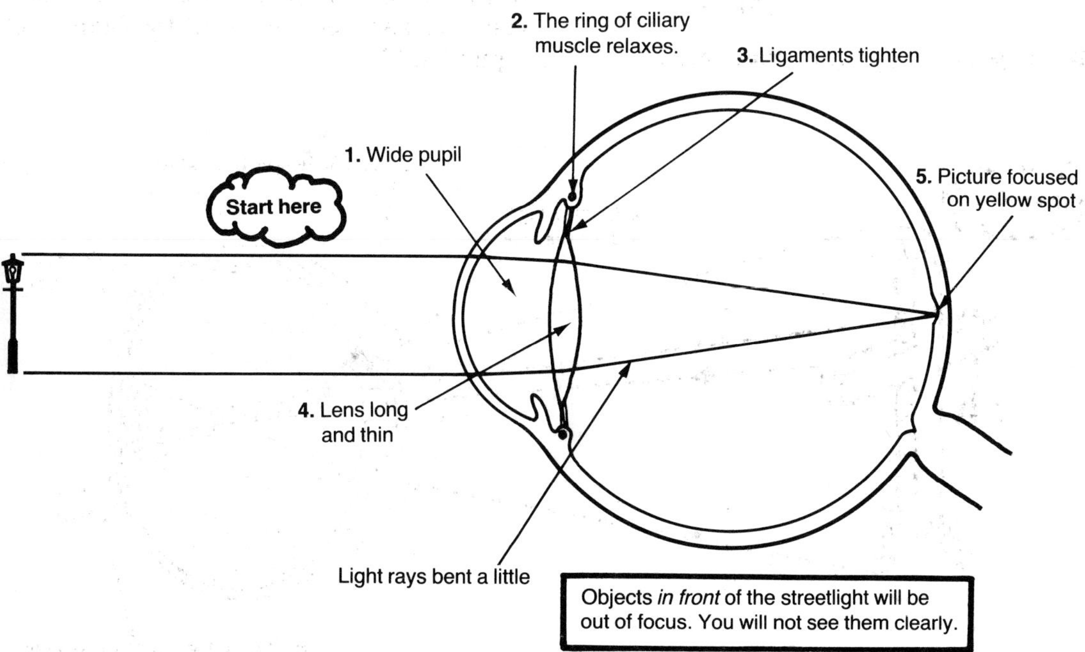

Figure 36.9 Looking at distant objects

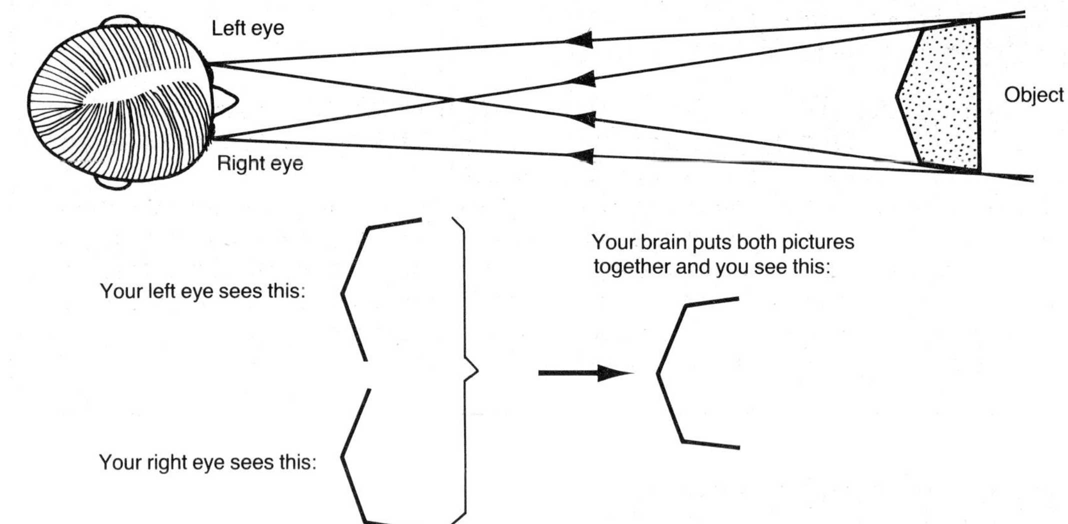

Figure 36.10 Stereoscopic vision

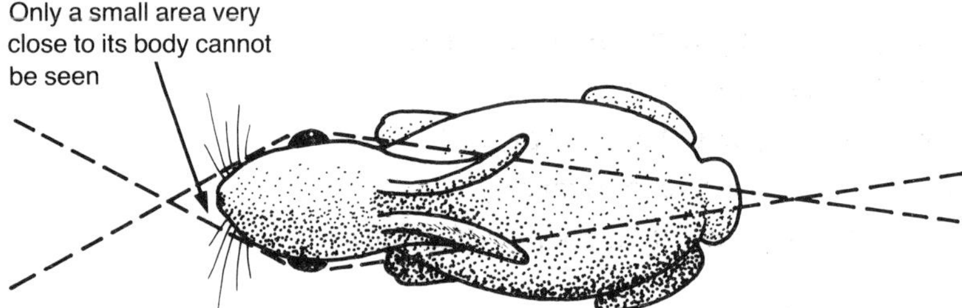

Figure 36.11 This hare can see all around itself!

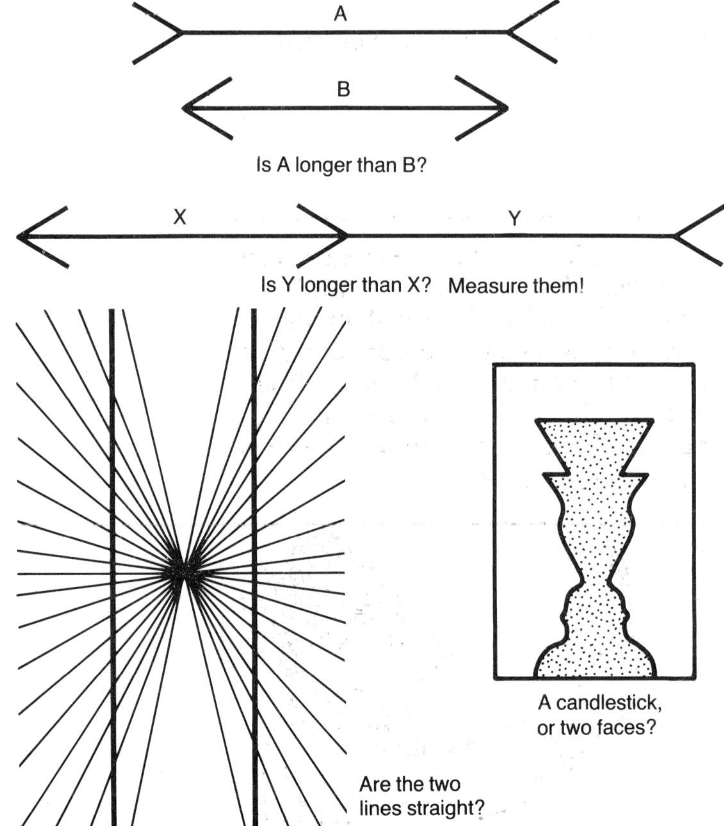

Figure 36.12 Are your eyes fooling you?

TWO PICTURES INTO ONE

Each eye sends your brain a slightly different picture of an object. This is called stereoscopic vision. It help us to guess distance and makes objects seem 'solid'. If you look through one eye, objects seem 'flat'. (See figure 36.10.)

Animals with eyes at the fronts of their heads have stereoscopic vision. They are usually carnivores. It is important for them to guess the distance to their prey because they have to catch it and kill it. Animals with eyes at the sides of their heads can see all round but they are not good at guessing distance. (See figure 36.11.)

Sometimes your brain is tricked and you don't see objects as they really are. (See figure 36.12.) This is called an optical illusion.

LOOKING AFTER YOUR EYES

If you cannot read a telephone directory held 48 cm from your eyes, you may need glasses. Try each eye separately. Always read with a good light shining onto your book.

Protection of your eyes from strong light is very important. Get a good pair of sunglasses! **Never** look at the sun through binoculars or lenses: you could blind yourself. You should always wear protective glasses if there is danger of something going into your eyes. This might happen in the school science laboratory or in the workshop.

Eyes sometimes become sore and infected. See your doctor if any soreness does not clear up in two days.

Summary

Light goes into your eye through the *pupil* and is focused by your *lens* onto your *retina*. The shape of your lens can be changed by your *ciliary muscles* so that you see a clear picture. When you look at near objects the ciliary muscles *contract* and your lens gets fatter. When you look at distant objects your ciliary muscles *relax* and your lens gets thinner. Your *iris* can open wide to let in more light. It can also get smaller to keep out too much bright light.

Each eye sees a slightly different picture which gives you *stereoscopic vision*. The picture on your retina is upside down but your brain turns it the right way up again.

Important words

Sclerotic	the strong outer coat of your eyeball.
Choroid	the dark-coloured middle layer of your eye.
Retina	the inner layer of your eye. It has light-sensitive cells in it.
Cornea	the clear covering over the front of your eye.
Blind spot	the place where the optic nerve goes out of your eye.
Yellow spot	part of your retina where you see things most clearly.
Iris	the coloured part of the front of your eye. It controls the size of your pupil.
Pupil	the opening in your iris which lets light go into your eye.
Ciliary muscle	a ring-shaped muscle inside the ciliary body.
Cones	cells in your retina that are sensitive to colour. They only work in bright light.
Rods	cells in your retina that are not sensitive to colour. They can work in dim light.

Things to do

1. Find your blind spot!

Close your left eye. Look at the cross with the right eye. Hold the page about 30 cm away from your eye. Slowly move the page towards yours eye. What happens to the spot? Why does this happen?

2. Work with a partner. One partner must hold up lengths of different coloured cotton against white paper. The other partner must stand at different distances from the paper. Can you guess the colour of the cotton? Is the colour of the paper important? Are some colours easier to guess than others?

3. Most people have one eye stronger than the other. Hold up a pencil at arm's length. Try to line the pencil up with something behind it. Close one eye. Now open that eye and close the other. When you are using your stronger eye the pencil does not seem to move. Which is your strongest eye?

Questions

A.

Join these sentences together using either the word 'and' or the word 'because', whichever is correct.

1. In dim light not much light gets into your eyes. Your pupils open wide.

2. Your pupils get wider in dim light. More light can get into your eyes.

3. The ligaments of your eye pull on the lens. Your ciliary muscles relax.

4. When you look at near objects your ciliary muscles contract. Your lens gets fatter.

B.

Figure 36.13 shows a front view of the right eye.

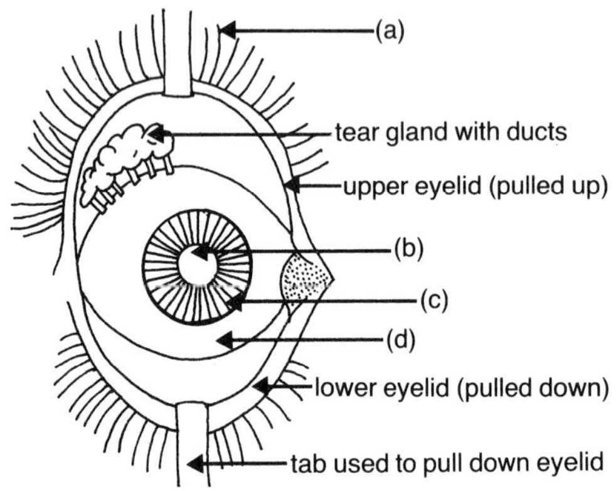

Figure 36.13

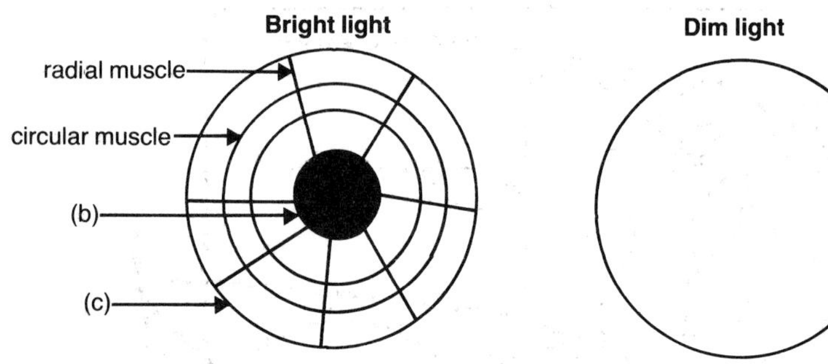

Figure 36.14

1. Name the parts labelled (a) to (d) on the diagram.

2. What is the main function of the tear gland?

3. Give *two* natural structures which protect the eye from damage.

4. What is the function of the part labelled (b)?

5. The inside of the eyeball viewed through the part labelled (b) is black. Give *one* reason for this.

6. Figure 36.14 shows a front view of parts of the eye labelled (b) and (c). Draw the outline diagram (below right) in your book and complete it to show what happens to the parts when the eye is in dim light.

7. Give *one* reason why the change described above (part **6**) must take place.

8. We cannot control the reaction shown in (part **6**). What name is given to this type of response?

9. Below is a list of parts of the eye of a mammal. Opposite this is a list of functions. Copy the parts of the eye into your book. Select the correct statement for each of the parts listed and write its letter alongside the right word. The first part has been completed as an example.

Part	*Function*
Suspensory ligament — H	A to keep the shape of the eye
Lens	B to focus light to a sharp image
Vitreous humour	C to produce a black and white image
Blind spot	D to give the most accurate image
Fovea (yellow spot)	E to produce a coloured image
Rod	F where nerve fibres leave the eye
Cone	G to carry nerve impulses to the brain
Optic nerve	H to hold the lens in position

(ALSEB)

TOPIC 37

THE EAR

THE PARTS OF YOUR EAR

Your ear has cells that are sensitive to sound. These cells help your brain to sort out sounds into:
1. high and low notes,
2. loudness,
3. the direction the sound comes from.
Your ear also helps you to keep your balance. (See figure 37.1.)

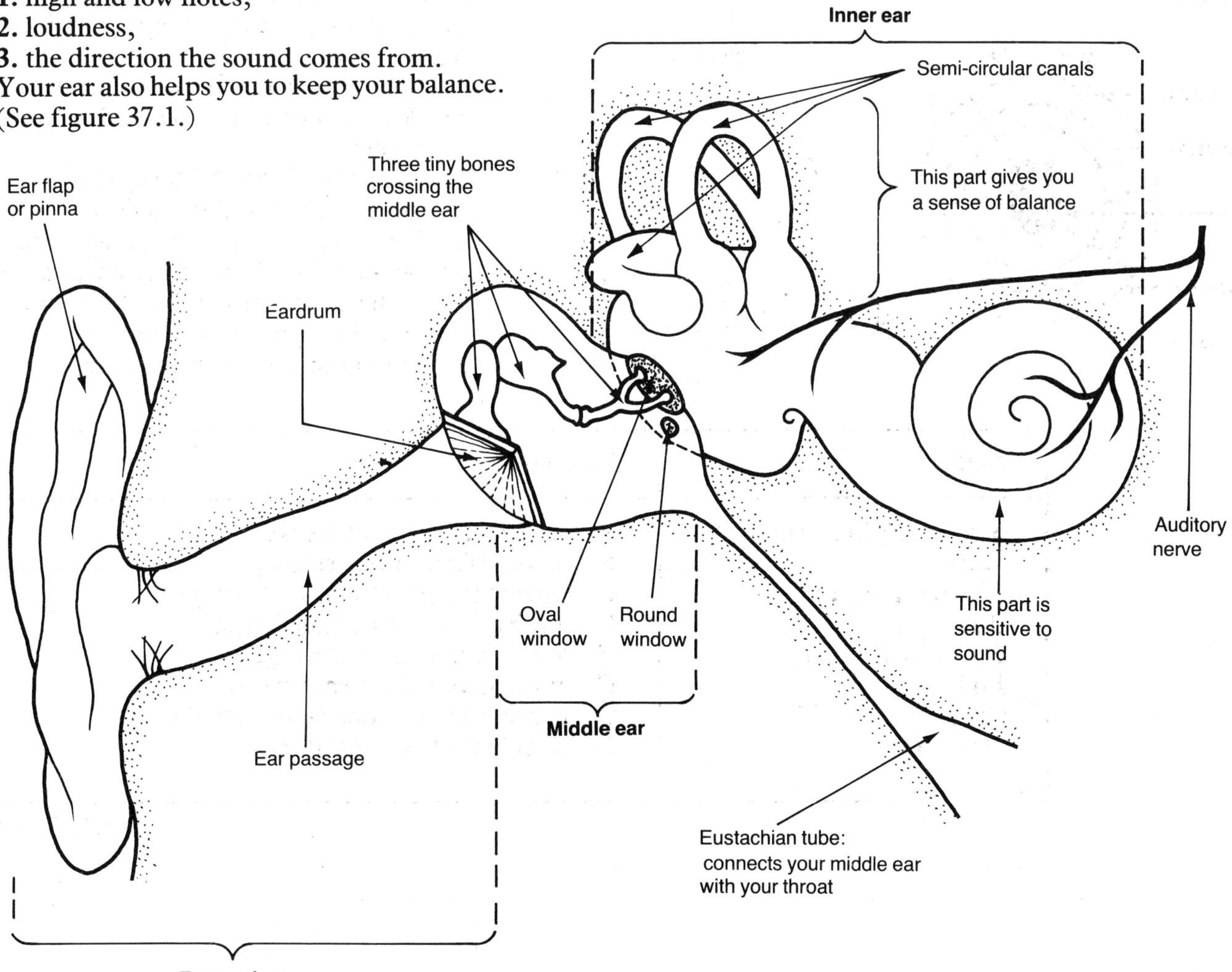

Figure 37.1

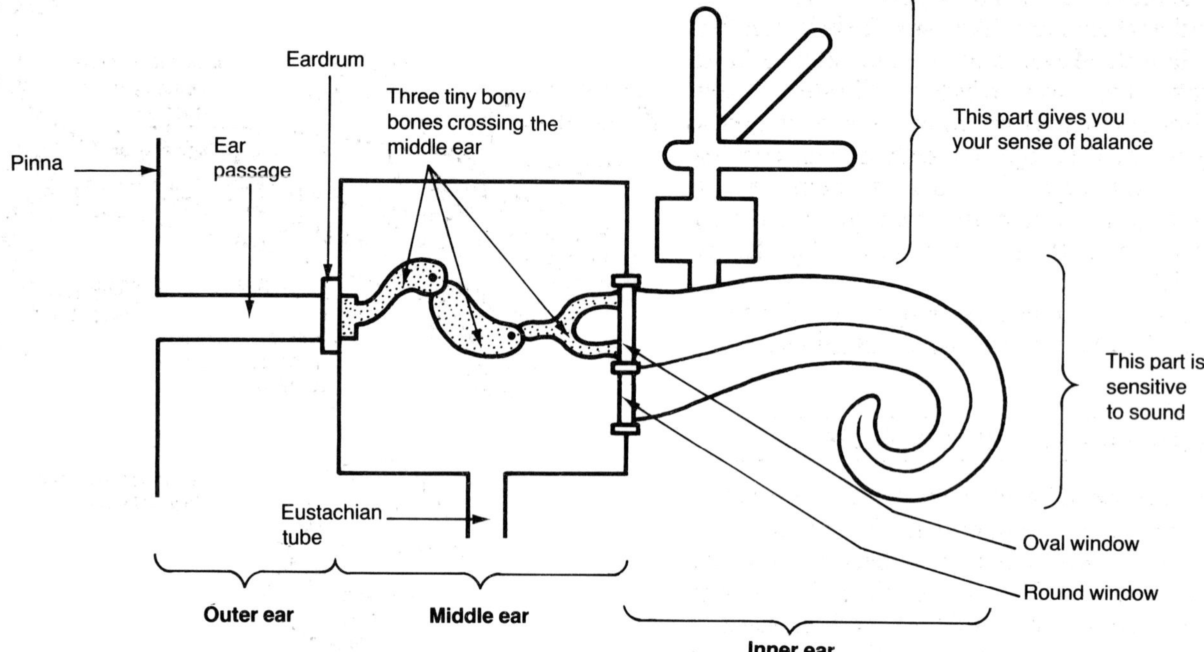

Figure 37.2 A simple picture of your ear

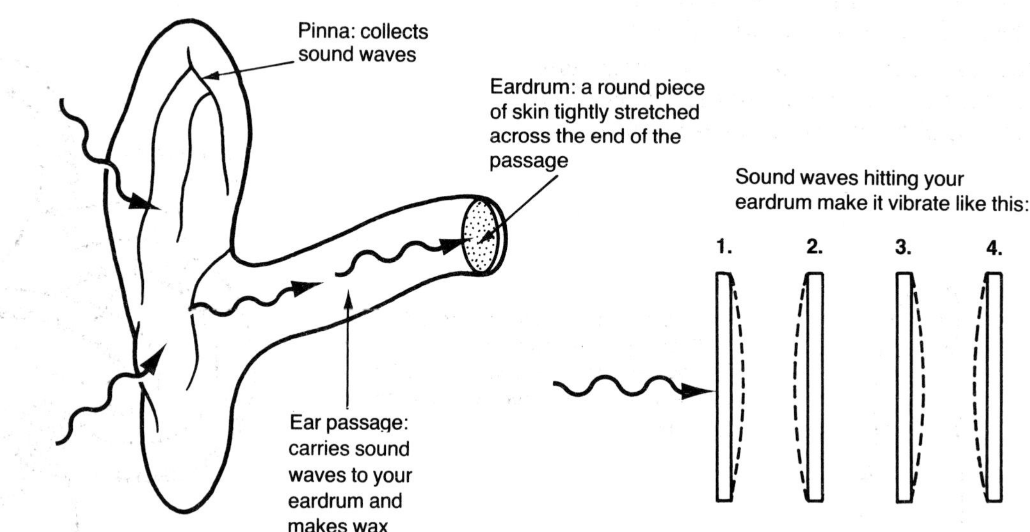

Figure 37.3 Your outer ear

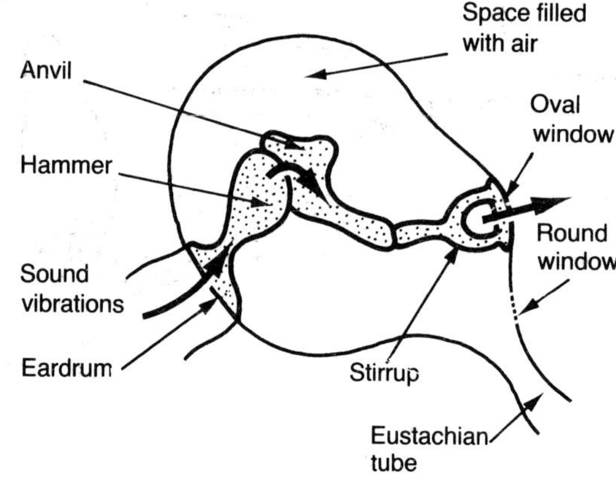

Figure 37.4 Your middle ear

Figure 37.2 is a simple picture of your ear. Compare this with Figure 37.1.

Horses, cats, rabbits and other animals, can turn the *pinna* towards a sound. This helps to make their hearing very sensitive. (See figure 37.3.)

Your middle ear is like a cave crossed by a bridge of three tiny bones. These are called *ossicles* and their names are: the hammer, the anvil and the stirrup bones. (See figure 37.4.) Vibrations travel from the eardrum to the *oval window*, by moving from one bone to the other.

Air pressure must be kept the same on each side of your eardrum. The *eustachian tube* helps this to happen because it connects with your throat.

Sound is sorted out by your *cochlea*. This is a tube which looks like a snail's shell. It is full of liquid. Movements of your stirrup bone make the oval window vibrate. These vibrations travel up your cochlea and back again. As this happens, cells in your cochlea are stimulated. This makes them send a message to your brain along your auditory nerve. You then hear sounds. (See figure 37.5.)

Your *round window* stops the vibrations after they have been sorted out into sounds.

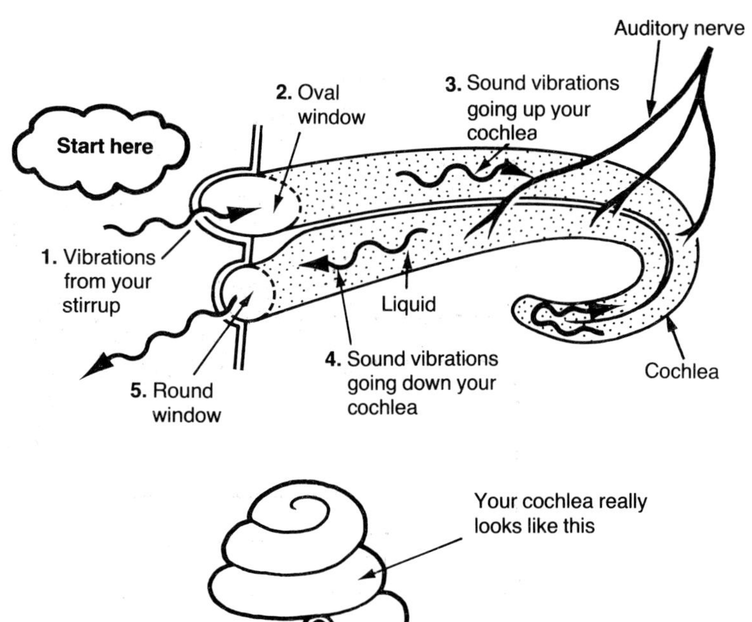

Figure 37.5 Sorting out sound – your inner ear

HOW DO YOU BALANCE?

Your sense of balance comes from sense cells in your semi-circular canals. These canals are full of liquid. When your head moves, the liquid stays still for a short time. This bends the sense cells over and they send messages to your brain. (See figure 37.6.) Your brain tells you:

1. how fast or slowly you are moving,
2. the position of your head and body.

Any movement of your head will stimulate sense cells in one or more of the canals. This is because of the way the canals are fixed.

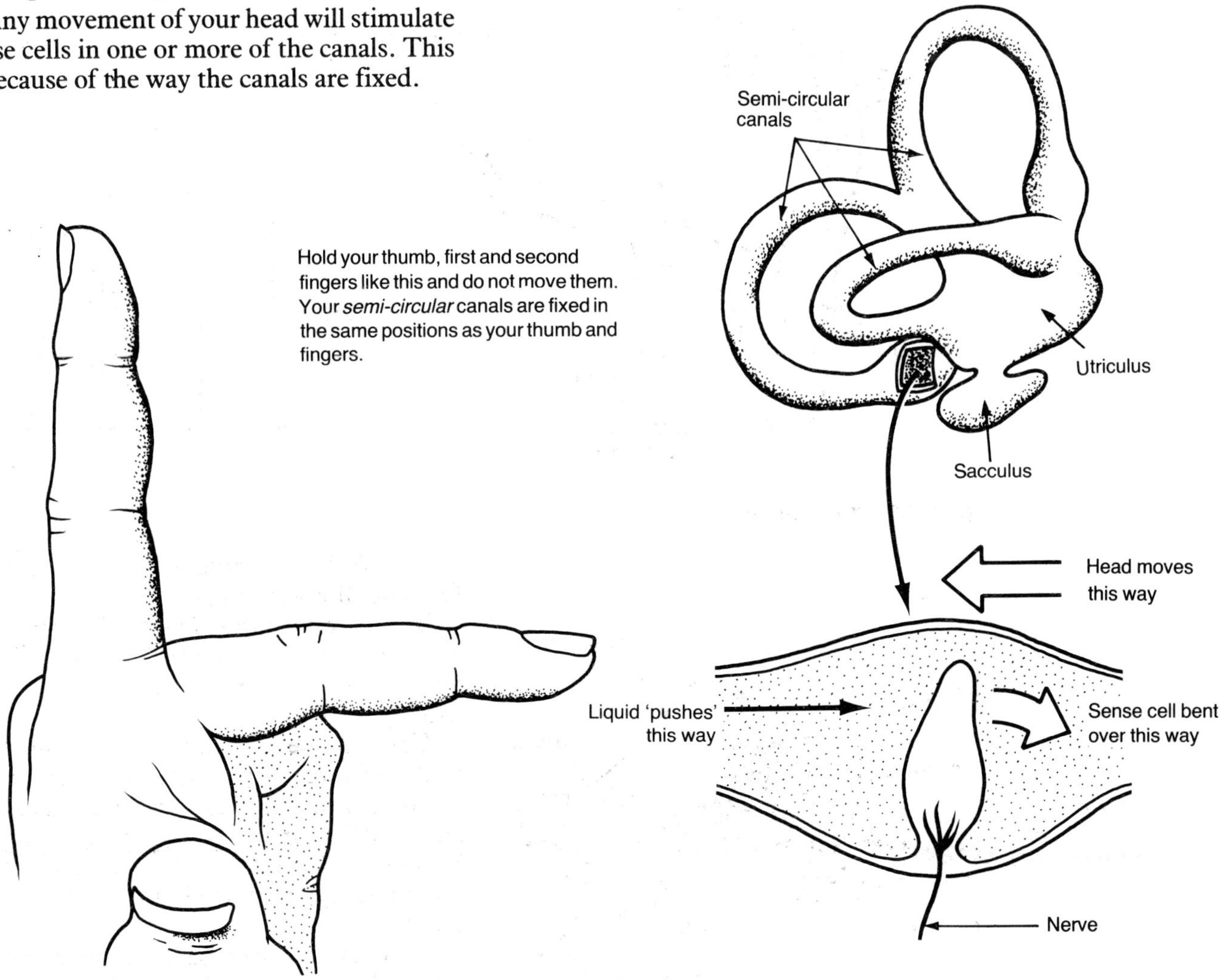

Hold your thumb, first and second fingers like this and do not move them. Your *semi-circular* canals are fixed in the same positions as your thumb and fingers.

Semi-circular canals

Utriculus

Sacculus

Head moves this way

Liquid 'pushes' this way

Sense cell bent over this way

Nerve

Figure 37.6 Sorting out balance – your inner ear

LOOKING AFTER YOUR EARS

Never put anything *anything* into your ear. You can damage your eardrum and cause deafness.

Loud noise can damage your hearing. If you cannot hear what someone is saying to you because of noise, that noise is putting your hearing in danger!

Fancy that!

Bats can fly in the dark by listening to their own squeaks! The squeaks bounce back off objects in the path of the bat. The bat's large ears collect the echo and the bat can then 'see' where the object is!

Summary

Your ears are affected by *sound* and also help you to keep your *balance*. Sound is collected by your *pinna* and goes down your *ear passage*. The sound makes your *eardrum* move or *vibrate*. These vibrations are carried by your *ossicles* to the *oval window*. The vibrations go along your *cochlea* where they are sorted out into different sounds. The cochlea sends messages about these sounds along your *auditory nerve* to your brain.

Your *semi-circular canals* help you to balance. Movements of your head stimulate sense cells in one or more of the canals. Messages from these sense cells are sent to your brain.

Important words

Pinna	a flap which helps to collect sound vibrations.
Eardrum	a thin skin stretched across your ear passage.
Oval window	a thin skin against which the stirrup fits.
Round window	a thin skin which stops the sound vibrations after they have travelled along your cochlea.
Eustachian tube	a tube which connects your middle ear with your throat.
Ossicles	the three bones (hammer, anvil and stirrup) which carry sound vibrations across your middle ear.
Semi-circular canals	three tubes, fixed at right angles to each other, which give you your sense of balance.
Cochlea	a coiled tube that sorts out sound vibrations and sends messages to your brain.

Things to do

Work in pairs. Blindfold your partner. Make a tapping noise at different positions around your partner's head. Ask your partner to say where each sound is coming from and keep a record of each guess. In which position can your partner hear best? Is it in front of his or her head, behind it, above it, or at the sides?

Questions

A.

Put each of these parts of sentences into the correct order.

1.	your cochlea is and your semi-circular canals are	like three half circles coiled like a snail's shell
2.	any movement of your head affects	your semi-circular canals the sense cells in
3.	your eardrum your eustachian tube	helps to keep the same air pressure on each side of

B.

Figure 37.7 shows the structure of an ear.

1. Name the parts labelled (A), (B) and (C).
2. (a) Where does the Eustachian tube end?
   (b) If you are on an aircraft which is taking off your ears may be felt to 'pop'. What causes the feeling?
3. In the middle ear on the diagram are structures labelled (D), (E) and (F).
   (a) Name any one of these structures and give its number.
   (b) Of what are these three structures made?
   (c) Write out the phrase which best describes the function of the structures: they amplify sound waves; they detect the loudness of a sound; they detect the changes in the position of the head.

Figure 37.7

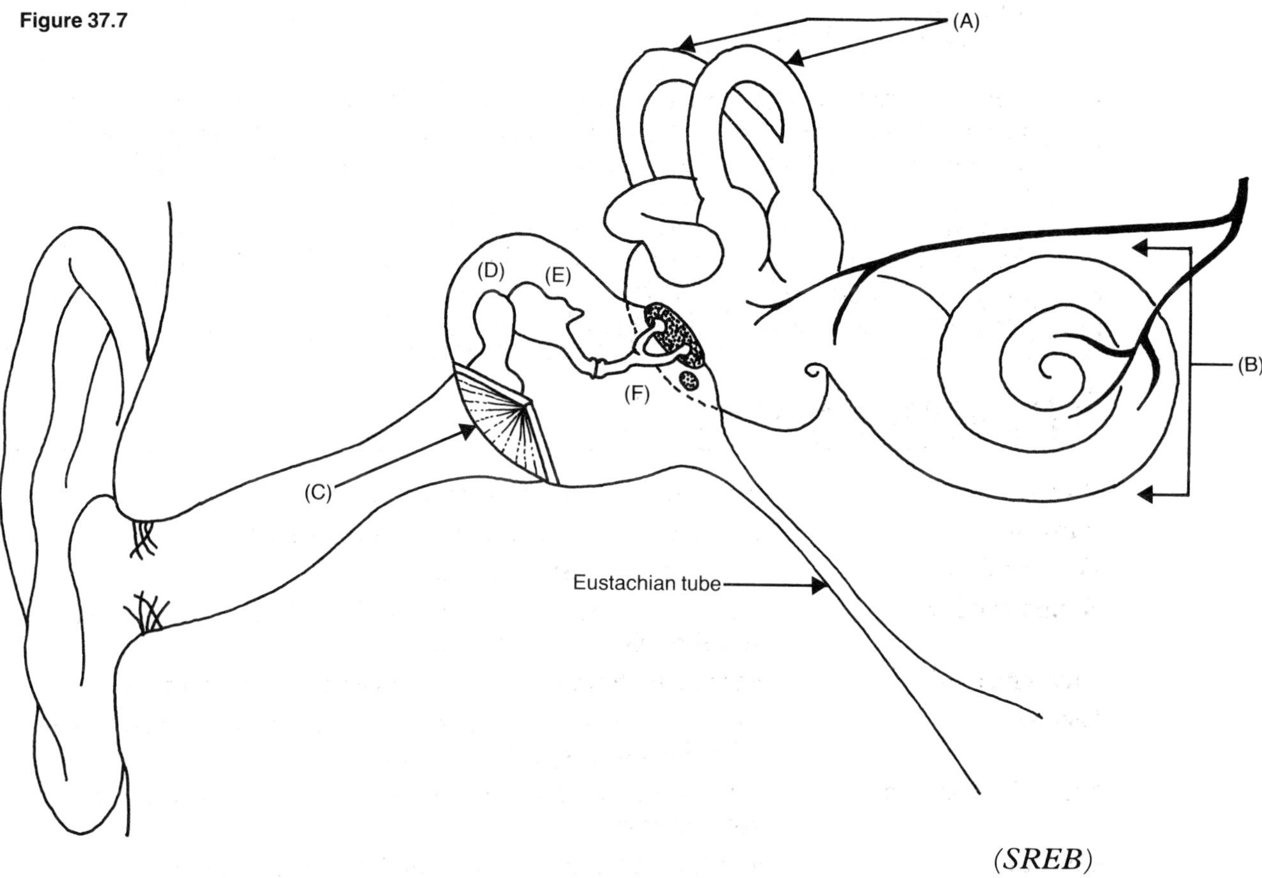

(SREB)

C.

1. What happens to sound waves as they travel through your outer, middle and inner ear?
2. What would happen if your ear passage was blocked with wax?
3. How can a throat infection spread to your middle ear?
4. Why are your semi-circular canals fixed at rights angles to each other?
5. How do the sense cells in your semi-circular canals work?

TOPIC 38

THE SENSE ORGANS OF YOUR NOSE, TONGUE AND SKIN

Your nose, tongue and skin have a lot of important sense organs in them. These send messages to your brain to tell you about your surroundings. Each sense organ is only sensitive to one kind of stimulus. A sense organ sensitive to heat will not tell you anything about touch. Your ears and eyes are special sense organs.

Fancy that!

Smell and taste are important to some people for their work! Cheese-graders, tea-tasters, perfume-makers and wine-tasters all need a good sense of smell and taste.

Smell and taste are more important to animals than to man. Dogs can pick out their owner's smell on an object he or she held for only 2 seconds! Male silk moths can smell the female 11 kilometres away!

Fish have taste buds all over their bodies!

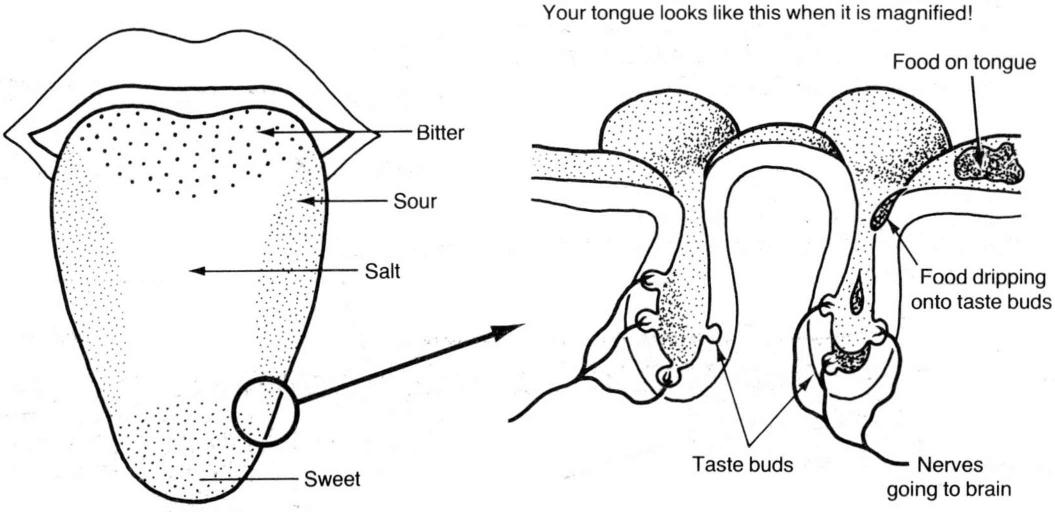

HOW DO YOU TASTE?

Your tongue has sense organs called *taste buds* which are sensitive to chemicals dissolved in water. There are only four kinds of taste buds in your mouth. This means that you only have four kinds of taste: salt, sour, bitter and sweet. You have groups of taste buds for each 'taste' on your tongue. (See figure 38.1.)

Figure 38.1

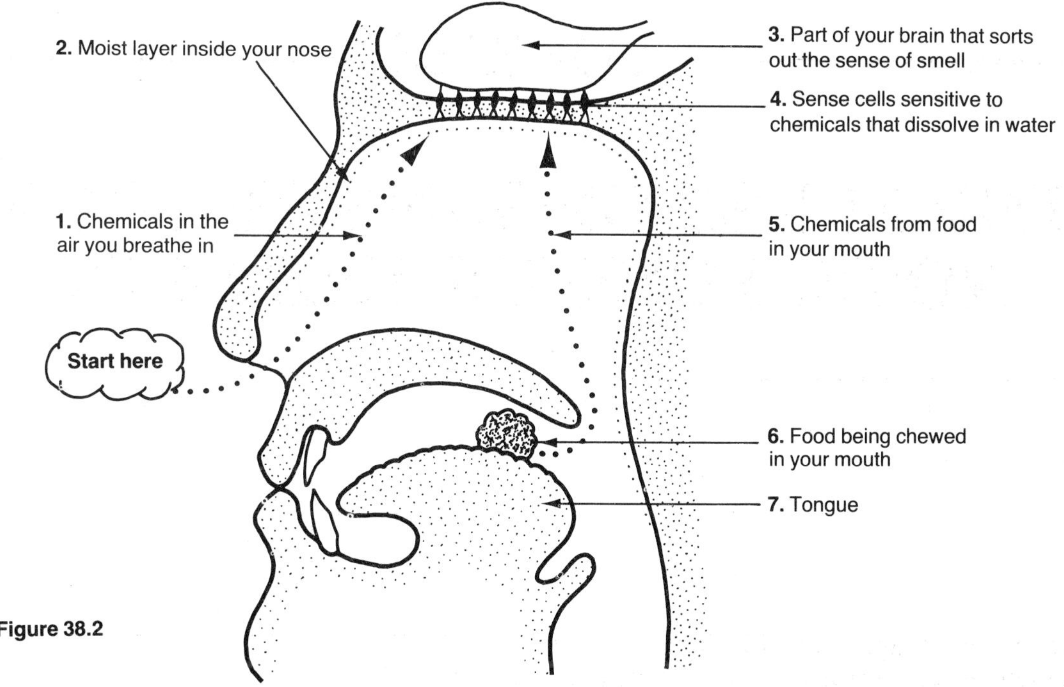

Figure 38.2

YOUR SENSE OF SMELL

Smell is important to your sense of taste. If you have a heavy cold, your food is tasteless. This is because the sense organs in your nose cannot tell you about the smell and flavour of your food.

Your sense of smell is easily tired. You soon get used to a smell and cannot tell if it is still there.

Chemicals which are given off by food or other substances go into the air. They then dissolve in the moist layer inside your nose. The sense cells in your nose are stimulated by the chemicals and send a message to your brain. Some chemicals from all food get into the air but more from hot food than cold. You would be surprised if you could smell a salad, but worried if you could not smell a stew cooking! (See figure 38.2.)

The forked tongue of a snake flicks out to pick up chemicals in the air. These chemicals are then 'tasted' in the snakes mouth.

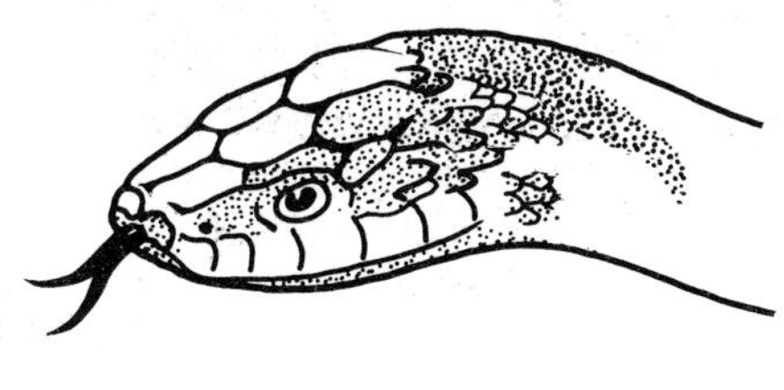

Figure 38.3

YOUR SKIN

Your skin has sense organs sensitive to touch, pressure, heat and pain. Some parts of your skin have more sense organs than other parts. Your finger tips have a lot of sense organs and are very sensitive to touch. Blind people 'read' by running their fingers over small raised dots arranged in patterns. This is called 'Braille'. (See figure 38.4.)

The boy in figure 38.5. is sucking a lollipop while sitting at a desk reading. The diagram shows just *some* of the messages sent to his brain by his sense organs! His brain sorts out the message and 'tells' him what is happening.

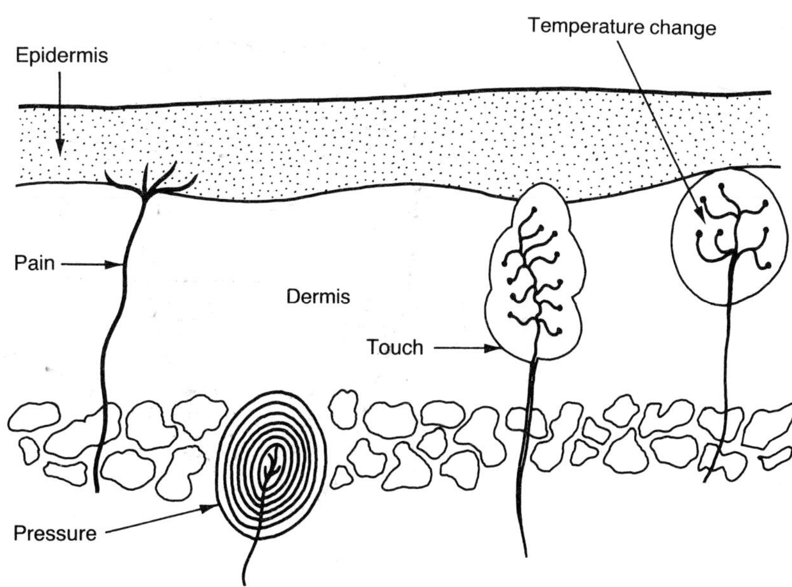

Figure 38.4 Sense organs of your skin

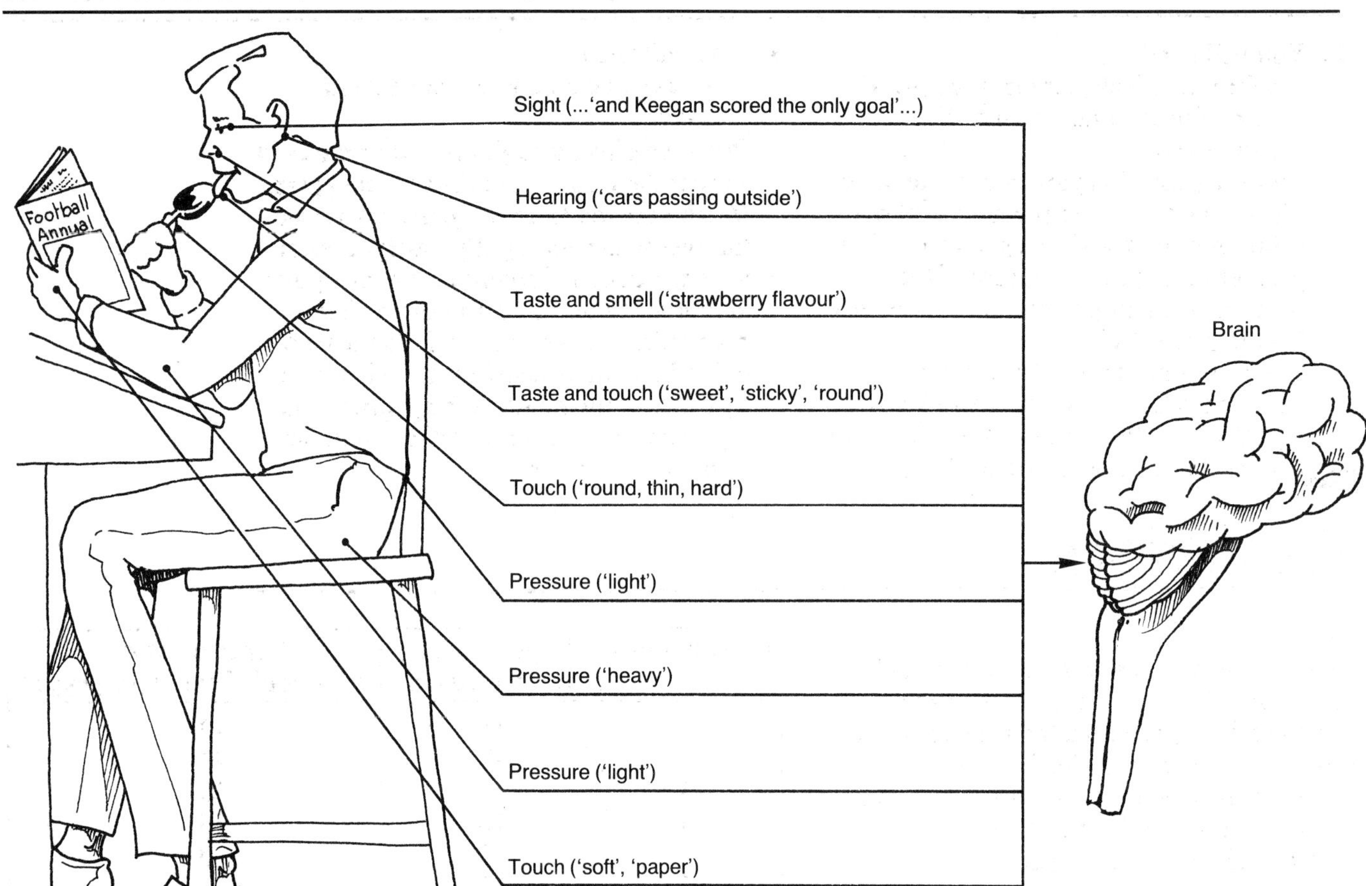

Figure 38.5

Summary

Sense organs are sensitive to *one* sort of stimulus. Sense organs in your nose and mouth tell you about the *chemicals* in the air and in your food. The sense organs in your tongue are called *taste buds* and they tell you about *salt*, *sour*, *bitter* and *sweet* tastes in your mouth. Your sense of smell also helps you to taste things. Sense organs in your skin are sensitive to *touch*, *pressure*, *pain* and changes of *temperature*.

Important words

Taste buds — sense organs in four groups on your tongue. Each group is sensitive to one sort of taste: sour, sweet, bitter or salt.

Things to do

1. You will need:

mashed-up apple, onion, potato, lemon and orange
a teaspoon
a blindfold

Work in pairs. One partner must wear a blindfold and pinch his or her nose (or wear a nose-clip). The other must feed him or her with each food in turn. Repeat without the nose-clip. Is it easier to guess the foods with or without the clip and why?

Do not eat in the laboratory! Do **1.** and **2.** in the home economics room or a classroom.

2. You will need:
   solutions of salt, lemon juice (sour), sugar (sweet) and tea (bitter)
   a glass rod

   Work in pairs. Get your partner to put out his tongue while you put a drop of one solution onto it with the glass rod. Your partner must guess the taste of the solution without putting his tongue into his mouth. Why?

   Try another part of his tongue with the same solution. Wash the rod and repeat with a different solution. Are your results the same as figure 38.1?

3. You will need:
   a piece of card about 6 cm x 3 cm
   2 pins

   Push the pins through the end of the card so that their points are about 2 cm apart. Work in pairs. Get your partner to close his eyes while you lightly touch his skin with the points. Sometimes use one point and other times use both points. How many pin pricks can he feel? Is the back of his hand more sensitive than his finger tips? Move the points to 1 cm apart and try again. Is it harder to tell the number of pin pricks now?

Questions

A.

An experiment was carried out in which blindfolded schoolchildren were asked whether food placed on their tongues was onion or potato or apple. A similar experiment was then performed, but this time the noses of the blindfolded schoolchildren were pegged.

The table of results given here shows the number of times each child guessed correctly (out of 20 attempts) for each of the experiments.

Pupil number	Experiment 1 Blindfolded only	Experiment 2 Blindfolded and nose-pegged
1	18	13
2	17	10
3	14	15
4	16	13
5	19	9
6	17	8
7	12	8
8	17	10
9	15	7
10	15	7

1. Calculate:
   (a) the total number of correct reponses in Experiment 1;
   (b) the total number of tests in Experiment 1;
   (c) the percentage of correct responses in Experiment 1.
2. Calculate:
   (a) the total number of correct responses in Experiment 2;
   (b) the total number of tests in Experiment 2;
   (c) the percentage of correct responses in Experiment 2.
3. In which of the two experiments was each pupil using:
   (a) mainly taste;
   (b) both taste and smell?
4. State three conclusions which can be drawn from these results.
5. Explain why the results obtained by pupil number 3 demonstrate the importance of using a large number of individuals in this type of investigation.
6. Name one other sense which could be helping each pupil to distinguish between the three types of food.

(EAEB)

TOPIC 39

HUMAN REPRODUCTION

Humans do not develop their reproductive systems properly until puberty starts. This happens between the ages of 11 and 17 in boys and 8 and 15 in girls. At puberty many changes happen to a young person's body. These changes are called secondary sex characteristics and are caused by sex hormones. The female sex hormones are made by *ovaries* and are called *oestrogens*. Male sex hormone is made by *testes* and is called *testosterone*. (See figure 39.1.)

The following changes happen at puberty.

In boys

1. Their testes start to make sperms.
2. Their voices 'break' or deepen.
3. Pubic hair grows around their sex organs.
4. Hair grows on the face, chest and arm-pits.

In girls

1. Their ovaries start to release eggs.
2. Their breasts start to grow.
3. Pubic hair grows around their sex organs.
4. Hair grows in their arm pits.

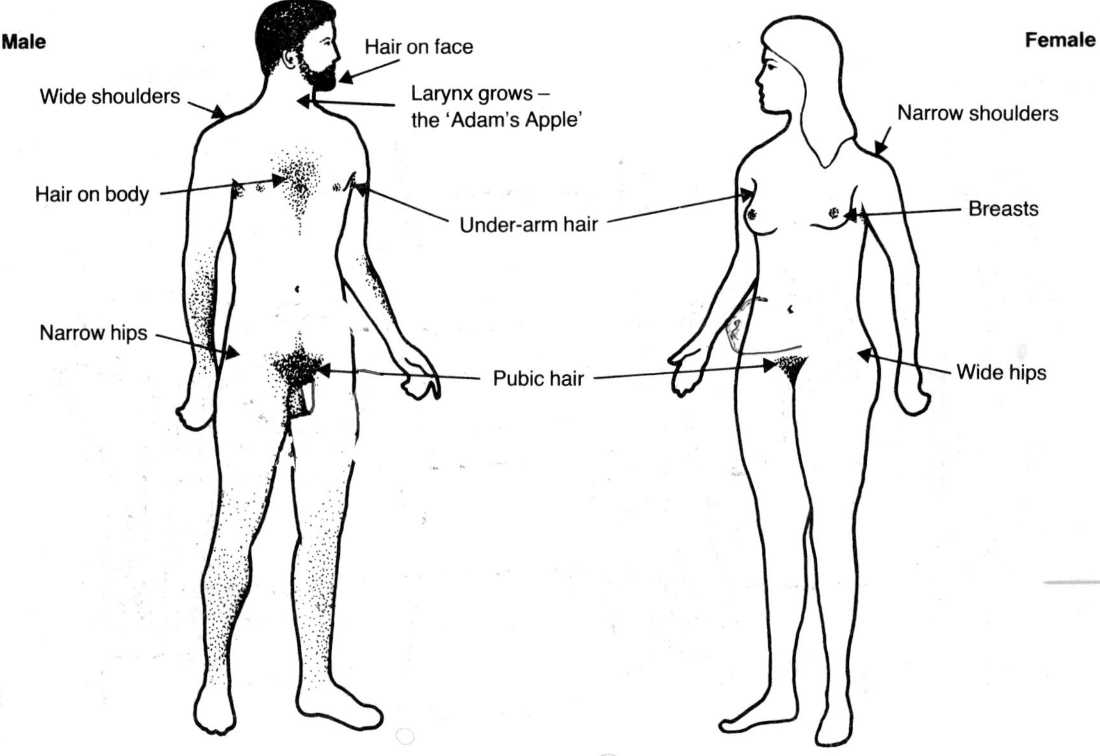

Figure 39.1 Secondary sex characteristics

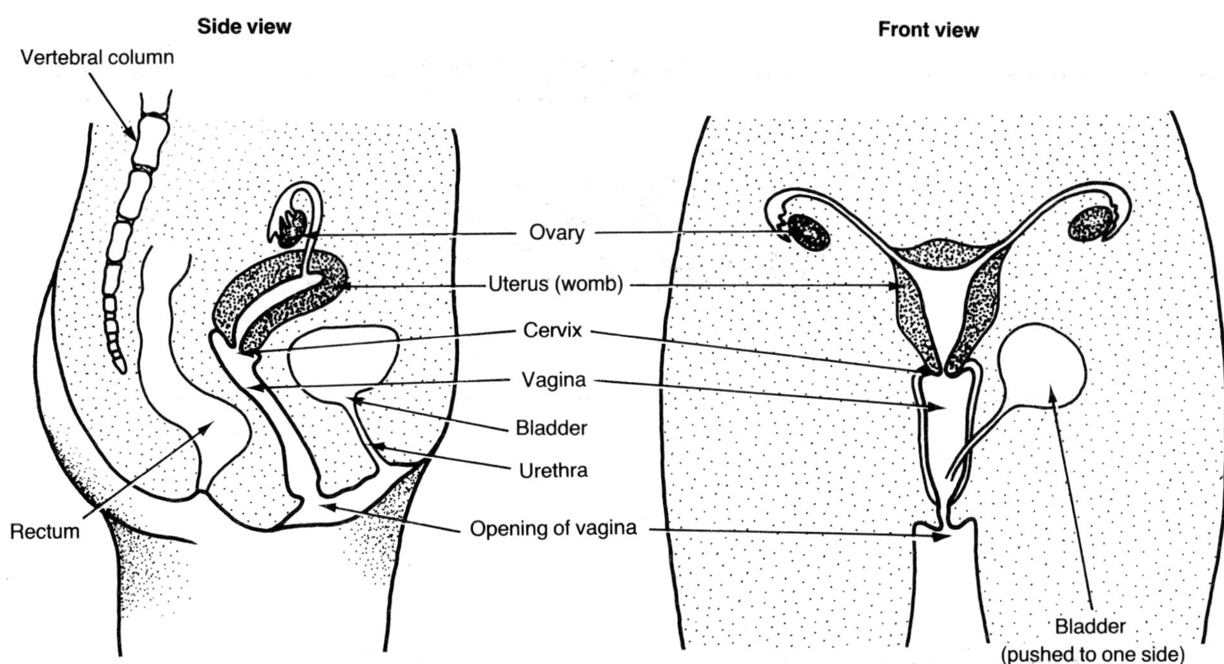

Figure 39.2 Female sex organs

FEMALE SEX ORGANS

Eggs or ova (singular: *ovum*) are made by a woman's ovaries. The eggs travel down her *oviducts* to her *uterus* or womb. A uterus is a thick-walled bag of muscle where a baby can develop. The cervix is a ring of muscle which closes a woman's uterus from her *vagina*.

MALE SEX ORGANS

Sperms are made by a man's testes which hang in a bag or scrotum outside his body. The sperms travel down the sperm tubes to a man's *urethra*. His prostate gland makes a fluid in which the sperms swim.

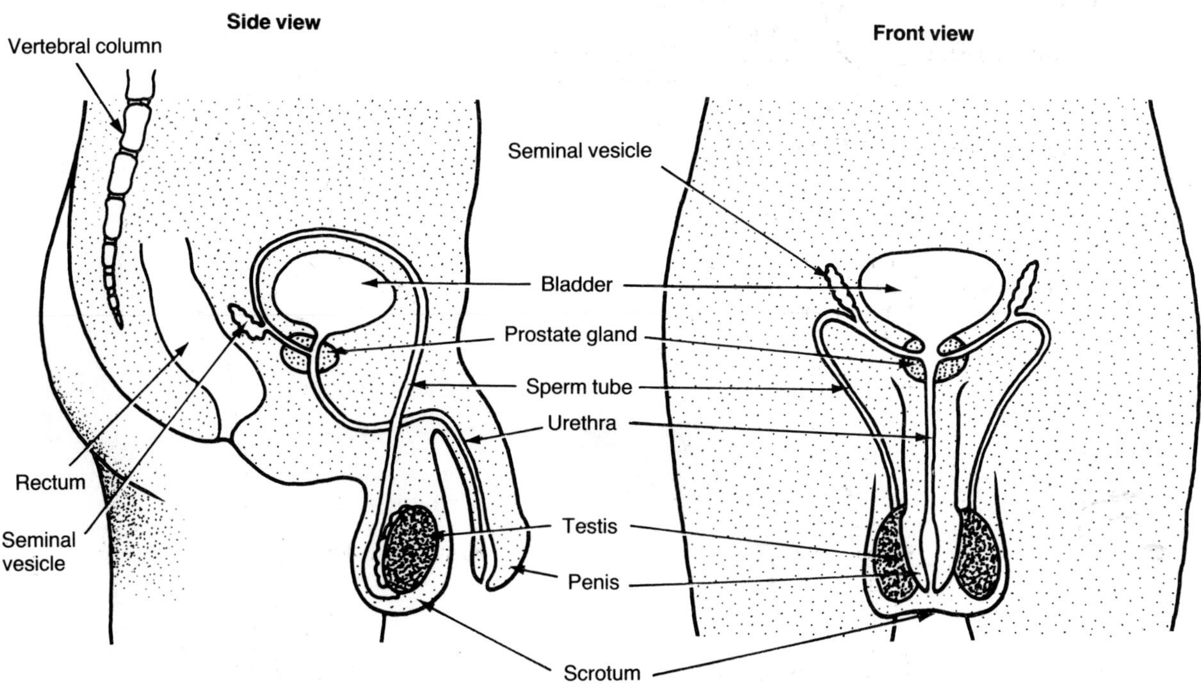

Figure 39.3 Male sex organs

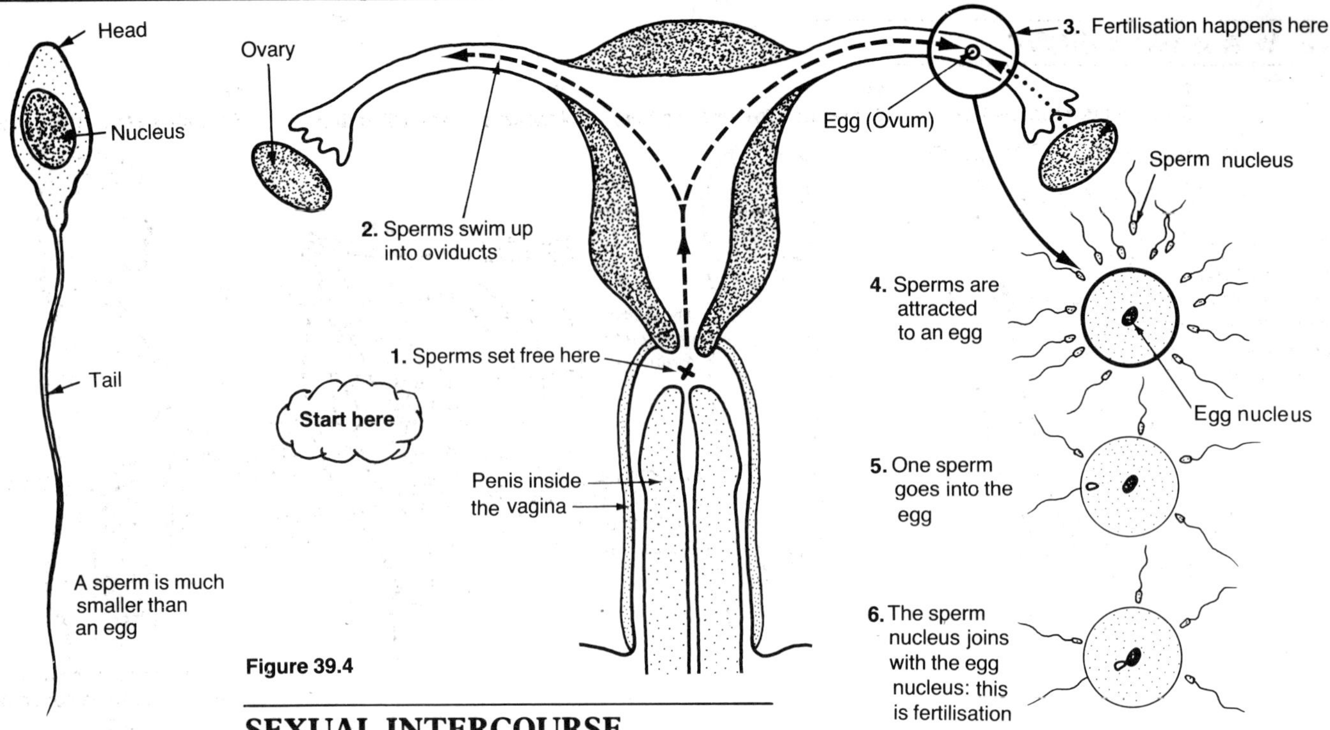

Figure 39.4

SEXUAL INTERCOURSE

In sexual intercourse a man's penis becomes stiff. This is because blood is pumped into it faster than it can get out. The man's penis is placed in the woman's vagina and moved up and down. This makes sperms shoot out of the penis into the vagina. The sperms swim up the woman's oviducts in a liquid made by the man's prostate gland and seminal vesicles. Chemicals in this liquid make the sperms move their tails. If there is an egg in the oviduct, *fertilisation* may happen. (See figure 39.4.)

WHAT HAPPENS TO A FERTILISED EGG

If one of a woman's eggs is fertilised she becomes *pregnant*. During pregnancy the egg develops and grows into a baby. It takes nine months for a baby to grow. The growing baby is protected from damage because it floats in liquid inside the *amniotic sac*. When the baby is ready to be born the woman's uterus starts to contract. This is called 'labour'. The amniotic sac breaks and the fluid runs out of the woman's vagina. The baby is pushed out of the woman's vagina head first. (See figure 39.5.) An *umbilical cord* still connects the baby with the placenta. The baby's umbilical cord is cut and tied by the doctor or midwife. The remains of the umbilical cord leave a scar on the baby which is called the navel or 'tummy button'. Sometimes a baby comes out feet first. This is called a breech birth and is more difficult than a normal birth.

Soon after a baby is born the placenta and the rest of its umbilical cord come out. This is called the afterbirth.

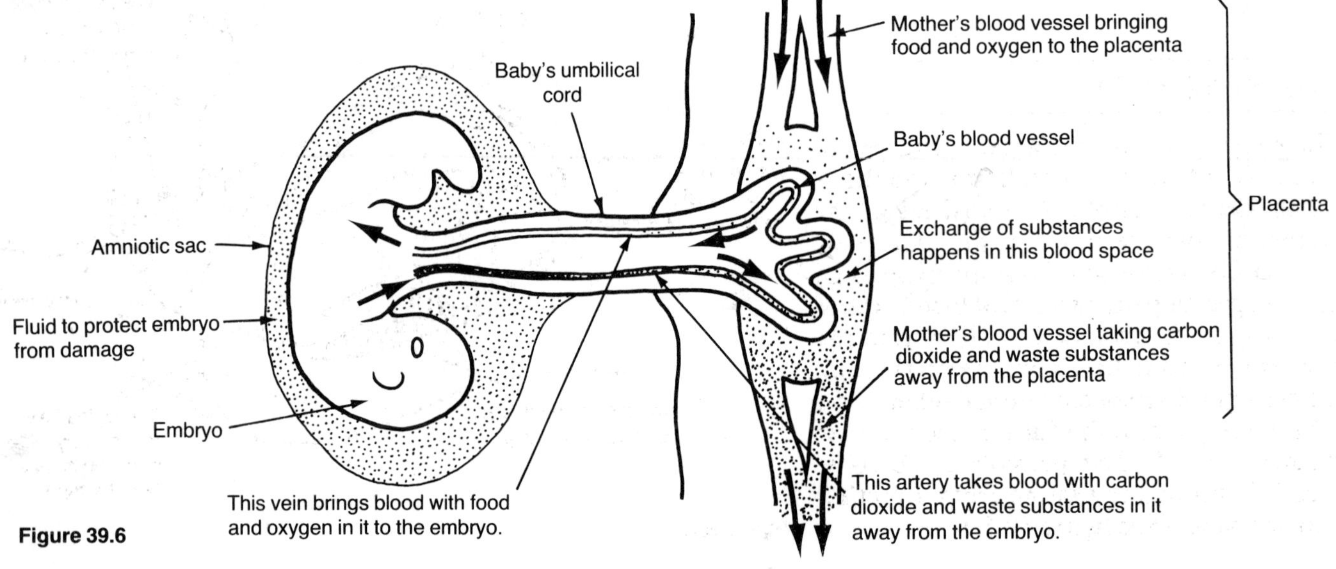

Figure 39.6

HOW A BABY GROWS

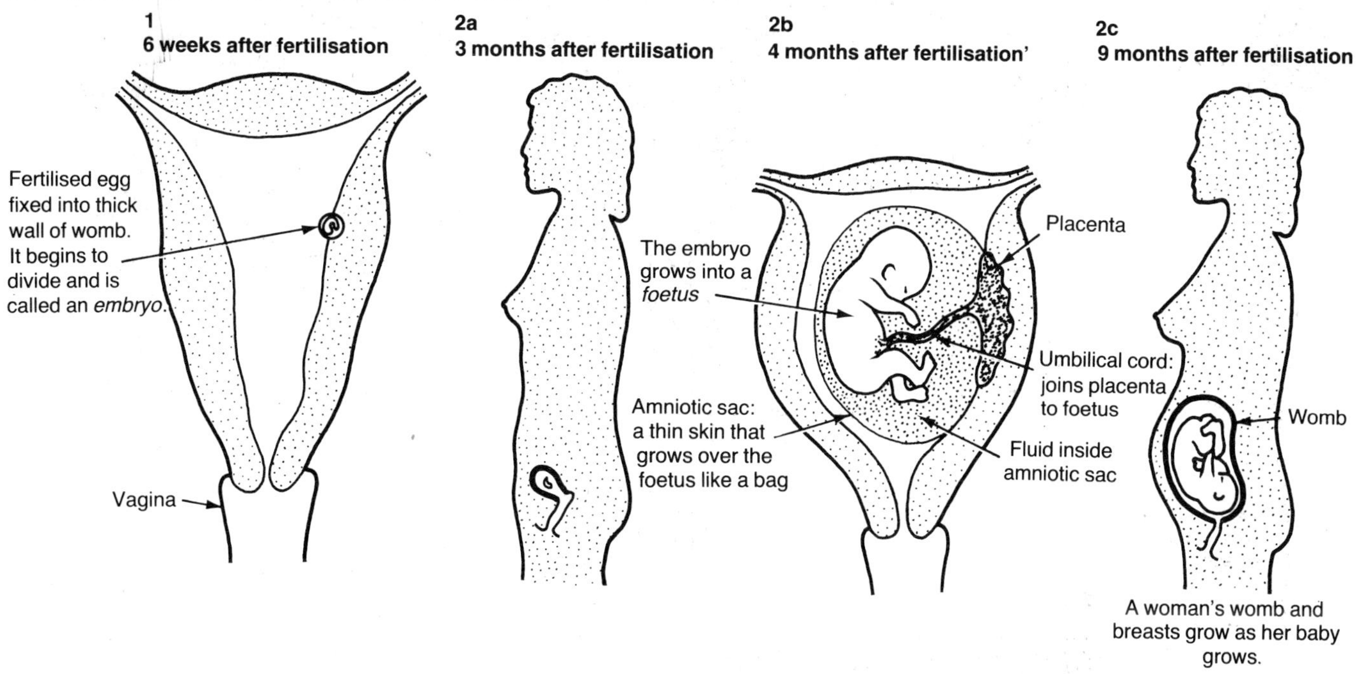

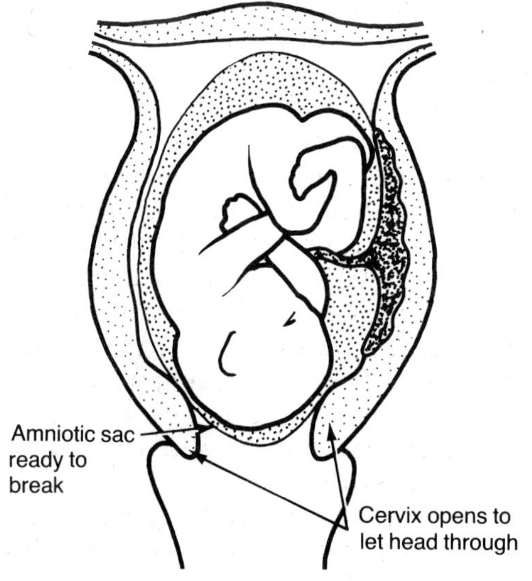

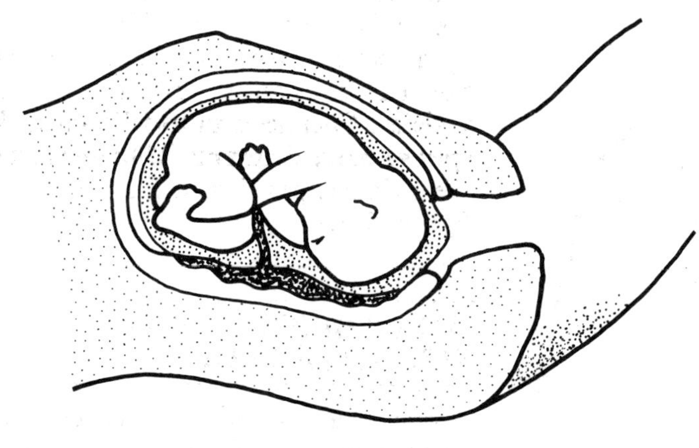

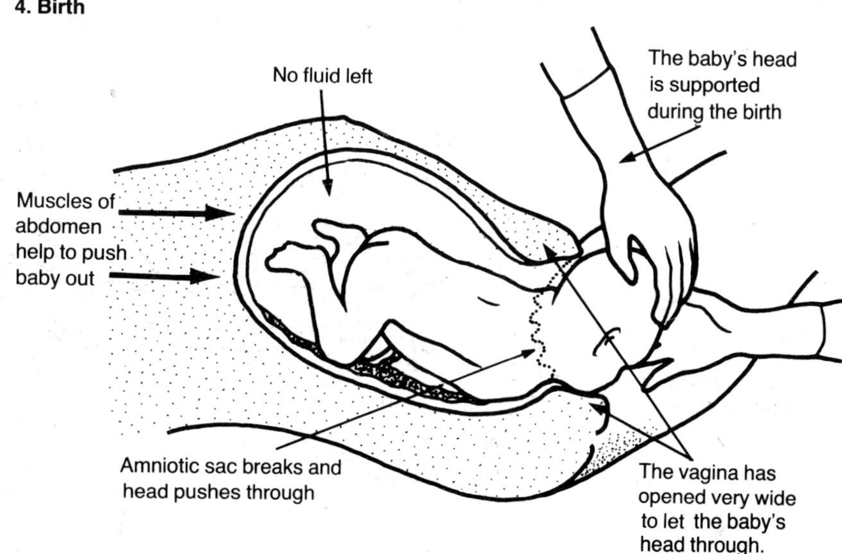

Figure 39.5

THE PLACENTA

The baby's *placenta* is a large, round pad of tissue. It is fixed to the wall of its mother's womb. On one side of a placenta there are the mother's blood vessels. On the other side there are blood vessels from the baby. The tissue separating the two sets of blood vessels is very thin. Oxygen and food go from the mother's blood to her baby's blood through the placenta. Carbon dioxide and other waste substances go from the baby's blood into its mother's blood. The placenta stops some harmful substances passing from a mother into her baby. (See figure 39.6.)

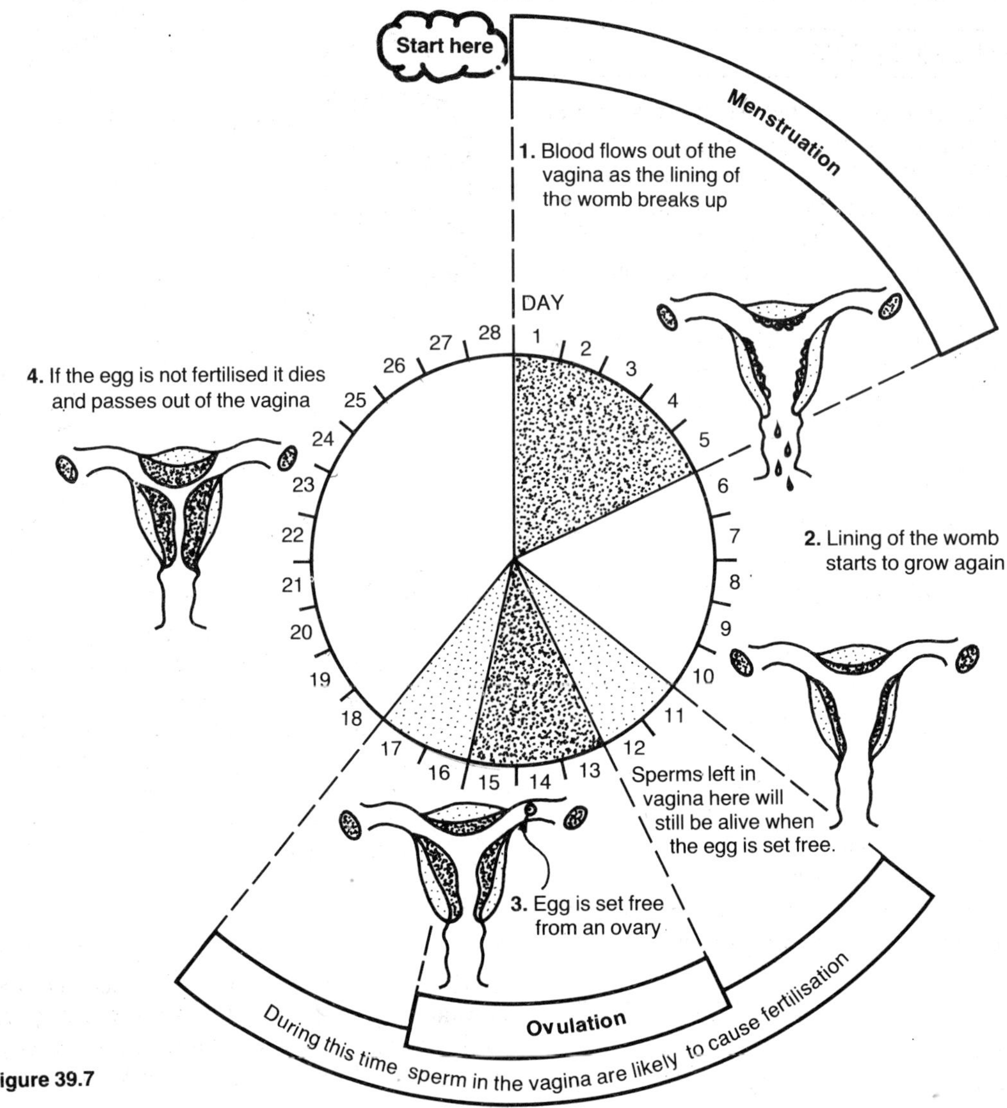

Figure 39.7

THE MENSTRUAL CYCLE

At puberty, girls start their 'periods' or *menstrual cycle*. A menstrual cycle usually lasts about 28 days. (See figure 39.7.)

During ovulation an egg is set free from one of a woman's ovaries. It travels slowly down her oviduct towards her uterus. The lining of a woman's uterus (womb) grows and a lot of blood vessels develop in it. This gets the womb ready in case an egg is fertilised.

An egg only lives for about 36 hours after ovulation. If the egg is not fertilised during this time it dies. About ten or twelve days later the thick lining of a woman's womb starts to break up and blood and dead cells flow out of her vagina. This is called a menstrual flow. Girls and women need to wear a sanitary towel or tampon at this time. A woman's menstrual flow lasts about five days. The 28 day cycle starts on the first day of the menstrual flow. If an egg is fertilised, menstruation does not happen. (See figure 39.8.)

Ovulation usually happens between days 13 and 15 of the 28 day cycle. Sperms can live up to three days in a woman's womb. This means that fertilisation can happen between days 11 and 17 of her 28 day cycle. If a woman becomes pregnant it is useful to know when the baby will be born. A doctor usually counts 40 weeks from the first day of a woman's last period to work this out.

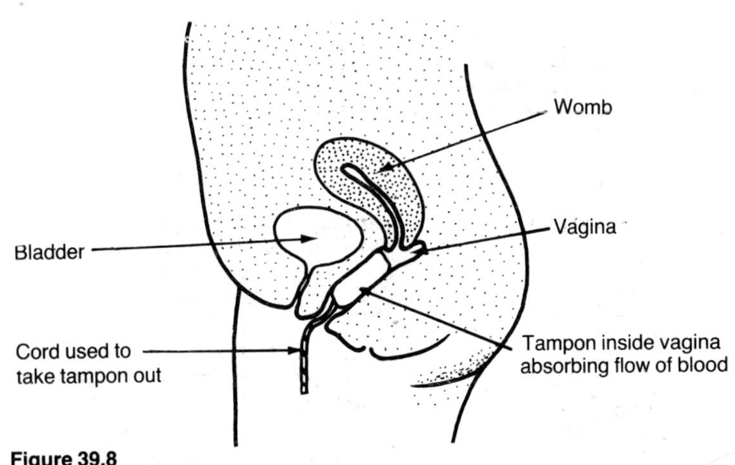

Figure 39.8

BIRTH CONTROL

Sexual intercourse just before, during or just after ovulation can cause pregnancy (see figure 39.7). People who want to control the size of their families may use *contraception* to stop a pregnancy. (See figure 39.9.) The main methods of contraceptions are as follows.

1. The pill; this is a very good method of contraception. A contraceptive pill contains hormones which stop eggs being set free from the ovaries. One pill must be swallowed on each of the days between the menstrual periods.
2. The sheath (or condon or French letter); this is like the finger of a glove. It is made of very thin strong rubber and it is put over a man's penis. The sheath stops sperms getting into a woman's womb.
3. The cap or diaphragm; this is made of soft rubber and fits over a woman's cervix. It stops sperms getting into her womb.
4. The coil or loop; this is a small piece of plastic which is put inside a woman's womb and left there. It stops an egg from fixing itself into her womb.

Of course, the only way to be certain of not getting pregnant is not to have sexual intercourse at all!

> **Fancy that!**
>
> About 1 hundred million sperms are released into the vagina during sexual intercourse! Only *one* of these will fertilise an egg!
>
> A fertilised human egg is about as big as the full-stop at the end of this sentence.

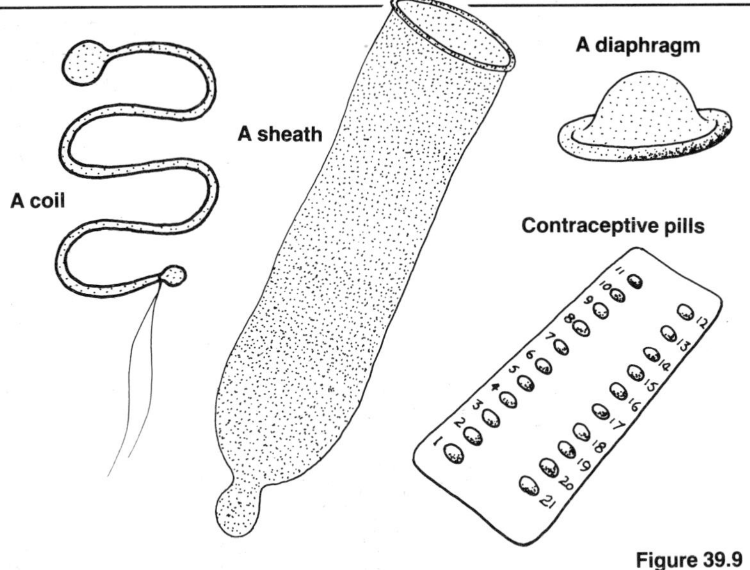

Figure 39.9

Room for all?

About every 50 years the number of people in the world doubles. More people live longer and more babies are being born. Many people cannot get enough food. Difficulty in finding food or living space has often caused wars and disease. Contraception is an important way of controlling the number of people in the world.

Parental care

A new-born baby is fed only on milk. It gets this from its mother's breasts. Milk can also be made-up from powdered milk and given to the baby in a bottle. Babies must be kept warm and clean and given milk every few hours.

TWINS

Figure 39.10 shows that there are two ways twins can happen. (See also page 261.)

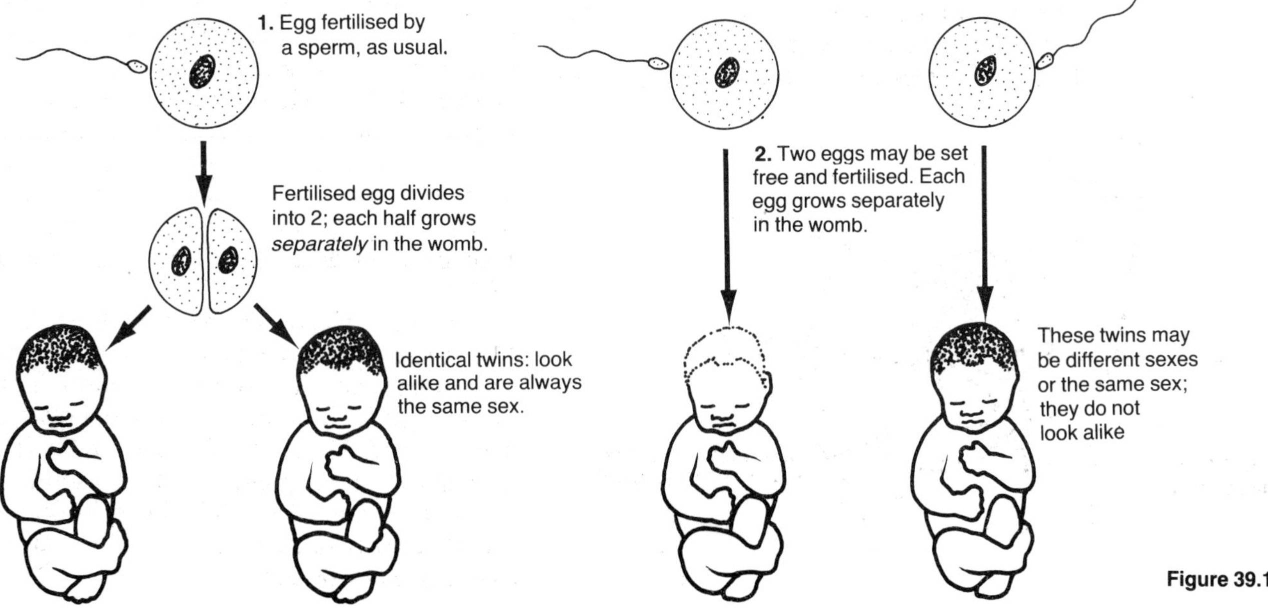

Figure 39.10

Summary

The human *reproductive system* becomes fully developed during *puberty* when the *secondary sex characteristics* appear. The changes which happen at puberty are caused by *hormones*. During *sexual intercourse* an *egg* may be *fertilised* by a *sperm*. A woman then becomes *pregnant*. The fertilised egg grows inside the *uterus* for *nine months*. When a baby is ready to be born the mother's uterus contracts as *labour* starts.

At puberty girls start their *periods* or *menstrual cycle*. Each cycle lasts about *28 days* and prepares the uterus for pregnancy. If an egg is not fertilised the lining of the uterus breaks up and blood comes out of the *vagina*. This is called *menstruation*. Sexual intercourse just before or after an egg is set free can cause pregnancy. Pregnancy can be stopped by using a method of *contraception*.

Important words

Oestrogens	female sex hormones made by a female's ovaries.
Testosterone	male sex hormone made by a male's testes.
Uterus	a hollow organ in which a baby develops in a female.
Vagina	a tube that receives sperm from a male in sexual intercourse.
Ovary	an organ that makes eggs in a female (plural: ovaries).
Testis	an organ that makes sperms in a male (plural: testes).
Oviduct	a tube leading from the ovary to the uterus in a female.
Penis	the male sex organ.
Urethra	a tube from the bladder to the outside of the body in males and females; in males it carries urine and sperm; in females it carries urine only.
Egg (or ovum)	a female sex cell (plural: ova).
Sperm	a male sex cell.
Fertilisation	the joining of an egg and sperm.
Pregnant	a woman who has a baby developing inside her.
Amniotic sac	a fluid-filled bag that grows around a developing baby to protect it.
Umbilical cord	a tube from a baby to the placenta.
Placenta	an organ that helps to feed a growing baby.
Menstruation	the sending out of blood and dead cells from a female's uterus every 28 days.
Contraception	stopping sperms from fertilising an egg.
Embryo	a very young animal growing in an egg or in its mother's body.
Foetus	a stage where the embryo of mammal begins to look like a young mammal.

Questions

A.

Put each of these parts of sentences into the correct order.

1.	fertilisation happens sperms are set free	in the vagina but in the oviducts
2.	before ovulation a few days	sperm left in the vagina can fertilise an egg

3.	after menstruation finishes about 8-10 days	an egg is set free from an ovary
4.	the vagina for about 5 days	during menstruation blood and dead cells come out of

B.

Figure 39.11 shows the variation in the thickness of the lining of the womb and events within the ovary during the menstrual cycle.

1. (a) During which days is the lining of the womb decreasing in thickness?
(b) Explain the reason for this decrease in thickness.

2. (a) During which days of the cycle is the womb lining at its thickest?
(b) Explain the importance of the lining being thick at this time.

3. (a) How many days after the start of the period has the ovary released the egg?
(b) Describe fully why sexual intercourse is likely to result in fertilisation during the part of the cycle described as 'most fertile'.

(EAEB)

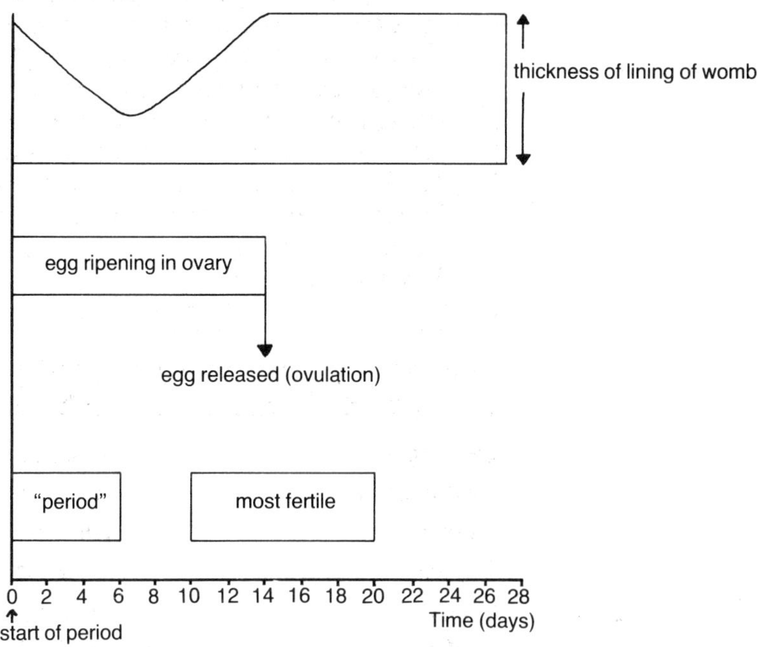

Figure 39.11

C.

Figure 39.12 shows the number of reported cases of Gonorrhoea affecting people of different ages in England in 1978.

1. (a) How many reported cases of Gonorrhoea were there in boys under the age of sixteen?
(b) How many cases of Gonorrhoea were there in girls under the age of sixteen?
(c) Suggest *one* reason why more girls than boys suffer from this disease under the age of nineteen.

2. (a) For which age group are there most reported cases of Gonorrhoea in males and females?
(b) Suggest *one* reason for there being a large number of cases in these age groups.

3. (a) Gonorrhoea is a sexually transmitted disease. Explain the meaning of *sexually transmitted*.
(b) State *three* ways in which a person can avoid catching the disease.

(EAEB)

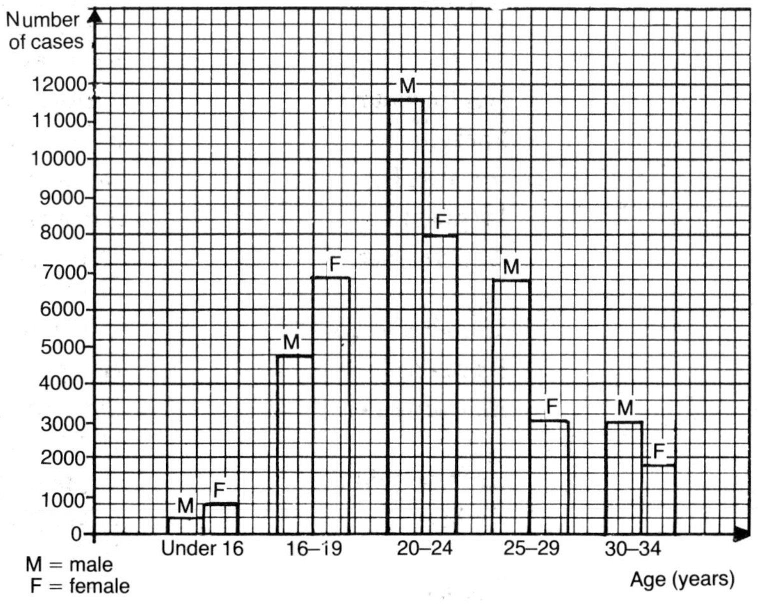

Figure 39.12

TOPIC 40

REPRODUCTION IN ANIMALS

Animals die from old age, disease or by being eaten. They need to reproduce to make new animals to replace the dead ones. Most animals reproduce by sexual reproduction and usually a male and a female animal are needed.

Male and female animals make sex cells or gametes. The male gametes are sperms and the female gametes are eggs. During sexual reproduction, a male sperm joins with a female egg. This is called fertilisation. In some animals fertilisation happens *outside* the body and this is called external fertilisation. Internal fertilisation happens *inside* the body of a female animal.

Some animals, such as earthworms, have both male and female reproductive organs in the same animal. There are no male or female animals. Each 'male–female' is called an *hermaphrodite*.

DIFFERENT WAYS OF GROWING UP

Some animals lay eggs. The young animals develop inside these eggs before they are ready to hatch. A lot of eggs may have to be laid as most of them may be eaten by other animals. (See figure 40.1.)

Some animals keep the fertilised eggs inside their bodies where they start to develop. This stops so many of the eggs being eaten by other animals. The eggs may be laid just before they are ready to hatch. In some snails, and lizards, the eggs can hatch inside the mother. The tiny young animals then crawl out and are 'born'. (See figure 40.2.)

Many animals do not lay eggs. In these animals the fertilised eggs grow and develop inside the body of the female. Because the

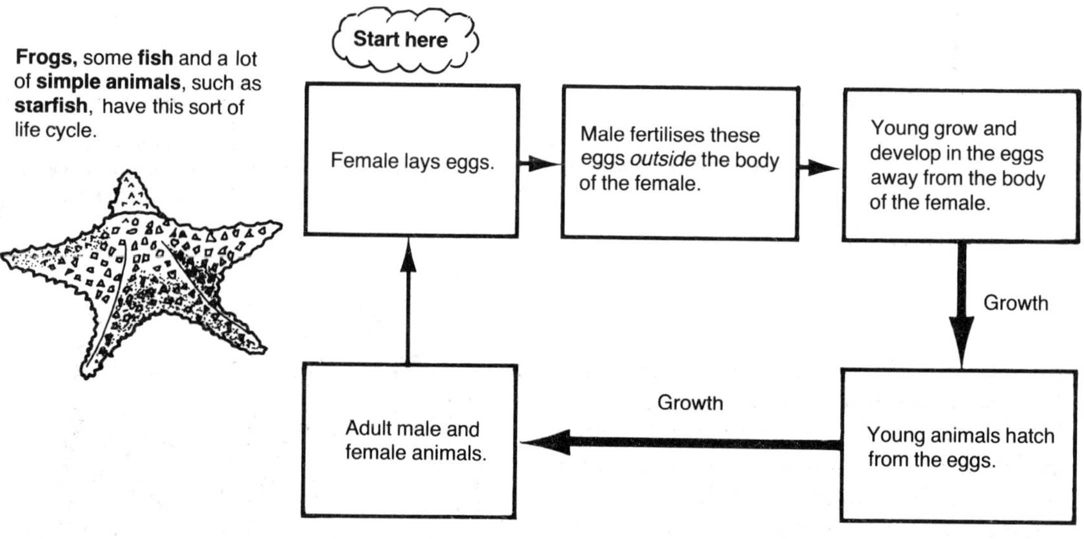

Figure 40.1

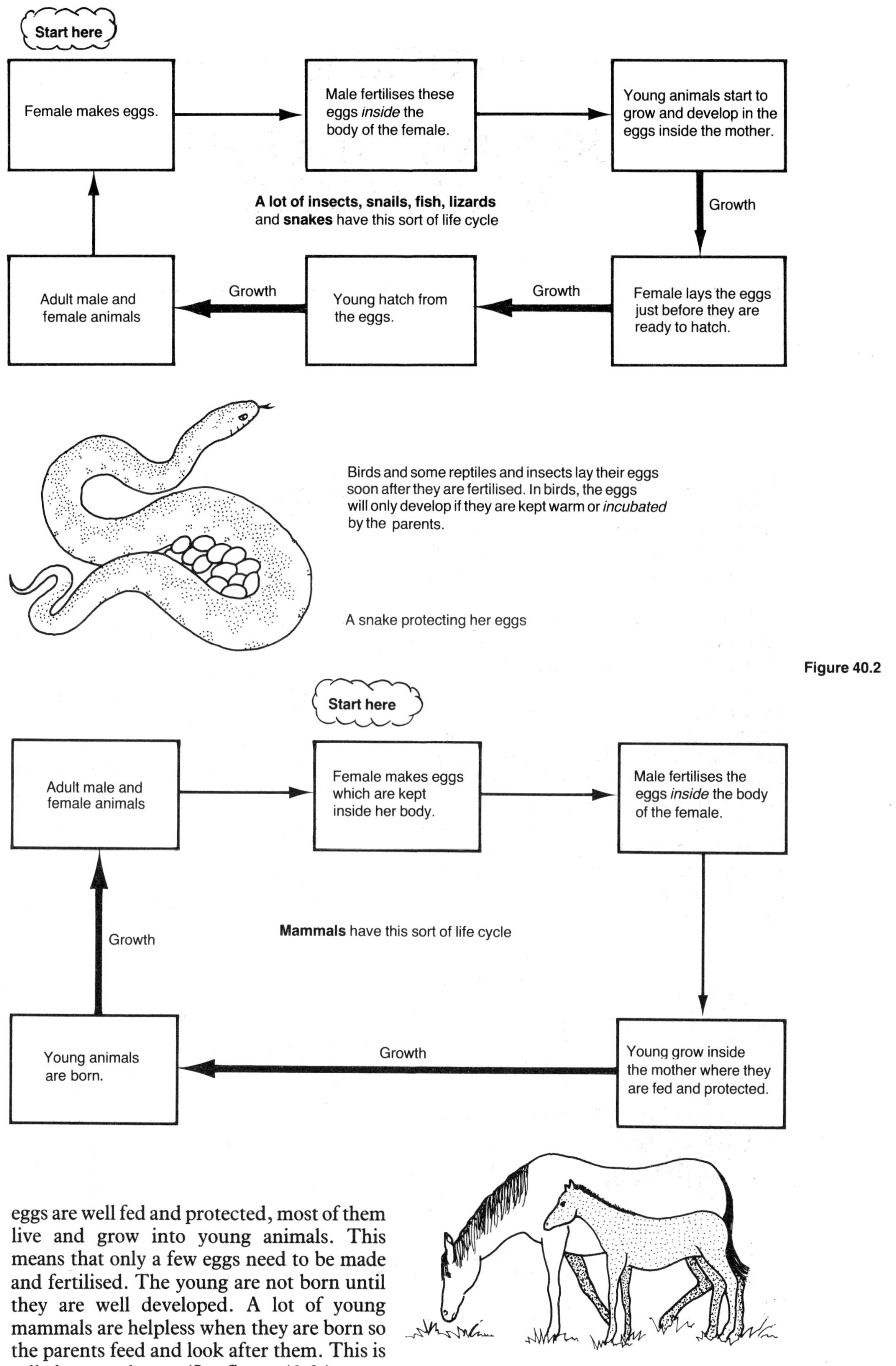

Figure 40.2

eggs are well fed and protected, most of them live and grow into young animals. This means that only a few eggs need to be made and fertilised. The young are not born until they are well developed. A lot of young mammals are helpless when they are born so the parents feed and look after them. This is called parental care. (See figure 40.3.)

A female horse (mare) with her foal

Figure 40.3

HOW FISH REPRODUCE

Most fish lay eggs but in some kinds the young are born ready to swim away.

In trout most of the eggs never grow into young animals. Out of 10,000 eggs laid, only about 250 live to be one year old!

Trout are good to eat! People rear them in concrete ponds in 'trout farms' and feed them on food pellets. (See figure 40.4.)

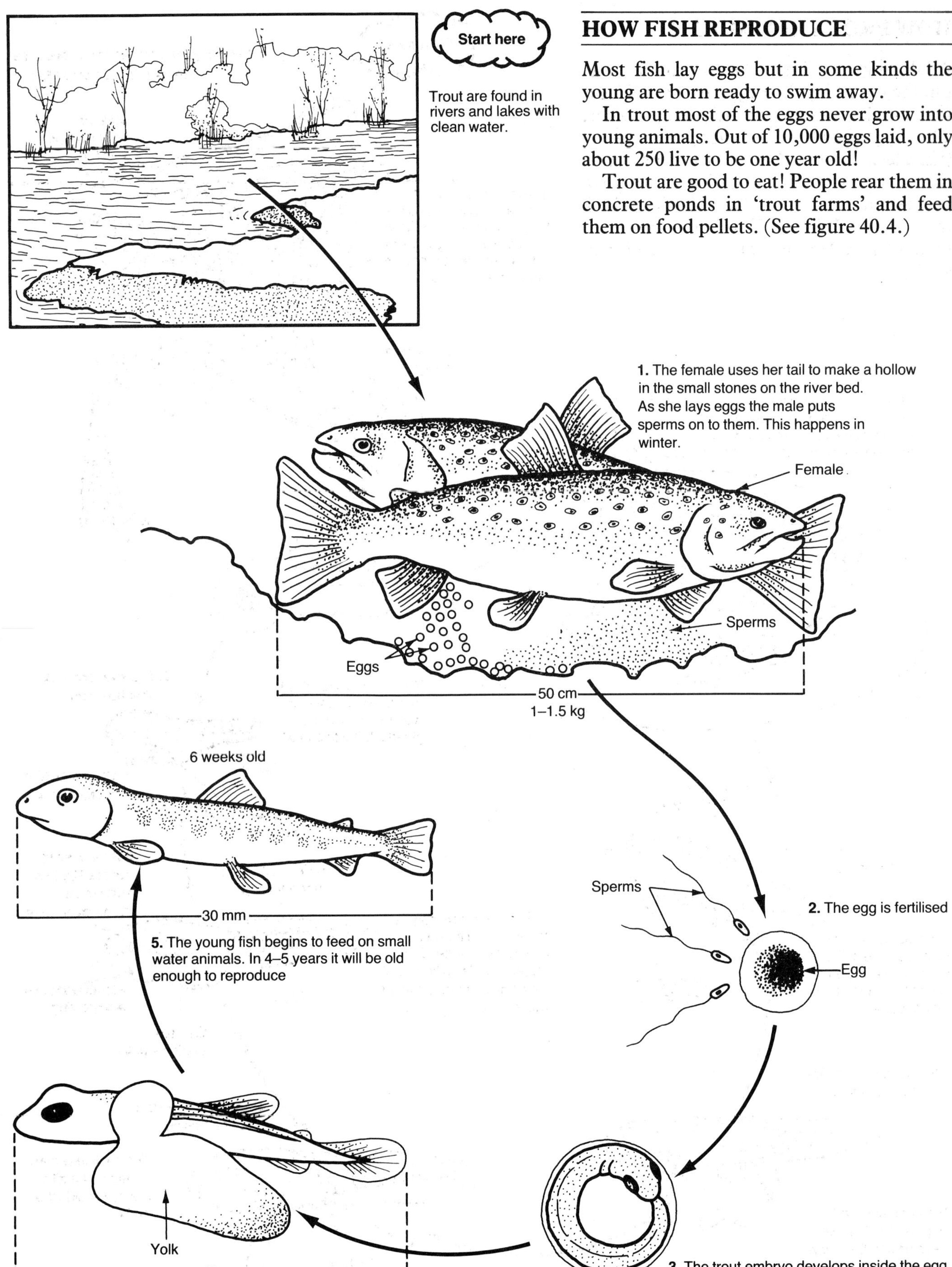

Figure 40.4

HOW FROGS REPRODUCE

Adult frogs can live on land or in the water but they must lay their eggs in water. This is because their young can only live in water. The eggs hatch into tadpoles or *larvae* (singular: *larva*). The larvae look quite different from the adults. The larvae grow and develop and they slowly begin to look more like adult frogs. This change from larva to adult is called *metamorphosis*. (See figure 40.5.)

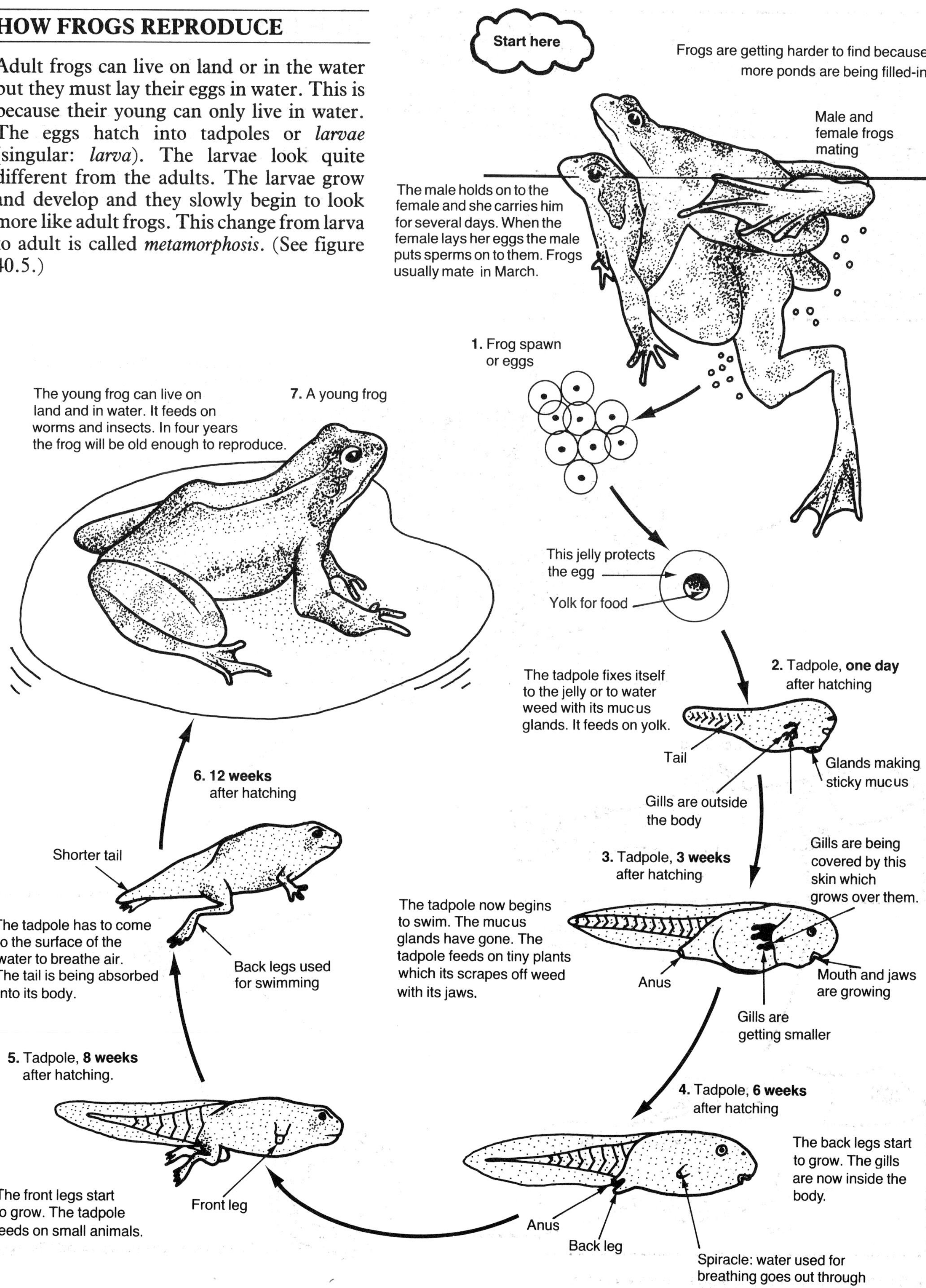

Figure 40.5

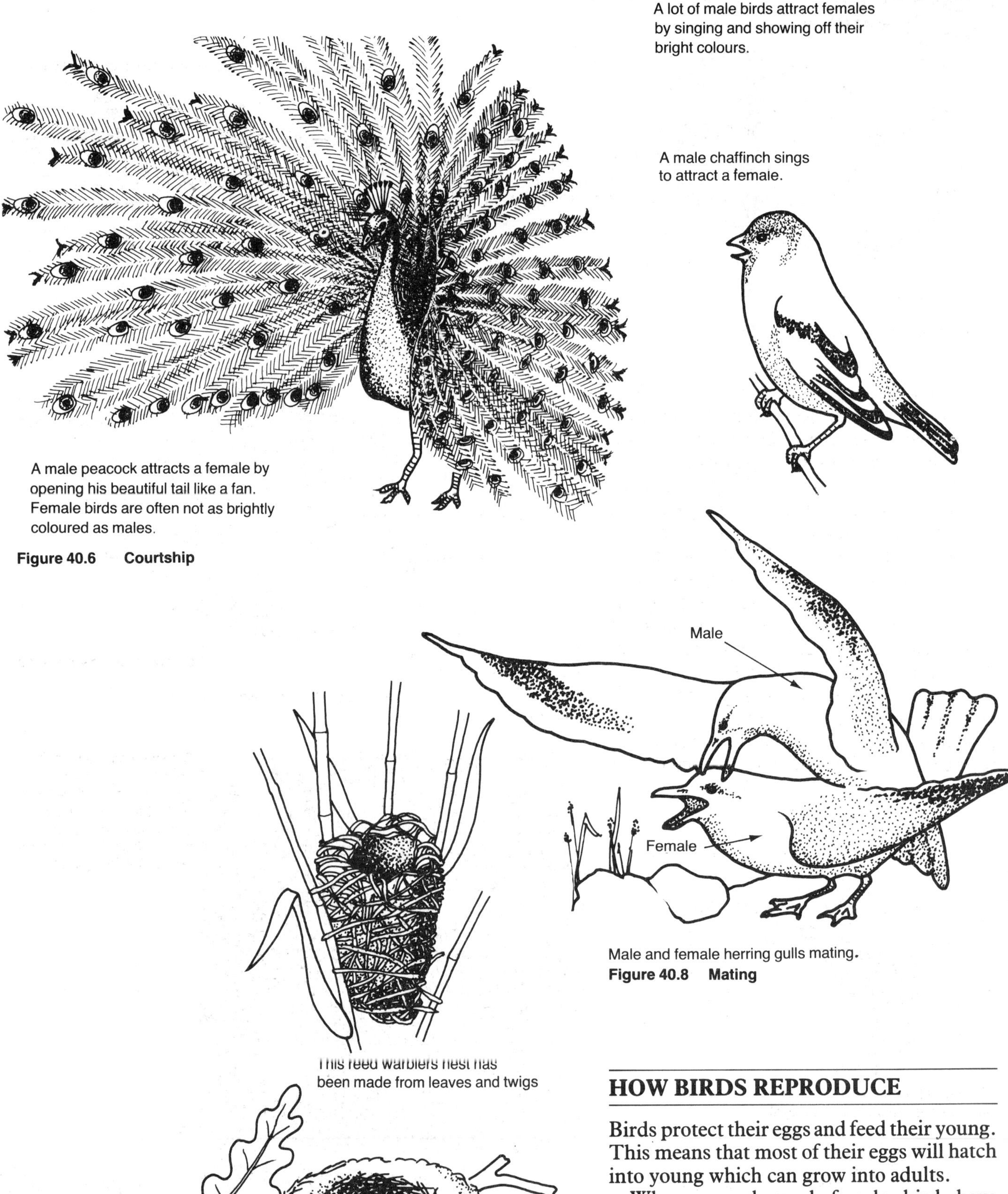

A lot of male birds attract females by singing and showing off their bright colours.

A male chaffinch sings to attract a female.

A male peacock attracts a female by opening his beautiful tail like a fan. Female birds are often not as brightly coloured as males.

Figure 40.6 Courtship

Male and female herring gulls mating.

Figure 40.8 Mating

This reed warblers nest has been made from leaves and twigs

The cup nest is a common shape. The chaffinch sticks bits of moss round the outside to hide the nest.

Figure 40.7 Nest building

HOW BIRDS REPRODUCE

Birds protect their eggs and feed their young. This means that most of their eggs will hatch into young which can grow into adults.

When a male and female bird have attracted each other, they build a nest. Birds makes their nests, using mud, grass, leaves or stones. The nests are often lined with soft feathers. (See figures 40.6 and 40.7.)

To fertilise the eggs, the male bird presses his reproductive opening to the reproductive opening of the female. Sperms are passed from the male to the female. Fertilisation is *internal*. (See figure 40.8.)

Figure 40.9 Egg-laying and incubation

The fertilised eggs are laid in the nest. The parents sit on the eggs to keep them warm. This is called incubation. If the eggs get cold, they will not develop. (See figure 40.9.)

The young chick or embryo develops inside the egg and uses the yolk for food. The *albumen* stops the egg from drying-up. Oxygen goes through the shell into the air space and it is carried to the embryo by blood vessels. Carbon dioxide goes out of the embryo in the other direction. The embryo floats in a bag of fluid. This protects it from damage. (See figures 40.9 and 40.10.)

The parents feed the young chicks until they are old enough to feed themselves. The parents also keep the chicks warm until their feathers grow. (See figures 40.11 and 40.12.)

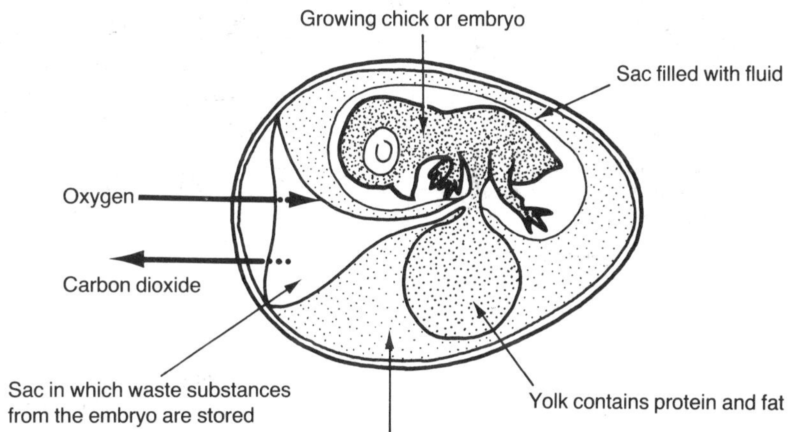

Figure 40.10 Development

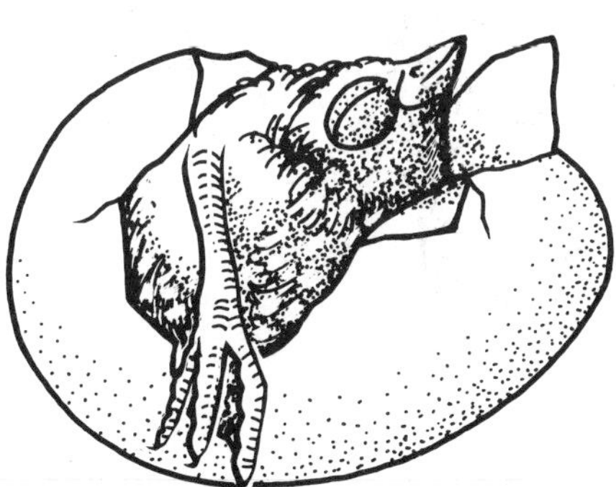

The chick breaks out of the egg. It leaves waste substances behind it in the egg shell.

Chicks are helpless when they are born. Their eyes are closed and they have few feathers to keep them warm.

Figure 40.11 Hatching

Blackbird chicks in their nest; their eyes have not opened yet and they have no feathers. The chicks are begging for food; those which do not beg are not fed by their parents.

Figure 40.12 Parental care

HOW INSECTS REPRODUCE

In some insects the eggs hatch into young called *larvae* (singular: *larva*). Larvae look very different from the adult insects which made them. The larvae eat a lot of food and grow quickly. When it is fully grown, a larva stops eating and changes into a *pupa*. The adult insect grows inside the pupa which splits open to let the adult crawl out. This sort of development is called *complete metamorphosis*. Butterflies, moths and flies develop in this way. Figure 40.13 shows what happens in a butterfly.

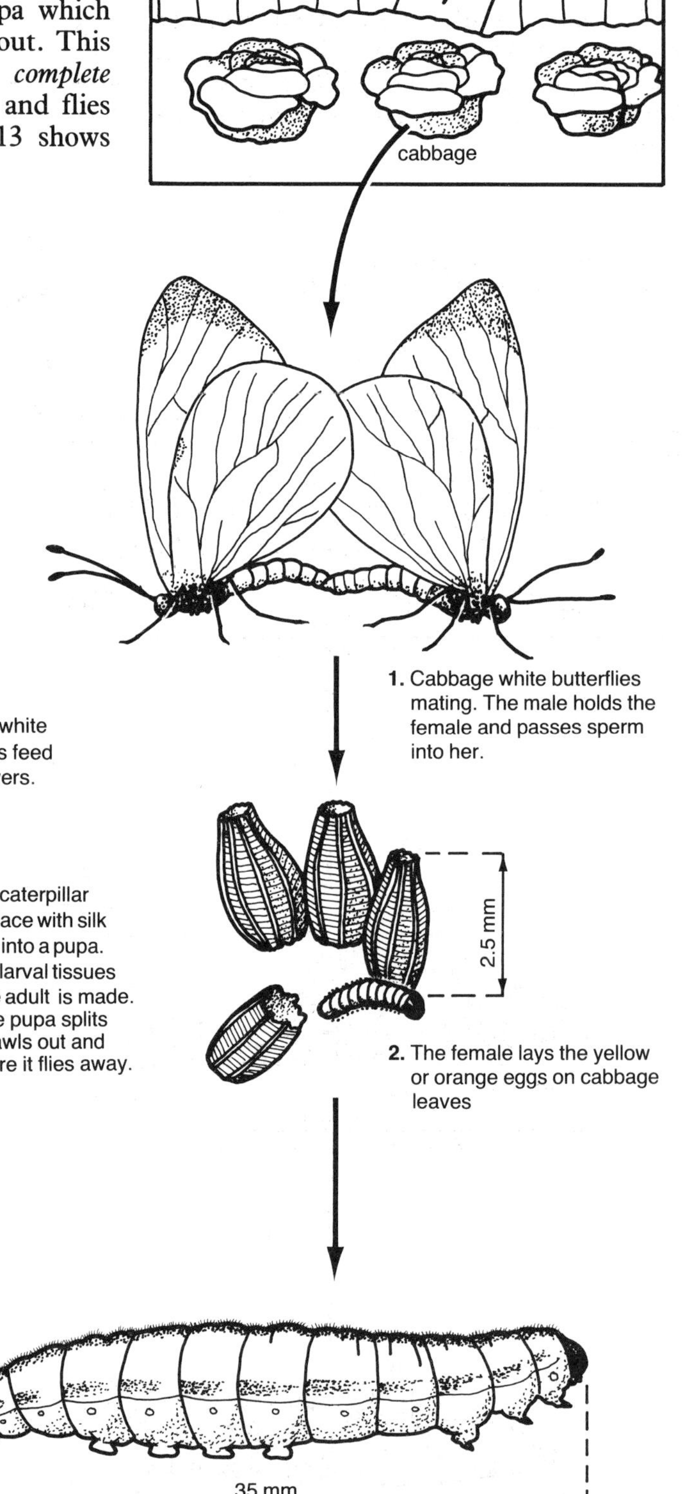

1. Cabbage white butterflies mating. The male holds the female and passes sperm into her.

2. The female lays the yellow or orange eggs on cabbage leaves

3. The larva is called a *caterpillar*. This eats the cabbage leaves and grows bigger. As it grows it splits its skin, or *moults*, a few times. It does this because its skin cannot stretch any more to keep up with its size. The caterpillars can eat all the leaves off a cabbage plant in a few days!

4. When it is full size a caterpillar fixes itself in a dry place with silk threads. It changes into a pupa. Inside the pupa the larval tissues break down and the adult is made. After 2–3 weeks the pupa splits open. The adult crawls out and dries its wings before it flies away.

5. A female cabbage white butterfly. The adults feed on nectar from flowers.

Figure 40.13

In some insects the eggs hatch into young called *nymphs*. These nymphs look like the adult insects that made them. The nymphs are smaller than the adults and they cannot reproduce. This sort of development is called *incomplete metamorphosis*. Cockroaches, grasshoppers and locusts develop in this way. Figure 40.14 shows what happens in locusts.

The number of locusts in an area can become very great. When this happens the locusts fly away in a swarm. When the swarm lands, the locusts eat all the plants in the area.

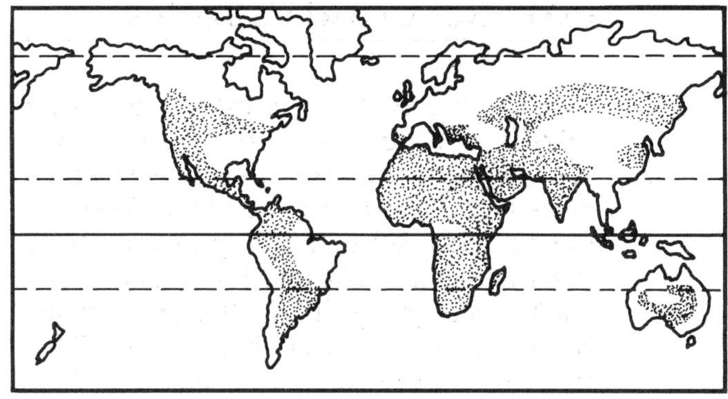

Where you might find locusts.

Locusts are found in many parts of the world. They cause a lot of damage to food crops.

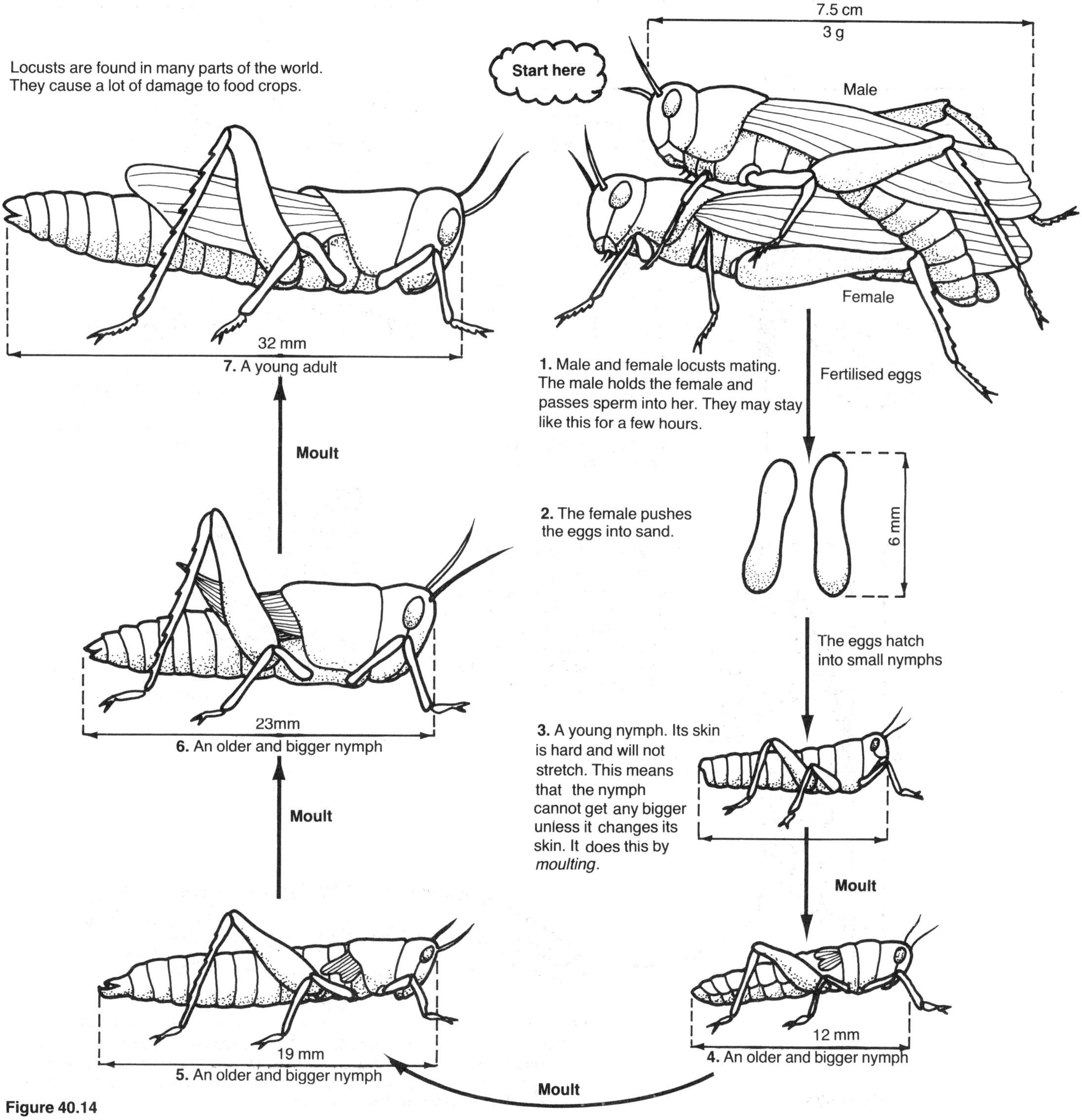

Start here

7.5 cm
3 g
Male
Female

1. Male and female locusts mating. The male holds the female and passes sperm into her. They may stay like this for a few hours.

Fertilised eggs

2. The female pushes the eggs into sand.

6 mm

The eggs hatch into small nymphs

3. A young nymph. Its skin is hard and will not stretch. This means that the nymph cannot get any bigger unless it changes its skin. It does this by *moulting*.

Moult

12 mm
4. An older and bigger nymph

Moult

19 mm
5. An older and bigger nymph

Moult

23mm
6. An older and bigger nymph

Moult

32 mm
7. A young adult

Figure 40.14

Summary

Most male and female animals reproduce by *sexual reproduction*. They do this using *sex cells* or *gametes*. During *fertilisation* a male gamete or *sperm* joins with a female gamete or *egg*. In some animals fertilisation happens *inside* the female's body but in other animals it happens *outside* her body. Some simple animals are *hermaphrodite* which means an animal makes both eggs and sperms.

In some animals the fertilised egg develops *outside* the female's body. In mammals a fertilised egg grows *inside* the female.

Most fish lay eggs but some give birth to young which are ready to swim away. Young trout feed on *yolk* inside the egg while they are growing.

Young frogs look different from the adults and can only live in water. These *tadpoles* or *larvae* grow into adults and this change is called *metamorphosis*.

Some insects lay eggs which hatch into larvae called *caterpillars*. These change into *pupae*. The adults hatch from the pupae and this kind of development is called *complete metamorphosis*. Some insects lay eggs which hatch into *nymphs* which look like their parents. This is called *incomplete metamorphosis*.

Birds *incubate* their eggs and feed and protect their young. This is called *parental care*.

Important words

Hermaphrodite	an animal that has both male and female organs of sexual reproduction.
Incubate	to keep eggs in the best conditions until they hatch.
Larva	a part of the life cycle of some simple animals and some vertebrates.
Pupa	a part of the life cycle of some insects.
Metamorphosis	the change of body form that happens in some animals as they develop from fertilised egg to adult.
Complete metamorphosis	a kind of life cycle where the egg hatches into a larva; this changes into a pupa which develops into the adult.
Incomplete metamorphosis	a kind of life cycle where the egg hatches into a nymph which develops into the adult.
Nymph	a young form of adult in some insect life cycles.
Moult	to split the skin and grow a new one to keep up with increase in body size.
Albumen	a thin, watery liquid containing protein, found in the eggs of some animals
Yolk	a substance found in the eggs of some animals and used as food by the embryo.

Fancy that!

The biggest swarm of locusts happened in 1889. It covered an area of 5180 km^2 and contained about 250 000 000 locusts! These would weigh about 50 800 tonnes!

A female codfish lays about 7 million eggs!

The biggest egg laid by a bird is that of the ostrich. The egg is 15–20 cm long and weighs up to 1780 g!

Questions

A.

1. What are the main differences between a larva and a pupa?
2. Why do insects moult as they grow?
3. Give *three* differences between the eggs of frogs and birds.
4. Which of these animals make a nest for their young: trout, horses, butterflies, frogs, gulls?

B.

Copy the table comparing the reproduction of *four* British wild vertebrates into your book and then complete it.

	Named example	How the sexes are attracted to each other	How mating takes place	Where fertilisation takes place
Fish				
Amphibian				
Bird				
Mammal				

(*SEREB*)

C.

Copy the table into your book and then complete it by writing the name of the class of vertebrates in the correct place. Give an example of each group found living wild in Britain.

Characteristics	Class of vertebrate	Example
Eggs are fertilised internally and laid with hard shells		
Lives in water for part of its life cycle		
Breathes by means of gills		
Young develop inside mother's body		
Has dry skin covered in horny scales		

(*SEREB*)

Explain what is meant by the following terms, using examples of animals you have studied: (a) breeding season; and (b) parental care.

TOPIC 41

CHROMOSOMES AND CELL DIVISION

A lot of living things start life as a *fertilised* egg cell or *zygote*. This cell divides to make two new cells. Each of these then divides to make two more cells. Cells divide like this until hundreds of thousands of cells have been formed. (See figure 41.1.) These cells make up the organs and tissues of the new organism. Cell division or *mitosis* happens in *every* cell at first.

Once organisms are fully grown only a few cells (apart from the sex cells) can still divide. In plants these cells are in places called meristems. These are at the ends of roots and shoots and in the cambium cells. Animals make new cells at several different places in their bodies, such as in bone marrow.

THE CHROMOSOMES

The nucleus in every cell contains *chromosomes*. (See figure 41.2.) These look like tiny pieces of cotton. Organisms which belong to different species have different numbers of chromosomes in their cells. Human cells always have 46 chromosomes, mouse cells always have 40 and broad bean cells always have 12.

Chromosomes are important because they are made up of *genes*. Genes control the way cells develop and grow.

Pairs of chromosomes are found in all cells except sex cells. The two chromosomes of each pair are the same size and shape. One chromosome of each pair comes from the mother and the other comes from the father. In human cells, 23 of the 46 chromosomes come from the mother and the other 23 come from the father. When cells divide during growth, every new cell must get a 'copy' of each pair of chromosomes.

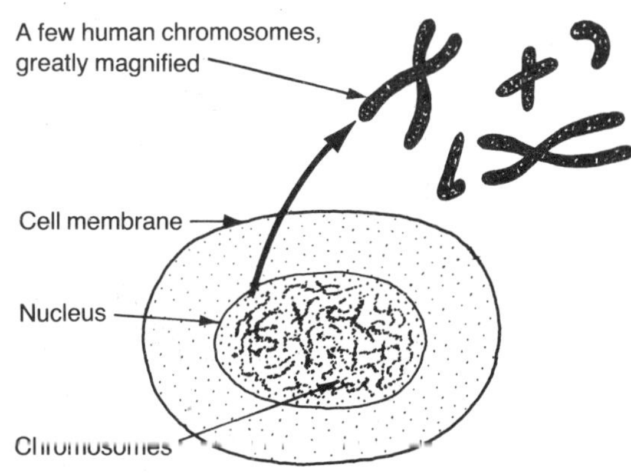

Figure 41.2.

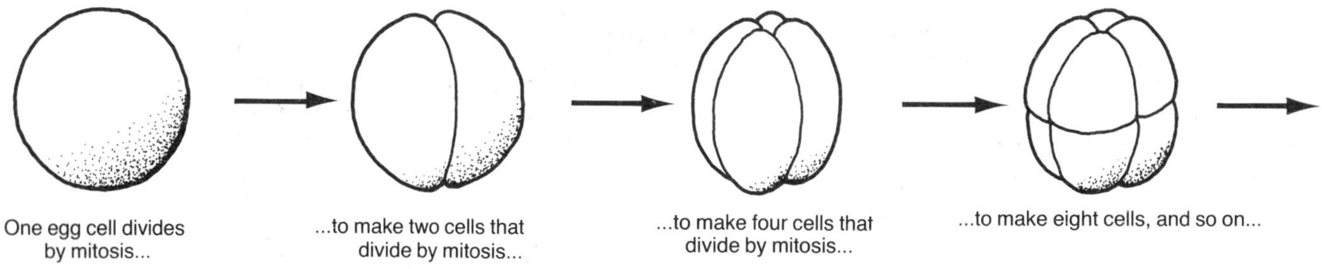

One egg cell divides by mitosis... → ...to make two cells that divide by mitosis... → ...to make four cells that divide by mitosis... → ...to make eight cells, and so on... →

Figure 41.1 How a fertilised egg divides

WHAT HAPPENS IN CELL DIVISION OR MITOSIS

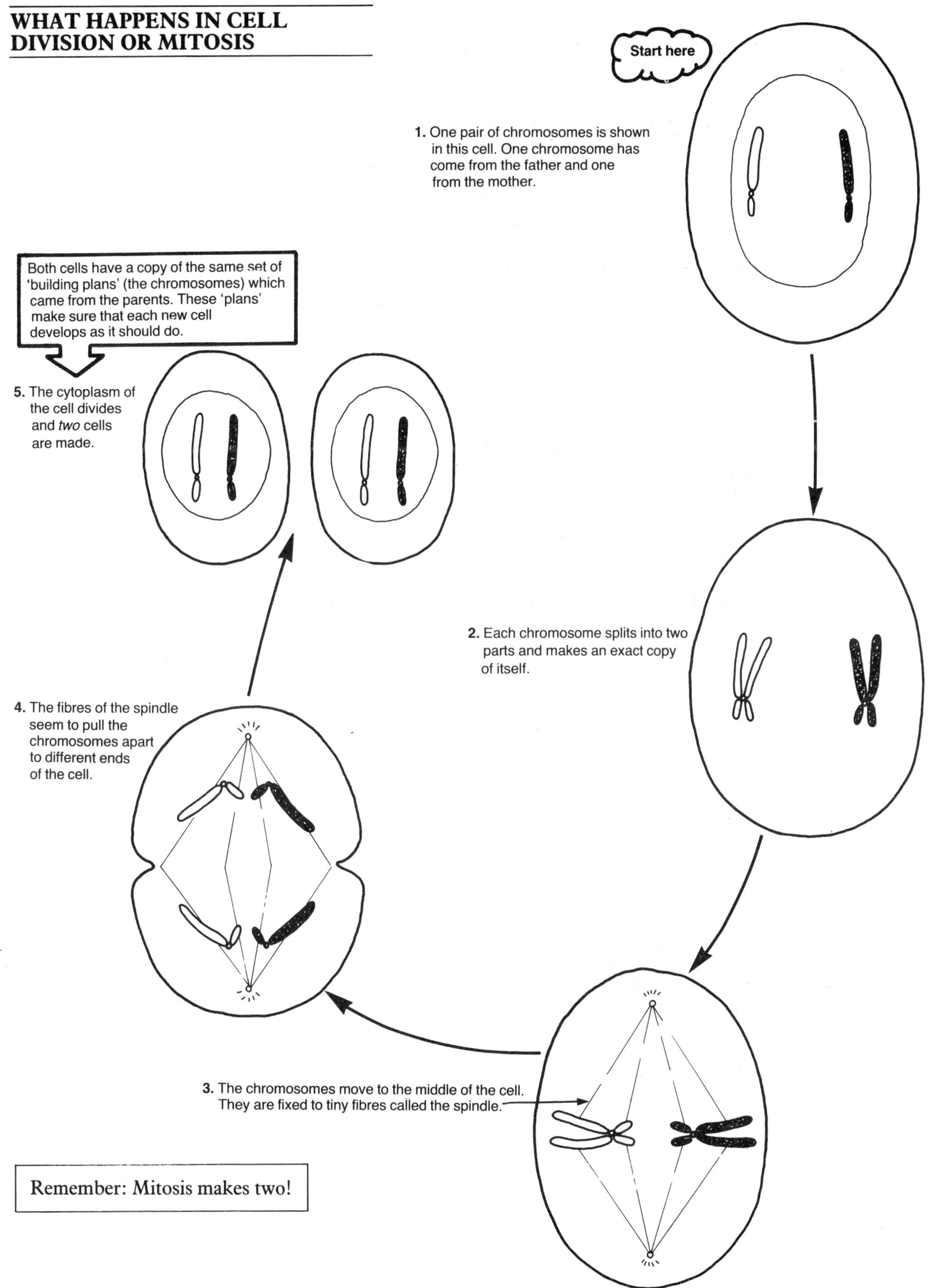

Remember: Mitosis makes two!

Figure 41.3. The dance of the chromosomes

HOW EGGS AND SPERMS ARE MADE

During sexual reproduction a male sex cell joins with a female sex cell. If each sex cell had 46 chromosomes, the fertilised egg would not develop properly. This is because the fertilised egg would have twice as many chromosomes as other cells. This does not happen because of how the sex cells are made. (See figure 41.4.)

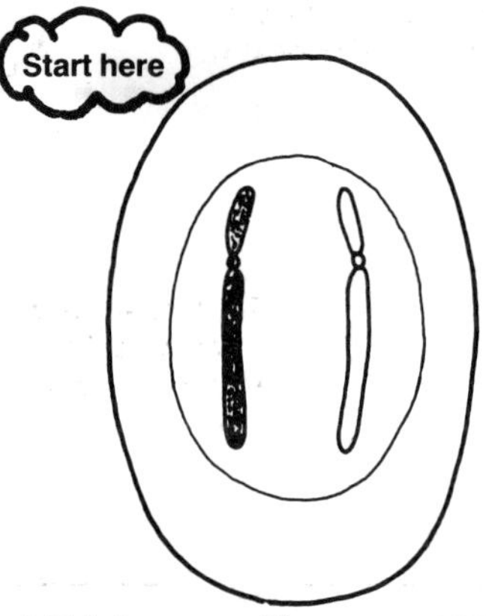

1. This is a sex cell from a sex organ such as an ovary or testis. The diagram shows what happens to only one of the pairs of chromosomes in this sex cell.
One chromosome has come from the mother and one from the father.

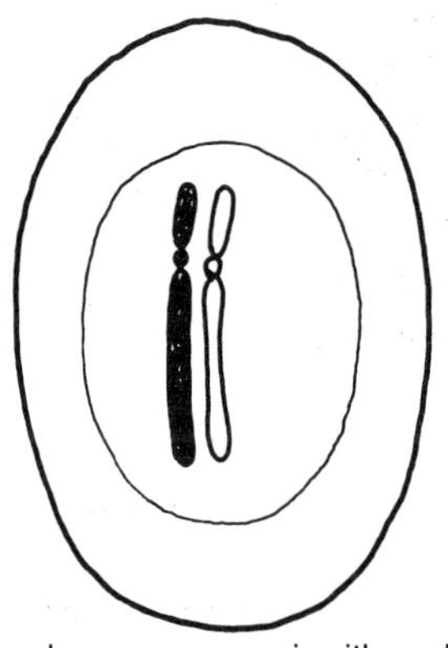

2. The chromosomes pair with each other. This happens with **all** chromosomes in the nucleus.

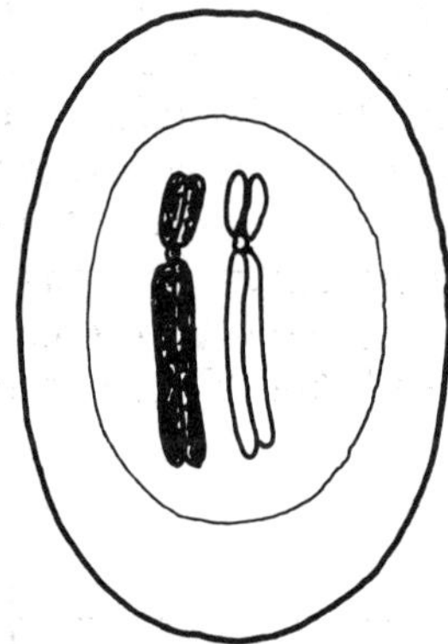

3. Each chromosome splits into two parts and makes an exact copy of itself.

4. The chromosomes swap pieces with each other. This is called 'crossing over'.

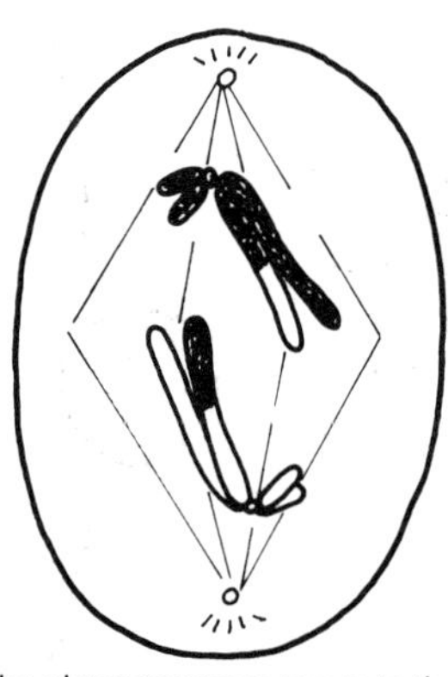

5. The chromosomes move to the ends of the cell on the spindle

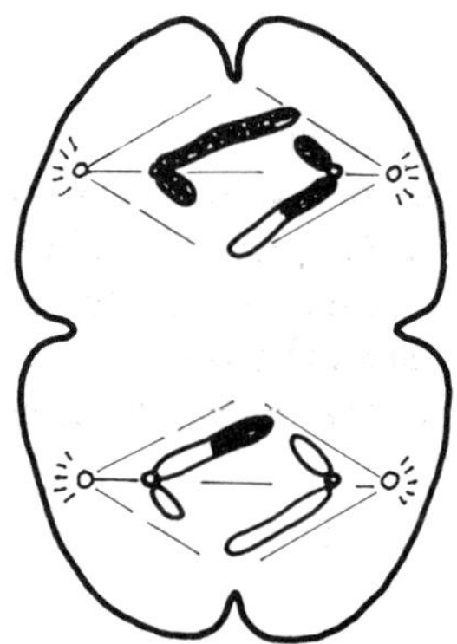

6. The two parts of each chromosome now move away from each other on new spindles. The cytoplasm starts to divide.

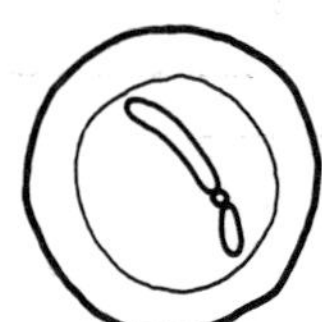

7. *Four* new cells are made. These develop into sex cells or *gametes*. In males the gametes are sperms and in females they are eggs.

Figure 41.4 How eggs and sperms are made

> Remember: Meiosis makes four!

1. This kind of cell division is called *meiosis*. It only happens in the *sex organs* of living things.
2. In meiosis, *four* sex cells are made (stage **7**) by the division of *one* (from stage **1**).
3. Each sex cell only has *half* the number of chromosomes (stage **7**) of the first cell (stage **1**).
4. Some of the chromosomes in the sex cells (stage **7**) are different from the chromosomes in the first cell (stage **1**). This is because of the 'crossing over' in stage **4**.

FERTILISATION

Because of meiosis, sex cells only have half their full number of chromosomes. When fertilisation happens two sex cells join together so the zygote has the full number of chromosomes. (See figure 41.5.)

In humans one of the pairs of chromosomes are *sex chromosomes*. These make the baby either a male or a female. All female cells have two sex chromosomes that look the same. These are called X chromosomes. All male cells have two sex chromosomes that look different. These are called X and Y chromosomes.

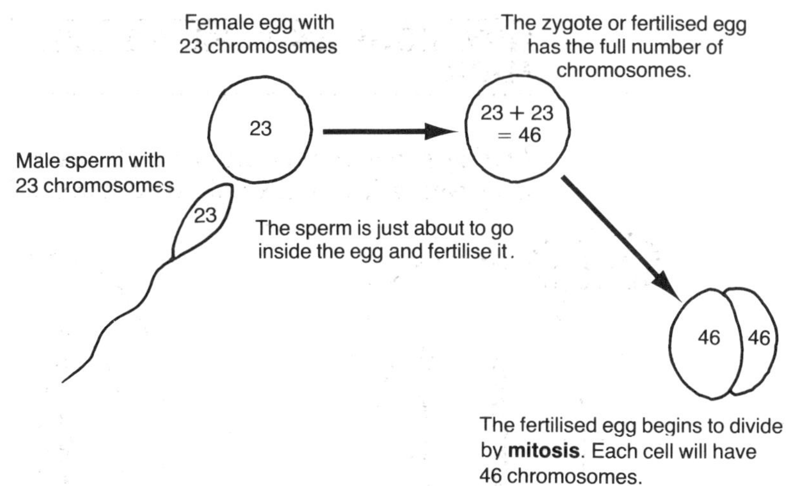

Figure 41.5.

The parents
Only the sex chromosomes are shown in these sex cells.

The gametes
Each of the sex cells make four new cells (stage 7, figure 41.4) but only two are shown. The other two have the same sex chromosomes as the ones shown here. **One** kind of egg is made but **two** kinds of sperm.

The children
The sex of the baby depends on which kind of sperm fertilises the egg. The table shows a way of working this out.

If a Y sperm fertilises the egg, the baby will be a boy. If an X sperm fertilises the egg, a girl will be born. There is an equal chance of either an X or a Y sperm fertilising the egg. This means there should be equal numbers of boys and girls born.

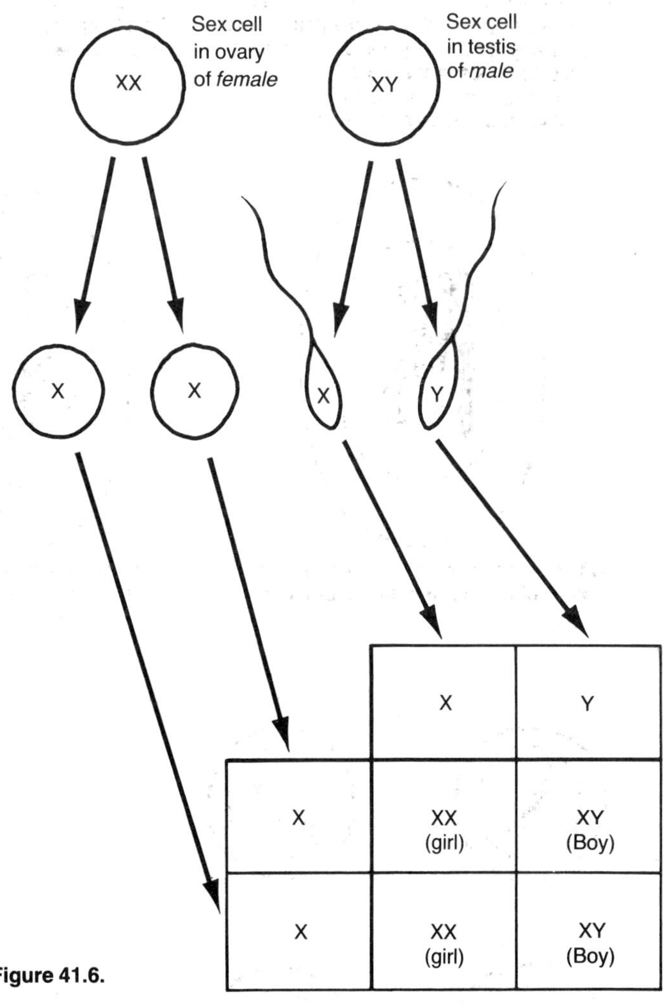

	X	Y
X	XX (girl)	XY (Boy)
X	XX (girl)	XY (Boy)

Figure 41.6.

Twins

If a woman produces two eggs at the same time and both are fertilised, twins are born. These twins may or may not be of the same sex and they will not look very much like each other.

Identical twins come from the same fertilised egg, which breaks into two separate parts by accident. These twins are always of the same sex and look very like each other. (See also p. 245.)

Summary

Most living things grow from a fertilised egg or *zygote*. This grows by cell division or *mitosis*. In young organisms, every cell divides but only a few types of cells can divide in older organisms.

Every nucleus contains *chromosomes*. Each species has its own number of chromosomes. Chromosomes are in pairs: one comes from the father and one from the mother. Both chromosomes of a pair have the same size and shape.

Gametes are sex cells and are made by a different kind of cell division called *meiosis*. This only happens in the sex organs. Meiosis *halves* the number of chromosomes. Each gamete has half as many chromosomes as the other cells of the organism. The full number of chromosomes is made up at *fertilisation*.

The sex of a young organism is determined by the *sex chromosomes*. Males have XY chromosomes and females have XX.

Important words

Gamete	a male or female sex cell.
Fertilisation	the joining together of a male and female sex cell.
Zygote	a fertilised female gamete.
Chromosome	a thread-like structure in the nucleus of a cell. It is made of a lot of genes.
Sex chromosomes	chromosomes that decide the sex of an animal.
Gene	(See Topic 42) a piece of chromosome that helps to control the characteristics of an organism.
Mitosis	the process by which a cell divides into two cells, each with the full number of chromosomes.
Meiosis	the process by which a cell divides to form sex cells, each with half the number of chromosomes.

Things to do

Figure 41.7 is a drawing of a set of chromosomes from a cell of an imaginary animal. Trace the drawings and cut the chromosomes out. Stick them in your book in pairs and number the pairs. Scientists do this when they study chromosomes. Give your animal a name!

Fancy that!

The greatest number of children produced by one mother is 69! These included sixteen sets of twins, seven sets of triplets and four sets of quadruplets!

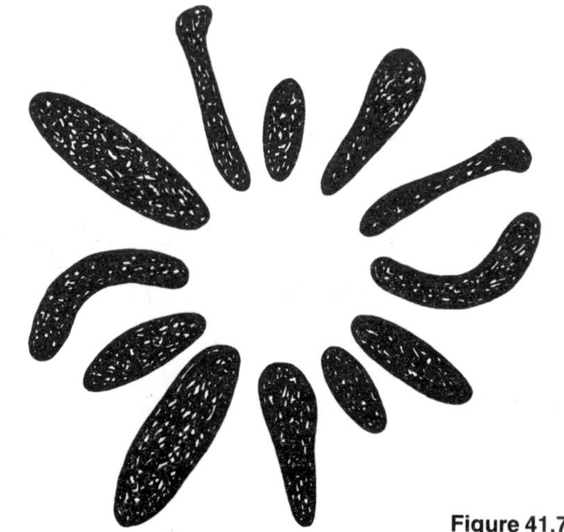

Figure 41.7

Questions

A.

Copy this into your book choosing the correct word from inside the brackets. Two kinds of cell division happen in living things. (Mitosis/Meiosis) is cell division which makes new cells needed for growth but (mitosis/meiosis) only happens in the (meristems/sex organs). In both sorts of cell division the (chromosomes/nuclei) make copies of themselves. In (mitosis/meiosis) the chromosomes are mixed up during (crossing-over/cell division) so that each of the (two/four) new cells has (half/double) the number of (chromosomes/nuclei) of other cells in the organism. All the new cells made in (mitosis/meiosis) have the same sort of (gametes/chromosomes) as the other cells.

B.

Join these sentences together using either the word 'and' or the word 'because', whichever is correct:

1. Sex cells do not have the full number of chromosomes. Meiosis is a different kind of cell division to mitosis.
2. The sex of a baby is decided by the male sperms. These can have either an X or a Y chromosome in them.
3. Cells made by mitosis have the full number of chromosomes. Cells made by meiosis have half the full number.
4. At fertilisation the full number of chromosomes appear. The chromosomes of the sperm are added to the chromosomes of the egg.
5. There are equal numbers of girls and boys born. There is an equal chance of either an X or Y sperm fertilising an egg.

C.

1. Apart from the sex cells every cell in a mouse has 40 chromosomes. How many are there (a) in the sperm, (b) in the egg before fertilisation, (c) in a fertilised egg?
2. What would happen if the male sex chromosomes were YY?
3. What would happen if the sex cells had the full number of chromosomes?
4. In meiosis it is sometimes said that two divisions happen. Say why you think this is correct or incorrect.
5. Explain why (a) identical twins are always of the same sex, (b) other twins can be of different sexes.

D.

1. What is a chromosome?
2. Copy the diagram below into your book. Write the symbols for the X and Y chromosomes in the circles.
3. What is the sex of the children arising from the zygotes (a), (b), (c) and (d)?

(EAEB, LREB, ULESEC)

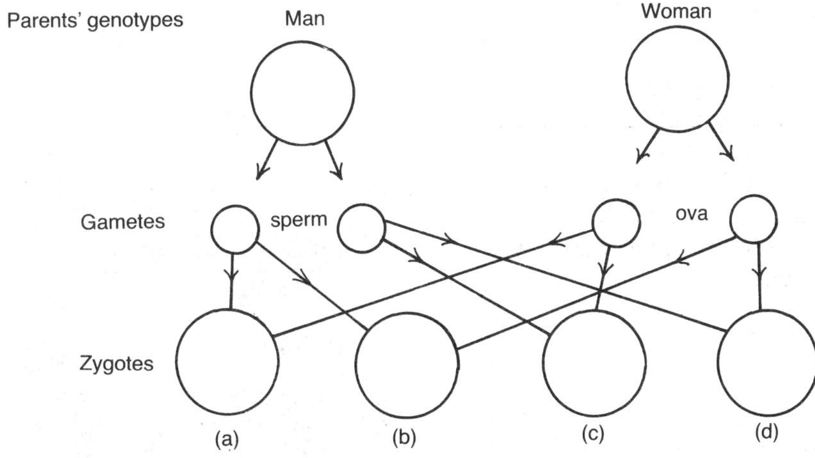

Figure 41.8

TOPIC 42

HEREDITY

All living organisms have some *characteristics* that make them like their parents. They have other characteristics that make them different from their parents. Characteristics are those things that help us to describe organisms. Some of these characteristics, such as height and shape, can be seen. (See figure 42.1.) Most characteristics cannot be seen because they are to do with how our bodies work.

All these characteristics are inherited, that is, they come from our parents. They are passed on to us in chromosomes. This happens when an egg joins with a sperm to make the first cell of a new human being.

In the study of heredity we find out how these characteristics are passed on.

WHAT IS INHERITED?

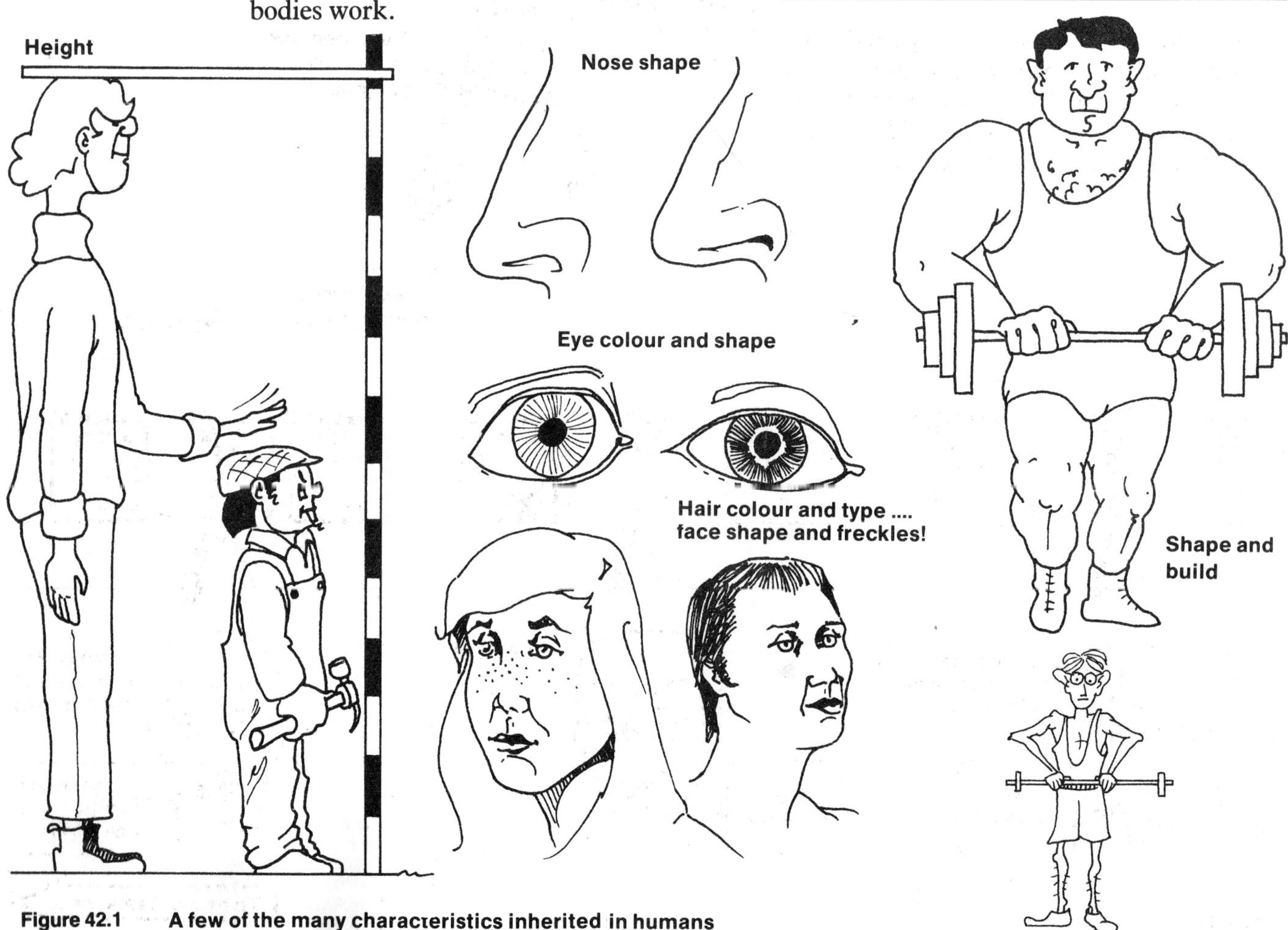

Figure 42.1 **A few of the many characteristics inherited in humans**

CHROMOSOMES AND GENES

All living organisms show differences like the examples of *variation* shown in figure 42.1. The *genes* carried on chromosomes cause this variation. Genes are too small to be seen even with a very powerful microscope. Genes are groups of chemicals and are a bit like gangs of workmen in a factory. Each gang does a certain job using its 'building plans' inherited from the parents. (See figure 42.2.) Most human characteristics are controlled by more than one gene.

Nearly all the characteristics of organisms are controlled by genes. They control important things such as how well your organs work. They also control things which are not so important such as the colour of your hair and the shape of your face. Genes, like chromosomes, are in pairs, except in sex cells or gametes. All the cells of an organism have the same pairs of genes. One gene of each pair comes from the mother and the other comes from the father. The pairs of genes are in the same place on the chromosomes. (See figure 42.3.)

Each partner in a gene pair may have the same 'building plans'. But sometimes the building plans are different. (See figure 42.4.)

To understand how genes are passed from parents to young we need to learn about what *Mendel* did. Gregor Mendel was a monk who found out the laws of heredity. He did his experiments with garden pea plants.

Figure 42.2

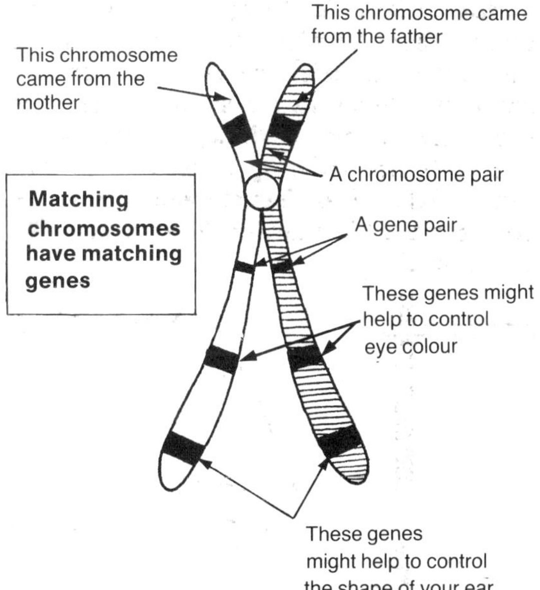

Figure 42.3

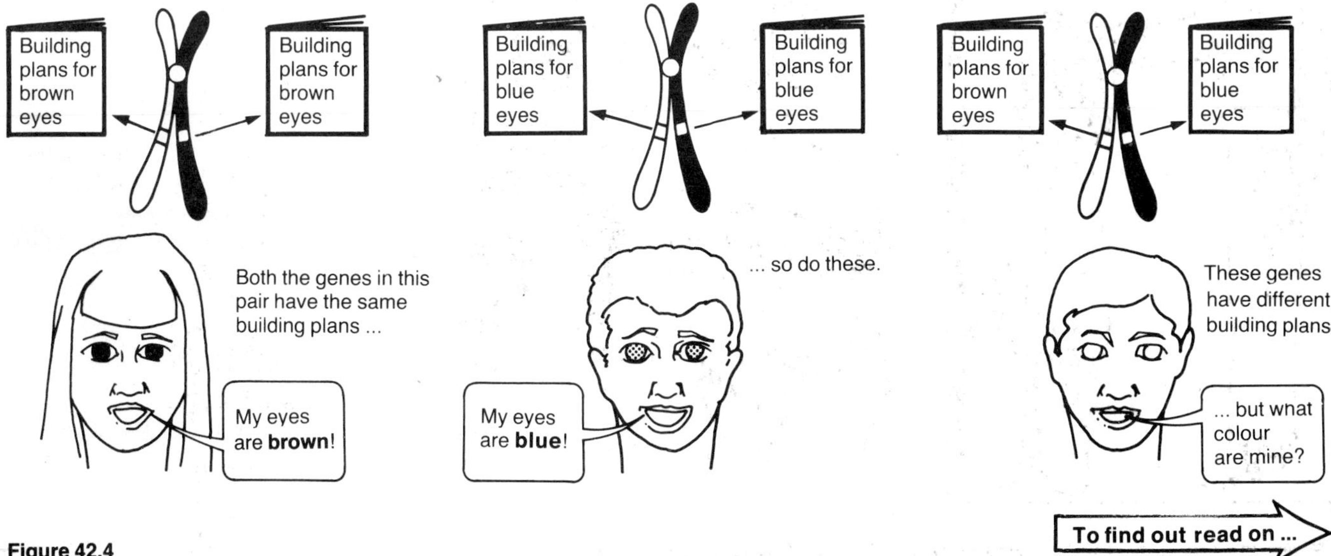

To find out read on ...

Figure 42.4

White flowers on a pure-breeding plant.

Red flowers on a pure-breeding plant.

The pollen was taken from the red flower to the white flower. Mendel found it could also be taken from the white flower to the red flower. The result was the same in each case.

The pods were collected from the white flowers. The seeds in these pods are the young of both plants. The seeds were then planted.

When the seeds grew, all the plants had red flowers. These plants from this first cross are called the F_1 generation

Figure 42.5 Mendel's first experiment

MENDEL'S EXPERIMENTS

Gregor Mendel started his experiments with pure-breeding plants or pure lines. Their seeds grow into plants which have the same characteristics as the parents. Pure lines of red flowered plants, for example, give seeds which grow into plants with red flowers. To get pure lines the plants are pollinated with their own pollen. (This is called self-pollination.)

In one experiment Mendel used pollen from red flowers to pollinate plants with white flowers. (See figure 42.5.) This is called a *cross*. The question Mendel asked was:

'What kind of flowers will I get in plants grown from this cross?'

The plants that Mendel grew from this cross all had red flowers. Red seemed to be 'stronger' than or *dominant* to white. Mendel called red the *dominant character*. White seemed to be 'weaker' than red and Mendel called white the *recessive* character

Mendel thought that *both* dominant and recessive characters were in the F_1 plants.

The next question Mendel asked was:

'If I cross these red flowers with each other will the recessive character show itself again?'

Figure 42.6 shows the results when Mendel tried this.

For this experiment Mendel used the F_1 plants from his first experiment.
He put pollen from the male parts of the flower onto the female parts of the same flower.

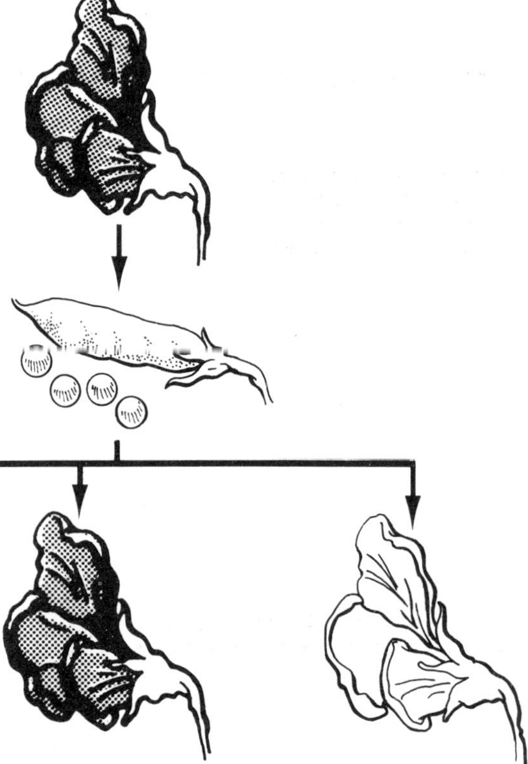

He collected and planted the seeds.

When the seeds grew, some of the plants had white flowers.
The recessive character (white) had shown itself again. The plants from this cross are called the F_2 generation and are the 'grandchildren' of the original pure breeding plants in the first experiment.

Figure 42.6 Mendel's second experiment

Mendel found that about 3/4 of the plants had red flowers and 1/4 had white flowers

WHAT MENDEL HAD FOUND

From his experiments Mendel found that:

1. Only one out of two colours (or characters) could be seen in the 'children', or F_1 generation. The other character seemed to 'hide'. The character which appeared was the dominant one. The other character was recessive.
2. The recessive character could be seen in some of the 'grandchildren' or F_2 generation. There were three times more grandchildren with the dominant character than with the recessive one.

BACK TO THE GENES!

You can explain the results of Mendel's experiments by looking at what happens to the genes. (See figures 42.7. and 42.8.)

The characteristic of red flowers is controlled by a gene. This gene is dominant and we can write it as R. The characteristic of white flowers is also controlled by a gene. This gene is recessive and we can write it as r.

Pairs of genes are found in all cells, except sex cells, (figure 42.3) so both parents must have *two* genes for flower colour, like this:

a plant with two genes RR has red flowers;
a plant with the two genes Rr has red flowers, this is because red is dominant to white;
a plant with the two genes rr has white flowers.

Because the chromosomes split in two in meiosis (Figure 41.4) the gametes or sex cells have only one gene for colour. This gene is either an R or an r.

At fertilisation the genes pair up again. The pairs are different from the gene pairs in the parents. The table shows a way of working this out. All these F_1 plants have red flowers because all of them have the dominant red gene.

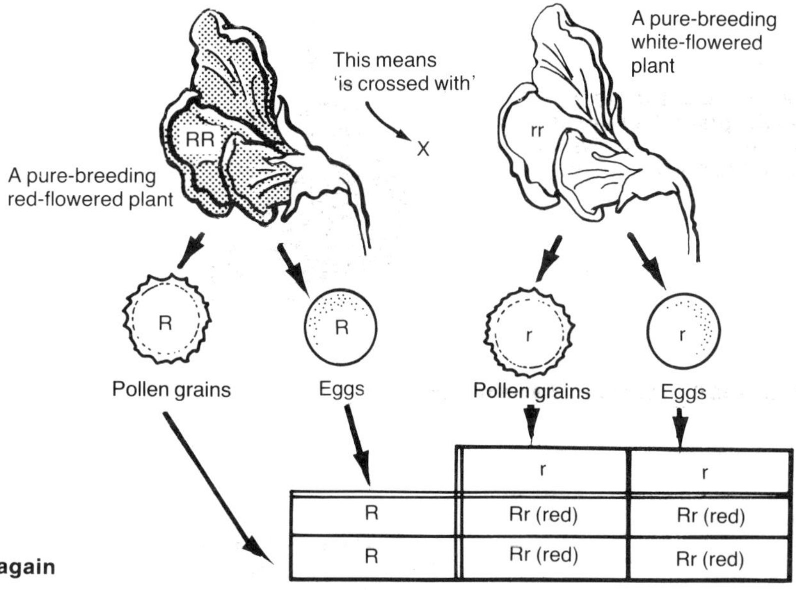

	r	r
R	Rr (red)	Rr (red)
R	Rr (red)	Rr (red)

Figure 42.7 Looking at Mendel's first experiment again

Flowers from the F_1 generation are fertilised with their own pollen. These plants all had a dominant and a recessive gene.

Three quarters of the F_2 plants have RR or Rr and are red. One quarter have rr and are white.

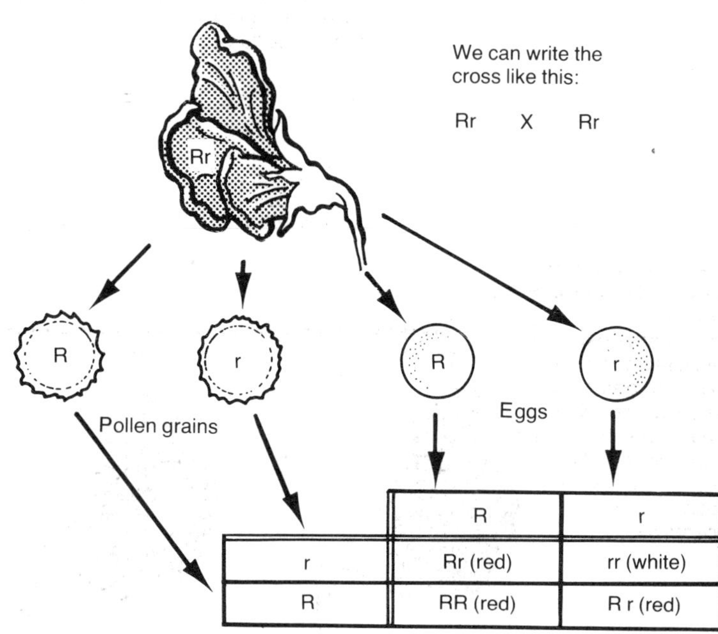

	R	r
r	Rr (red)	rr (white)
R	RR (red)	R r (red)

Figure 42.8 Looking at Mendel's second experiment

HOW EYE COLOUR IS INHERITED

Mendel's results help us to work out the eye colour of the boy on page 265. The boy has a gene for brown eyes and a gene for blue eyes in his body cells. The gene for brown eyes is dominant (B). The gene for blue eyes is recessive (b). The boy must have *brown* eyes! But what about the rest of us (see figures 42.9 and 42.10)?

Fancy that!

Different kinds of animals and plants can be bred by making crosses between parents with certain characteristics. This is how all the different kinds of dogs have been bred!

If both parents have brown eyes each cell in their bodies *might* have the pair of genes Bb. (They are carrying the gene for blue eyes but it does not show up in them.)

The sex organs will make eggs and sperms. Some eggs and sperms have genes for brown eyes. Other eggs and sperms have genes for blue eyes.

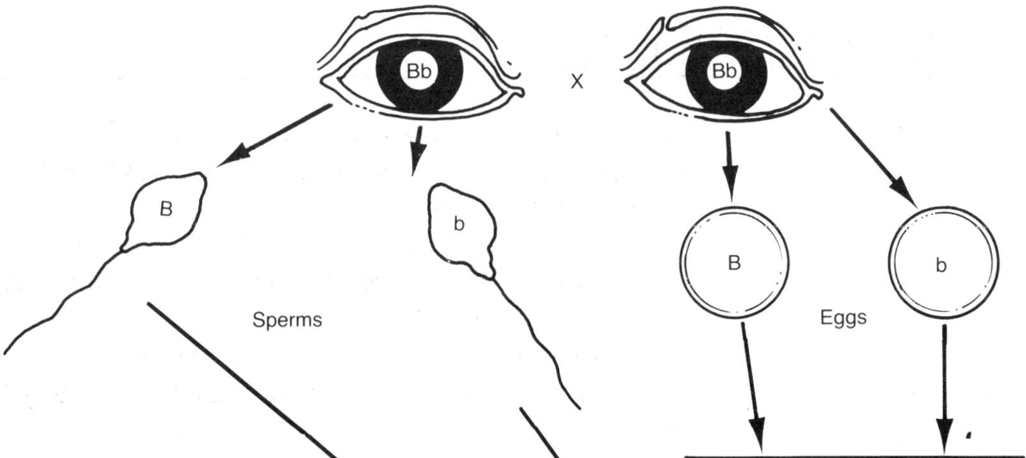

The children are three times more likely to have brown eyes than blue eyes.

Bb × Bb

Sperms: B, b — Eggs: B, b

	B	b
b	Bb (brown eyes)	bb (blue eyes)
B	BB (brown eyes)	Bb (brown eyes)

Figure 42.9

If one parent has brown eyes, each cell in his or her body *might* have the pair of genes BB. If the other parent has blue eyes each cell must have the pair of genes bb.

The sex organs will make eggs and sperms. All the sperms have the same genes as each other. All the eggs have the same genes as each other.

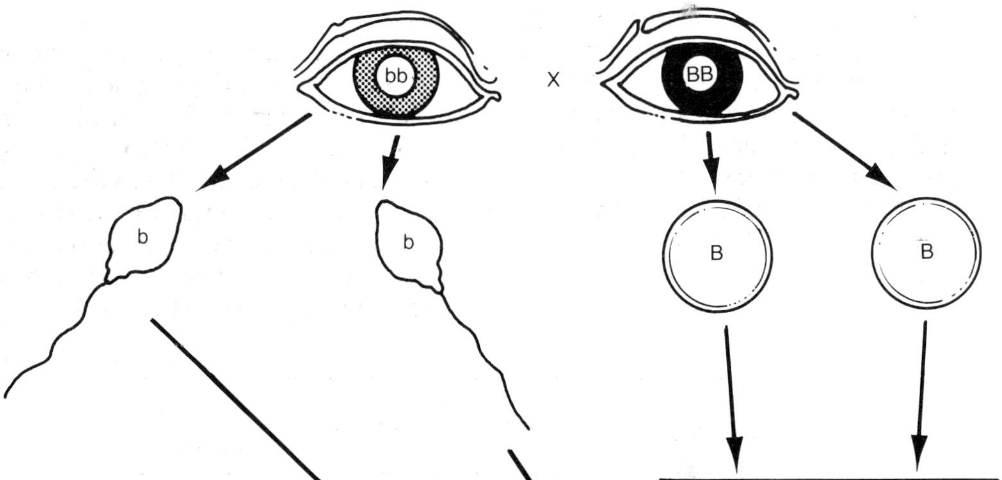

All the children will have brown eyes.

bb × BB

Sperms: b, b — Eggs: B, B

	B	B
b	Bb (brown eyes)	Bb (brown eyes)
b	Bb (brown eyes)	Bb (brown eyes)

Figure 42.10

Summary

Characteristics of organisms are those things which help us to describe the organisms. Characteristics are *inherited* from the parents in the sex cells or gametes. These are made during meiosis in the sex organs of the parents.

Gametes have *genes* which control the development of characteristics in the young. Pairs of genes are found in all cells (except in gametes) and one gene in each pair comes from each parent.

Mendel used pea plants to find out how genes are inherited. Somes genes are *dominant* and always show up in the young. Other genes are *recessive* and may not show up in the young.

Important words

Characteristic	anything which helps us to describe an organism.
Gene	a piece of chromosome which helps to control the characteristics of an organism.
Variation	differences between the characteristics of organisms.
Mendel	the person who discovered how characteristics are passed on from one organism to the next.
Dominant	a gene which always shows itself in the young.
Recessive	a gene which does not always show itself in the young.

Things to do

Mendel found that some of his plants were three times more likely to have red flowers than white ones. This 3 to 1 proportion only shows when there are a lot of young. You can find this out for yourself!

You need about 300 beads of one colour (say red) and 300 of another colour (say white). Mix 150 red beads with 150 white beads and put them in a box. The beads should be the same size. Put the rest of the beads into another box.

One box is a 'female flower' and the other is a 'male flower'. The beads are the 'eggs' and 'pollen'.

Without looking, pick one bead out of each box. Put them side by side. This is the 'fertilised egg' or 'zygote.

Write down the colours of the flowers the zygotes will produce in a table, as shown below.

Put the beads back into the boxes you took them from. Mix them up again and pick out two more. Carry on doing this. From time to time count up the number of red and white flowers. After a while you will find that there are about three times more red flowers than white ones. Best results come with really big numbers! If everyone in your class can do this, add together all the results.

Egg	Pollen	Zygote	Colour of flowers
White	White	rr	White
Red	White	Rr	Red
Red	Red	RR	Red

Questions

A.

These sentences describe one of Mendel's experiments. Put the sentences into their correct order. Work with a partner and each write out some of the sentences on strips of paper. Swap the strips of paper round to find the best order. Copy this into your book.

1. Seeds from the F_1 flowers were planted.
2. Pollen from the red flowers was used to pollinate the white flowers.
3. Mendel carried out an experiment with pure lines of pea plants with red and white flowers.
4. Seeds from the pollinated flowers were planted.
5. The F_1 flowers were self pollinated.
6. Three quarters of the F_2 plants had red flowers.
7. The F_1 plants all had red flowers.

B.

1. Use the diagrams on page 268 to find out what colour eyes the children of the following couples will have:

   (a) The mother has brown eyes and is Bb. The father has blue eyes and is bb.
   (b) The mother has blue eyes and is bb. The father has blue eyes and is bb.

   (c) What would happen if the father's and mother's genes were the other way around in (a) and (b)?
2. In sheep black wool is recessive to white wool. Someone asks you which genes a black sheep and a white sheep have. Explain why you can only be sure of your answer for one.

C.

In a breeding experiment, pure breeding black mice were mated with pure breeding brown mice. All the first generation of offspring had black fur. (Copy Figures 42.11 and 42.12 into your book.)

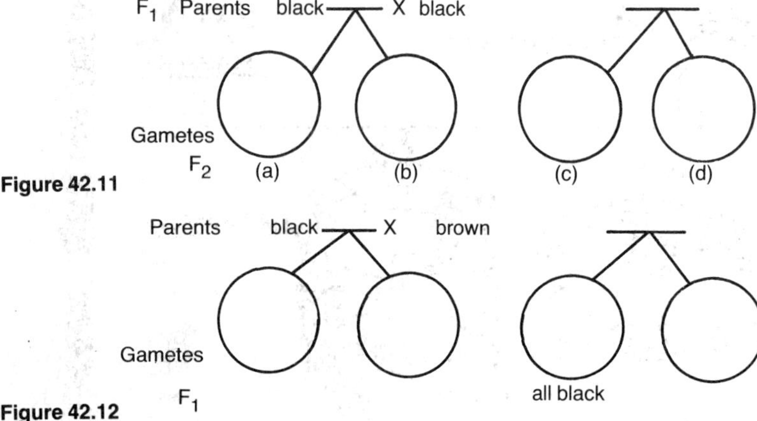

Figure 42.11

Figure 42.12

1. Using the symbols B for black gene (allele) and b for brown gene (allele), complete figure 42.11 for the cross.
2. When the black F_1 offspring were bred together they produced offspring of both colours. Use the same symbols to complete figure 42.12
3. What are the colours of the fur of the animals (a), (b), (c) and (d)?
4. What ratio of black to brown animals would you expect to obtain in the F_2 generation?
5. Give *one* reason why no brown offspring were obtained in the F_1.
6. Black F_2 offspring will not all be pure breeding black. Briefly describe a breeding experiment you would carry out to decide whether a black mouse was pure breeding.

(ALSEB)

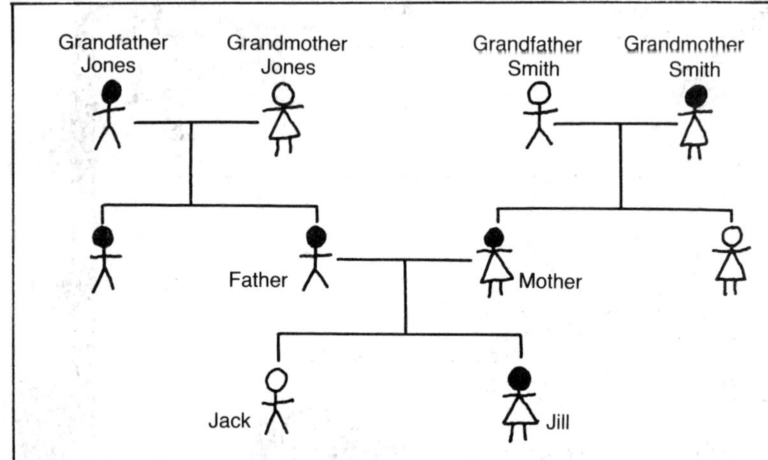

Figure 42.13

D.

Study the family tree in figure 42.13, in which dark hair is shown by • and red hair by ○. If B stands for the allele for dark hair and b stands for the allele for red hair, the genetic make-up of Grandmother Smith can be written as Bb.

1. What symbols give the genetic make up of: (a) Jack; (b) his mother, and (c) his father?
2. Explain with the aid of symbols B and b how Jack can be red-haired when both his parents are dark.
3. What evidence is there that Grandmother Smith is carrying an allele for red hair?

(NREB)

TOPIC 43

EVOLUTION

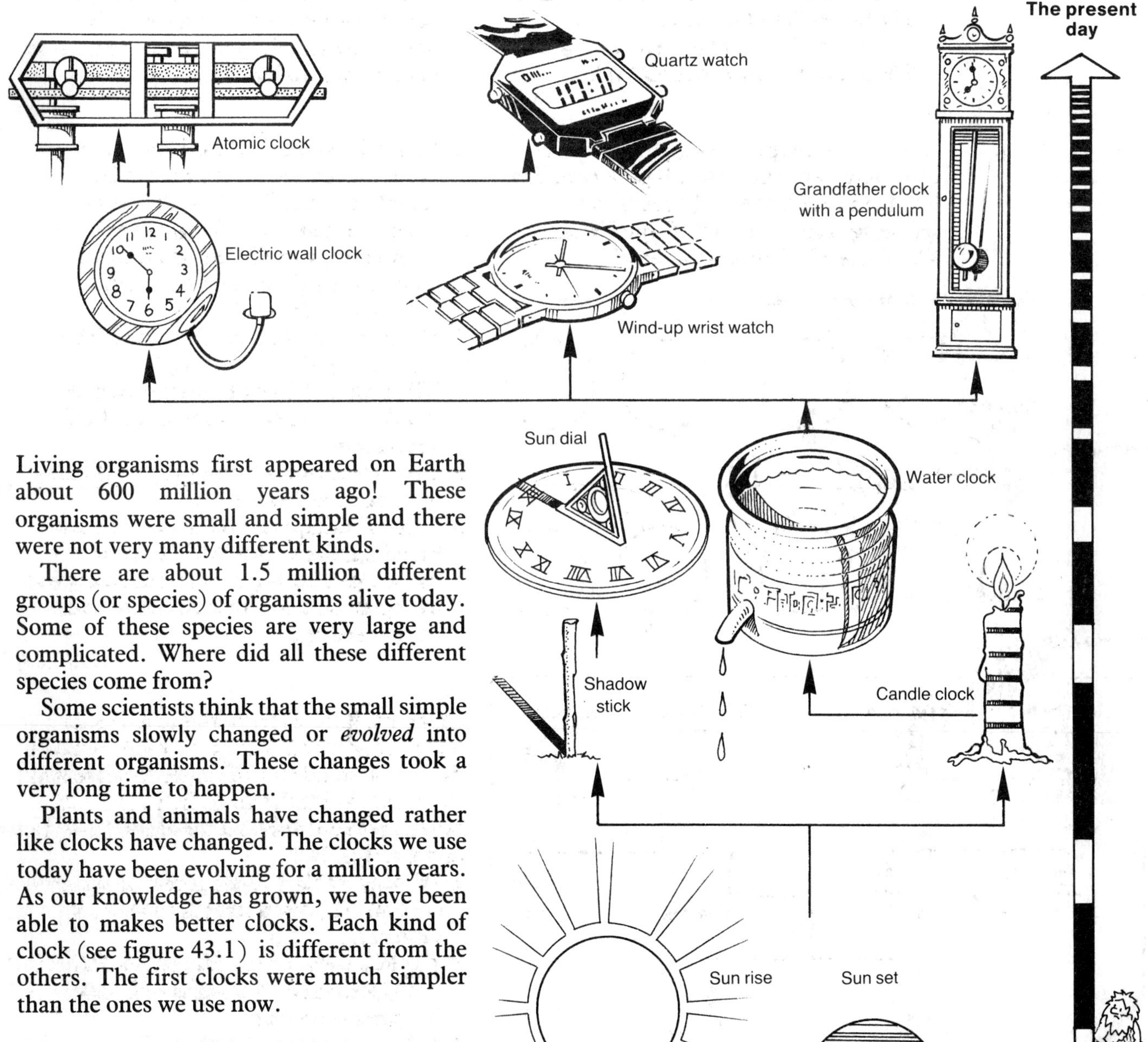

Figure 43.1 How clocks have evolved

Living organisms first appeared on Earth about 600 million years ago! These organisms were small and simple and there were not very many different kinds.

There are about 1.5 million different groups (or species) of organisms alive today. Some of these species are very large and complicated. Where did all these different species come from?

Some scientists think that the small simple organisms slowly changed or *evolved* into different organisms. These changes took a very long time to happen.

Plants and animals have changed rather like clocks have changed. The clocks we use today have been evolving for a million years. As our knowledge has grown, we have been able to makes better clocks. Each kind of clock (see figure 43.1) is different from the others. The first clocks were much simpler than the ones we use now.

FOSSILS

We can no longer see some species that lived millions of years ago because they have become extinct (or died out). They may have died out because they could not survive when conditions on Earth changed. We know that these organisms used to live on Earth because the remains of some of them are found in rocks. These remains, or *fossils*, are often dug up when the rocks are pushed to the surface. (See figure 43.2.)

Figure 43.3 shows how vertebrates might have evolved. The first vertebrates were fish that lived more than 400 million years ago. Fossils show that other vertebrates seem to have evolved slowly from these fish. Most present-day animals are quite different from the animals of 400 million years ago. A few present-day animals seem to have changed very little. Today, you can see only the groups of animals shown on the right hand side of figure 43.3. The other species died out long ago. Figure 43.3 also shows how conditions on Earth changed as animals evolved.

Figure 43.2

1. This strange fish lived several hundred million years ago. When it died its body fell into soft mud at the bottom of the sea.

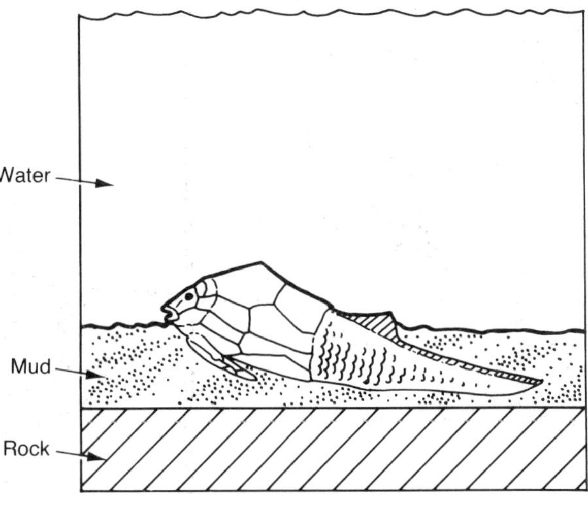

2. Time passed and the soft flesh rotted. The hard skeleton did not rot. Salts in the water changed the skeleton into stone and it became a fossil. The fossil was covered with more mud.

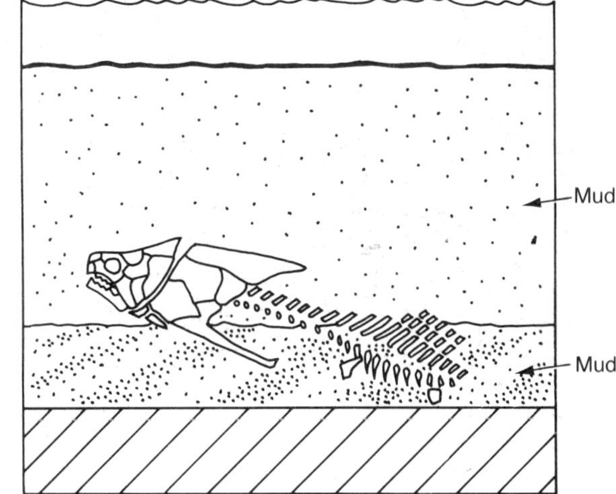

3. The mud began to harden into rock which was slowly pushed up above the sea.

4. The fossil fish was found by someone on holiday at Bognor Regis! It was 280 million years old!

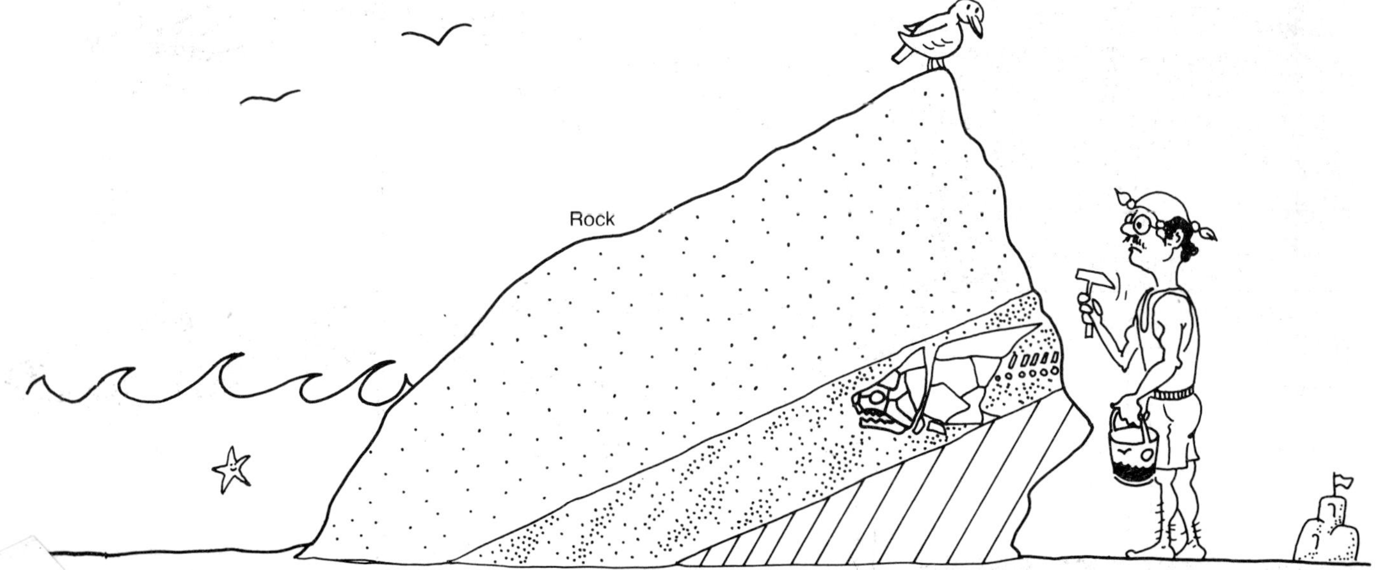

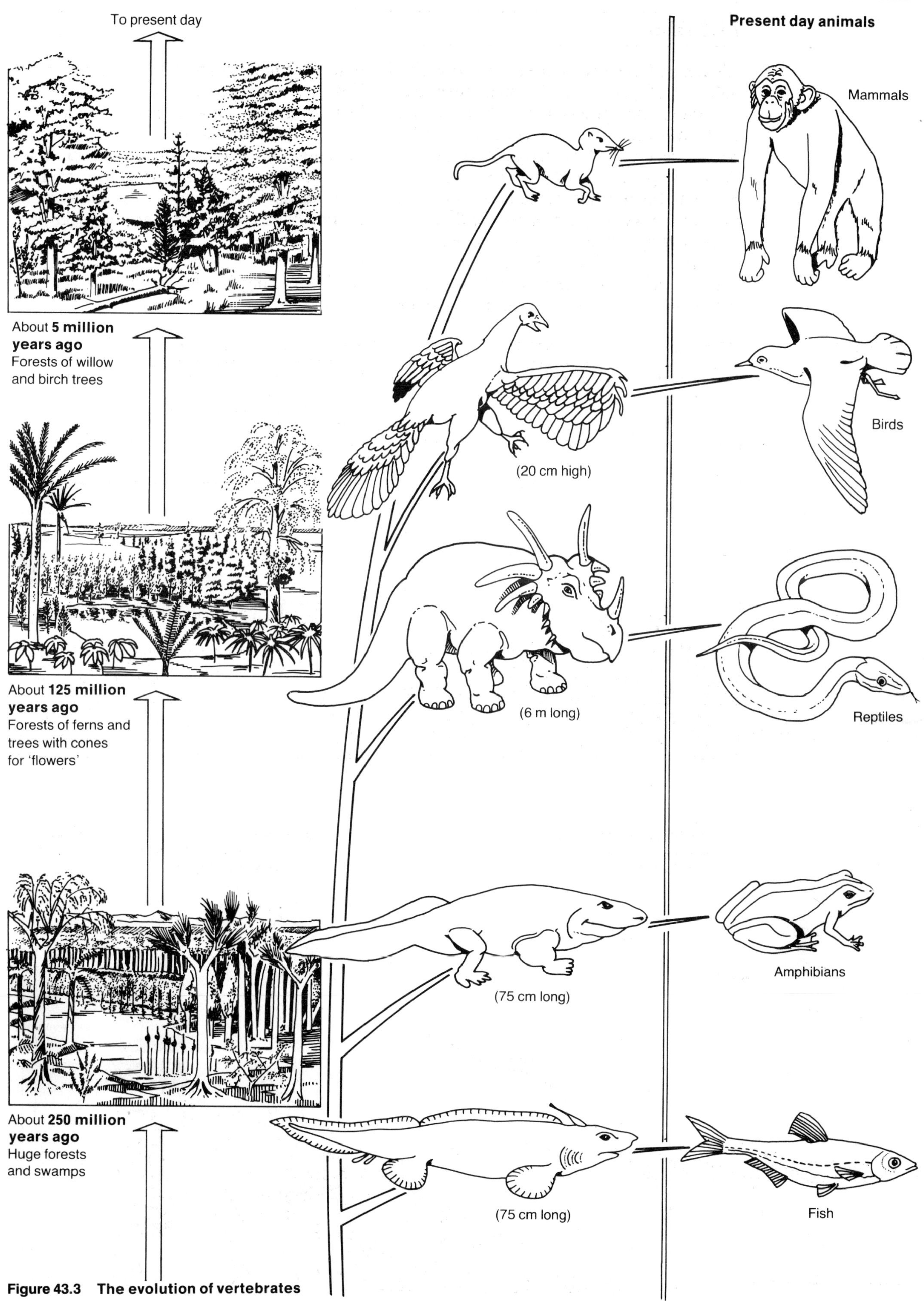

Figure 43.3 The evolution of vertebrates

HOW HORSES EVOLVED

From looking at fossils of horses we know that during their evolution (see figure 43.4):

1. they have got bigger,
2. their legs have got longer,
3. their feet have changed,
4. their teeth have changed.

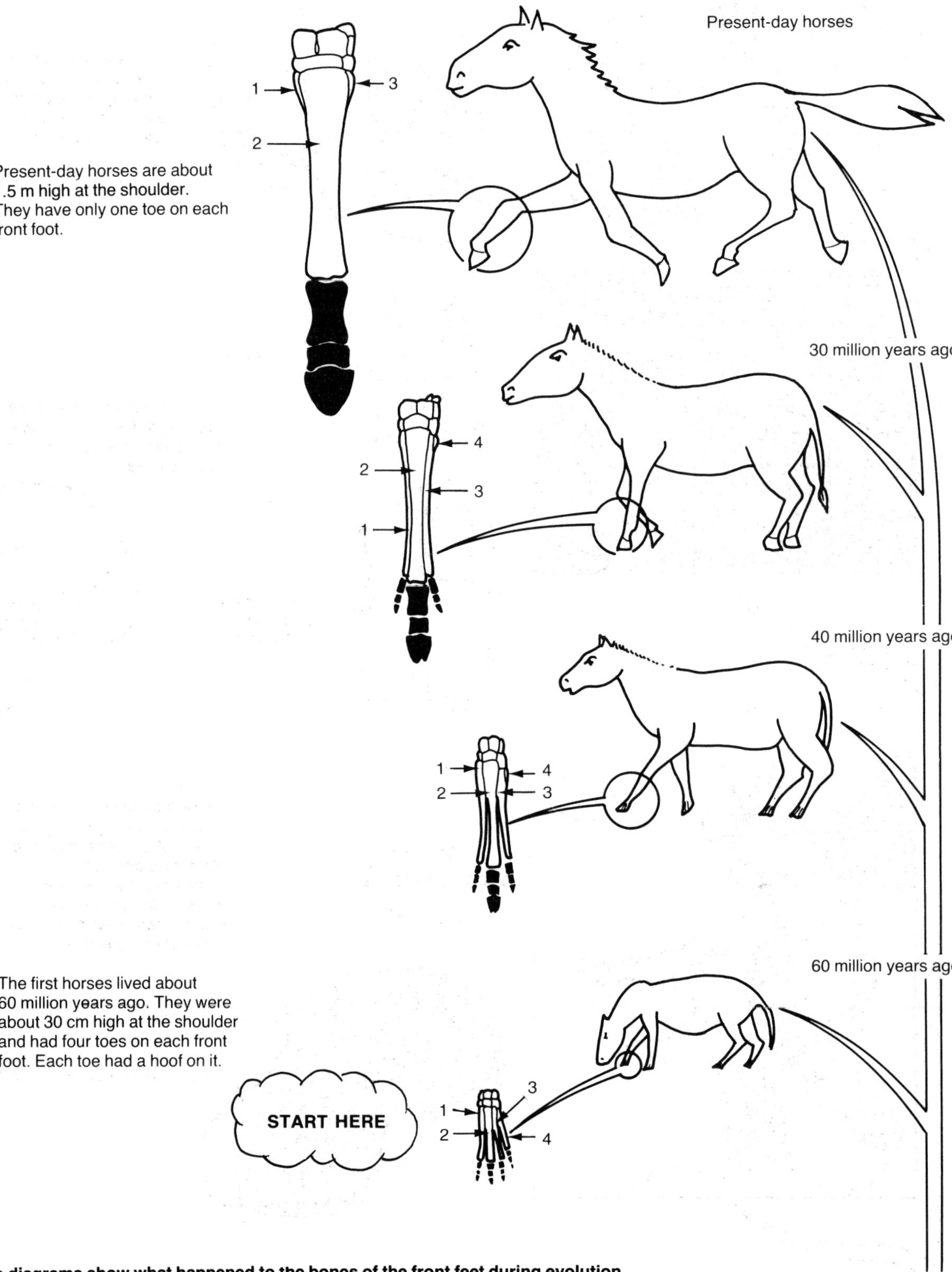

Figure 43.4 The diagrams show what happened to the bones of the front feet during evolution. Can you say what these changes were from looking at the diagram?

HOW HUMANS EVOLVED

From looking at human fossils we know that during our evolution (see figure 43.5):
1. we have got taller,
2. we have learned to stand upright,
3. we have developed a large brain.

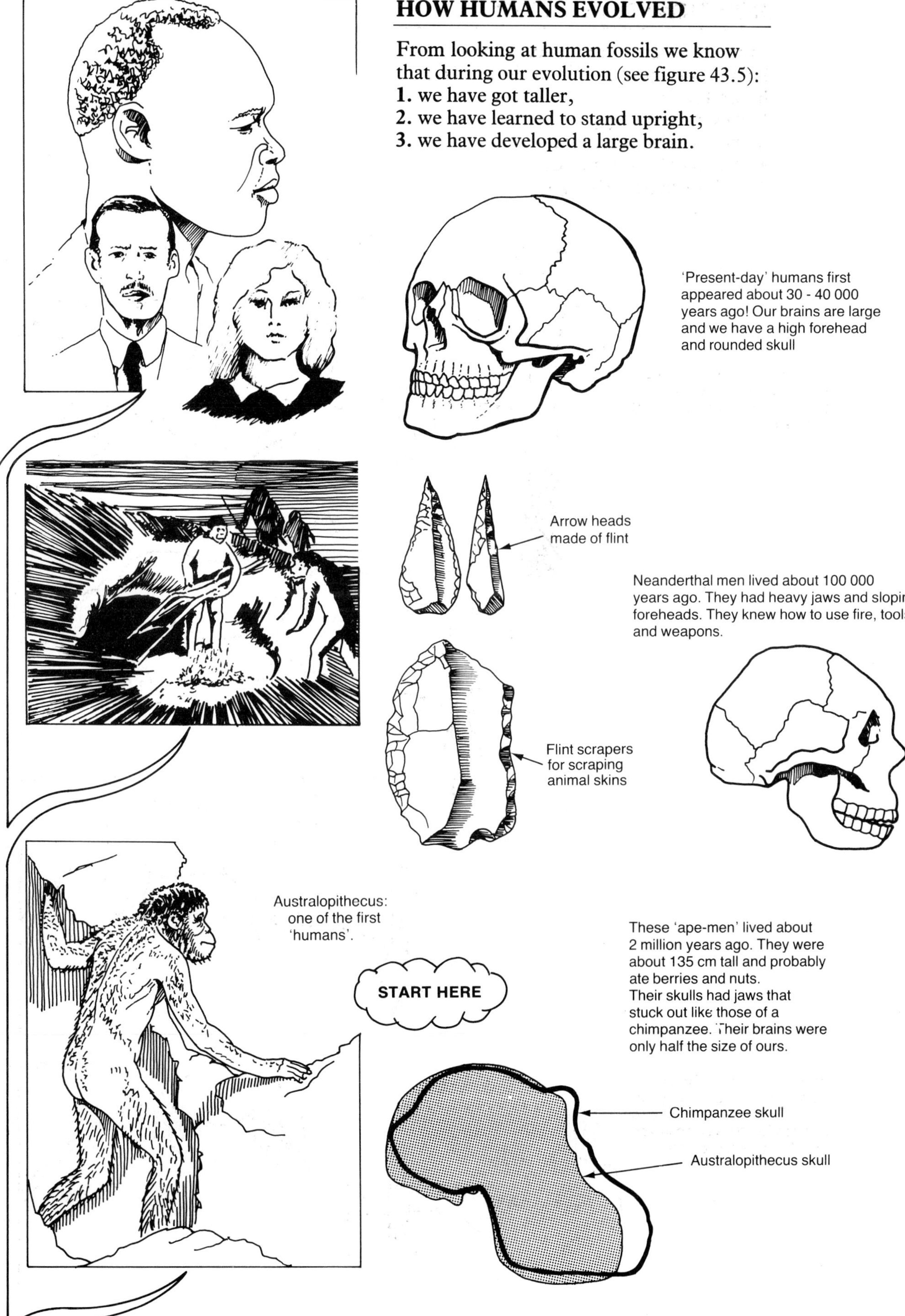

Figure 43.5

HOW HAS EVOLUTION HAPPENED?

In 1859, *Charles Darwin* explained how evolution might have happened. Darwin thought that *natural selection* was important in controlling how one species evolved from another.

HOW NATURAL SELECTION WORKS

Darwin thought that all organisms are different from each other in many ways. Even organisms from the same species are different. This variation betweeen living things can help them to survive or it can cause them to die. Darwin knew that all young animals and plants do not grow into adults. A lot of them die for different reasons and there must be a struggle to survive.

Organisms that 'win' the struggle will grow into adults and reproduce themselves. Organisms that 'lose' the struggle will die before they reproduce. Darwin called this natural selection because Nature is 'choosing' the organisms best able to survive. Natural selection works by choosing the fittest organisms to survive. This is called 'survival of the fittest'.

The tall plants in figure 43.6 can get plenty of light. Their big leaves do not let much light through to the short plants which cannot grow well or reproduce because of the poor light. The short plants will probably die.

Figure 43.6

The tall plants have 'won' the struggle to survive and are reproducing. Two characteristics which help them to survive are:

1. tallness,
2. big leaves.

The characteristics have been selected because they make the tall plants more likely to survive.

The tall and short plants in figure 43.7 are growing on high ground. Strong winds break off the big leaves and some stems of the tall plants. Because of this they cannot grow well or reproduce. The tall plants will probably die.

The short plants are not damaged by the strong winds because they are closer to the ground. The tall plants have 'lost' the struggle to survive. Two characteristics which do *not* make them fit to survive are:

1. tallness
2. big leaves

Figure 43

Organisms pass on many useful characteristics to their young in the sex cells. These characteristics 'collect' in a species as it evolves over millions of years. The variations that the characteristics cause in a species sometimes make it evolve into a new species.

> Some characteristics help organisms to win the struggle for survival. The same characteristics in different conditions may cause organisms to lose the struggle for survival and die. The characteristics best fitted to survive are chosen by natural selection.

HOW SELECTION CAN CHANGE A SPECIES

Golden retriever

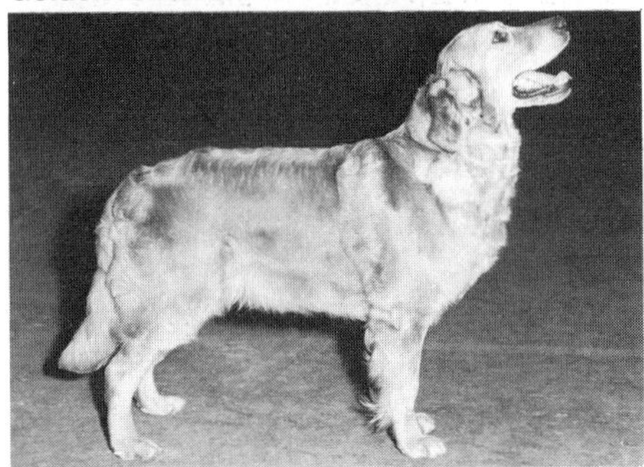

Pekinese

Fox terrier

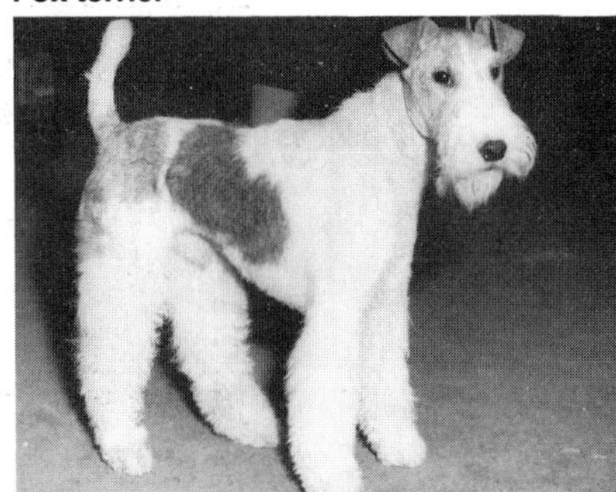

Darwin showed that we can use *artificial selection* to change animals and plants to make new varieties. We do this by choosing organisms which have characteristics useful to us and *breeding* from them.

The varieties of dog in figure 43.8 have all been bred by choosing certain characteristics in the parents.

The varieties of cabbage in figure 43.9 have been bred by choosing certain characteristics found in wild cabbage. The new varieties have characteristics which make them more useful for food than wild cabbage.

> Species can be changed by artificial selection in a few years. Darwin thought that natural selection could have done the same thing in millions of years.

Long-haired dachshound

Figure 43.8 Four different varieties of pure bred dog

MUTATIONS

Darwin did not know that the characteristics important in natural selection are controlled by genes. Genes sometimes change by *mutation*. Organisms which inherit mutated genes may look different. This new characteristic may be useful and may be 'chosen' by natural selection. The new characteristic will then help the organism to survive. However, most mutations are harmful and can cause the organism to die.

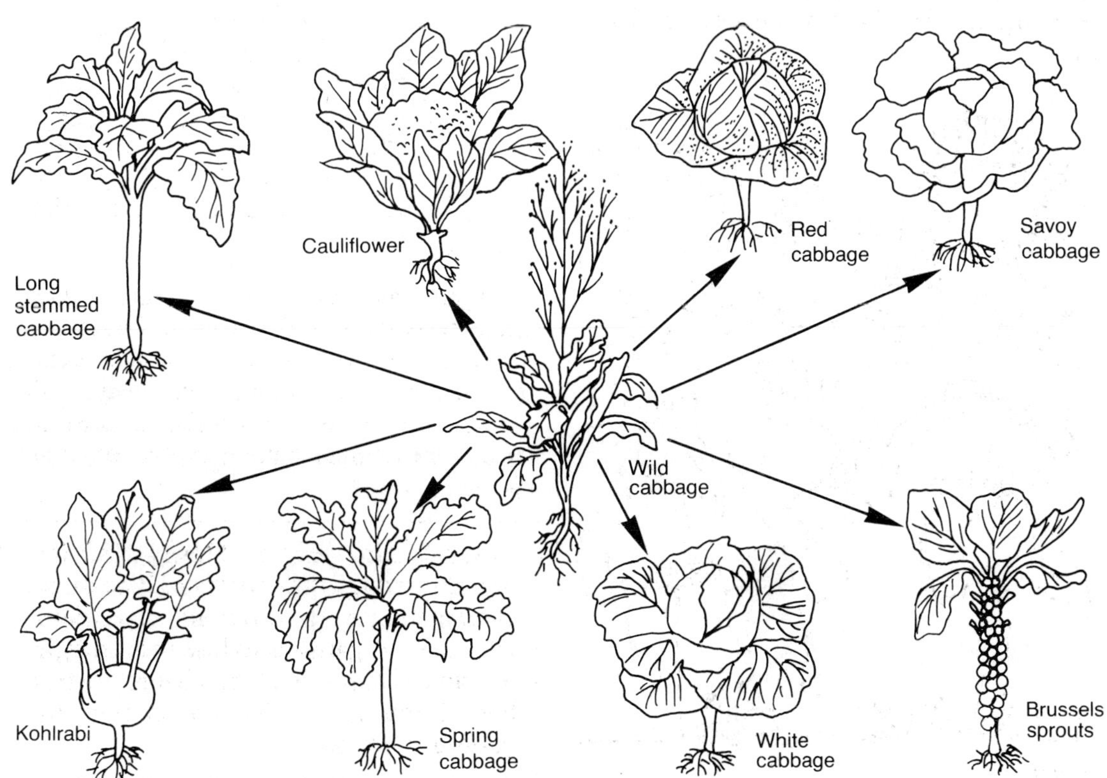

Figure 43.9

MUTATIONS IN MOTHS

Some moths have a gene that makes them a light colour. Sometimes this gene mutates so the young are darker than their parents. In dirty cities the *dark* moths cannot be seen easily by the birds that try to eat them. So in cities the birds eat the *light* moths. There are a lot of dark moths in cities because they can survive to reproduce better than the light moths. In country areas there are more *light* moths than *dark* moths. This is because the dark moths get eaten. The light moths are harder for birds to see against the cleaner background. In the two photographs below, which moths are the easiest to see?

Mutations help to speed up the changes that happen in evolution.

Fancy that!

Tyrannosaurus was one of the biggest carnivores ever to have lived. It was a reptile called a dinosaur and measured 6 m high and 15 m long!

Both light and dark "Peppered moths" on clean bark (left) and sooty bark (right).

Summary

The first animals and plants on Earth were small, simple organisms. Over millions of years they slowly changed into different organisms with new characteristics. This is called *evolution*. *Fossils* show us how organisms have changed as they evolved.

Charles Darwin said that characteristics that are useful help organisms to survive. He called this *natural selection*. These useful characteristics are passed on from parents to young.

Genes control the characteristics of organisms. Sometimes genes change by *mutation*. This may cause a new characteristic to appear which may be useful. Many new kinds of organism have been bred by *artificial selection*.

Important words

Evolution	the changes by which different kinds of organisms have developed from simpler organisms.
Fossil	the remains or shape of an organism that lived a long time ago.
Natural selection	the survival of organisms best fitted to the conditions they live in.
Darwin	the man who first thought that evolution happened by natural selection.
Artificial selection	producing new kinds (or varieties) of organism by breeding from parents with useful characteristics.
Breeding	producing young by crossing selected parents.
Mutation	a sudden change that happens in the genes of an organism.
Species	a group of organisms of the same kind which can breed together to produce young.

Questions

A.

1. What are the differences between natural selection and artificial selection?
2. Suppose you have a collection of tadpoles in a jar. Write down the ways in which the tadpoles might be different from each other. Which of these variations do you think (a) might be useful, (b) might be harmful, (c) will make no difference to the survival of the tadpoles?
3. 'Survival of the fittest' is important in natural selection. What do you think Darwin meant by the word 'fittest'?
4. Penicillin is an antibiotic that kills some disease-causing bacteria. When penicillin was first used it killed nearly all these bacteria. Many bacteria cannot now be killed by penicillin. Explain why you think this has happened.
5. How do we know that (a) present-day horses can run faster than the first 'horses' (b) the first 'horses' lived on soft, wet ground, (c) present-day humans have a larger brain than the first 'humans'.

TOPIC 44

SORTING OUT LIVING THINGS

CLASSIFYING THINGS

There are about 1 million different groups of animals and about 350 thousand different groups of plants. Sorting out all these organisms into groups can be a problem! To do this scientists collect together organisms which have the same characteristics. These organisms are then put into the same group. This is called classification. The books in your school library are classified into groups. This helps you to find any book quickly.

People who collect stamps usually classify them into groups. They could group the stamps on this page using the characteristics of:

1. size and shape,
2. whether there is a picture of an animal or a plant,
3. country which made the stamp,
4. cost of the stamp.

The method a person chooses to classify his stamps depends on how his stamp collection is used. Any of the four methods would be correct.

In the same way, different methods can be used to classify organisms. The characteristics we normally use to classify organisms are all to do with their structure. Firstly we group living organisms into animals and plants. Then we put these into smaller groups like this:

The smallest group of animals or plants is the *species*.

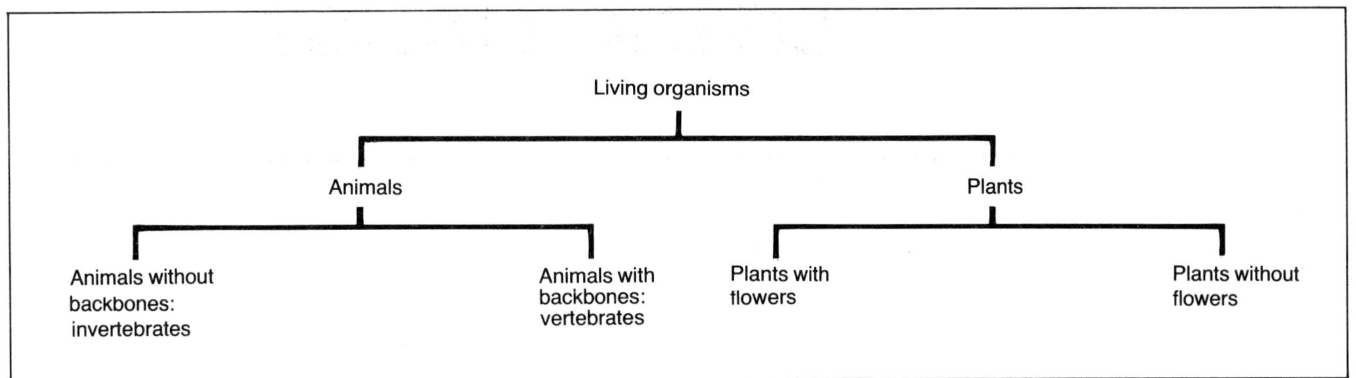

ANIMALS WITHOUT BACKBONES (Invertebrates)

Protozoa

These are animals made of one cell. You will need a microscope to see them! Most of them live in water but some live in damp soil or inside other animals.

Amoeba moves using pseudopodia. Paramecium moves using tiny hairs or cilia.

Vorticella is fixed with a long coiled stalk.

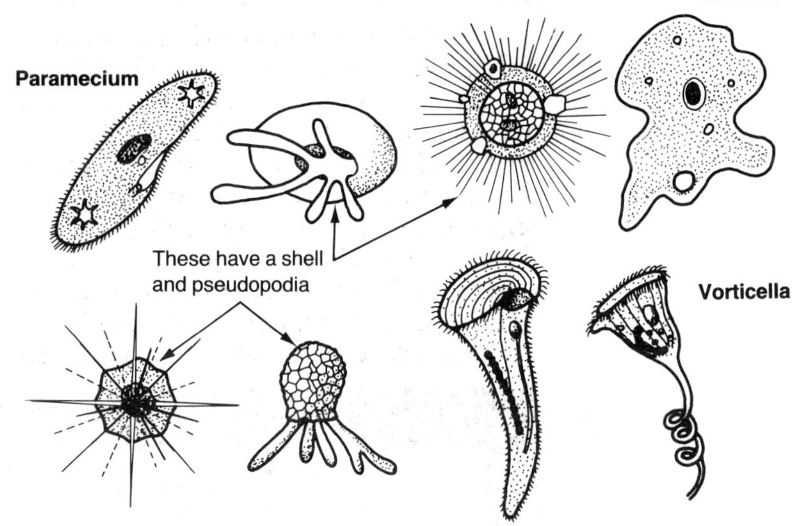

Figure 44.1

Coelenterates

Coelenterates have a hollow body like a bag. The opening to the 'bag' is the mouth which is surrounded by tentacles. The animal pushes food into its mouth with its tentacles. Waste food also leaves its body through its mouth.

Coelenterates all live in water. Sea anemones and jellyfish live in the sea. Jellyfish float but sea anemones are fixed to rocks. Look for sea anemones in rock pools. Try dropping a small piece of meat onto the tentacles and watch how they catch it! Hydra live in ponds and streams and can be green, brown or white. They are usually fixed to pondweed.

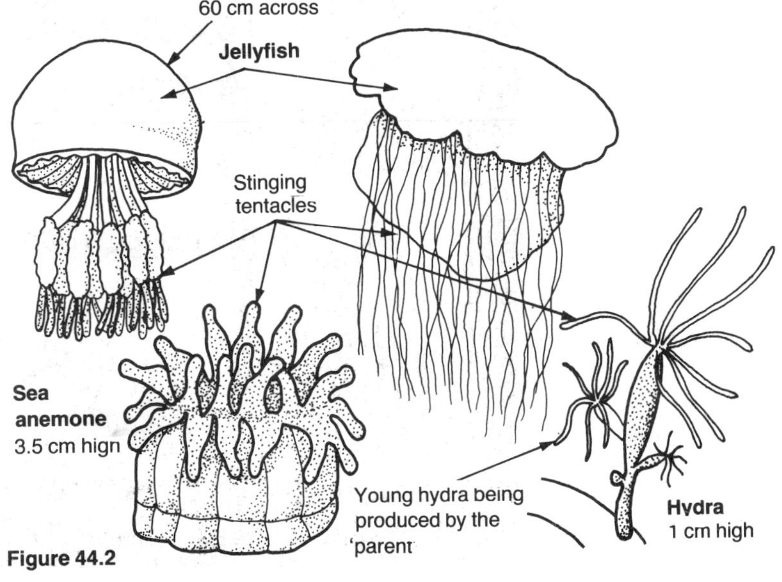

Figure 44.2

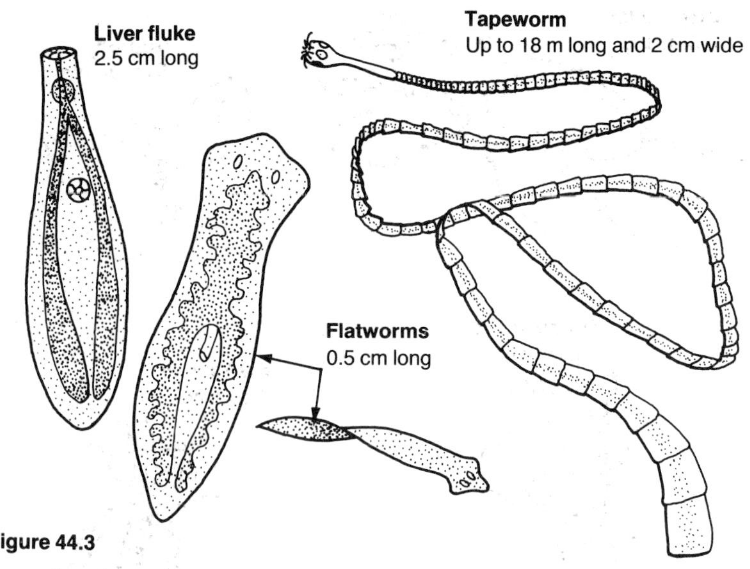

Figure 44.3

Flatworms

Tapeworms and flukes are parasites and they live inside humans and animals such as sheep and cattle. Tapeworms fix themselves to the wall of the digestive system using hooks and suckers.

Flatworms live in freshwater and move over mud and weeds. They eat small crustaceans and worms. Look for them under stones in ponds and streams!

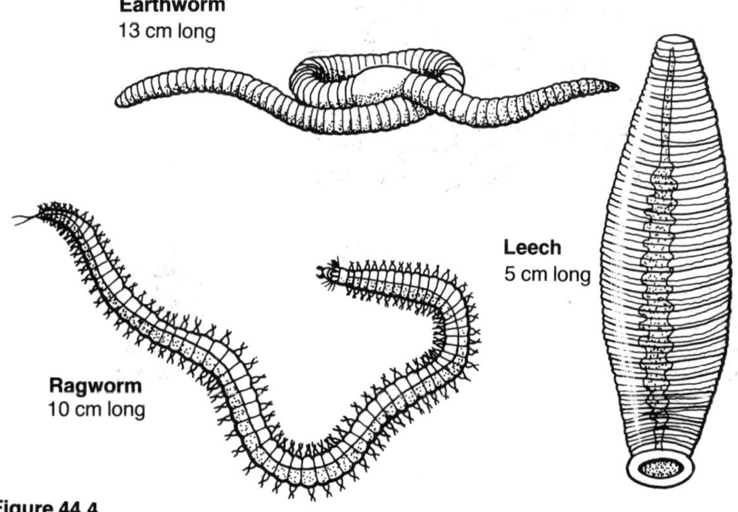

Figure 44.4

Segmented worms

These animals have round bodies made of rings or segments.

Earthworms live in soil. They feed by eating soil and digesting some of the substances in it. Earthworms are important animals because they improve the soil. They do this by mixing the soil and helping it to drain.

Leeches live in fresh water, sea water, forests and swamps. Many leeches are parasites and feed by sucking blood from vertebrates.

Ragworms are often brightly coloured. You can find them on the sea shore!

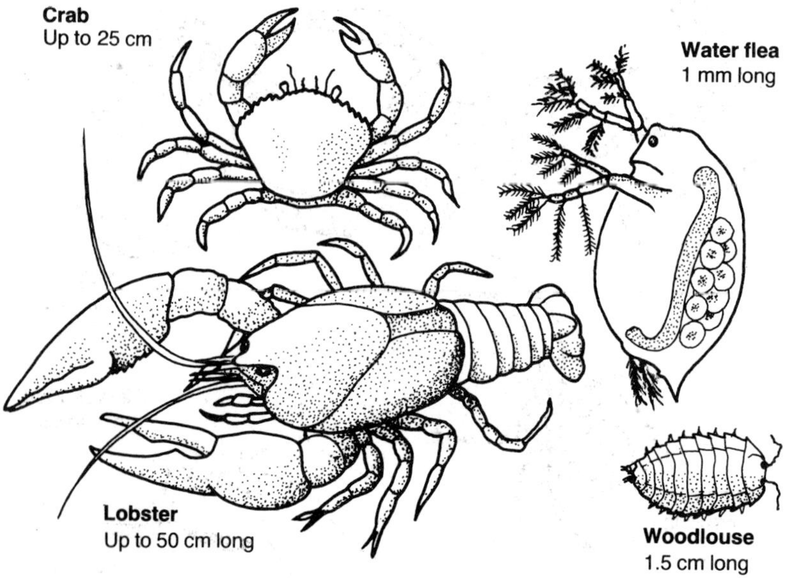

Figure 44.5

Crustaceans

Crustaceans have a hard layer or exoskeleton on the outsides of their bodies. The exoskeleton protects the soft parts of the animal.

Crabs and lobsters have five pairs of legs which they use for walking. You can find crabs in rock pools on the sea shore but lobsters live in deeper water.

Water fleas and woodlice have a thinner exoskeleton than crabs or lobsters. Water fleas swim using jerky movements of their legs. With a microscope you can watch the heart of a water flea beating. Woodlice live under stones and bark where the air is always damp.

Insects

Most insects have wings. All insects have a body made of three parts: a head, thorax and abdomen. The wings and three pairs of legs are fixed to the thorax.

Insects are an important group of animals. Insects such as mosquitoes, lice, fleas and flies spread disease. Insects such as locusts and aphids damage plants which we grow for food. Some insects such as bees, silk 'worms' and ladybirds are useful insects.

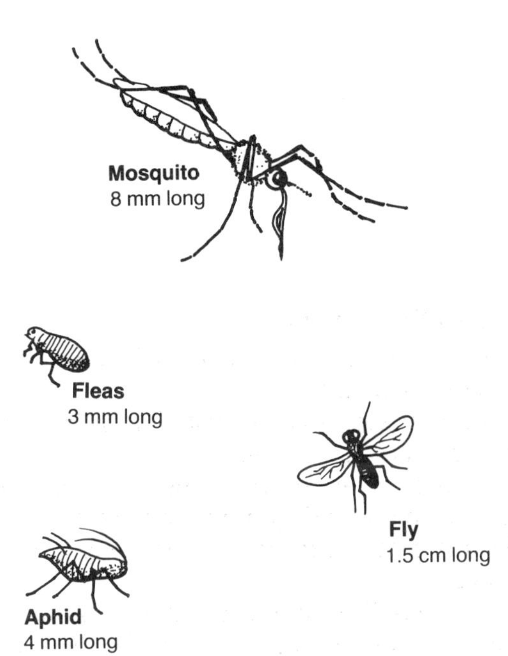

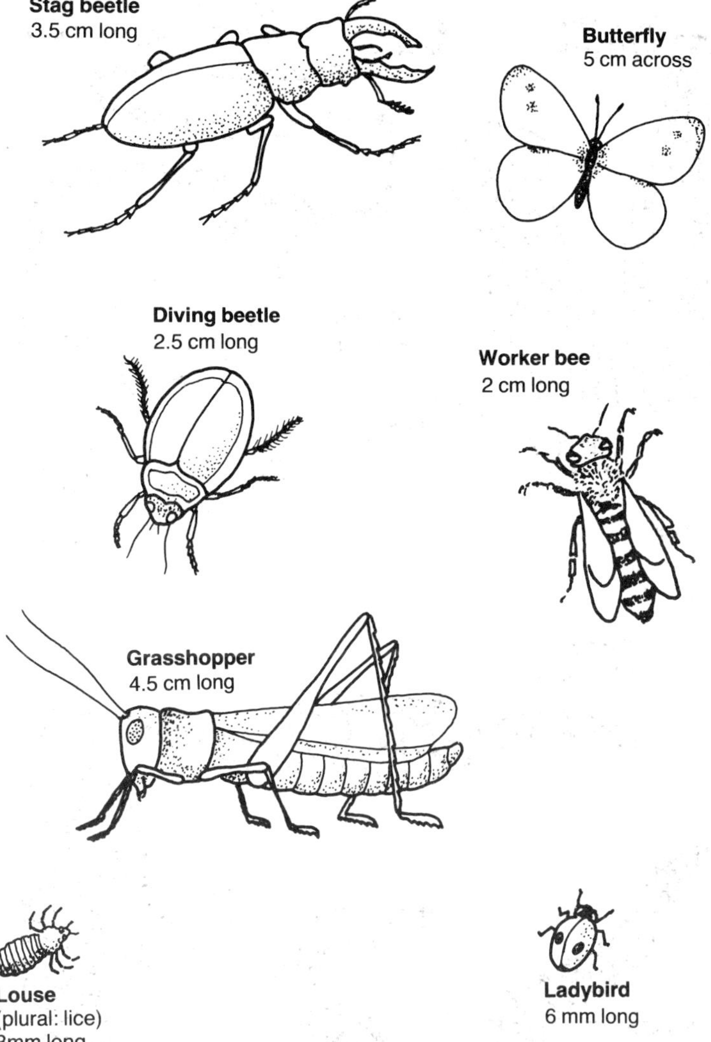

Figure 44.6

Arachnids

Arachnids have four pairs of legs and their bodies are made of two parts.

Some spiders spin webs to catch their food but other spiders hunt for food. Some can even catch small birds!

Scorpions live in hot countries and have a poisonous sting in their tails. They feed on insects.

Harvestmen are common in summer and have long legs. They feed on insects.

Some ticks are parasites and live on other animals.

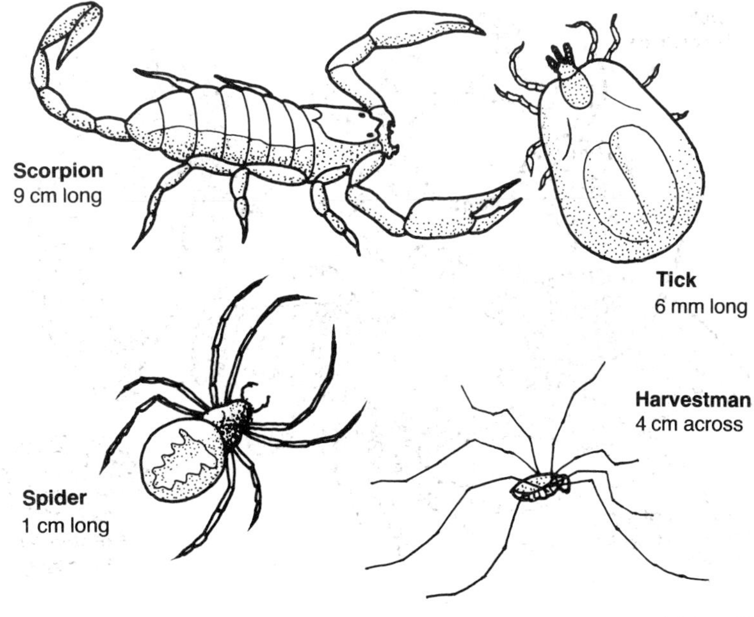

Figure 44.7

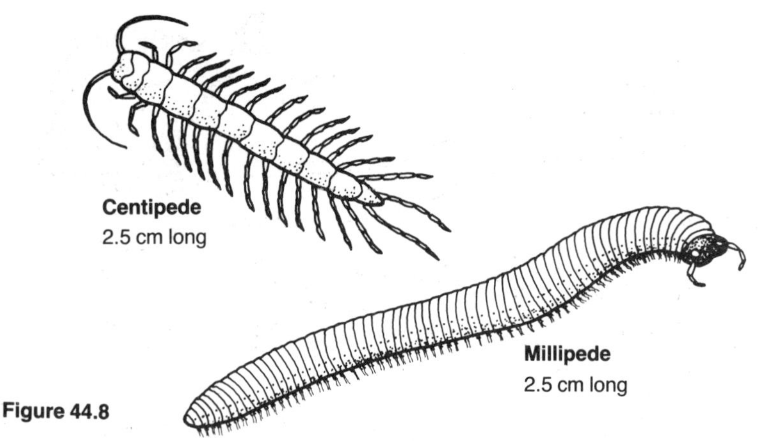

Figure 44.8

Myriapods

Myriapods have a lot of legs. Their bodies are made of many segments.

Centipedes have one pair of legs on each segment. They are carnivorous and eat other small animals.

Millipedes have two pairs of legs on each segment. It is interesting to watch all these legs moving! They are herbivorous and eat plants. They can be a pest in the garden.

Look for both centipedes and millipedes under stones!

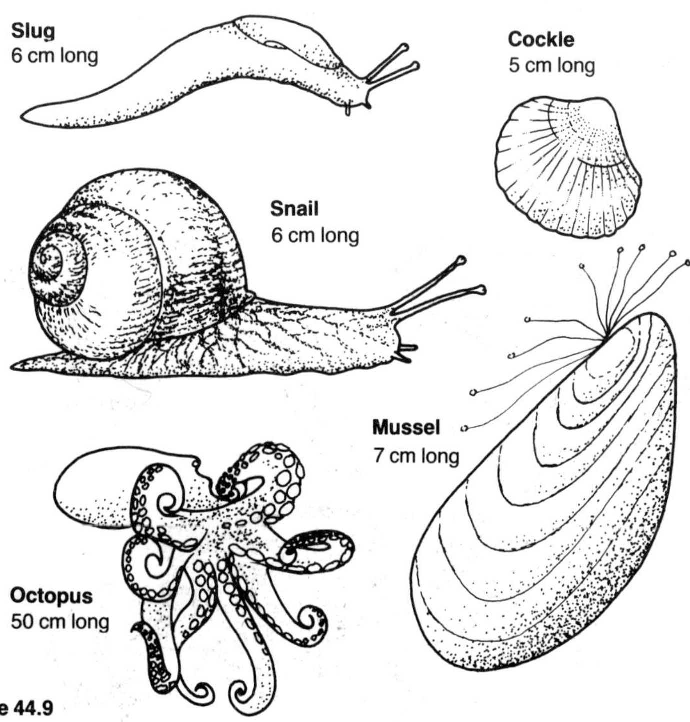

Figure 44.9

Molluscs

Molluscs have soft bodies which may be protected by a shell.

Snails and slugs are common in gardens where they eat plants. You can see where snails and slugs have been because they leave a trail of slime!

Mussels and cockles live on the sea shore. Mussels are dark blue in colour and they are fixed to rocks. Cockles live buried in sand.

An octopus has eight arms. These have suckers and are used to catch food.

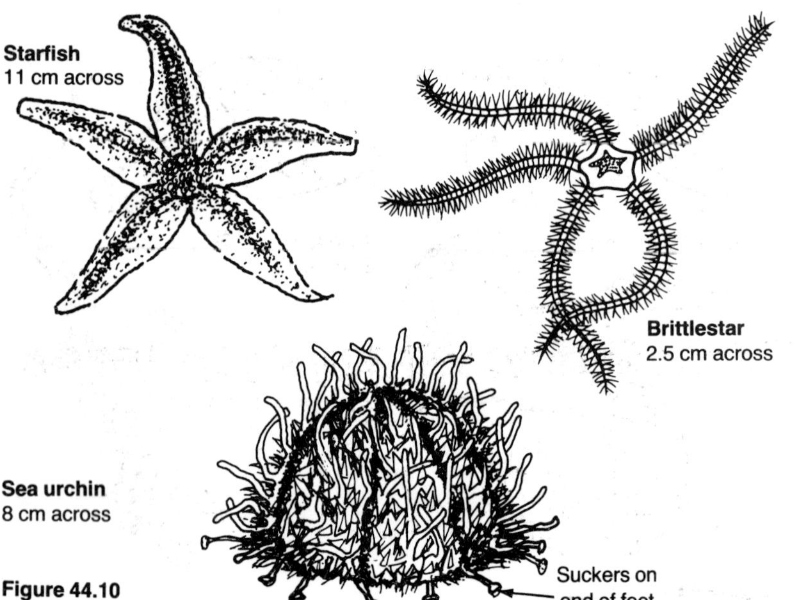

Figure 44.10

Echinoderms

Echinoderms all live in the sea. They have spiny skins covered with little tubes. The suckers on the ends of these tubes help the animals to move.

Starfish and brittle stars have five arms. The mouth is where the arms meet. Sea urchins have a round body and the five arms are joined together so they do not look like separate arms.

ANIMALS WITH BACKBONES: (Vertebrates)

Fish

Fish live in water and have a streamlined body covered with scales. They use their fins for balance and movement in swimming. Fish breathe with gills and most of them reproduce by laying eggs. Most fish have a skeleton made of bone.

Plaice and mackerel live in the sea and are good to eat! Mackerel are fast-swimming carnivorous fish. Plaice have flat bodies and lie on the sea bottom.

Sharks have a skeleton made of a substance called cartilage and are carnivores.

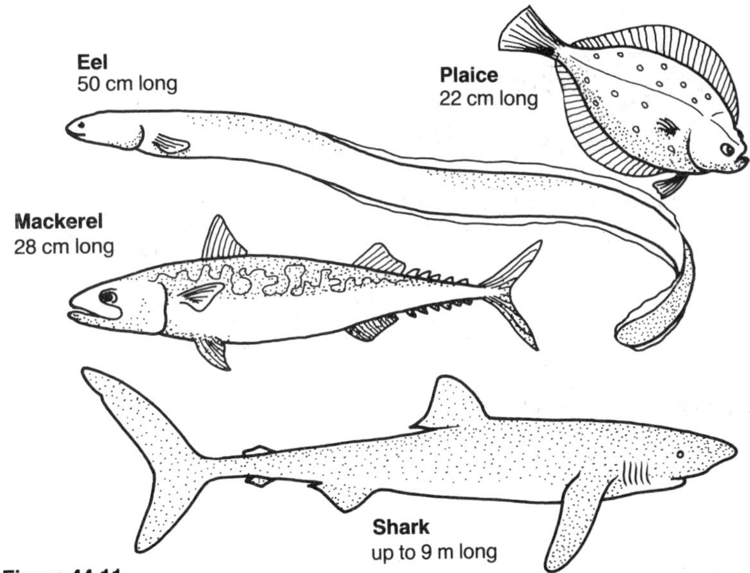

Figure 44.11

Amphibia

Amphibia have thin skins which are smooth and moist. They lay their eggs in water but the adults can live on land or in water.

The eggs grow into larvae which develop into adults. The larvae breathe using gills but adults breathe using lungs.

Frogs live in or near pools and streams. They eat insects, spiders, millipedes, slugs, snails and worms. Frogs are useful animals in gardens!

Toads have a thicker skin than frogs and can live in drier places.

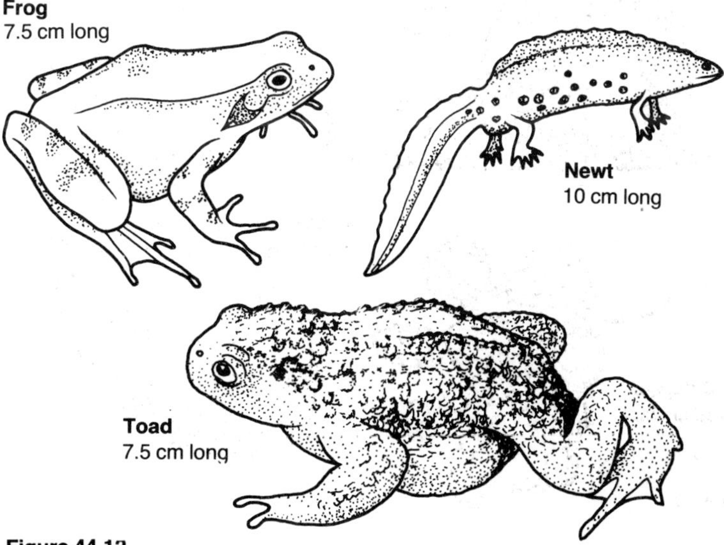

Figure 44.12

Reptiles

Reptiles have thick, dry skins covered with scales. Most of them live on land but some can live in water as well as on land. Reptiles breathe with lungs and reproduce by laying eggs which have tough shells.

Turtles and tortoises are protected by a shell. Turtles live in the sea but lay their eggs on land. Some tortoises live on land but others live in freshwater.

Most lizards are carnivorous. Some live in water and others on land. Many lizards can change colour!

Snakes have no legs. A lot of them have a poisonous bite.

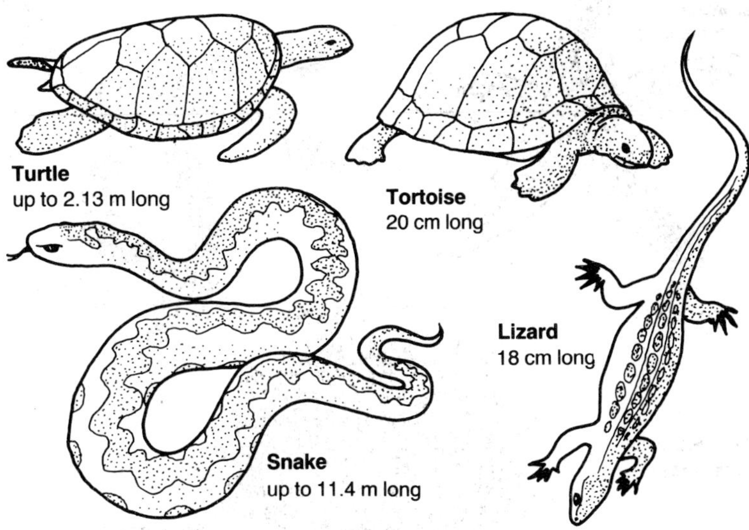

Figure 44.13

Figure 44.14

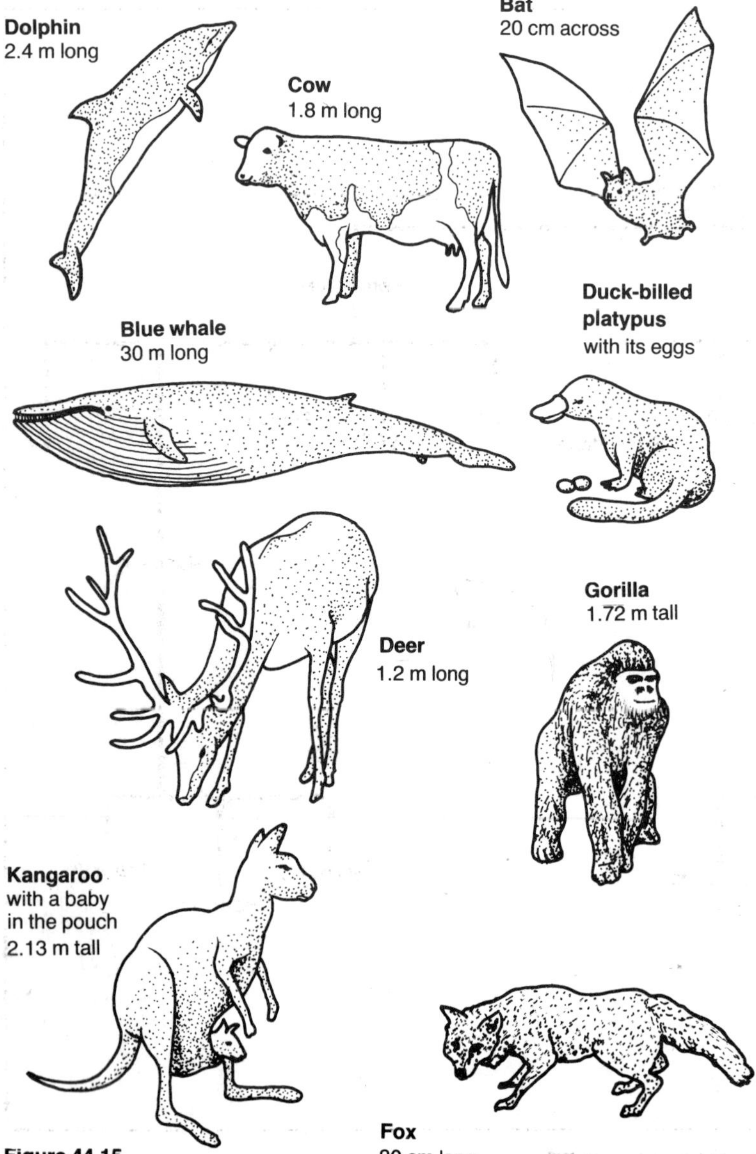

Figure 44.15

Birds

Birds have a warm body which is always kept at the same temperature. Their bodies are covered with feathers. All birds have wings but some cannot fly. Birds have a beak which they use for feeding and they lay eggs protected by hard shells.

Swallows come to Britain in March and leave in November. They feed on insects. Tawny owls only fly at night. They eat small birds, mice and insects.

Ostriches cannot fly but they can run very fast. Their eggs weigh about 1.65 kg!

Homing pigeons can find their way back even when they are let go many miles from home!

Mammals

Mammals have a warm body which is always kept at the same temperature. Their bodies are covered with hair or fur. The young mammals feed on milk which is made in the breasts or mammary glands of the female.

Different mammals can run, hop, jump, fly, swim, climb and burrow! There are three groups of mammals:

1. mammals that lay eggs,
2. mammals that keep their young in pouches,
3. mammals that keep their young inside their bodies.

Egg laying mammals

This is a small group of simple mammals. The duck-billed platypus lives in rivers in Australia. Its eggs are laid in burrows and the young are fed on milk when they hatch.

Mammals with pouches

Kangaroos and koala bears carry their young in a pouch on the stomach. Their babies are born before they are fully developed.

They crawl out from inside the mother and go into the pouch. They stay in the pouch feeding on milk until they are old enough to look after themselves.

Mammals that keep their young inside their bodies

These are called placental mammals because the young are joined to the mother with a placenta. The placenta is inside the mother's body and it helps to feed the young. After they are born the young feed on milk from the mother. Gorillas, bats, deer, cows foxes and humans are placental mammals.

HOMEOTHERMIC AND POIKILOTHERMIC ANIMALS

All invertebrates are poikilothermic (cold-blooded) animals. Fish, amphibia and reptiles are cold-blooded vertebrates. The body temperature of all these animals is about the same as the temperature of their surroundings.

Birds and mammals are homeothermic (warm-blooded) vertebrates. The body temperature of these animals is always about the same. In very hot weather, their body temperature is cooler than the surroundings. In cold weather, their body temperature is warmer than the surroundings.

Warm-blooded animals can move around when cold-blooded animals may not be able to because their bodies are not at the right temperature.

Parental care

Birds and mammals produce fewer young than many other animals. This is because the parents look after the young so that most of them survive. This is called parental care.

Most other animals do not have parental care. They have to produce a lot of young so that a few will survive. Most of the young will be eaten by other animals. Having parental care and being warm-blooded have helped birds and mammals to be successful.

SUMMARY OF ANIMAL CLASSIFICATION

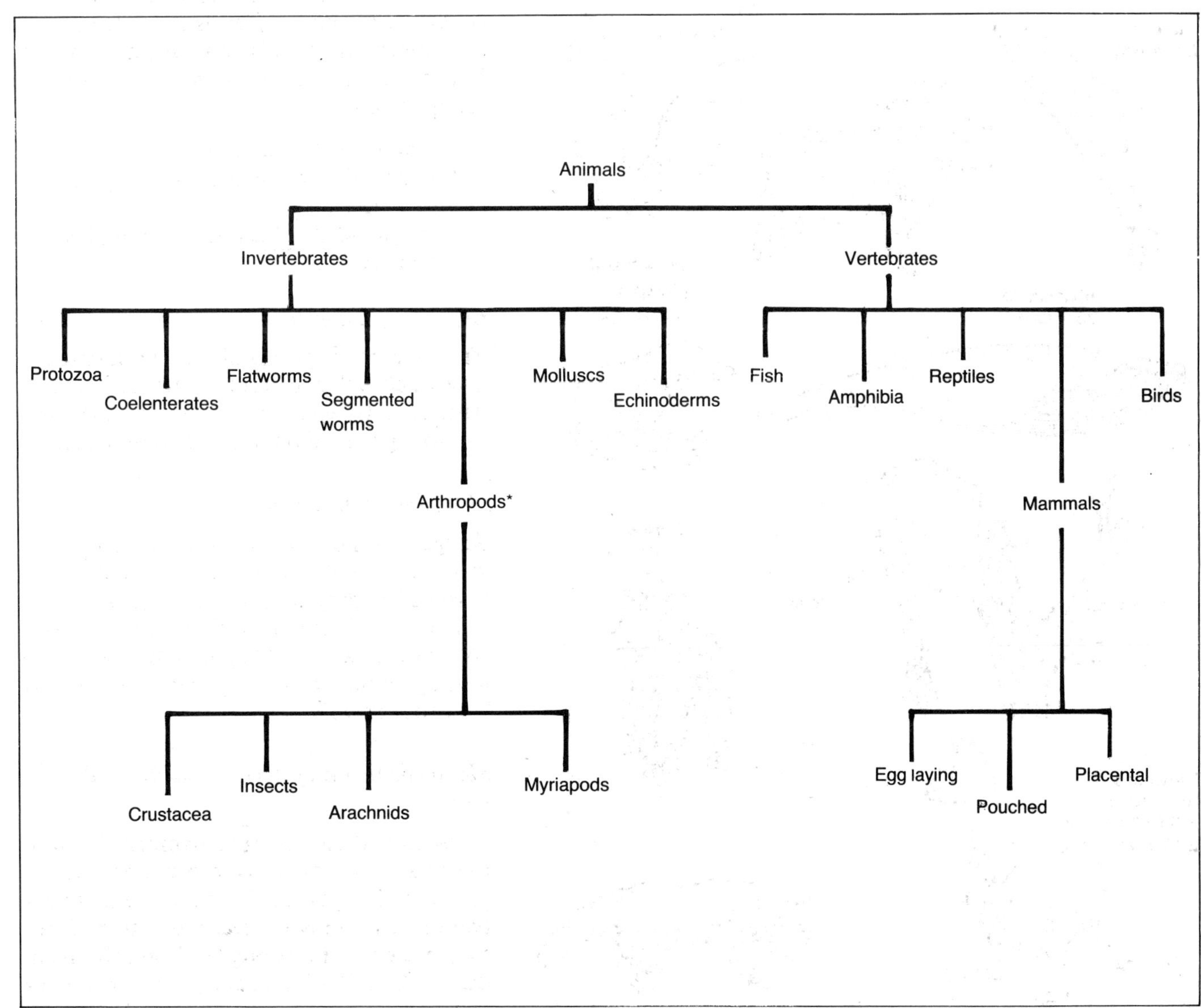

* *Arthropods* are a big group made up of animals which have an exoskeleton and jointed legs

Figure 44.16

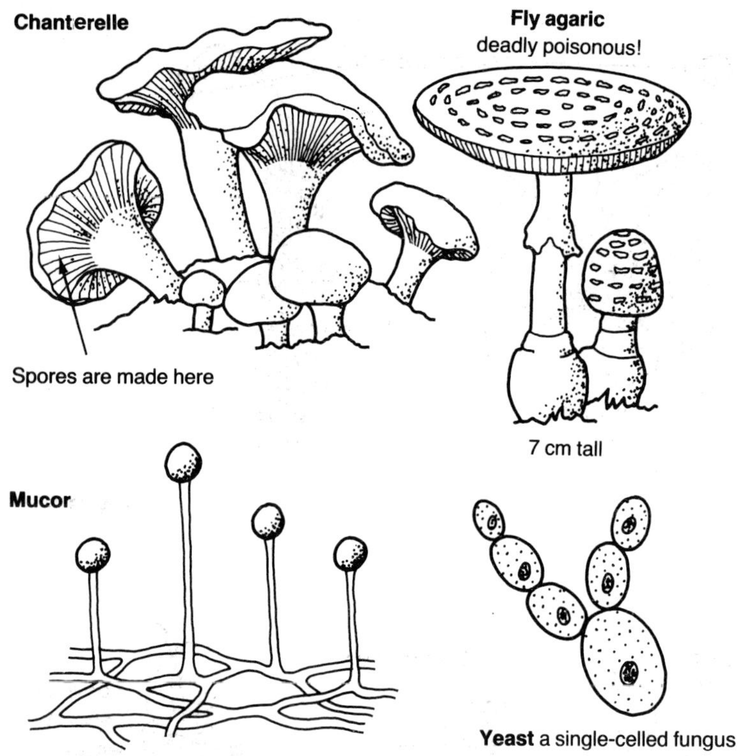

Figure 44.17

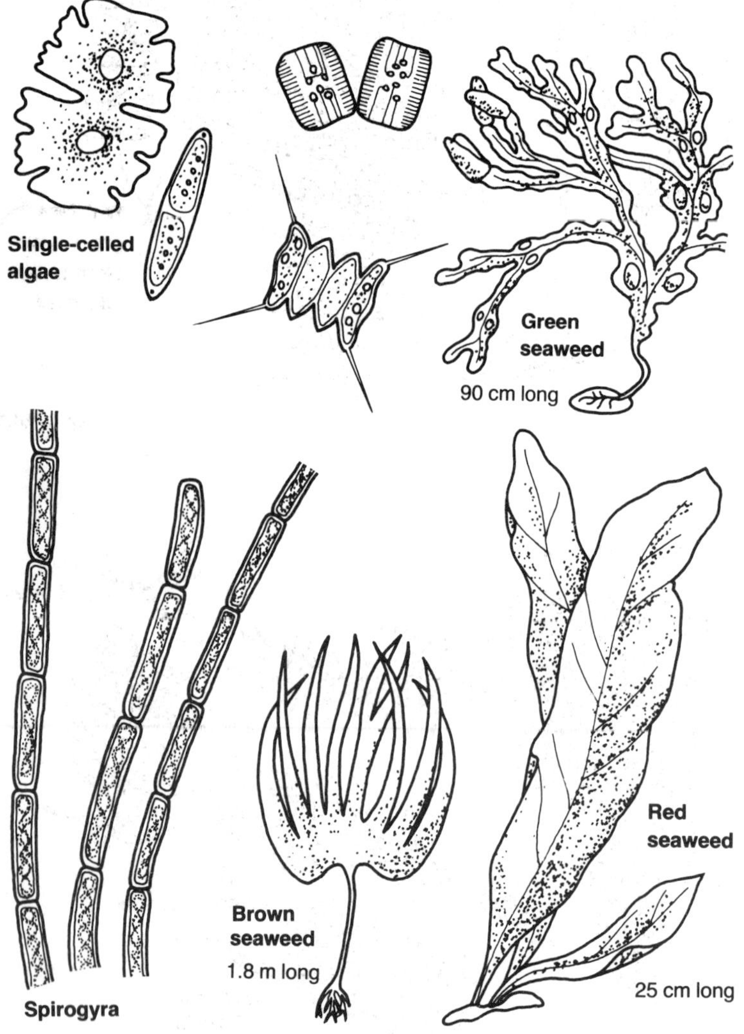

Figure 44.18

PLANTS WITHOUT FLOWERS

Fungi

Fungi cannot make their own food unlike green plants. This is because fungi have no chlorophyll (or green substance) which helps green plants to make their food. Some fungi are saprophytes and feed on dead organisms. Other fungi are parasites and feed on living organisms.

Fungi reproduce by spores. Fungi are important plants because some of them help to make dead organisms decay. The substances from the dead organisms can then be used by other living organisms for new growth.

Algae

Most algae live in water. Some of them are very small and you can only see them with a microscope. These small algae are important food for a lot of animals such as fish, crustacea and molluscs. Other algae such as seaweeds are quite big plants.

Substances in seaweeds are used to make some foods like ice-cream!

The light-green slimy substance in pools in summer is an alga called Spirogyra.

Liverworts and mosses

These are small green plants which grow in damp places. Look for them on old walls, between paving slabs and in blocked gutters! They reproduce by spores made in spore cases.

Liverworts are flat, leaf-like plants. At one time people thought that they cured liver diseases!

Mosses grow in groups closely packed together. You will see that they are very beautiful when you look at them closely.

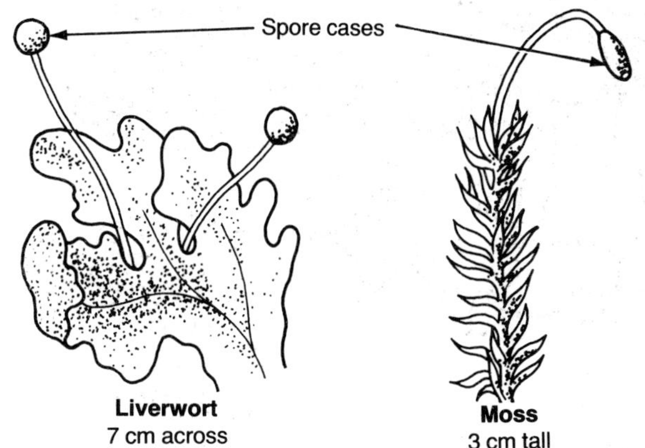

Figure 44.19

Ferns and Horsetails

Ferns reproduce using spores made on the backs of their leaves. Bracken ferns cover hillsides in many parts of the country and are important weeds. They are difficult to get rid of and they stop farmers from ploughing the land.

Horsetails reproduce using spores which are made in simple cones. Look for Horsetails on waste ground and in damp places!

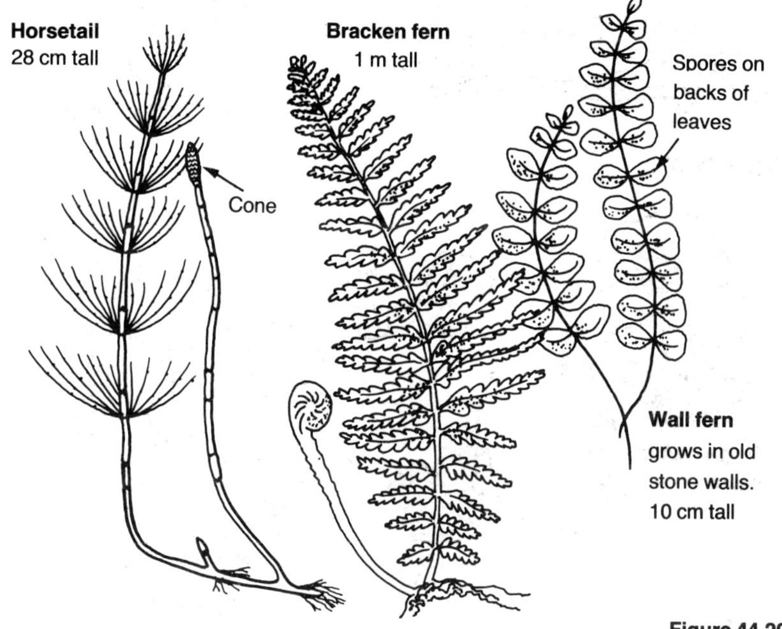

Figure 44.20

Plants with cones

Trees which have seeds made inside cones are called conifers. Most conifers keep their leaves in winter and are called evergreens. The larch is a deciduous conifer because it drops its leaves in winter.

Large areas of land are planted with conifers because they grow quickly. Their wood is used in building and furniture making.

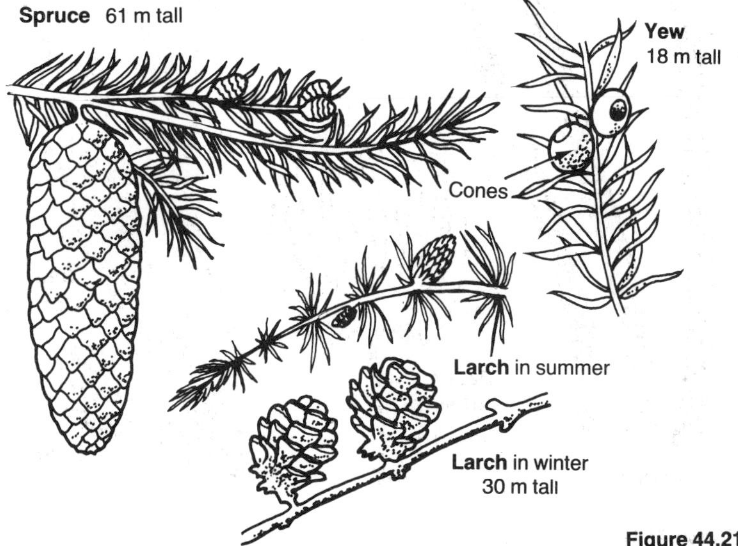

Figure 44.21

PLANTS WITH FLOWERS

These plants reproduce with seeds made inside flowers. The male sex cells are called pollen grains and they are made in the anthers. The female sex cells are called ova and they are made in the ovary. After fertilisation the ova grow into seeds inside the ovary.

Plants which grow from seeds that have one seed leaf or cotyledon are called monocotyledons.

Plants which grow from seeds that have two seed leaves are called dicotyledons.

Monocotyledons

These plants have narrow leaves. A lot of important food plants such as wheat, barley, rice, corn and oats are monocotyledons.

Dicotyledons

This is the biggest group of flowering plants. They have wide leaves with a network of veins.

The smallest dicotyledons have stems that die in winter. These are called herbaceous plants. Daisies, dandelions, buttercups and dead nettles are herbaceous.

Bigger dicotyledons have stems that do not die in winter. These are called shrubs. Bushy plants like privet are shrubs.

The biggest dicotyledons are trees such as oak, elm and ash.

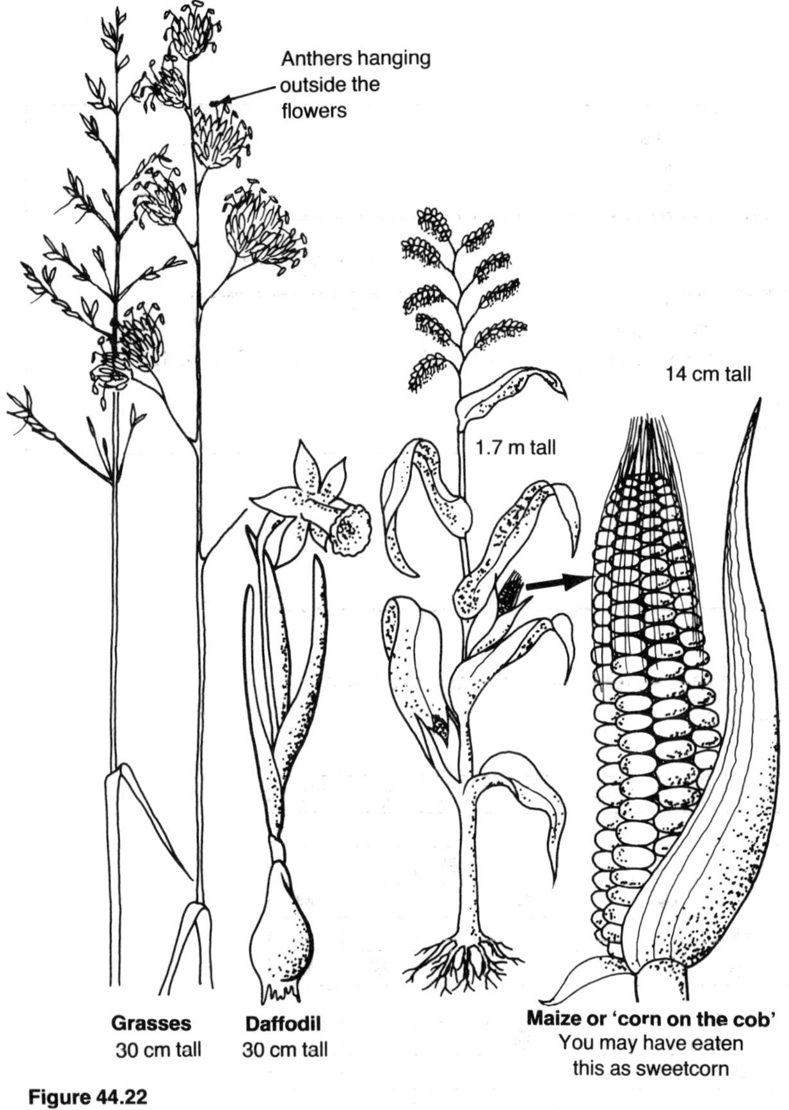

Figure 44.22

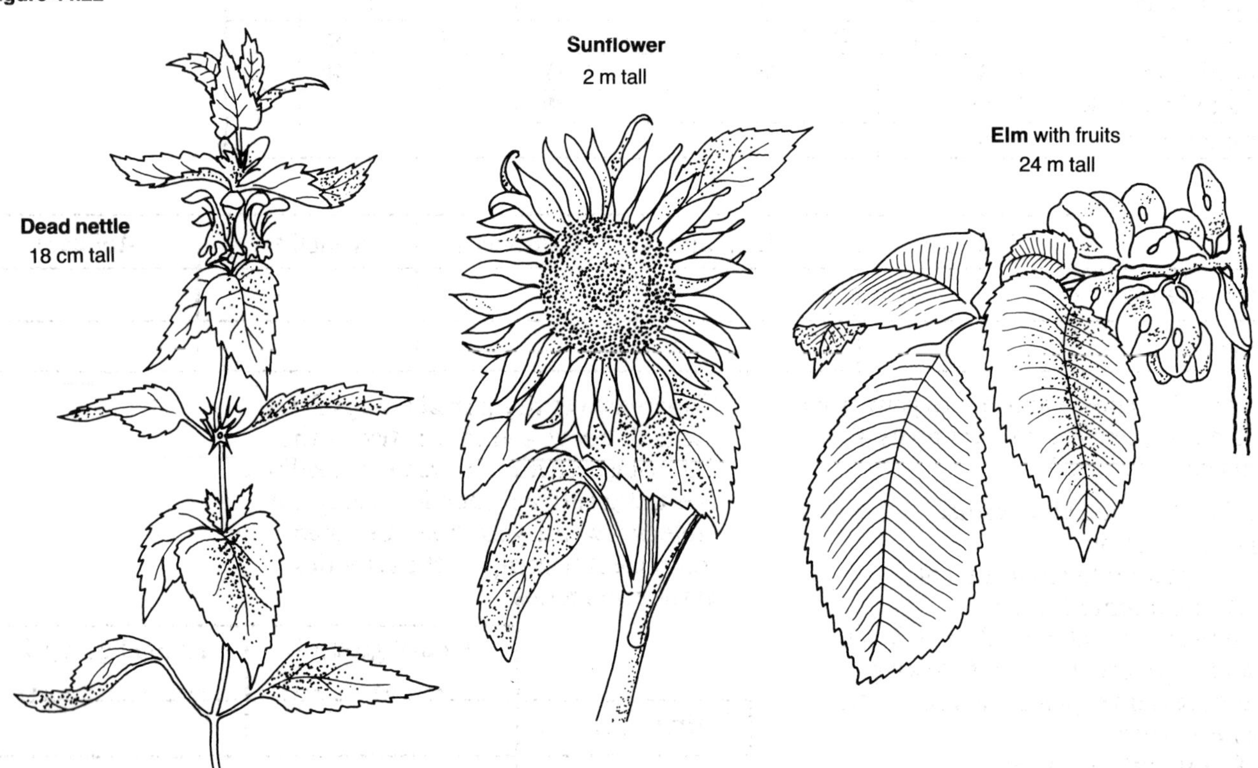

Figure 44.23

SUMMARY OF PLANT CLASSIFICATION

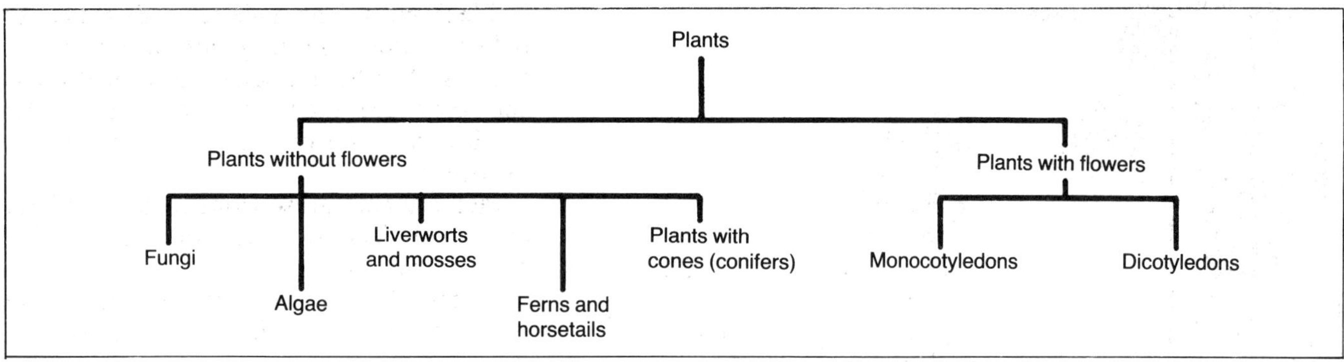

Figure 44.24

Questions

A.

The chart gives some clues about vertebrate animals . Animals (a) – (e) have many clues but animals (f) – (k) have fewer clues. Write down what you think each sort of animal might be.

	(a)	(b)	(c)	(d)	(e)	(f)	(g)	(h)	(i)	(j)	(k)
hair	●										
feathers									●		
scales		●	●			●		●			●
moist, damp skin					●						
legs	●	●		●	●					●	●
wings				●							
fins			●					●			
eggs laid in water			●		●	●					
eggs laid on land		●		●							
cold-blooded		●	●							●	
warm-blooded	●			●			●			●	
young fed on milk	●						●				
young born alive	●										

B.

	Protozoa	Coelenterata	Arthropoda	Annelida	Mollusca
Named example					
Habitat					

Copy the table shown above into your book and then complete it using examples of animals you have studied.

1. Explain the following terms:
(a) Classification:
(b) Adaptation to environment;
(c) Asexual reproduction.

2. Give the names of animals which you would expect to have the following structures and explain why the structures are necessary:
(a) Contractile vacuole;
(b) Stinging cells.

3. Choose two of the animal groups from the table above and choose two of the following activities: movement, feeding, breathing and reproduction. Copy the table below into your book and then complete it to compare the activities in the two groups.

	Animal group 1	Animal group 2 ....
Activity 1		
Activity 2		

(SEREB)

C.

Look at the six diagrams of well known invertebrates in figure 44.25.

1. What is an invertebrate?
2. Five of the animals belong to the Phylum Arthropoda. Which of the animals does not?
3. To which Phylum does the odd one out belong?
4. Name *one* other animal that belongs to the same Phylum as the odd one out.
5. Arthropods can be divided into four main groups or classes. These groups are called Arachnids, Crustaceans, Insects and Myriapods. Describe one feature that all Arthropods have in common.
6. The pictures in the figure 44.25 show five Arthropods. Which *two* belong to the same class?
7. To which group or class do they belong?
8. Give a reason for your answer.
9. The following are all plants:

a geranium	green algae
moss	daffodil
fern	pine tree
mushroom	oak tree
honeysuckle	

Select *one* of these plants to match each of the statements below.

(a) Reproduces asexually and produces bulbs as well as reproducing sexually and producing seeds.
(b) Does not contain chlorophyll and so it cannot photosynthesise.
(c) A deciduous tree.
(d) A climbing plant.
(e) An aquatic plant.

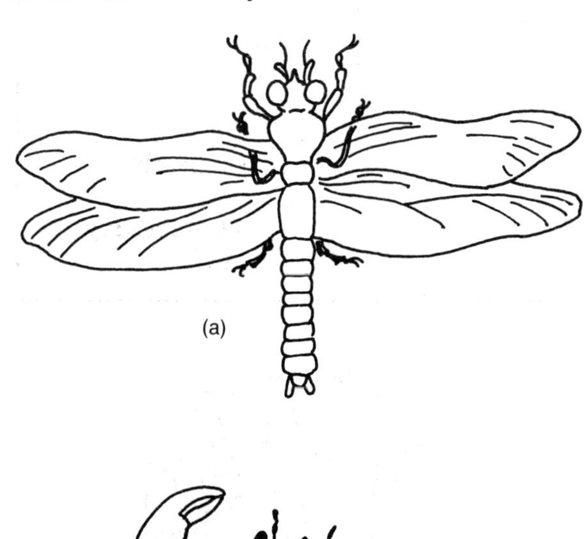

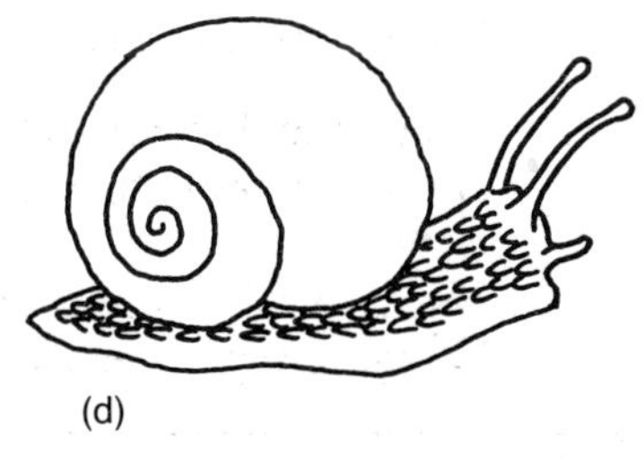

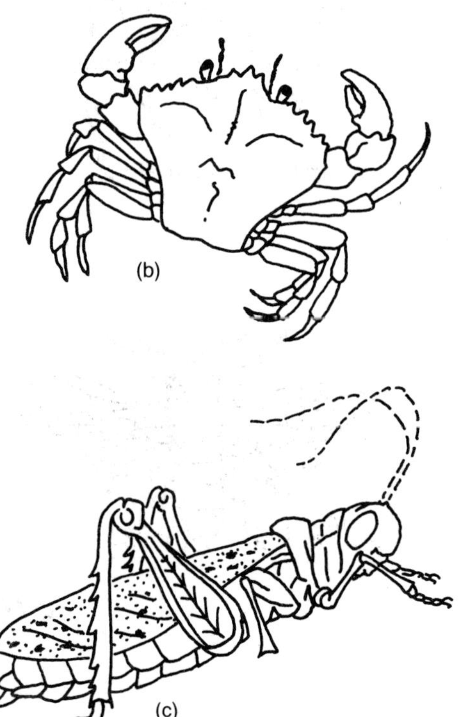

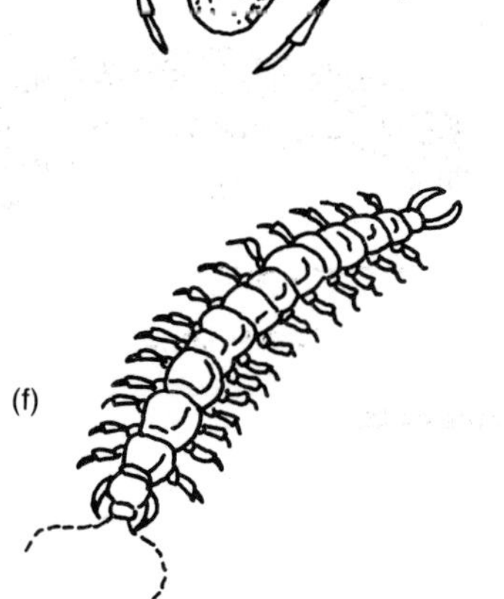

Figure 44.25

(SREB)

D.

A key is a means of identifying organisms. The key shown here enables the identification of some insect pests which are illustrated in figure 44.26. The key operates by selecting features which differ for each insect. By examining the features of the animals in figure 44.26 and working through the key, identify the insects.

1.	Wings present Wings absent	go to 6 go to 2
2.	Antennae long Antennae not obvious	go to 3 go to 5
3.	Piercing mouthparts present Piercing mouthparts not visible	...... aphid go to 4
4.	Three projections from end of abdomen Fewer than three projections from end of abdomen	...... silverfish ...... springtail
5.	Three pairs of legs More than three pairs of legs	...... grass grub lava ...... porina moth lava
6.	One pair of wings Two pairs of wings	go to 7 go to 8
7.	Abdomen fewer than 6 segments Abdomen more than 6 segments	...... carrot fly ...... soldier fly
8.	Wings partly membranous Wings entirely membranous	...... vegetable bug ...... sawfly

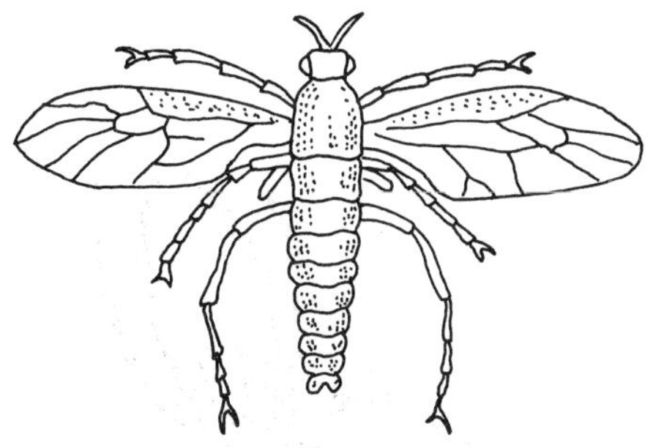

(a) right side only is shown

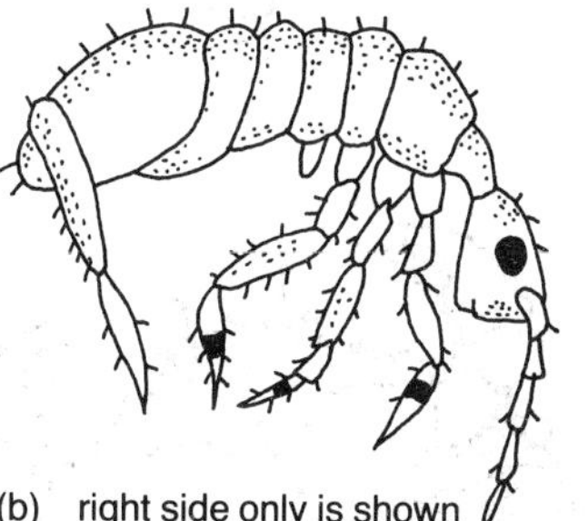

(b) right side only is shown

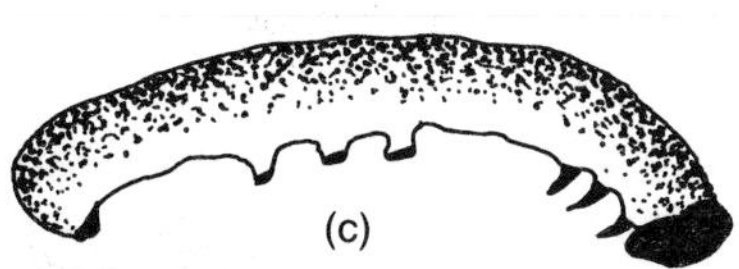

(c)

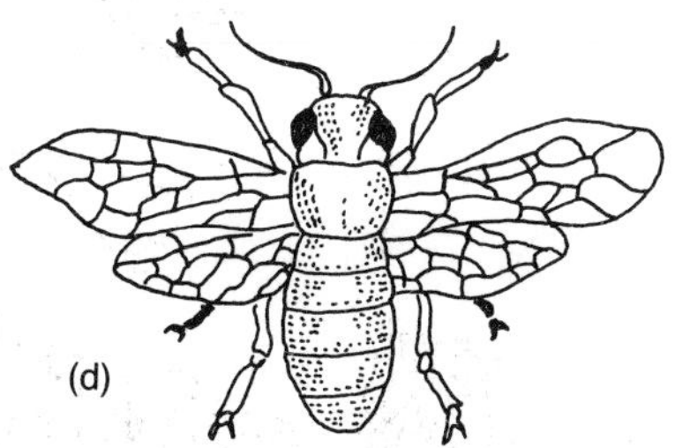

(d)

Figure 44.26

(WJEC)

PROJECT WORK

In this section you will find some suggestions for investigations which need more time than usual. You could try some of them on your own at home. The care with which you do these investigations will affect the kind of results you obtain.

RIVER WATCH

Pollution of rivers by detergents

River water often contains detergents which come from waste water used for washing.

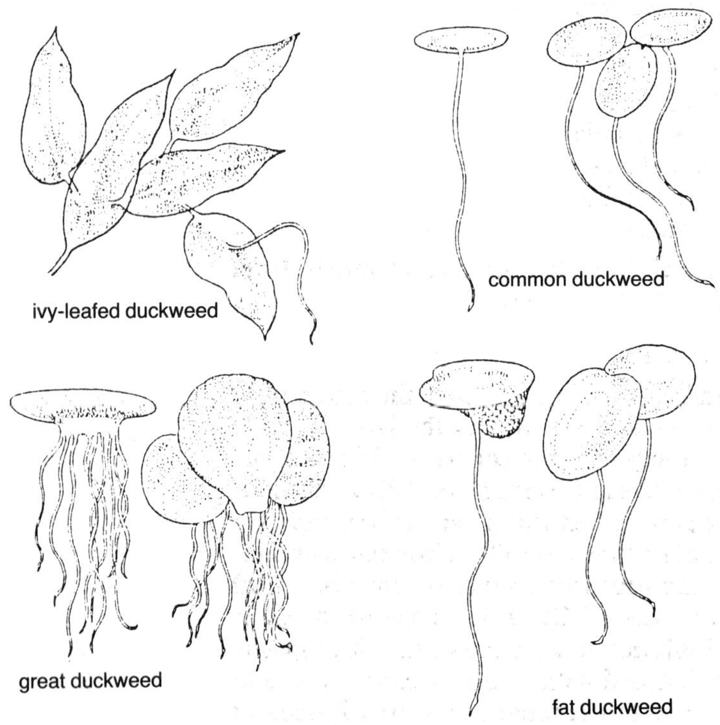

You may have seen rivers with clumps of white detergent foam floating on them. Detergents can cause damage to plants which live in rivers.

Duckweed is a small plant commonly found floating on the surface of ponds and canals. It can also be found in parts of rivers where the water is still or slow moving. It is an important food for many animals which live in these environments. There are four different kinds of duckweed in Britain (illustrated below). In this investigation you can find out the effects of detergents on the growth of duckweed.

What you need

Collect a few duckweed plants which should all be the same sort. You will also need four large jam jars, an artist's paintbrush and some household detergent (washing-up liquid).

What to do

Wash the jars out thoroughly. Partly fill each jar with 100 cm^3 of water taken from where you collected the duckweed. If you cannot do this, use tap water which has been boiled and allowed to get cold. Add one drop of plant food (such as 'Baby Bio') to each jar and stir. Add one drop of detergent to the first jar, two drops to the second jar and three drops to the third jar. Label the jars in each case. Stir each solution once. Leave the fourth jar as a control without any detergent in it. Add ten duckweed plants to each jar. Make sure they are all of a similar size. Place the jars where they can get plenty of light. Leave the plants for a week.

After the week is over:

1. Count the number of leaves in each jar.
2. In each case, estimate the green area of each leaf as a percentage of the whole leaf area. You can find the leaf area by placing a piece of clear plastic ruled with millimetre squares over each leaf. Plot a graph of the total percentage green area of the leaves in each jar against the amount of detergent. What does this graph tell you about the effect of your detergent on the growth of duckweed?

Other things to do

1. Do the investigation again using washing powders. Is there a difference between the effects of ordinary and biological washing powders on the growth of duckweed?
2. Look at the leaves of duckweed from your control jar under the low power of a microscope. The chloroplasts look like green oval discs. Now look at the leaves of duckweed taken from the detergent and washing powder solutions. Is there any difference in the number and shape of the chloroplasts in leaves from different solutions?
3. Are the different kinds of duckweed affected by detergents or washing powders in the same way?

The effects of fertilisers on rivers

Many rivers receive large amounts of fertilisers washed out from fields by rain. Waste water put into rivers from sewage works also contains many plant nutrients. When this happens the water is said to be enriched. The large amounts of extra nitrates and phosphates in the water make plants grow very quickly. When these plants die, they decay and cause all the oxygen in the water to be used up. Shortage of oxygen can cause the death of all the fish and invertebrate animals in the river. In this investigation you can find out how enrichment affects the growth of duckweed.

What you need

Collect a few duckweed plants, which should all be the same sort. You will also need four large jam jars, an artist's brush and some fertiliser. A liquid fertiliser such as 'Baby Bio' is suitable.

What to do

Wash the jars thoroughly and partly fill each with 100 cm^3 of boiled water which has been allowed to go cold. Add one drop of 'Baby Bio' to the first jar, two drops to the second jar and three drops to the third jar. Leave the fourth jar without any fertiliser as a control. Stir the solutions. Use the paintbrush to float ten duckweed plants in each jar. Count and make a note of the number of leaves in each jar; it should be about the same for each. Put the jars on a window ledge and leave for a few weeks. Each week, count the number of leaves in each jar. Draw a graph of the number of plants in each jar against the number of days. In which jar are the plants growing fastest? What does the graph tell you about the effect of fertilisers on the growth of duckweed?

Other things to do

Do the investigation again using other kinds of duckweed. Do the different kinds of duckweed grow at the same rate?

AIR WATCH

The air we breathe is polluted by many man-made substances. In this investigation you can find out the effects of two of these substances: sulphur dioxide and smoke or dust particles.

Air pollution caused by sulphur dioxide

Sulphur dioxide is a gas given off by some fuels as they burn. It is harmful to living things and to buildings.

What you need

5 large jam jars
cress seeds
cotton wool
5 plastic bags
5 rubber bands
5 small glass tubes
Campden tablets
citric acid

You can buy the last two materials from home brewing stores.

What do do

Number the jars 1 – 5. Soak the cotton wool in water and put it into the jars. Sprinkle cress seeds over the cotton wool in each jar. Put the jars in a warm place. When the seeds have germinated and are about 2cm high, fill four glass tubes ¾ full of citric acid solution. Put one tube into each of the four jars. Add half a crushed Campden tablet to the citric acid solution in jar 1 and cover with a plastic bag fastened with a rubber band. Now add one crushed Campden tablet to jar 2, one and a half tablets to jar 3 and two tablets to jar 4.

Cover each jar with a plastic bag as soon as you have added the crushed tablets. The citric acid and Campden tablets react together to set free sulphur dioxide gas. Fill the fifth tube with water and put it into the last jar. Cover this jar with a plastic bag. This is the control.

Look at the seedlings each day for a week. Record how many seedlings are dead in each jar on each day. Plot a graph of the number of dead seeds in each jar on each day. What does the graph tell you about the effects of sulphur dioxide on cress seedlings? Why do you think sulphur dioxide is a harmful gas?

Air pollution caused by smoke and dust

Smoke comes from burning fuels and dust comes from many different sources. Smoke and dust particles can collect in our lungs in heavily polluted air. Buildings and clothes need frequent cleaning duc to smoke and dust. In this investigation you can find out about these pollutants in your environment.

What you need

a ruler
a magnetic compass
some sheets of white paper
a felt-tip pen
tissue paper

What do do

Use your ruler and felt-tip pen to make two marks 30cm apart on the inside of a window. Wrap a small piece of paper around the edge of a ruler. Grip the ruler in both hands and scrape it down the window between the two marks. Press the ruler hard against the window and only scrape between the two marks. Remove the paper and write on it 'Inside' and the date and place. Now scrape the outside of the window between the two marks using a new piece of paper. Repeat this with four other windows which face in different directions. Now take one of the paper scrapes and lay it on the bench. Find out how many pieces of white tissue paper (or greaseproof paper) you need to cover the mark to make it disappear. Write this number down and repeat this for your other scrapes.

1. Which windows had the most pollution?
2. Which direction did these dirty windows face?
3. How can you account for this?
4. Were the outsides of the windows dirtier than the insides?

Other things to do

1. Repeat your investigation at a different time of year, for example, in summer and winter. Are there seasonal differences in pollution?
2. Put a *thin* smear of Vaseline on some microscope slides and place them on external window ledges. After a week, look at them under the low power of a microscopc. Describe the particles you see.

INDEX

Page numbers in *italics* refer to pages which contain figures.